The Engineering of Knowledge-based Systems

Theory and Practice

Avelino J. Gonzalez
University of Central Florida

Douglas D. Dankel
University of Florida

An Alan R. Apt Book

Prentice Hall, Englewood Cliffs, New Jersey 07632

Library of Congress Cataloging-in-Publication Data

González, Avelino J.
    The engineering of knowledge-based systems / Avelino J. González,
Douglas D. Dankel.
        p.   cm.
    "An Alan R. Apt book."
    Includes bibliographical references and index.
    ISBN 0-13-276940-9
    1. Expert systems (Computer science)   I. Dankel, Douglas D.
II. Title.
QA76.76.E95G665   1993
006.3'3--dc20
                                                    92-38279
                                                    CIP

To my late father, Avelino Sr.,
whose presence and encouragement
I always felt
and to my mother, who never let me forget.

Avelino J. Gonzalez

To all PWAs. Their struggle in life
is an inspiration to us all.

Douglas D. Dankel

Publisher: Alan Apt
Production Editor: Mona Pompili
Copy Editor: Martha Williams
Cover Designer: Maureen Eide
Prepress Buyer: Linda Behrens
Manufacturing Buyer: Dave Dickey
Supplements Editor: Alice Dworkin
Editorial Assistant: Shirley McGuire

 © 1993 by Prentice-Hall, Inc.
A Simon & Schuster Company
Englewood Cliffs, New Jersey 07632

The author and publisher of this book have used their best efforts in preparing this book. These efforts include the development, research, and testing of the theories and programs to determine their effectiveness. The author and publisher shall not be liable in any event for incidental or consequential damages in connection with, or arising out of, the furnishing, performance, or use of these programs.

Printed in the United States of America

10 9 8 7 6 5 4 3 2 1

ISBN 0-13-276940-9

Prentice-Hall International (UK) Limited, *London*
Prentice-Hall of Australia Pty. Limited, *Sydney*
Prentice-Hall Canada, Inc., *Toronto*
Prentice-Hall Hispanoamericana, S.A., *Mexico*
Prentice-Hall of India Private Limited, *New Delhi*
Prentice-Hall of Japan, Inc., *Tokyo*
Simon & Schuster Asia Pte. Ltd, *Singapore*
Editora Prentice-Hall do Brasil, Ltda., *Rio de Janeiro*

Preface

1 INTRODUCTION

In the early 1970s, researchers in Artificial Intelligence (AI) recognized that the general problem-solving methods and searching techniques developed over the previous ten years were insufficient to solve the difficult research and application-oriented problems of the day. They realized that what was required was specific knowledge about the particular, limited application domains of interest rather than broad general knowledge which applied across many domains. This recognition led to the development of *knowledge-based* (i.e., *expert*) systems. Since its inception, knowledge-based systems technology has grown into a dominant topic in the AI technical literature. From the simple concept in the mind of a researcher in a laboratory has emerged a rapidly evolving multimillion dollar industry of practical applications.

The arrival of this technology has had a major impact in industry and government. Knowledge-based systems are currently found in a broad diversity of fields ranging from accounting and banking to engineering design and medical diagnosis, with numerous applications currently under development. Applications range from simple knowledge-based systems like AUDITOR, an assistant to a professional auditor which evaluates a client's potential for defaulting on a loan [Dungan, 1983]; to I&W, which assists an intelligence analyst in predicting when and where an armed conflict will next occur [Kiremidjian, 1983]; to XCON, a VAX computer configuration system developed and used by Digital Equipment Corporation (DEC) [McDermott, 1982]. Systems are implemented on personal computers, dedicated workstations, and mini- and mainframe computers.

To support the diversity of applications and the range of their sizes, many support organizations have formed. These organizations include hardware manufacturers who build computers on which to develop systems efficiently, software developers who build tools to facilitate their construction, and consultants who assist not only in the selection of hardware and software, but also in the development of these systems themselves.

But why are knowledge-based systems so popular at this time? What is it about them that has grabbed the attention of business as well as the scientific community? To answer these questions requires an understanding of their structure as well as their relationship with other technological innovations of the present time. In this book we provide an in-depth examination of what knowledge-based systems are, how information is represented within these systems, and how these systems are constructed. Before we plunge into a description of knowledge-based systems, however, it would be good to see what has been accomplished in the field over the last 10 to 15 years. The amount of space in this preface dedicated to such a historical perspective does not do justice to the accomplishments which have occurred. Nevertheless, we shall have to be content with a quick review of a number of significant systems and a more in-depth glance at one major system now in commercial operation.

Numerous knowledge-based systems have been developed over the last two decades and many more are currently under development. Some of the "classic" systems merely served to show the applicability of this new technology in some new domain, while others evolved into commercially applied systems. The following descriptions illustrate the diversity of developed systems.

PROSPECTOR [Duda, 1978]   Assists geologists in identifying geological formations which may contain mineral deposits. It was developed by SRI International between 1974 and 1983 and did not mature into a commercial system.

XCON [McDermott, 1982]   Assists in the configuration of newly ordered VAX computer systems. XCON was developed by Digital Equipment Corporation (DEC) in conjunction with Carnegie-Mellon University. It is presently used internally by DEC.

MYCIN [Shortliffe, 1976; Buchanan, 1984b]   Medical diagnostic system which determines the infectious agent in a patient's blood and specifies a treatment for this infection.

GUIDON [Clancey, 1979, 1983]   Instructional program teaching students therapies for patients with bacterial infections. GUIDON is a descendant of MYCIN and was developed as a research tool at Stanford University. It is not commercially available.

LES [Scarl, 1987]   Monitors and diagnoses the process of loading liquid oxygen (commonly referred to as LOX) into the space shuttle's main tank. It was developed by MITRE Corporation and NASA-KSC (NASA-Kennedy Space Center). LES never developed into a commercial application; however, the concepts developed in LES have been featured in another NASA-developed knowledge-based system called KATE (Knowledge-based Autonomous Test Engineer). KATE is presently being applied to the environmental control system in the Orbiter Maintenance and Refurbishment Facility at the Kennedy Space Center.

ISIS [Fox, 1984]   Generates a job shop schedule for a factory floor. It uses a technique called *constraint-directed reasoning*, which allows certain constraints to determine the sequence of operations needed to complete a job within the specified schedules. It evaluates the alternative sequences which are suggested to pick the best. It was developed by Carnegie-Mellon University and Westinghouse Electric Corporation in Pittsburgh and is presently being used by Westinghouse.

DELTA/CATS [Bonissone, 1983]   This is a rule-based diagnostic system for troubleshooting electric diesel locomotives. It was developed by the General Electric Company of Schenectady, NY, and is presently being used internally by the General Electric Company.

STEAMER [Hollan, 1984]   A simulation-based system developed to instruct naval propulsion engineering students in the operation of a shipboard steam propulsion plant. It was developed by the U.S. Navy in collaboration with BBN Corporation and is currently used in the training of naval personnel.

INTERNIST/CADUCEUS [Miller, 1982]   One of the largest medical systems developed, INTERNIST assists the physician in making multiple and complex diagnoses in internal medicine. It was developed at the University of Pittsburgh and is not currently in commercial use.

COOKER [AInteractions, 1985]   Assists in the maintenance of soup-making equipment. Developed by Texas Instruments for the Campbell Soup Company, it uses a personal computer as the delivery platform and is currently in use within the Campbell Soup Company.

AUTHORIZER'S ASSISTANT [Leonard-Barton, 1988]   Assists the credit authorization staff determine the credit level for credit card customers. The system takes information from a number of databases and approves or disapproves a telephone request from a merchant to authorize a large purchase from a cardholder. It was developed by Inference Corporation and American Express Company and is currently used by American Express Company.

GENAID [Gonzalez, 1986]   Remotely monitors and diagnoses the status of large electrical generators in real time. It issues a diagnosis with a confidence factor whenever the machine is operating outside its normal operating conditions. It was developed by Westinghouse Electric Corporation with assistance from Texas Utilities Generating Company and Carnegie-Mellon University and is presently in commercial operation at various sites throughout the United States.

But how does the field of knowledge-based systems relate with AI? This question merits a closer look.

2 RELATIONSHIP TO AI

Very often, knowledge-based systems and AI are mistakenly assumed to be one and the same. One reason for the mistaken assumption is that the field of knowledge-based systems is the branch of AI which has, by far, seen the most success in terms of practical applications. Such thinking is fairly common among nontechnical people. The news media contributes to this phenomenon since the term *artificial intelligence* is more dramatic and sensational than *knowledge-based systems*. The former has often been used where the latter was intended.

While the use of knowledge has always been one of a set of techniques employed by AI practitioners, the knowledge used by the early AI systems tended to be very general in nature. The development of knowledge-based systems was marked by the realization that general knowledge was not sufficient to solve the difficult problems, and that high quality, domain-specific knowledge was the alternative.

But what exactly is meant by AI?

A good definition of AI is quite elusive simply because human intelligence is not completely understood. The various textbooks on AI provide diverse definitions emphasizing the different perspectives which their author(s) feel the field entails. Nevertheless, one general definition [Tanimoto, 1987] which provides a good broad view of the field is:

Artificial intelligence is a field of study that encompasses computational techniques for performing tasks that apparently require intelligence when performed by humans. Such problems include diagnosing problems in automobiles, computers and people, designing new computers, writing stories and symphonies, finding mathematical theorems, assembling and inspecting products in factories, and negotiating international treaties. It is a technology of information processing concerned with processes of reasoning, learning, and perception.

Historically computers have excelled at performing rather simple, repetitive tasks such as complex arithmetic calculations or database storage and retrieval. What these repetitive tasks have in common is that they are *algorithmic* in nature. That is, they involve a precise and logically designed set of instructions which yield a single correct answer. Humans, on the other hand, excel at solving problems using symbols rather than numbers, such as when planning a schedule of tasks or understanding a poem. AI, in more specific terms, is the science which provides computers with the ability to represent and manipulate such symbols so they can be used to solve problems not easily solved through algorithmic models.

The term *artificial intelligence* was coined by John McCarthy in 1956 during a workshop which he organized at Dartmouth College. This so-called Dartmouth Conference brought together John McCarthy, Marvin Minsky, Allan Newell, and Herbert Simon, four individuals who pioneered AI research. While this event is generally considered to be the birth date of AI, some research had already been ongoing during the previous ten years. Research began in earnest after this workshop, starting initially in academic centers throughout the world.

The early emphasis in AI research was on game playing and machine translation of natural languages. In game playing, researchers have developed a number of chess-playing programs over the years including MacHack by Richard Greenblatt (1967), Chess 3.0 by David Slate and Larry Atkin (1970), Chess 4.0 (1976), and Belle (1983), the latter of which has a tournament rating of 2552 [Hsu, 1990]. Other programs have included a checkers-playing program developed by A. L. Samuel which defeated R. W. Nealey, "one of the nation's foremost players" [Samuel, 1963]; a backgammon program by Hans Berliner in 1979 which defeated the reigning world champion [Berliner, 1980]; and a checkers-playing program called Chinook which in 1991 placed second in the U.S. National Open, winning the right to challenge for the world title [Peterson, 1991; Schaeffer, 1991].

The efforts in machine translation of natural languages were not nearly as successful. Originally, researchers felt that there was a one-to-one correspondence between words in one language and words in another. To translate from one language to another required, so they thought, merely finding the corresponding words and changing word orders slightly.

One example of direct word-for-word translation which illustrates the obstacles faced by researchers is the case of Braniff International Airways, which in the early 1980s advertised the desirability of flying in the leather upholstery found in the seats of their aircraft. While presumably successful in convincing English-speaking travelers to fly with them, such was not the case when they translated the ads into Spanish for the large Hispanic market of the Southwest. Their motto, "fly in leather," when directly translated into Spanish, unwittingly exhorted the Spanish-speaking travelers to "fly naked." Because of similar difficulties, the machine translation efforts were abandoned in the mid-1960s.

In the late 1960s and early 1970s, other areas of research within the field of AI emerged. One of them, of course, was knowledge-based systems. The others included natural language understanding, learning, planning, robotics, vision, and neural networks.

3 OBJECTIVE OF THIS TEXTBOOK

The objective of this textbook is to serve as an introduction to the branch of AI known as knowledge-based systems. The book has been divided into two major sections, each discussing one of the major aspects of knowledged-based systems: *The Theory*, discussing their internal structure and organization, and *The Practice*, discussing issues dealing with their development and use. These two sections are preceded by Chapters 1 and 2 which introduce the basic concepts of knowledge-based systems—a definition of what we mean by the term "knowledge-based systems" and a discussion of their general internal structure.

The Theory (Chapters 3 through 9) covers topics such as logic, rule-based reasoning (forward and backward chaining), frames and objects, blackboard architectures, uncertainty management, and alternative techniques in knowledge-based systems. As the name suggests, *The Practice* (Chapters 10 through 17) is more practical in nature, covering the development of knowledge-based systems. The focus is on the relationship between knowledge engineering and software engineering. Covered are such topics as selection of a good candidate project for a knowledge-based system, how to select the project resources, how to elicit knowledge from an expert, how to use some of the available packages which facilitate the knowledge engineering, and how to verify and validate the knowledge base. This section also includes a preview of techniques on the horizon of knowledge-based systems to prepare you for the changes ahead.

The format of this book is intended to facilitate its use in courses using one of two different approaches. Those courses emphasizing the engineering and design of systems can concentrate on *The Theory*. In this approach, the chapters of the book should be followed in the order presented; first the theoretical aspects of knowledge engineering, then the practical aspects of building a system. This approach is well suited for a course where students will actually build their own knowledge-based shells and use those shells to create some application system. Most likely this course would involve two semesters or quarters where the first concentrates on the theoretical issues and the second involves the development of some application.

Alternatively, this book can be used in courses that emphasize the use of knowledge-based systems as tools by concentrating on the practical issues of knowledge-based systems development. After covering the first two chapters, these courses will next examine Chapters 10 to 17, *The Practice*, before proceeding to Chapters 3 to 9, *The Theory*. The optional chapter sections in Chapters 5 and 6 should be eliminated to allow time to concentrate on the development of a practical application, since these courses typically will be only one semester or quarter in length.

Included with the text are a series of diskettes containing:

1. A demonstration version of the TI Personal Consultant Plus shell
2. A copy of version 5.0 of the CLIPS knowledge-based system shell.

4 ACKNOWLEDGMENTS

We would like to acknowledge in this section the people who helped us by reviewing this book at all stages. They are Dr. Dale Isner, Dr. Larry Hall, Dr. Uma Gupta, Dr. Glenn Blank, Dr. Bruce W. Porter, Dr. Larry Medsker, Dr. Bill Mettrey, Mr. Mark Fishman, Dr. Gordon Novak, Dr. Lois Bogess, Dr. Soheil Khajenoori, as well as many others. Additionally, we would like to acknowledge the editorial department of Prentice Hall who guided us by the hand in this our first effort at publishing a book of this magnitude. Specifically, we would like to recognize the editor, Alan Apt. Lastly, we would like to thank our colleagues at our respective departments at the University of Central Florida and the University of Florida who supported us during the process and our students who served as "guinea pigs" on the early drafts of this book.

Avelino J. Gonzalez
Douglas D. Daniel

Contents

1 Introduction to Knowledge-based Systems

1.1 INTRODUCTION

When confronted with a problem, humans employ various types of knowledge in an attempt to solve it. For example, consider a lawn mower that will not start. Our general knowledge about lawn mowers allows us to classify this problem into a particular problem domain (e.g., is it a gas or electric mower?). More specific knowledge about trouble-shooting small internal combustion engines deals with the individual circumstances of this problem (e.g., if it is a gas mower, is there gas in the gas tank?).

What is not immediately obvious, however, is another class of knowledge: general problem-solving knowledge about how to apply these other two forms of knowledge in problem solving.

The *intelligent program* of a knowledge-based system consists of an *inference engine* and a *knowledge base*. Closely associated with this intelligent program is a *data* or *fact base*. See Figure 1.1. The inference engine manipulates the knowledge represented in the knowledge base to develop a solution to the problem(s) described by the information in the database. The inference engine contains the general problem-solving knowledge (i.e., how do we approach the solution of this problem?) while the knowledge base contains the knowledge about this particular problem (i.e., how does a lawnmower work? how do we diagnose the problem?). The database, on the other hand, contains the problem-specific data (i.e., the initial information on the problem as well as information progressively derived as we solve it).

The power of knowledge-based systems evolves from this clear separation of the knowledge from its use. This separation allows us to develop different applications by having to create only a new knowledge base for each application. The generic reasoning technique (i.e., the inference engine) is not modi-

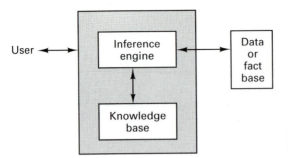

FIGURE 1.1 The General Structure of a Knowledge-based System

fied. For example, the basic trouble-shooting approach used in medical diagnosis is similar to that used by a mechanic in diagnosing a fault in an automobile. Only the domain is different. Once the generic knowledge is encoded, it can be applied to either domain, thereby greatly simplifying the development process.

Knowledge has many different forms. Some knowledge consists simply of facts, while others identify relationships between facts. Some knowledge is algorithmic while other knowledge is *heuristic*.[1] No matter what form the knowledge takes, to use it for problem solving in the computer, we must represent it within a program and must create some means of interpreting it.

Five major knowledge representation schemes are commonly used in knowledge-based systems: logic, rules, associative (i.e., semantic) networks, frames, and objects. Each uses different types of reasoning techniques to interpret and apply its knowledge. Chapter 3 examines logic systems and their applicability to knowledge-based systems. Chapters 4 and 5 examine rule-based systems that use the concept of data-driven reasoning and goal-directed reasoning. The other representations (associative networks, frames, and objects) and their corresponding reasoning schemes are examined in Chapter 6.

In each of these chapters we examine a particular knowledge representation scheme, as well as inference technique(s) commonly used with them. We discuss their organization, advantages, and disadvantages. Which of these knowledge representation and manipulation schemes should be used for any particular problem is determined by the characteristics of the problems to be solved. Each of these is suited for a different type of problem. What you must do is understand the characteristics of each so you can make an intelligent choice among them. Remember that these representation schemes are just tools and any tool can be abused. The key is to use a tool intelligently.

The objectives of this chapter are to provide a definition for the term *knowledge-based systems* and to identify how knowledge-based systems differ from conventional software in purpose, architecture, and development. We begin with a discussion of the traditional computing techniques and follow it

---

[1]"A heuristic is a rule of thumb, strategy, or trick used to improve the efficiency of a system which tries to discover the solutions of complex problems" [Slagle, 1971].

with a definition and description of one of the theoretical underpinnings of artificial intelligence (AI) in general and knowledge-based systems in particular: the concept of searching through a *problem space* (a representation of the problem and all potential solutions paths) to find a particular solution. We then compare knowledge-based systems to programs using search as well as to conventional algorithmic programs. Finally, we discuss the general advantages and disadvantages for knowledge-based systems.

Chapter 2 describes the structure of knowledge-based systems in general as viewed by different people with different levels of relationship to the knowledge-based system.

1.2 ALGORITHMIC METHODS IN COMPUTING

Traditional computer programming involves the development of a suitable mathematical or logical model that describes a domain, or a part of one. A solution to many problems can be derived through the use of such a model. With the existence of this model, a structured sequence of steps can be developed that is guaranteed to find a solution to the problem in a finite length of time. Such procedures are called *algorithms* and they form the basis for conventional software systems.

To illustrate an algorithmic solution to a problem, let us assume that we are visiting Paris for the first time and are trying to locate *la Tour Eiffel*, the Eiffel Tower. We know our current location is at the Sorbonne University, on Boulevard St Michel, and we also know what the tower looks like. See the section of a map of Paris shown in Figure 1.2. What we desire is a path through the city from our current location to the tower. To find the route to the Eiffel Tower algorithmically, we absolutely require a map (a model of the route system of the city!) and the specific directions on how to use it.

But what if a map is unavailable and we do not speak French? Clearly, no algorithm is available and we must, therefore, find an alternative solution method.

1.3 SEARCH AS THE FOUNDATION OF ARTIFICIAL INTELLIGENCE

The early researchers in artificial intelligence (AI) had as their main objective the solution of problems that were difficult to solve through (existing) computational techniques, yet were easily solved by the human brain, a slower and, in many ways, a much more limited device. These problems generally either had no known algorithmic solutions or else very complex ones that were not practical to implement on a computer. Nevertheless, these problems were regularly solved by humans with their "inferior" processing capabilities.

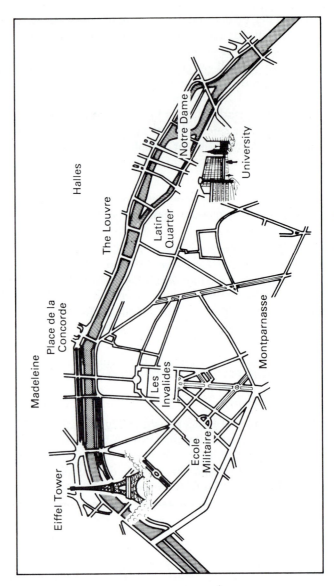

FIGURE 1.2 A Partial Map of Paris

The answer, of course, was to develop new problem-solving techniques, similar to those used by humans, and to implement them in a computer. One of the most important of these was *search*.

Searching through data structures has always been a fundamental concept in computer algorithms. The searches that AI researchers developed, however, were different since they were used to search a *problem space*, not for any particular piece of data, but rather for a path connecting the initial description of the problem to a description of the desired state of the problem (i.e., the solved problem). This path represents the solution steps of the problem. The process of searching for a solution to the problem develops a *solution space* (i.e., that portion of the problem space which is actually examined).

Unlike a data structure that is predefined and already in existence when the search begins, problem spaces are generally, although not always, *procedurally defined*. That is, the entire problem space is not created and then searched but, rather, is created as it is being explored. Procedures are used to define the next possible states in the space to which the search can proceed from the current state. Only the explored paths need to be explicitly defined.

To illustrate the concepts of a problem space and a solution space, suppose that your automobile fails to start one morning—a problem that many of us have encountered. Your initial problem state is that your car fails to start. Your desired goal or final state is the car's starting when you turn the ignition switch. There are many possible problems that can cause your car to fail to start and each of these problems might have several different solutions. All of these problems and their solutions define the problem space, a portion of which is shown in Figure 1.3.

In this figure the arcs represent actions that can be taken and the nodes represent possible results that can occur from these actions. Note that not all possible results are represented (e.g., when you turn the key, the engine might turn over), and the paths from the initial state to the goal state assume that only one problem exists.

Determining which problem is present and taking an appropriate corrective action is the process of problem diagnosis and repair. This process finds the appropriate path from the initial state to the goal state, thereby providing a solution to the problem. Searching the problem space to find this path, however, can be difficult.

The first step in solving this problem might be to see whether the engine will turn over. The information obtained defines a new state in the solution space that you get to by turning the ignition key and seeing what results. For this example, let us say that the engine does not turn over. This new state is, therefore, described by the facts:

THE CAR DOES NOT START AND ITS ENGINE DOES NOT TURN OVER.

See Figure 1.4a. Scanning the problem space we find a possible next step in the solution is determining the viability of the battery. Should you find the

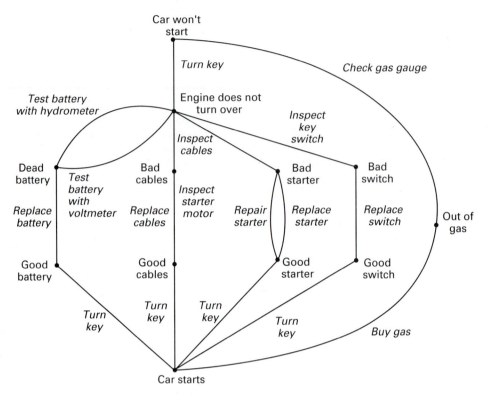

FIGURE 1.3 Network Representation of a Portion of a Problem Space

battery to be defective, you can replace it and the problem can be said to be solved. Note, there are many other possible steps that you could have taken, such as determining the status of the starter motor, but for one reason or another, you choose to explore the path that examines the battery. Two methods can be used to test the battery: measuring the charge on the battery with a hydrometer or measuring its charge using a voltmeter as you turn the ignition switch. These two methods are shown in Figure 1.4b as dashed lines. You decide to use the hydrometer and discover that the battery is in good shape. See Figure 1.4c.

The new and current state is that the car does not start, the engine does not turn over, and the battery is fully charged. This state is incompatible with the potential solution (i.e., replacing the battery) so you have reached a dead end for this possible solution. As a result you must go back and consider other potential problems for why the engine does not turn over. One such problem is that your car may have a bad starter motor (Figure 1.4d). When you inspect the starter motor you discover that it has a broken lead. Correcting this problem can be performed by taking one of two actions: replacing the motor or re-

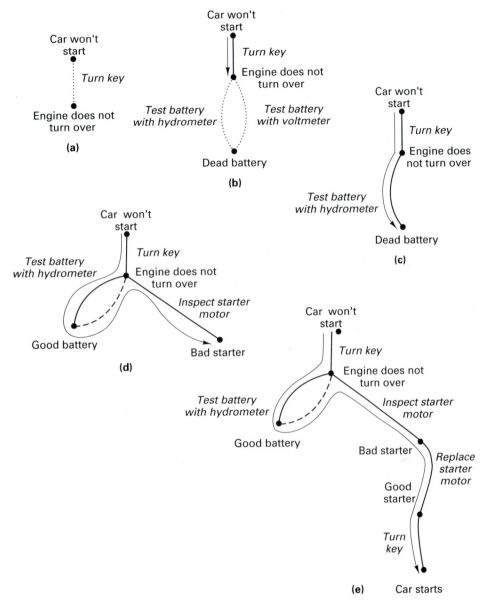

FIGURE 1.4   Step-by-Step Exploration to a Problem Solution

pairing the leads. You choose to replace the entire motor. Upon completion of the repair, you verify that you have reached the final state by turning the ignition key and finding that the car now starts and the problem is solved. See Figure 1.4e. Although the procedures that defined succeeding states

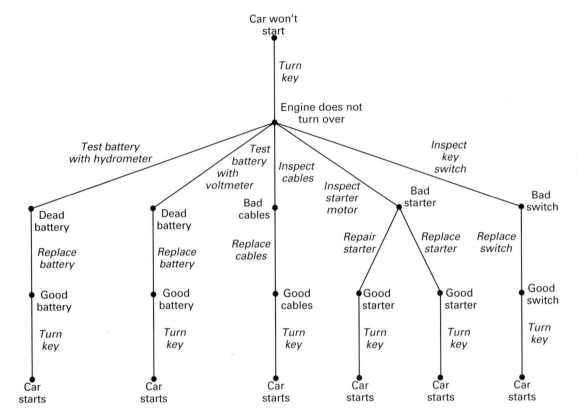

FIGURE 1.5 Tree Representation of a Problem Space

were somewhat fuzzy, it is clear that search was used to traverse this solution space.

A problem space can be represented as either a *network* or a *tree*. A network (or graph) is a nonempty set of nodes, a set of edges or links, and a mapping from the set of edges to pairs of nodes [Tremblay, 1984]. As an example see Figure 1.3. Each node is a state of the problem. The edges specify actions that can be taken to move from one state to another. Traversal through the network is achieved by moving between nodes, hopefully moving ever closer to the goal state. A set of operators define the legal "movements" that can be made from any one state to another.

A tree is a directed, acyclic network in which each node has a single parent. The root of the tree is the initial problem and each leaf represents a potential solution. See Figure 1.5. A tree is similarly searched by traversing the nodes of the tree. A set of operators define the legal movements within the tree and a path from the root to a leaf represents a solution to the problem.

1.3.1 Searching a Problem Space

Let us return to the problem of locating the Eiffel Tower. Suppose that we are in Paris without a map and are unable to speak French. How can we search for and locate the Eiffel Tower?

Because of the conceivably infinite number of possible routes that could be taken (some of which could be by way of China!), we need to bound the area of our search. With our limited knowledge of Paris, we know that the Eiffel Tower is located within two physical barriers: the autoroute to the south and the Seine River on the north, east, and west. Reaching either of these will be considered a dead end, resulting in our traveling in some alternative direction.

Governing our search is a set of operators that defines the legal paths we can follow. These operators are the traffic laws which state that upon reaching any intersection, we have a choice of continuing on the same street to the next intersection or turning into any other street at this intersection. To simplify our search, let us assume that there are no one-way streets.

Various methods can be used to search for our goal. For example, we could randomly turn at any street, hoping that sooner or later we will bump into the Eiffel Tower. While this *random* search should ultimately find the Eiffel Tower, it may take an infinite amount of time because the arbitrary manner with which we select a path to follow can result in paths being taken multiple times.

Because a random search cannot guarantee that it will explore all paths in the problem space and thereby find a solution, we need some alternative method that will be more systematic in the manner in which it explores the domain. One such approach is to follow exhaustively every street to its end (i.e., the river, the autoroute, or a dead end). When an end is encountered we find a parallel road and follow it in the opposite direction, regardless of whether we are moving closer to or farther from our goal. Eventually (if Paris followed a grid system) this approach will consider all locations in our problem space, a definite improvement over the uncontrolled process of the random search. This type of systematic search is called a *blind search* since it uses no knowledge of how close we are to a solution in picking the path to follow from our current location to a new location. For some applications, it can be quite effective.

Alternatively, we can use our knowledge of what the tower looks like to improve the efficiency of our search. Assuming that the tip of the Eiffel Tower can be seen from everywhere in our problem space (which is actually *not* a true assumption!), we can look up and take whatever street appears to take us in its general direction. This is called a *directed search*, because we are neither randomly or blindly searching for our goal. Directed or knowledge-based searches form the foundation of AI.

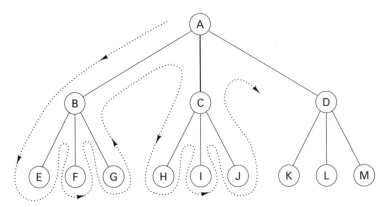

FIGURE 1.6   Depth-first Search of a Tree

One difference to note between the Eiffel Tower and the automobile re-pair problems is how each of these problem's search spaces is defined. Trying to locate the Eiffel Tower involves searching a space that is predefined by the roads within Paris, while repairing the automobile involves a procedurally de-fined space. Problem space searches are typically more like the latter.

There are a number of different search methods, blind as well as di-rected. Depending on the application, one may be better suited than others. The next sections discuss some of these methods.

1.3.2 Depth-first Search

Depth-first search is a blind systematic search that expands one path to its conclusion before examining any other path. This single path is followed until it either reaches the goal or a dead end. When a dead end is encountered, depth-first search *backtracks* to the last node of the solution space to see whether that node has any unexplored paths. If it does, the search proceeds down one of these paths until either the goal or another dead end is reached. If there are no more unexplored paths from a node, depth-first search backs up to its parent node and repeats this process until a solution is found or all paths reach dead ends. Figure 1.6 diagrams the order (i.e., A, B, E, F, G, C) in which nodes are examined using depth-first search.

1.3.3 Breadth-first Search

Breadth-first search is also a blind, systematic search technique. While depth-first search proceeds down a path until a dead end or the goal is encountered, a breadth-first search investigates all nodes at the same hierarchical level in the tree before proceeding to the next level. Figure 1.7 depicts the order (i.e., A, B, C, D, E, F) in which nodes are examined using this approach.

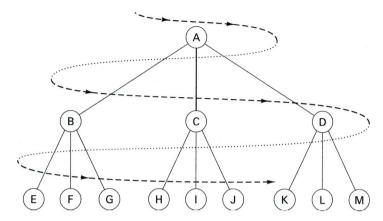

FIGURE 1.7   Breadth-first Search of a Tree

1.3.4 Beam Search and the Use of Knowledge

Beam search is a *directed* variation of a breadth-first search where only a limited number of nodes are expanded when you proceed from one level of the search tree to the next. A *beam width*, w, specifies the number of nodes to be considered. All successors of the nodes on the current level are created and evaluated (scored) according to some knowledge, called a *heuristic*. The best *w* nodes are kept while all others are pruned from the search tree. This search is *directed* or *heuristic* since it uses a *heuristic function* to determine the best path to select when expanding the solution space. Heuristic functions work by estimating or measuring how far nodes are from the goal or determining which paths from a particular node appear more promising to follow by estimating or measuring their ability to reach the goal.

1.3.5 Hill-climbing Search

Hill climbing is a directed variation of depth-first search. In hill climbing you explore the solution space in a depth-first manner pursuing the path that appears to decrease the remaining distance from the goal the most. For example, in our search for the Eiffel Tower we might, whenever we encounter an intersection, use "as-the-crow-flies" knowledge—look for the tower and follow the road that appears to lead most directly toward it. Our assumption in this approach is that if a road leads in the general direction of the tower, it will provide the shortest path. The difficulty with using this approach is that we may select a street that is a dead end. When we reach the end of this street we will have no way to back out of the dead end since to do so will increase our distance from our desired goal.

Hill climbing is an excellent technique to use in solving many problems, but it suffers from a number of difficulties that become very obvious when the problem involves parameter optimization [Winston, 1992]. To illustrate these problems consider the task of finding the highest point in a large hilly field in a dense fog. Your only tools are a compass to aid your selection of a direction to pursue and an altimeter for measuring your height. Your task is to wander through this field (adjusting your north-south and east-west parameters) until you find the highest point. At each location in exploring this field you measure the height of your current position, then take steps from this point in various directions, measuring the height at each of these new points. The problems that you can encounter are discussed below and illustrated in Figure 1.8 [Winston, 1992].

Foothill: The foothills problem occurs when there are a number of small hills within the field that surround the tallest hill. When you encounter a foothill, you progress up its sides to its peak where you then stay since every direction you step from this point is lower. This peak is a local maximum rather than the global maximum within the field.

Plateau: The plateau problem occurs when the field is generally very flat and contains only a few very sharp peaks. As you explore the field, every point appears to be the same height unless you are lucky enough to encounter one of these peaks. The plateau provides no information to guide you toward the global maximum (or even local maximums).

Ridge: In the ridge problem, you find a path that leads you up the slope of the ridge, but once are on the edge of the ridge you cannot find the proper direction to continue on toward the peak. The difficulty is that the ridge is very sharp (its sides slope off very quickly on both sides) and the number of directions that you are considering is not large enough to find a point higher on the ridge.

1.3.6 Branch and Bound Search

Branch and bound search, another directed search method, is very similar to hill climbing. While hill climbing always follows a path from the most recently examined node, branch and bound search follows a path from the most promising node in the solution tree regardless of where this node might be in the tree.

To illustrate how this search works, consider the road network shown in Figure 1.9 where travel times between the nodes are shown on the arcs. Suppose that we want to find not merely a path between Gainesville and Key West, but rather the shortest path. Starting at Gainesville we would find all of Gainesville's immediate successors. This is shown in Figure 1.10a where the cost of travel (e.g., the travel time) to the leaf nodes is given in parentheses. Jacksonville has the lowest cost so it is expanded next giving Figure 1.10b (note that the path back to Gainesville is not included since it will result in a

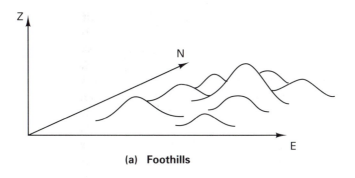

(a) Foothills

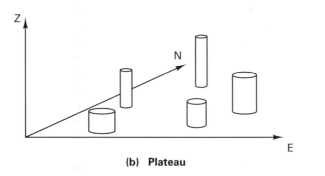

(b) Plateau

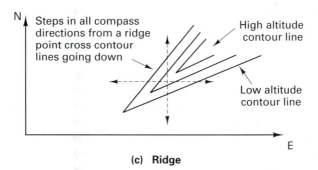

(c) Ridge

FIGURE 1.8   The Problems of Hill Climbing

loop). When this expansion is done we now have two nodes labeled Orlando in our tree. Because we are interested in finding only the shortest path, we can ignore the path to Orlando with a cost of 3. Continuing in this manner we will eventually develop the tree shown in Figure 1.10f, which identifies the shortest path as Gainesville–Orlando–Miami–Key West.

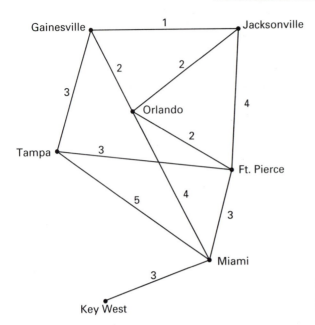

FIGURE 1.9   Road Network
Representing Distances between
Various Cities

The difficulty with searching in this manner is that a significant portion of the full search tree is developed to find the shortest path. There is information that is not being used that could reduce the search effort—the estimated cost in traveling from any node to the goal.

1.3.7 Best-first Search

Suppose that we are able to provide an estimate at every node of how far we are from the solution. In best-first search we look at the unexpanded nodes' estimates and continue our search from the node with the smallest estimate. Note that this is very similar to what we are doing in hill climbing, except that in hill climbing we always expand from our current position.

Recall our search for the Eiffel Tower. If we can see the tower from every point in Paris and if we always try to move closer to the tower from our current position, we are performing hill climbing. If on the other hand, we mark every road intersection with an estimate of how far we are from the Eiffel Tower and always try the next available path from the intersection that appears closest to the tower, we are performing best-first search.

While finding a solution using either of these methods does not guarantee that the solution is the shortest path, best-first search typically does better. The problem with best-first search is that it does not take into account how far we have traveled to get to the current intersection, which branch and bound does do. Combining best-first and branch and bound together gives us A*.

1.3.8 A* Search

Suppose that we have knowledge that allows us to estimate the cost of travel between each node and our desired goal. A smart trip planner would use these estimates in searching for the shortest path by computing an estimated total trip cost:

$$Estimated\ Total\ Trip\ Cost =$$

$$Cost(trip\ from\ Gainesville\ to\ Current\ Node) +$$

$$Estimated\ Cost(trip\ from\ Current\ Node\ to\ Key\ West)$$

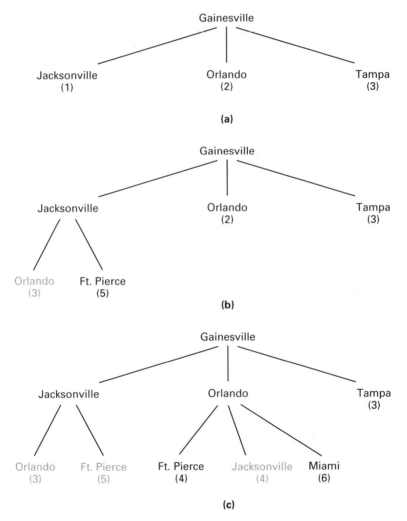

FIGURE 1.10   Step-by-Step Development of a Branch and Bound Search Tree

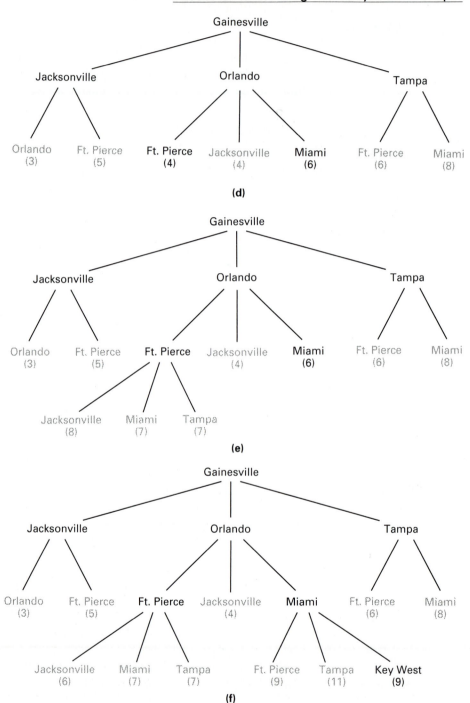

(d)

(e)

(f)

FIGURE 1.10 (Continued)

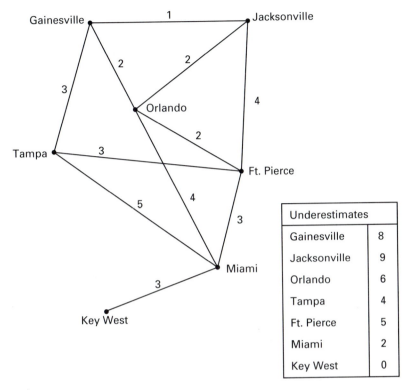

FIGURE 1.11   Road Network Representing Distances between Various Cities with Estimated Distance

This estimated cost would then be used to determine the particular path to follow. If our estimated costs are very close to the actual costs, the solution tree that we develop might have very few unnecessary paths. But if an estimated cost significantly overestimates the actual cost, we might never find the optimal path. We, therefore, desire to have estimated costs that are as close as possible to the actual costs. In most instances it is very difficult to obtain really good estimates so we instead make the restriction that estimated costs should always be greater than zero but never greater than the actual cost. If our estimates obey this restriction, we are guaranteed to always find the lowest cost path and our search is called an A* search.

Figure 1.11 shows the graph representing travel distances that we used in finding a best-first search path. This figure also includes the estimated travel cost from each city to our goal, Key West. Note that each of the estimated travel distances is less than the actual distance, thereby satisfying our condition for performing this search. The estimate for Key West is zero, since it is our goal. Figure 1.12 details the step-by-step expansion of the search tree. First the tree is grown to include all nodes connected directly to

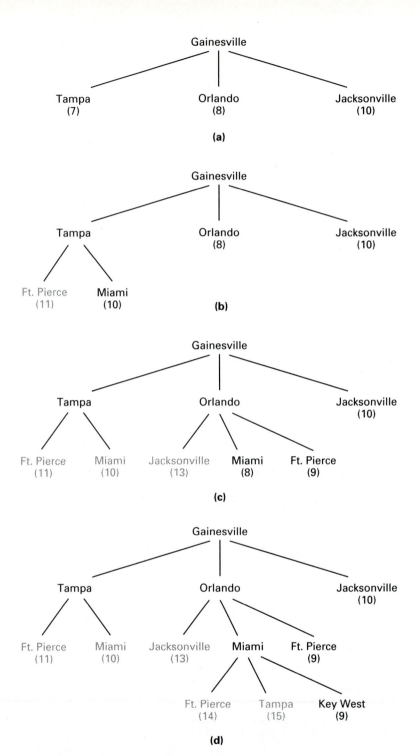

FIGURE 1.12 Step-by-Step Development of the A* Algorithm Search Tree

Gainesville. See Figure 1.12a. Estimated trip costs are computed for each of these nodes and the one with the lowest estimate, Tampa, is selected for expansion. This process continues until the tree shown in Figure 1.12d is developed. Note in this figure that the cost to Key West is computed to be 9 and that the costs to all other nodes in the tree are greater than or equal to this value. If any nodes had a lower cost, we would have had to continue expanding those nodes. This assures us that we have found the lowest cost solution to our problem. If you compare the development of this search tree to the development of the search tree for best-first search, you will note that we have expanded fewer nodes in finding the solution to the problem. The closer the estimates are to the actual cost, the fewer nodes that will be expanded.

1.4 EXPERTISE AND HEURISTIC KNOWLEDGE

In the early 1970s, some researchers in AI recognized that the general problem-solving methods and searching techniques described above that were developed over the previous ten years were insufficient to solve the difficult research and application-oriented problems of the day. They realized that what was required was specific knowledge about the particular, limited application domains of interest rather than broad *general knowledge* that applied across many domains. This recognition led to the development of knowledge-based (e.g., expert) systems. Since its inception, knowledge-based systems technology has grown into a major topic in the AI technical literature. From a simple concept in the mind of a researcher in a laboratory has emerged a rapidly evolving multimillion dollar industry of practical applications.

The knowledge represented in knowledge-based systems is that of experts in the domain. A part of an expert's knowledge consists of cause-and-effect relationships. These relationships or rules of thumb originate from the expert's past experiences and are commonly called *heuristics*. They represent informal knowledge, or shortcuts, that allow an expert to quickly reach a solution to a problem without having to perform a detailed analysis of a particular situation, because either an analysis of a similar problem was successfully performed previously, or the relationship may have been learned as a result of a past failed attempt to solve a similar problem. The expert may not remember, or even know, all the details of the original problem analysis, but she recognizes that a particular approach worked once for a similar problem and that this same approach will probably work again for the problem at hand. Consider the following example that illustrates this concept.

A motorist suddenly notices a backfiring noise in his automobile while stopped at a light. Although he doesn't know what it is, he has been driving this particular automobile for a long time, and remembers a similar situation that occurred several months earlier. At that time he took the car to his mechanic for repair, and

the mechanic told him that the problem was simply a loose vacuum hose connection in the engine that caused air in-leakage, resulting in the backfiring. The mechanic even showed him which hose caused the problem. Thus, the motorist stops
the car, opens the hood, discovers that the same hose is loose, and proceeds to
reconnect it. When the car is restarted, he discovers that it no longer backfires.

The motorist did not methodically analyze the operation of his engine to
determine the malfunction. He may not even know how an internal combustion engine operates. The motorist also did not search for a solution using any
of the search methods described earlier in this chapter. Instead, he used heuristic knowledge based on his prior experience to determine that the problem
was with the vacuum hose. The use of this type of heuristic knowledge is what
makes knowledge-based systems such a powerful tool.

A heuristic, then, *often* provides a correct solution to some problem. However, since it does not represent an exhaustive in-depth analysis, it occasionally gives incorrect answers or even fails to give any answers at all. This failure
to always be successful is based on its use of an "acceptable" choice rather than
the *true* correct answer. Heuristics represent an acceptable choice rather than
the correct choice because (1) the number of possibilities that must be examined is too large, (2) the algorithmic evaluation function applied to each possibility to determine if it is the correct answer is too complex, or (3) the
algorithmic evaluation function is unknown and must be approximated.

As will be seen, the use of heuristics in knowledge-based systems is
markedly different from the heuristic functions described in the previous sections for use in heuristic searches. The heuristic functions described above
represent general knowledge used to guide a search. Heuristics in knowledge-
based systems refer to the heuristic knowledge used by an expert in the solution of a problem. The latter is more domain-specific and deeper in nature.

An expert is a person who possesses skills that allow him to draw upon
past experiences and quickly focus on the core of a given problem. While a nonexpert may approach a problem in a systematic manner, employing a specific
procedurally oriented methodology (if one indeed exists), this approach may be
too complicated and subject to errors or else it may take an unacceptable
amount of time and effort. This blind use of the methodology may result from
limited understanding of the domain and its cause and effect relationships. An
expert, on the other hand, has a much higher success rate in solving problems
because he has acquired a set of powerful cause-and-effect relationships based
on experience. An expert is able to utilize this basic knowledge to recognize
quickly the salient features of the problem, categorize it according to these
characteristics, and correctly devise a solution.

The differences between heuristic and algorithmic techniques can be further illustrated through another real-world example. Consider the following:

A prospective home buyer arrives for a meeting with a residential building contractor carrying a set of architectural plans describing the design of a house. This

buyer desires an estimate of the cost of the house before committing to employ the contractor.

A contractor typically determines the price of the house by performing a detailed cost analysis. This involves carefully calculating the amount of material necessary to build the house; calling a building supply warehouse to obtain material prices; evaluating quotations from subcontractors on the cost of their labor; determining the appropriate contractors' fees; allowing a reasonable contingency figure, and so forth. This process has the advantage of nearly guaranteeing a correct result (assuming no computational errors are made) and entails very little risk for the contractor. The disadvantage, however, is that this process involves a significant amount of effort and time. What if this particular buyer needs a quotation today?

An experienced contractor (an expert!) has another option. He compares the size of this home to ones that he recently completed. By finding a home that has approximately the same square footage, he can obtain a rough estimate (based on his previous experience) for the price per square foot. He then looks for differences between the homes that might raise or lower the estimate. These differences might include additions like a swimming pool (raising his estimate by $15,000), modifications like pine kitchen cabinets rather than oak (decreasing his estimate by $1,500), or deletions such as two bathrooms rather than three (decreasing his estimate by $6,000). After evaluating these differences, he is able to make an estimate in only 30 minutes.

Obviously the advantage of the expert's approach is that he is able to give a timely quotation. The disadvantage is the possibility that a miscalculation will invalidate the estimate. But if the individual is a true expert, this is unlikely to occur.

The first approach is algorithmic: thorough, detailed, and highly accurate, but possibly inadequate due to its development time and effort. The second method is heuristic: not as thorough or detailed, but probably just as accurate and developed within acceptable limitations on time and effort. Thus, while the results of an algorithmic process are always precise and accurate, it is often the case that a heuristic estimate of almost equal accuracy can be made with significantly less effort. But only experts are capable of doing the latter and, often, a greater risk of being wrong exists.

1.5 KNOWLEDGE-BASED SYSTEMS—A DEFINITION

The stage has now been set for the definition of a knowledge-based system. In general terms, a knowledge-based system can be defined to be:

A computerized system that uses knowledge about some domain to arrive at a solution to a problem from that domain. This solution is essentially the same as that concluded by a person knowledgeable about the domain of the problem when confronted with the same problem.

If the definition of knowledge-based systems given above is followed strictly, however, many conventional software systems could be incorrectly categorized as knowledge-based systems.

For example, consider programs written in a conventional programming language (e.g., FORTRAN, PASCAL) that calculate currents and voltages in an electric circuit, analyze the stress factors in bridge trusses, calculate loan default risk, or simulate traffic flow in a city to determine the best traffic light configurations. All of these programs perform the same analysis as an expert in the field (albeit much faster!) and use the same knowledge (i.e., formulas).

Programs such as these have been around for years and yet they are not considered knowledge-based systems. The reason is that there is considerably more to knowledge-based systems than simply duplicating the knowledge and expertise of a human expert from a specific domain. A better definition of knowledge-based systems, therefore, is required to resolve this inconsistency. Knowledge-based systems are different from general search systems and from conventional software because of several fundamental concepts.

A knowledge-based system reflects the problem solving abilities of a human expert within some domain and uses these abilities to solve problems in much the same manner as the human expert. We now modify this general definition to describe more precisely what is meant by a knowledge-based system.

Three fundamental concepts of knowledge-based systems distinguish them from conventional algorithmic programs and from general search-based programs:

1. The separation of the knowledge from how it is used
2. The use of highly specific domain knowledge
3. The heuristic rather than algorithmic nature of the knowledge employed

The first idea traces historically from the General Problem Solver (GPS) [Newell, 1963], developed during the late 1950s and early 1960s. GPS solved problems by finding a sequence of operators that eliminated the difference between the initial state of a problem and one of the desired goal states. These operators represented general knowledge about what operations were possible within the domain. GPS used generic search techniques to find the right sequence of operators that would progressively decrease the distance between the original state and the goal state of the problem.

The second underlying concept was initially exploited during the late 1960s and early 1970s in the development of DENDRAL and Meta-DENDRAL [Lindsay, 1980]. DENDRAL infers the molecular structure of unknown compounds from mass spectral and nuclear magnetic response data, while Meta-DENDRAL assists in the determination of the dependence of mass spectrometric fragmentation on substructural features.

The third concept of using heuristic knowledge arose from the ability of humans to solve difficult problems without the continuous use of models

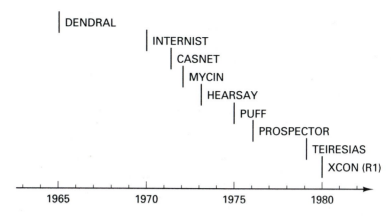

FIGURE 1.13   Approximate Starting Dates for Development of the Early Knowledge-based Systems

or algorithms. This concept was the common string of consistency between the early AI researchers and the development of the field of knowledge-based systems.

However, it was not until the development of the MYCIN system at Stanford University in the early 1970s [Shortliffe, 1976; Buchanan, 1984b] that these concepts were merged, creating the field of knowledge-based systems. As mentioned in the Foreword, MYCIN is a knowledge-based system developed to diagnose and specify treatments for blood disorders through a "conversation" with a physician. It directs this conversation by asking questions about the signs and symptoms of the patient and by requesting the performance of certain laboratory tests. Once the condition of the patient has been determined, the system recommends a drug treatment to correct the disorder.

Significant in MYCIN's development was the adherence of the researchers to the first two of the fundamental concepts shown above that were actually not fully recognized at that time. Their adherence to these principles led them to realize that the basic structure used in manipulating knowledge to arrive at a diagnosis and treatment within MYCIN (called the *inference mechanism*) could be used with knowledge from other domains (e.g., lung disease [Aikins, 1983], structural analysis [Bennett 1978], geology [Bonnet 1983], and software development [Underwood, 1981]) to perform the same style of diagnostic analysis. By removing the domain-specific knowledge (on diagnosis and treatment of blood disorders), they were left with the *essential* elements of MYCIN, or the *empty* shell of MYCIN called *EMYCIN*. This discovery proved to be quite significant in the evolution of knowledge-based systems.

A number of knowledge-based systems developed during the 1970s demonstrated the wide applicability of the techniques developed in DENDRAL and MYCIN to other domains. These other domains were medicine (CASNET, INTERNIST, PUFF, TEIRESIAS), spoken language understanding

(HEARSAY), geology (PROSPECTOR), and manufacturing (XCON). Figure 1.13 shows the historical progression of the various knowledge-based systems developed during the 1970s. Refer to the Foreword for the descriptions of some of these systems.

1.6 KNOWLEDGE-BASED SYSTEMS AND THE VARIOUS TYPES OF EXPERTISE

The word *expert* can be used to describe people possessing many different levels of skills or knowledge. A person can be an expert at a particular task irrespective of how sophisticated that area of expertise is. For example, there are expert bus drivers just as there are expert brain surgeons. Each of them excels in the performance of tasks in their respective field.

Thus, the concept of expertise must be classified for different types of domains. The skill levels of experts from different domains should not be compared to each other. All experts require the same basic cognitive skills. The difference is in the depth of their expertise when compared to others from their own domains (i.e., a highly skilled bus driver has greater abilities than a novice driver, just as an expert brain surgeon has greater skills than an intern).

The types of expertise of interest in knowledge-based systems can be classified into three distinct categories. Knowledge-based systems have had varying degrees of success when representing knowledge from each of these categories. These categories, discussed in the following subsections, are (1) associational (black box), (2) motor skills, and (3) theoretical (deep) knowledge.

1.6.1 Associational Knowledge

Knowledge-based systems excel in representing *associational* knowledge. This level of skill reflects heuristic ability or knowledge that is acquired mostly through observation. The expert may not understand what happens inside a black box, but he can associate the inputs with specific outputs.

In technical fields, it is usually desirable for an expert to have a detailed understanding of the underlying theory within that field. But is this absolutely necessary? What about the television technician who is considered an expert repairman, but who does not understand all of the complex internal workings of a transistor or a picture tube? This individual may have excellent associational understandings of these devices and, based on experience, may be able to fix almost any problem encountered. However, if she encounters a new, previously unseen problem, she may not know how to proceed. The knowledge used by this individual is typically in the form of rules (IF - THEN relationships) that cover most, if not all, of the possible situations. This type of expertise is the most commonly used throughout this book.

1.6.2 Motor Skills

Motor skill knowledge is physical rather than cognitive-oriented; therefore, knowledge-based systems cannot easily emulate this type of expertise. Humans learn these skills by repeatedly performing them. While some people have greater abilities for these types of skills than others, real learning and expertise result from persistent practice. For example, consider the tasks of

> driving an automobile
> riding a bicycle
> hitting a baseball
> downhill snow skiing

When you observe experts performing these activities, you notice that their reactions seem spontaneous and automatic. These reactions result from the experts' continual and persistent practice. For example, when a skilled baseball player bats he instinctively reacts to a curve ball, adjusting his swing to connect with the ball. This appropriate reaction results from encountering thousands of curve balls over many years. A novice batter might recognize that a curve ball was thrown but, due to a lack of practice, reacts slower and as a result, may strike out.

One reason why knowledge-based systems are poorly suited for solving problems requiring this type of knowledge is based, in part, on the limited capabilities of robotic technology. While present day robots can represent the required knowledge and can successfully use it for reasoning, their visual capabilities generally cannot quickly capture the necessary data and the manipulators cannot react with the required speeds. While robots can tie knots in ropes [Inoue, 1985], they are still many years from being expert at playing baseball.

1.6.3 Theoretical (Deep) Knowledge

Finding a solution to a technical problem often requires going beyond our basic understanding of the domain. We must apply creative ingenuity, ingenuity that is based on our theoretical knowledge of the domain. This type of knowledge allows experts to solve problems that have not been seen before and, therefore, are not associational in nature.

Such deeper, more theoretical knowledge is acquired through formal training and hands-on problem solving. Typically, this type of knowledge is possessed by engineers and scientists who have many years of formal training. Because of its theoretical and technical nature, this expertise is very easily forgotten unless continually used. As you have most likely determined, this knowledge cannot be easily duplicated in conventional knowledge-based systems at present. Model-based reasoning systems are a notable attempt to encapsulate this deep knowledge and reason with it. Such systems are discussed in Chapter 9.

1.7 FEATURES OF KNOWLEDGE-BASED SYSTEMS

Knowledge-based systems have a number of distinct advantages as well as disadvantages when compared to other solutions such as conventional software or human problem solvers.

1.7.1 Advantages

Knowledge-based systems have a number of advantages that encourage their development and use.

1. *Wide distribution of scarce expertise:* Knowledge-based systems reproduce the knowledge and skills possessed by experts—individuals who are considered to be experts because so few possess their specialized knowledge. This ability to reproduce an expert's knowledge allows for wide distribution of this expertise at a reasonable cost. For example, a company may have an expert on the legal aspects of federal tax laws. If the company has various groups that need this expertise, it may profit by developing a knowledge-based system on tax laws structured on the knowledge and skills of their tax expert, thereby providing all these groups unlimited access to the expert's skills. While the development of this system may not be trivial, it may be less costly than hiring additional tax lawyers to handle the heavy demand.

2. *Ease of modification:* The fundamental concept of the separation of knowledge from the reasoning mechanism eases the process of modifying the knowledge. This is an important feature in heuristic programming where changes may occur frequently. The tax expert system illustrates this feature since tax legislation changes every year. Ease of modification is a very desirable feature in these situations.

3. *Consistency of answers:* Different human experts often present dissimilar answers to the same problem. The same human expert may even provide slightly different results on various occasions. In some cases, these variations are minor inconsistencies with little or no consequence; in others, they are major flaws resulting from the poor health, emotional disposition, or stress of the expert. Knowledge-based systems, on the other hand, are always consistent in their problem-solving abilities, providing uniform answers at all times. There are no emotional or health considerations that can vary their performance.

4. *Perpetual accessibility:* Knowledge-based systems provide (almost) complete accessibility. They work 24 hours a day, weekends, and holidays. They take no sick leave or vacation.

5. *Preservation of expertise:* In situations where the turnover of experts is high, where an expert is in poor health, or about to retire, the experience and proficiency of an individual can be preserved for posterity in a knowledge-based system.

6. *Solution of problems involving incomplete data:* Knowledge-based systems, partially by virtue of their heuristic nature, are capable of solving problems where complete or exact data do not exist. This is an important feature because complete and accurate information on a problem is rarely available in the real world.

7. *Explanation of solution:* Partly due to their heuristic nature, knowledge-based systems track the knowledge used to generate solution(s). Thus, inquisitive or doubting users can query the system for explanations about how conclusions were derived. These explanations assist the user by clarifying and justifying the results and, additionally, provide a rudimentary form of tutoring, allowing the user to become more competent.

1.7.2 Disadvantages

Knowledge-based systems are not, however, the panacea some consider them to be. They have shortcomings of which a potential user needs to be aware:

1. *Answers may not always be correct:* Experts often make mistakes, so it is expected that knowledge-based systems will also make mistakes. These errors, however, can prove to be very expensive as might be the case with a tax expert system or a system monitoring a nuclear reactor.

2. *Knowledge limited to the domain of expertise:* Knowledge-based systems always endeavor to deduce a solution, regardless of whether or not the problem at hand is within the system's field of expertise. They have limited knowledge of what they know and when they know it. As a result, misleading or incorrect answers may be generated, which an unsuspecting user may take as fact. Humans, in contrast, know the limits of their knowledge and, as a result, qualify their answers or do not attempt to solve problems outside the boundaries of their expertise.

3. *Lack of common sense:* Common-sense knowledge can be difficult to represent in knowledge-based systems. Some measure of common sense can be represented, but it must be done explicitly. For example, it is commonly known that under normal circumstances, it is impossible to have water at a temperature of 20° Fahrenheit. An expert system would not know this, since this fact is more common-sense knowledge than domain knowledge. If the user specified a water temperature of 20° Fahrenheit,

the system would unknowingly plow ahead to derive an answer, not realizing that the value is sure to be incorrect. Compensation can be introduced by teaching the system explicitly that fresh water temperatures
below 32° Fahrenheit (at atmospheric pressures) are physically impossible and, therefore, incorrect. However, one would have to explicitly enter all such knowledge, which can be impractical in many situations.

In summary, knowledge-based systems provide an excellent approach for
solving a large class of problems, but each application must be chosen carefully so this technology is appropriately applied. In Chapter 11 we discuss the
topic of project selection in greater depth.

1.8 GenAID—A CASE STUDY

Since the creation of MYCIN, a great number of knowledge-based systems
have been developed. Some of these were originally intended to be research
prototypes, whose purpose was merely to show the applicability of the technology or to illustrate an alternative problem-solving strategy within the application domain. Other systems reached a certain stage in their development
and, for a variety of reasons (e.g., cost, lack of management interest) did not
progress into operational systems.

A minority of systems have reached operational status and are presently
in use [Feigenbaum, 1988]. These systems include XCON (see Foreword), one
of the earliest operational systems, and the Authorizer's Assistant, developed
by American Express Co. (also discussed in the Foreword). These systems were
developed for internal use within the sponsoring or developing organization,
where a highly skilled, forgiving set of users could be expected.

One of the earliest (if not the earliest) knowledge-based systems developed as a commercial product (i.e., for external users) was the Westinghouse
GenAID system [Gonzalez, 1986]. This system was developed in the early 1980s
by Westinghouse Electric Corporation, a manufacturer of large power generating equipment. Westinghouse decided that a market existed for an aid to
help its customers decrease the downtime of their turbine generators through
the early detection of potentially serious abnormal operating conditions.

From a financial standpoint, this domain presents the potential for significant cost savings. A large, base-loaded (i.e., continuously-operated) power
plant during the peak load seasons (winter and summer) has a typical downtime cost ranging from $60,000 to $250,000 *per day*, depending on the size and
the type of the plant. This daily cost reflects just the difference in cost for replacement power needed to supply their customer's load (since that power
must come from less efficient plants in their own system or must be purchased
from neighboring utilities, usually at a premium). It does not take into account the cost of repairing the broken unit. The magnitude of this problem be-

comes apparent when you realize that a major incident can cause downtimes ranging from three to six months!

The basis of the GenAID product was that many of these so-called major incidents actually started out as relatively minor faults that went undetected for a comparatively long period of time. This neglect caused the problem to become serious and, henceforth, led to a major incident. Had the problem been detected early, corrective action could have been taken to drastically reduce the outage from several months to two or three days (or even less).

Power generation equipment is typically well instrumented with sensors that are monitored continuously by a data acquisition system. If the data were to be inspected periodically by a knowledgeable individual (an expert), these incipient failures could be detected in time to take corrective action. The problem is that typical power plant personnel do not have the expertise to be able to interpret properly these sets of readings. By providing this expertise to a typical power station, presumably, major incidents could be avoided.

Westinghouse first attempted to solve this problem with a microprocessor-based system using probabilistic analysis. The system worked well for up to ten possible malfunctions, but had a number of serious limitations. These included a difficulty in representing knowledge and the inability to handle more than one malfunction at a time. Additionally, computations became too complex for the system when more than ten malfunctions were represented. For these reasons, the focus of the research turned to knowledge-based systems which, at the time (1979), was a fairly obscure technology.

In 1980, Westinghouse embarked on the development of a tool that would ease the representation of the knowledge concerning malfunctions and their repair. The resulting product, called Process Diagnostic System (PDS), was jointly developed by the Westinghouse R&D Laboratories in Pittsburgh and the Robotics Institute at Carnegie-Mellon University. The first piece of equipment chosen for commercial application of on-line diagnostics was the electric generator. GenAID, which stands for Generator Artificial Intelligence Diagnostics, represents the combination of PDS and the specific diagnostic knowledge used by experts to detect problems in these generators. GenAID resides at a central location in Orlando, FL, where it accepts data directly from the plant site on a semicontinuous basis and diagnoses any developing malfunctions in real time. Because of limitations in the sensors monitoring the generators, the input data have some associated uncertainty that causes the results produced by GenAID to rarely be absolutely certain. As a result, all diagnoses produced are qualified by a numeric value representing the likelihood of the problem being present. These results are transmitted to the plant site over a data link for use by the plant operators.

Development on the GenAID knowledge base began in 1983 with limited service starting one year later. The development was completed in 1987. As of 1990, there were ten generators connected to the system with four others in the process of installation.

In its short existence, GenAID has been successful in diagnosing a number of problems that might have otherwise gone undetected and resulted in serious incidents. As a result, Westinghouse has proceeded to extend this concept to other pieces of equipment, such as the steam turbine, that it manufactures.

1.9 DEVELOPMENT OF KNOWLEDGE-BASED SYSTEMS

Development of a knowledge-based system differs from that of standard software. While the latter's requirements can be rather easily defined, in most cases this is not as easily done for problems suitable for solution by knowledge-based systems. Human expertise is difficult to define and even more difficult to elicit. Thus, it is incumbent on the developer of a knowledge-based system to maintain close contact with the expert(s) throughout the entire development process. It is this constant and almost continuous interaction that separates knowledge-based systems development from that of conventional software.

The desirable qualities for knowledge-based systems development personnel are also quite different. Instead of solely possessing knowledge of computers and programming languages, the developers of knowledge-based systems must depend equally upon intuition and personal qualities, such as the ability to get along well with others, to be successful. Their knowledge of computers and languages is not to be discounted; however, many of the techniques they employ are different from those used in developing standard software.

Whereas the conventional software developer has been given the name of software engineer, the knowledge-based systems developer is called a *knowledge engineer*, and the development process has been dubbed *knowledge engineering*. A definition of the knowledge engineering process is:

> The acquisition of knowledge in some domain from one or more non-electronic sources, and its conversion into a form that can be utilized by a computer to solve problems that, typically, can only be solved by persons extensively knowledgeable in that domain.

During the development of a knowledge-based system, a knowledge engineer faces many challenges unlike those seen by her counterparts in software engineering. As the name implies, knowledge engineering is heavily related to problem-solving knowledge.

Note that this definition of knowledge engineering makes no mention of the development of the underlying program utilizing the knowledge to solve the problem. The job of a knowledge engineer, like that of other engineers, is to use existing and available tools to solve a problem. Nevertheless, should an adequate tool not be available, the knowledge engineer should possess the appropriate skills to develop one.

Knowledge engineering, however, involves more than merely translating the knowledge from human terms to a machine-readable form. Knowledge engineering expertise involves recognizing what knowledge is being used to solve a problem, categorizing this knowledge, and determining the best way to represent it. This last step is of utmost significance since improperly represented knowledge may ultimately doom a knowledge-based system development project. One problem is that the impact of a poor representation may not be immediately felt. The developer may expend significant effort creating a system that, ultimately, must be completely redeveloped due to the use of a poor knowledge representation paradigm.

The methodology of knowledge engineering is rapidly progressing. Beginning in Chapter 10, we present some of the practical aspects of this evolving field. Further explorations and refinements within this field will ultimately transform these techniques from their current state as an art into a true science.

1.10 CHAPTER REVIEW

The fundamental underpinnings of artificial intelligence are based on the concept of searching through a problem (or solution) space. Various types of search techniques are described in this chapter. These search techniques can be divided into three general categories: random, blind, and directed. AI makes its most significant contribution in the directed category.

The difference between knowledge-based systems and conventional software is that conventional software uses algorithms to solve problems, while knowledge-based systems solve problems where algorithmic solutions either do not exist or are very costly to implement. Knowledge-based systems use heuristic knowledge instead. Various examples are given that describe this difference.

There are three basic types of expertise:

1. **Associational expertise.** The internal workings of a device or system are not understood, but its symptomatic behavior is used to solve problems. This is the type of expertise best represented in knowledge-based systems.
2. **Motor skills expertise.** This is expertise requiring motor skills to carry it out. A person becomes better at these tasks by practicing them over and over again. Sports and physical tasks are examples of this type of expertise. Knowledge-based systems are not suited to represent this type of knowledge.

3. Theoretical expertise. The internal workings of a system or device are well understood. This allows experts with this knowledge to solve problems that they might never have seen before. Advances in representing this kind of knowledge in knowledge-based systems is continuing.

But while knowledge-based systems are not solutions for every problem, they do have several advantages including their

1. Ability to widely distribute the scarce resource of an expert's knowledge
2. Ease of modification
3. Consistency of answers
4. Perpetual accessibility
5. Preservation of expertise
6. Ability to solve problems involving incomplete data
7. Ability to explain solutions

These advantages are not without some disadvantages:

1. Their answers may not always be correct.
2. Their knowledge is limited to the domain of expertise.
3. Their lack of common sense.

To provide an indication of a good, successful knowledge-based system application, we described the Westinghouse GenAID system, its purpose, and operation.

This chapter set the groundwork for *The Practice* section of this book by introducing the concept of knowledge-based systems development. Knowledge engineering, as it is called, is different from more traditional software engineering and is the subject of the last eight chapters of this book.

1.11 PROBLEMS

1-1. Classify the following types of knowledge as "associational," "motor skill," or "theoretical." Explain your classification.
 (a) Repairing a broken vase
 (b) Repairing a flat tire on a bicycle
 (c) Tying a shoe lace
 (d) Replacing a burned out light bulb
 (e) Writing a computer program
 (f) Debugging a computer program
 (g) Assembling a model car from a set of instructions

 (h) Baking a cake

1-2. Identify five commonly used heuristics to get into a house or apartment when you are locked out. Why is each of these a heuristic?

1-3. Consider a jigsaw puzzle. Identify a set of heuristics that can be used in assembling the puzzle.

1-4. Finding a path from one location to another within any city involves the use of heuristics since traffic patterns vary from hour to hour and day to day. Pick two places in your city (e.g., your apartment and campus) and identify a set of heuristics based upon the time of day that you use daily when traveling from one to the other.

1-5. Consider the following maze.
  (a) How would you search this maze for a solution using a blind, depth-first search? Why is this blind? Why is this depth-first?
  (b) How would you search this maze using a blind, breadth-first search? Why is this breadth-first?

Start

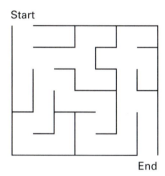

End

1-6. "It is possible for a depth-first search to find a shorter solution path for a problem than a breadth-first search." Explain why you agree or disagree.

1-7. "Using heuristics always helps you find a solution to a problem quicker than searching blindly." Explain why you agree or disagree.

1-8. Consider the sliding tile problem shown below. The objective is to get all the tiles in numeric order as shown in the figure on the right. Several different heuristics can be employed when attempting to

solve this problem. These heuristics include counting the number of tiles that are misplaced (the figure on the left has six tiles misplaced), counting the number of squares each tile must move through to get in its proper position (the figure on the left has a total of six tile moves to get in proper order), and summing the absolute values of the differences between each tile's value and the value that should be in the tile's position (if we assume a value of zero in the empty tile position, the figure on the left has a sum of 18). When the value of any of these heuristics reaches zero, you have a solution.
  (a) Using the tile problem on the left, perform a branch and bound search using each of these heuristics.
  (b) Which heuristic appears to have the best performance?
  (c) Construct your own heuristic which is better than all of these. *Hint:* Your heuristic can be a composite of several simple heuristics including the ones discussed.

	1	3
5	2	6
4	7	8

$\Longrightarrow$

1	2	3
4	5	6
7	8	

1-9. In Figure 1.12 node B is expanded before node C. Why is its estimated cost value lower than C's?

1-10. What happens in the A* algorithm if the heuristic estimates are all zero? What search is this?

2 ■ Knowledge-based Systems Structure

2.1 INTRODUCTION

In this chapter we examine the internal structure of knowledge-based systems. Knowledge-based systems are complex computer programs that can be viewed from several different perspectives. They remind us of the story of the five blind men from Hindustan who encountered an elephant for the first time. After each touched the elephant, he described it from his uniquely different point of view—"it's a snake" (the trunk), "it's a spear" (a tusk), "it's a fan" (an ear), "it's a tree" (a leg), and "it's a wall" (the body). Similarly, a knowledge-based system appears quite different depending on your perspective.

Each blind man experienced some limited element of all of the features that comprise the elephant and formed his impression based on this constrained information. When learning about knowledge-based systems, we must be careful to gain exposure to the whole, not just some limited features. Without this perspective, we will be like the blind men, having formed an incomplete and imprecise understanding of what a knowledge-based system really is and, as a result, will be unable to utilize its power effectively and efficiently.

In this chapter, we present three points of view that are commonly taken of these systems. These views represent the three different types of individuals who interact with a knowledge-based system: the end user, the knowledge engineer, and the tool builder. Each of these individuals has a unique view of what a knowledge-based system is. We present these three views, in order, from the simple to the complex.

2.2 SYSTEM COMPONENTS—END-USER'S VIEW

The simplest point of view is that of the end user, the individual for whom the knowledge-based system is being developed. See Figure 2.1. From his perspective, a knowledge-based system consists of three components: the *intelligent program*, the *user interface*, and a *problem-specific database*. Let us examine each of these components in turn.

2.2.1 The Intelligent Program

To the end user, the intelligent program contains all of the intelligence of the system. He typically has no comprehension of how this program operates and, most likely, does not really care. The system is simply a black box that operates according to some unknown logic and derives the results that he wants. The later chapters of this book provide several examples of these intelligent programs. The development of these intelligent programs is the responsibility of the knowledge engineer and the expert with whom she interacts.

2.2.2 The User Interface

The user interface serves to provide the end user with a friendly means of communicating with the intelligent program. It does this by providing convenient interaction using menus, natural language, and/or graphical displays. This interface can be used for the following purposes:

1. Enabling the intelligent program to pose questions to the user about the problem at hand
2. Providing explanations about why it (the intelligent program) is asking particular questions

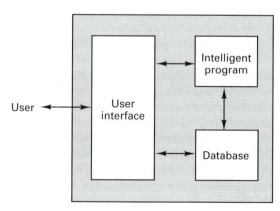

FIGURE 2.1   User's View of a Knowledge-based System

3. Allowing the user to query the intelligent program as to why or how a particular decision was made
4. Displaying the derived results
5. Providing graphic output for the derived results
6. Allowing the user to save or print the results

A user interface may perform many other functions. The above list is only a sample.

While an end user does not really worry much about the intelligent program, he can be quite picky about the user interface. Its design must be carefully considered so that it is properly matched to the target users. For example, if the intended user is an individual who is highly computer literate, the interface features probably need not be quite as sophisticated as those intended for users who are unfamiliar with computer technology.

Knowledge-based system projects have been known to fail due to inadequate design of their user interface. The emphasis in the development of a knowledge-based system has traditionally been with the expert and trying to represent his knowledge. Often, however, the end users are not consulted about their needs at any point in the development process. Consequently, they may refuse to use a developed system despite its intelligence and helpfulness. Development of the user interface belongs with the knowledge engineer, although what she is able to do depends greatly upon what the tool builder has provided. We discuss this topic further in later chapters of this book.

2.2.3 The Problem-specific Database

The final component visible to the end user is the problem-specific database. The database contains all of the information provided by the user about the current problem and all conclusions that the intelligent program has been able to derive. These conclusions include both the final ones representing the solution required by the user and intermediate ones that act as stepping stones in the intelligent program's path to the ultimate conclusion. For example, when trying to diagnose a case of the flu, a physician needs to determine whether the patient's temperature is "high." Such an intermediate conclusion can be reached after measuring the actual patient's temperature (e.g., 101° F). The actual temperature is a known input, the qualified temperature value of "high" is an intermediate conclusion, and the diagnosis of "flu" is the final conclusion.

This database fully describes (from the user's point of view) all facts that are currently known about this problem and serves as the description of the problem for the intelligent program. This data may in some cases actually be derived by a data management system that interfaces directly with the knowledge-based system. In other cases, however, it may be a set of sensor readings collected automatically by a data acquisition system or simply a group of answers provided by the end user in response to queries generated by the intelligent program itself.

As with all computer systems, a knowledge-based system depends on accurate data describing the problem—erroneous data can result in drawing inaccurate conclusions. Although it is true that knowledge-based systems can operate with imprecise, incomplete, and often incorrect data, it is obvious that the more correct, precise, and complete the data are, the better the results that the system derives. The gathering of the initial data for this database is the responsibility of the user. The intelligent program derives the intermediate and the final conclusions as the result of its operation on these initial data and places these results in the database. The knowledge engineer is responsible for defining the knowledge that the intelligent program must possess to "understand" these data.

2.3 SYSTEM COMPONENTS—KNOWLEDGE ENGINEER'S VIEW

The job of the knowledge engineer is to build a knowledge-based system by interacting with a domain expert. Through a series of interviews with the expert, the knowledge engineer gleans the knowledge possessed by the expert so that it can be incorporated within a knowledge-based system.

From the knowledge engineer's view, a knowledge-based system consists of two major components: the *intelligent program* and the *development shell*. See Figure 2.2. The intelligent program is the product developed for the end user. It is identical to the one the end user sees except that, from the standpoint of the knowledge engineer, we can open the black box and see what is inside. The development shell is a set of tools that eases the creation of the knowledge within the intelligent program.

2.3.1 Intelligent Program

In Chapter 1 we introduced the idea that one fundamental characteristic of all knowledge-based systems is the clear and clean separation between the knowledge that the system is using and the program that utilizes it for problem solving. The two components that compose the intelligent program are, therefore, a *knowledge base* and an *inference engine*.

2.3.1.1 The knowledge base.   The knowledge base represents the most important component of a knowledge-based system. It contains all of the relevant, domain-specific, problem-solving knowledge that has been gathered by the knowledge engineer from the various sources available to her. This knowledge can be viewed from two perspectives: its nature and its format.

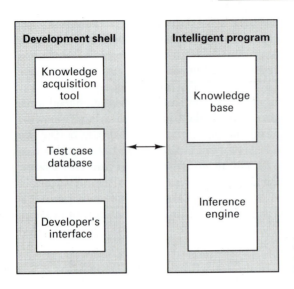

FIGURE 2.2 Knowledge Engineer's View of a Knowledge-based System

The nature of the knowledge refers to whether the knowledge is algorithmic or heuristic. Most knowledge-based applications occur in domains where algorithmic problem-solving approaches either do not work well or do not exist. The knowledge instead consists of many "rules of thumb" that have been learned and developed over years of practical problem solving. This knowledge must be extracted from the domain-specific expert through the process of knowledge extraction. Chapters 13 through 15 detail this process.

The format of the knowledge refers to how this knowledge is represented internally within the knowledge-based system so that it can be used in problem solving. Several knowledge representation schemes are commonly used: predicates, rules, associative networks, frames, and objects. Each of these schemes has different advantages and disadvantages, and a knowledge engineer must be aware of them when developing a knowledge-based system. The details of these schemes are discussed in Chapters 3 through 6.

2.3.1.2 The inference engine.   The second component of the intelligent program is the inference engine. The inference engine is the interpreter of the knowledge stored in the knowledge base. It examines the contents of the knowledge base and the data accumulated about the current problem and derives additional data and conclusions.

The set of problems that a particular knowledge-based system is designed to cover can be viewed as a very large graph. See Figure 2.3. On one side of the graph are a series of nodes representing all of the signs, symptoms, characteristics, and features of interest that are used as inputs when attempting to solve these problems. On the other side are nodes representing all of the possible solutions to the problem. All other nodes are the intermediate

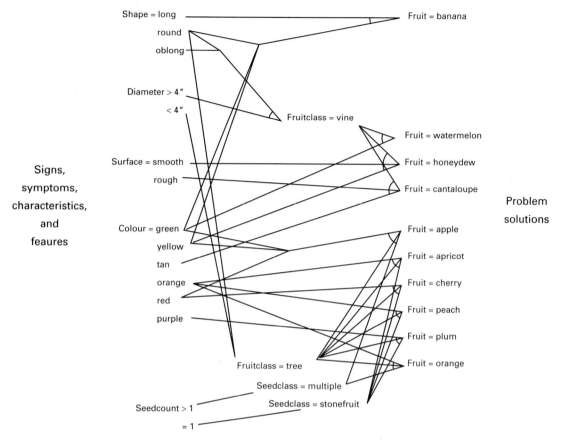

FIGURE 2.3   Problem Description Graph

conclusions discussed above. The arcs connecting the nodes in the graph depict the knowledge used by the expert during problem solving that has been gathered from the expert and stored in the knowledge base. Thus, this knowledge specifies how new conclusions can be deduced from existing facts (or earlier derived conclusions). The process of deriving a solution to a problem can be viewed simplistically as one of finding a connection between the inputs and a conclusion.

The inference engine attempts to find connections between the features and the solutions. The creation of these connections can occur in several different ways. The inference engine might attempt to work from the features to the solutions (called *forward reasoning*), from the solutions to the features (*backward reasoning*), or from both ends simultaneously (*bidirectional reasoning*). The particular method used depends upon characteristics of the problem domain and the reasoning of the expert. More details on these reasoning schemes are provided in Chapters 4 and 5.

Although there are various means for representing knowledge in a knowledge base (e.g., rules, frames), it should be obvious that the inference engine must support the representation scheme appropriate for the application and use by the system developer. This problem is actually much more significant than it appears, since many inference engines use the same knowledge representation paradigms but implement them using different methods or syntax. This problem is alleviated somewhat by the existence of development shells.

2.3.2 The Development Shell

The development shell assists the knowledge engineer in structuring, debugging, modifying, and expanding the knowledge gathered from the expert. A development shell typically contains three components: a *knowledge acquisition tool*, a *test case database*, and the *developer's interface*. Depending on the type and size of the knowledge-based system, some of these components are not always necessary, although all are helpful. Nevertheless, we describe them all below.

2.3.2.1 Knowledge acquisition tool.
The knowledge acquisition tool assists the knowledge engineer in the construction of the knowledge base. The knowledge engineer has interacted with the expert and has acquired knowledge from this expert. She must now take this knowledge and represent it within the knowledge-based system. In its simplest form, this tool acts solely as a knowledge base editor. It merely provides a view of the knowledge and allows the knowledge engineer to make whatever changes are desired.

In its most complicated form, this tool provides a wide range of features. It assists the knowledge engineer in locating "bugs" within the knowledge base, it compares existing knowledge to new knowledge attempting to "second guess" what the knowledge engineer really means should she not be as precise and exact as required, and it provides bookkeeping functions to keep a record of all modifications that have been made, who made them, when they were made, and why they were made. A tool that provides these features can greatly assist the knowledge engineer and significantly shorten the development time of a knowledge-based system.

2.3.2.2 Test case database.
The knowledge acquisition tool enables the knowledge engineer to make potentially significant changes to the knowledge base by deleting or modifying existing knowledge or adding new knowledge. The deletion of existing knowledge might eliminate important relationships, just as the modification of existing knowledge might change important relationships, and the addition of new knowledge might introduce contradictions. Any of these could compromise the correctness of the overall knowledge base.

Therefore, checks must be made to ensure that these changes improve rather than degrade the problem-solving abilities of the knowledge-based system.

To aid the knowledge engineer in verifying that these changes are improvements, many knowledge-based systems include a test case database. This database consists of sample problems that have been successfully executed on the knowledge base. Whenever a change to the knowledge base is made, we can execute these test cases to verify that degradation of the knowledge base has not occurred.

2.3.2.3 Developer's interface.   The final component of the development shell is the developer's interface. This is the same as the interface seen by the end user discussed previously, except that it contains additional features to assist the knowledge engineer in the development process.

The developer's interface allows the knowledge engineer to exercise the knowledge base as it is being modified and tested. This permits the knowledge engineer to see exactly how the system will operate when delivered to the end user. Features within this interface include the ability to question the system about what portions of the knowledge are currently being used in the problem-solving process; explanations about why certain questions are being asked; details on why and how particular results are derived; and a convenient interaction using menus, natural language, and/or graphical displays. When combined with the features of the knowledge acquisition tool, this provides the knowledge engineer with a powerful environment for developing a knowledge-based system.

2.4 SYSTEM COMPONENTS—TOOL BUILDER'S VIEW

The tool builder has a view of a knowledge-based system that is very similar to that of the knowledge engineer. He is very concerned with providing an adequate set of tools for the knowledge engineer to ease the knowledge engineer's task in building the knowledge-based system. From an external point of view, the tool builder perceives a system in the same way as that of the knowledge engineer. He differs from the knowledge engineer in his focus. See Figure 2.4.

When examining the knowledge base, he worries about what problems the knowledge engineer will try to solve using this system. This, in part, requires that he be concerned about what knowledge representation scheme(s) will provide the knowledge engineer with the greatest flexibility in representing knowledge from this domain. Some questions that should be asked to help in ascertaining this are:

1. Can the knowledge be represented using rules, associative networks, frames, or will it require some combination of these schemes?

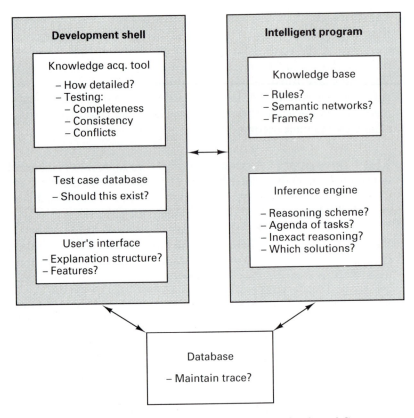

FIGURE 2.4 Tool Builder's View of a Knowledge-based System

2. What is the most suitable reasoning scheme for the inference engine to use in processing the knowledge and data?

3. Should backward, forward, bidirectional, or some alternative reasoning scheme be provided?

4. Is the problem being solved complex—consisting of many small sub-tasks—that might necessitate maintaining an agenda of potential tasks that need completion?

5. How should the system deal with inexact knowledge and data? Various uncertainty management schemes have their own advantages and disadvantages. Chapter 8 provides details on the four most commonly used numerical methods.

6. Should all derived solutions be presented or only the "best" solution?

The tool builder is additionally concerned with what features and tools the system should provide to the knowledge engineer within the development shell:

1. How detailed should the explanations be?
2. Should a test case database be maintained?
3. Should a trace of the execution be maintained so the user can see what knowledge was considered and what knowledge was actually used?
4. Should the knowledge base be automatically tested for completeness of coverage, consistency, and/or conflicting knowledge?
5. How detailed should the knowledge editor be?
6. What features should the user interface provide?

The answers to these various questions determine the structure of the resulting knowledge-based system. In Chapters 3 through 8 we examine many of these issues in detail so you will gain the skills needed to function as a tool builder, or to select an appropriate tool intelligently.

2.5 KNOWLEDGE-BASED TOOLS

In the course of this chapter, we have repeatedly referred to the "tools" used to build knowledge-based systems. We now define that term, expand upon it, and rename it, since we use it frequently in the following chapters.

Generally, there are two methods for developing a knowledge-based system. These are (1) using a "tool," or (2) developing a system from scratch.

A development tool is a software package that contains some or all of the components and features that we described in the knowledge engineer's view of a system, except the knowledge. The knowledge engineer uses this package to develop a knowledge base and possibly a specialized user interface. Such tools are commonly called *expert system shells*. However, we do not particularly like the term *expert system*, because it limits the scope of knowledge-based systems to applications where expert-level knowledge is required. Thus, we refer to these tools as *knowledge-based shells* or simply *shells*.

2.5.1 Shells

Numerous shells are commercially available. They range in price from less than one hundred dollars to tens of thousands of dollars. They also range widely in the number of features that they offer. It is not our intent to make a commercial comparison of the various shells. We will, however, roughly classify them according to the knowledge representation paradigms that they support. These are:

1. Inductive shells
2. Rule-based shells
3. Hybrid shells
4. Special purpose shells

Inductive shells are the simplest. In these systems the knowledge engineer specifies example cases as a matrix of known data (or premises) and their resulting effects (or conclusions). This matrix is then converted into a decision tree or a set of *IF-THEN* statements. The advantage of inductive systems is that knowledge acquisition is performed through the specification of these examples. While all problems do not lend themselves to this approach, for those that do, the task of the knowledge engineer is one of selecting the proper examples to present to the inductive tool. This is often simpler than distilling the knowledge from these examples. Inductive systems are the subject of further discussion in Chapter 15.

Rule-based shells range from the simple to the complex. Some simple rule-based shells are really nothing more than decision trees with good user interfaces. These shells are limited to solving fairly simple problems. Other rules-based shells are quite sophisticated. They structure the rules into subsets and provide extensive rule-editing features. No matter what degree of sophistication is involved, however, the knowledge within these shells is expressed as *IF-THEN* rules that describe situations that might occur and conclusions that can be drawn if the situations become true. Appendices A and B discuss two different types of rule-based shells, the Personal Consultant Plus system developed by Texas Instruments and the CLIPS system developed by NASA.

The more sophisticated shells, called *hybrid shells*, support multiple knowledge-representation paradigms, as well as various reasoning schemes. These systems allow the knowledge engineer to represent knowledge not only as rules but also as associative networks, frames, and/or objects, thereby giving the knowledge engineer great latitude in developing a proper knowledge structure. Because these various representation paradigms require different reasoning schemes, these systems are typically quite complex, as well as powerful.

Such shells can be quite expensive and usually require specialized workstations, but some implementations on microcomputers do exist. Their biggest advantage is that they are applicable to a wide range of problems since they are a generic tool.

Special purpose shells also exist that were specifically designed for particular types of problems. For example, one type of special purpose shells specializes in the diagnosis of process control systems. However, it should be noted that because it is designed for a highly specialized domain, it cannot be comfortably used for many other types of problems.

2.5.2 Developing a System from Scratch

Developing a system from scratch involves considerably more time and effort than selecting a preexisting shell. This results from the knowledge engineer performing not only her normal function as a knowledge gatherer, but the function of tool builder as well. The result may in fact be the development of a new shell that may greatly resemble other commercially available shells.

While this additional effort is a serious disadvantage, there are some distinct advantages to this approach. One is that the knowledge engineer is not tied to the constraints imposed by the tool builder. The tool builder tries to satisfy a large cross section of the marketplace since he is building a generic tool and may thus compromise on the features and capabilities that are implemented. By building her own tool, the knowledge engineer becomes a tool builder as well and, as such, designs a system that meets her requirements while making no compromises. Finally, when bugs appear in the shell, the knowledge engineer does not need access to another individual (the tool builder) for support in correcting these bugs since she was the developer.

Generally speaking, however, for any well-defined problem, the available commercial shells should be investigated thoroughly before considering the development of a system from scratch because of the time and effort required to develop a shell.

2.6 CHAPTER REVIEW

A knowledge-based system can be viewed from three different perspectives: an end-user's, a knowledge engineer's, and a tool developer's.

Each of these individuals sees a knowledge-based system with increasing levels of detail. An end user, being concerned only with solving a problem with the knowledge-based system, considers it to be a black box, generally labeled an *intelligent program*, with which he communicates through the user interface. Depending on the nature of the system, he may also have to develop a database that defines some inputs to the system.

A knowledge engineer, being the developer of the knowledge-based system, sees considerably more detail, since the black box of the intelligent program becomes transparent. This program is subdivided into a knowledge base (which she develops) and an inference engine. The knowledge engineer generally considers the inference engine to be a black box in its own right. The knowledge engineer sees the intelligent program, not through the user interface but through the development shell that is designed to ease her work. This development shell (also called an environment), was supplied by the tool builder and includes features such as a knowledge acquisition environment, a test case database, and a development interface.

The most complex point of view of the knowledge-based system comes from the perspective of a tool developer. He develops the inference engine as well as the development shell. Involved in this development effort are decisions concerning how general should the tool be. A general tool is useful for a larger cross section of applications with the potential cost of decreased power and/or efficiency. Conversely, a highly specialized tool limits the market applicability, but includes enhanced features that may be quite attractive to this segment of the market.

2.7 PROBLEMS

2-1. List and discuss the features that you, as an end user, would like to have in the following systems:
  - **(a)** Diagnostic assistant for a physician in general practice
  - **(b)** Diagnostic assistant for an automobile mechanic
  - **(c)** System for scheduling classes at a university
  - **(d)** Academic advisor for a college student
  - **(e)** Stock market advisor
  - **(f)** Aircraft design assistant
  - **(g)** Coaching assistant to help a football coach call plays during a game
  - **(h)** On-line diagnostic system for a turbine generator (such as GenAID)
  - **(i)** Local weather forecaster's assistant

2-2. What are the desirable features that are common to most of the systems described in Problem 2-1?

2-3. What features are specific for only a few of the above systems?

2-4. Could any of the systems described in Problem 2-1 be implemented using conventional programming techniques?

2-5. For those systems in Problem 2-4 that were considered to be solvable using conventional programming techniques, which are more easily implemented using knowledge-based techniques (based on your limited knowledge about knowledge-based systems)?

2-6. Given your limited exposure to knowledge-based systems, list any other types of problem-solving systems that could more easily be implemented using knowledge-based system techniques.

2-7. Identify all of the end-user features that you would like to see in the systems you specified in your answer to Problem 2-6.

2-8. Discuss the features that you would like to see in the knowledge acquisition shell for the systems listed in Problem 2-1 and in the systems listed in your solution to Problem 2-6.

2-9. Identify for the CLIPS shell discussed in Appendix A the advantages and disadvantages to its (a) user interface and (b) knowledge acquisition shell.

2-10. Identify for the Personal Consultant Plus (PC Plus) shell discussed in Appendix B the advantages and disadvantages to its (a) user interface and (b) knowledge acquisition shell.

2-11. Does CLIPS or PC Plus have a better user interface? Why?

2-12. Does CLIPS or PC Plus have a better knowledge acquisition shell? Why?

2-13. If you had to select either CLIPS or PC Plus to solve a knowledge-based problem, which would you select based only on its user interfaces and knowledge acquisition shell? Why?

3 ▰ Logic and Automated Reasoning

3.1 INTRODUCTION

The field of artificial intelligence is deeply rooted in logic. Logic is quite significant within the context of AI, and especially knowledge-based systems, because it provides a formalism for the two important concepts in knowledge-based systems: (1) *representation of knowledge* and (2) *automation of the inferencing process.*

Some of the earliest efforts within AI occurred in theorem proving and deductive reasoning, both based heavily on predicate logic. More recently, formal logic, as predicate logic, has been successfully used for developing knowledge-based systems as a language that provides a reasoning mechanism and a means of representing knowledge—all in one package. Formal logic has served as a theoretically satisfying foundation for its many variations that have been implemented in knowledge-based systems and that also populate the research literature, such as fuzzy logic, and so forth.

The study of logic is generally attributed to the ancient Greeks, specifically Socrates, Plato (as contained in *The Republic*), and Aristotle. Logic originated as a method to propose arguments in oratory that could be defended through a generally accepted set of rules of reasoning. These rules were used to evaluate the truth of the presented arguments in light of other statements known to be true and would irrefutably accept these arguments as either true or false.

Further developments in logic, however, were slow to form. It was not until the nineteenth century when George Boole, a British mathematician, adapted the laws of conventional algebraic manipulation and operations to logical statements that the field began to flourish. Boole defined a new algebra (now called *Boolean algebra*) that used *truth tables* to evaluate the truth value of compound logical statements. His mathematical treatment of these statements formed much of the foundation of subsequent advances in logic and is used even today in the design of computers.

This chapter starts its discussion of logic by introducing *propositional logic*. A more general format for representing statements, known as *predicate logic*, that is more widely used in logic-based AI is then described. This is followed by a discussion of automated reasoning as defined in predicate logic, including the various types of inference that are typically used to automate the reasoning process in knowledge-based systems. Finally, we briefly discuss PROLOG, a programming language based on predicate logic, which pulls together all the features described within this chapter.

3.2 PROPOSITIONAL LOGIC

Propositional logic is one of the oldest as well as one of the simplest forms of logic. Using a primitive representation language, it allows us to depict and manipulate (e.g., reason about) facts about the world. Propositional logic assists this reasoning by providing a mechanism that enables us first to evaluate *simple statements* and, subsequently, *complex statements* formed through the use of propositional connectives (e.g., *and, or*). This mechanism determines the truth of a statement from the truth values assigned to the original simple statements.

A *proposition* is a simple statement having a value of either *true* (T) or *false* (F). Simple statements are typically used to express some state or fact about the world. For example, consider the following facts:

```
             Today is Friday
          It rained yesterday
               It is cold
```

Propositional logic allows us to assign a truth value to each of these entire statements, but has no facilities to analyze the individual words that compose the statements. Consequently, the representation of the above statements as propositions might be

```
             today-is-friday
             yesterday-rain
               it-is-cold
```

Propositions can also be combined with other propositions in order to express more complex concepts about the world. For example,

```
        (Today is Friday) and (It is cold)
```

can be expressed in propositional logic as

Today–is–friday and it–is–cold

A *well-formed formula (wff)* is either a simple or compound proposition that is meaningful and whose truth value can be properly determined. Examining the above statement, we can see that this wff is a compound proposition composed of two simple propositions (each of which is also a wff) joined together through the logical *and* connective. Each of these wff's (both the two simple wff's and the compound wff) has an associated truth value. Propositional logic provides a mechanism for assigning a truth value to the compound proposition based upon the truth values of the individual simple propositions and the nature of the connective involved.

The basic connectives of propositional logic are shown in Table 3.1. The truth tables for the three basic operators are depicted in Table 3.2.

TABLE 3.1   BASIC PROPOSITIONAL LOGIC CONNECTIVES

English name	Connective name	Connective symbol
Conjunction	AND	$\wedge$
Disjunction	OR	$\vee$
Negation	Not	$\sim$
Material implication	If-Then	$\rightarrow$
Material equivalence	Equals	$\equiv$

TABLE 3.2   TRUTH TABLE FOR OR, AND, AND NOT OPERATORS

p	q	Disjunction $p \vee q$	Conjunction $p \wedge q$	Negation $\sim p$
T	T	T	T	F
T	F	T	F	F
F	T	T	F	T
F	F	F	F	T

The material implication connective can be thought of as a conditional such that

if $A \rightarrow B$ is to be true,
then whenever A is true, B must always be true.

Table 3.3 shows the truth table for this operator. The last two lines of this table can be quite perplexing to a student, so let's discuss them a little further.

TABLE 3.3   TRUTH TABLE FOR MATERIAL
IMPLICATION CONNECTIVE

		Material implication	Material equivalence
p	q	$p \rightarrow q$	$p \equiv q$
T	T	T	T
T	F	F	F
F	T	T	F
F	F	T	T

What these lines state is that when p is not true, q can be either true or false without altering the validity of the clause, since the operator cannot make any inferences about q's value.

Various equivalences in propositional logic merit description. See Table 3.4. These are very similar to those of Boolean algebra (where $\wedge$ is the symbol for *meet* and $\vee$ is the symbol for *join*) and the Boolean algebra of sets (where $\wedge$ is more specifically the symbol for *intersection* and $\vee$ is the symbol for *union*).

TABLE 3.4   EQUIVALENCES IN PROPOSITIONAL LOGIC

Idempotent Laws	$A \rightarrow B \equiv \sim A \vee B$
	$A \wedge \sim A \equiv F$
	$A \vee \sim A \equiv T$
Commutative Laws	$A \wedge B \equiv B \wedge A$
	$A \vee B \equiv B \vee A$
Distributive Laws	$A \wedge (B \vee C) \equiv (A \wedge B) \vee (A \wedge C)$
	$A \vee (B \wedge C) \equiv (A \vee B) \wedge (A \vee C)$
Associative Laws	$A \wedge (B \wedge C) \equiv (A \wedge B) \wedge C$
	$A \vee (B \vee C) \equiv (A \vee B) \vee C$
Absorptive Laws	$A \vee (A \wedge B) \equiv A$
	$A \wedge (A \vee B) \equiv A$
DeMorgan's Laws	$\sim(A \wedge B) \equiv \sim A \vee \sim B$
	$\sim(A \vee B) \equiv \sim A \wedge \sim B$

The equivalences of Table 3.4 help in manipulating complex statements by replacing portions of them with an equivalent statement of a form more appropriate for some desired reduction to be performed later. For example, the wff

$$\sim(A \wedge B) \vee B$$

can be manipulated using the above identities into a simpler but equivalent representation as follows:

```
(~A ∨ ~B) ∨ B      DeMorgan's Law
~A ∨ (~B ∨ B)      Associative Law
~A ∨ T             Idempotent Law
T                  Identity Law
```

Familiarity with the above equivalences can also lead to minimal rules when developing rules in a knowledge-based system as is shown in later chapters.

3.3 PREDICATE LOGIC—A MEANS OF REPRESENTING KNOWLEDGE

Propositional logic's weakness is its limited ability to express knowledge. There are many complex statements about the world that lose much of their meaning when represented in propositional logic. For instance, the statements

```
The Pacific Ocean contains water
                and
Florida is a state within the U.S.A.
```

are assigned a *true* value in propositional logic without making any statements about "oceanhood" or "statehood." Furthermore, not all statements in English can be represented meaningfully in propositional logic. For example, representing the statement

```
All men are mortals
```

in propositional logic would be something like

```
all—men—are—mortals
```

This is not a meaningful representation because propositional logic does not support an inference method that, given the true proposition

```
Socrates—is—a—man
```

could infer

```
Socrates—is—mortal
```

The reason for this is that the statement "All men are mortals" includes a *quantifier* (all), which cannot be adequately described in propositional logic. Similar statements include:

All children like ice cream
Some dogs like cats

Thus, a more general form of logic is desired that is capable of representing all of the details expressed in statements such as the ones above and that provides the capabilities for dealing with these details. Predicate logic is this form.

3.3.1 Predicates and Terms

Predicate logic is based on the idea that sentences (propositions) really express relationships between objects as well as qualities and attributes of such objects. These objects can be people, other physical objects, or concepts. Such relationships or attributes are called *predicates*. The objects are called the *arguments* or *terms* of the predicate. The use of terms allows a predicate to express a relationship about many different objects rather than just a single object. Like propositions, predicates have a truth value, but unlike propositions, their truth value depends upon their terms: A predicate can be true for one set of terms, yet false for another. For instance, if the following predicate is true

```
color(grass, green)
```

the same predicate but with different terms may not necessarily be true

```
                color(grass, red)
                        or
                color(sky, yellow)
```

So, you can see that by using predicates we can express more complex statements about the world than we could with propositions.

Predicates can also be used to represent action or an action relationship between two objects. For example, we can define the predicate *bite* to represent the relationship between two terms: the first representing an animate object performing the act of biting (e.g., a dog) and the second an object being bitten (e.g., a letter carrier). The predicate represents an action taken by the first term toward the second. For example,

```
bite(rover, mr-jones)
```

The truth of this statement depends upon the particular terms used within the predicate.

Likewise, we can also define predicates that assign an abstract quality to its term(s). For example, the predicate *mortal* has a single term and can be used to describe the mortality of John Smith:

```
mortal(john-smith)
```

Other examples using predicates to represent truths in the world are the following:

```
weather(tuesday, snow)
bird(albatross)
loves(john, mary)
reads(john, treasure-island)
football-game(dolphins, cowboys, 17, 14)
```

The assumption that we have used in expressing predicates (and propositions for that matter) up to this point is that a predicate's truth value is based on its relationship to the real world. Naturally, being practical people, we would prefer that a predicate be in agreement with the description of the world as we know it, but there is no requirement that this be so. Simply stating a predicate as true is sufficient for it to be considered true in predicate logic. For example, we can write a predicate that indicates that France is in Asia:

```
part-of(france, asia)
```

While this is obviously not true in the real world, predicate logic does not know this since it knows nothing about geography. Predicate logic is only concerned with sound argumentation methods. Such argumentations are called the *rules of inference* for this logic. If we are given a set of facts that we accept as true, these rules guarantee that only true consequences are derived. So if we assert that the predicate

```
part-of(france, asia)
```

is true, then it will be considered *logically* true, since its real truth value is not of primary consequence. Such truths, stated and assumed to be logically true, are called *axioms* and require no justification in order to establish their truth.

The connectives that were introduced for propositional logic are also valid in predicate logic. Indeed, propositional logic is merely a subset of predicate logic. The truth tables for conjunction, disjunction, negation, material implication, and material equivalence all hold in predicate logic as they did in propositional logic.

While we have seen a substantial increase in flexibility between representing truths with predicates as compared to propositions, the power of predicate logic does not stop here.

3.3.2 Variables and Quantifiers

Up to this point each argument in a predicate has stood for one specific object. Such arguments are called *constants*. Predicate logic allows us, however, to have arguments that represent objects which at the moment may be unknown. Called *variables*, they represent a quantum leap in the power and flexibility for predicate logic over propositional logic.

Using the above example, we could use the variable X to represent any color as follows:

```
color(grass, X)
```

The variable X could take the value of "green" resulting in the predicate's being true. Or, X's value could be "red" resulting in the predicate's being false. Variables can also be quantified. The two quantifiers typically used in predicate logic are:

1. The *universal* quantifier, ∀, which indicates that the wff, in its scope, is true for all allowable values of the variable it quantifies. For example,

$$∀ X . . .$$

states that "for all X, it is true that. . . . "

2. The *existential* quantifier, ∃, which indicates that the wff, in its scope, is true for some value or values in the domain. For example,

$$∃ X . . .$$

states that "there exists an X, such that. . . . "

Some examples of quantified predicates are:

```
∀ X, [child(X) → likes(X, ice-cream)].
  ∀ Y, [mammal(Y) → birth(Y, live)].
∃ Z, [letter-carrier(Z) ∧ bite(rover, Z)].
```

From a representational point of view, however, quantifiers are difficult to use. It is, therefore, desirable to replace them with some equivalent representation that is easier to manipulate. Implementation of an equivalent to the universal quantifier can easily be accomplished by assuming that all variables not in the scope of a quantifier are universally quantified. Thus, universally quantified variables are simply denoted by a variable.

The existential quantifier is somewhat more difficult to replace. To do this we must first discuss the third type of term allowed under predicate logic, the *function*.

A *function* maps its arguments (i.e., the constants or variables of the function) from one domain to another (possibly the same) domain. The result of a mapping is called the *value* of the function. The act of replacing the function and its argument(s) by its value is called the *evaluation* of the function.

The existential quantifier guarantees the existence of one (or more) instances (i.e., particular values) of the quantified variable making the clause true. If we assume that a function exists which can determine the values of the variable that makes this true, we can simply remove the existential quantifier and replace its variables by a function returning these values. When solving actual problems, this function (called a *Skolem function*) must be known and defined.

3.3.3 Unification

As in propositional logic, whenever a predicate wff is to have its truth value assigned, it can simply be *asserted* as being true (e.g., through an axiom found in a database defining our problem). Often, however, we may want to know the truth value of a statement (e.g., some predicate). If connectives are used within the statement, the component predicates need to be evaluated to determine whether the overall statement is true. We must, therefore, search through the set of axioms to see whether the component predicates are found to be true. A component predicate is said to be true if it *matches* a true statement, or axiom, found in our database.

The process of matching some statement to the set of known axioms is trivial in propositional logic since two propositional logic expressions can match only if they are syntactically identical. In predicate logic it is more complicated, however, because the predicates can use variables as their terms. We will refer to such predicates as *patterns*. Unification is the process of computing the proper substitutions to make when determining if two predicate logic expressions or patterns match.

The matching or *unification* process involves the following steps:

1. Any predicates in the pattern that do not contain variables must have an exact match in the database of axioms for the pattern to be considered matched.

2. If a predicate contains a variable, this variable must be *bound* to an actual value. This *binding* is done by searching the database of axioms and selecting those axioms that match the pattern in every way except for the variable. The variable is then *bound* to the value in the corresponding position of the axiom. It is possible that more than one axiom can match a given predicate. If this occurs, all of these values are considered potential matches and are treated separately.

3. The matching process continues under the assumption that the value of this variable is the bound value wherever else it appears.

4. The logical connectives are applied between all of the predicates to determine the value of the statement.

This matching process is probably best explained by considering some examples.

Suppose that we have a predicate logic system for determining gender of individuals within a family. This system might have the following statements in its database of axioms:

```
                    female(alina)
                   female(nicole)
                      male(aj)
      wife_of(nicole, aj)      ;nicole is the wife_of aj
      son_of(nicholas, aj)     ;nicholas is the son_of aj
       son_of(philip, aj)      ;philip is the son_of aj
      son_of(alex, nicole)     ;alex is the son_of nicole
```

Given the above axioms, we now propose a statement and want to determine whether it is true or not:

$$\exists\ X,\ female(X)$$

Within this statement, the term X (and any "word" within logic statements having a capitalized first letter from this point on) is a variable and the statement (also called *a query*) is a pattern. Predicate logic determines the statement's truth value by attempting to find a match for the pattern in its database of axioms.

When we examine the statements, we see that the first and second axioms have the identical predicate, as well as having only a single term. Since the variable X can take any value matched, the query is true for both the values of *alina* and *nicole*.

To further illustrate the power of unification consider the following statement consisting of three components:

$$\exists\ X,\ \exists\ Y,\ \exists\ Z,\ [son\_of(X,\ Y)\ \wedge\ son\_of(Z,\ Y)\ \wedge\ male(Y)]$$

The first component matches successfully with the last three axioms in our database, providing the following substitution instances or unifications:

```
              [nicholas/X, aj/Y]
               [philip/X, aj/Y]
              [alex/X, nicole/Y]
```

where the notation **P/Q** identifies that **P** is substituted for the variable **Q** in the original statement. The second component can similarly match the last three axioms to provide the following unifications:

```
[nicholas/Z, aj/Y]
 [philip/Z, aj/Y]
[alex/Z, nicole/Y]
```

but note that these two sets of unifications cannot each stand by themselves. The original statement **AND**s these components together and the two components share a common variable, *Y.* Therefore, all possible combinations of these two groups must be formed where *Y* has the same value. This results in the following unifications:

```
[nicholas/X, aj/Y, nicholas/Z]
[nicholas/X, aj/Y, philip/Z]
[philip/X, aj/Y, nicholas/Z]
 [philip/X, aj/Y, philip/Z]
 [alex/X, nicole/Y, alex/Z]
```

Finally, the last component is compared to the database to find its unifications:

```
[aj/Y]
```

When this is integrated with the results of the unification of the first and second components it yields

```
[nicholas/X, aj/Y, nicholas/Z]
[nicholas/X, aj/Y, philip/Z]
[philip/X, aj/Y, nicholas/Z]
 [philip/X, aj/Y, philip/Z]
```

See [Luger, 1989] for a more precise statement of the actual unification algorithm.

The concept of variables and matching is quite powerful. It becomes extremely useful in Chapter 4 when it is reintroduced in a more sophisticated form as *pattern matching.*

3.3.4 Converting English Statements into wff's

To this point we have seen how to manipulate wff's in a logic system, but knowledge of our world is rarely stated using logic initially. Instead, knowledge is typically expressed verbally or through English text, so a critical question is, how do we generate wff's from English sentences? This can be rather difficult to do and yet is extremely important in the development of knowledge-based systems.

To illustrate this process, let us consider some examples. Suppose that we are trying to determine grades for students in an artificial intelligence course. We might express a portion of our grading knowledge by the following English sentence:

> *If the student's average grade is greater than 90%,*
> *then the student will get an A in the course.*

This can immediately be represented in predicate logic as follows:

```
∀ Name , ∀ X, [student(Name) ∧ avg-grade(Name, X) ∧ ge(X, 90)
        → final-grade(Name, "A")]
```

Not all English statements can be converted into logic as easily. For instance, in natural language the "and" can represent temporal sequence as well as causality. Consider the sentence "I sat down in the driver's seat and I started the car." Since the conjunction operator is commutative we should be able to state "I started the car and I sat down in the driver's seat" without any loss of meaning. Yet, this does not convey the same meaning as the original English sentence. The reason is that "and" in this case is not the conjunctive operator, but rather an indicator of temporal sequence. Likewise, the disjunction operator can be ambiguous between inclusive and exclusive uses, and double negatives do not always cancel each other.

3.4 LOGICAL INFERENCES AND AUTOMATED REASONING—MANIPULATING THE KNOWLEDGE

Our discussion in the last two subsections focused on representing knowledge as statements in predicate logic. But as stated in the introduction to this chapter, the essence of predicate logic is making logical inferences. This gives rise to the thought of automated reasoning, where new truths can be logically derived from existing axioms, a key concept in knowledge-based systems.

There is, however, a plethora of terminology that can be confusing, so let us begin this discussion by first defining two terms: *reasoning* and *inference*. These terms have very similar meaning as evidenced by their definitions in Webster's Dictionary [Webster, 1960]:

infer: to conclude or decide from something known or assumed; derive by reasoning; draw as a conclusion.

reason: to think coherently and logically; draw inferences or conclusions from facts known or assumed.

The process of *reasoning*, therefore, involves *making inferences* from known facts. Automated reasoning, thus, is described by the following statement:

> *Given a set of premises known (or thought to be*
> *true) and a reasoning method, certain conclusions*
> *(or beliefs) can be inferred to also be true.*

Making inferences involves the derivation of new facts from a set of true facts. Predicate logic provides a set of *sound rules of inference* with which we can perform logical inferences. The best known of these is *modus ponens* [Stanat, 1977]:

> *If the statements p and (p → q) are known to be true,*
> *then we can infer that q is true.*

As we see in Chapter 4, modus ponens is the basis for rule-based reasoning. To illustrate its use, consider the following English statement:

> If someone is snorkeling then they are wet.

Representing this in predicate logic, we have

$$\forall \ X, \ [\text{snorkeling}(X) \ \rightarrow \ \text{wet}(X)]$$

If the statement

$$\text{snorkeling}(\text{alex})$$

is found in the database, then through modus ponens (and the unification algorithm!), we can infer

$$\text{wet}(\text{alex})$$

Modus tolens, another important rule of inference, states [Stanat, 1977]

> *If (p → q) is known to be true, and q is false, then p is false.*

Considering our example, if the above relationship is true (i.e., $\forall X$, [*snorkeling*(X) → *wet*(X)]), and if alex is not wet, then he was not snorkeling. In predicate logic, this is represented as

$$\sim\text{wet}(\text{alex})$$

which implies, through modus tolens,

$$\sim\!\texttt{snorkeling(alex)}$$

This reflects the last entry in our truth table of Table 3.2.

We have seen that modus ponens and modus tolens provide the foundation for making inferences. But this is not the entire story. The question now becomes, "What are the appropriate reasoning methods that can be applied to a set of premises?" There are three basic reasoning methods: (1) deduction, (2) abduction, and (3) induction.

3.4.1 Deduction

Webster's Dictionary [Webster, 1960] defines *deduction* as

> Reasoning from a known principle to an unknown, from the general to the specific, or from a premise to a logical conclusion.

Deduction has been concisely defined as "logically correct inference" [Charniak, 1985]. This means that deduction from true premises is guaranteed to result in true conclusions. Deduction is the most widely accepted, understood, and recognized of the three basic inference methods. It is the basis of both propositional and predicate logics. As an example, consider the following sentence, which is similar to the one about Alex and snorkeling:

> IF   *you have an object A that is larger than some object B*
> *and object B is larger than another object C*
> THEN   *we can state that object A is larger than object C*

which in predicate logic would be represented as

$$\forall \; A, \; \forall \; B, \; \forall \, C, \; [\texttt{larger(A, B)} \; \wedge \; \texttt{larger(B, C)} \rightarrow \texttt{larger(A, C)}]$$

If our list of axioms contains the axioms

$$\texttt{larger(house, car)}$$
$$\texttt{larger(car, cat)}$$

then through deductive reasoning, the wff

$$\texttt{larger(house, cat)}$$

can be derived and added to our list of axioms.

3.4.2 Abduction

Defined by C. S. Peirce, an early twentieth-century logician, [Sowa, 1984], *abduction* is the reasoning method commonly used for generating explanations. Unlike deduction, it does not guarantee that a true conclusion results and, thus is not a sound logical inference. For this reason, it is called an *unsound rule of inference*. Nevertheless, it is a quite useful technique.

Although we may not realize it, we use abduction often in our daily lives. Diagnosis, for example, is the process of explaining something that is either taking place or has already occurred and, as a result, depends heavily on abduction. Since diagnosis is a common application for knowledge-based systems, it is expected that the latter will make extensive use of abduction.

In order to explain abduction, let us make use of the "snorkeling" example from above. Assume that we have the rule

$$\forall \ X, \ [\texttt{snorkeling(X)} \ \rightarrow \ \texttt{wet(X)}]$$

Suppose that alex comes into the house "wet as a fish." This is represented in predicate logic as

$$\texttt{wet(alex)}$$

Using abduction, we could conclude that

$$\texttt{snorkeling(alex)}$$

Note, however, that this is not guaranteed to be true. There could certainly be other reasons why alex is wet (e.g., he walked home in the rain, he had a water-balloon fight with his friends, he went swimming but not snorkeling).

Given the following:

$$(A \rightarrow B)$$
$$B \text{ is true}$$

abduction allows us to say

$$A \text{ is possibly true}$$

and, therefore, provides one possible explanation for *B* being true. In light of this, abduction provides a perfect opportunity to introduce the subject of reasoning under uncertainty. It is clear from this example that the reason alex is wet may not necessarily be because he went snorkeling. There may be some level of probability for which this statement is true based on past history or just common sense. For example, if it is raining heavily when alex came in, we may attach a low probability to the *snorkeling(alex)* predicate. But if there is a swimming pool in the backyard, the weather is sunny and hot, and alex is wearing a bathing suit and carrying a mask and fins, then it is more likely that he was snorkeling.

But these restrictions such as raining heavily, or wearing a bathing suit, and so forth, which are placed on the left-hand side of the operator, are considerably more constraining than those in deduction where the only restriction was that alex be a member of the domain for that predicate.

In abduction, we begin with a conclusion and proceed to derive the conditions that would make the conclusion valid. In other words, we try to find an *explanation* for the conclusion.

3.4.3 Induction

Induction is the third major reasoning method. Webster's dictionary [Webster, 1960] defines induction as

Reasoning from particular facts or individual cases to a general conclusion

Inductive inference forms the basis of scientific discovery. The most common form of inductive reasoning is as follows:

P(a) is true
P(b) is true

then by induction we can conclude that

$$\forall\, X,\ P(X) \text{ is true}$$

Consider our example of alex again. If we observe alex over a period of time we might note that whenever alex is wet, it turns out that he has gone snorkeling. This might be based on only one or two observations or, possibly, on hundreds of cases. We might apply inductive reasoning in this situation to induce that

$$\forall\ X,\ [\texttt{wet(X)} \rightarrow \texttt{snorkeling(X)}]$$

Obviously, this is not always true. But what if we have made the slightly different observation

$$\forall\ X,\ [\texttt{snorkeling(X)} \rightarrow \texttt{wet(X)}]$$

This would actually be true for all X (assuming that X can swim, X is in water using a mask and fins, and X's body is not covered by a "dry" suit).

Induction is an important form of inference because learning and discovery are based on it. Like abduction, induction is not a sound logical inference. Many consider abduction to be just a form of induction. Induction is a key technique in machine learning and *knowledge acquisition*, topics discussed in more detail in Chapter 13.

3.4.4 Automated Theorem Proving and Resolution

Resolution is a form of inferencing based on the sound rule of inference by the same name. The *Resolution Rule* states:

> *IF*   *(A $\lor$ B) is true and (~B $\lor$ C) is true,*
> *THEN*   *(A $\lor$ C) is true.*

The process of resolution operates by finding two clauses (e.g., $A \lor B$ and $\sim B \lor C$) that are *resolved* to produce a new clause (i.e., $A \lor C$) called the *resolvent*. This resolvent details the minimum that we know to be true from the original two clauses. If both the original clauses are known to be true, then it must be that either B or $\sim B$ is true. If B is true then C must be true to ensure that the second clause is true. If $\sim B$ is true, then A from the first clause must be true by a similar argument. The result of this is that minimally either A or C must be true.

A resolvent is determined by finding two clauses that contain the same literal. In one clause the literal is in a positive form (i.e., B) while in the other it is in a negative form (i.e., $\sim B$). Since these literals contradict, a new clause is created by combining all of the other literals from the clauses.

Resolution can be generalized so that there are as many disjuncted literals as desired, including only one [Winston, 1992]. It is necessary when performing resolution that only one of the literals in a clause be the negation of a literal in another clause.

Let us now see how this works by reexamining the snorkeling example. Suppose we have the following two predicates:

```
∀ X, [snorkeling(X) → wet(X)]
          snorkeling(charlie)
```

Before resolving these predicates, it is necessary to transform them into clause form (i.e., logical statements having no quantification). The Idempotent Law from Table 3.4 states

```
∀ X, [p(X) → q(X)] ≡ ~p(X) ∨ q(X)
```

Using this law on our first predicate

$$\forall \ X, \ [\texttt{snorkeling(X)} \rightarrow \texttt{wet(X)}]$$

results in

$$[\sim\texttt{snorkeling(X)} \ \lor \ \texttt{wet(X)}]$$

Unifying X with *charlie* and combining this with our second predicate, [i.e., *snorkeling(charlie)*], the application of resolution results in

$$\texttt{wet(charlie)}$$

as the derived truth.

It can be seen from the above example that resolution achieves the same objective as modus ponens as well as modus tolens. In fact, these two are considered special cases of resolution.

Theorem proving was one of the earliest research areas in AI. Logic Theorist [Newell, 1963], developed during the mid-1950s, was a successful early attempt to automate the logical proof of mathematical theorems. There are many implementations of theorem proving, but the most common ones use resolution to prove that predicates are true using the principle of *refutation*. In refutation we attempt to prove that a statement is true by initially assuming that it is false. This is done by purposely negating the statement that we want to prove true and adding this negated statement to our base of axioms. This addition introduces a potential *contradiction* into our logic system. If the original statement is really true, we should be able to find a contradiction between our assumed negative statement and the other axioms in our world. The theorem prover, therefore, attempts to prove a statement's validity by using resolution to produce a contradiction with the given axioms. This contradiction occurs when resolution produces an empty clause, which has a value of false. Since false cannot be true, a contradiction must exist—a contradiction introduced by the addition of the negated statement to our base of axioms [Rich, 1991]. If a contradiction is found, then through refutation the original statement must have been true.

The following steps implement a theorem prover using refutation/resolution [Luger, 1989].

1. Transform all of the axioms into clause form using the Idempotent Laws.
2. Add to the set of axioms the negation of the statement (goal) to be proven.
3. Use the resolution rule of inference to combine axioms to "cancel" out any literals and their negations.

4. Continue this process until a contradiction (i.e., an empty clause) is generated. Since there is a contradiction, one or more of the axioms are false. Since all but the originally negated statement are real axioms, they cannot be false. Only the negated one can be and is false, thus proving the original statement.

Let us look at an example of proving a theorem through refutation/resolution and arriving at the same conclusion through modus ponens. For this example assume that all people who live in the United States are U.S. residents, and all U.S. residents pay taxes. Stating this knowledge in predicate form results in the following logical statements:

$$\forall \ X, \ [\texttt{live-in-US(X)} \ \rightarrow \ \texttt{resident-of-US(X)}] \tag{1}$$
$$\forall \ Y, \ [\texttt{resident-of-US(Y)} \ \rightarrow \ \texttt{taxpayer(Y)}] \tag{2}$$

If we now know the fact

live-in-US(charlie)

logical statement 1, through unification binds X to *charlie*, and modus ponens causes the following new axiom to be derived:

resident-of-US(charlie)

Again through unification, the axiom *resident-of-US(charlie)* matches with predicate (2) and binds `charlie` to Y. Modus ponens will once again derive the following new axiom:

taxpayer(charlie)

Using resolution/refutation we can prove the above theorem through the following procedure:

1. Convert all of our predicates and known facts to clause form: predicate (1) becomes

[~live-in-US(X) ∨ resident-of-US(X)]

predicate (2) becomes

[~resident-of-US(Y) ∨ taxpayer(Y)]

and our one known fact is already in clause form

live-in-US(charlie)

2. Add to these clauses the negation of what we want to prove

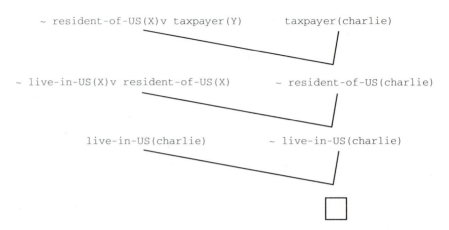

FIGURE 3.1   Unification Tree

~taxpayer(charlie)

3. Resolve the clauses together:

> taxpayer(Y)   in clause (2) unifies with and
> ~taxpayer(charlie)   leaving the resolvent
> ~resident-of-US(charlie)

that in turn unifies with resident-of-US(X) in clause (1) leaving

~live-in-US(charlie)

which combines with our original known fact, resulting in an empty clause which represents a contradiction. See Figure 3.1. Since the original axioms (our two predicates and one fact) must all be true by definition, then the negation

~taxpayer(charlie)

is invalid, making charlie a taxpayer.

Resolution/refutation is the basic theorem-proving mechanism used by the language PROLOG, which is described in Section 3.5.

3.4.5 Monotonic Versus Nonmonotonic Reasoning

Deductive reasoning is a monotonic form of reasoning that produces arguments that preserve truth. In monotonic systems all of the axioms used are either basic (e.g., atomic or known to be true by themselves) or can be derived from other facts known to be true. Axioms are not allowed to change, since once a fact is known to be true, it is always true and can never be modified or retracted. Thus, in monotonic reasoning, the world of axioms continually increases in size.

However, not all problem-solving situations are monotonic. Consider a football game where the Tampa Bay Buccaneers are playing the Miami Dolphins and the following facts are known to be true:

quarter(fourth)
leading(bucs)

One standard strategy used in football is that if a team has the lead in the latter part of the game, this team should play good defense and not take risks so they can maintain their lead (i.e., play conservatively). Expressed in predicate logic, this can be represented as

∀ Team, [leading(Team) ∧ quarter(fourth)] →
strategy(Team, conservative)

From these facts we can deduce

strategy(bucs, conservative)

But suppose that the Dolphins suddenly score a touchdown and take the lead? Obviously, we have a problem since the state of our world has changed. We must add the fact

leading(dolphins)

to our problem description, a change that introduces a conflict—two teams cannot both lead in scoring at the same time of the same game. Somehow the fact, leading(bucs), must be removed. Not only must this fact be removed but all facts derived from this fact must also be removed; otherwise the Buc's coach would be obliged to continue playing conservatively, an improper strategy if they are to regain the lead and win the game.

Monotonic reasoning does not allow axioms to be retracted from the world of axioms. Once an axiom is *asserted* into the world, it is always going to remain true. For that reason, monotonic reasoning is not suitable for many real-world problems.

Another aspect of monotonic reasoning is that if more than one logical inference can be made at some specific time and one of these inferences is performed, the remaining inferences will still be applicable after this inference is made. In other words, the making of a logical inference, which may assert another axiom into the world, does not impair the ability of other inferences to be subsequently made.

Monotonic reasoning is also not suitable if *default reasoning* is required. In default reasoning, certain assumptions are made that are not explicitly stated in the system. For example, if we say that we went to a restaurant last night, you would probably draw the conclusion that we in fact ate at the restaurant, even though that is not explicitly stated (abductive thinking!). The problem with default reasoning is that assumptions are often made which later prove to be untrue when more information is received (e.g., our later stating that we went to the restaurant to assist a friend whose car would not start). The obvious course of action is to deassert the assumption and replace it with the correct statement. Predicate logic is monotonic in nature and does not support this action of deassertions.

As you can probably imagine, this is a significant problem because humans are always making assumptions that, if proven to be unfounded, are easily corrected. Additionally, changes always take place in the course of human events that invalidate previous truths.

Nonmonotonic reasoning is a way around this problem. It simply allows the *retraction* of truths that are present in the system whenever contradictions arise forcing the reestablishing of beliefs. Obviously, the number of axioms in a nonmonotonic system can both increase and decrease. Likewise, the applicability of an operator cannot be guaranteed after a logical inference is made because that inference could have retracted the axiom that matched the operation.

But the concept of nonmonotonic reasoning adds complexity to our knowledge-based system development. Its implementation is not as simple as retracting facts whose truth values have changed from true to false. This is because facts that were either derived or assumed and, which later turn out to be retracted, may have contributed to the derivation of other facts. The retraction of the first facts may make facts derived later unfounded. *Truth maintenance systems (TMS)* are designed to maintain the integrity of the database at all times by keeping track of all derivations made and ensuring that the derivations in the database are based only on truths. TMSs retract any other derived fact that depended on the validity of retracted fact(s). In our example about football strategy, the originally retracted fact is

```
leading(bucs)
```

Since this fact was originally used to derive

```
strategy(bucs, conservative)
```

its retraction leaves the above expression unfounded, requiring that it also be retracted.

Nonmonotonic reasoning systems are potentially more useful than traditional monotonic ones. Default reasoning, developed by R. Reiter [Reiter, 1980; Rich, 1991], allows for the making of assumptions and the subsequent retraction of these assumptions if they later prove to be incorrect. Most of the real-world applications of knowledge-based systems discussed in this book are nonmonotonic in nature.

3.5 PROLOG

The PROLOG language is an implementation of predicate logic for computing. PROLOG and LISP are generally considered to be the major AI languages. One of their basic differences is that PROLOG is a declarative language, while LISP is procedural. When compared to PROLOG, LISP is a lower-level language in which many features (e.g., search, matching) have to be programmed whereas PROLOG has many of these built-in.

PROLOG (which stands for PROgramming in LOGic) was developed in the late 1970s by Alain Colmerauer at the University of Marseilles [Colmerauer, 1973; Maier, 1988]. It is based on Robinson's work on resolution in the 1960s [Robinson, 1965] and is a contemporary of a previous attempt at logic programming in 1971 at MIT called Microplanner. Whereas PROLOG has not replaced LISP as the language of choice among the majority of AI researchers in the United States, it has a considerable following in Europe and Japan.

The objective of this section is *not* to teach PROLOG as a language. Instead, our objective is to introduce the basic structure and philosophy of PROLOG so you can fully appreciate the features of predicate logic described earlier in this chapter. This introduction, additionally, reveals some of the basic operations of knowledge-based systems since PROLOG exhibits some similar features. In particular, PROLOG introduces a technique called *backtracking* that is similar to *backward chaining*, a technique that tries to prove a query (e.g., fact) is true by searching a knowledge base for supporting evidence for this conclusion.

3.5.1 A Basic Introduction

PROLOG is based on predicate logic. It uses resolution to prove theorems about whether proposed solutions to problems can be found either directly from a set of known axioms or indirectly through logical inference. PROLOG employs depth-first search in its attempt to prove theorems, which are simply queries made by the user to the system. The *instantiations* (i.e., bound values) of variables that make the query true are typically displayed. PROLOG also allows side effects, such as the assertion of new axioms, the retraction of axioms, display of results, mathematical calculations, as well as populating and accessing data structures.

PROLOG, unlike predicate logic however, assumes that if something is not explicitly stated as an axiom, then it is false. This is called the *closed-world assumption* (CWA). The CWA states that if a theorem were true, an axiom would exist stating it as being true. If the axiom does not exist, we can assume that the theorem is false. This permits a conceptually satisfying way to interpret the negation connective because by using the CWA assumption we can avoid having to store explicitly all negative axioms about our domain, the set of which would certainly exceed all of the axioms known to be true.

Two difficulties exist for the CWA: We may actually have an incomplete set of knowledge or our inference process may not be powerful enough to determine that an axiom is true. Despite these problems, PROLOG uses the CWA to derive the fact that some axiom is false rather than stating that it cannot be inferred from the known axioms.

As in LISP, there are various dialects of PROLOG. Unlike LISP, however, a standard implementation (like Common LISP) has not as yet emerged. Edinburgh PROLOG (Clocksin and Mellish) is closest to a standard, but numerous variations exist, including some that are only partial implementations (e.g., Turbo PROLOG).

The keys to understanding PROLOG involve three basic concepts. The first two correspond to knowledge representation, while the third represents the basic search mechanism used by PROLOG in responding to a query. These are (1) *facts,* (2) *rules,* and (3) *backtracking.*

Since we have discussed predicate logic, the first two terms are merely new labels for concepts already seen. We discuss each of these terms in order. To understand facts fully, however, we must first state that PROLOG is a nonmonotonic language. This is where PROLOG makes its first major deviation from pure predicate logic.

3.5.2 Facts

Facts in PROLOG are axioms. The collection of all the facts in the system is called the *database* or the *fact base.* The mere presence of a fact (which could be the negation of some truth) in the database causes that fact to be considered to be true. PROLOG's syntax for representing facts is identical to what we have used in our discussion of predicate logic. Some examples of PROLOG facts are:

```
daytime
nighttime
wet(alex)
snorkeling(alex)
loves(mary, george)
child-of(alina, nicole)
male(nicholas)
rises(sun, twice)
```

Note that when each of these facts is asserted, it must be followed by a period. For example,

$$\text{color-of(sports-car, red)}.$$

The period at the end of a fact is the part of PROLOG's syntax that identifies the end of a clause.

3.5.3 Rules

A *rule* is the name for an implication operation in PROLOG. Rules are considered to be axioms and are the means through which new facts are derived to substantiate queries. The implication operator symbol in PROLOG is :-. Thus instead of

$$(A \rightarrow B) \qquad \text{(i.e., A implies B)}$$

PROLOG uses

$$B :- A. \qquad \text{(i.e., B such that A)}$$

This statement format is referred to as a *Horn Clause*. PROLOG requires that all logical assertions be expressed in the uniform format of Horn Clauses rather than arbitrary logical expressions. This simplifies PROLOG's interpreter since only one rule of inference is needed (resolution) rather than all of the other rules of inference if the knowledge were instead expressed using quantifiers.

The predicate on the left-hand side of the rule is called the rule's *head*, while the right-hand side is referred to as the *body* of the rule. The right-hand side has to be satisfied before the left-hand side is derived. Note that this is just the opposite of what we have seen in the previous sections of this chapter, where the predicates on the left-hand side were the premises and those on the right were the conclusions.

Variables in PROLOG are identical to variables we defined in predicate logic (i.e., a symbol starting with a capitalized letter). The value of a variable becomes bound when it is matched within any predicate. This binding holds for the scope of that variable (e.g., throughout an entire rule). This binding is, however, only temporary. It holds only within the scope of the rule.

Rules can have multiple premises, which are combined using conjunction or disjunction. A conjunction (the AND operator) of premises is indicated by a comma between the premises. A disjunction (the OR operator) is indicated by a semicolon separating the premises. Disjunctions are less commonly used since they can also be represented by writing several rules. Negation of a predicate is indicated by use of the *not* function. Thus,

$$b :- a, c, d, \text{not}(e).$$

represents a conjunction of premises *a, c, d,* and the negation of *e.* A disjunction

$$b :- a; c; d; not(e).$$

can also be expressed as a sequence of separate rules:

```
b :- a.
b :- c.
b :- d.
b :- not(e).
```

3.5.4 Backtracking and the Inference Process in PROLOG

PROLOG has a built-in mechanism for performing the inferences required to solve a problem. This mechanism, which employs unification, is based on the premise that the user specifies a query or a goal and the interpreter searches through its database (composed of facts and rules) either directly finding, or indirectly deriving, a fact that satisfies the query. Failure to find a match results in a value of false for the query.

PROLOG attempts to satisfy a posed query by employing unification as a pattern-matching algorithm. A depth-first search is made of the database for the rule or fact that will allow the query to be matched.

While searching, PROLOG abandons fruitless search paths and keeps track of the location in the database where an instantiation of a variable was made (sometimes called *place markers*) so it can return to this point to avoid repeating work unnecessarily. This backtracking process is best illustrated through an example. See Figure 3.2. Please note that the numbers in parentheses to the right of each fact are not part of the PROLOG grammar, but rather, a simple numbering of the facts to assist in this example.

To pose a query in some PROLOG implementations, you must identify a statement as a query by preceding it with a question mark and a dash. For example,

```
?- brothers(nicholas, philip).
```

The backtracking process begins by searching the database for a fact or a rule head that matches this predicate-form query. The search for a match is performed in a depth-first manner, making the order of the facts and rules in the database quite important. All facts using a particular predicate name must be placed above the rules that use this predicate. This is illustrated in Figure 3.2 where fact 20 (defining a particular *sisters* relationship) is placed above the rule that derives the *sisters* relation.

```
child_of(alex, nicole).              (1)
child_of(alina, nicole).             (2)
child_of(nicholas, leah).            (3)
child_of(philip, leah).              (4)
child_of(melanie, cathy).            (5)
child_of(leslie, cathy).             (6)
child_of(sarah, cathy).              (7)
child_of(angela, cathy).             (8)
male(alex).                          (9)
male(philip).                       (10)
male(nicholas).                     (11)
female(alina).                      (12)
female(leah).                       (13)
female(nicole).                     (14)
female(angela).                     (15)
female(sarah).                      (16)
female(leslie).                     (17)
female(melanie).                    (18)
female(cathy).                      (19)
sisters(nicole, leah).              (20)
sisters(X, Z) :- child_of(X, Y), child_of(Z, Y),
                 female(X), female(Z).
brothers(X, Z) :- child_of(X, Y), child_of(Z, Y),
                  male(X), male(Z).
```

FIGURE 3.2   Sample PROLOG Fact Base

In the search for this predicate, no matching fact is found, but the second rule does match. The satisfaction of this rule requires the instantiation of several variables. The initial instantiations, bound by the query above, are:

$$X = \text{nicholas}$$
$$Z = \text{philip}$$

After the unification algorithm makes these variable bindings, PROLOG attempts to satisfy the four conjoined premises of the rule in order from left to right. Skipping the details of the internal operation, it can clearly be seen that

```
child_of(nicholas, Y)
```

must first be satisfied. This is done by treating it as a subquery in a manner identical to the original query. Searching through the database we find one fact (i.e., fact 3) that directly satisfies the subquery if the variable Y is bound to *leah*. This completes the matching of the first subquery (or subgoal).

Since the predicates in the premise are And'ed together, all must be satisfied before the rule is executed. Thus, the second predicate in the premise is now attempted. Note that all of the variables in this predicate have already been bound to values, so we are searching for child_of(philip, leah)

This subgoal is satisfied by fact 4. Proceeding to the next subgoal with instantiation

male(nicholas)

we find a match with fact 11. Finally, the last subgoal to be satisfied is

male(philip)

This subgoal is matched by fact 10. The final result provided by PROLOG to our original query will simply be

TRUE

Obviously, this is a rather simple case. Let us examine another example where the matching fails the first time. This shows a little more of the power of backtracking. Suppose that our query, in this case, is

?- brothers(alina, alex).

The interpreter begins by searching the database from the top to find either a fact or a rule head that matches the predicate in our query. Because this fact is not in our database, the first match that is found is the second rule. The following bindings result:

X = alina
Z = alex

The first predicate of the right-hand side of the rule becomes our new subgoal to be satisfied. Replacing the variables with their bindings, this subgoal is now:

child_of(alina, Y)

This matches fact 2, creating the binding

Y = nicole

The second predicate in the premise of the rule becomes our next subgoal that must be satisfied. With the variables substituted by their respective bindings, this subgoal is child_of(alex, nicole)

This subgoal matches fact 1. The next subgoal is

male(alina)

which cannot be found in the database either as a fact or a rule. Therefore a failure occurs. Rather than announcing a result of FALSE, PROLOG backtracks to see if other variable bindings can result in a satisfaction of this goal. PROLOG first backtracks to the previously satisfied subgoal and unbinds the variable instantiations made within it. This predicate is

child_of(Z, Y)

which with variable instantiations is

child_of(alex, nicole)

Since no variable bindings were made in this clause, it cannot unbind any variables and must backtrack one more step to

child_of(alina, nicole).

The variable Y is now uninstantiated. The variable $Z = alex$ cannot be unbound because it was bound in the original query. When PROLOG made the initial binding to Y it put a place marker in the database at the point where the match was found. Now it returns to this place marker to continue looking for another suitable binding for the variable.

Because *alex* and *alina* are the only children of *nicole*, the search is unable to find any other matches. There are no other bindings for Y that would make *alina* a male. Therefore, the query fails and PROLOG returns

FALSE

Although this second example shows some backtracking, it still does not indicate the full power of the PROLOG backtracking mechanism. Let us, therefore, consider a third example. In this example we ask who are sisters in the above database. This query is

?- sisters(A, B).

Now the task of the interpreter is not only to identify whether the query is true or false. It must also identify which variable instantiations cause the query to be true. Here is where various implementations of PROLOG work differently: Some of the older implementations search only until they find a single set of variable bindings that cause the query to be true, even though other matches may exist. In these implementations, the user must prompt the system to look for additional solutions. Although this prompt is easy to make (typically by entering a semicolon), other implementations of the language do not force the user to provide input, but rather automatically generate all possible combinations. We assume in our discussion below that PROLOG finds all possible solutions without additional user input.

To find all sisters our search of the database begins at the top looking for any direct matches. Fact 20 is the only direct match so PROLOG immediately announces success by stating

```
A = nicole
B = leah
```

PROLOG continues its search by returning to the place marker in fact 20. The only additional match that it finds is to the first rule's head, which matches the predicate *sisters*. Unifying the variables A with X and B with Y, it then pursues the first subgoal

```
child_of(X, Y)
```

Since no variables are currently bound, PROLOG searches for a fact that can match this subgoal. It finds an immediate match with fact (1) and instantiates the following variables:

```
X = alex
Y = nicole
```

The second subgoal in the rule now becomes

```
child_of(Z, nicole)
```

which matches fact 2, thus instantiating

```
Z = alina
```

The third subgoal

```
female(alex)
```

is now pursued and since it is not matched, it fails. This failure starts the backtracking process. PROLOG backtracks to the point where the variable (X) was bound (to *alex*). This binding is undone, causing PROLOG to search for another possible binding. But none is found since nicole does not have any other children. PROLOG then unbinds *Y* from the value *nicole* and looks for a new match.

The next possible match occurs with facts 3 and 4, binding

```
X  =  nicholas
Y  =  leah
Z  =  philip
```

but unfortunately, these bindings also fail since they are not females, so the backtracking continues with

```
X  =  melanie
Y  =  cathy
Z  =  leslie
```

which results in a complete match. The other combinations of sisters that are matched are

```
A  =  melanie,    B  =  sarah
A  =  melanie,    B  =  angela
A  =  leslie,     B  =  sarah
A  =  leslie,     B  =  angela
A  =  sarah,      B  =  angela.
```

It should be mentioned that PROLOG also computes the following matches:

```
A  =  sarah     B  =  melanie
A  =  leslie    B  =  melanie
A  =  sarah     B  =  leslie
A  =  angela    B  =  leslie
A  =  angela    B  =  sarah
A  =  angela    B  =  melanie
```

Let us consider one final example. Suppose that *nicole* had another baby boy named *eric*. Thus, the following two facts are added to the database of Fig. 3.2:

```
child_of(eric, nicole)                                      (21)
male(eric)                                                  (22)
```

Given the query

```
?- brothers(A, B)
```

the system matches only on the first rule, which creates the subgoal

child_of(X, Y)

and binds

X = alex
Y = nicole

Continuing with the second subgoal results in the binding

Z = alina

Pursuing our search with these instantiations results in failure. Backtracking now unbinds variable *Z* looking for another child of *nicole* who would be a male. A match is found in fact 22

Z = eric

which results in a complete match. The PROLOG interpreter then presents these initial results of the query:

A = alex
B = eric

Continuing with the backtracking eventually yields an additional answer of

A = nicholas
B = philip

3.5.5 The CUT

PROLOG is not pure in its approach to declarative programming. In an effort to increase its efficiency, as well as to allow it to solve certain problems, PROLOG has implemented an approach that gives the programmer some control over the backtracking process. This control mechanism is called the *CUT* operation.

The backtracking process in PROLOG is designed always to begin after a failure and to proceed incessantly until the goal is found or until there are no more possibilities to explore. Yet in some circumstances, this exhaustive searching may not be necessary or even desirable. The CUT serves as a means of limiting the backtracking at a certain point. This may be because PROLOG already has found an answer and does not need another one, because any further progression along this predicate will be fruitless, or because of the way the predicate is written, any further backtracking will result in a wrong answer.

The CUT is a *built-in predicate* in PROLOG (i.e., it has an intrinsic meaning), which always succeeds the first time it is reached. It can be likened to a fence that can be "crossed" only going from left to right. Unlimited backtracking can take place before the fence is crossed and, likewise, for any backtracking on its right. However, when the backtracking process attempts to cross back through the fence (i.e., going from right to left) it fails. This causes the entire predicate, as well as any subgoal of the parent predicate that caused this predicate to be set up as a subgoal, to fail as well. The CUT is represented in PROLOG as the exclamation symbol, !. Its operation is best described through an example.

Suppose that we have the following rules:

```
a :- b, c, !, d, e.
a :- g, h, i.
```

and we introduce the following query:

```
?- a.
```

Let us assume that the predicate a is not found within the database, but some of the subgoals within these two rules are. PROLOG starts the execution of this query by searching for the predicate a, which it fails to find, but it does find the first rule above. It then sets up as subgoals each of the predicates in the right-hand side of this rule. As a result, PROLOG first tries to satisfy the subgoal b.

As long as the CUT predicate is not our current subgoal (which will immediately succeed), normal backtracking can take place as necessary between b and c. However, once the CUT succeeds, whatever variables were bound in b and c are now set and cannot be unbound. Further backtracking can now occur between predicates d and e. If predicates d and e cannot be satisfied, PROLOG attempts to backtrack through the CUT, which results in an immediate failure for *the overall original query* without even attempting the second rule! Once the CUT was passed, PROLOG dropped from consideration the second rule for proving a. But had b and c failed to be satisfied, PROLOG would have considered the second rule since the CUT had not yet been encountered.

Let us look at a more complex example of the CUT (courtesy of Glenn Blank).[1] Suppose that we own a computerized dating service and have as our goal matching the common interests of men and women. Our database looks as follows:

[1]Personal communication from Dr. Glenn Blank, 1992.

```
person(tom, male, [travel, books, computers, baseball]).
person(sue, female, [wines, books, computers, travel]).
person(jill, female, [swimming, travel, stamps]).
```

with our matching relationships being as follows:

```
matchmaker :-
        person(M, male, Minterests),
        person(W, female, Finterests),
        common-interests(Minterests, Finterests),
        write(M, "might like ", W), nl,
        fail.


common-interests(Intl, Int2) :-
        member(I, Intl),
        member(I, Int2).
```

Note that in the predicates above, we are assuming the presence of a *member* predicate that succeeds when the first argument is a member of the structure represented by the second argument. Although this is not a primitive in standard PROLOG, it is commonly included in many versions or can be easily defined. The predicate *fail* is a primitive that causes the interpreter to search for another match after it has found one.

If we provide the interpreter with the following query

```
?- matchmaker
```

it tries to find all the different combinations of matches between the men and women in the database for each of their interests. It will, as a result, return the following solutions:

```
tom might like sue
tom might like sue
tom might like sue
tom might like jill.
```

The cause of the redundancy between *tom* and *sue* is that they share three common interests, (travel, books and computers). To eliminate this redundancy, we place a CUT at the end of the common-interest predicate as shown below:

```
common-interests(Intl, Int2) :-
        member(I, Intl),
        member(I, Int2),
        !.
```

This causes the solution *"tom likes sue"* to appear only once, which is what we want. But at the same time it allows the matching process to continue to produce *"tom likes jill"* as a second match for *tom*.

However, if we place the CUT in *matchmaker,* right after the *common-interest* subgoal, then it will never report the match between *tom* and *jill*, which is not a desirable side effect. Therefore, care needs to be taken when deciding where to place the CUT.

3.6 ADVANTAGES AND DISADVANTAGES OF PREDICATE LOGIC AS A BASIS FOR A KNOWLEDGE-BASED SYSTEM

As we have seen in our examination of PROLOG, logic programming can be a powerful formalism for developing a knowledge-based system. It is an established means of representing knowledge and its built-in reasoning mechanism using deduction is theoretically founded. Nevertheless, there are some aspects of predicate logic that makes it very inflexible and possibly inappropriate for dealing with certain types of problems:

1. *Managing uncertainty.* One major disadvantage of predicate logic is the availability of only two levels of truth: **true** and **false**. There is no in-between. This is because pure deduction always guarantees that the inference is absolutely true.

   We know, however, that many problems in the world are not black and white. For example, the sentence

   > Most people of southern Italian heritage have dark hair.

   is not easily represented in predicate logic because there is no mechanism to represent the quantifier *most*. Nevertheless, uncertainty management techniques such as certainty factors can be and have been implemented many times in PROLOG, significantly mitigating this disadvantage.

2. *Monotonic versus nonmonotonic reasoning.* Predicate logic, being a monotonic reasoning formalism, is often not suitable for real-world problem domains since in these domains assumptions are typically made or truths legitimately change with the passage of time. PROLOG compensates for this deficiency by providing a mechanism for removing facts from the database, but this operation makes PROLOG something other than a pure predicate logic system.

3. *Declarative versus procedural programming.* Predicate logic, as implemented in PROLOG, is a declarative programming language where the programmer need only be concerned with knowledge expressed in terms of the implication operator and axioms. As mentioned above, predicate logic has its own methodology for searching and matching, which works

on declared axioms and relationships. The deductive mechanism of predicate logic arrives at an answer (if one is feasible) by using exhaustive search and matching.

Whereas this exhaustive search may be highly appropriate for some problems, it can introduce some inefficiencies at run time. Predicate logic, being a purely declarative formalism, suffers from this. Because of the CUT operation, PROLOG is not purely declarative. It can, however, be made purely declarative if the CUT is not used.

3.7 CHAPTER REVIEW

Predicate logic, a powerful extension of propositional logic, allows more flexibility and power in the representation of knowledge. Whereas propositional logic can represent only simple statements having a truth value of **true** or **false,** predicate logic permits the expression of relationships between objects or abstract quantities. *Predicates* are these relationships, and their arguments (or *terms*) are the objects that these relationships tie together. Predicate logic also supports the use of variables, which bind a predicate's arguments to successively different values. Through the use of variables and *Skolem functions*, predicate logic also supports the concept of quantification, something propositions cannot do. The main quantifiers are the "There exists. . . . " (called the existential quantifier, and represented by the symbol $\exists$), and the "For all . . . ," (called the universal quantifier, and represented by the symbol $\forall$).

Predicate logic (like propositional logic) can determine the truth value of complex clauses, called *well-formed formulas* (wff's), which are composed of various predicates (or propositions) connected by logic operators such as the conjunction (AND or $\wedge$), the disjunction (OR or $\vee$), the negation (NOT or $\sim$), or the material implication ($\rightarrow$) among others. *Truth tables* describe the truth value to be assigned to the wff for various connectives as well as values for the individual component predicates.

Like propositional logic, predicate logic serves as an implementation of automated reasoning. Logic defines sound *rules of inference* that allow the logical inference of new truths from existing truths. The most significant of these, for knowledge-based systems, is *modus ponens*, which states:

> *If the statements p and (p $\rightarrow$ q) are known to be true,*
> *then we can infer that q is true.*

Modus ponens forms the basis for *deductive reasoning*, which is reasoning from known facts to unknowns. Deduction always guarantees a true conclusion if the initial facts or premises are true. It is the most widely accepted as well as recognized reasoning method.

Modus tolens, another sound rule of inference, states:

If the statement $(p \rightarrow q)$ is true and q is false,
then we can infer that p is false.

A third sound rule of inference is called *resolution*. Resolution uses refutation to prove a desired statement. Refutation attempts to create a contradiction with the negation of the original statement, thus showing that the original statement is true. Resolution is a powerful technique for proving theorems in logic and forms the basic inferencing technique in PROLOG, a computational implementation of predicate logic.

A second method of reasoning is called abduction. Abduction attempts to derive a rule's premises from observing its conclusions. For example, medical diagnosis generally tries to explain the symptoms felt by the patient by finding a disease whose effects are similar to the symptoms. When properly performed, abduction can lead to correct inferences (and eventual treatment), but abduction does not guarantee a correct answer, since it is not considered a logical inference technique.

The last method discussed is induction, which forms the basis for learning. Induction is performed by observing facts and generalizing from them. Induction is also an unsound rule of inferencing because it cannot guarantee a correct answer.

A close facsimile of predicate logic is implemented in the language PROLOG. It differs from pure predicate logic in that it is not completely declarative (because of the CUT) and is nonmonotonic in nature.

3.8 PROBLEMS

3-1. Write a well-formed formula (wff) for the following English sentences. Make use of quantifiers if deemed necessary:
  (a) He who laughs last laughs best.
  (b) If Joe doesn't get home before midnight, he will be grounded for a month.
  (c) If we score a touchdown now, we will win the game.

3-2. Consider each of the following statements. Some of these can be converted into predicate logic statements while others cannot. Convert those that can and state why the others cannot.

  (a) Molly is a cow.
  (b) Cows never have a color of purple.
  (c) John does not like Molly.
  (d) Most cows are brown.
  (e) A cow's weight in pounds is 1.6 times the square of its girth in inches.
  (f) Cows nurse their young.
  (g) There are no cows in Antarctica.
  (h) The features of bulls and cows are quite similar.
  (i) Cows have four legs.
  (j) Molly gives milk.

3-3. Consider the following English statements:

1John likes to go only to sports events involving individual competition.

It is safe to assume that a sports event is basketball unless explicitly told otherwise.

Basketball is a sports event involving team competition.

The O'Connell Center rarely hosts sports events involving individual competition.

People do not do things that will cause them to be in situations that they do not like.

(a) It should be possible to deduce the following statement from those provided above. Explain precisely in English how you would do this.

John does not go to the O'Connell Center very often.

(b) Assume that we have, as a minimum, the following predicates:

like(X,Y)	X likes Y
type(X,Y)	X is a type of Y
hosts(X,Y)	X hosts Y
go(X,Y)	X goes to Y
do(X,Y)	X does Y

What problems would we encounter in trying to translate the statements above into logic. Write a two- or three-sentence explanation for each statement.

3-4. The following are a set of facts concerning a murder. Covert each into predicate logic using the relations: dead(X), sex(X,Y), know(X,Y), hate(X,Y), victim(X), murder(X).

The victim is dead.

The victim is female.

John and Steve knew the victim.

The victim knew Tom and John.

The murderer knew the victim.

Sue is the victim.

John hated Sue.

Steve hates Tom.

Tom hates John.

The victim knew someone who hated the murderer.

3-5. Consider the following logic statements:

∀ X, [panther(X) → feline(X)]
∀ X, [house−cat(X) → feline(X)]
∀ X, [house−cat(X) → docile(X)]
∀ X, [feline(X) → carnivore(X)]
∀ X, [carnivore(X) → food(X, meat)]
∀ X, [horse(X) → herbivore(X)]
∀ X, [herbivore(X) → food(X,plants)]

(a) Using modus ponens derive all possible relations from the following facts:

    panther(sam)
    house−cat(rubble)
    lion(leo)

(b) Using abduction and the following statement, what could kitty be?

        food(kitty, meat)

(c) Convert all of the logic statements into clauses.

(d) Attempt to prove all of the following statements using resolution:

house−cat(rebel) ∧ food(rebel, meat)
horse(wilber) ∧ food(wilber, meat)

3-6. Assume the following facts:

Rob only eats vegetarian meals.

Vegetarian meals contain no meat.

Cotes de Boeuf contains meat.

All meals at the French Truffle are vegetarian.

Carte du Jour is a meal at the French Truffle.

Use resolution to answer the question, "What meal would Rob like?"

3-7. Given the following facts:

$$p \rightarrow q$$
$$q \wedge r \rightarrow s$$
$$t \wedge u \rightarrow r$$
$$u \rightarrow w$$
$$w \rightarrow x$$

$$t \rightarrow y$$
$$y \rightarrow u$$
$$r \rightarrow p$$
$$q \rightarrow m$$

(a) Use modus ponens to show that s is true when t is true.

(b) Use resolution to show that s is true when t is true.

(c) Use resolution to show that m is true when u is true.

3-8. Suppose that we know the following to be true:

$$p \wedge q \wedge {\sim}r$$
$$p \wedge {\sim}q$$
$$p \wedge q \wedge r$$

Prove that p is true using resolution.

3-9. Write a computer program that performs resolution on a set of clauses.

3-10. Given the following set of PROLOG facts:

```
job(smith,clerk).
job(dell,stock-person).
job(jones,clerk).
job(putnam,assistant-manager).
job(fishback,clerk).
job(adams,stock-person).
job(phillips,manager).
job(stevens,vice-president).
job(johnson,president).
boss(clerk,assistant-manager).
boss(stock-person,assistant-
  manager).
boss(assistant-manager,manager).
boss(manager,vice-president).
boss(vice-president,president).
```

determine PROLOG's response to the following queries:

(a) ?- job(phillips,X), boss(X,Y), job(Z,X).

(b) ?- boss(stock-person,X); boss(president,X).

(c) ?- boss(stock-person,X); boss(clerk,X).

(d) ?- job(X,clerk), boss(clerk,Y), job(Z,Y).

3-11. Repeat Problem 3-10. Assume that we have the additional fact:

```
boss(X,Z) :- boss(X,Y),
             boss(Y,Z).
```

3-12. [hard] Consider each of the following English statements:

Garfield is a cat.

Garfield is a cartoon character.

All cats are animals.

All animals are beings.

Everyone loves someone.

All cats either love or hate dogs.

Someone only tries to hurt someone they do not love.

Odie is a dog.

Garfield tried to hurt Odie.

(a) Convert each of these statements into predicate logic.

(b) Convert each of these predicate logic statements into a clause.

(c) Show "Garfield does not love Odie" using resolution.

4 ■ Introduction to Rule-based Reasoning

4.1 INTRODUCTION

Rule-based systems are the most commonly used as well as the most misunderstood of the different types of knowledge-based systems. The classical systems described in the Foreword and Chapter 1, such as Dendral, MYCIN, R1/XCON, and GenAID from the first generation of knowledge-based systems, were all rule based. As a result, most knowledge-based systems are rule based. While many disadvantages of rule-based systems have recently become apparent as they are being used more for new and different applications, their popularity, simplicity, and similarity to human reasoning still make them a powerful tool in many domains.

Rule-based systems are often misunderstood because the conditional approach they use for representing and manipulating knowledge is similar to the conditional structures found in many conventional programming languages. Many ill-conceived knowledge-based system applications employ a rule-based paradigm to achieve what could more easily be done using the conditional features provided within conventional languages. Rules and conditional structures are not the same, and this chapter and Chapter 5 demonstrate why this is so.

Rule-based systems are also often confused with logic systems. Granted, many similarities exist and the foundation of rule-based inference is based in logic. Rule-based systems, however, diverge from pure logic systems, and these distinctions make a strong case for a different identity for rule-based systems. This chapter also discusses these differences.

In this chapter we describe rule-based systems by discussing the structure of rules, the two inference methods commonly used in rule-based reasoning (i.e., forward and backward reasoning), and the two basic architectures used to organize rules and perform inferencing. We also present the advantages and disadvantages of rule-based systems. Chapter 5 continues this discussion by describing more specific details of rule-based systems.

4.2 WHAT ARE RULES?

Rules are an important knowledge representation paradigm. If you question skilled problem solvers about how they solve problems or what causes them to draw certain conclusions, they typically respond with knowledge expressed in a rule format. For instance:

> *Well, I noticed that A, B, and C were present in this problem and these three facts imply that D is true.*
> or
> *If A, B, and C are present, then you can conclude D.*

People find it natural to express knowledge using this format. This is especially true for domain knowledge they have accumulated over time that has resulted in internal empirical associations (i.e., heuristics). Rules, therefore, represent knowledge using this *IF-THEN* format. The *IF* portion of a rule is a *condition*, (also called a *premise* or an *antecedent*), which tests the truth value of a set of facts. If these are found true, the *THEN* portion of the rule (also called the *action*, the *conclusion*, or the *consequent*) is inferred as a new set of facts.

Rules can be used to express a wide range of associations. They can express situations and actions that must be taken in these situations:

> *If dark clouds are rolling in from the west and the wind is increasing and lightning strikes are occurring, then you should seek cover in a building.*

> *If you are driving a car and an emergency vehicle approaches, then you should slow down and pull to the side of the road to allow the emergency vehicle to pass.*

> *If you are baking a cake and a toothpick when stuck into the cake and removed has no batter on it, then you should remove the cake from the oven.*

They can express premises and conclusions that can be drawn from those premises:

> *If your temperature is above 99°, then you are running a fever.*

> *If the outside temperature is below freezing and the gas gauge on your car does not register empty and the engine turns over but will not start, then it is highly likely that you have a frozen gas line.*

If the gram stain of the organism is gramneg and the morphology of the organism is coccus, then there is strongly suggestive evidence that the identity of the organism is Neisseria [Buchanan, 1984b].

They also can express antecedents and their consequences:

If X is a cat, then X is an animal.

If the tub's drain is clogged and the water is left running, then the floor will become wet.

If the electric bill is past due and your credit rating is bad, then your lights will be turned off.

The categorization (i.e., situation-action, premise-conclusion, or antecedent-consequent) of a rule does not matter. The fact that the knowledge is being expressed as a rule is important.

Rule-based systems are often also called *production systems*, an idea that dates from Post [Post, 1943] and the Markov algorithm. The basic underlying concept of these systems [Waterman, 1978, 1986a; Lenat, 1977] is this idea of condition-action pairs or rule knowledge as described above.

Rule-based systems are by far the most popular knowledge representation technique within existing or developing knowledge-based systems. This can be attributed to the excellent ability of rules to represent heuristic knowledge. Rule-based systems also tend to be easy to implement and to understand once implemented. Additionally, as we discussed above, rules are a natural and very common format used by experts to express problem-solving knowledge in many types of domains.

4.3 RULE-BASED INFERENCE

Rule-based systems use the modus ponens rule of inference described in Chapter 3 to manipulate rules. This means that given

```
fact A is true and
operation A → B is true,
then fact B is derived to be true
```

Using search techniques and *pattern matching*, rule-based systems automate these reasoning methods and provide the logical progression from initial data to the desired conclusions. This progression causes new facts to be derived and leads to a solution of the problem. Thus, the process of problem solving in knowledge-based systems is to create a series of inferences that create a "path" between the problem definition and its solution. This series of inferences is progressive in nature and is called an *inference chain*.

To illustrate this idea, consider the following very simple example. Suppose we are building a knowledge-based system for forecasting the weather over the next 12 to 24 hours in Florida during the summer. Among many others, it would contain the following rule:

```
RULE 1:  IF    the ambient temperature is above 90° F
         THEN  the weather is hot
```

While rule 1 does not say much by itself, the advantage of a rule-based system is that a group of rules can be created to form a rule chain capable of reaching a more meaningful conclusion. Adding the following two rules illustrates this idea:

```
RULE 2:  IF    the relative humidity is greater than 65%
         THEN  the atmosphere is humid

RULE 3:  IF    the weather is hot and the atmosphere is humid
         THEN  thunderstorms are likely to develop
```

Facts, on the other hand, are statements considered true within the knowledge-based system. Practically speaking, facts represent the data used by the system. Let us suppose that the following facts are true:

```
            The ambient temperature is 92° F
                          and
            The relative humidity is 70%
```

Rules 1 and 2 would "see" these facts and deduce the following new facts:

```
            The atmosphere is humid
                      and
            The weather is hot
```

which *satisfy* the premises of rule 3, causing it to derive the new fact:

```
            Thunderstorms are likely to develop
```

Of course, in this simple example, a single rule could have been written to reach the same conclusion directly:

```
RULE 1-A:  IF    the ambient temperature is above
                 90° F and
                 the atmospheric relative humidity
                 > 65%
           THEN  thunderstorms are likely to develop
```

Nevertheless, the example shows how a chain of rules would work. Additionally, there may be other rules that use the facts *"The weather is hot"* and *"The atmosphere is humid"* for other purposes, making a good case for keeping the three rules separate.

Rule-based systems differ from logic in the following major ideas:

1. They are generally nonmonotonic.

2. They accept uncertainty in the deductive process.

As explained in Chapter 3, nonmonotonic reasoning is the concept by which derived facts can be retracted when they are no longer true. This represents a more realistic view of the world.

As defined in logic, deduction always carries complete certainty in its inferences. Deduction is also considered to infer from the general to the specific (i.e., from cause to effect). Unfortunately, in the real world, the cause and effect relationships are not always completely understood and, thus, cannot always be said to be certain. In the thunderstorm example, the inference progresses from the cause to the effect, which describes deduction. Yet, since our understanding of the meteorological phenomenon is incomplete, we hedge our bets and assign a measure of uncertainty to the conclusion derived (i.e., thunderstorms are *likely*).

4.4 THE REASONING PROCESS

The reasoning process of rule-based systems is a progression from a set of data toward a solution, answer, or conclusion. How we obtain our result, however, can vary significantly. In some situations, humans find it most natural to progress from the initial data to a final answer. This approach makes good sense whenever little data are required and/or there are many possible conclusions.

Alternatively, applications exist where many pieces of data are available and only a small portion of them is relevant. It would be highly inefficient to consider all of the data, most of which would be irrelevant anyway. A good example of this is when we go to our physician. We tell him/her only about our abnormal symptoms (e.g., headache, nausea) rather than providing all the data that imply our good health. A good doctor determines a possible diagnosis based on the limited initial data that we provide and then tries to prove the hypothesis by asking additional questions.

Thus, there are two means of progressing toward conclusions:

1. Start with all the known data and progress naturally to the conclusion (*data driven* or *forward chaining*).

2. Select a possible conclusion and try to prove its validity by looking for supporting evidence (*goal driven* or *backward chaining*).

Let us illustrate these ideas through an example. Suppose we have a task of identifying different varieties of fruit. We might describe the knowledge used in this identification process through a set of rules that examine the physical characteristics of the fruit. This knowledge could consist of the following set of rules:

```
Rule 1:  IF    Shape  =  long and
               Color  =  green or yellow
         THEN  Fruit  =  banana

Rule 2:  IF    Shape  =  round or oblong and
               Diameter  >  4 inches
         THEN  Fruitclass  =  vine

Rule 3:  IF    Shape  =  round and
               Diameter  <  4 inches
         THEN  Fruitclass  =  tree

Rule 4:  IF    Seedcount  =  1
         THEN  Seedclass  =  stonefruit

Rule 5:  IF    Seedcount  >  1
         THEN  Seedclass  =  multiple

Rule 6:  IF    Fruitclass  =  vine and
               Color  =  green
         THEN  Fruit  =  watermelon

Rule 7:  IF    Fruitclass  =  vine and
               Surface  =  smooth and
               Color  =  yellow
         THEN  Fruit  =  honeydew

Rule 8:  IF    Fruitclass  =  vine and
               Surface  =  rough and
               Color  =  tan
         THEN  Fruit  =  cantaloupe

Rule 9:  IF    Fruitclass  =  tree and
               Color  =  orange and
               Seedclass  =  stonefruit
         THEN  Fruit  =  apricot

Rule 10: IF    Fruitclass  =  tree and
               Color  =  orange and
               Seedclass  =  multiple
         THEN  Fruit  =  orange
```

```
Rule 11:IF    Fruitclass = tree and
              Color = red and
              Seedclass = stonefruit
      THEN    Fruit = cherry

Rule 12:IF    Fruitclass = tree and
              Color = orange and
              Seedclass = stonefruit
      THEN    Fruit = peach

Rule 13:IF    Fruitclass = tree and
              Color = red or yellow or green and
              Seedclass = multiple
      THEN    Fruit = apple

Rule 14:IF    Fruitclass = tree and
              Color = purple and
              Seedclass = stonefruit
      THEN    Fruit = plum
```

Note that each rule describes some characteristics of the different types of fruit through a series of *parameters*. When used in the premises, these parameters identify values that are necessary for the rules to execute. When used in the conclusions, these parameters identify values that will be derived when the rules execute. In this regard, parameters are similar to variables in programming languages with each having a specific set of values that are acceptable.

The knowledge expressed in the rules above is shown pictorially in Figure 4.1 using an *and-or tree*, which graphically expresses the AND and OR operators. Data provided by a user are given on the left side of this figure and conclusions drawn by the rules on the right. Some links between the data and a particular conclusion have a short curved arc at the intersection point of various links. This represents a conjunction of the links, and the parameter where the links meet is an *AND-parameter* (i.e., its validity depends on the correctness of <u>all</u> the connected links). The connected links not having a short arc, on the other hand, represent the disjunction of the links, meaning that the truth of one of the links is sufficient to establish the truth of the parameter being pointed at. This parameter is called an *OR-parameter*. This graphical format clearly details the connections that exist between rules via the parameters. Note the presence of *intermediate facts* or parameters (e.g., *fruitclass*), which are facts located between the data provided by the user and the final goals or conclusions. Intermediate facts are derived from the information provided initially by the user that are in turn used to derive the final results or conclusions. Generally, these facts can be derived through the application of some rules rather than being requested directly from the user.

This brings us back to the idea of data-driven and goal-driven reasoning. These are means of using the knowledge contained within a knowledge base.

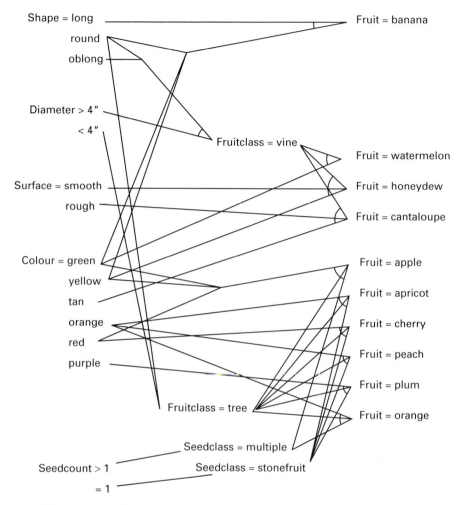

FIGURE 4.1 Graphical Representation of the Fruit Identification Knowledge Base

In data-driven reasoning, a rule is selected for execution when its premises (i.e., the rule's IFs) are satisfied. Progress is made forward from the data toward a solution of the problem. This reasoning approach is ideally suited for problem domains involving synthesis, such as design, configuration, planning, and scheduling. In these problem domains the data drive the solution approach and, potentially, many different but equally acceptable solutions exist. When using forward chaining to solve our fruit classification problem, we would start with an initial set of data that have been gathered from observing a piece of fruit and progress toward the classification.

In goal-driven reasoning, a goal is selected and the system seeks to verify its validity by finding supporting evidence. This approach is ideally suited for

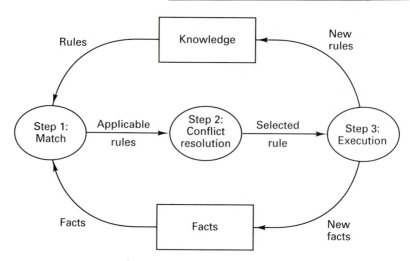

FIGURE 4.2   Forward Reasoning Inference Process

diagnostic problems that have a small number of conclusions that can be drawn. In our fruit identification problem, backward reasoning starts with a hypothesis of what the fruit is and we see if the characteristics of the actual fruit support this hypothesis. The system requests inputs only when they are needed. When it finds the answer, it can stop the execution or go on to satisfy another goal.

Now that we have a very basic idea of how reasoning can be performed using rules, let us examine additional details about how these methods actually work.

4.4.1 Forward Reasoning

In forward reasoning, we start from a set of data collected through observation and work toward a conclusion. We check each of the rules to see if the observed data satisfy the premises of any of these rules. If a rule is satisfied, the rule is executed, deriving new facts that might then be used by other rules to derive additional facts. This process of checking the rules to see if they are satisfied is called *rule interpretation*.

Rule interpretation is performed by the inference engine in a knowledge-based system. Rule interpretation, or inference, in forward reasoning involves the repetition of the basic steps shown in Figure 4.2 [Davis, 1983]:

1. *Matching.*   In this step, the rules in the knowledge base are compared to the known facts to decide which rules are *satisfied*. By satisfied we mean that all of the situations, premises, or antecedents of the rule have been found true.

2. *Conflict Resolution.*   It is possible that the matching phase will find multiple rules that are satisfied. Conflict resolution involves selecting the rule with the highest priority from the set of all rules that have the potential to be executed (i.e., those whose premises have been satisfied).

3. *Execution.*   The last step in rule interpretation is the execution (or *firing*) of the rule. This execution can result in one of two possible outcomes: A new fact (or facts) can be derived and added to the fact base, or a new rule (or rules) can be added to the set of rules (the knowledge base) that the system considers for execution.

In this manner, execution of the rules proceeds in a forward manner (from the *if*s to the *then*s) toward the final goals.

To illustrate this process, let us consider the fruit identification rules. For this example, we must specify a particular interpreter, similar to the one just presented, that clarifies the process of conflict resolution. This interpreter consists of the following steps:

1. [Matching] Find all rules whose premises are true and mark them as being applicable.

2. [Conflict Resolution] If more than one rule applies, then deactivate any whose actions add a duplicate result to the database.

3. [Action] Execute the action of the lowest numbered applicable rule. If none applies, then halt.

4. [Reset] Reset the applicability of all rules and return to step 1.

Note that the matching phase of the inference engine involves examining the knowledge base to see if the specified parameters have been given the values shown within the rule.

For this example, consider the database to consist of the following facts:

Database:
```
Diameter = 1 inch
Shape = round
Seedcount = 1
Color = red
```

Figure 4.3 details a trace of the execution of this system. In execution cycle 1 the inference process finds that two rules apply, rules 3 and 4. Since both rules will derive new facts, the lowest numbered of these rules is selected and executed deriving *fruitclass = tree*. Note that for illustration purposes only the newly derived facts are specified when a rule executes rather than the entire database. In each execution cycle, one rule is selected for execution and its specified conclusion is derived and added to the database. In cycle 4 we

Execution cycle	Applicable rules	Selected rule	Derived fact
1	3, 4	3	Fruitclass = tree
2	3, 4	4	Seedclass = stonefruit
3	3, 4, 11	11	Fruit = cherry
4	3, 4, 11	—	—

FIGURE 4.3   Trace of Rule-based Execution

discover that all of the applicable rules have been executed (i.e., their conclusions are already derived and present within the database). As a result, no rules are selected and execution halts. The final conclusion derived by the system is that the fruit must be a cherry.

4.4.2 Backward Reasoning

The inference mechanism, or rule interpreter for backward reasoning, differs significantly from that of forward reasoning. While both processes involve an examination and application of rules, backward reasoning starts with a desired conclusion and decides if the existing facts support the derivation of a value for this conclusion. As a result, backward reasoning corresponds very closely to depth-first search. The system starts with a database of known facts that is typically empty:

Known Fact Base: ( )

A list of goals (or conclusions) is provided for which the system attempts to derive values. These goals are specified in the order that the developer feels is best to pursue. For our fruit identification problem, there is only a single goal:

Goals: (fruit)

Backward reasoning uses this list of goals to coordinate its search through the rule knowledge base. This search consists of the following steps:

1. Form a stack initially composed of all of the top-level goals defined in the system.
2. Consider the first goal from the stack. Gather all rules capable of satisfying this goal.
3. For each of these rules, examine in turn the rule's premises:
   a. If all premises for a rule are satisfied (i.e., each premise's parameter has its specified value contained in the database), then execute this

rule to derive its conclusions. Since a value has been derived for the current goal, remove this goal from the stack and return to step 2.

b. If a premise of a rule is not satisfied (i.e., one of the premise's parameter's values does not exist within the database), look for rules that derive the specified value for the parameter used in this premise. If any can be found, then consider this parameter to be a subgoal, place it on the top of the stack, and go to step 2.

c. If step b cannot find a rule to derive the specified value for the current parameter, then query the user for its value and add it to the database. If this value satisfies the current premise then continue with this rule's next premise. If the premise is not satisfied, then consider the next rule.

4. If all rules that can satisfy the current goal have been attempted and all have failed to derive a value, then this goal remains undetermined. Remove it from the stack and go back to step 2. If the stack is empty (i.e., all top-level goals have been tried), then halt and announce completion.

To illustrate backward reasoning, let us assume the piece of fruit that we are examining is a cherry. Let us now trace the execution of the rules to see if they are able to derive *cherry* as the value for *fruit*. The trace of execution begins with the single top level goal: *fruit*.

Step 2 specifies that all rules that can derive this goal should be gathered. This list of rules consists of rules 1, 6, 7, 8, 9, 10, 11, 12, 13, and 14. Execution starts with the first of these rules, rule 1. The first premise of this rule (*shape = long*) is examined and no value for *shape* is found in the database. Since no rules can derive a value for the premise *shape*, the inference mechanism asks the user for its value:

What is the value for shape?

We respond with the value of *round* which is added to the database:

Known Fact Base:
((shape = round))

Rule-based systems generally follow the closed-world assumption described in Chapter 3. Therefore, since the proper value for this premise was not found, this value causes rule 1 to fail. Execution then proceeds to rule 6. The first premise of this rule (*fruitclass = vine*) is examined and no value for this parameter is found in the database. A search of the rules determines that rules 2 and 3 are capable of deriving values for *fruitclass*, so we temporarily suspend our processing for *fruit* and add this parameter to the stack:

Goals: (fruitclass fruit)

After collecting the two rules (rules 2 and 3) that can derive values for *fruit-class*, we examine the first of these to see if it is satisfied. The first premise of rule 2 asks if the value of *shape* equals *round* or *oblong*. Since the *shape* does exist in the database and does have a value of *round*, we proceed to the next premise. A value for *diameter* does not exist and no rules derive its value so we ask the user for a value:

What is the value of diameter?

The user responds with *1 inch* which changes the database to:

Known Fact Base:
```
( (shape = round)
  (diameter = 1 inch) )
```

Rule 2 fails since its second premise is not satisfied. The interpreter now examines rule 3. Both premises of this rule are satisfied by the values in the database so this rule derives *fruitclass = tree* which is added to the database:

Known Fact Base:
```
( (shape = round)
  (diameter = 1 inch)
  (fruitclass = tree) )
```

Since a value for *fruitclass* has been found, this goal is removed from the goal list and we return to the goal *fruit*, continuing with rule 6. Because the value derived for *fruitclass* does not satisfy the first premise of this rule, we proceed to the next rule, rule 7.

Both rule 7 and rule 8 fail since both of their first premises (i.e., *fruitclass = vine*) are not satisfied. The next rule, rule 9, has its first premise (*fruitclass = tree*) satisfied, so we examine the next premise, *color = orange*. The value for *color* is not in the database and no rules can derive it so the inference process asks the user for its value:

What is the value of color?

to which we respond *red*. This value causes rules 9 and 10 to fail. Finally we reach rule 11. The first two premises are satisfied by values in the database so we proceed to the third premise, *seedclass = stonefruit*. Since no value exists in the database for this parameter and no rules derive it, the inference process asks the user for a value:

What is the value of seedclass?

to which we respond *stonefruit*, satisfying rule 11 and allowing it to fire. Having derived *cherry* as the value for *fruit*, our final database is:

Known Fact Base:
```
( (shape = round)
  (diameter = 1 inch)
  (fruitclass = tree)
  (color = red)
  (seedclass = stonefruit)
  (fruit = cherry) )
```

Since *fruit* has a value, it is removed from the goal stack. The stack is now empty, so the backward reasoning process halts with the appropriate value derived for *fruit*.

4.5 RULE-BASED ARCHITECTURES

The type of knowledge described with rule-based systems varies significantly in complexity. Sometimes the conclusions drawn by rules can be facts that match the premises of other rules precisely. In these instances we can visualize a knowledge base as a network of interconnected rules and facts.

In other cases, the conclusions drawn are more general. As a result, we cannot form a visualization of the knowledge base as a network. Instead, we are forced to think of the conclusions drawn by rules as a collection of facts that might or might not match the various patterns described by other rule premises.

As a result, there are two basic structures and organizations to the knowledge contained within a rule-based system (1) *inference networks* and (2) *pattern-matching systems*. The following subsections examine these two structures in more detail to clarify their differences further.

4.5.1 Inference Networks

An inference network can be represented as a graph in which the nodes represent parameters that are facts obtained as raw data or derived from other data (i.e., intermediate parameters). Each parameter (fact) makes a statement about some aspect of the problem under analysis and can serve as an antecedent or consequent of a rule. These statements can range from the final conclusion of a system to simple, observed, or incrementally derived intermediate facts. Each of these parameters can have one or more associated values, where each value has a corresponding measure of uncertainty representing how credible the particular value is for that parameter.

The rules in the system are represented within this graph by the interconnections between the various nodes. This knowledge is used by the infer-

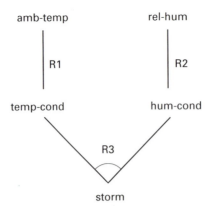

FIGURE 4.4 A Sample Inference Network

ence process to propagate results throughout the network. Note that all of the interconnections between the various nodes of the inference network are known prior to the execution of the system. As a result, all of the interconnections can be stated explicitly prior to run-time, which minimizes searching for facts that match premises. They also simplify the implementation of the inference engine and the handling of explanations. When inference is performed, values are derived and set for the various parameters. This is similar to deriving new facts and placing them within a fact base. Because the explicit interconnections are shown, the conflict resolution problem is reduced to simply maintaining a list of newly matched rules for subsequent firing. Thus, it is easy to decide what resulting actions need to be taken whenever some fact is derived.

Consider the weather example discussed earlier. This small set of rules could be implemented as the inference network shown in Figure 4.4. Note that the ambient temperature and relative humidity are parameters with unique numeric values that might be set by an external data acquisition system. These inputs are called *amb-temp* and *rel-hum*, respectively, within the figure. Rules 1 and 2 use the values of these parameters in an attempt to satisfy their premises. If these rules successfully execute, they derive and set the values of two other parameters, *temp-cond* and *hum-cond*, which hold symbolic values representing the qualitative conditions of the atmosphere, (i.e., *hot* and *humid*, respectively). These last two parameters are then used by rule 3 to derive a value for the last parameter, *storm*.

MYCIN, PROSPECTOR, and GenAID are examples of large knowledge-based systems that successfully employed the inference network architecture. All three are related to either diagnostics (MYCIN and GenAID) or classification (PROSPECTOR) in a science or engineering-based domain.

The Personal Consultant system, discussed in Appendix B, is a rule-based system shell that uses the inference network architecture.

4.5.2 Pattern-matching Systems

Pattern-matching systems use extensive searches to match and execute the rules, deriving new facts. They typically use sophisticated implementations of pattern matching to bind variables, constrain the permissible values to be matched to a premise, and determine which rules to execute. Relationships between rules and facts are formed at run-time based on the patterns that match the facts.

A pattern-matching system depends on matching the premises of a rule to existing *facts* to determine which rules have their premises satisfied by the facts and can, therefore, execute. The result of rule execution is most often an assertion of newly derived facts into the *fact base*. The premises of a rule are *patterns*, which may be either simple or complex. These patterns are satisfied when a search through the database of facts discovers any facts that match them.

While the argument can be made that facts in a pattern-matching system are equivalent to the parameters in an inference net, the use of multifield facts, multifield patterns, variables, and the potential for multiple instantiations for each variable, make this architecture significantly different from an inference net.

Pattern matching is an important and powerful idea in automated reasoning that we saw for the first time in PROLOG. The pattern-matching features of rule-based systems can become quite intricate, allowing complex constraints within the rule's premises. These restrictions can specify elaborate patterns that do not have identical matches within the fact base. The facts instead match these patterns because the facts adhere to elements within these involved restrictions. The typical features included within pattern-matching systems are classified as one of the following five types:

1. *Pattern connectives.* Pattern connectives are the relationships that connect the individual patterns (or premises) together to form the overall condition of the rule. Individual patterns are typically AND'ed or OR'ed. More complicated relationships can be specified using a combination of conjuctions and disjunctions. The default connective is usually the conjunction.

2. *Wildcard.* A wildcard is a term within a pattern that is similar to a variable. It can match any atomic symbol or number within a fact, but no binding occurs as a result. The wildcard is used to match symbols that are superfluous to the current pattern. No binding is performed to the wildcard since its corresponding position is to be ignored. Two wildcard symbols are typically provided: ? and $. The first, ?, is used to represent a single field in a fact, while the second, $, represents zero or more fields. To illustrate their use consider the following example. Suppose that we

are building a knowledge base describing houses. Each house might be described within this fact base by a four-tuple: the type of house being represented, its color, number of stories, and square footage. For example,

(contemporary brown 2 2835)
(ranch red 1 1565)

If we are interested in a contemporary house that has a certain square footage, but do not care about its color or number of stories, we might use one of the following patterns (among others):

(contemporary ? ? ⟨var1⟩)
(contemporary $ ⟨var1⟩)

3. *Field constraints.* Often, there is a need to constrain the values of a field in a pattern for a successful match. These constraints allow the pattern to specify values that should not be allowed within a field (using the not, ~, symbol) or alternative values that would be acceptable (using the disjunctive, I, symbol). For instance, in the house example, if we were interested in a ranch house that was definitely not a red color we might specify the pattern

(ranch ~red ? ⟨var1⟩)

Or if we desired a contemporary house that was either gray or white

(contemporary gray|white ? ⟨var1⟩)

4. *Mathematical operators.* Mathematical operators are used both in the premises and in the conclusions (action) of a rule. Once a variable is bound, various operations can be performed with it. For example, in our house database, we may have a rule that calculates the average square footage for each story of a house and derives it as a new fact:

```
RULE 10   IF    (⟨var1⟩ ? ⟨var2⟩ ⟨var3⟩)
          THEN (assert (avg–size ⟨var1⟩
                              (⟨var3⟩/⟨var2⟩)))
```

5. *Test feature.* This feature is a variation of the field constraints used with the mathematical operators and pattern connectives to test the value of a field. Various testing operations are typically provided. For example, a more complicated form of the average-square-footage-per-floor rule might find the average square footage per floor for the house with the largest number of floors:

```
RULE 11   IF    (⟨var1⟩ ? ⟨var2⟩ ⟨var3⟩)
                (⟨var4⟩ ? ⟨var5⟩ ⟨var6⟩)
                (test (not (⟨var5⟩ > ⟨var2⟩))))
          THEN (assert (avg–size ⟨var1⟩
                              (⟨var3⟩/⟨var2⟩)))
```

Rule 11's use of the NOT operation makes it a little tricky to understand. To pass this test, there cannot be any house that has more floors than the house matched by the first pattern.

Commercially available pattern matchers, such as the one found in CLIPS, contain additional as well as more advanced features than the simple ones illustrated above. Some of these features are discussed in greater detail in Appendix A.

4.5.3 Evaluation of the Architectures

Rule-based systems that use pattern matchers are extremely flexible and powerful. They are more applicable for domains where the possible solutions are either unbound or large in numbers, such as design, planning, and synthesis. In these domains, there are no predetermined relationships between the rules and the facts. While the patterns used by these systems are extremely flexible in the types of knowledge that they can express, they are awkward to diagram on paper and, typically, do not easily support reasoning with uncertainty. Additionally, the use of search to find applicable rules makes pattern matchers inefficient in large implementations. Despite these disadvantages, several knowledge-based systems (e.g., XCON) and shells (e.g., OPS-5, ART, CLIPS, and KEE) are based on the pattern-matching architecture.

Inference networks, on the other hand, are quite useful for domains where the number of different alternative solutions is limited, e.g., the classification of elements in the natural sciences and diagnostic problems. An inference network is easier to implement, but less powerful because all the relationships between rules and facts have to be known ahead of time, thus precluding the ability to synthesize new relationships during the inference process.

Another advantage to inference networks is that they more easily allow for the explanation of the solution derived by the system. This is because the predetermined chain of rules can be easily traced to explain the problem-solving process followed. In a pattern-matching system, there are no such explicitly defined relationships. All the paths must be dynamically "remembered" as the inference engine carries out the rule execution.

4.6 DISADVANTAGES OF RULE-BASED SYSTEMS

Several problems exist with rule-based systems. These problems fall into one of three categories: (1) infinite chaining, (2) addition of new, contradictory knowledge, and (3) modification of existing rules.

The first two problems result from the *Great Myth of Rule-Based Systems* [Davis, 1983]:

If the system does not work properly, then all that you need to do is add more rules.

4.6.1 Infinite Chaining

When adding a rule, take care to ensure that infinite looping (forward chaining) or infinite backward chaining does not occur. Figure 4.5 provides an example for each of these cases.

```
RULE 23: IF    sickle-cell-risk (?person)
         THEN  sickle-cell-risk (son(?person))

RULE 57: IF    sickle-cell-risk (father(?person))
         THEN  sickle-cell-risk (?person)
```

FIGURE 4.5 Infinite Chaining Rules

Rule 23 illustrates infinite looping as it can occur in forward chaining. Suppose that John has a risk of carrying sickle cell anemia. This rule states that his son also has a similar risk. So the application of this rule would derive *sickle-cell-risk (son(John))*. Note that this fact in the database now also matches the premise of the rule so we would derive *sickle-cell-risk (son(son(John)))*. This again satisfies the premise. As you can see, our system will hang on this rule, continually deriving the risk of sickle cell for all future generations of John's male descendants.

Rule 57 illustrates the same process for backward chaining. Suppose that we are attempting to derive whether Tom has a risk of sickle cell anemia. This rule states that Tom's risk is dependent on his father's risk. So we set a subgoal of deciding if *sickle-cell-risk(father(Tom))* is true. Rule 57 states that this can be determined by looking at this person's father so a second subgoal is set of *sickle-cell-risk(father(father(Tom)))*. In a fashion similar to that which occurs in forward chaining, this process now infinitely loops.

Note that while these two examples illustrate infinite chaining within a single rule, it is possible and much more likely for the same situation to occur through several rules. For example, see Figure 4.6. Such situations are typically very hard to detect through a simple examination of the knowledge base as you can see by this example.

4.6.2 Addition of New, Contradictory Knowledge

In rule-based systems it is possible to introduce new knowledge to fix some problem in the knowledge base, which in turn introduces a contradiction. See Figure 4.7.

RULE 15: IF   mortgage rates are high and new construction is
                 increasing
          THEN   it is a buyer's market

RULE 34: IF   inflation is high and
                 The prime rate is greater than 12%
          THEN   mortgage rates are high

RULE 130: IF   money is hard to borrow and it is a buyer's market
                 and short-term interest rates are greater than 13%
          THEN   inflation is high

FIGURE 4.6   Infinite Chaining through Multiple Rules

RULE 107: IF   it is raining
          THEN   not (weather is sunny)

RULE 109: IF   location is Florida
          THEN   not (weather is cloudy)

RULE 96: IF   time of day is late afternoon
          THEN   weather is sunny or
                 weather is cloudy

FACTS: time of day is late afternoon
          location is Florida

FIGURE 4.7   Introduction of Contradictions

Rule 96 states very general information about late afternoon weather. The given set of facts satisfy both this rule and rule 109. Combining their derived results provides a final conclusion that the weather is sunny.

Now suppose that the rule shown in Figure 4.8 is added to the knowledge base. Combining the results of rules 96, 107, 109, and 120, we encounter a contradiction where the identity of the weather is not derived. Note that rules 96, 107, and 109 work properly together and rules 96, 109, and 120 do also. It is only when all four rules are combined that a problem occurs. Situations such

---

RULE 120: IF   time of day is late afternoon and
                 location is Florida
          THEN   it is raining

FIGURE 4.8   An Additional Rule

as these can be extremely difficult to locate and correct as a knowledge base becomes larger and increasingly more complex.

4.6.3 Modifications to Existing Rules

Another difficulty that can exist with rule-based systems occurs when making modifications to existing knowledge. Suppose that we are modifying a rule base that contains knowledge about the treatment of diseases. The rule base as initially constructed might have contained many rules of the format shown in Figure 4.9 [Davis, 1983]. This rule states that if we have identified the organism causing the current infection to be either strep (streptococcus) or gonorrhea, then we should prescribe penicillin as a treatment.

```
RULE 302: IF    organism = strep or
                organism = gonorrhea
          THEN prescription = penicillin
```

FIGURE 4.9   The Specification of Penicillin as a Treatment

When specifying this rule, the knowledge engineer and expert failed to recognize that some individuals have an allergic reaction to penicillin. This might imply modifications to the knowledge base as shown in Figure 4.10 [Davis, 1983]. Rule 302 now merely indicates that penicillin is a treatment for these organisms. Rule 342 questions whether penicillin is indicated and whether it is unknown that the patient has an allergy to this drug. If these conditions are satisfied, the rule specifies to ask if the patient is allergic. Finally, rule 367 tests to see if penicillin is indicated and the patient is not al-

---

```
RULE 302: IF    organism = strep or
                organism = gonorrhea
          THEN indicated-drug = penicillin

RULE 342: IF    indicated-drug = penicillin and
                unknown (allergy-to = penicillin)
          THEN ask (allergy-to = penicillin)

Rule 367: IF    indicated-drug = penicillin and
                not (allergy-to = penicillin)
          THEN prescription = penicillin
```

FIGURE 4.10   Modified Rules to Deal with Allergies to Penicillin

lergic to penicillin. If both conditions are satisfied, the rule at last prescribes penicillin as a treatment.

This modification, however, leads to the specification of many additional rules. Patients can be allergic to aspirin, tetracycline, and so forth. Each of these allergies would require a modification like the one shown in Figure 4.10. A knowledge engineer who thinks carefully about this problem will recognize that a single modification, using variables, could handle all of these cases as shown in Figure 4.11 [Davis, 1983].

```
RULE 342 : IF   indicated–drug  =  ?drug and
                unknown (allergy–to  =  ?drug)
          THEN  ask (allergy–to  =  ?drug)

RULE 367 : IF   indicated–drug  –  ?drug and
                not (allergy–to  =  ?drug)
          THEN  prescription  =  ?drug
```

FIGURE 4.11   Alternative Modification to the Rule Base to Deal with All Allergies

4.6.4 Additional Disadvantages

Three additional disadvantages to rule-based systems must be mentioned:

1. *Inefficiency:* The execution of pattern-matching rule representations is highly inefficient. During every cycle of the inference engine, each rule in the knowledge base is examined to see whether it applies to the current situation. Some improvements have been made in this area such as the *Rete algorithm* of OPS-5, described in Chapter 5, and the subdivision of knowledge bases into partitions in the TI Personal Consultant, but an adequate solution to this problem remains to be found.

2. *Opacity:* It is very difficult to examine a developed knowledge base and determine what actions are going to occur when. The division of knowledge into small distinct packets, while making each rule easier to deal with individually, creates a global perspective that is hard to comprehend.

3. *Coverage of domain:* There are domains that contain so many variations of the inputs that they would require knowledge bases containing tens of thousands of rules. Developing such a knowledge base would be an extremely difficult process, even while ignoring the problems of its verification and maintenance. For example, consider air traffic control. A knowledge-based system to assist air traffic controllers would be a significant aid for the industry. This is a good application area since the knowledge is generally heuristic in nature and controllers tend to think

in terms of rules. However, such a system would need to consider and represent a nearly infinite number of situations given the potential number of aircraft in the air at once (and all of their features—types, locations, speeds, etc.), the weather conditions, and any emergencies that are present.

4.7 ADVANTAGES OF RULE-BASED SYSTEMS

While the disadvantages detailed above do exist, rule-based systems have remained the most commonly used knowledge representation scheme for knowledge-based systems. This has resulted from their three significant advantages:

1. *Modularity:* Rule-based knowledge is highly modular. Ignoring the caveats expressed above, each rule is a distinct separate unit of knowledge that can be added, modified, or removed independently of the other rules that exist. This gives the knowledge engineer great flexibility in developing a knowledge base since she can develop some portion, test that portion, then add it to the existing knowledge base, slowly expanding the knowledge base into its final form.
2. *Uniformity:* All knowledge in the system is expressed in exactly the same format. This eases the development of the knowledge base by the knowledge engineer since a uniform representation requires less shifting of thought on her part.
3. *Naturalness:* Rules are a natural format for expressing knowledge within some domain. Experts logically think about problems and their solutions using the existing situations to point to the desired conclusions.

4.8 CHAPTER REVIEW

Rule-based systems are the most common type of knowledge-based system. This is partly due to the natural expression of knowledge by humans as condition/action relationships. Thus, it is no surprise that most major knowledge-based systems built at this time are based on rules.

Rules represent conditional knowledge that is quite similar to the way humans express it. They express knowledge as a two-part relationship. The first part is a conditional test, called the *IF,* the *premise,* or the *antecedent.* If the test is satisfied through a true match with known facts, then the second part, called the *THEN,* the *action*, or the *consequent*, is executed. Rules look like conditional statements in conventional languages, but unlike the latter, rules are applied in a totally different manner, making rule-based systems declarative.

Rules are applied in two ways: *data driven* and *goal driven*. If the number of inputs is limited, many inputs are acquired automatically, and/or the number of possible conclusions is large, then rules are applied in a *data-driven* fashion. *Forward chaining* (as it is also called) progresses from the initial facts, to intermediate facts, and ultimately to a solution or set of solutions. Modus ponens provides the basis for this reasoning.

Alternatively, if the number of possible final conclusions (called *goals*) is limited, and/or input values are not acquired automatically, then reasoning backwards from a goal is more efficient. In *goal-driven reasoning*, or *backward chaining*, the rules are applied only to derive values for goals or for intermediate facts used later to set values to these goals. This process is called *tracing a goal*. Tracing stops when a goal is either found true or proven to be unsupported because no rule can derive the goal's value.

There are two major architectures for implementing knowledge-based systems: *pattern-matching systems* and *inference nets*. These architectures define how the rules are expressed and related to the facts, as well as how the matching of the premises to the facts is performed.

Pattern-matching systems use extensive searches to match and execute the rules, deriving new facts. They typically use sophisticated implementations of pattern matching to bind variables, constrain the permissible values to be matched to a premise, and determine which rules to fire. Relationships between rules and facts are formed at run-time based on the patterns that match the facts.

Inference nets, on the other hand, are less flexible and less powerful, but more efficient because the relationships between the rules and the parameters are formed prior to run-time. These predefined relationships minimize the search for matching facts to premises and for executing the rules. They also simplify the implementation of the inference engine and the handling of explanations.

While both architectures will work with either backward or forward chaining, pattern matchers have traditionally been forward chainers, while backward chainers have been inference nets.

The advantages of rule-based systems are (1) modularity, (2) uniformity, and (3) naturalness.

The disadvantages of rule-based systems, on the other hand, include (1) infinite chaining, (2) existence of contradictory knowledge, (3) inconsistent addition of new rules, (4) inefficiency, (5) opacity, and (6) combinatorial explosion for some applications.

This chapter sets the stage for the discussion of the actual rule-based inferencing techniques, forward and backward chaining, which are the subject of the next chapter.

4.9 PROBLEMS

4-1. Does the order of the rules have any effect on the derived results in forward reasoning? Justify your answer.

4-2. Does the order of the rules have any effect on the derived results in backward reasoning? Justify your answer.

4-3. For each of the following, state why or why not a forward reasoning approach would be suitable.

(**a**) A monitor for the printing of a newspaper for problems with the printing press.

(**b**) A diagnostic system for ignition problems in an automobile.

(**c**) A monitoring system that makes corrections to the process of producing gasoline in a refinery. Note that this is a continuous process where raw materials flow in on one end of the refinery and gasoline and waste products flow out the other.

(**d**) An automatic pilot for a low-altitude aircraft flying over unknown terrain. This system is able to monitor the terrain though radar, sonar, and visual input.

(**e**) A diagnostic system for a printer problem with your personal computer. You issue the print command and nothing happens.

(**f**) A system to determine why your lawn mower will not start.

(**g**) A system to determine the appropriate action for a weapons officer to take in a nuclear attack submarine.

(**h**) An air traffic controller which provides the appropriate directions to aircraft.

(**i**) A design system that helps with the process of designing a bicycle.

(**j**) A scheduling system for games in a Little League baseball season.

(**k**) A financial investment advising system.

(**l**) A system for driving an automobile automatically.

4-4. For each subproblem mentioned in Problem 4-3, state why or why not a backward reasoning approach would be suitable.

4-5. For each subproblem mentioned in Problem 4-3, state why or why not an inference network approach would be suitable.

4-6. For each subproblem mentioned in Problem 4-3, state why or why not a pattern-matching approach would be suitable.

4-7. All programming languages support some form of IF-THEN control construct. Why should we not use this construct to build a knowledge-based system? What does a rule-based shell provide that is not contained within a programming language?

4-8. What does a programming language provide that is not exhibited by a forward chaining knowledge-based system?

4-9. In the discussion of pattern matching we gave two patterns that would find a contemporary house and its square footage, ignoring its color and number of stories:

```
(contemporary ? ? ⟨var1⟩)
(contemporary $ ⟨var1⟩)
```

Create three additional patterns capable of performing this match that do not use any additional variables.

4-10. Consider the house knowledge base presented in the section on pattern matchers. Suppose that the following fact is in our fact base:

```
(spanish red tile-roof
 2-car-garage 2-story 2500)
```

Which of the following are legitimate patterns and to what will the variables be matched?

```
(spanish ? ? 2-car-garage ? ⟨var1⟩)
(⟨var1⟩ $ 2-car-garage $ ⟨var2⟩)
(⟨var1⟩ ? 2-car-garage ? ⟨var2⟩)
```

```
(⟨var1⟩ $ 2–car–garage ? ⟨var2⟩)
(spanish $ 2–story ⟨var1⟩)
(? red $ $ 2–story ⟨var1⟩)
($ ⟨var1⟩ $ ⟨var2⟩ $)
```

4-11. Implement the fruit identification knowledge base using CLIPS.

4-12. Implement the fruit identification knowledge base using PC Plus.

5 ■ Details of Rule-based Reasoning

5.1 INTRODUCTION

How does a rule-based system use modus ponens, deduction, and/or abduction to manipulate the knowledge represented as rules? The two primary methods briefly introduced in the last chapter are *forward-* or *data-driven reasoning* and *backward-* or *goal-directed reasoning*. A third method called *bidirectional reasoning,* which we will not discuss, combines the above two. Which of these methods is best suited for a particular problem depends on the characteristics of that problem. Traditionally, pattern-matching systems have been associated with forward reasoning while backward-reasoning systems typically have been implemented as inference networks. But this is only a historical tendency and in no way limits what can be accomplished. This chapter presents four examples of forward and backward reasoning and examines how forward- and backward-reasoning systems can be implemented.

5.2 FORWARD REASONING

As discussed in the last chapter, forward reasoning is the process of working from a set of data toward the conclusions that can be drawn from this data. A rule is eligible for execution when its *premises* (i.e., the rule's IF) are satisfied. Progress is made forward from the data toward a solution of the problem. The conclusions of rules can be used to match the premises of other rules, firing them if successfully matched.

One set of applications suited for forward reasoning includes monitoring and diagnosing real-time process control systems where data are continually being acquired, modified, and updated. These applications have two important characteristics:

1. The need for a quick response to changes in the input data.
2. Few predetermined relationships existing between the input data and the conclusions drawn.

Typically, these systems use forward reasoning inference networks because of the required efficiency in execution.

Another set of applications suited for forward reasoning includes design, planning, and scheduling where the synthesis of new facts based on the rules' conclusions occurs. In these applications there are many potential solutions that can be derived from the input data. Because these solutions cannot be enumerated, the rules express knowledge as general patterns and the precise connections, or inference chains, between these rules cannot be predetermined. As a result, these applications use forward-reasoning pattern-matching systems due to the implicit flexibility of the pattern-matching approach.

In the following subsections we examine the idea of forward reasoning, the Rete algorithm (used within pattern-matching systems to ease the combinatorial explosion of searching for satisfied rules), various conflict resolution schemes, and the coding of a general forward-reasoning system.

5.2.1 Example 1 of Forward Reasoning

The residents of Low Lands, Florida, have discovered that their long sought retirement village is within the flood plain of the Suwannee River. Because of the frequent floods that occur each spring, they requested Dr. Paul Peters of Experts Technology, Limited, to build a knowledge-based system to alert them whenever a flood warning or evacuation order should be given.

After careful consideration and analysis of their problem, Dr. Peters determined that a total of 10 parameters and 18 rules are required to define and solve this problem. See Figure 5.1. Because this knowledge is relatively simple, the interconnections between the parameters and rules can be detailed using an inference network as shown in Figure 5.2. Recall that an inference network is a graph where the nodes represent various parameters (observed or derived data) and the interconnections between the nodes represent the rule knowledge of the system. The knowledge of these systems forms a true network of interconnections because all of the interconnections between the various nodes are known prior to the execution of the system and can be stated explicitly. In this figure, the circles represent the input parameters, while the rectangles are parameters that are both intermediate and final conclusions. The round-cornered blocks represent intermediate conclusions. Rules are shown as lines connecting the parameters.

When writing these rules, Dr. Peters had to associate confidence factors (CF values) with several of the rule conclusions. Since confidence factors are

PARAMETER	POSSIBLE VALUES
month	any month of the year
upstream precipitation	none, light, heavy
weather *forecast*	sunny, cloudy, stormy
river *height*	measurement in feet
season	dry, wet
local *rain*	none, light rain, heavy rain
river *change*	none, lower, higher
river *level*	low, normal, high
flood warning	yes, no
evacuation order	yes, no

```
R1        IF    month = may . . . oct
          THEN  season = wet

R2        IF    month = nov . . . april
          THEN  season = dry

R3        IF    upstream = none AND
                season = dry
          THEN  change = lower

R4        IF    upstream = none AND
                season = wet
          THEN  change = none

R5        IF    upstream = light
          THEN  change = none

R6        IF    upstream = heavy
          THEN  change = higher

R7        IF    level = low
          THEN  flood = no AND
                evac = no

R8        IF    change = none | lower AND
                level = normal | low
          THEN  flood = no AND
                evac = no

R9        IF    change = higher AND
                level = normal AND
                rain = heavy
          THEN  flood = yes (CF = 0.4) AND
                evac = no
```

FIGURE 5.1   Parameters and Rules for the Flood Warning and Evacuation Knowledge Base

```
R10              IF     change = higher AND
                        level = normal AND
                        rain = light
                 THEN   flood = no AND
                        evac = no

R11              IF     change = higher AND
                        level = high AND
                        rain = none | light
                 THEN   flood = yes (CF = 0.5) AND
                        evac = yes (CF = 0.2)

R12              IF     change = higher AND
                        level = high AND
                        rain = heavy
                 THEN   flood = yes AND
                        evac = yes (CF = 0.8)

R13              IF     height < 10
                 THEN   level = low

R14              IF     height >= 10 AND <= 16
                 THEN   level = normal

R15              IF     height > 16
                 THEN   level = high

R16              IF     forecast = sunny
                 THEN   rain = none

R17              IF     forecast = cloudy
                 THEN   rain = light

R18              IF     forecast = stormy
                 THEN   rain = heavy
```

FIGURE 5.1   (Continued)

described in more detail in Chapter 8, assume for now that these values represent the likelihood or certainty that a particular conclusion is correct.

Dr. Peters also determined that forward reasoning is the most appropriate method for reasoning about this problem's solution because of the following important problem characteristics:

1. The data used by this system can be gathered from a set of sensors, requiring no interaction with the users of the system.
2. The system must continually monitor the data collected by the sensors to determine if a warning should be given.

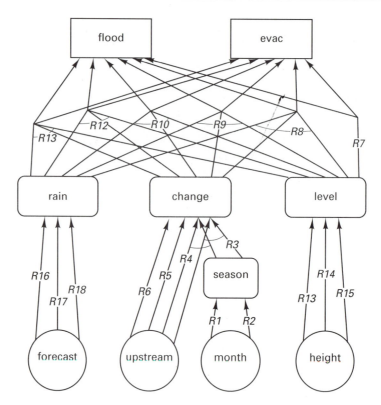

FIGURE 5.2   Inference Network for the Flood Warning and Evacuation Knowledge Base

Because all of the interconnections between the rules can be explicitly defined, Dr. Peters was able to encode this knowledge using an internal representation that exploits this explicitness to simplify rule execution. This internal representation details for each rule:

1. The rule number
2. Parameters used within the premises of the rule (called upstream elements)
3. Parameters used within the conclusions of the rule (called downstream elements)
4. The set of premises
5. The set of conclusions

and for each parameter:

1. The name of the parameter
2. A list of rules that derive a value for this parameter (called set-by)

3. A list of rules that use this parameter in their premises (called premise-for)

4. The value(s) of this parameter (and their associated confidence factors) if known

For example, rule R1 and parameter *change* are described internally as

```
Rule:                       R1
Upstream-elements:          month
Downstream-elements:        season
Premises:                   month = may . . . oct
Conclusions                 season = wet

Parameter:                  change
Set-by:                     (R3 R4 R5 R6)
Premise-for:                (R8 R9 R10 R11 R12)
Values:                     —
```

This solution approach requires maintaining two additional lists that identify which of the parameters are input data and which parameters are conclusions of the system:

```
Input data:      (month upstream forecast height)
Conclusions:     (flood evac)
```

Because all the interconnections among the rules can be stated explicitly, it is easy to determine what actions need to be taken whenever some parameter obtains a value. The algorithm required is the basic breadth-first search technique described in Chapter 1. Figure 5.3 provides the details of this algorithm.

Let us now apply this algorithm to the sample knowledge base provided in Figure 5.1 to determine the derived results. Step 1 of the algorithm requests values for each input data parameter. Assume that the following values are obtained:

```
month =       may
upstream = light
forecast = cloudy
height =       15
```

Step 2 requires that we build a queue of rules. From the diagram of Figure 5.2 we can see this queue would be:

```
Q = (R1  R2  R3  R4  R5  R6  R13  R14  R15  R16  R17  R18)
```

1. Assign values to all input nodes from the external sources providing information to the knowledge-based system.
2. Form a queue, Q, containing all rules that use the values of these input nodes in their premises.
3. Until there are no more rules in Q:
   a. Examine the first rule in Q, comparing its premises with the values of the appropriate parameters to decide if the premises of the rule are satisfied.
   b. If the premises of the rule are not satisfied, remove the rule from Q and go back to a.
   c. If the rule is matched:
      i.   execute the rule, setting the rule's downstream elements to the values specified by the rule,
      ii. decide which rules use the downstream elements just set within their premises,
      iii. add these rules as the last rules within Q if they are not already in Q, even if their premises are not fully satisfied,
      iv. delete the original rule from the front of the Q and return to step a.
4. Output the values of the hypotheses that have been identified as conclusions.
5. If this application involves a real-time process control, go back to step 1 and start the process again.

FIGURE 5.3   Forward-Reasoning Inference Network Algorithm

Step 3 specifies that we examine the first of these rules, R1, to see if its premise is satisfied. The value, *may*, of the parameter *month* does satisfy the premise of R1 so it is executed deriving *season* = *wet*. Additionally, we see that *season* is used as a premise in R3 and R4, but since these rules are already in Q we do not add them. R1 is removed from Q and the next rule, R2, is tried. The premise of this rule fails to be satisfied so it is removed and we proceed to the next rule, R3. Both this rule and the next rule, R4, fail to be satisfied so they are removed from Q. Finally, when R5 is tried, we discover that its premise is satisfied, deriving *change* = *none*. The value of parameter change is used by R8, R9, R10, R11, and R12, all of which are not in Q so Q becomes

Q = (R6 R13 R14 R15 R16 R17 R18 R8 R9 R10 R11 R12)

and the known facts (i.e., parameters with assigned values) are

```
month    =    may
upstream =    light
forecast =    cloudy
height   =    15
season   =    wet
change   =    none
```

This process continues until Q is empty. At this time our database of known facts becomes:

```
month    =    may
upstream = light
forecast = cloudy
height   =    15
season   =    wet
change   =    none
level    =    normal
rain     =    light
flood    =    no
evac     =    no
```

Assuming that this knowledge base is examining a real-time application (which a flood and evacuation system would be), this system now returns to step 1 and acquires a new set of input data parameter values and the process repeats.

Forward-chaining systems implemented as inference networks are very good for applications involving monitoring and diagnosing real-time process control systems where data are continually being acquired, modified, and updated automatically. Forward-chaining inference networks are also preferred in domains (e.g., scientific classification) where the relationships between facts are easily predetermined. GenAID and PROSPECTOR are good examples of forward-chaining inference network systems.

Forward-chaining systems implemented as inference networks are not suited for applications that involve interactive problem solving such as diagnosis and classification where the acquisition of data is done through a keyboard query of a human. For these cases, a more selective approach such as backward reasoning is necessary to minimize the number of queries.

Let us now consider a more complicated example that requires the use of a pattern matcher.

5.2.2 Example 2 of Forward Reasoning

Suppose that John Smith, a student, is changing apartments and needs to move several household items. These items, shown in Figure 5.4, have several important characteristics of which he needs to be aware when packing: Some items are much heavier than others, some occupy more space (specified in the figure using generic space units), some are easily broken, and others are malleable and can occupy many different shaped spaces. John wants to ensure that all of the items survive the move unbroken and is not interested in finding the optimal scheme for packing all of the items since he is making only a very short move.

ITEM	COUNT	WEIGHT	SIZE	FRAGILE?	PLIABLE?
Books	7	heavy	2	no	no
Lamp	2	medium	8	yes	no
Dishes	1 set	medium	5	yes	no
Coat	2	light	3	no	yes
VCR	1	medium	4	no	no
TV	1	heavy	10	yes	no
Glasses	1 set	medium	4	yes	no
Jeans	4	light	2	no	yes
Shirts	8	light	1	no	yes

FIGURE 5.4   Items to Be Packed by the BOXER System

To assist this process, John develops a small knowledge-based system called BOXER to direct his packing process. Note that this problem is one of synthesis, since there are many possible combinations to use in packing all his things; therefore, forward reasoning is quite applicable. This process also requires a pattern matcher since the objects and the boxes can be described by a list of values that detail the object's (or box's) properties.

Recognizing the characteristics specified above for the various objects, John develops four primary steps in his BOXER system:

1. Box the fragile items, first taking care to pad each of these items.
2. Box the heavy-weight items, ensuring that these items are not placed with fragile items.
3. Box the medium-weight items, again ensuring that these items are not placed with fragile items.
4. Box the light-weight items, putting them wherever there is room.

To simplify BOXER's reasoning, John has collected enough boxes all of the same size (10 space units) in which to pack his possessions.

Given these constraints, John creates the following set of rules to direct BOXER's actions:

```
RULE 1  IF    Step is box-fragile-items
              There is a fragile item to box
              There is an empty box or a box
                 containing only fragile items
              The fragile item has not been padded
        THEN  Pad the fragile item
```

```
RULE 2   IF    Step is box-fragile-items
               There is a fragile item to box
               There is an empty box or a box
                  containing only fragile items
               The fragile item has been padded
               The box's free space >= the
                  fragile item's size
         THEN  Put the fragile item in the box
               Decrease the box's free space by
                  the fragile item's size

RULE 3   IF    Step is box-fragile-items
               There is a fragile item to box
         THEN  Start a fresh box

RULE 4   IF    Step is box-fragile-items
         THEN  Discontinue box-fragile-items
               Start box-heavy-items

RULE 5   IF    Step is box-heavy-items
               There is a heavy item
               There is an empty box, a box that
               does not contain fragile items, or
                  a box that contains < 4 heavy items
               The box's free space >= the item's size
         THEN  Put the heavy item in box
               Decrease the box's free space by
                  the heavy item's size

RULE 6   IF    Step is box-heavy-items
               There is a heavy item
         THEN  Start a fresh box

RULE 7   IF    Step is box-heavy-items
         THEN  Discontinue box-heavy-items
               Start box-medium-items

RULE 8   IF    Step is box-medium-items
               There is a medium item
               There is an empty box or a box
                  with no fragile items
               The box's free space >= the medium item's size
         THEN  Put the medium item in box
               Decrease the box's free space by
                  the medium item's size

RULE 9   IF    Step is box-medium-items
               There is a medium item
         THEN  Start a fresh box
```

```
RULE 10 IF    Step is box-medium-items
        THEN  Discontinue box-medium-items
              Start box-light-items

RULE 11 IF    Step is box-light-items
              There is a light item
              There is a box whose free space >=
                 the light item's size
        THEN  Put the light item in box
              Decrease the box's free space by
                 the light item's size

RULE 12 IF    Step is box-light-items
              There is a light item
        THEN  Start a fresh box

RULE 13 IF    Step is box-light-items
        THEN  Discontinue box-light-items
              Halt
```

You should notice several important characteristics of these rules. First, each rule checks to see which step of the packing process is currently active. By keeping track of the steps, the system subdivides the knowledge into smaller groups. Only when all of the objects of a certain type have been processed (see rule 4) does the system move to the next step of packing. The collection of step change rules (rules 4, 7, 10, and 13) ensure that all fragile items are processed first, all heavy items thereafter, and so forth. Second, each rule has different premises that must be satisfied. Each rule is specifying some specific set of premises that must be satisfied before its actions are to be performed and some satisfying premises are just more complex than others. Third, if you examine a subset of the rules (e.g., rules 1 to 4) you notice that the premises for some rules are subsets of the premises within other rules. This means that one set of data can actually satisfy several rules and since only one rule can be executed at a time, some *conflict resolution scheme* must be employed to determine which actual rule will be executed.

To get a better understanding of how forward reasoning works to solve this problem, let us create an actual set of data, describe a conflict resolution scheme, and simulate this system's execution. A subset of John's possessions, detailed in Figure 5.4, might be described in a database as shown in Figure 5.5. Note that this database includes one additional fact expressing the particular step in which the BOXER system starts. Included at the end of the figure is a description of the format for representing the various boxes as they are filled with items.

Because the system starts in the state *box-fragile-items* and there are three fragile items, the system has several rules that are satisfied or instantiated:

State:	box-fragile-items				
Unboxed Items:	*Number:*	*Weight:*	*Size:*	*Fragile?:*	*Pliable?:*
book	1	heavy	2	no	no
book	2	heavy	2	no	no
lamp	1	medium	8	yes	no
dishes	1	medium	5	yes	no
coat	1	light	3	no	no
tv	1	heavy	10	yes	no
pants	1	light	2	no	yes
pants	2	light	2	no	yes
shirt	1	light	1	no	yes
shirt	2	light	1	no	yes
Box Number:	*Contains:*			*Free Space:*	

FIGURE 5.5   Items to Box

Rule 3   for   lamp 1
Rule 3   for   dishes 1
Rule 3   for   tv 1
Rule 4

Several different conflict resolution schemes can be used to resolve which of these instantiations is selected for execution. Typical schemes are discussed in Section 5.4. For this discussion, we base our selection on two ordered criteria: (1) Always select the rule instantiated with the largest number of premises and (2) should multiple instantiations still exist, select the rule instantiated with the data closest to the top of the database. In this instance, rule 3 has the larger number of premises and of its three instantiations the first is selected since lamp 1 is closest to the top of the database. The execution of this rule results in the database shown in Figure 5.6.

The inference process now repeats by finding all rule instantiations:

Rule 1   for   lamp 1 and box 1
Rule 1   for   dishes 1 and box 1
Rule 1   for   tv 1 and box 1
Rule 3   for   lamp 1
Rule 3   for   dishes 1
Rule 3   for   tv 1
Rule 4

and selecting the instantiation that has the largest number of matched clauses and the data values closest to the top of the database:

State:	box-fragile-items				
Unboxed Items:	Number:	Weight:	Size:	Fragile?:	Pliable?:
book	1	heavy	2	no	no
book	2	heavy	2	no	no
lamp	1	medium	8	yes	no
dishes	1	medium	5	yes	no
coat	1	light	3	no	no
tv	1	heavy	10	yes	no
pants	1	light	2	no	yes
pants	2	light	2	no	yes
shirt	1	light	1	no	yes
shirt	2	light	1	no	yes
Box Number:	Contains:			Free Space:	
1	-			10	

FIGURE 5.6   Database after Execution of Rule 3 with Lamp 1

Rule 1   for   lamp 1 and box 1

The execution of this rule results in the database shown in Figure 5.7.
The inference process repeats for a third time finding the following instantiations:

State:	box-fragile-items				
Unboxed Items:	Number:	Weight:	Size:	Fragile?:	Pliable?:
book	1	heavy	2	no	no
book	2	heavy	2	no	no
lamp (padded)	1	medium	8	yes	no
dishes	1	medium	5	yes	no
coat	1	light	3	no	no
tv	1	heavy	10	yes	no
pants	1	light	2	no	yes
pants	2	light	2	no	yes
shirt	1	light	1	no	yes
shirt	2	light	1	no	yes
Box Number:	Contains:			Free Space:	
1	-			10	

FIGURE 5.7   Database after Execution of Rule 1 for Lamp 1 and
Box 1

Rule 1   for   dishes 1 and box 1
Rule 1   for   tv 1 and box 1
Rule 2   for   lamp 1 and box 1
Rule 3   for   lamp 1
Rule 3   for   dishes 1
Rule 3   for   tv 1
Rule 4

Rule 2 has the largest number of clauses so it is executed with its matched data resulting in the database of Figure 5.8.

The inference process continues in this manner until all the fragile objects are boxed as shown in Figure 5.9. At this point, only rule 4 is instantiated. The execution of this rule causes the system to enter the *box–heavy–items* state. In the *box–heavy–items* state the books are packed in a box resulting in the database of Figure 5.10 and a switch to the *box–medium–items* state.

Since no medium-weight objects remain, the BOXER immediately executes rule 10 causing a switch to the *box–light–items* state where all of the light items are boxed. The final database is shown in Figure 5.11.

As can be seen from the BOXER example, forward reasoning implemented in pattern-matching systems is typically employed in applications where synthesis of new conclusions is desired, such as design, planning, and scheduling. The fact that predefined links between rules and parameters cannot be defined as in inference networks allows great flexibility by not constraining the conclusions drawn.

State:	box-fragile-items				
Unboxed Items:	*Number:*	*Weight:*	*Size:*	*Fragile?:*	*Pliable?:*
book	1	heavy	2	no	no
book	2	heavy	2	no	no
dishes	1	medium	5	yes	no
coat	1	light	3	no	no
tv	1	heavy	10	yes	no
pants	1	light	2	no	yes
pants	2	light	2	no	yes
shirt	1	light	1	no	yes
shirt	2	light	1	no	yes
Box Number:	*Contains:*			*Free Space:*	
1	lamp (padded) 1			2	

FIGURE 5.8 Database after Execution of Rule 2 for Lamp 1 and Box 1

State:	box-fragile-items				
Unboxed Items:	*Number:*	*Weight:*	*Size:*	*Fragile?:*	*Pliable?:*
book	1	heavy	2	no	no
book	2	heavy	2	no	no
coat	1	light	3	no	no
pants	1	light	2	no	yes
pants	2	light	2	no	yes
shirt	1	light	1	no	yes
shirt	2	light	1	no	yes

Box Number:	Contains:			Free Space:	
1	lamp (padded) 1			2	
2	dishes (padded) 1			5	
3	tv (padded) 1			0	

FIGURE 5.9   Database after Boxing All Fragile Objects

State:	box-medium-items				
Unboxed Items:	*Number:*	*Weight:*	*Size:*	*Fragile?:*	*Pliable?:*
coat	1	light	3	no	no
pants	1	light	2	no	yes
pants	2	light	2	no	yes
shirt	1	light	1	no	yes
shirt	2	light	1	no	yes

Box Number:	Contains:			Free Space:	
1	lamp (padded) 1			2	
2	dishes (padded) 1			5	
3	tv (padded) 1			0	
4	book 1, book 2			6	

FIGURE 5.10   Database after Boxing All Heavy Objects

State:					
Unboxed Items:	*Number:*	*Weight:*	*Size:*	*Fragile?:*	*Pliable?:*
-					

Box Number:	Contains:	Free Space:
1	lamp (padded) 1, pants 1	0
2	dishes (padded) 1, coat 1, pants 2	0
3	tv (padded) 1	0
4	book 1, book 2, shirt 1, shirt 2	4

FIGURE 5.11   Database after Boxing All Objects

Many commercial forward-chaining systems use the pattern-matching structure (e.g., CLIPS, ART, and KEE). They employ a complex form of premise and fact representation that requires a pattern-matching algorithm to determine whether a rule's premise is satisfied and, if so, execute any variable bindings that may be required. This can be a complicated and inefficient process. The Rete algorithm is used to remedy this situation.

5.2.3 The Rete Algorithm

As presented in the example above, a pattern-matcher, forward-reasoning system is extremely inefficient. The *match, conflict resolution,* and *execute* cycle implies that all of the rules are compared to all of the facts in the fact base to decide which rules belong in the conflict set. If we have r rules in our knowledge base, f facts in our data base, and an average of p premises in each rule, we will perform $r*f^p$ comparisons to our fact base on every cycle to determine which rules can be executed. If we assume that our knowledge base contains 150 rules (a typical number for a small- to medium-size system), 20 facts exist in the fact base, and each rule has an average of 4 premises, then $150*20^4$ or 24,000,000 comparisons would be made on every cycle!

This inefficiency is, in part, due to being unable to determine how often a given rule can be satisfied by the facts in the database. A larger contributing factor to this inefficiency is, however, the manner in which premises and facts are compared. The code that is typically written assumes that significant changes are occurring to the database whenever a rule executes, an assumption that is usually false. Typically, a very limited number of changes occur in the database. As a result, the rules that can potentially execute on any cycle change very little. Rather than comparing rules to facts to see which rules are satisfied we should instead maintain a list of satisfied rules and determine how this satisfaction list changes due to the addition and deletion of facts. This approach is exploited by the *Rete algorithm.*

The Rete algorithm involves the development of two networks: a *pattern network* and a *join network.* To illustrate part of its operation, consider the following rule:

```
TEST 1: IF    ((cat ?c small ?h ?n1)
               (dog ?c ?q medium ?n2)
               (cat ?c large ?h ?n3)
               (dog ?c ?q long ?n4) )
        THEN ( ... )
```

where each premise has the following format:

```
(animal-type color size hair-length name)
```

The *pattern network* consists of a set of trees formed from all of the premises in all of the rules. The root of each tree is the first item within each premise pattern. Each node in the tree represents an additional item within the premise. The first two premises form the trees shown in Figure 5.12. Note that the variables named *?c* on each of these paths currently are completely different variables.

When the third premise is added to the network, the algorithm recognizes that a tree already exists starting with *cat*. The algorithm reuses as much of the existing network as possible in adding this premise, only creating a new path within the tree when the existing tree nodes do not correspond with the new item from the premise. A similar action occurs when the fourth premise is added. This results in the network shown in Figure 5.13.

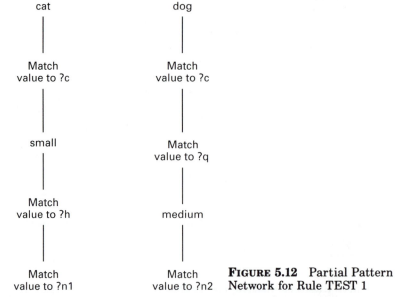

FIGURE 5.12 Partial Pattern Network for Rule TEST 1

Once the pattern network, shown in Figure 5.13, is developed, the algorithm builds what is called the *join network*. The join network connects the various leaf nodes of the trees together (in the order in which they occur as clauses) and compares similarly named variables to ensure that they have the same values. See Figure 5.14. The first join compares the values assigned to the two variables *?c*, the second compares values of the *?h* and *?c* variables, and the third compares the values of the *?c* variables.

Note that in the second comparison the values of both *?h* and *?c* must be examined. At first glance this does not seem necessary. To illustrate why this must be done, consider the following database facts:

```
1.   (cat    yellow    large     short     rebel)
2.   (cat    calico    large     short     rubble)
3.   (cat    calico    small     short     kitty)
4.   (dog    brown     medium    long      charlie)
```

```
5.    (cat    brown     small     medium    prince)
6.    (dog    brown     small     short     sam)
7.    (dog    calico    medium    medium    butch)
8.    (dog    brown     large     medium    star)
9.    (dog    calico    medium    long      tramp)
```

Each of these facts is first *parsed* through the pattern network. For example, the first element of the first fact is found to match the *cat* on the top of the first tree. The second element of this fact is then bound to the variable *?c*. The third element matches the value *large*, so the fourth element is bound to *?h* and the fifth to *?n3*. Note that when the second fact is parsed, the variable *?c* is bound to an additional value. In the pattern network variables can have multiple values. Their values are merely dependent on which facts are able to successfully pass the required values (e.g., *cat*) within the trees.

If you examine the sixth fact you will find that it can only be parsed down the tree headed by *dog* as far as the variable *?q* because the next element in this fact does not match either path below this point. Figure 5.15 illustrates the results of parsing all of these facts through the pattern network.

Remember that this example deals with only a single rule. When multiple rules exist, the Rete algorithm builds a similar set of pattern and join networks. If similar patterns exist with several rules, the algorithm reuses as much of the existing networks as is possible.

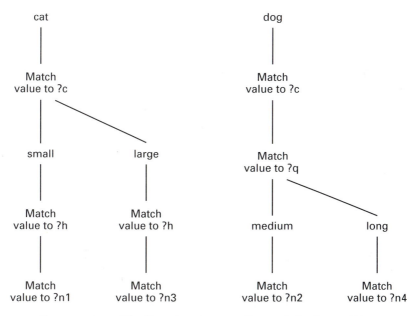

FIGURE 5.13   The Complete Pattern Network for Rule TEST 1

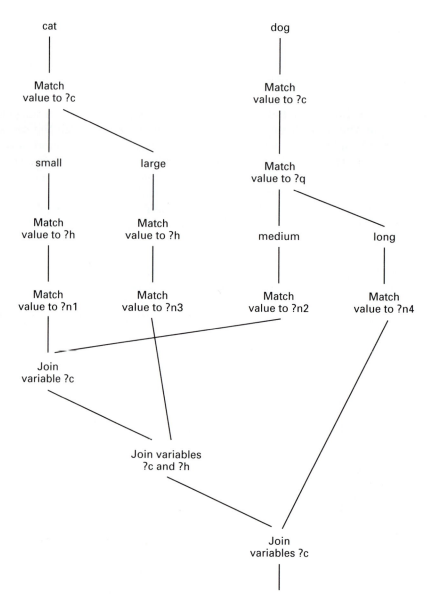

FIGURE 5.14 The Complete Pattern and Join Network for Rule TEST 1

Once all of the facts are parsed through the pattern network, the facts which emerge are passed to the join network where the values of the various variables are compared for similar values. Facts 3 and 5 are successfully parsed down the leftmost path through the trees. The *?c* bindings of these two

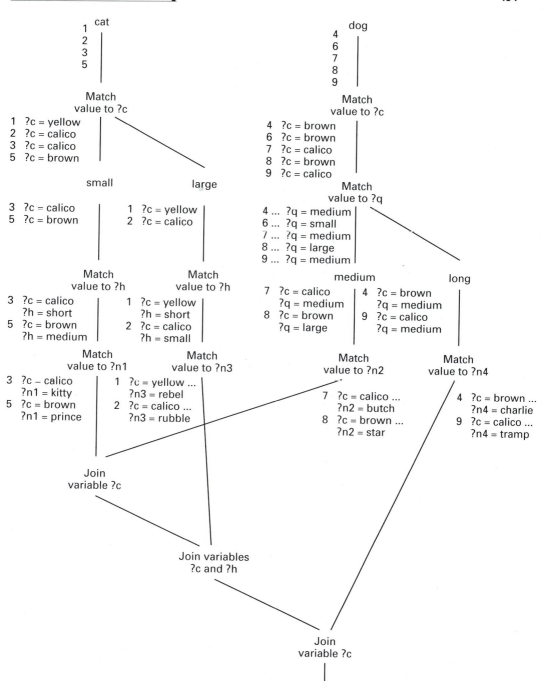

FIGURE 5.15 Facts Parsed through the Pattern Network

facts are now compared for matches with the facts that have parsed down the third path (i.e., facts 7 and 8). The *?c* variables for facts 3 and 7 are found to have the same value (i.e., *calico*) so they are joined together and facts 5 and 8 are also found to have the same value (i.e., *brown*) so they are joined.

These two joined groups are then compared to facts 1 and 2 from the second path through the pattern network. Fact 2 is found to have the same value for both the *?c* and *?h* variables as the joined group of facts 3 and 7 resulting in a new joined group of facts 2, 3, and 7. This group is then compared to facts 4 and 9 from the rightmost path through the pattern network to form the final joined group of facts 2, 3, 7, and 9 as shown in Figure 5.16. This cluster of facts satisfies the rule and allows it to be placed in the set of rules that are currently capable of being executed.

When a rule is executed, its actions can add, delete, or modify facts on the fact list. Each of these actions changes the parsed and joined facts within the pattern and join networks. By merely updating these facts within the network, a forward-reasoning system using the Rete algorithm can quickly determine all rules that can execute.

5.2.4 Conflict Resolution Schemes

Many different conflict resolution schemes are used in forward reasoning. These schemes have resulted from the specific needs of many diverse applications. We can divide them into four broad categories based on the following criteria:

1. Number of rules to execute
2. Order of the rules
3. Complexity of the rules
4. Order of the data

Systems that fall in the first category have a specific number of rules that should be executed during each cycle. In all of the examples shown above, the number of rules that were executed during any given cycle was limited to one. In some applications more than a single rule might be applied. In the extreme case, all rules that are found to be applicable will be executed.

The remaining three categories always apply when a limited number of rules, typically one, is to be executed on each execution cycle. Each of these categories uses some algorithm to determine the specific rule(s) (of the set of satisfied rules) that should be executed.

Systems using the second category of conflict resolution determine which rule should be applied by the position of the rule in relationship to other rules. Different applications require selecting different rules. For example, always select (1) the lowest numbered rule, (2) the first applicable rule following the

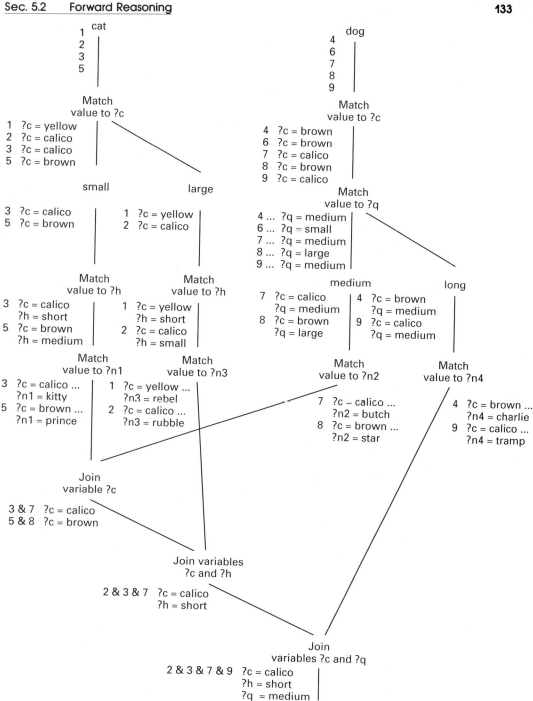

FIGURE 5.16   Results of Passing Facts through the Join Network

one that fired on the last cycle, (3) the lowest numbered rule that will derive a new fact, and so forth.

A possible alternative to examining the order of the rules is to examine their complexity. Rules vary in complexity through the number of premises or conditions that are tested. Complex and specific rules typically have numerous premises while general rules have few premises. A conflict resolution strategy might always select the most complex rule for execution, thereby always trying to attack the most refined portion of the problem. Alternatively, it may select the most general rule thereby trying to find broader, more general solutions first.

Systems utilizing the final category examine the order of the data to decide which rule to select. Ordering schemes include executing the rule that matches the oldest data, the newest data, or another data-ordering criterion.

While we have presented these schemes as distinct methods, they are often combined. As we saw in the BOXER system, looking at just the most complex rule was not sufficient to perform conflict resolution.

5.2.5 Coding Forward Reasoning (optional)

In this section we present a general set of simple and concise routines implementing forward reasoning. Note that these routines are more similar to the pattern-matching algorithm detailed above because the relationships between the rules and the facts are not known ahead of time, which requires searching for matches between the premises and all the facts in the database.

Before detailing the code, let us first describe an internal representation format for facts and rules that is capable of representing all of the knowledge expressed in the fruit identification example of the last chapter. This representation format is described in Figure 5.17. Each fact is a triple consisting of the verb **is** or some numeric operator, an *attribute*, and a *value* for the attribute. The database consists of a list of zero or more facts. Each rule is a 5-tuple: the rule's *name*, the word **if**, a list of *premises*, the word **then**, and a list of *conclusions*. A knowledge base consists of a list of one or more rules.

The process of forward reasoning, as implemented below, is somewhat different from what we described in BOXER. It consists of sequentially examining each rule in a knowledge base to find the first one capable of deriving

```
fact                 ::=  (is attribute value)|
                          ( numeric-op attribute value)
numeric-op           ::=  = | > | < | >= | <=
data base            ::=  (fact *)
rule                 ::=  (name if (fact *) then (fact *))
knowledge base       ::=  (rule⁺)
```

FIGURE 5.17 BNF Description of a Database and Knowledge Base

facts that are currently not known. Every time such a rule is found, it is immediately executed and the cycle starts again. Because this code stops searching for a rule to execute when it encounters the first satisfied rule that has not executed yet, there is never more than one eligible rule placed on the agenda simultaneously. Thus, there is no need for conflict resolution. However, an execution price must be paid by this approach—potentially all rules must be examined on each rule execution cycle.

The inference process is performed by the five functions shown below. The function **forward** initiates the forward-reasoning process. It loops as long as new facts are being derived and returns **T** if any facts are derived.

```
(defun forward ()
   (let (derived-fact?)
      (loop
         (cond ((not (execute-rule))
                    (return derived-fact?))
                (t (setq derived-fact? t)) ) ) ) ))
```

Execute-rule searches through the knowledge base (rule-list) looking for a rule that derives a new fact.

```
(defun execute-rule ()
   (do ((rules rule-list (cdr rules)))
       ((null rules) nil)
       (if (eval-rule-f (car rules)) (return t)) ))
```

Eval-rule-f examines an individual rule to see if it executes. This is done by checking to see if the rule's premises are in the database (fact-list) and calling **derive-new-fact?** to see if one of the rule's conclusions is currently not in the database.

```
(defun eval-rule-f (rule)
   (do ((ifs (caddr rule)
             (if (member (car ifs)
                           fact-list :test #'equal)
                  (cdr ifs)
                  (return nil)))
        (thens (caddr (cddr rule))))
       ((null ifs) (derive-new-fact? thens)) ))

(defun derive-new-fact? (facts)
   (do ((new-fact? nil)
        (facts-arg facts (cdr facts-arg)))
       ((null facts-arg) new-fact?)
       (cond ((member (car facts-arg)
                        fact-list :test #'equal))
```

```
                        (t (display-results (car facts-arg))
                            (setq new-fact? t)
                            (setq fact-list
                                    (cons (car facts-arg) fact-list))
            ) ) ))
```

The final function, **display-results,** merely prints a message every time a new fact is derived.

```
            (defun display-results (derived-fact)
                (terpri)
                (princ "The value of ")
                (princ (cadr derived-fact))
                (princ " is ")
                (princ (caddr derived-fact)) )
```

To illustrate processing this forward-reasoning code, let us implement the fruit identification system of the last chapter. Note that in the English description of these rules several contain premises with alternative values (e.g., *color = green or yellow* in premise 2 of rule 1). To express this knowledge we break these rules into two separate rules (rule 1a and 1b) where each checks a different value. One possible expression of this set of rule knowledge is

```
(setq rule-list
     '( (Rla  IF    ((is shape long)
                     (is color green))
             THEN  ((is fruit banana)) )

        (Rlb  IF    ((is shape long)
                     (is color yellow))
             THEN  ((is fruit banana)) )

        (R2a  IF    ((is shape round)
                     (> diameter 4))
             THEN  ((is fruitclass vine)) )

        (R2b  IF    ((is shape oblong)
                     (> diameter 4))
             THEN  ((is fruitclass vine)) )

        (R3   IF    ((is shape round)
                     (< diameter 4))
             THEN  ((is fruitclass tree)) )

        (R4   IF    ((= seedcount 1))
             THEN  ((is seedclass stonefruit)) )

        (R5   IF    ((> seedcount 1))
             THEN  ((is seedclass multiple)) )
```

```
(R6   IF    ((is fruitclass vine)
            (is color green))
      THEN  ((is fruit watermelon)) )

(R7   IF    ((is fruitclass vine)
            (is surface smooth)
            (is color yellow))
      THEN  ((is fruit honeydew)) )

(R8   IF    ((is fruitclass vine)
            (is surface rough)
            (is color tan))
      THEN  ((is fruit cantaloupe)) )

(R9   IF    ((is fruitclass tree)
            (is color orange)
            (is seedclass stonefruit))
      THEN  ((is fruit apricot)) )

(R10  IF    ((is fruitclass tree)
            (is color orange)
            (is seedclass multiple))
      THEN  ((is fruit orange)) )

(R11  IF    ((is fruitclass tree)
            (is color red)
            (is seedclass stonefruit))
      THEN  ((is fruit cherry)) )

(R12  IF    ((is fruitclass tree)
            (is color orange)
            (is seedclass stonefruit))
      THEN  ((is fruit peach)) )

(R13a IF    ((is fruitclass tree)
            (is color red)
            (is seedclass multiple))
      THEN  ((is fruit apple)) )

(R13b IF    ((is fruitclass tree)
            (is color yellow)
            (is seedclass multiple))
      THEN  ((is fruit apple)) )

(R13c IF    ((is fruitclass tree)
            (is color green)
            (is seedclass multiple))
      THEN  ((is fruit apple)) )

(R14  IF    ((is fruitclass tree)
            (is color purple)
            (is seedclass stonefruit))
      THEN  ((is fruit plum)) ) ) )
```

To execute the above knowledge base using the forward-reasoning code, we must provide a fact base of initially known facts. Consider the following fact base:

```
(setq fact-list
         '((is color red)
           (is shape round)
           (= seedcount 1)
           (< diameter 4)
      ) )
```

This fact base causes the following execution results to be displayed:

```
The value of FRUITCLASS is TREE
The value of SEEDCLASS is STONEFRUIT
The value of FRUIT is CHERRY
T
```

5.3 BACKWARD OR GOAL-DIRECTED REASONING

Backward chaining is better suited for applications having many more inputs than possible conclusions. The ability to trace the logic backwards from the few conclusions to the many inputs makes it more efficient than forward chaining. A good application for backward chaining is diagnosis (e.g., medical diagnosis) where the human interfaces directly with the knowledge-based system and supplies the data through the keyboard. Most diagnostics systems have been implemented using an inference network architecture since the relationships between the facts are typically well known.

Classification problems are also ideally suited for backward chaining. This type of problem can be implemented using either inference networks or pattern matchers depending upon the complexity of problem's data.

5.3.1 Example 1 of Backward Reasoning

Consider the following knowledge base that helps us select a beverage and main course for a meal:

```
RULE 1    IF    guest-age < 21
          THEN  alcohol-indicated = no

RULE 2    IF    guest-age >= 21
          THEN  alcohol-indicated = yes

RULE 3    IF    alcohol-indicated = yes AND
                meal = formal
          THEN  drink = wine
```

```
RULE 4    IF    alcohol-indicated = yes AND
                guest = boss
          THEN  drink = wine

RULE 5    IF    alcohol-indicated = yes AND
                guest = neighbor
          THEN  drink = beer

RULE 6    IF    drink = wine AND
                dinner = fish
          THEN  wine-type = white

RULE 7    IF    drink = wine AND
                dinner = red-meat
          THEN  wine-type = red

RULE 8    IF    guest = boss AND
                day = friday
          THEN  dinner = fish

RULE 9    IF    guest = boss AND
                day <> friday
          THEN  dinner = red-meat

RULE 10   IF    guest-age < 21
          THEN  dinner = pizza

RULE 11   IF    guest-age >= 21
          THEN  dinner = fish

RULE 12   IF    alcohol not indicated
          THEN  drink = soda
```

where the parameters used (and their acceptable values) are

```
guest-age: positive integer between 15 and 100
alcohol-indicated: yes/no
meal: formal/informal
drink: wine/beer/soda
guest: boss/neighbor/friend
dinner: fish/veal/red-meat/poultry/pizza
day: monday/tuesday/ ... /sunday
```

   Suppose that instead of initially observing our dinner situation and specifying all of the features that we observe, we allow the system to ask us about
these features when they become important in deriving results. This approach
often proves to be more cost effective to operate since the user is not burdened
with attempting to find every fact about the situation that might prove useful.
Rather, the system takes this responsibility by questioning the user about
these facts when they are needed within the reasoning process.

In this reasoning scheme, called backward reasoning, the system starts with no data attached to any of the parameters:

Known Fact Base: ( )

Since the system is unable to function without some high-level guidance, a list of goals (or possible conclusions) that the system can derive is provided. These goals are specified in the order that the developer feels is best to pursue. For example,

Goals: (drink wine–type dinner)

The inference mechanism for backward reasoning is significantly different from that of forward reasoning. While both processes involve an examination and application of rules, the backward-reasoning process must be coordinated through this list of specified goals. Backward reasoning, therefore, consists of the following steps:

1. Form a temporary stack initially composed of all of the top-level goals defined in the system.
2. Set the goal to be traced equal to the top goal on the stack. If the stack is empty (i.e., all top-level goals have been tried), halt and announce completion.
3. Gather all rules capable of satisfying this goal.
4. Consider each of these rules in turn:
   a. If all premises are satisfied (i.e., each premise's parameter has its specified value within the database), then fire this rule to derive its conclusions. Do not consider any more rules for this goal. Its value is now given by the current rule's conclusion. If the goal presently being traced is a top-level goal, then remove it from the stack, and return to step 2. If it is a subgoal, then remove this subgoal from the stack and return to the processing of the previous goal that was temporarily suspended.
   b. If a value is found in the database for a premise's parameter that does not match the premise's parameter's value, fail to execute this rule successfully.
   c. If any premise is not satisfied (i.e., the premise's parameter is not defined within the database), do rules exist that will derive a value for the parameter? If yes, then consider this parameter to be a subgoal, temporarily suspend the execution of this rule, push the parameter onto the top of the stack, and go back to step 2 recursively.

d. If step 4c is unable to find any rules to derive the specified value for the current parameter, ask the user for its value and add it to the database; then go to step 4a and consider the next premise of the rule.

5. If all rules that can satisfy the current goal have been attempted and all have failed to derive a value, then this goal remains undetermined. Remove it from the stack and go back to step 2.

Let us now trace the execution of the rules for planning a dinner and beverages with the given goals and interpreter. For this example, suppose that it is Tuesday and we have invited our 30-year-old neighbor for a casual meal. Since the list of goals has already been determined, our trace starts with step 2, the selection of the first top-level goal: *drink*.

Step 3 specifies that all rules deriving this goal should be gathered and placed on a stack. This stack initially consists of rules 3, 4, 5, and 12. The first of these rules (rule 3) is examined to see if it can successfully execute in step 4. The first parameter of this rule, *alcohol-indicated*, is examined to see if it is present in the database, which it is not. Since this parameter does not currently have a value, we execute step 4c which recursively creates *alcohol-indicated* as a subgoal and goes back to step 2. We find that two rules, rules 1 and 2, can derive a value for *alcohol-indicated*.

The first of these (rule 1) is selected and the database is examined to see if this rule's first (and only) premise is present. Again, we discover that a premise's parameter's value is not in the database, so we gather rules that can derive a value for that parameter. We discover that there are no rules that can derive a value for the guest's age, so (using step 4d) we are forced to ask the user for a value, for which the user enters 30. This parameter and its value are added to the database and we return to the previously suspended goal and our examination of rule 1. Rule 1 fails on the value provided by the user, so the second rule that can derive *alcohol-indicated* (rule 2) is tried.

The system examines the parameter in the first premise of rule 2 (*guest-age*) and discovers that it has a value in the database (30) that satisfies the rule's premise. Since no other premises are present, rule 2 successfully executes deriving *alcohol-indicated = yes*.

The system now returns to the second premise of rule 3, *meal = formal*. The system discovers that the parameter of this premise does not have a value defined in the database and that no rules can derive it, so the user is questioned for its value (*casual*). Again, this parameter and its value are added to the database. This value does not satisfy the premise, so rule 3 fails.

The system finds that the next available rule to derive a value for drink is rule 4. This rule's first premise, *alcohol-indicated = yes*, is satisfied, so the second premise, *guest = boss*, is tried. No rules can derive a value for the parameter in the premise, so the user is again questioned for a value (*neighbor*) that is added to the database. This value causes rule 4 to fail requiring the system to try the next available rule, rule 5. Both of rule 5's premises are in the database so this rule executes, deriving a value of *beer* for the parameter *drink*.

If you continue the trace of this knowledge base, you will find that the following parameters are endowed with the values given below:

Database:
```
( (dinner = fish)
  (drink = beer)
  (guest = neighbor)
  (meal = casual)
  (alcohol-indicated = yes)
  (guest-age = 30) )
```

Note that the system is unable to derive a value for the parameter *wine-type* since the type of drink to serve is not wine. Also note that the system never requests a value for *day*, since this premise is used only in rules 8 and 9 when the guest has been determined to be the boss.

5.3.2 Example 2 of Backward Reasoning

The game of baseball can be quite complicated even to someone somewhat familiar with it. A knowledge-based system that is able to recommend a strategy for a particular situation can be quite useful for an inexperienced coach or manager.

For instance, it is widely known that the third base coach always provides the signals to the batter and to the base runners to tell them what they should do. Each has few options: The batter can "swing away," "sacrifice fly," "sacrifice bunt," "take a pitch," or "hit-and-run," while the runner can run ("steal the next base") or not. While the options are few, the circumstances which lead to the decision are many. Many variables are involved, such as the score, the inning, the batter at the plate, the number of outs, and whether there are any base runners and how fast are they. The following expresses a small portion of the knowledge used by a third base coach in deciding what signal to provide to the batter and the base runner(s), if any:

```
RULE 1:   IF    there is no one on base AND
                the batter is good
          THEN  swing away

RULE 2:   IF    we lead by greater than 3 runs AND
                it is the 7th inning or later
          THEN  swing away
```

```
RULE 3:   IF    a fast runner is on 1st base AND
                there is no one on 2nd base
          THEN  attempt to steal 2nd base

RULE 4:   IF    a fast runner is on 2nd base AND
                there is no one on 3rd base
          THEN  attempt to steal 3rd base

RULE 5:   IF    a fast runner is on 1st base AND
                a good hitter is at bat AND
                the pitcher and the batter are opposite-handed
          THEN  hit-and-run

RULE 6:   IF    the score is tied or
                we are behind by 1 run AND
                there are less than 2 outs AND
                it is the 8th or 9th inning AND
                a fast runner is on 3rd base
          THEN  sacrifice fly

RULE 7:   IF    a poor hitter is up AND
                a fast runner is on 1st base AND
                there are less than two outs
          THEN  sacrifice bunt

RULE 8:   IF    there are runners on base AND
                a good hitter comes to bat AND
                there are two outs
          THEN  swing away

RULE 9:   IF    a batter is batting less than .240
          THEN  he is a poor batter

RULE 10:  IF    a batter is batting more than .300
          THEN  he is a good batter

RULE 11:  IF    a runner has stolen more than 30 bases
          THEN  he is a fast runner

RULE 12:  IF    a runner has stolen less than 10 bases
          THEN  he is a slow runner
```

Although the number of inputs required by this knowledge base are not large per se, when this knowledge is encoded below we find that a number of different patterns are required. If a knowledge-based system is truly being developed for this and other tasks within the baseball world, we will need to encode additional data, some of which are not pertinent to the signal decision. Thus, our inputs are quite expansive while our number of conclusions are limited, making it is better to employ backward chaining to develop a recommendation.

   To use this knowledge in making decisions about the game situation, we must have a format for representing the knowledge expressed within these rules. The format that we will use is a list, or database, of various facts where each fact expresses some important data about the game situation. The first of these facts describes general information about the game, base runners, and the batter

   (game *inning outs runners–on–base score–margin batter–up*)

where

   inning is an integer greater than 1 (and typically less than or equal to 9) identifying the particular inning of the game.

   outs is the current number of outs that exist within this inning.

   runners–on–base is a list of the players on each base. For example, the situation of Smith at first, Jones at third, and no one at second base, would be expressed as

   (smith nil jones)

   score–margin is the difference between your team's and your opposing team's score. A positive number indicates you are leading the game, a negative number that you are losing, and a value of zero that the score is tied.

   batter–up is the name of the player whose turn it is to bat.

   Also significant is information on the other team. Since left-handed batters do better against right-handed pitchers, (and vice versa) it is important to know the pitching arm of the pitcher. This fact is represented as

   (pitcher *name arm*)

where

   name is the name of the pitcher and

   arm is whether the pitcher is right-handed (right) or left-handed (left).

   Next, the third base coach must know the capabilities of each of his players—both as batters and as base runners. For example, he may be willing to let a fast runner attempt to steal a base, but not a slow runner. Each player in the game on the coach's team is represented, therefore, as

   (player *name average side stolen*)

where

name is the name of the player,

average is the player's batting average,

side is whether the batter is a right- or left-handed hitter, and

stolen is the player's number of stolen bases.

Players' descriptions also include two additional facts:

```
(batter name skill)
(runner name skill)
```

where

name is the name of the player and

skill is his/her playing level (good or poor for batters; fast or slow for runners) at this task.

Finally, we must have some format for expressing the results or signals given by the third base coach. These signals will be expressed as

```
(signal individual action)
```

where

individual identifies either the runner or batter and

action is the specific operation that he/she is to perform.

Given this structure for the knowledge describing a game situation, let us now encode the knowledge expressed within the rules. Given the complexity of the representation of each fact, we will use a pattern-matching scheme. Let us first define the notation that will be used to write the rules.

1. A rule is expressed as a list

```
( rule #
    premises
 ==>
    conclusions)
```

where

\# is the number of the rule

premises is the set of premises (facts) to be matched for this rule to be considered for execution

==> is a separator placed between the premises and conclusions of a rule

conclusions is the set of actions to take if this rule is selected for execution

2. A question mark in the pattern designates a wild card (i.e., the value in this position of a fact does not matter)

3. Variables are designated by <*an–atom*>

4. Any tests that must be performed on some variable are defined by a list starting with the symbol *test*. This list contains a description of the specific test to be preformed.

Given this representation, the rules become:

```
(RULE 1
            (game ? ? (<rnr1> <rnr2> <rnr3>) ? <batter>)
            (test ((and (null <rnr1>)
                        (null <rnr2>)
                        (null <rnr3>))))
            (batter <batter> good)
    ==>
            (signal <batter> swing–away))

(RULE 2
            (game <inn> ? ? <margin> <batter>)
            (test (> <inn> 7))
            (test (> <margin> 3))
    ==>
            (signal <batter> swing–away))

(RULE 3
            (game ? ? ( <rnr1> <rnr2> ?) ? ?)
            (test (and (null <rnr2>) (not (null <rnr1>))))
            (runner <rnr1> fast)
    ==>
            (signal <rnr1> steal–base))

(RULE 4
            (game ? ? (? <rnr2> <rnr3>) ? ?)
            (test (and (null <rnr3>) (not (null <rnr2>))))
            (runner <rnr2> fast)
    ==>
            (signal <rnr2> steal–base))

(RULE 5
            (game ? ? (<rnr1> ? ?) ? <batter>)
            (runner <rnr1> fast)
            (batter <batter> good)
            (player <batter> ? <hand> ?)
            (pitcher ? <handl>)
```

```
                       (test (not (equal <hand> <hand1>)))
       ==>
                       (signal <batter> hit-and-run))

       (RULE 6
                       (game <inn> <outs> (? ? <rnr3>) <margin> <batter>)
                       (test (> <inn> 7))
                       (test (< <outs> 2))
                       (test (or (= <margin> 0) (= <margin> 1)))
                       (runner <rnr3> fast)
       ==>
                       (signal <batter> sacrifice-fly))

       (RULE 7
                       (game ? <outs> (<rnr1> ? ?) ? <batter>)
                       (runner <rnr1> fast)
                       (batter <batter> poor)
                       (test (< <outs> 2))
       ==>
                       (signal <batter> sacrifice-bunt))

       (RULE 8
                       (game ? <outs> (<rnr1> <rnr2> <rnr3>) ? <batter>)
                       (batter <batter> good)
                       (test (= <outs> 2))
                       (test (not (and (null <rnr1>)
                                       (null <rnr2>)
                                       (null <rnr3>))))
       ==>
                       (signal <batter> swing-away))

       (RULE 9
                       (player <batter> <avg> ? ?)
                       (test (< <avg> .240))
       ==>
                       (batter <batter> poor))

       (RULE 10
                       (player <batter> <avg> ? ?)
                       (test (> <avg> .300))
       ==>
                       (batter <batter> good))

       (RULE 11
                       (player <runner> ? ? <bases>)
                       (test (> <bases> 30))
       ==>
                       (runner <runner> fast))

       (RULE 12
                       (player <runner> ? ? <bases>)
                       (test (< <bases> 10))
       ==>
                       (runner <runner> slow))
```

The goals of this system are, in order: *swing-away*, *steal-base*, *hit-and-run*, *sacrifice-fly*, and *sacrifice-bunt*. These actions are expressed in an internal form as

```
((signal <batter> swing-away)
 (signal <runner> steal-base)
 (signal <batter> hit-and-run)
 (signal <batter> sacrifice-fly)
 (signal <batter> sacrifice-bunt))
```

To illustrate the operation of this system, let us now create a small example database describing a game situation where it is the bottom of the ninth inning, the score is tied, and Henderson is at bat:

```
( (player   mays        .237   left     35)
  (player   mantle      .278   right     2)
  (player   maris       .356   right     0)
  (player   aaron       .300   left     31)
  (player   robinson    .289   right    32)
  (player   katzson     .220   left     10)
  (player   henderson   .308   right    86)
  (player   gonzalez    .380   right    36)
  (player   dankel      .178   left      0)
  (pitcher  ryan     right)
  (game  9   0 (nil    nil    nil)  0    henderson) )
```

As you should recall from the other examples, a backward-chaining system attempts to satisfy the goals by taking each in turn, comparing it to conclusions drawn by the various rules, and examining the rules that can derive these goals to see if their premises are satisfied by the known facts. In this example, let us assume that the inference engine continues to be applied until either any single goal is satisfied or all of the goals have been tried and none are successful.

Applying this process to this knowledge base, we start by examining the first goal of this system, (*signal* <batter> *swing-away*) to see if it can be satisfied by any rules. We discover that it can by three rules: 1, 2, and 8. The first of these rules (rule 1) has three premises. The first premise matches the game fact with <rnr1>, <rnr2>, and <rnr3> instantiated to *nil* and <batter> instantiated to *henderson*. The second premise of this rule, the *test*, is satisfied by the values associated with <rnr1>, <rnr2>, and <rnr3>. The final premise, however, is not found in the database, so the inference engine applies backward chaining to see if there is a way to derive this fact.

The system discovers that only rule 10 can derive this premise if its conclusion <batter> variable is instantiated to *henderson*, so the system checks to see if this rule's premises are satisfied. The first premise matches the fact (*player henderson .308 right 86*) from the database with *<avg>* instantiated to *.308*. The second premise, the *test*, is satisfied so the rule derives (*batter henderson good*) which satisfies the final premise of rule 1 causing it to derive its conclusion, the first goal, of

```
(signal henderson swing-away)
```

stopping the tracing process.

Let us now assume that Henderson is successful in getting on base and is currently on first. The next batter is Katzson so our game situation is described as

```
(game 9 0 (henderson nil nil) 0 katzson)
```

We start with the original goal list by examining the first goal, (*signal <batter> swing-away*). The same set of rules (1, 2, and 8) can satisfy this goal so we start with the first of these, rule 1. The second premise of this rule is not satisfied since Henderson is on first base, so we attempt rule 2. This rule is also not satisfied since the third premise will fail (our margin is 0 which is not greater than 3). When rule 8 is attempted, we match the first premise but do not have a fact to match the second premise, (*batter katzson good*). Checking the rules we discover that rule 10 matches this premise, so we check to see if this rule's premises exist. A match is found for the first premise but the second premise fails since Katzson's average, .220, is less than *.300* required by this rule.

Since no rules can satisfy this goal, (*signal <batter> swing-away*), it is now discarded and the next goal is attempted. This goal is

```
(signal <runner> steal-base)
```

Rules 3 and 4 match this goal. The first of these, rule 3, is tried. The first premise of this rule matches the game fact in the database instantiating *<rnr1>* to *henderson* and *<rnr2>* to *nil*. The second premise is also satisfied. The third premise is not found in the database, but a rule, rule 11, is found that can derive it. When we attempt to execute this rule with *<runner>* bound to *henderson* we satisfy the first premise with *<bases>* instantiated to *86*. This value satisfies the second premise, so this rule is successfully executed and the final premise of rule 3 is matched, so rule 3 executes deriving

```
(signal henderson steal-base)
```

Let us assume that Henderson is successful in stealing second base. Our game situation is updated to reflect the fact that Henderson is now on second:

```
(game 9 0 (nil henderson nil) 0 katzson)
```

Starting the goal list again, we discover that the first goal is still not satisfied, so it is discarded. The second goal, (*signal* <*runner*> *steal–base*), is then tried. It is matched by rules 3 and 4. Rule 3's second premise is not satisfied by the game situation, so it is discarded and rule 4 is attempted. The first premise of this rule causes <*rnr2*> and <*rnr3*> to be instantiated to *henderson* and *nil*, respectively. The second premise is satisfied, so we try the third. This is not found in the database but can possibly be derived by rule 11. Attempting this rule succeeds and the final premise of rule 4 is matched deriving the signal

```
(signal henderson steal–base)
```

Let us assume that Henderson again steals successfully and is now at third base. The game situation changes to

```
(game 9 0 (nil nil henderson) 0 katzson)
```

and the execution begins once again with the list of goals.

The first goal matches the same three rules (rules 1, 2, and 8) and, again, none is successfully executed, so the first goal is discarded. Neither of the two rules (rules 3 and 4) that match the second goal, (*signal* <*runner*> *steal–base*), are satisfied, so it is also discarded. The third goal, (*signal* <*batter*> *hit–and–run*), matches rule 5, but its second premise, (*runner nil fast*), cannot be successfully matched so this rule fails causing the third goal to be discarded.

The fourth goal, (*signal* <*batter*> *sacrifice–fly*), is now tried. Only rule 6 matches this goal, so we see if its premises are satisfied. The first premise matches the game fact instantiating <*inn*> to 9, <*outs*> to 0, <*rnr3*> to *henderson*, <*margin*> to *0*, and <*batter*> to *katzson*. The test premises 2, 3, and 4 are all satisfied, so we try the fifth and final premise, (*runner* <*rnr3*> *fast*). This premise is not found in the database, but can be derived by rule 11. When this rule is attempted, we discover that it is successfully executed, causing (*runner henderson fast*) to be derived, satisfying the fifth premise of rule 6. This results in rule 6 executing and deriving

```
(signal katzson sacrifice–fly)
```

Katzson successfully hits a sacrifice fly when given this signal, scoring Henderson from third base, resulting in our winning the game.

Although we have not been completely rigorous in our treatment of pattern matching or, for that matter, baseball strategy, you can see from this example how a backward-chaining system can be used with pattern matching to solve problems where the data are quite complex and a limited number of conclusions can be drawn.

5.3.3 Coding a Backward-reasoning System (optional)

Using the same knowledge representation format presented for forward reasoning, we can encode a simple backward-reasoning system in the following manner. As in forward reasoning, this code does not correspond precisely to either of the algorithms presented above. It is, however, closer to that discussed in the pattern-matching backward-reasoning section. Note that these functions use three global values: **hypotheses**, containing the list of goals to be satisfied; **fact-list**, containing the database of known facts; and **rule-list**, containing the list of all rules in the knowledge base.

The function **backward** is the main function. It calls **find-hypothesis-value** to derive values for all of the hypotheses, then displays their values by calling **display-results**.

```
(defun backward ()
   (mapc  #'display-results
          (mapcar #'find-hypothesis-value hypotheses)))
```

Find-hypothesis-value tries to determine a hypothesis's value by looking it up in the list of known facts (by calling **value-from-facts**), deriving it (by calling **value-from-rules**), or, if all else fails, asking the user (by calling **ask-user**).

```
(defun find-hypothesis-value (hypothesis)
   (let (rules)
        (cond ((value-from-facts hypothesis fact-list))
              ((setq rules (find-rules hypothesis rule-list))
               (value-from-rules hypothesis rules))
              (t (ask-user hypothesis)) )) )
```

Value-from-facts searches through the list of known facts looking for the hypothesis's name. Since hypotheses are allowed to have only a single value, once the hypothesis's name is found, that hypothesis and its value are returned from the list.

```
(defun value-from-facts (hypothesis facts)
   (cond ((null facts) nil)
         ((equal hypothesis (caar facts)) (car facts))
         (t (value-from-facts hypothesis (cdr facts))) ))
```

Ask-user merely questions the user for a value of the hypothesis in question. This fact is then added to the list of facts and is returned by the function as its value.

```
(defun ask-user (hypothesis)
   (let ((answer))
      (terpri)
      (princ "Please enter a value for ")
      (princ hypothesis)
      (princ ": ")
      (setq answer (list hypothesis 'is (read)))
      (princ "Thank you!")
      (setq fact-list (cons answer fact-list))
      answer))
```

Find-rules searches through the list of rules looking for a rule that can derive a value for the current hypothesis.

```
(defun find-rules (hypothesis rule-list)
   (let (rules)
      (loop
         (cond ((null rule-list)
                (return (reverse rules)))
               ((good-rule? hypothesis (car rule-list))
                (setq rules
                      (cons (car rule-list) rules)) ) )
         (setq rule-list (cdr rule-list)) )))
```

Good-rule examines an individual rule to see if it can derive a value for a particular hypothesis. It uses **in-then?** to search through the list of conclusions for the presence of the hypothesis.

```
(defun good-rule? (hypothesis rule)
   (in-then? hypothesis (caddr (cddr rule))))
```

```
(defun in-then? (hypothesis then)
   (cond ((null then) nil)
         ((equal hypothesis (caar then)))
         (t (in-then? hypothesis (cdr then)) )))
```

Value-from-rules examines a list of rules that can derive a value for a specific hypothesis. Each of these rules is examined to see if it can successfully derive a value for the hypothesis by calling **eval-rule**.

```
(defun value-from-rules (hypothesis rules)
   (cond ((null rules) nil)
         ((eval-rule hypothesis (car rules)))
         (t (value-from-rules hypothesis (cdr rules))))))
```

Eval-rule examines all of the premises of a rule to see if they are satisfied by calling **find-hypothesis-value**. If the proper value exists for all of the premises, this function adds all of its conclusions to the facts that are known to be true (i.e., to fact-list). Otherwise, this function returns a value of **nil** to identify that it has been unsuccessful in executing.

```
(defun eval-rule (hypothesis rule)
   (let ((ifs (caddr rule))
         (thens (caddr (cddr rule))) )
      (loop
         (cond ((null ifs)
                (setq fact-list (append thens fact-list))
                (return (value-from-facts hypothesis thens)))
               ((equal (car ifs) (find-hypothesis-value
                                   (caar ifs)))
                (setq ifs (cdr ifs)))
               (t (return nil)) )) ))
```

Finally, we have **display-results** that merely takes a given fact and displays it and its value on the screen for the user.

```
(defun display-results (derived-fact)
   (terpri)
   (princ "The value of ")
   (princ (car derived-fact))
   (princ " is ")
   (princ (caddr derived-fact)) )
```

To illustrate the operation of this code we have implemented a small knowledge base dealing with animal identification [Winston, 1992]:

```
(setq rule-list

'( (R1   IF    ((body-cover is hair))
         THEN ((class is mammal)) )

   (R2   IF    ((baby-food is milk))
         THEN ((class is mammal)) )
```

```
(R3      IF    ((body-cover is feathers))
         THEN  ((class is bird)) )

(R4      IF    ((transportation-means is fly)
                (birth is eggs))
         THEN  ((class is bird)) )

(R5      IF    ((class is mammal) (food is meat))
         THEN  ((kind is carnivore)) )

(R6      IF    ((class is mammal)
                (teeth-type is pointed)
                (toe-type is claws)
                (eye-direction is forward))
         THEN  ((kind is carnivore)) )

(R7      IF    ((class is mammal) (toe-type is hoofs))
         THEN  ((kind is ungulate)) )

(R8      IF    ((class is mammal) (food is cud))
         THEN  ((kind is ungulate)
                (toe-count is even)) )

(R9      IF    ((kind is carnivore)
                (color is tawny)
                (fur-pattern is dark-spots))
         THEN  ((animal is cheetah)) )

(R10     IF    ((kind is carnivore)
                (color is tawny)
                (fur-pattern is black-stripes))
         THEN  ((animal is tiger)) )

(R11     IF    ((kind is ungulate)
                (leg-length is long)
                (neck-length is long)
                (color is tawny)
                (fur-pattern is dark-spots))
         THEN  ((animal is giraffe)) )

(R12     IF    ((kind is ungulate)
                (color is white)
                (fur-pattern is black-stripes))
         THEN  ((animal is zebra)) )

(R13     IF    ((class is bird)
                (transportation-means is walk)
                (leg-length is long)
                (neck-length is long)
                (color is black-and-white))
```

```
          THEN  ((animal is ostrich)) )

(R14    IF    ((class is bird)
              (transportation-means is swim)
              (color is black-and-white))
          THEN  ((animal is penguin)) )

(R15    IF    ((class is bird)
              (type-of-flier is good))
          THEN  ((animal is albatross)) ) ) )
```

Note that we must initialize the fact-list to **nil** and hypotheses to our top-level goal of animal:

```
          (setq fact-list nil)
          (setq hypotheses '(animal))
```

Suppose that the animal we are trying to classify has the following observed characteristics: has forward pointing eyes, is a tawny color, is covered with hair, has pointed teeth, eats meat, and has black stripes in its hair. The execution of these functions produces the following interaction (user input is given in italics):

```
(backward)
Please enter a value for BODY-COVER: hair
Thank you!

Please enter a value for FOOD: meat
Thank you!

Please enter a value for COLOR: tawny
Thank you!

Please enter a value for FUR-PATTERN: black-stripes
Thank you!

The value of ANIMAL is TIGER
((ANIMAL IS TIGER))
```

Try executing this knowledge base with different data values to see what conclusions it draws.

5.4 CHAPTER REVIEW

There is a fundamental difference in the nature of forward- and backward-reasoning systems. There is also a less fundamental, but nevertheless significant difference in the inference net and pattern-matching architectures described in Chapter 4. Backward chaining systems are typically, although not solely, implemented using inference networks. Likewise, forward chainers are typically (not solely) implemented as pattern matchers.

Applications suitable for forward chaining require a quick response to changes in the input data and have a limited number of relationships between the input data and the conclusions. Examples of such applications include monitoring and diagnosis of real-time systems. The inference net is the preferred architecture for such systems because of the need for efficiency and speed of operation in a real-time environment.

Planning, scheduling, and design also require forward-chaining systems because of their potentially large number of possible solutions. The use of pattern matching eases the representation of the knowledge required in such systems.

The Rete algorithm increases the efficiency of pattern-matching systems. It uses two networks: a *pattern network* and a *join network*. The pattern network consists of a set of trees formed from all of the premises in all of the rules. The root of each tree is the first item within each premise. The join network connects the various leaf nodes of the trees together (in the order in which they occur as clauses) and compares similarly named variables to ensure that they have the same values.

Backward chaining is better suited for applications having more inputs than conclusions. The ability to trace backwards from the conclusions to the inputs makes it more efficient than forward chaining. Backward chaining is ideally suited for diagnostic applications. Most diagnostics systems are implemented using an inference network architecture since the relationships between the facts are typically well known.

Classification problems are ideally suited for backward chaining using either inference networks or pattern matchers depending upon the complexity of problem's data.

5.5 PROBLEMS

5-1. Trace the execution of the dinner selection knowledge base in Section 5.3.1 when the guest is your boss, the day is Friday, and your boss is 45. What happens if your boss is 18 instead?

5-2. The forward-reasoning process has several places where bottlenecks can occur.
   (a) Identify these bottlenecks.
   (b) For each of these bottlenecks identify whether the Rete algorithm is able to provide some relief.

   (c) How does the Rete algorithm provide relief for these bottlenecks?

5-3. What are the potential bottlenecks in the Rete algorithm?

5-4. Implement the dinner example from Section 5.3.1 using PC Plus.

5-5. Implement the animal identification example from Section 5.3.3 using PC Plus.

5-6. Implement the BOXER example using CLIPS.

5-7. Given the rules developed in your solution to Problem 5-6, draw a Rete network that represents the knowledge in these rules.

5-8. Suppose that you are given the Rete network developed in Problem 5-7 and the following set of facts that have been asserted in the order shown. Enter the facts into the network, indicating what information is stored at each node of the network.

Unboxed
Items:	Number:	Weight:	Size:	Fragile?:	Pliable?:
book	1	heavy	2	no	no
monitor	1	heavy	6	yes	no
diskettes	1	light	3	yes	no
book	2	medium	1	no	no
shirt	1	light	1	no	yes
cds	1	medium	2	no	no
cd player	1	medium	1	yes	no
shirt	2	light	1	no	yes
records	1	light	3	yes	no

5-9. Implement the BOXER example using the code provided in Section 5.2.5.

5-10. Implement the fruit identification example using the code provided in Section 5.3.3.

5-11. Suppose that you are given the following set of items for the BOXER system to pack.

Unboxed
Items:	Number:	Weight:	Size:	Fragile?:	Pliable?:
computer	1	heavy	6	yes	no
TV	1	medium	5	yes	no
monitor	1	heavy	6	yes	no
diskettes	1	light	3	yes	no
records	1	light	3	yes	no
stereo	1	medium	5	yes	no
picture	1	light	2	yes	no
dishes	1	medium	4	yes	no

(a) Simulate the execution of the system.

(b) Note how inefficiently Boxer has packed the items. This inefficiency can be corrected by changing the order of the facts or developing a new set of rules. Modify the set of rules so they are more efficient in the number of boxes used.

Code-oriented Problems

5-12. Modify the forward-reasoning code of Section 5.2.5 to permit numeric comparisons. This extension will allow you to fully implement the fruit identification knowledge base so premises such as (seedcount > 1) will be satisfied by the fact (seedcount = 3).

5-13. Modify the forward-reasoning code provided in Section 5.2.5 so rule names are printed with each fact derived.

5-14. Modify the backward-reasoning code and knowledge representation so each parameter knows what are acceptable values and does not allow the user to enter an illegal value.

5-15. Continue the extension in Problem 5-12 so a user can enter "?" when he does not know what values are acceptable for a parameter. The system should display a list of all acceptable values.

5-16. Modify the backward-reasoning code so a prompt can be specified for each parameter if the knowledge engineer so desires. If a prompt is not specified the system should generate an appropriate prompt as it now does.

5-17. Add a question answering facility that will work with either the forward- or backward-reasoning code that allows a user to question the system at the end of execution about any parameter and the parameter's values. This facility should allow the user to ask, "How did parameter X obtain its value of Y?" A message should be printed that identifies the rule successfully deriving the value or that prints the value obtained by user input.

5-18. Add the capability to answer "Whynot" questions, such as, "Why did parameter X not obtain a value of Y?" to the code in Section 5.3.3. An appropriate message should be printed to explain why a rule that could have derived that value failed to execute successfully.

5-19. Develop a knowledge editor similar to that used in the T.I. PC Plus Shell to aid the user in developing a knowledge base.

5-20. Add a pattern-matching capability similar to that found in CLIPS to the code contained in Section 5.2.5.

5-21. Add a pattern-matching capability similar to that found in CLIPS to the code contained in Section 5.3.3.

6

Associative Networks, Frames, and Objects

6.1 INTRODUCTION

In this chapter we examine three alternative knowledge representation schemes: *associative (semantic) networks*, *frames*, and *objects*. These schemes offer the ability to represent structured knowledge about physical or conceptual objects more easily than rules. They have become increasingly popular within knowledge-based systems as the limitations of rule-based systems have become apparent. Each offers its own unique features for representing structured knowledge, such as the parts that compose objects and relationships between objects. We start our discussion with the simplest of these representations, associative networks, which form the basis for the other two.

6.2 ASSOCIATIVE (SEMANTIC) NETWORKS

Semantic networks were originally developed by Quillian [Quillian, 1968] for representing knowledge within English sentences. He was interested in creating a knowledge representation format that would allow the *meaning* or semantics of words to be represented so these meanings could be used to perform tasks in a humanlike manner. The two specific tasks that he examined were (1) comparing and contrasting the meanings of two words and (2) processing text to create an understanding of its meaning. Today, the term *associative networks* is more widely used to describe these networks since they are used to represent more than just semantic relations. They are widely used to represent physical and/or causal associations between various concepts or objects.

6.2.1 General Introduction

An *associative* or semantic network is a labeled, directed graph. The nodes in the network are used to represent various concepts or objects, and the arcs or links connecting the nodes represent the various relationships or associations that hold between the concepts.

An important feature of any associative network is the associative links that connect the various nodes within the network. It is this feature that makes associative graphs different from simple directed graphs. To understand the difference better, let us consider the directed graph shown in Figure 6.1 that represents the airline flights between cities serviced by Fly-by-Night Airlines. The links of this network merely provide information about acceptable traffic flow. Since all links within the network represent the same semantic information, this graph is a simple directed graph rather than an associative graph.

To better illustrate the basic features of an associative network, consider Figures 6.2 and 6.3 that were created by Quillian [Quillian, 1968]. Figure 6.2 defines his associative links. These relationships provide the structure for understanding the meaning represented within an associative graph that defines a particular concept. The power of an associative network is derived from the richness of its underlying relationships. Without these relationships the network is merely a collection of unrelated facts. The relationships provide a cohesive structure for interpreting the structure and inferring new facts.

Quillian defined a concept (i.e., word) through a graphical description. This graphical description defines a particular concept by connecting the meanings of the various words used to provide a dictionary definition of this concept. This graph can be viewed as one plane in an interconnected network of planes, where each plane defines a separate concept and the interconnections between the planes show the relationships between the concepts. Figure 6.3 [Quillian, 1969] illustrates Quillian's definition of the word *food*. As identified in Figure 6.2 the dashed links show the connections to related concepts (e.g., *BEING 2, THING*). The letters *A* and *B* represent a thing and a being, respectively. The numeric values identify a particular definition for that concept when more than one definition exists.

Within knowledge-based systems, associative networks are most commonly used to represent semantic associations (e.g., taxonomies). In the more technically oriented applications, they can be used to express both physical and causal structures of systems.

As an example of how associative networks can be used to express the physical structure of a system, consider Figure 6.4, which provides a theoretical diagram of the ignition system of a Triumph TR-7. Three semantic relationships are used within this diagram: *Part-of (P.O.)*, *Connected-to (C.T.)*, and *Number-of (#OF)*. The *Part-of* relation details the part/subpart relationship (e.g., the battery is part-of an ignition system, the positive pin is part-of the

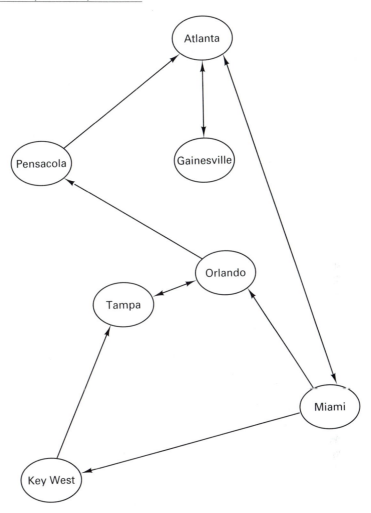

FIGURE 6.1   Fly-by-Night Airlines Flights between Cities

battery). The *Connected-to* relation identifies the electrical connectivity of the ignition system (e.g., the primary winding of the coil is connected to both the secondary winding and the output terminal, the secondary winding is connected to the distributor's rotor). The *Number-of* relationship specifies the number of occurrences of particular objects within the system.

Inextricably involved with two of these semantic relationships (i.e., *Part-of* and *Connected-to*) is the concept of transitivity: The rotor is *Part-of* the distributor and the distributor is *Part-of* the ignition system, which implies that the rotor is *Part-of* the ignition system. Similarly, the fact that the positive pin of the battery is *Connected-to* the ignition switch and the ignition switch is

Associative link (type-to-token and token-to-token, used within a plane)

1.   B names a class of which A is a subclass (only where A is a type node).

2.   B modifies A (only where A is a token node).

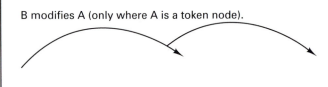

3.   A, B, and C form a disjunctive set.

4.   A, B, and C form a conjunctive set.

5. and 6.   B, a subject, is related to C, an object, in the manner specified by A, the relation. Either the link to B or to C may be omitted in a plane, which implies that A's normal subject to object is to be assumed.

Associative link (token-to-type, used only between planes)

6.

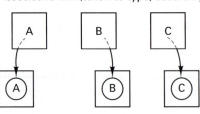

A, B, and C, are token nodes for, respectively, A, B, and C.

FIGURE 6.2   Quillian's Associative Link Types

Food: 1. That which living being has to take to keep it living and for growth. Things forming meals, especially other than drink.

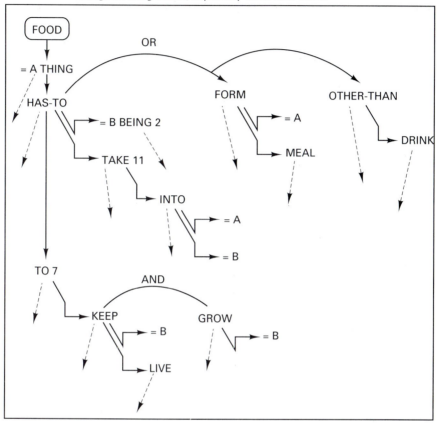

FIGURE 6.3   Quillian's Semantic Network for "Food" (where the dotted lines point to other definitions)

Connected-to the primary winding of the coil implies electrical connectivity between the positive pin and the primary winding. Note that we must be very careful in how we define the semantics associated with *Connected-to*. While the explicit use of this relationship within this figure identifies that two objects are directly connected to each other electrically, the application of transitivity derives only electrical connectivity between two objects, not that they are directly connected. This raises the issue: Is this relationship truly transitive? We can answer this only by asking the question, what are the semantics of the relationship? If this relationship means that the two objects are directly connected, then the relationship is not transitive, while if it means only electrical connectivity, then it is.

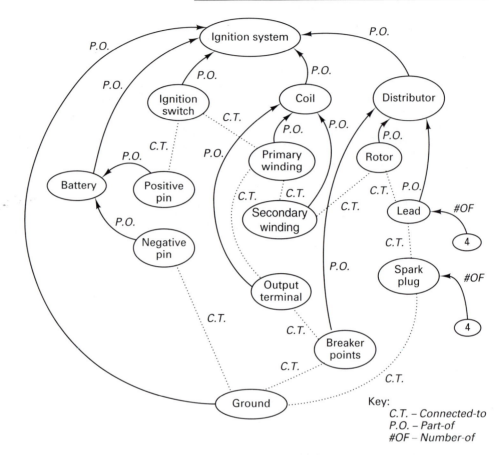

FIGURE 6.4   TR-7 Ignition System

To further illustrate this problem, consider Figure 6.5. The *is-a* relationship within the figure is used to specify membership in some larger class of objects. By inheritance of properties we can derive that since 1956 MGAs are rare cars, they are collected by car collectors. If we assume transitivity across

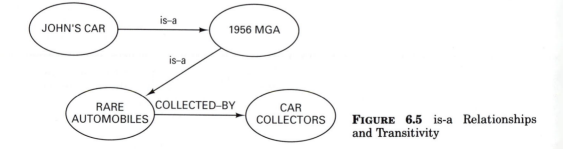

FIGURE 6.5   is-a Relationships and Transitivity

is-a, it is possible to derive that John's car is collected by car collectors, a statement which is most likely false. In part, this incorrect interpretation is due to an inappropriately defined and used *is-a* relationship. This relationship traditionally has been misused to represent several different relations including *instance-of, set-member, subclass-of, has-properties-of, has-structures-of*, and *is-equivalent-to*—all of which are different! In our example, *is-a* is really describing two relationships: set membership (i.e., *set-member* or an individual belongs within a set) and set inclusion (i.e., *subclass-of* or one set is wholly contained within another), when it should be used only to represent a single relationship. See [Woods, 1975] and [Brachman, 1979] for an additional discussion on this problem of defining and interpreting semantic primitives.

As mentioned above, associative networks can also be used to express causal relationships. A more complicated network representing a set of causal relationships that was developed by Chuck Reiger [Reiger, 1977; Davis, 1983] is detailed in Figures 6.6 and 6.7. This network describes the cause-and-effect

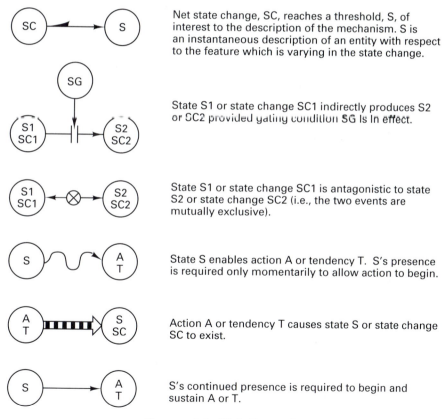

Net state change, SC, reaches a threshold, S, of interest to the description of the mechanism. S is an instantaneous description of an entity with respect to the feature which is varying in the state change.

State S1 or state change SC1 indirectly produces S2 or SC2 provided gating condition SG is in effect.

State S1 or state change SC1 is antagonistic to state S2 or state change SC2 (i.e., the two events are mutually exclusive).

State S enables action A or tendency T. S's presence is required only momentarily to allow action to begin.

Action A or tendency T causes state S or state change SC to exist.

S's continued presence is required to begin and sustain A or T.

FIGURE 6.6   Link Semantics

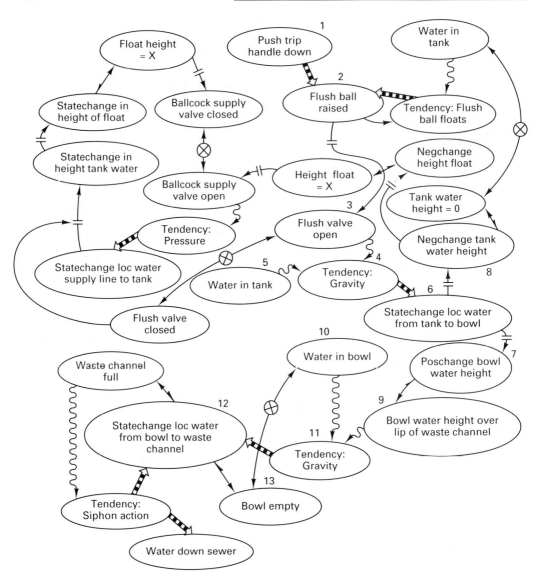

FIGURE 6.7 Associative Network Description of a Reverse-trap Toilet

relationships existing in the operation of a common reverse-trap toilet. Note
that the nodes of this associative network represent events rather than objects
and the links describe interevent causal interactions that are necessary (and
believed close to sufficient) to describe our underlying concepts of the causality
within the physical mechanisms being described. The following paragraph
provides a partial interpretation of the network shown in Figure 6.7.

Pushing down on the trip handle of the toilet (node 1) causes the flush ball to be raised (2). The raising of the flush ball directly causes the flush valve to open (3) which allows gravity (4) to force the water from the tank (5) into the bowl (6). The water flowing into the bowl directly causes two actions: a positive change in the position of the bowl water height (7) and a negative change in the tank water height (8). The positive change in the bowl water height results in a threshold that forces water over the lip of the waste channel (9). This action combined with water being in the bowl (10) and gravity (11) results in bowl water flowing into the waste channel (12), eventually emptying the bowl (13) [which is mutually exclusive with the state of water being in the bowl (10)]. An understanding of the rest of the network should be determined easily.

By representing this knowledge explicitly within an associative network, a knowledge-based system obtains a higher level of understanding for the actions, causes, and events that occur within this domain. This higher level of understanding allows the system to reason more completely about problems that exist within this domain (e.g., Why does the toilet not flush when the handle is pushed?) and to develop better explanations in response to user queries (e.g., What is the purpose and role of the flush ball?).

6.2.2 Associative Network Example

To further illustrate how an associative network might be used, let us reexamine Figure 6.4. Suppose that we would like to develop code which will allow us to reason about electrical connectivity and part/subpart relationships within this diagram. First, we must develop a representation capable of accurately detailing all of the relationships within this figure. One possible encoding would be to use triples for the *Part-of* and *Connected-to* relations:

```
(part-of   super-structure   sub-structure)
   (connected-to   object1   object2)
```

Note that we must clearly identify the semantics associated with each of these relationships. The *Part-of* relationship is transitive (since sub-subparts are part of the larger structure), but is not commutative (since there is a definite order associated with the superstructure and substructure). The *Connected-to* relationship, however, is both transitive and commutative. These additional facts can be stated using the tuples

```
(transitive x)
(commutative x)
```

Given these relationships, we can express the knowledge within Figure 6.4 as the following set of facts:

```
(setq known-facts
  '((part-of  ignition-system  ground)
    (part-of  ignition-system  battery)
    (part-of  ignition-system  ignition-switch)
    (part-of  ignition-system  coil)
    (part-of  ignition-system  distributor)
    (part-of  battery  positive-pin)
    (part-of  battery  negative-pin)
    (part-of  coil  output-terminal)
    (part-of  coil  primary-winding)
    (part-of  coil  secondary-winding)
    (part-of  distributor  breaker-points)
    (part-of  distributor  rotor)
    (part-of  distributor  lead)
    (number-of  lead  4)
    (number-of  spark-plug  4)
    (connected-to  ignition-switch  positive-pin)
    (connected-to  primary-winding  ignition-switch)
    (connected-to  negative-pin  ground)
    (connected-to  ground  breaker-points)
    (connected-to  ground  spark-plug)
    (connected-to  primary-winding  secondary-winding)
    (connected-to  primary-winding  output-terminal)
    (connected-to  output-terminal  breaker-points)
    (connected-to  secondary-winding  rotor)
    (connected-to  rotor  lead)
    (connected-to  lead  spark-plug)
    (transitive  connected-to)
    (transitive  part-of)
    (commutative  connected-to) )  )
```

Given the above relationships, how might we use this knowledge to answer questions about the diagram? Or to state this question differently, what sort of questions would we like to answer using this knowledge? On the most simplistic level we might wish to query about the existence of a simple relationship:

```
(connected-to  rotor  ground)
;; Is the rotor connected to ground?
```

or

```
(part-of  ignition-system  positive-terminal)
;; Is the positive terminal part of the ignition
;; system?
```

On a more complicated level, we might query about logical combinations of simple relationships:

```
(and   (connected-to   positive-pin   ground)
       (connected-to   negative-pin   ground)
       (or  (part-of   distributor   positive-pin)
            (part-of   distributor   negative-pin) ) )
;; Are both the positive pin and negative pin connected
;; to ground and is either of them part of the ignition
;; system?
```

Finally, we might want to be able to retrieve facts from the fact base about the relationships between various parts:

```
(and   (connected-to   battery   (* x))
       (part-of   distributor   (* x)) )
;; What parts connected to the battery are part of the
;; distributor?
```

where (* x) identifies that we would like to retrieve and assign to the variable x all values that satisfy the current pattern's position.

One top-level function is required to interface to this implementation—the **find** function. This function is given the semantic relationships that we are attempting to verify. It applies any logical operations that are specified between the various clauses and returns a truth value identifying whether or not the specified relation(s) exist in the fact base. This function, as implemented in the following optional section, can be used to answer all but one of the above queries:

```
(find   '(and (connected-to rotor ground))
        ;; Is the rotor connected to ground?
  )
```

returns **T**,

```
(find   '(and (part-of ignition-system positive-terminal))
        ;; Is the positive terminal part of the ignition
        ;; system?
  )
```

also returns **T**, and

```
(find   '(and (connected-to positive-pin ground)
              (connected-to negative-pin ground)
              (or (part-of distributor positive-pin)
                  (part-of distributor negative-pin)))
```

```
                      ;; Are both the positive pin and negative pin
                      ;; connected to ground and is either of them
                      ;; part of the ignition system?
            )
```

returns **nil** because neither the *positive-pin* nor the *negative-pin* are part of the *distributor*. Note that because of the way the code is developed below, the expression given to the **find** function must start with an **AND** or **OR** relation even if it consists of a single clause (as in the first two examples above).

The **find** and its related functions as defined in the following section are incapable of solving the final example:

```
    (find  '(and (connected-to battery (* x))
                 (part-of distributor (* x)))
            ;; What parts connected to the battery are part
            ;; of the distributor?
    )
```

since they are unable to perform the complicated variable pattern matching expressed. This extension to **find** is left as a chapter problem.

6.2.3 Coding Associative Networks (optional)

The implementation of the code to recognize logical combinations of relations within our database is accomplished through a series of functions. Before these functions can be executed, an initialization function, **initialization**, must be executed. This function modifies the fact base by adding inverse facts for all commutative facts. The addition of these facts simplifies the actions that must be performed by the remaining functions. This initialization function applies one function, **commut**, which creates the needed commutative facts.

```
(defun initialization ()
   (let ((commut-facts (matcher '(commutative *) known-facts)))
       (setq known-facts
           (append known-facts
               (apply 'append
                   (mapcar
                       '(lambda (itm)
                           (commut (matcher (list (cadr itm) '* '*)
                                           known-facts)))
                       commut-facts)))) ) )
```

```
(defun commut (1st)
   (mapcar '(lambda (itm)
              (list (car itm)(caddr itm)(cadr itm)))
          lst) )
```

On the topmost level is the **find** function. This function is given the semantic relationships that we are attempting to verify as a logical combination
of clauses. It checks for a prefixed *and* or *or* then **mapcar's eval-clause**
across the relationships (clauses).

```
(defun find (p-list)
   (cond ((null p-list) t)
         ((equal (car p-list) 'and)
          (and-lst (mapcar 'eval-clause
                           (cdr p-list)
                           (dupl nil (length (cdr p-list))))))
         ((equal (car p-list) 'or)
          (or-lst (mapcar 'eval-clause
                          (cdr p-list)
                          (dupl nil (length (cdr p-list))))))
         ((atom (car p-list))
          (printc "error: bad list")
          nil)
         (t (and-lst (mapcar 'eval-clause
                             p-list
                             (dupl nil (length p-list))))) )) )
```

The **eval-clause** function verifies that each pattern has a match in the
database of known facts. Because embedded *ands* and *ors* can occur, it must
check for these embedded clauses and recursively evaluate them. Should a
pattern not be directly found in the database a check is made to see if the relationship of the pattern is transitive. Should the pattern be transitive, the
transitive semantics are applied through a call to **trans-eval-clause**. Note
the second argument for this function, *depth-list*. This argument keeps
track of all visited nodes as the function performs a depth-first search of transitive relations.

```
(defun eval-clause (clause depth-list)
   (cond ((equal (car clause) 'and)
          (and-lst (mapcar 'eval-clause
                           (cdr clause)
                           (dupl nil (length (cdr clause))))) )
         ((equal (car clause) 'or)
          (or-lst (mapcar 'eval-clause
                          (cdr clause)
                          (dupl nil (length (cdr clause))))) )
         ((matcher clause known-facts))
```

```
((and (matcher (list 'transitive (car clause))
                known-facts)
       (not (member (cadr clause) depth-list))
       (trans-eval-clause clause depth-list)) )
  (t   nil) ) )

(defun trans-eval-clause (clause depth-list)
  (let ((facts (matcher (list (car clause)
                              (cadr clause)
                              '*)
                        known-facts)))
    (or-1st (mapcar 'eval-clause
                    (modify facts (caddr clause))
                    (dupl (cons (cadr clause) depth-list)
                          (length facts)))) ) )
```

The **matcher** function is given a single pattern and a list of facts. It retrieves all facts which match the particular pattern. Multiple facts might be
matched since the pattern might contain a wildcard, *, which can match any
value.

```
(defun matcher (pat f-list)
  (apply 'append
         (mapcar '(lambda (item)
                    (cond ((match-fact pat item)
                           (list item))))
                 f-list)) )
```

The **match-fact** function compares a single fact with a pattern to see if
there is a match.

```
(defun match-fact (pat data)
  (cond ((and (null pat) (null data)) t)
        ((or (null pat) (null data)) nil)
        ((or (equal (car pat) '*)
             (equal (car pat) (car data)))
         (match-fact (cdr pat) (cdr data))) ) )
```

The **modify** function is used by transitive relationships to construct a
new set of patterns that must be examined. The transitive relationship for
some fact, *(rel fact-a fact-c)*, is attempted to be proven by first locating
all facts of the form *(rel fact-a fact-b)*. These facts are then rewritten by
the **modify** function into the format *(rel fact-b fact-c)*. *1st* contains the
list of retrieved facts that must be rewritten and *itm* contains *fact-c*.

```
(defun modify (1st itm)
  (mapcar '(lambda (1st-itm)
```

```
          (list (car lst—itm)
                (caddr lst—itm) itm))
     lst) )
```

The final two functions, **and-lst** and **or-lst**, take a list of true and false values and apply a logical AND or OR to them:

```
(defun and—lst (lst)
   (cond ((null lst) t)
         ((car lst) (and—lst (cdr lst)))
         (t nil)) )

(defun or—lst (lst)
   (cond ((null lst) nil)
         ((car lst) t)
         (t (or—lst (cdr lst)) )) )
```

The final function is **dupl**, which creates a list containing cnt copies of lst.

```
(defun dupl (lst cnt)
   (cond ((zerop cnt) nil)
         (t (cons lst (dupl lst (1— cnt)))) ) )
```

The code presented in this section represents only a limited application and use of associative networks. Reasoning about the semantics of a flush toilet expressed in Figure 6.7 would require a completely new and more complicated set of interpretive routines since the underlying semantics of the relationships are significantly different.

6.2.4 Advantages and Disadvantages of Associative Networks

Associative networks have two advantages over the rule- and logic-based systems discussed in the previous three chapters.

1. *Explicit and succinct:* Networks allow the statement of important associations explicitly and succinctly. For example, in Figure 6.5 the *is-a* link between *JOHN'S CAR* and *1956 MGA* clearly identifies the connection between these two entities. Because the property of inheritance is associated with this link type, all of the parts that compose a *1956 MGA* are contained within *JOHN'S CAR* so these parts would only need to be represented once within the network.

2. *Reduced search time:* Because nodes are directly connected to related nodes rather than being expressed as relationships in a large database, the search time for particular facts can be greatly reduced.

The disadvantages for associative networks include:

1. *No interpretation standards:* No standard interpretation exists for knowledge expressed within a network. The interpretation of a network depends solely on the programs that manipulate the network. When examining a network it is very difficult to interpret what is represented. Does the node *1956 MGA* represent the concept of a particular automobile, the class of all 1956 MGAs, or a typical 1956 MGA? Each of these interpretations supports different types of inferences.

2. *Invalid inferences:* Often invalid inferences can be drawn from the knowledge contained within the network. Remember from Figure 6.5 that it could be possible to derive that John's car is collected by car collectors when in actuality this statement is most likely false.

3. *Combinatorial explosion:* Exploring an associative network using routines similar to the ones developed in Section 6.2.2 results in a combinatorial explosion. This is especially true when some relationship is false, since many or all of the relations in the network must be examined to show that the relationship is false.

6.3 FRAMES

Recognizing that associative networks, rules, and logic do not provide the ability to group facts into associated clusters or to associate relevant procedural knowledge with some fact of group of facts, Marvin Minsky developed the representation scheme called *frames* [Minsky, 1975]. This knowledge representation scheme attempts to account for our ability to deal with new situations (either objects or actions), which are encountered each day, by using our existing knowledge of previous events, concepts, and situations.

6.3.1 General Introduction

Consider the situation of renting an automobile. While you have experience in driving many different types of automobiles, you might not have driven the particular type of automobile assigned to you. Nevertheless, you do have several expectations about the automobile based upon previous ones that you have driven and rented. You expect that the gas tank is full, the car has a steering wheel, the tires are properly inflated, the key is in the car, the car will start, and so forth. This knowledge includes not only information about the physical structure of the automobile, but also information about how to use this knowledge and what to do if your expectations are not confirmed.

A frame provides the structure or framework for representing this knowledge acquired through previous experience. Using a collection of knowledge consisting of a frame name and a set of attribute-value pairs, a frame represents a stereotypical situation (i.e., an object or process) from the world.

The attributes of the attribute-value pairs are often called *slots* while the values are called *fillers*. The fillers can additionally be subdivided into *facets*, each having their own associated values. The following example illustrates this structure.

Figure 6.8 contains a small frame describing general information about an automobile. This frame indicates that automobiles have attributes (slots) for their manufacturer, country of manufacture, color, model, reliability, miles per gallon, year, and owner. Several possible facets can be associated with each slot. These facets include *Range* (the set of possible values for this slot), *Default* (the value to assume if none is explicitly stated), *If–Needed* (procedure(s) for determining the actual value), *If–Added* (procedure(s) to execute when a value is specified for the slot), and *If–Changed* (procedure(s) to execute if the value of the slot is changed). These procedures, also called *daemons* or *demons*, represent a powerful concept in frames—the ability to combine procedural knowledge within the declarative knowledge structure of the frame.

Notice that the frame described in Figure 6.8 is a generic or prototypical frame describing automobiles. While it provides information that we associate with all automobiles, it does not describe any particular automobile in

```
Generic AUTOMOBILE Frame
    Specialization-of: VEHICLE
    Generalization-of: (STATION-WAGON COUPE SEDAN)
    Manufacturer:
        Range: (FORD MAZDA BMW SAAB)
        Default: MAZDA
    Country-Of-Manufacture:
        Range: (USA JAPAN GERMANY SWEDEN)
        Default: JAPAN
    Model:
        Range: ()
    Color:
        Range: (BLACK WHITE BURGUNDY PERSIAN-AQUA)
        If-Needed: (EXAMINE-TITLE or CONSULT-DEALER or
                    LOOK-AT-AUTOMOBILE)
    Reliability:
        Range: (HIGH MEDIUM LOW)
    Miles-Per-Gallon:
        Range: (0 - 100)
    Year:
        Range: (1940 - 1990)
        If-Changed: (ERROR: Value cannot be modified)
    Owner:
        Range: Person-Name
        If-Added: (APPLY-FOR-TITLE and OBTAIN-TAG and PAY-SALES-TAX)
```

FIGURE 6.8   Generic Frame for an Automobile

detail. Particular automobiles are "created" using this generic frame even if they are different in some features (i.e., they are a coupe rather than a sedan). This feature of frames is illustrated by the *Generalization-of* slot in the generic frame. Likewise, this generic frame is in turn a specialization of a more general frame, the VEHICLE frame. This is indicated by the *Specialization-of* slot.

When you examine the description of coupe in Figure 6.9, you are immediately struck with its simplicity. Because this frame describes a generalized subclass of automobiles, it does not need to represent all features shared by automobiles and coupes. It must, rather, simply identify those characteristics that distinguish it from a generic automobile. This provides significant economy within the overall representation.

Suzie Smith's new Mazda RX-7 might be described, for example, by the frame shown in Figure 6.10. Note that this frame is a *Specialization-of* a COUPE, which in turn is a *Specialization-of* an AUTOMOBILE, which in turn is a *Specialization-of* a VEHICLE. Most of the information describing Suzie Smith's RX-7 is inherited from the generic AUTOMOBILE frame with the COUPE frame adding a slot called *Doors*. Should information about Suzie's car not be explicitly represented (e.g., the *Country-Of-Manufacture*), the procedures associated with the frame system will define precisely how this information should be determined. Other information (i.e., the number of doors on Suzie's car) is not explicitly stated in her car's representation but is inherited from the more general frames (i.e., COUPE, AUTOMOBILE, and VEHICLE) by using the first explicit value found in the search up through the hierarchy.

Frames attempt to represent general knowledge about classes of objects, knowledge that is true for a majority of cases. Often the specific objects or concepts being represented as instances of a frame violate properties contained in the general frame. This allows frame systems to represent the complexities of the real world where boundaries between classes are often fuzzy (e.g., a penguin is a bird yet it does not fly—a characteristic associated with "all" birds). An important concept of frames is that properties associated with higher-level, or more general, frames are considered to be fixed, while the lower-level frames may vary but follow the general framework described by the higher frames. When a conflict in values occurs (e.g., penguins don't fly but birds do), the more specialized value takes precedence over the general value.

```
Generic COUPE Frame
    Specialization-of: AUTOMOBILE
    Generalization-of: (SUZIE-SMITH'S-AUTOMOBILE
                        JOHN-DOE'S-AUTOMOBILE)
    Doors: 2
```

FIGURE 6.9 The COUPE Frame

```
SUZIE-SMITH'S-AUTOMOBILE Frame
    Specialization-of: COUPE
    Manufacturer: MAZDA
    Country-Of-Manufacture:
    Model: RX-7 GSL
    Color: Black
    Reliability: HIGH
    Miles-Per-Gallon: 26
    Year: 1990
    Owner: SUZIE SMITH
    Doors:   ()
```

FIGURE 6.10   Specific Frame for an Automobile

Frame-based systems have gained increasing acceptance since they allow the packaging of declarative knowledge (the basic structure of the frame) with procedural knowledge (the *If-Needed, If-Added,* and *If-Changed* facets of the slots). This general approach has been used to develop other knowledge representation schemes (e.g., scripts [Schank, 1977]), several general knowledge representation languages (e.g., KRYPTON [Brachman, 1983], and FRL [Goldstein, 1977]), and expert system shells (e.g., KEE [Fikes, 1985]).

6.3.2 A More Detailed Example

To illustrate how frames might be encoded, consider the following example. Suppose that we wish to develop a small knowledge base to keep track of individuals at our university. This knowledge base must be capable of representing the different facts or attributes associated with different types of individuals. For example, people have general attributes such as parents, spouses, addresses, and names while staff members of the university have additional facts about their office location, office phone number, and official duties. Figure 6.11 presents the hierarchy of these different categories of people and Figure 6.12 shows the various features associated with these categories as frames.

In this example, we have simplified the representation by not identifying restrictions on the values (e.g., their type and number of occurrences allowed) for the various features (or slots) of these frames. Note that frames lower in the hierarchy have only those slots that are different from higher-level frames specified. For example, `students` have four facts about them (e.g., a major, advisor, school year, and courses) which distinguish them from `university-persons`. Similarly, `man` differs from a generalized `person` by having a value of `male` for `gender`.

Another property of frames is illustrated in Figure 6.13. This frame represents a faculty member at the university, Dr. Tom Thomas. Suppose that we require information about Dr. Thomas's duties at the university. Examining

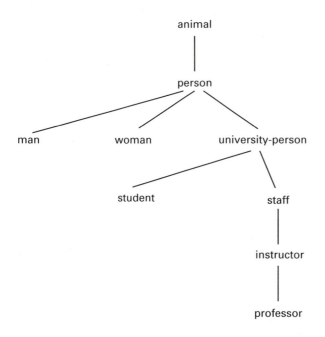

FIGURE 6.11 Hierarchy of Categories of People

his frame, we discover that it does not specify the specific duties that he performs. Because frames are a hierarchical representation that utilize inheritance, we are able to make use of values stored with other frames of the knowledge base to answer this question. If we search up through the frame hierarchy (from Dr. Thomas's *Specialization-of* slot to the *professor* frame) we discover that a *Duties* slot does exist. We are able to retrieve the values of "research teaching advising" from this slot of the *professor* frame and can assume that these are his duties since no others are associated with his frame.

The implementation of frames presented in the next section provides two manners for creating frames. To explicitly create a frame you reference either of the frame-defining functions, **frmdef** or **frmdefq**. The major difference between these two functions is that **frmdefq** does not require the quoting of its arguments. For example, the following two calls create exactly the same frame structures:

```
(frmdefq  instructor   staff
     (dept)
     (courses)
     (duties  (:value  teaching))  )

(frmdef  'instructor   'staff
     '( (dept)
        (courses)
        (duties  (:value teaching))  )  )
```

```
person FRAME
   Specialization-of: animal
   Gender:
   Parent:
      If-Added: add-inverse add-spouse-inverse
      If-Removed: remove-inverse
   Children:
      If-Added: add-inverse add-spouse-inverse
      If-Removed: remove-inverse
   Spouse:
      If-Added: add-symmetric
      If-Removed: remove-symmetric
   Address:
      If-Needed: get-spouse-addr
   Name:
   Age:
   Height:
   Weight:

man FRAME
   Specialization-of: person
   Gender: male

woman FRAME
   Specialization-of: person
   Gender: female

university-person FRAME
   Specialization-of: person
   Id-Number:

student FRAME
   Specialization-of: university-person
   Major:
   Advisor:
   Year:
   Courses:

staff FRAME
   Specialization-of: university-person
   Office:
   Office-Phone:
   Duties:
```

FIGURE 6.12   Frame Descriptions of the People Categories

```
instructor FRAME
   Specialization-of: staff
   Dept:
   Courses:
   Duties: teaching

professor FRAME
   Specialization-of: instructor
   Advisees:
   Duties: research teaching advising
```

FIGURE 6.12   (Continued)

```
Dr. Tom FRAME
   Specialization-of: professor
   Gender: male
   Address: Box 50, Paradise, FL
   Name: Dr. Tom Thomas
   Age: 40
   Height: 70
   Weight: 160
   ID-Number: 123456789
   Office: 501 Weil
   Office-Phone: 392-1990
   Dept: CS
   Courses: CS101 CS121
   Advisees: John
```

FIGURE 6.13   Dr. Tom Thomas's Frame

In this example, *instructor* is the name of the specific frame being created, *staff* is the frame's ancestor in the frame hierarchy, and *dept*, *courses*, and *duties* are the names of slots within the frame. The last slot, *duties*, has a specified facet called *:value*. This is a special facet that always contains the explicit value for a slot (which in this case is *teaching*).

The frames described in Figure 6.12 are implemented in Figure 6.14 using the calls to these two frame functions. This figure also includes the various functions acting as demons within these frames. Figure 6.15 details the function calls to create four frames describing individuals from our university world.

```
(frmdefq person animal
    (gender)
    (parent (:if-added add-inverse add-spouse-inverse)
            (:if-removed remove-inverse))
    (children (:if-added add-inverse add-spouse-inverse)
              (:if-removed remove-inverse))
    (spouse (:if-added add-symmetric)
            (:if-removed remove-symmetric))
    (address (:if-needed get-spouse-addr))
    (name) (age) (height) (weight) )

(frmdefq man person
    (gender (:value male)) )

(frmdefq woman person
    (gender (:value female)) )

(frmdefq university-person person
    (id-number) )

(frmdefq student university-person
    (major) (advisor) (year) (courses) )

(frmdefq staff university-person
    (office) (office-phone) (duties) )

(frmdefq instructor staff
    (dept) (courses)
    (duties (:value teaching)) )

(frmdefq professor instructor
    (advisees)
    (duties (:value research teaching advising)) )

;;; supporting functions (demons)

(defun add-inverse (frm slt dat)
    (if (equal slt 'children)
        (frmput dat 'parent :value frm)
        (frmput dat 'children :value frm) ) )
```

FIGURE 6.14   Code to Implement the Generalized Frames in Figure 6.12

```
(defun add-spouse-inverse (frm slt dat)
    (cond ((and (equal slt 'children)
                (frmvalues frm 'spouse))
           (frmput dat 'parent
                   :value (car (frmvalues frm 'spouse)))
           (frmput (car (frmvalues frm 'spouse))
                   'children :value dat))
          ((frmvalues frm 'spouse)
           (frmput dat 'children
                   :value (car (frmvalues frm 'spouse)))
           (frmput (car (frmvalues frm 'spouse)) 'parent
                   :value dat)) )
```

FIGURE 6.14 (Continued)

```
(defun remove-inverse (frm slt dat)
    (if (equal slt 'children)
        (frmremove dat 'parent :value frm)
        (frmremove dat 'children :value frm) ) )

(defun add-symmetric (frm slt dat)
    (frmput dat slt :value frm) )

(defun remove-symmetric (frm slt dat)
    (frmremove dat slt :value frm) )

(defun get-spouse-addr (person addr)
    (frmget-local (car (frmget-local person 'spouse :value)) addr
                  :value) )

(frmdefq dr-tom professor
    (gender (:value male))
    (address (:value (box 50 paradise fl)))
    (name (:value (dr tom thomas)))
    (age (:value 40))
    (dept (:value cs))
    (height (:value 70))
    (id-number (:value 123456789))
    (courses (:value cs101 cs121))
    (weight (:value 160))
    (office (:value 501weil))
    (office-phone (:value 3921990))
    (advisees (:value jane)) )
```

FIGURE 6.15 Creation of Four Frame Instances

```
(frmdefq dr-sue professor
    (gender (:value female))
    (address (:value (box 93 bird-nest fl)))
    (name (:value (dr sue smith)))
    (age (:value 38))
    (dept (:value cs))
    (height (:value 66))
    (id-number (:value 234567890))
    (courses (:value cs512 cs324))
    (weight (:value 130))
    (office (:value 305weil))
    (office-phone (:value 3927845))
    (advisees (:value john)) )

(frmdefq john student
    (gender (:value male))
    (parent (:value craig roberta))
    (address (:value (304 syme gainesville fl)))
    (name (:value (john james)))
    (age (:value 18))
    (height (:value 74))
    (weight (:value 230))
    (id-number (:value 567345789))
    (major (:value cs))
    (advisor (:value dr-sue))
    (year (:value freshman))
    (courses (:value cs101 engl02 phyl34 econl04)) )

(frmdefq jane student
    (gender (:value female))
    (parent (:value paul clare))
    (name (:value (jane anderson)))
    (age (:value 20))
    (height (:value 68))
    (weight (:value 130))
    (id-number (:value 137491298))
    (major (:value cs))
    (advisor (:value dr-tom))
    (year (:value junior))
    (courses (:value cs505 cs421 art263 stat344 bus532)) )
```

FIGURE 6.15 (Continued)

       If all we could do was create frames, they would be very uninteresting, so we need several additional interface functions that allow us to assign new values to a particular facet of a frame's slot:

```
(frmput frame-name slot-name facet-name value)
```

delete values from the facet of a particular frame's slot:

```
(frmremove frame-name slot-name facet-name value)
```

retrieve the *:value* of a frame's slot:

```
(frmvalues frame-name slot-name)
```

and display an entire frame:

```
(frmdisplay frame-name)
```

       Given these definitions, we can now utilize the created frames to answer the following questions about our university world (note that user input is in italics):

```
;; What is John's address?
(frmvalues 'john 'address)
>> ((304 SYME GAINESVILLE FL))
    ;; his address is directly retrieved

;; What does John's frame look like?
(frmdisplay 'john)
>>
Frame  JOHN
    slot  GENDER:
       :VALUE=  MALE
    slot  PARENT:
       :VALUE=  CRAIG ROBERTA
    slot  ADDRESS:
       :VALUE=  (304 SYME GAINESVILLE FL)
    slot  NAME:
       :VALUE=  (JOHN JAMES)
    slot  AGE:
       :VALUE=  18
    slot  HEIGHT:
       :VALUE=  74
    slot  WEIGHT:
       :VALUE=  230
    slot  ID-NUMBER:
       :VALUE=  567345789
```

```
       slot  MAJOR:
          :VALUE=  CS
       slot  ADVISOR:
          :VALUE=  DR-SUE
       slot  YEAR:
          :VALUE=  FRESHMAN
       slot  COURSES:
          :VALUE=  CS101 ENG102 PHY134 ECON104
       slot  AKO:
          :VALUE=  STUDENT
  JOHN


;; What is Jane's address?
(frmvalues 'jane 'address)
>> NIL
  ;; she has no address specified and none can be
  ;; inherited


;; What does Jane's frame look like?
(frmdisplay 'jane)
>>
Frame  JANE
    slot  GENDER:
       :VALUE=  FEMALE
    slot  PARENT:
       :VALUE=  PAUL CLARE
    slot  NAME:
       :VALUE=  (JANE ANDERSON)
    slot  AGE:
       :VALUE=  20
    slot  HEIGHT:
       :VALUE=  68
    slot  WEIGHT:
       :VALUE=  130
    slot  ID-NUMBER:
       :VALUE=  137491298
    slot  MAJOR:
       :VALUE=  CS
    slot  ADVISOR:
       :VALUE=  DR-TOM
    slot  YEAR:
       :VALUE=  JUNIOR
    slot  COURSES:
       :VALUE=  CS505 CS421 ART263 STAT344 BUS532
    slot  AKO:
       :VALUE=  STUDENT
  JANE
```

```
;; state that John and Jane become married
(frmput 'john 'spouse :value 'jane)
>> JANE

;; What is Jane's address now?
(frmvalues 'jane 'address)
>> ((304 SYME GAINESVILLE FL))
   ;; her address is derived from John's address by a
   ;; demon

;; state that they have a child
(frmput 'john 'children :value 'mark)
>> MARK

;; see that Jane's child, Mark, is properly derived
;; through a demon
(frmvalues 'jane 'children)
>> (MARK)

;; see who are Mark's parents
(frmvalues 'mark 'parent)
>> (JOHN JANE)

;; What does John's frame look like now?
(frmdisplay 'john)
>>
Frame  JOHN
    slot  GENDER:
        :VALUE=  MALE
    slot PARENT:
        :VALUE=  CRAIG ROBERTA
    slot  ADDRESS:
        :VALUE=  (304 SYME GAINESVILLE FL)
    slot  AME:
        :VALUE=  (JOHN JAMES)
    slot  AGE:
        :VALUE=  18
    slot  HEIGHT:
        :VALUE=  74
    slot  WEIGHT:
        :VALUE=  230
    slot  ID-NUMBER:
        :VALUE=  567345789
    slot  MAJOR:
        :VALUE=  CS
    slot  ADVISOR:
        :VALUE=  DR-SUE
    slot  YEAR:
```

```
            :VALUE=   FRESHMAN
      slot  COURSES:
            :VALUE=   CS101 ENG102 PHY134 ECON104
      slot  AKO:
            :VALUE=   STUDENT
      slot  SPOUSE:
            :VALUE=   JANE
      slot  CHILDREN:
            :VALUE=   MARK
JOHN

;; What does Jane's frame look like?
(frmdisplay 'jane)
>>
Frame  JANE
      slot  GENDER:
            :VALUE=   FEMALE
      slot  PARENT:
            :VALUE=   PAUL CLARE
      slot  NAME:
            :VALUE=   (JANE ANDERSON)
      slot  AGE:
            :VALUE=   20
      slot  HEIGHT:
            :VALUE=   68
      slot  WEIGHT:
            :VALUE=   130
      slot  ID-NUMBER:
            :VALUE=   137491298
      slot  MAJOR:
            :VALUE=   CS
      slot  ADVISOR:
            :VALUE=   DR-TOM
      slot  YEAR:
            :VALUE=   JUNIOR
      slot  COURSES:
            :VALUE=   CS505 CS421 ART263 STAT344 BUS532
      slot  AKO:
            :VALUE=   STUDENT
      slot  SPOUSE:
            :VALUE=   JOHN
      slot  CHILDREN:
            :VALUE=   MARK
JANE

;; What does Mark's frame look like?
(frmdisplay 'mark)
>>
```

```
Frame  MARK
   slot  PARENT:
      :VALUE=  JOHN JANE
MARK

;; John and Jane are divorced
(frmremove 'john 'spouse :value 'jane)
>> T

;; Jane no longer has John as a spouse or his address
(frmvalues 'jane 'spouse)
>> NIL
(frmvalues 'jane 'address)
>> NIL

;; What does John's frame look like now?
(frmdisplay 'john)
>>
Frame  JOHN
   slot  GENDER:
      :VALUE=  MALE
   slot  PARENT:
      :VALUE=  CRAIG ROBERTA
   slot  ADDRESS:
      :VALUE=  (304 SYME GAINESVILLE FL)
   slot  NAME:
      :VALUE=  (JOHN JAMES)
   slot  AGE:
      :VALUE=  18
   slot  HEIGHT:
      :VALUE=  74
   slot  WEIGHT:
      :VALUE=  230
   slot  ID-NUMBER:
      :VALUE=  567345789
   slot  MAJOR:
      :VALUE=  CS
   slot  ADVISOR:
      :VALUE=  DR-SUE
   slot  YEAR:
      :VALUE=  FRESHMAN
   slot  COURSES:
      :VALUE=  CS101 ENG102 PHY134 ECON104
   slot  AKO:
      :VALUE=  STUDENT
   slot  SPOUSE:
      :VALUE=
```

```
    slot   CHILDREN:
        :VALUE=   MARK
JOHN

;; What does Jane's frame look like?
(frmdisplay 'jane)
>>
Frame   JANE
    slot   GENDER:
        :VALUE=   FEMALE
    slot   PARENT:
        :VALUE=   PAUL CLARE
    slot   NAME:
        :VALUE=   (JANE ANDERSON)
    slot   AGE:
        :VALUE=   20
    slot   HEIGHT:
        :VALUE=   68
    slot   WEIGHT:
        :VALUE=   130
    slot   ID-NUMBER:
        :VALUE=   137491298
    slot   MAJOR:
        :VALUE=   CS
    slot   ADVISOR:
        :VALUE=   DR TOM
    slot   YEAR:
        :VALUE=   JUNIOR
    slot   COURSES:
        :VALUE=   CS505 CS421 ART263 STAT344 BUS532
    slot   AKO:
        :VALUE=   STUDENT
    slot   SPOUSE:
        :VALUE=
    slot   CHILDREN:
        :VALUE=   MARK
JANE
```

The following optional section contains details on how the various functions utilized in this example are actually coded.

6.3.3 Implementation of Frames (optional)

Before discussing the code [Finin, 1986] capable of creating the example presented above, we need to discuss four global variables. These variables keep track of names of all created frames, *framelist*, and identify actions

performed during the system's operation: *finherit*, *fdemons*, and
fdefault. *finherit* determines if values that are not specified in instances of frames can be inherited from their "parents." Recall the example in
Figure 6.13 that presented the specific frame representing Dr. Tom Thomas.
His frame did not specify his duties, but through inheritance we were able to
search through the hierarchy of frames to retrieve the values of "research
teaching advising" from the *professor* frame. *fdemons* determines if
demons provided within the various slots are applied when the values of the
slot are set (*If–Added* demons), retrieved (*If–Needed* demons), or deleted
(*If–Removed* demons). Finally, *fdefault* determines if a default value
should be used when you request a value for a slot and no value is present.
Initially, we assume that no frames exist and all of the system operations are
legal so each of these variables is assigned the following values:

```
(setq *framelist* nil)    ; no frames initially exist
(setq *finherit* t)       ; try inheritance if you cannot
                          ; find value
(setq *fdemons* t)        ; apply any demons which might
                          : exist when appropriate
(setq *fdefault* t)       ; use the default values if
                          ; present and the actual value
                          ; is not known
```

The creation of a frame involves referencing one of two functions: **frmdef** or
frmdefq. As stated in the last section, the major difference between these two
functions is that **frmdefq** does not require that its arguments be quoted. The
definitions for these functions are

```
(defun frmdef (frm parent defn)
   ;; defines a frame by setting its values
   ;;   and linking to parent
   (rplacd (frmframe frm) defn)
   (frmput parent 'specializes :value frm)
   (frmput frm 'ako :value parent) )

(defmacro frmdefq (frm parent &rest defn)
   ;; allows definition of frame without quotes
   '(frmdef (quote ,frm)
            (quote ,parent)
            (quote ,defn)) )
```

When a new frame is created, **frmframe** and **frmcreate** are used to initially create the frame by placing its name on *framelist* and building the
association list to hold all of the frame's slots and facets. This association list

is placed in a property slot called *frame* attached to the atom with the frame's name

```
(defun frmframe (frm)
    ;; returns structure representing specified frame,
    ;; creating it if needed
    (or (get frm 'frame)
        (frmcreate frm)) )

(defun frmcreate (frm)
    ;; creates frame with name frm
    (setq *framelist* (if (member frm *framelist*)
                          *framelist*
                          (cons frm *framelist*)))
    (setf (get frm 'frame) (list frm)) )
```

Alternatively, a frame is created implicitly by simply attempting to obtain some value from it. For example,

```
(frmget 'john 'parent :value)
```

creates the frame *john* if it does not already exist. **frmget** uses the global variables, when needed, to retrieve the frame's slot's facet's value by referencing either **frmvalues**, which retrieves values from :value facets, or **frmgetl**, which retrieves values from all other facets.

```
(defun frmget (frame slot facet
               &key (inherit *finherit*)
                    (demons *fdemons*)
                    (default *fdefault*))
    ; retrieve frame's slot's facet's value
    (if (equal facet :value)
        (frmvalues frame slot
                   :inherit inherit
                   :demons demons
                   :default default)
        (frmgetl frame slot facet inherit)) )

(defun frmgetl (frame slot facet inherit?)
    ;; retrieve frame's slot's facet's value by
    ;; inheritance, possibly
    (or (frmget-local frame slot facet)
        (if inherit?
            ;; search up inheritance structure for value
            ;; one parent at a time
            (some #'(lambda (parent)
                        (frmgetl parent slot facet t))
                  (frmparents frame)))) )
```

```
(defun frmvalues (frame slot
                    &key (inherit *finherit*)
                         (demons *fdemons*)
                         (default *fdefault*)
                         (finitial frame))
  ;; retrieve frame's slot's :value facet
  (or (frmget-local frame slot :value)
      (and default
           (frmget-local frame slot :default))
      (and demons
           (some #'(lambda (demon)
                     (funcall demon finitial slot))
                 (frmget-local frame slot
                               :if-needed)))
      (and inherit
           (some #'(lambda (parent)
                     (frmvalues parent slot
                                :inherit t
                                :demons demons
                                :default default
                                :finitial finitial))
                 (frmparents frame)))) )

(defun frmget-local (frame slot facet)
  ;; returns the :value facet for a frame's slot
  ;; without inheritance or demons
  (cdr (assoc facet
              (cdr (assoc slot
                          (cdr (frmframe frame)) )) ))
)
```

Adding values to the facet of a frame's slot is performed by **frmput** which, if the :value facet is changing, applies appropriate demons by referencing **frmput-value** or simply adding the facet's value by referencing **frmput-add**.

```
(defun frmput (frame slot facet datum
                &key (demons *fdemons*)
                     (inherit *finherit*))
  ;; add datum to the specified frame's slot's facet
  (cond ((member datum
                 (frmget-local frame slot facet))
         datum)
        ((equal facet :value)
         (frmput-value frame slot datum demons inherit))
        (t
         (frmput-add frame slot facet datum)
         datum)) )
```

```
(defun frmput-value (frame slot datum demons? inherit?)
    ;; adds datum to frame's slot's value
    ;; then run any demons which apply
    (frmput-add frame slot :value datum)
    (if demons?
        (mapcar #'(lambda (demon)
                    (funcall demon frame slot datum))
                (frmget frame slot :if-added
                        :inherit inherit?)))
    datum)

(defun frmput-add (frame slot facet datum)
    ;; adds datum to the given frame's slot's facet
    (rplacd (last (frmfacet frame slot facet))
            (list datum)) )
```

These functions use a series of auxiliary functions to perform the operation of storing values. These functions include **frmfacet** and **extend**:

```
(defun frmfacet (frame slot facet)
    ;; returns the frame's slot's facet's value,
    ;; creating it if necessary
    (extend facet (extend slot (frmframe frame))) )

(defun extend (key alist)
    ;; like assoc, but adds key KEY if not
    ;; already in the alist ALIST
    (or (assoc key (cdr alist))
        (cadr (rplacd (last alist)
                      (list (list key)) )) ) )
```

Removing information is achieved through two functions, **frmremove** and **frmerase**. **frmremove** removes a specific datum from a frame's slot's facet and applies appropriate demons, while **frmerase** completely removes a frame from the knowledge base.

```
(defun frmremove (frame slot facet datum
                  &key (demons *fdemons*)
                       (inherit *finherit*))
    ;; remove datum from frame's slot's facet
    (when (member datum (frmget-local frame slot facet))
        (delete datum (frmfacet frame slot facet))
        (if (and (eq facet :value)
                 demons)
            (mapcar #'(lambda (demon)
                        (funcall demon frame slot
                                 datum))
```

```
                       (frmget frame slot :if-removed
                                  :inherit inherit)) )) )

(defun frmerase (frm)
    ;; removes a frame from the world. Note: This can
    ;; remove a frame on any level of the tree
    ;; First, delete this frame from the parents'
    ;; SPECIALIZES slot
    (mapcar #'(lambda (parent)
                  (frmremove parent 'specializes :value frm))
            (frmget frm 'ako :value))
    ;; Next, delete frm from its children
    (mapcar #'(lambda (child)
                  (frmremove child 'ako :value frm))
            (frmget frm 'specializes :value))
    ;; Then, move all of the children of this frame up
    ;; to the parent
    (mapcar #'(lambda (parent)
                  (mapcar #'(lambda (child)
                               (frmput parent
                                       'specializes
                                       :value child)
                               (frmput child 'ako
                                       :value parent) )
                          (frmget frm 'specializes :value)))
            (frmget frm 'ako :value))
    (delete frm *framelist*)
    (remprop frm 'frame) )
```

To see the frames that exist in the knowledge base, use the **frmdisplay** function:

```
(defun frmdisplay (frm) ; displays a frame
    (format t "~%Frame  ~S" frm)
    (mapcar
       #'(lambda (slot)
             (format t "~%   slot  ~S:" slot)
             (mapcar
                #'(lambda (facet)
                      (format t "~%       ~S=" facet)
                      (mapcar
                         #'(lambda (datum)
                               (format t " ~S" datum))
                            (frmget frm slot facet)))
                   (frmfacets frm slot)))
          (frmslots frm))
       frm)
```

A small set of additional functions is required to interface with the frame's structure. These include **frmparents** (which retrieves parents of a frame), **frmslots** (which retrieves a frame's slots), **frmfacets** (which retrieves the facets of a frame's slot), and **some** (which applies functions from a list until one successfully executes.

```
(defun frmparents (frm)
    ;; retrieves the parents of the specified frame
    (frmget-local frm 'ako :value))

(defun frmslots (frm)
    ;; retrieves the slot names in a frame
    (mapcar 'car (cdr (frmframe frm))) )

(defun frmfacets (frm slot)
    ;; retrieves the facets of the frame's slot
    (mapcar 'car
            (cdr (assoc slot (cdr (frmframe frm)) )) ) )
```

Several problems exist with this implementation. We are unable to specify the type or number of values that are allowed for any slot. It would, therefore, be possible to create a spouse with a name of "123" or to have John married to both Sue and Jane. Corrections to these difficulties are addressed as problems at the end of the chapter.

6.3.4 Frames in Knowledge-based Systems

In the previous sections we described how knowledge can be represented using frames. The examples show a simple application of frames for answering questions. While this can be considered a rudimentary knowledge-based system, it does not really illustrate the full problem-solving capability of frame systems. In fact, frames are the preferred knowledge representation scheme used in *model-based* and *case-based reasoning*. These reasoning methods are described in Chapter 9.

Many hybrid systems (i.e., those simultaneously supporting frames and rules) use frames to represent structured knowledge and rules to reason about this frame knowledge. Frames additionally can be used to implement the representation of rule-based knowledge. This is done by implementing each rule as a frame where the premise, action, and other elements of the rule (i.e., certainty factor) are represented as slots. Another use of frames is the representation of factual knowledge within a rule-based system—all facts (whether initial facts, intermediate results, or final conclusions) can be implemented within frames using slots like *:value*, *:certainty-factor*, *:possible-values*, and so forth. This use of frames has occurred in the implementation of inference net systems [Fox, 1983].

You may also notice similarities between frame systems and database management systems. Whereas both represent "data" (through the frame's "slot" and the database's "field"), frames represent knowledge while databases typically represent only data. Current database research is examining their application to the representation of knowledge (containing inheritance and demons) similar to that of a knowledge-based system.

6.3.5 Advantages and Disadvantages of Frames

The advantages of frame-based systems include:

1. *Facilitation of expectation-driven processing:* A frame-based system, through the use of demons, is able to specify actions that should take place when certain conditions arise during the processing of information. While this might appear to be very similar to what happens in rules, it is significantly more powerful. In a rule-based system the rules must be repeatedly tested to see if they apply. In contrast, the demons of a frame-based system lay in wait until they are needed and "triggered." Only then are they executed.

2. *Organization of knowledge:* The knowledge possessed by a frame-based system is significantly more structured and organized than the knowledge within an associative network. When storing or retrieving information, this structure allows the system to quickly direct attention to the appropriate slots within the required frames, thereby facilitating the recall of information from the knowledge base and improving the speed of the inference process.

3. *Self driven:* The frames can be structured so they are able to determine their own applicability in given situations. Should a particular frame not apply, it can then suggest other frames that are appropriate in the given situation.

4. *Storage of dynamic values:* Dynamic values of variables during the execution of a knowledge-based system can be easily stored in frame slots. This can be especially useful when applying knowledge-based systems to simulations, planning, diagnostic problems, or database front-ends.

The disadvantages of the frame-based approach include:

1. *Departures from prototypes:* Many real-world situations involve objects that depart considerably from the prototypes. This increases the complexity of the system since each particular instance of an object has unique features that must be represented. For example, a frame representing a bicycle may define that a bicycle has two wheels. How do we deal with representing three-wheel bicycles or a bicycle with training wheels? What about a recumbent bicycle?

2. *Accommodation of new situations:* When new objects or situations are encountered, a frame-based system does not have the prototypes built to guide the representation of these instances. This severely limits the applicability of these systems.

3. *Detailing heuristic knowledge:* It is difficult to use frames to describe heuristic knowledge that is much more easily represented with rules. For example, a medical diagnostic system could use frames to represent a typical patient, a general disease, and the specific characteristics of particular diseases, but it would be difficult to represent how specific symptoms relate to each other and are used to diagnose a patient with the disease without expressing this knowledge using the rule representation format.

6.4 OBJECTS

While Minsky, Schank, and others explored the use of frames for representing knowledge in the 1970s, another group of researchers took an alternative, object-oriented approach. In frames, programs and data are treated as two separate but related entities. Data are defined through variables that are grouped into records or higher level structures. Code is similarly defined through statements into a hierarchy of procedures and functions. The two are related to each other through the code since this code manipulates and interprets the structures representing the data. The data can be processed independently and differently by separate procedures with each imposing a distinct interpretation. Similarly, segments of code can be viewed as *black boxes* that perform certain actions.

6.4.1 General Introduction

Unlike frames the object-oriented approach creates a tight bond between the code and data rather than separating them into two complex, separate structures. Small chunks of code and data are tightly coupled together with each of these chunks loosely tied to each other. While this approach seems unnatural, it actually corresponds more closely to our actual view of entities within the real world and provides a much firmer basis for program development.

An object is defined to be a collection of information (i.e., the data) representing an entity within the real world and a description of how this information is manipulated (i.e., the code or *methods*). For example, if we are developing a system to reason about terrorist attacks, we would be concerned about the particular terrorist event, the group instigating the event, and the leader of the attack. Each of these would be represented in an object-oriented system by a *class* of objects. The specific event, group, and leader would be instances from each of these classes. The methods, referenced through *messages*, would manipulate these instance objects to provide or derive specific data (e.g., Who is the immediate target? What is the symbolic value of the target? What is the estimated bomb size? Who received the warning? What are the strategic objectives of the group?) used in reasoning about the attack.

Several principles of the object-oriented approach make it well suited for representing knowledge.

1. *Abstraction:* Abstraction is ignoring aspects of some entity that are not relevant to the current problem so that you can concentrate more fully on those aspects that are. The object-oriented approach encourages the developer to use both procedural and data abstraction to simplify her view of the problem. In procedural abstraction, an operation (i.e., sorting) is viewed by its users as though it is a single entity even though it is actually achieved through some sequence of lower-level operations. Data abstraction is similar—an object (i.e., a car) is viewed as a single object rather than as a composite of all of its individual parts. The suppression of the lower-level details allows us to reason about the operation or object at hand more efficiently.

2. *Encapsulation* or *information hiding:* Each component of a program should hide a single design decision with each program interface revealing as little as possible about its inner workings. By hiding information, you help minimize the quantity of rework that must be performed when developing a new system.

3. *Inheritance:* Inheritance is receiving characteristics or properties from an ancestor. Inheritance allows us to express the common characteristics possessed by a collection of different classes of objects once. The special characteristics of each object are then expressed for that object only. This is identical to the inheritance of features within frames.

4. *Polymorphism:* Polymorphism involves "the ability of an entity to refer at run-time to instances of various classes. . . . " [Meyer, 1988] and the ability to overload operators. Polymorphism of objects, for example, allows an instance of a particular class (e.g., the class of people) to be assigned a value from a more restricted class (e.g., the class of infants). Polymorphism in operators, or operator overloading, allows the developer of a system to create a common interface to all of the various objects used within the domain. A "new" message can be used to create new instances of various object classes since a method by this name has been defined in each class. This allows each class to respond to the same message in its own unique way. For example, the sign "+" could be considered an addition operator if its arguments are numerical, or it could represent the concatenation of two strings if the two arguments are strings. Its definition simply depends on the type of arguments that the operator is provided. Polymorphism provides greater flexibility in our use of the hierarchy of classes and operators.

6.4.2 Historical Perspective

The concepts of object-oriented programming originated in the language Simula during the late 1960s and early 1970s. This language was used to model concurrent processes like those found in a factory assembly line. While exhibiting the concepts of objects, classes, and their associated methods, this language did not provide encapsulation and polymorphism.

Later in this period, the Learning Research Group at Xerox Palo Alto Research Center (PARC) started development of the *Smalltalk* language. Since this language was being designed for use by nonprogrammers on a special purpose graphics workstation, the system developers felt that an object-oriented approach would be the most natural and appropriate. Starting with only an external object-oriented structure, the language evolved through four versions to become totally object-oriented in Smalltalk-80 [Krasner, 1983].

In 1977 Bobrow and Winograd developed KRL (Knowledge Representation Language) [Bobrow, 1977] that used frame-like structures called *conceptual objects* to represent prototypes and their associated properties. A key component of these "objects" is that the properties appearing interesting or important depend upon how you perceive the object and intend to use it. For example, a screwdriver is viewed by a carpenter as a tool for inserting screws, by a painter as a device for prying a lid off a paint can, and by a cyclist as a tire iron. In this case, all individuals are viewing the object as some form of tool. A tree, on the other hand, is viewed by a lumber salesperson for its board feet, by an electric company employee for the damage it can cause to power lines, and by a homeowner for the shade it provides in the summer, the number of leaves that drop in the fall, its wind-breaking ability in the winter, and its flowers in the spring.

Another key component of these conceptual objects was that they were intended to be viewed in relation with other objects from the domain. Thus, the process of describing an object becomes one of comparing it to similar yet slightly different objects. For example, a manx is just like any other cat except it has short hair and no external tail. This ability to describe complex objects by comparison to other known objects simplifies the representation process since no one can agree on a set of primitive concepts or how these primitives might be combined to form more complicated structures.

6.4.3 Object-oriented Extensions to LISP

Because AI researchers in North America have great familiarity with LISP, several extensions have been made to its different dialects to give LISP an object-oriented capability. This has been implemented in an object-oriented extension to Scheme called SCOOPS, in the Symbolics Flavors system, as Xerox PARC's CommonLOOPS, and Common LISP's CLOS. This section reviews each of these efforts.

6.4.3.1 General features.   Each object-oriented LISP extension has introduced several important innovative features including *mixins* (multiple inheritance that causes the class structure to become a network rather than a tree);
method combination (including both primary and demon methods, which facilitate modification of existing methods and eliminate the need to rewrite entire methods); and *multimethods* (messages that are sent to any number of
objects rather than a single object). Below we discuss each of these features as
they appear in these various languages to illustrate the evolution of object-
oriented features within LISP.

Before examining each of these object-oriented LISP systems, let us
briefly consider the concept of method inheritance, a common feature in all
object-oriented systems.

Suppose that we have a problem involving reasoning about various vehicles. Our world might include automobiles, bicycles, and airplanes. Classes
for each of these object types would be defined using some function like *def-
struct* as follows. (Note the particular function name and format will vary depending upon the particular object oriented-implementation used.)

```
(defstruct (car)
   start-x-pos
   start-y-pos
   end-x-pos
   end-y-pos
   start-time
   end-time
   miles-per-gallon)

(defstruct (bicycle)
   start-x-pos
   start-y-pos
   end-x-pos
   end-y-pos
   start-time
   end-time
   number-of-gears)

(defstruct (airplane)
   start-x-pos
   start-y-pos
   start-z-pos
   end-x-pos
   end-y-pos
   end-z-pos
   start-time
   end-time)
```

Each of these classes might have methods defined that compute the total distance traveled and the speed of the object:

```
(defmethod   (car distance)
   (sqrt
      (+ (expt   (- end-x-pos   start-x-pos) 2)
         (expt   (- end-y-pos   start-y-pos) 2) )))

(defmethod   (bicycle distance)
   (sqrt
      (+ (expt   (- end-x-pos   start-x-pos) 2)
         (expt   (- end-y-pos   start-y-pos) 2) )))

(defmethod   (airplane distance)
   (sqrt
      (+ (expt   (- end-x-pos   start-x-pos) 2)
         (expt   (- end-y-pos   start-y-pos) 2)
         (expt   (- end-z-pos   start-z-pos) 2) )))
```

Note the heavy redundancy within the definition of each object (they all have the properties *end-x-pos*, *start-x-pos*, *end-y-pos*, *start-y-pos*, *start-time*, and *end-time*) and the methods for computing distance traveled for the car and the bicycle are identical. All this redundancy can be eliminated by defining a higher-level class called *vehicle* and defining the other classes as follows:

```
(defstruct (vehicle)
   start-x-pos
   start-y-pos
   end-x-pos
   end-y-pos
   start-time
   end-time)

(defstruct (car (include: vehicle))
   miles-per-gallon)

(defstruct (bicycle (include: vehicle))
   number-of-gears)

(defstruct (airplane (include: vehicle))
   start-z-pos
   end-z-pos)
```

The definitions of car, bicycle, and airplane now identify that they should include all that is defined for a vehicle (through the use of *include:*). Each of these, therefore, now includes the properties of *end-x-pos*, *start-x-pos*, *end–y–pos*, *start–y–pos*, *start–time*, and *end–time* in addition to their other properties. This ability to inherit features of higher-level classes also applies to the methods. We can define a generalized distance method in the *vehicle* class that applies to two-dimensional motion. Since the *car* and *bicycle* classes inherit from this class, they will inherit this method and use it to compute the distance traveled. Since airplanes travel in three dimensions, we must define another, specialized method for the *airplane* class (as we did in the first example). This new method ends up being used to compute airplane distances since its association with the airplane class causes it to be the first method encountered when we start searching the class hierarchy.

Instances of these classes are created in the following manner:

```
(setq my-mazda (make-instance 'car))
```

One final, general characteristic of classes should be noted. From an external view, we do not know the internal structure of the classes. Values associated with the instances (be they given as properties or computed through methods) are all retrieved in the same manner:

```
(funcall my-mazda ':start-x-pos)
            or
(funcall my-mazda ':distance)
```

As a result, the classes defined above for the different types of vehicles could have alternatively been implemented using polar coordinates or any other coordinate system desired instead of Cartesian coordinates. This concept of information hiding is an important feature of object-oriented systems.

There are many object-oriented systems that have and are being created. SCOOPS, developed by Texas Instruments, is an object-oriented extension to Scheme, a LISP dialect developed by Guy Steele and Gerry Sussman at M.I.T. SCOOPS supports two important features, *mixins* and *active values* (also known as procedural attachments), which are not supported by some object-oriented languages.

The first commercially available object-oriented extension to LISP to gain widespread popularity was Symbolics Flavors. The concepts of Symbolics Flavors evolved from the Flavors system created by the LISP Machine project at M.I.T. during the 1970s. Symbolics Flavors supports both mixins and method combination. The implementation of mixins in Symbolics Flavors is basically identical to that of SCOOPS.

Xerox PARC also developed an object-oriented extension to LISP called CommonLOOPS. Because of their research in the development of Smalltalk, CommonLOOPS best illustrates how object-oriented programming can be molded to fit in a LISP environment.

CommonLOOPS departs from the other LISP implementations by providing several built-in classes similar to the classes defined by Smalltalk. A number of these classes are metaclasses, classes used to define how other classes behave.

The newest and most widely accepted object-oriented extension to LISP is the *Common LISP Object System (CLOS)* [Keene, 1988]. CLOS, as a language standard, defines conventions to be supported by a wide range of Common LISP implementations, thus allowing CLOS programs to be easily ported from one implementation to another. CLOS was adopted as a part of Common LISP by the committee that is creating the ANSI Standard Common LISP and is a conservative composite of the features of all the other systems described above. It was designed to implement what was desirable in each of the older systems, leaving behind what was not. They did not try to significantly extend the ideas and concepts of object-oriented programming, but rather wished to standardize those features and techniques that were well defined and understood within the programming community.

As a result of the great flexibility provided within CLOS, it is easy for new users to be overpowered by all there is to learn. You should realize that typical applications require only a small portion of these techniques, If you use CLOS, become familiar with all that it has to offer so you can select the appropriate subset for your application.

6.4.4 Advantages and Disadvantages

In the general introduction on objects we provided characteristics that distinguish objects from other representations. These characteristics embody the advantages for using this form of knowledge representation and are repeated here for completeness.

1. *Abstraction:* Ignoring aspects of some entity that are not relevant to the current problem so that you can concentrate more fully on the relevant aspects.
2. *Encapsulation* or *information hiding:* Each component of a program should hide a single design decision with each program interface revealing as little as possible about its inner workings.
3. *Inheritance:* Receiving characteristics or properties from an ancestor.
4. *Polymorphism:* Overloading of operators. Polymorphism allows the developer of a system to create a common interface to all of the various objects used within the domain.

Two other advantages also exist for the object-oriented approach:

5. *Reusability of code:* By using demons and inheritance, the developer of a system is able to save development time and effort.

6. *More leverage in working with large programs:* A significant time savings occurs in developing object-oriented systems since the programs are being built out of existing `parts` that communicate with each other rather than starting the development from scratch.

While these characteristics allow objects to model our view of the world more closely than rules or associative networks, they are not without their disadvantages. These disadvantages for objects are similar to those for frames:

1. How do we deal with departures from the norm?
2. How do we deal with new situations that have not been previously encountered?

6.5 CHAPTER REVIEW

An associative network is a labeled, directed graph that symbolizes the associations between various concepts. The nodes in the network represent the concepts while the arcs represent the relationships. They were originally developed to represent the relationships expressed in natural language. Because of this ability to express relationships, associative networks look very much like the inference net architecture that we discussed in Chapters 4 and 5. The main difference between associative and inference nets is that associative nets are generally used to represent static relationships, which are always enforced. The concept of premises that may or may not be satisfied (i.e., match) is somewhat foreign in the associative network context. Unlike inference nets, associative nets typically support inheritance as well as transitivity.

Frames are another, very similar means of representing structured knowledge. They have the ability to cluster knowledge (or data) into associated clusters of significance. Their main features are inheritance and procedural attachments called *demons* that can be automatically called to assist in the derivation of values for slots in the frame. The main differences between the frames and associative nets are that associative nets generally do not permit the clustering of associations and do not support demons.

Objects represent a third similar type of knowledge representation paradigm. There are many similarities between frames and objects. They both serve to cluster associated knowledge, support inheritance and abstraction, and support the concept of procedural attachments. It has been suggested that the only difference between them is their names, but this is not true.

While frames' demons are conceptually similar to objects' methods, they serve only to compute values for the various slots or to maintain the integrity of the knowledge base whenever an action by one frame affects another. Objects' methods are more universal since they provide any type of general computation needed and support encapsulation and polymorphism.

6.6 PROBLEMS

6-1. Develop a set of semantic primitives similar to Reiger's that describe the operation of a(n)

   (a) washing machine

   (b) lawn mower

   (c) bicycle

   (d) stereo system (components only)

   (e) telephone

   (f) automobile (major components only)

   (g) heating system in a house controlled by a thermostat

   (h) cruise control mechanism on an automobile

Given these semantic primitives, develop an associative network describing how this object operates.

6-2. Create a set of frames to represent the following various household pets: gerbils, hamsters, cats, and dogs. Make certain that your set is general enough to describe the following set of pets:

   (a) Max, a tailless gerbil

   (b) Tiny, a very large and overweight hamster

   (c) Butch, a chihuahua

   (d) Precious, a manx (tailless) cat

   (e) Ralph, a Russian wolfhound

6-3. How could the set of frames that you created in Problem 6-2 be used to classify each of specific pets mentioned?

6-4. What would happen if you were asked to classify Fluffy, a chinchilla, or Stretch, a boa constrictor?

6-5. Create a frame to describe a general classroom. Make this frame general enough to describe a classroom at your university and a classroom at the high school that you attended.

6-6. Consider the classroom where your Knowledge-based Systems Class is held. Answer the following questions about this room while not in the room:

   (a) How many door does the room have? Do the doors have windows in them? What color are the doors?

   (b) How many windows?

   (c) How many blackboards?

   (d) What is the color of the walls in the room?

   (e) Are there coat racks on the walls? If so, where?

   (f) Where is the light switch?

   (g) Is there a pencil sharpener mounted on a wall of the room?

The next time you have class, compare your answers to the actual room. Why did you fail to get all of the answers correct?

6-7. Extend the frame implementation of university people to include *Graduate–Student* and *Undergraduate–Student* frames.

6-8. Using the frame representation system described in this chapter, develop a knowledge-based system to assist a new car salesman order cars from the factory. The salesman is faced with the problem that when a new model automobile is introduced, he has to learn all the different possible combinations of optional equipment that can coexist as well as those that can't. This system will help him to ask the customer the right questions when filling out the factory order form. We will define three models of the Dragon, Belchfire Motor Co.'s new model in the mid-size category: the LH (the 4-door basic model), the LX, (the 5-door luxury model), and the GT, (the 2-door sporty coupe version). The following tables represent the standard equipment for each and the options.

Equipment	LH	LX	GT
2.2L/4cyl Engine	std	n/a	n/a
3.3L/6cyl	opt	std	n/a
3.3L/6cyl Turbo	opt	opt	std
Auto transmission	opt[b]	std	opt
Air conditioning	opt[a]	std	std
AM radio	std	std	std
AM/FM radio	opt	std	std
AM/FM w/ cassette	opt	opt	opt

Power steering	opt	std	opt
Performance package	n/a	opt[c]	std
Power brakes	opt	std	opt
Tinted glass	opt	opt	std
Anti-lock brakes	opt[d]	opt	opt[d]

opt: optional; std: standard; n/a: not available

[a]Air conditioning available only with 6 cyl engines and tinted glass.

[b]Auto transmission available only with power steering and power brakes.

[c]Performance package available only with turbo-charged engine.

[d]Only available with power brakes.

Implementation-oriented Problems

6-9. Modify the associative network routines to include a conditional or (COR), exclusive or (EXOR), and conditional and (CAND) logical relation.

6-10. Modify the associative network code to eliminate the **dupl** function.

6-11. (Hard) Modify the associative network code to eliminate the **initialization** function.

6-12. Modify the associative network routines so they are able to bind variables in a pattern and return the matched values.

6-13. Extend the associative network code so that it is capable of dealing with inheritance across an *is–a* arc.

6-14. Extend the frame implementation so it performs type checking on the values specified for the various slots by adding a *:type* facet to all slots. For example, a *salary* slot in the *staff* frame could be restricted to only numeric values or the year slot in *Undergraduate–Student* could be restricted to values of *Fresh–man*, *Sophomore*, *Junior*, and *Senior* while the same slot for *Graduate–Student* could be restricted to *masters* and *phd*.

6-15. The frame system as currently implemented allows a person to have more than one spouse since no check is made on the number of acceptable values for the slot. Add *:max* and *:min* facets that will allow you to specify upper and lower limits on the number of values that a slot can have.

6-16. Examine the implementation of frames. It currently does not support multiple inheritance. Extend the implementation so you could define a *Teaching–Fellow* frame that inherits from both *Instructor* and *Graduate–Student*. What potential problems occur for retrieving values from inherited slots? What schemes could possibly be used to determine a value? What are the advantages and disadvantages of each?

7 ▊ Blackboard Architectures

7.1 INTRODUCTION

In Chapters 4 and 5 we introduced the ideas of forward and backward reasoning, the two most commonly used reasoning methods. Recall that forward reasoning starts from a set of data and attempts to derive plausible conclusions. This method has been found well suited for real-time and/or process monitoring applications where data are changing over time. Backward reasoning, on the other hand, starts with a set of premises and attempts to find data which support these premises. This method is well suited for diagnostic applications where explanations of the system's operation might be requested by the user. While these two methods are commonly preferred, a different method, *opportunistic reasoning*, has increasingly been recognized as an important alternative for certain classes of problems.

In opportunistic problem solving, knowledge is not applied strictly in a forward- or backward-reasoning manner. Instead, knowledge is applied at the most opportune time and in the most auspicious fashion. Rather than trying to satisfy certain subgoals, the system reasons opportunistically—the particular reasoning method used at any instant of time is determined dynamically based upon what was last discovered by the system. This form of reasoning is highly suited for applications where the problem-solving knowledge can be partitioned into independent modules that then cooperate in solving a problem.

In this chapter we examine one implementation of opportunistic problem solving called a *blackboard architecture*. We start by presenting the framework or structure that these systems have.

7.2 THE BLACKBOARD FRAMEWORK

The process of opportunistic problem solving can best be illustrated through an example. Suppose that a faulty communications satellite that has fallen out of its normal orbit has been rescued and repaired by a space shuttle crew. A group of scientists is attempting to decide how to return this satellite to its normal orbit. Each of these individuals is very knowledgeable (i.e., an expert) in some different and very small aspect of the problem, but none is knowledgeable about more than one area. For example, one is an expert in astronomy, another in rocket propulsion, a third in operation of the satellite itself, a fourth in communications, and the fifth is the shuttle astronaut who just repaired the satellite. Each of these experts can help the others in solving the entire problem by opportunistically applying his knowledge during the most appropriate time in the problem-solving process. Complicating their interaction is that they are physically located in different places and are consulting with each other through a computer link. The computer link does not allow the individuals to talk directly to each other; instead they must communicate one at a time through a central "message center" using written messages describing partial solutions, observations, and so forth.

At the start of the problem-solving process, a statement of the existing problem is displayed by the message center. When a participant feels that he can contribute to the solution, he sends his observations and/or conclusions to the message center. Each expert observes the messages written by others and considers those messages that impact his decision making. Some of these experts are able to offer immediate suggestions on what to do since their knowledge applies directly to the information currently in the message center. Others, however, are forced to wait, possibly for an extended time, before their expertise is needed and can be applied.

Initially a question is posed on the message center about what is the optimal new orbit to which the satellite should be deployed. The astronomer, perceiving that the question is in his realm of expertise, quickly responds with "200 miles, but how are we going to get it there?" The astronaut states that is well beyond the range of the shuttle, so shuttle transport to the higher orbit is not a viable alternative. The satellite designer responds that the satellite has three small guidance motors that could be used, but he doesn't know whether they are sufficiently powerful to take the satellite to its determined orbit. The propulsion expert inquires about the type and size of the engine, to which the designer responds with the needed information. Upon review of these data, the propulsion expert decides that it has only sufficient fuel to make it halfway to the correct orbit. The astronaut suggests that if the shuttle could lift the satellite to a high enough orbit, the satellite could then successfully propel itself the rest of the way. The communications expert determines the particular sequence of commands to give from ground control to ignite the engines once the astronauts have launched the satellite from the shuttle. This provides the final key to the problem's solution.

A blackboard system operates in a very similar manner. Instead of using human experts, the contributors are a set of knowledge sources that are each very knowledgeable about solving some aspect of the total problem. Additionally, the message center is replaced with a "blackboard."

This blackboard problem-solving scheme has no predefined priority schedule determining how and when the individual knowledge sources are allowed access to the blackboard. Each source is self-initiating, determining when it has something to contribute to the problem solution. An entire problem is solved by each source merely examining the observations and conclusions offered by the others and providing input when their expertise identifies that it is most appropriate. The solution is therefore built incrementally, based on the cooperative behavior of these knowledgeable sources.

While this example illustrates the basic problem-solving process used within blackboard systems, it fails to address how such systems can be implemented on present day sequential computers. To illuminate how the problem-solving process is controlled we need to modify our view of the above methodology. This modification, in turn, provides sufficient structure to clarify how blackboard systems can possibly be implemented.

Using the analogy of a blackboard, imagine that our experts are together in a classroom but are not allowed to talk directly with each other. They can communicate, however, by writing on the classroom's blackboard. However, since there is only one piece of chalk, only one individual is able to access the blackboard at any instant. To control the experts in their glee of problem solving we introduce a monitor who oversees the solution of the problem. The monitor determines who is given access to the chalk and blackboard at any one time. She polls all experts about what they can contribute to the developing solution. She then evaluates what they propose using some criteria, selects one expert to make some contribution to the developing solution, and provides him with the chalk, allowing his contribution to be added to the blackboard. The problem-solving process of these cooperating experts is now precisely and sequentially controlled with only one expert given access to the blackboard at any instant. The criteria used by the monitor to evaluate the experts' proposed contributions can be predetermined or can be developed while the problem solution evolves. In either case, the monitor is empowered with significant influence over how the solution evolves.

As described through this example and illustrated in Figure 7.1 [Nii, 1986], a blackboard system consists of three major components: the knowledge sources, the blackboard, and the control. Let us now examine each of these in more detail.

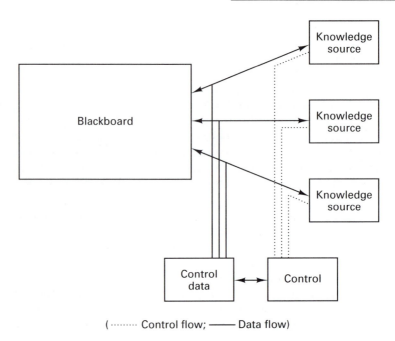

(········ Control flow; ─────── Data flow)

FIGURE 7.1   The Blackboard Model

7.2.1 The Knowledge Sources

The knowledge sources contain the domain knowledge required to solve a problem. This knowledge (typically represented as frames, procedures, or rules) is partitioned into separate and distinct units. Individually these units can solve specific parts of the total problem. Together they are capable of co-operatively solving the entire problem.

Each knowledge source has specific preconditions that must be satisfied for that knowledge source to be applicable. For example, in a software development blackboard system, a software testing knowledge source can be applied only after code is written and a design knowledge source can be applied only after the requirements are specified. Each knowledge source is responsible for determining if and when its own individual conditions are satisfied. When they are and the source is authorized by the control to execute, the knowledge source takes information from the blackboard, interprets these data, arrives at a conclusion, and updates the problem representation by modifying the blackboard. The knowledge sources are able to make only explicit modifications to this representation of the problem or information used by the control (that is sometimes located on the blackboard). They are also the only elements of the system that can modify the blackboard.

7.2.2 The Blackboard

The blackboard provides a location for the various knowledge sources to communicate, indirectly, with each other. It holds the various pieces of data describing the problem that have been collected from the domain and the problem's solution state that has been produced by the knowledge sources.

These data (consisting of input data, partial and/or alternative solutions, final solutions, and, possibly, control data) can be hierarchically organized. This organization aids the analysis process since data on one level of the hierarchy typically serve as input to some knowledge source that derives output for another level. Each level of the hierarchy might use a different representation of the problem and, therefore, might require a completely different vocabulary of terminology to describe its representation of the problem and its solution state.

For example, if a blackboard system is developing a program from a set of specifications and requirements, it might represent the program on the different levels of the hierarchy as a set of pseudo-English statements about the problem's requirements, a set of module headers with pre- and postconditions, a flow chart, and coded modules. Each level utilizes different representations since each is communicating different details about the problem and its solution, yet all are useful in the development of a solution because the details that they introduce are needed to solve the problem.

Not only can the blackboard be organized into a hierarchy, but the blackboard can also consist of different blackboard panels. These panels might contain hierarchically organized, parallel descriptions of the problem and its solution using different but analogous representations. Such a scheme was used within the CRYSALIS system [Terry, 1983].

7.2.3 The Control

The control coordinates the knowledge sources as they proceed to examine the current state of the blackboard, recommends actions that they can take, and performs these actions to make various changes to the description of the problem and its solution. The control decides which actions will occur at the various points of the problem-solving process by monitoring the changes that appear on the blackboard. The control utilizes various kinds of information in making its decision on what is the current *focus of attention*. This information can be represented along with the other data on the blackboard or it can be maintained in a separate control data area as illustrated in Figure 7.1.

The current focus of attention determines what actions take place within the blackboard system. The focus of attention candidates are (1) a particular knowledge source to be activated next, (2) a particular blackboard object that should be examined next, or (3) a combination of a knowledge source and a blackboard object. Since the control selects the focus of attention independent of what this focus does, any type of reasoning (e.g., data driven, control driven) can be performed. This is why the reasoning process is opportunistic.

Hayes-Roth and Hewett [Hayes-Roth, 1988a] define the behavioral goals for intelligent control in a blackboard system to be those that solve the control problem; that is, determining which action to implement at a certain point in the problem-solving process from a set of possible actions that attempt to solve the total problem. These goals are defined as follows:

1. The control must decide which of the possible actions to implement, when these actions should be performed, and must carry out these actions as specified.

2. Not all desirable actions are feasible and not all feasible actions are desirable. The control must examine the set of actions it should perform and the set of actions it can perform to decide what actions it will perform.

3. When attacking a problem, sometimes specific actions are warranted while at other times more general actions apply. A system must be aware of the granularity of its control heuristics and decide which are most appropriate for the subproblem at hand.

4. Problem-solving actions have attributes that seriously affect their usefulness under specific circumstances. For example, the building contractor discussed in Chapter 1 had two possible problem-solving actions that he could use in estimating a house's cost: in one (the methodical approach), accuracy was the main attribute, while in the other (the heuristic approach), timeliness was the main attribute. The method that he used depended upon which characteristic was more significant. A good control system is knowledgeable about the attributes as they affect the solution to the problem and varies its solution approach appropriately.

5. The characteristics of a problem change as it is being solved. Control heuristics are designed to assist in solving particular subproblems, not all subproblems. Therefore, a system must be able to evaluate its control heuristics to determine which still apply, which should be added, and which should be discarded in attacking the current subproblem.

6. Many different control heuristics may be applicable at any one time during problem solving, some complementary and others contradictory in their priorities. A system must decide how to integrate these heuristics into a single action.

7. There is often a significant advantage to understanding the global issues involved in a problem rather than concentrating on the solution of local subproblems. A system should look strategically rather than tactically when planning actions.

8. At every step, the control must decide whether to perform actions that produce part of the solution to the domain problem or part of the solution to the control of solving this domain problem. The priorities of both must be examined to determine the most appropriate action.

When the generic blackboard architecture called BB1 (discussed later in this chapter) was developed, the developer addressed each of these goals.

7.2.4 Execution of Blackboard System

The execution of a blackboard system consists of the following steps [Nii, 1986]:

1. A knowledge source makes some change to the blackboard and a record of these changes is made in the control data area.
2. Each knowledge source examines the relevant information on the blackboard, determines what actions it can take, and indicates these actions to the control.
3. The control examines the information provided by the first two steps and, as a result, selects a focus of attention.
4. The control prepares the particular focus of attention for execution:
   a. If the focus of attention is a knowledge source, then some item on the blackboard is identified for it to examine.
   b. If the focus of attention is a blackboard object, then some knowledge source must be selected to process the object.
   c. If the focus of attention is a knowledge source and an object then the system is ready for execution.
5. At this point, both a knowledge source and blackboard object have been examined so the system returns to step 1 to execute and make appropriate changes on the blackboard.

The only item not specified in the above sequence is how the system stops execution. Some criteria are provided at the creation of the system by which it is able to judge that a solution to the problem has been found. These criteria are usually embedded within one of the knowledge sources.

Now that we have a basic understanding of the structure of a blackboard system, let us examine their development and applications from a historical standpoint.

7.3 HISTORICAL PERSPECTIVE

The first reference to the term "blackboard" occurred during 1962 in a paper by Allen Newell:

Metaphorically we can think of a set of workers, all looking at the same black-board: each is able to read everything that is on it, and to judge when he has some-thing worthwhile to add to it. [Newell, 1962]

Newell, at this time in AI history, was very concerned about the organi-zation of the existing artificial intelligence systems. These systems tended to be highly structured and, as a result, very rigid in their operation. The pro-gramming structures used to build these systems stimulated their developers to view problem solving as a methodology where only one event is processed at any instant of time, when in actuality, problem solving typically involves many different operations occurring at any instant in time, with a multitude of di-verse types of information being used to guide this process. What was needed was a structure similar to:

... that of Selfridge's Pandemonium (Selfridge, 1959): a set of demons, each in-dependently looking at the total situation and shrieking in proportion to what they see that fits their nature. . . . [Newell, 1962]

This structure involved a collection of independent and isolated routines with a common data structure that all the routines could access. A blackboard proved to be a perfect analogy for this organization.

Herb Simon, a colleague of Newell's, arrived at the idea of a black-board from a different point of view. Simon was interested in how discov-eries are made—how ideas evolve from a simple germ into a complete theory. He discussed in a paper originally written in 1966 [Simon, 1977] the idea of a hierarchy or tree of goals and subgoals that grows and develops during the process of solving some problem. As the solution unfolds the prob-lem solver examines various features of the problem environment and remem-bers some of these by storing them in memory. "I will call the informa-tion about the task environment which is noticed in the course of problem solution and fixated in permanent (or relatively long-term) memory the 'black-board.' . . ."

These concepts evolved into the idea of rule-based production systems and eventually led to the development of OPS-5. The concept was also com-municated to D. R. Reddy and D. L. Erman who had just started the Hearsay project and were in need of a system design that would provide flexible control in the domain of natural language speech understanding. Many concepts that are considered integral parts of a blackboard architecture evolved during the development of this project. Its development and structure spawned numerous other systems and architectures as detailed in Figure 7.2 [Nii, 1986]. Let us, therefore, start our examination of various blackboard systems with the Hear-say project. This discussion is followed by an examination of CRYSALIS, AGE, and blackboard development architectures.

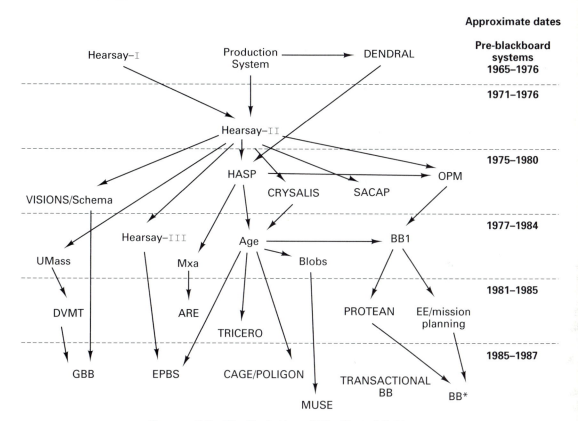

FIGURE 7.2 The Evolution of Blackboard Systems

7.4 HEARSAY

The Hearsay project was a five-year, DARPA-sponsored speech-understanding research program at Carnegie-Mellon University (CMU) which started in 1971 [Erman, 1980]. The goal of the project was to develop a system that could recognize spoken utterances from a limited vocabulary in near real time.

CMU developed a total of three systems during this period. The first, which became known as Hearsay-I, was a very limited system that demonstrated the viability of the proposed architecture more than it solved the speech recognition problem. Several weaknesses existed within this system including limited parallelism, an inability to express relationships among the alternative sentence hypotheses, and problems with the use of a built-in problem-solving strategy that limited their ability to easily make modifications and to make comparisons with other strategies. These weaknesses were addressed in the development of Hearsay-II, which also expanded the task domain.

The second and most successful of the three systems was HARPY. It had a very high performance in recognizing the utterances. This was attributed to its "hard-wired" knowledge base. While it made some interesting contributions to speech recognition, its requirement of considerable predefined task-specific knowledge limited its applicability to other task domains.

The final system of the three, developed as the Hearsay-II project, had the goal to develop a system that would [Erman, 1980]:

- accept connected speech
- from many
- cooperative speakers of the General American Dialect
- in a quiet room
- using a good-quality microphone
- with slight tuning per speaker
- requiring only natural adaptation by the user
- permitting a slightly selected vocabulary of 1000 words
- with a highly artificial syntax and highly constrained task
- providing graceful interaction
- tolerating less than 10 percent semantic error
- in a few times real time on a 100-million-instructions-per-second machine
- and be demonstrable in 1976 with a moderate chance of success.

The specific task domain that they used as an application area was answering queries about, and retrieving documents from, a collection of computer science abstracts in artificial intelligence. The typical types of commands given to this system included:

Which abstracts refer to hill climbing?
Are any by Newell and Simon?
List those articles.

The system was designed to be independent of this or any other application domain. By specifying a different sentence syntactic structure, vocabulary, and underlying semantics, the system could be transported to this new domain.

If we examine the process of speech understanding, we discover that it is very complex because of two sources of uncertainty or error. Errors are first introduced through the speaking process. These errors occur in the translation of an idea that the speaker intends to say to the actual uttered sound wave. In the ideal case a spoken sentence will be produced exactly as it would be written on the printed page. Speakers, however, rarely produce such perfect sentences. Instead they introduce several problems for the listener. Typical problems include pauses during the production of the sentence, extraneous sounds from the environment, inappropriate word choices or grammar, and unnecessary repetition of phrases within the sentence. These problems make it impossible to map directly from the sound waves into a sequence of words.

The second source of errors occurs on the listener's part. The listener must perform roughly the inverse of what the speaker did in uttering the sentence. The sound waves must be interpreted to determine what phonemes were uttered. These phonemes must be connected to form syllables, then transformed into words, phrases, a sentence, and finally the conceptual structures (e.g., meaning) representing the speaker's intentions.

Each of these transformations provides opportunities for the introduction of errors. Because of the large number of errors that can be introduced during the understanding process, a speech understanding system must consider a potentially large number of alternative interpretations, evaluating each as a possible solution.

At each level (phoneme, syllable, word, phrase, sentence, and conceptual structure) the system has potential interpretations of what was said. What might appear highly probable at a particular level, may prove to be highly improbable at the next level. For example, the speaker might have uttered "Find papers on how to recognize speech," shown phonetically in Figure 7.3a. Because of errors introduced in all parts of both the production and recognition processes, it is possible that the various phonemes shown in Figure 7.3b, among others, could have been "heard." These could lead to at least the set of words shown in Figure 7.3c. The listener must combine these various interpretations of the fragments of what was heard into, on the highest level, a probable conceptual structure. At each point of the process, the system determines the likelihood or credibility of what it is generating. While it is possible that the system could determine that the most probable sentence uttered was "Find papers on how to wreck a nice beach" on the sentence level (see Figure 7.3d), that sentence would probably fail to be rated higher than the truly uttered sentence on the conceptual level.

A total of 13 different knowledge sources are utilized within the Hearsay-II system as shown in Figure 7.4 [Erman, 1980]. This figure details where these various knowledge sources obtain information (e.g., the location or level within the blackboard identified by the circles) and where they place their results (identified by the arrows). A short description of each of these knowledge sources is provided in Figure 7.5 [Erman, 1980]. Note that several of the knowledge sources work in a bottom-up fashion (e.g., as in the case of SEG which takes acoustical signals and produces sound segments) while others work in a top-down manner (e.g., taking specific words and generating

"Find papers on how to recognize speech"
fīnd pāpərs òn hàu tə rekəgnīz spēch
(a)   Phonetic Level, Intended

$$\text{fīnd}^{p}_{k}\bar{a}^{p}_{h}\text{ərsònhàutərek}^{\dot{a}}_{\bar{a}}\text{gnī}^{zsp}_{sb}\bar{e}\text{ch}$$

(b)   Phonetic Level, Potentially Heard

$$\text{fīnd}^{p}_{k}\bar{a}^{p}_{h}\text{ərsònhàutərek}^{\dot{a}}_{\bar{a}}\text{gnī}^{zsp}_{sb}\bar{e}\text{ch}$$

find	fīnd	
fine	fīn	
paper	pāpər	
papers	pāpərs	
caper	kāpər	
capers	kāpərs	
her	hər	
hers	hərs	
on		òn
how		hàu
out		aùt
to		tə
recognize		rekəgnīz
wreck		rek
a		ā
nice		nīs
speech		spēch
beach		bēch

(c)   Alternative Word Choices

fīnd pāpərs òn hàu tə rek əg nīz spēch
fīnd pāpərs òn hàu tə rek ā nīs bēch

find papers on how to wreck a nice beach
(d)   A Potential Interpretation

FIGURE 7.3   Partial Processing of a Sample Sentence

alternative phonetic sequences). By cooperating with each other, these knowledge sources operate opportunistically.

The Hearsay-II blackboard is divided into seven levels, each corresponding with some intermediate level of the decoding process (see Figure 7.4). The knowledge sources generate new hypotheses to place on the blackboard or modify existing hypotheses that exist on the blackboard by examining information at their specified input level. In this way the blackboard allows

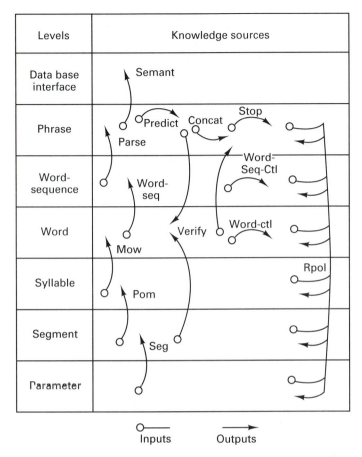

FIGURE 7.4   The Levels and Knowledge Sources of Hearsay-II

communication between the various knowledge sources by serving as the depository of all information about the current problem and all of its potential solutions (both intermediate and final). For a discussion of a specific example of the operation of Hearsay-II you should consult [Erman, 1980, 1988].

Table 7.1 [Erman, 1980] summarizes the performance of Hearsay-II. The use of opportunistic problem solving proved to improve significantly both the obtained results and processing speed. Hayes-Roth and Lesser [Hayes-Roth, 1977] compared the Hearsay-II opportunistic approach to a nonopportunistic approach and found that the opportunistic approach had a 29 percent error rate vs. a 48 percent rate for the nonopportunistic while using less than half the processing time.

Signal Acquisition, Parameter Extraction, Segmentation, and Labeling:
  * SEG: Digitizes the signal, measures parameters, and produces a labeled segmentation.

Word Spotting:
  * Pom: Creates syllable-class hypotheses from segments.
  * Mow: Creates word hypotheses from syllable classes.
  * Word-Ctl: Controls the number of word hypotheses that Mow creates.

Phrase-Island Generation:
  * Word-Seq: Creates word-sequence hypotheses that represent potential phrases from word hypotheses and weak grammatical knowledge.
  * Word-Seq-Ctl: Controls the number of hypotheses that Word-Seq creates
  * Parse: Attempts to parse a word sequence and, if successful, creates a phrase hypothesis from it.

Phrase Extending:
  * Predict: Predicts all possible words that might syntactically precede or follow a given phrase.
  * Verify: Rates the consistency between segment hypotheses and a contiguous word-phrase pair.
  * Concat: Creates a phrase hypothesis from a verified contiguous word-phrase pair.

Rating, Halting, and Interpretation:
  * Rpol: Rates the credibility of each new or modified hypothesis, using information placed on the hypothesis by other knowledge sources.
  * Stop: Decides to halt processing (detects a complete sentence with a sufficiently high rating, or notes the system has exhausted its available resources) and selects the best phrase hypothesis or set of complementary phrase hypotheses as the output.
  * Segmant: Generates an unambiguous interpretation for the information-retrieval system which the user has queried.

FIGURE 7.5 Functional Description of the Speech-Understanding Knowledge Sources

7.5 CRYSALIS

The Crysalis system [Terry, 1983] was developed through a cooperative effort between protein crystallographers at the University of San Diego and computer scientists in the Heuristic Programming Project at Stanford University during the late 1970s and early 1980s. Their objective was to build a system capable of determining the three-dimensional structure of protein molecules by examining X-ray diffraction data from crystals of the protein and the protein's amino acid sequence (which was possibly incomplete or out of order).

TABLE 7.1   HEARSAY-II PERFORMANCE

Number of speakers	One
Environment	Computer terminal room (>65 dB)
Microphone	Medium-quality, close-talking
System speaker-tuning	20–30 training utterances
Speaker adaptation	None required
Task	Document retrieval
Vocabulary	1011 words, with no selection for phonetic discriminability
Language constraints	Context-free semantic grammar based on protocol analysis, with static branching factor of 10
Test data	23 utterances, brand-new to the system and run "blind." 7 words/utterance average, 2.6 seconds/utterance average, average fanout[1] of 40 (maximum 292)
Accuracy	9 percent sentence semantic errors[2], 19 percent sentence error (i.e., not word-for-word correct)
Computing resources	60 MIPSS (million instructions per second of speech) on a 36-bit PDP-10

[1]The static branching factor is the average number of words that can follow any initial sequence as defined by the grammar. The fanout is the number of words that can follow any initial sequence in the test sentences.

[2]An interpretation is semantically correct if the query generated for it by the SEMANT KS is identical to that generated for a sentence which is word for word correct.

While the researchers were unable to solve the complete problem as originally proposed, they did solve a significant part of it. In doing so, they made two important contributions: (1) They were the first to use multiple hierarchies (blackboard panels) on a blackboard and (2) they addressed the difficult control problem within blackboard systems from the perspective of rule-based systems.

The task of protein crystallography involves many steps as detailed in Figure 7.6 [Terry, 1988]. First, the protein to be analyzed must be chemically isolated from other proteins. A crystal must be grown from this protein. This crystal is bombarded with X-rays and the position and intensity of the defracted waves are studied. Each atom within the crystal contributes to the produced waves, thereby providing a unique pattern for each protein. The problem with examining these data is that the defraction pattern is too imprecise (intensities cannot be determined with complete accuracy and the resolution of this defraction data is too low) to be used to derive directly the protein's structure. Therefore, mathematical and chemical methods must be employed to estimate some of the data and these are then used to calculate an electron density map (EDM). This EDM is used to derive a model of the

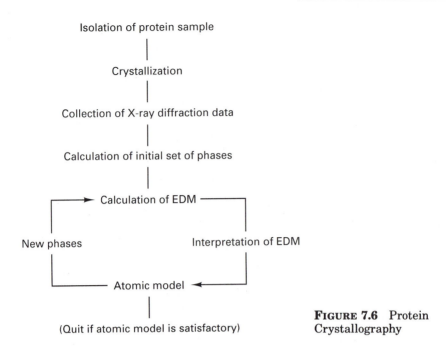

FIGURE 7.6 Protein Crystallography

protein's structure. Feedback is then employed to calculate, from the derived model, a more accurate set of data that are used to calculate a new EDM.

The process can be equated to having a poor (e.g., out of focus) picture of the shadows of a set of objects and a description of the set of objects that might be casting the shadows. You observe these shadows, attempting to determine where objects are likely to be. A model of the locations of the objects is built (the EDM). This model is used to calculate which specific objects might be at each point (the protein's structure). This is turn is used to build a new EDM. This process continues until the developed atomic model satisfactorily accounts for the original collected data.

The system utilized two abstract hierarchies (e.g., blackboard panels) to organize logically the different types of data needed in solving a particular problem. See Figure 7.7 [Terry, 1988]. The first, the *density panel*, contained all of the data produced by the signal processing algorithms initially used to process the X-ray defraction data. This set of data corresponds to the output from the low-level signal processing algorithms used in image understanding. The second, the *hypothesis panel*, contained information developed during the interpretation process. The system built partial solutions on the hypothesis panel using information present at any level of the density panel.

The knowledge used by the system was organized into a series of knowledge sources, each containing a set of rules. Unlike Hearsay, these knowledge sources were not self-selecting—they did not have preconditions to satisfy

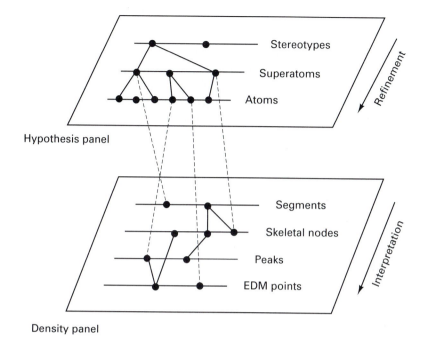

Hypothesis panel

Density panel

FIGURE 7.7 The Crysalis Blackboard Panels with Their Primary
Directions of Inference

that could identify to the control when they had something to contribute to
the problem solution. Instead, the system utilized a three-tiered control structure consisting of strategy, task, and object knowledge sources. The highest
level knowledge source was the strategy knowledge source consisting of
29 rules. Task level knowledge consisted of 112 rules divided among 9 knowledge sources, while object level knowledge consisted of 461 rules in 56 knowledge sources.

Execution of these knowledge sources progressed top-down from the
strategy knowledge source to the objects. The strategy-level knowledge source
examined the entire problem space trying to focus on a particular region. Once
a region was selected, the strategy-level knowledge source selected a particular task-knowledge source for execution. This task-knowledge source then
executed a sequence of object-knowledge sources. When operations at any level
were completed, control was returned to the next higher level to continue
its operations.

Each of these knowledge sources narrowed the focus of the problem using
a divide-and-conquer strategy starting with the original overall problem to a
region (through a strategy knowledge source) to specific nodes within the region (through a task knowledge source) then, finally, to the individual nodes
(through an object knowledge source). Because of the clearly defined top-down

approach used within Crysalis, its opportunistic application of knowledge is not obvious or apparent. In actuality, opportunistic problem solving is utilized only in the selection of which node to process next.

Crysalis's problem domain violated numerous criteria used to select an appropriate application domain for a knowledge-based system. These included a significant lack of (1) experts who could provide knowledge and test the system's solutions and approach, (2) theoretical knowledge about the relationship between the structures and functions of proteins, and (3) knowledge about reasoning in 3-D space. As a result, the system did not reach its goal of building complete stereo models of proteins. It was, however, in a few cases able to build models that mapped more than 75 percent of the amino acid residues in the data. This is equivalent to finding partial solutions on the middle level of the blackboard hierarchy. While only able to progress this far in a solution, it did solve a significant portion of the problem—one that took experts months to solve.

7.6 AGE

AGE (Attempt to GEneralize) was developed at Stanford University's Heuristic Programming Project in the late 1970s and early 1980s. Its objective was "to demystify and make explicit the art of knowledge engineering. . . ." [Nii, 1988] by attempting to describe the knowledge used by knowledge engineers when building a knowledge base, thereby making this knowledge explicit so others could use it to solve problems. Its developers were attempting to gather the knowledge utilized in the construction of the numerous systems developed in the Heuristic Programming Project (and knowledge generated at other laboratories) with the hope of developing "a *collection of building-block programs* combined with an *intelligent front-end* that will assist the user in constructing knowledge-based programs" [Nii, 1988]. By packaging these commonly used AI programs together, they hoped to decrease the development time of knowledge-based systems and improve the dispersion of AI techniques by helping non-AI trained individuals develop knowledge-based programs.

In attempting to build a knowledge-based software development laboratory, they tackled two problems: (1) determining which problem-solving techniques were knowledge-based, rather than domain-specific techniques and (2) developing an intelligent agent to guide the user in applying these techniques in problem solving. To solve these problems effectively the resulting system must itself be a knowledge-based system consisting of expertise about building knowledge-based systems plus an environment that enables users to play with different approaches.

AGE was intended to assist individuals who had little knowledge of AI in the construction of knowledge-based systems, but was initially developed for AI researchers who were capable of developing their own systems. While it can be argued that these individuals did not need such a system, AGE did provide them with two distinct advantages: (1) preprogrammed basic system components and (2) an opportunity to experiment with different techniques without extensive reprogramming. The intent of the developers was to expand the system at a later time to help less knowledgeable users.

Development of AGE followed two paths. First was the development of tools to assist a user develop different knowledge-based programs. This required preprogrammed modules that could be easily combined to form the underlying structure of a knowledge-based system. Second, they needed to develop a structure for intelligent interactions with the user about how these tools are used and what ones to use in particular applications.

AGE initially provided a basic blackboard model as detailed in Figure 7.8 [Nii, 1988]. This structure consisted of the blackboard, various knowledge sources, and a control mechanism as detailed below.

The blackboard.   The blackboard was designed to provide a means of communication between the various knowledge sources in the form of a hierarchical data structure. Its structure was developed to support both inductive and deductive reasoning for hypotheses using a flexible knowledge hierarchy that could range from being very flat (e.g., only two or three levels deep) to very complex (e.g., consisting of several blackboard planes). The hypotheses for some problem could be known *a priori*, not known until a specific problem was being solved, or some combination of the two.

The knowledge sources.   The knowledge sources were designed to be separate and distinct, containing task domain knowledge and responding to changes on the blackboard. The knowledge in the knowledge sources was represented in a rule format consisting primarily of *"knowledge of specifics* and the *knowledge of ways and means of dealing with the specifics"* [Nii, 1988].

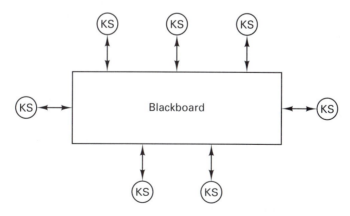

FIGURE 7.8   AGE's Blackboard Model

Each knowledge source had several properties including, among others, a set of preconditions required for invoking the knowledge source, the specific region within the problem domain where the rules of this knowledge source apply, and a strategy for using these rules. Facilities were provided to allow the user to divide the problem-specific knowledge into as many distinct knowledge sources as desired. The knowledge sources could also be organized hierarchically, as the knowledge sources of Crysalis were, if needed.

The control mechanism.   The control mechanism was structured to allow the user to specify how knowledge sources were invoked and how items on the blackboard were selected as the focus of attention. In designing this component of the system they tried to provide the users with the ability to express many different types of control knowledge even though the explicit specification of control knowledge had been attempted only within a few systems up until this time. The control components that needed to be specified included the input of data, the selection of a focus of attention, the selection of an appropriate knowledge source, the application of that knowledge source, and conditions for terminating the system. Preprogrammed control mechanisms for both expectation- and event-driven reasoning were provided.

Note that the structure of AGE did not prescribe the specific structure of the blackboard, how knowledge was to be represented within the knowledge sources (other than in a rule format), or how the system actually operates (e.g., its low level operation). These details were developed by the system designers as they interacted with AGE through its intelligent front-end. This front-end provided both tutorial (e.g., the structure and use of the current system components, the system's organization, and how new components can be constructed) and development knowledge (e.g., a guide through the various decision points of a system's development).

AGE was applied to a number of different problems including the solution of cryptogram problems, bidding in the game of bridge, and diagnosis of pulmonary function disorder. While showing the viability and applicability of a generalized framework, it raised a number of further research issues including how best to interact with users, the adequacy of rule-based representations, and what is the best structure for explanation facilities.

7.7 BLACKBOARD DEVELOPMENT ENVIRONMENTS

Hearsay, Crysalis and AGE represent classical, early blackboard systems that are significant because of their groundbreaking influences on the concept of blackboards. More recently, however, there have been significant advances in the development of blackboard application environments. These advances represent to blackboard systems what expert system shells mean to knowledge-based systems: the development of environments that provide the tools necessary to build a blackboard system application more easily. Hearsay-III, which we previously introduced, is one of these environments. Two other systems are the Generic Blackboard System (GBB) and the BB1 system.

The GBB system, developed at the University of Massachusetts (Amherst) in the early 1980s, was designed to facilitate the development of blackboard systems. The resulting system was unique in the following ways [Corkill, 1988]:

1. The insertion and retrieval of blackboard objects were made highly efficient. Blackboard objects are elements placed on the blackboard or used to manipulate these elements. For example, goals, hypotheses, and knowledge-source activation records are considered to be blackboard objects. The efficient insertion and retrieval of these objects is a critical issue for applications involving thousands of objects.

2. The specification of the insertion and retrieval structure of the blackboard was isolated from the specification of the blackboard and its objects. By cleanly separating these specifications a new blackboard database structure could be defined without impacting the other components of the blackboard. This provided a level of abstraction above the definition of the insertion/retrieval structure.

3. Objects composed of discrete elements were defined using a generic composite blackboard object.

4. The retrieval of blackboard objects was performed through a special, highly efficient pattern-matching language.

5. The control and database support subsystems were clearly separated, allowing the database subsystem to sustain alternative control schemes.

As can be seen, the major emphasis of the GBB system was on database efficiency.

On the other hand, the BB1 system's main focus was the generalization of the control capabilities of the blackboard system. It implements all the goals for intelligent control defined in Section 7.2.3.

The BB1 system organizes blackboard objects in two ways:

1. Partitions blackboard objects into levels of abstraction with attributes and links to other objects

2. Links objects to other objects by means of relations

BB1 allows multiple blackboards as well as multiple levels within a blackboard and multiple objects at each level [Hayes-Roth, 1988]. A typical application might have *problem* blackboards, *solution* blackboards, *knowledge* blackboards, and/or *control* blackboards. Each of these holds different facets of the problem, such as the problem's definition, potential actions that could solve the problem, and control actions as well as other elements that lead to the ultimate solution of the problem.

Knowledge sources in BB1 represent potential actions that could be taken to solve the problem as well as how to implement those actions. BB1 defines three types of knowledge sources: (1) Task KSs, which describe actions that solve a subproblem, (2) control KSs, which describe actions that solve the control problem, and (3) learning KSs, which define actions that affect the system's knowledge.

The execution cycle of the BB1 architecture is [Hayes-Roth, 1988a]:

1. Execute the appropriate KS action, which produces changes to blackboard objects.
2. Modify the agenda to account for the actions caused by the action that was just performed.
3. Determine which new action is the most appropriate to execute under the present circumstances.

BB1 puts everything in the blackboard, thus requiring no internal data structures. Even those blackboard objects that deal with the control problem are placed on the blackboard. This generality allows it to be used for many different applications, yet it leaves many issues to the developer, so that application development becomes a burdensome task for the developer.

Other blackboard development environments exist besides the three discussed above, such as MXA [Tailor, 1988], BLOBS [Zanconato, 1988], MUSE [Reynolds, 1988], and BB* [Hayes-Roth, 1988b] among others. Examine the literature for further information about these and other systems.

7.8 ADVANTAGES AND DISADVANTAGES

The most significant advantage of blackboard systems is that they fill a void in our problem-solving techniques:

1. *Suitable for a diversity of problems:* Blackboard architecture has proven to be ideally suited for a diversity of problems that have several underlying common characteristics:
   a. These problems typically have many diverse forms of input data, some of which might be noisy, which must be integrated to form a problem solution. This causes these problems to have large solution spaces and require many diverse and independent (or semi-independent) pieces of knowledge to cooperate in forming a solution. As a result, this usually prohibits the use of more standard solution techniques.
   b. Unlike other problem domains that we have examined, these problems do not have clearly defined goals around which to structure the solu-

tion and determine a reasoning path. This, in part, ensues from the many different forms of data required to describe the problem and knowledge that must cooperate to form a solution. Consequently, these problems require the use of multiple lines of reasoning that are pursued opportunistically.

  c. Blackboards are ideally suited for distributed environments. Each knowledge source could, potentially, be located on a different processor with a controller (also located on a separate processor) coordinating their activities.

Other less significant advantages are:

  2. *Hierarchical organization:*   The blackboard architecture is ideally suited for representing knowledge hierarchically. While not always used in this manner, this organization allows a diversity of ideas to be integrated together into a solution environment.

  3. *Data abstraction:*   Abstracted data can be used to represent portions of the problem, thereby reducing the computational needs of the system and simplifying the reasoning process since all of the details are not needed at all points of the reasoning process.

  4. *Postponement of decisions:*   The blackboard allows the developer of a system to postpone decisions. Data can collect on the blackboard until an appropriate combination occurs rather than partial data being gathered and the system being forced to categorize them when a high degree of uncertainty still exists about their classification.

  5. *Loose coupling of knowledge and its use:*   When developing a knowledge source, the system developer need not worry about where (e.g., which knowledge source) to send the processed information. All information is merely written to the blackboard where any knowledge source has an equal chance to process it further.

While blackboard systems do provide a number of distinct advantages and several useful characteristics that are extremely helpful in solving particular classes of problems, they are not without disadvantages:

  1. *Expensive:*   Blackboard systems are typically expensive to build and run. Few commercial blackboard systems (e.g., GBB) are available. While they provide a structure to attack very difficult and complex problems, blackboard systems are almost always "hand tailored" for particular applications, making their development and operation complex. As a result, they should not be used to solve problems when simpler models will suffice.

  2. *Difficult to determine partitioning of knowledge:*   It can be extremely difficult to determine an appropriate partitioning of a problem to cast it into the blackboard framework. This can result in a much more involved and costly development cycle, since problems in the underlying structure of the knowledge base might not become apparent until late in the development resulting in a major overhaul of the system.

7.9 CHAPTER REVIEW

The blackboard architecture provides a vehicle for implementing *opportunistic reasoning*. Opportunistic reasoning is a useful problem-solving paradigm to employ when the combination of various sources of knowledge is necessary to solve a highly complex problem. In such instances, no single person (or source of knowledge) has sufficient expertise to solve the problem completely, but instead, can solve only part of it.

The framework of a blackboard system includes: (1) the *blackboard*, (2) the *knowledge sources*, and (3) the *control*.

The blackboard represents the common database through which all knowledge sources communicate. All partial solutions by any of the knowledge sources are posted onto the blackboard for other knowledge sources to see. The knowledge sources contain the partial knowledge required to solve the pieces of the problem. They respond opportunistically to the data posted on the blackboard. Knowledge sources can be thought of as individual knowledge-based systems, each containing an inference mechanism and knowledge base. There is no requirement that these knowledge sources be homogeneous, however. For example, some knowledge sources could be rule-based systems, while others could be logic-based or frame-based. Likewise, the inference process of the various knowledge sources could differ significantly. Some employ the traditional modus ponens, while others use model-based reasoning, case-based reasoning, and so forth (techniques described in Chapter 9). The control is charged with determining which of the knowledge sources is best suited to contribute next to the emerging solution of the problem at hand.

Blackboard systems are complex in nature and should be used only when the more traditional knowledge-based systems are insufficient. They generally excel at solving problems with weak constraints.

7.10 PROBLEMS

7-1. Determine an application in diagnosis that could benefit from use of a blackboard system. Design the system on paper by:

(a) Determining the various knowledge sources.

(b) Determining the criteria used by the control to decide which knowledge source has priority.

(c) Deciding what information the control needs to make the above decision.

(d) Specifying a termination criterion.

(e) Describing why a blackboard architecture serves this problem better than a conventional knowledge-based system.

7-2. Consider the problem of planning and scheduling college courses. Assume that not all courses are taught every semester, prerequisites prohibit students from taking some courses before others, classes must be scheduled in rooms of an appropriate size, and, because certain classes are traditionally taken during the same semester, certain classes cannot be scheduled during the same hour. Is this problem suited for a blackboard architecture? If so, perform the same actions as prescribed in Problem 7-1.

7-3. Consider the problem of natural language understanding. English has certain rules defining how words can be combined to form legal sentences (the syntax of English), sentences have particular meanings based on the words they contain (the semantics of the sentence), and the sentences fit in an overall conversation (the pragmatics of the sentence). The meaning that we associate with a sentence is influenced by an appropriate combination of all of these elements. Detail the various components prescribed in Problem 7-1 that would be required to solve this problem using a blackboard architecture.

7-4. Why is it important that the knowledge sources remain separate? Why should they not be combined into one large knowledge base?

7-5. Why is a control component important within a blackboard system? Could the control be viewed as just another knowledge source within the system? How is it different?

7-6. Why was a blackboard architecture required in the HEARSAY project to solve the problem of spoken natural language understanding? Why was the knowledge partitioning approach used within the EMycin shell or the T.I. PC Plus system not sufficient?

8 ■ Uncertainty Management

8.1 INTRODUCTION

Most tasks requiring intelligent behavior have some degree of uncertainty associated with them. Knowledge-based systems exhibit intelligent behavior by modeling the empirical associations and heuristic relationships that experts have built over time rather than precise algorithms having clear-cut solutions. This results in the natural expectation that they exhibit the ability to reason with uncertainty as well. In fact, these systems need to be able to deal with uncertainty about the results that are being derived and, possibly, the data that have been collected to use in deriving these results.

The types of uncertainty that can occur in knowledge-based systems may be caused by problems with the data. For example,

1. Data might be missing or unavailable.
2. Data might be present but unreliable or ambiguous due to measurement errors, multiple conflicting measurements, and so forth.
3. The representation of the data may be imprecise or inconsistent.
4. Data may just be user's best guess.
5. Data may be based on defaults and the defaults may have exceptions.

Alternatively, the uncertainty may be caused by the represented knowledge since it might

1. Represent best guesses of the experts that are based on plausible or statistical associations they have observed.

2. Not be appropriate in all situations (e.g., may have indeterminate applicability).

Given these numerous sources of errors, most knowledge-based systems require the incorporation of some form of uncertainty management. When implementing some uncertainty scheme you must be concerned with three issues:

1. How to represent uncertain data.
2. How to combine two or more pieces of uncertain data.
3. How to draw inference using uncertain data.

The issues involved are often very subtle, yet they can have significant impact on the operation of and conclusions drawn by a system. Some individuals have even argued that the limited abilities of knowledge-based systems to deal with uncertainty are restricting their performance [Mamdani, 1985]. As a result of these concerns, many researchers have and are examining reasoning with uncertainty, attempting to develop the ultimate method that can deal with all of its nuances.

This chapter presents a summary of four different numerically oriented methods which have been developed to deal with uncertainty, identifying some of the particular advantages and disadvantages associated with each method. It should be noted that several symbolic approaches (including Cohen's Theory of Endorsements [Cohen, 1985] and Fox's semantic system [Fox 1986a; 1986b]) have also been developed that are not discussed here. To present an unbiased view of these methods, we present them in alphabetical order starting with the Bayesian approach.

8.2 BAYESIAN APPROACHES

The oldest and best defined technique for managing uncertainty, Bayes' Rule, is based on classical probability theory. This technique has been widely used both in computer science for computer-based decision aids and in other fields that use quantitative analysis.

8.2.1 Background

To understand the Bayesian approaches to uncertainty we need to review some fundamental probability theory. Suppose that x_i is some event. The collection of all events, called the sample space, is defined as the set X, where

$$X = \{x_1, x_2, \ldots, x_n\}$$

The probability that event x_i occurs is denoted $p(x_i)$. Every probability function, p, must satisfy the following three conditions:

1. The probability of any event x_i is nonnegative. The probability of an event could be 0 (the event will not occur), 1 (the event must occur), or any value in between.
2. The total probability of the entire sample space is 1 (e.g., some event in the collection of all of the events will occur—we just do not know which one).
3. If some set of events $x_1, x_2, \ldots, x_k$ are mutually exclusive, then the probability that at least one of these events will occur is the sum of all of their individual probabilities.

The complement of some event, denoted $\sim x_i$, represents event x_i not occurring. It should be obvious that:

$$p(x_i) + p(\sim x_i) = 1 \tag{1}$$

since the complement of an event represents all events excluding x_i.

Suppose that we have two events, x and y, from some sample space. We are often interested in the relationship that exists between x and y, that is, what is the likelihood that event y will occur if x occurs. This is called the conditional probability and is written $p(y \mid x)$. The probability that both events will occur, the joint probability, is denoted $p(x \wedge y)$ where $\wedge$ is the logical and operator. By definition,

$$p(y \mid x) = \frac{p(x \wedge y)}{p(x)} \tag{2}$$

provided that $p(x)$ is nonzero. Similarly,

$$p(x \mid y) = \frac{p(y \wedge x)}{p(y)} \tag{3}$$

and since, by definition,

$$p(y \wedge x) = p(x \wedge y) \tag{4}$$

we can derive from Equation (3) that

$$p(x \wedge y) = p(x \mid y)*p(y) \tag{5}$$

Substituting this result into Equation (2) yields

$$p(y \mid x) = \frac{p(x \mid y)*p(y)}{p(x)} \tag{6}$$

which is Bayes' Rule.

If we know the conditional probabilities of an event happening given another event, we can intuitively see that the probability of the first event happening independently of the second is

$$p(x) = p(x \wedge y) + p(x \wedge \sim y)$$

Since we know

$$p(x \wedge y) = p(x \mid y)*p(y) \tag{5a}$$

and we can derive

$$p(x \wedge \sim y) = p(x \mid \sim y)*p(\sim y) \tag{5b}$$

it follows that

$$p(x) = p(x \mid y)*p(y) + p(x \mid \sim y)*p(\sim y) \tag{7}$$

Substituting this value into Equation (6) allows us to now define Bayes' Rule
in a somewhat different form:

$$p(y \mid x) = \frac{p(x \mid y)*p(y)}{p(x \mid y)*p(y) + p(x \mid \sim y)*p(\sim y)} \tag{8}$$

8.2.2 Bayes' Rule and Knowledge-based Systems

As we have seen, rule-based systems express knowledge in an IF-THEN
format:

IF X is true
THEN Y can be concluded with probability p

If we observe that X is true, then we can conclude that Y exists with the specified probability. For example,

IF   the patient has a cold
THEN   the patient will sneeze (0.75)

But what if we reason abductively and observe Y (i.e., the patient sneezes)
while knowing nothing about X (i.e., the patient has a cold)? What can we conclude about it? Bayes' Rule describes how we can derive a probability for X.
Within the rule given above [and equation (6)], Y (y in the equation) denotes
some piece of evidence (typically referred to as E) and X (x in the equation)
denotes some hypothesis (H) giving

$$p(H \mid E) = \frac{p(E \mid H)*p(H)}{p(E)} \tag{9}$$

or

$$p(H \mid E) = \frac{p(E \mid H)*p(H)}{p(E \mid H)*p(H) + p(E \mid \sim H)*p(\sim H)} \qquad (10)$$

To make this more concrete, consider whether Rob has a cold (the hypothesis) given that he sneezes (the evidence). Equation (10) states that the probability that Rob has a cold given that he sneezes is the ratio of the probability that he both has a cold and sneezes, to the probability that he sneezes. The probability of his sneezing is the sum of the conditional probability that he sneezes when he has a cold and the conditional probability that he sneezes when he doesn't have a cold—in other words, the probability that he sneezes regardless of whether he has a cold or not. Suppose that we know in general

$p(H)$　　　= p(Rob has a cold)
　　　　　= 0.2

$p(E \mid H)$　= p(Rob was observed sneezing | Rob has a cold)
　　　　　= 0.75

$p(E \mid \sim H)$ = p(Rob was observed sneezing | Rob does not have a cold)
　　　　　= 0.2

then

$$p(E) = p(\text{Rob was observed sneezing})$$
$$= (0.75)(0.2) + (0.2)(0.8)$$
$$= 0.31$$

and

$$p(H \mid E) = p(\text{Rob has a cold} \mid \text{Rob was observed sneezing})$$

$$= \frac{(0.75)*(0.2)}{(0.31)}$$

$$= 0.48387$$

Or Rob's probability of having a cold given that he sneezes is about 0.5. We can also determine what his probability of having a cold would be if he was not sneezing:

$$p(H \mid \sim E) = \frac{p(\sim E \mid H)*p(H)}{p(\sim E)}$$

$$= \frac{(1 - 0.75)*(0.2)}{(1 - 0.31)}$$

$$= 0.07246$$

So knowledge that he sneezes increases his probability of having a cold by approximately 2.5, while knowledge that he does not sneeze decreases his probability by a factor of almost 3.

8.2.3 Propagation of Belief

Note that what we have examined so far is very limited since we have only considered when each piece of evidence affects only one hypothesis. This must be generalized to deal with "m" hypotheses and "n" pieces of evidence, the situation normally encountered in real-world problems. When these factors are included Equation (10) becomes

$$p(H_i \mid E_1 E_2 \ldots E_n) = \frac{p(E_1 E_2 \ldots E_n \mid H_i)*p(H_i)}{p(E_1 E_2 \ldots E_n)}$$

(11)

$$= \frac{p(E_1 \mid H_i)*p(E_2 \mid H_i)* \ldots p(E_n \mid H_i)*p(H_i)}{\sum_{k=1}^{m} p(E_1 \mid H_k)*p(E_2 \mid H_k)* \ldots *p(E_n \mid H_k)*p(H_k)}$$

This probability is called the posterior probability of hypothesis H_i from observing evidence $E_1, \ldots, E_n$. Note that this equation is derived based on the assumption that the pieces of evidence are conditionally independent given some hypothesis. This assumption often causes great difficulties for this and the other methods discussed in this chapter. For example, two symptoms, A and B, might each independently indicate that some disease is 50 percent likely. Together, however, it might be that these symptoms reinforce (or contradict) each other. Care must be taken to ensure that such a situation does not exist before using the Bayesian approach.

To illustrate how belief is propagated through a system using Bayes' rule, consider the values shown in Table 8.1. These values represent (hypothetically) three mutually exclusive and exhaustive hypotheses (H_1, the patient, Rob, has a cold; H_2, Rob has an allergy; and H_3, Rob has a sensitivity to light) with their prior probabilities, $p(H_i)$'s, and two conditionally independent pieces of evidence (E_1, Rob sneezes and E_2, Rob coughs), which support these hypotheses to differing degrees.

TABLE 8.1   PRIOR AND CONDITIONAL VALUES

	$i = 1$ (cold)	$i = 2$ (allergy)	$i = 3$ (light sensitive)
$p(H_i)$	0.6	0.3	0.1
$p(E_1 \mid H_i)$	0.3	0.8	0.3
$p(E_2 \mid H_i)$	0.6	0.9	0.0

If we observe evidence E_1 (e.g., the patient sneezes), we can compute posterior probabilities for the hypotheses using Equation (11) (where $n = 1$) to be:

$$p(H_1 \mid E_1) = \frac{0.3*0.6}{0.3*0.6 + 0.8*0.3 + 0.3*0.1} = 0.4$$

$$p(H_2 \mid E_1) = \frac{0.8*0.3}{0.3*0.6 + 0.8*0.3 + 0.3*0.1} = 0.53$$

$$p(H_3 \mid E_1) = \frac{0.3*0.1}{0.3*0.6 + 0.8*0.3 + 0.3*0.1} = 0.06$$

Note that the belief in hypotheses H_1 and H_3 have both decreased while the belief in hypothesis H_2 has increased after observing E_1. If E_2 (e.g., the patient coughs) is now observed, new posterior probabilities can be computed from Equation (11) (where $n = 2$):

$$p(H_1 \mid E_1 E_2) = \frac{0.3*0.6*0.6}{0.3*0.6*0.6 + 0.8*0.9*0.3 + 0.3*0.0*0.1} = 0.33$$

$$p(H_2 \mid E_1 E_2) = \frac{0.8*0.9*0.3}{0.3*0.6*0.6 + 0.8*0.9*0.3 + 0.3*0.0*0.1} = 0.67$$

$$p(H_3 \mid E_1 E_2) = \frac{0.3*0.0*0.1}{0.3*0.6*0.6 + 0.8*0.9*0.3 + 0.3*0.0*0.1} = 0.0$$

Hypothesis H_3 (e.g., sensitivity to light) has now ceased to be a viable hypothesis and H_2 (e.g., allergy) is considered much more likely than H_1 (e.g., cold) even though H_1 initially ranked higher.

8.2.4 Advantages and Disadvantages of Bayesian Methods

The Bayesian methods have a number of advantages that indicate their suitability in uncertainty management. Most significant is their sound theoretical foundation in probability theory. Thus, they are currently the most mature of all of the uncertainty reasoning methods. They also have well-defined semantics for decision making.

While Bayesian methods are more developed than the other uncertainty methods, they are not without faults.

1. They require a significant amount of probability data to construct a knowledge base. For example, a diagnostic system having 50 detectable conclusions (p) and 300 relevant and observable characteristics (q) requires a minimum of 15,050 ($p*q + p$) probability values assuming that all of the conclusions are mutually exclusive, the characteristics are conditionally independent for each conclusion, and all characteristics are truth values. If the conclusions are not mutually exclusive and/or the characteristics not conditionally independent (traits that are normally

true), a significantly larger number of probability values is required. Additionally, an entire calculation could be brought to a grinding halt if one single probability number is missing. While Bayesian networks reduce the number of required probabilities, the number still increases rapidly as the number of nodes and links increase [Clark, 1990].

2. What are the relevant prior and conditional probabilities based on? If they are statistically based, the sample sizes must be sufficient so the probabilities obtained are accurate. If human experts have provided the values, are the values consistent and comprehensive?

3. Often the type of relationship between the hypothesis and evidence is important in determining how the uncertainty will be managed. Reducing these associations to simple numbers removes relevant information that might be needed for successful reasoning about the uncertainties. For example, Bayesian-based medical diagnostic systems have failed to gain acceptance because physicians distrust systems that cannot provide explanations describing how a conclusion was reached (a feature difficult to provide in a Bayesian-based system).

4. The reduction of the associations to numbers also eliminates using this knowledge within other tasks. For example, the associations that would enable the system to explain its reasoning to a user are lost, as is the ability to browse through the hierarchy of evidences to hypotheses.

8.3 CERTAINTY FACTORS

During the development of Mycin, researchers found the Bayes' model of uncertainty inadequate for a number of reasons [Shortliffe, 1979]:

1. The medical area often lacks the large quantities of data and/or the numerous approximations/assumptions required by Bayes' theorem. Physicians seem to use reasoning methods that work without requiring such historical information and these methods generally provide accurate results even though the results are based on limited data.

2. There is a need to represent medical knowledge and heuristics explicitly, which cannot be done when using probabilities. This allows a system to generate explanations about its problem-solving process. Representing knowledge explicitly is important since it allows the physicians to see how the program is operating and better accept its reasoning and results.

3. Physicians appear to reason by capturing evidence that supports or denies a particular hypothesis. This information is gathered independently and appears to be a very different technique than that used by Bayes' analysis.

For these reasons the certainty factor (CF) formalism was developed. The formalism is based loosely on Bayes's analysis and varies slightly in its implementation from system to system. The discussion below is based on its original implementation in Mycin.

8.3.1 Certainty Factor (CF) Formalism

Knowledge in a expert system using the certainty factor (CF) formalism is expressed as a set of rules having the format:

$$\text{IF} \qquad \text{EVIDENCE}$$
$$\text{THEN} \quad \text{HYPOTHESIS (CF)}$$

where EVIDENCE is one or more facts known to support the derivation of HYPOTHESIS. The value of CF denotes the belief in HYPOTHESIS given that EVIDENCE is observed. This rule does not make any statement or claim about the belief or confidence in HYPOTHESIS not being true should EVIDENCE not be present (as we saw in the Bayesian approach).

The CF formalism makes use of three distinct values that are "defined in terms of hypothesized mathematical relationships governed by prior and posterior probabilities" [Clark, 1990]:

1. The measure of belief, $MB[h,e]$, which is a value between 0 and 1 representing the degree to which the belief in hypothesis h is supported by observing evidence e. This value is computed to be

$$
\begin{aligned}
MB[h,e] &= 1 & \text{if } p[h] = 1 \\
&= \frac{p[h \mid e] - p[h]}{1 - p[h]} & \text{otherwise}
\end{aligned}
\tag{12}
$$

2. The measure of disbelief, $MD[h,e]$, which is a value between 0 and 1 representing the degree to which the disbelief in hypothesis h is supported by observing evidence e. This value is computed to be:

$$
\begin{aligned}
MD[h,e] &= 1 & \text{if } p[h] = 0 \\
&= \frac{p[h] - p[h \mid e]}{p[h]} & \text{otherwise}
\end{aligned}
\tag{13}
$$

3. The certainty factor, CF, which is a composite of MB and MD ranging between -1 (h's denial) and 1 (h's confirmation). This value is computed to be

$$
CF = \frac{MB - MD}{1 - \min(MB,MD)}
\tag{14}
$$

8.3.2 Propagation of Certainty Factors

During the execution of a knowledge base, multiple rules are typically capable of deriving the same hypothesis or conclusion. As a result, there must be some mechanism for combining each rule's CF with any others that have been derived to result in a single CF for that hypothesis. For example, suppose that hypothesis h_1 currently has a CF value of CF_{old} and a rule in our knowledge base executes and derives h_1 with a new CF of CF_{new}. These two values are then combined under the CF formalism to determine a revised CF for the hypothesis of interest, in this case h_1, by using the following equations:

$$CF_{revised}(CF_{old}, CF_{new}) =$$

$$= CF_{old} + CF_{new}(1 - CF_{old}) \qquad \text{if both } CF_{old} \text{ and } CF_{new} > 0 \qquad (15)$$

$$= -CF_{revised}(-CF_{old}, -CF_{new}) \qquad \text{if both } CF_{old} \text{ and } CF_{new} < 0 \qquad (16)$$

$$= \frac{CF_{old} + CF_{new}}{1 - \min(\mid CF_{old} \mid, \mid CF_{new} \mid)} \qquad \text{if one of } CF_{old} \text{ and } CF_{new} < 0 \qquad (17)$$

Note that in Equation (15), the difference between 1 and CF_{old} (the amount of uncertainty associated with our hypothesis) is decreased relatively by CF_{new}. This allows the CF value to asymptotically approach 1.0. Should the CF have a value of 1.0, CF_{new} will in effect be ignored. Equation (16) treats the case of negative CFs identically to positive CFs. Finally, Equation (17) is the casting of Equation (14) from the domain of belief measurements into CFs. This equation provides a balancing of positive and negative results and is designed to prevent situations where a single strong piece of denying evidence could outweigh several weaker pieces of confirming evidence or vice versa.

8.3.3 Dealing with Uncertain Evidence

The assumption under which Equations (15) to (17) are based is that we have absolute confidence in the evidence or premises used to derive these values. Suppose, however, that we have the typical situation that exists within a knowledge-based system where a hypothesis from one rule is used as the evidence of another. In this case, we often do not have absolute confidence in the evidence. For example, consider the following rules:

```
RULE001     IF     A
            THEN   Q (CF = .75)
```

```
RULE002    IF    B  AND
                 C  AND
                 D
           THEN  Q  (CF = 0.7)
RULE003    IF    E  OR
                 F  OR
                 G
           THEN  Q  (CF = 0.6)
```

If premises A through G are all known to be true with absolute confidence, then each rule would derive hypothesis Q with its respective CF value. But should any of these premises be derived by another rule (or given by the user) with something less than absolute confidence (e.g., having an associated CF), Q's derived confidence must also be lower. The following three rules of combination are applied should this occur:

1. The resulting CF for the rule's hypothesis would be the product of the hypothesis' CF expressed within the rule and the CF of the rule's evidence. (See RULE001.)
2. If the rule consists of a conjunction of premises (i.e., RULE002), the resulting CF for the rule's hypothesis is the product of the hypothesis' CF expressed within the rule and the minimum CF associated with the premises (i.e., the various evidences).
3. If the rule consists of a disjunction of premises (i.e., RULE003), the resulting CF for the rule's hypothesis is the product of the hypothesis' CF expressed within the rule and the maximum CF associated with the premises.

8.3.4 Certainty Factor Example

To illustrate how certainty factors propagate, consider the following example about a murder trial [Park 1988]. In this trial, the defendant is being accused of first degree murder (the hypothesis). The jury must weight the evidence presented by the prosecutor and by the defense attorney to decide whether to convict or to clear the defendant. As an open-minded jury, the jurors start the trial with a CF of 0.0 for the first degree murder hypothesis (e.g., they don't have any evidence on which to base any conclusions). This is represented by the box shown in Figure 8.1.

The prosecution first introduces evidence to support their hypothesis. Their initial piece of evidence is that the defendant's fingerprints were on the murder weapon. Their implication is:

```
RULE001 IF    the defendant's fingerprints are on the murder
              weapon,
        THEN  the defendant is guilty.
```

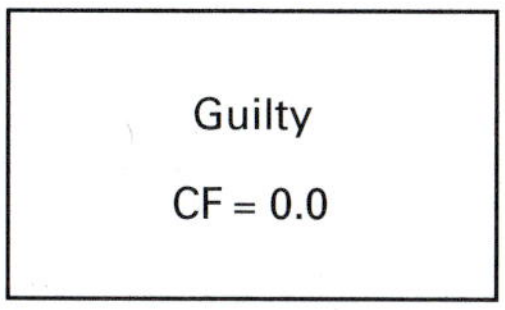

Guilty

CF = 0.0

FIGURE 8.1 Initial Certainty Factor in Guilty Verdict

However, the mere presence of the fingerprints on the murder weapon (a handgun) does not conclusively prove that the defendant committed the crime. The weapon may have been stolen from him or the defendant may have used the weapon for target practice at a firing range prior to the crime. Thus, a certainty factor less than absolute confidence, 1.00, must be associated with the above conclusion:

$$CF_{\text{rule1's conclusion}} = 0.75$$

The piece of evidence about the fingerprints is reported by an expert witness who is very believable (i.e., a college professor), so the jurors assign great credibility to the evidence being true:

$$CF_{\text{evid1}} = 0.90$$

The combined certainty factor for the rule, its impact on the hypothesis, is now

$$CF_{\text{comb1}} = CF_{\text{rule1's conclusion}} * CF_{\text{evid1}}$$

$$= 0.75 * 0.90 \tag{18}$$

$$= 0.675$$

This value becomes CF_{new} in Equations (15) to (17). Using these formulas, the revised CF for the "Guilty" hypothesis is calculated to be

$$CF_{\text{revised}} = CF_{\text{old}} + CF_{\text{new}} * (1 - CF_{\text{old}})$$

$$= 0.0 + 0.675 * (1 - 0.0) \tag{19}$$

$$= 0.675$$

The introduction of this evidence is depicted in Figure 8.2.

The next piece of evidence from the prosecution is a statement by a witness (the defendant's mother-in-law) that the defendant had a motive for the slaying. The implication is

```
RULE002 IF    the defendant has a motive
        THEN  the defendant is guilty of the crime
```

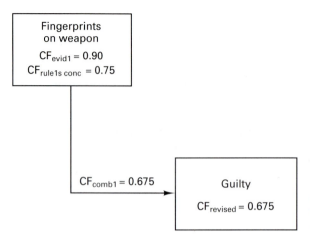

FIGURE 8.2 Certainty Factor in Guilty Verdict after Introduction of Fingerprint Evidence

However, motive is not a crime and, more often than not, does not lead to a crime; therefore, a lower certainty factor is associated with this rule's conclusion:

$$CF_{rule2\text{'s conclusion}} = 0.60$$

Since the witness is the defendant's mother-in-law and she hates the defendant, the jurors do not see her as a credible witness. As a result they only assign a certainty factor of 0.50 to her testimony.

$$CF_{new} = CF_{comb2} = CF_{rule2\text{'s conclusion}} * CF_{evid2}$$

$$= 0.60 * 0.50$$

$$= 0.30$$

This new belief is now propagated to the "Guilty" hypothesis using Equation (15):

$$CF_{revised} = CF_{old} + CF_{new} * (1 - CF_{old})$$

$$= 0.675 + 0.30 * (1 - 0.675) \qquad (20)$$

$$= 0.7725$$

This is shown in Figure 8.3.

The prosecution at this point rests their case, giving the defense a chance to introduce contradictory evidence. They present a single piece of evidence: a person who provides an alibi for the defendant. This witness states that he was with the defendant at the time when the murder occurred. This implication is

```
RULE003 IF    the defendant has an alibi
        THEN  he is not guilty
```

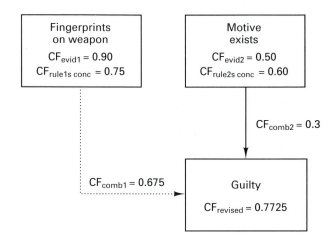

FIGURE 8.3   Certainty Factor in
Guilty Verdict after Introduction
of Motive Evidence

Since witnesses providing an alibi are known to lie sometimes, the conclusion of this rule has an associated certainty factor of 0.80. Since it acts to
decrease belief in the hypothesis (that the defendant *is* guilty), it is considered
a negative value. Thus

$$CF_{rule3's\ conclusion} = -0.80$$

The witness providing this information happens to be a respected judge, so the
jurors consider him to be highly credible and assign a certainty factor of 0.95
to the evidence:

$$CF_{evid3} = 0.95$$

The combined certainty factor from this rule is

$$CF_{comb3} = CF_{evid3} * CF_{rule3's\ conclusion}$$
$$= 0.95 * (-0.80) \tag{21}$$
$$= -0.76$$

Combining this result with the previous result using Equation (17) provides

$$CF_{revised} = \frac{CF_{old} + CF_{new}}{1 - \min(\ |\ CF_{old}\ |\ ,\ |\ CF_{new}\ |\ )}$$
$$= \frac{0.7725 - 0.76}{1.0 - 0.76} \tag{22}$$
$$= 0.052$$

Given this result, the jury would find it difficult to convict the defendant. The entire inference net is shown in Figure 8.4.

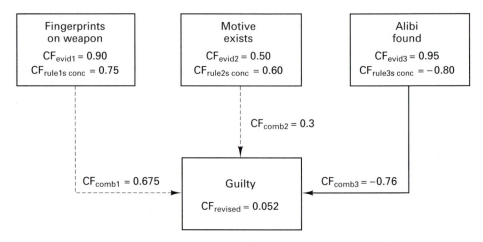

FIGURE 8.4   Confidence Factor in Guilty Verdict after Introduction of Alibi Evidence

8.3.5 Advantages and Disadvantages of Certainty Factors

The CF formalism has been quite popular with expert system developers since its creation because

1. It is a simple computational model that permits experts to estimate their confidence in conclusions being drawn.
2. It permits the expression of belief and disbelief in each hypothesis, allowing the expression of the effect of multiple sources of evidence.
3. It allows knowledge to be captured in a rule representation while allowing the quantification of uncertainty.
4. The gathering of the CF values is significantly easier than the gathering of values for the other methods. No statistical base is required—you merely have to ask the expert for the values.

Many systems, including Mycin, have utilized this formalism and have displayed a high degree of competence in their application areas. But is this competence due to these systems' ability to manipulate and reason with uncertainty or is it due to other factors?

Clancey examined this question with regard to Mycin in two ways [Buchanan, 1984a]. First, he modified the CF numbers to see how changes in these values would affect the derived results. Second, he turned off the CF reasoning portion of Mycin. In both cases he found that Mycin was able to derive correct diagnoses to most test cases. This revealed that the knowledge described within the rule contributes much more to the final, derived results than the CF values associated with this knowledge.

Other criticisms of this uncertainty reasoning method include among others:

1. Nonindependent evidence can be expressed and combined only by "chunking" it together within the same rule. When large quantities of nonindependent evidence must be expressed, this proves to be unsatisfactory [Clark, 1990].
2. CF values are unable to represent efficiently and naturally certain dependencies between uncertain beliefs [Heckerman, 1987].
3. The CF value associated with a rule is dependent on the strength of association between the evidence (e.g., premises) and the hypothesis (e.g, conclusions). As new knowledge about some domain is uncovered and is added to or deleted from a knowledge base, the CF values of existing knowledge will change, making knowledge base changes involved and complex [Heckerman, 1988].

Given these difficulties, it has been argued [Gordon, 1984] that Mycin, the system that developed certainty factors, would have been better served by the Dempster-Shafer theory of evidence.

8.4 DEMPSTER-SHAFER THEORY OF EVIDENCE

The Dempster-Shafer theory evolved during the 1960s and 1970s through the efforts of Arthur Dempster [Dempster, 1967] and one of his students, Glenn Shafer [Shafer, 1976]. This theory was designed as a mathematical theory of evidence where a value between 0 and 1 is assigned to some fact as its degree of support. It is like the Bayesian methods but is more general since the belief in a fact and its negation need not sum to one (as is the case with probability-based theories) and, in fact, the situation can exist where both values are 0 (reflecting that no information is available to make a judgment either way). It also more accurately represents the process of gathering evidence by allowing belief values to be associated with sets of facts as well as individual facts.

8.4.1 Definition of Terms

Given a set of possible conclusions to be drawn

$$\Theta = \{\theta_1, \theta_2, \ldots, \theta_n\}$$

that are mutually exclusive and exhaustive, we can define the following terms and make the following statements:

1. The "Frame of Discernment" is the power set, 2^{Θ}, of the set of possible conclusions, that is $(\phi, \{q_1\}, \{q_2\}, \{q_3\}, \ldots, \{q_n\}, \{q_1\,q_2\}, \{q_1\,q_3\}, \ldots, \{q_1\,q_n\},$ $\{q_2\,q_3\}, \ldots, \{q_2\,q_n\}, \ldots, \{q_1\,q_2\,q_3\}, \ldots, \{q_1\,q_2\,q_n\}, \ldots, \{q_1\,q_2\,q_3 \cdots q_n\})$

2. A mass probability function, m, assigns a numeric value from the range [0,1] to every item in the Frame of Discernment with the value 0 assigned to the empty set (e.g., $m(\phi) = 0$) since we know that one of the set of conclusions is true. The sum of these numbers, the total probability mass, should be 1.

3. If A is an element of the Frame of Discernment, (e.g., describing the set of possible conclusions $\{q_a\,q_b\,q_c\}$) then the value $m(A)$ is that portion of the total mass probability (e.g., 1.0) that is assigned to A. This value cannot be further subdivided to assign values to the various subsets of A. It also does not include the values assigned to the various subsets of A.

4. The belief, *Bel*, in a subset A is the sum of all of the mass probabilities, $m(B)$, assigned to all of the proper subsets B of A or, for example,

$$Bel(\{q_a, q_b, q_c\}) = m(\{q_a\}) + m(\{q_b\}) + m(\{q_c\}) + m(\{q_a, q_b\}) + $$
$$m(\{q_a, q_c\}) + m(\{q_b, q_c\}) + m(\{q_a, q_b, q_c\})$$

Since the belief in this subset is the *likelihood* that one of its members is the conclusion, the summation of all of the values associated with each of its subsets properly expresses our total belief in the subset A. Note that the $Bel(\Theta) = 1$ (see statement 2 above) since we know that one of the elements of Θ is the conclusion.

5. The certainty associated with a particular subset, A, is defined by the belief interval

$$[Bel(A)\ P^*(A)]$$

where $Bel(A)$, as defined above, is the measure of our total belief in A and its subsets and where $P^*(A)$ is:

$$P^*(A) = 1 - Bel(A^c)$$

or a measure of our failure to doubt A. This interval expresses our range of certainty about our belief in the particular subset. For example, a range of [0.240 0.245] leaves little doubt about the belief (it is very close to 0.240) while a range of [0.2 0.6] expresses much uncertainty (it could be as low as 0.2 and as high as 0.6) about our belief in the particular subset.

6. Given two mass probabilities, m_1 (representing a preexisting certainty state associated with hypothesis subsets X) and m_2 (representing some new evidence associated with hypothesis subsets Y), we can combine these into a third, m_3 (representing the certainty state associated with C, the intersection of X and Y), using Dempster's combination rule:

$$m_3(C) = \frac{\sum_{X \cap Y = C} m_1(X) * m_2(Y)}{1 - \sum_{X \cap Y = \phi} m_1(X) * m_2(Y)}$$

Because the above definitions and statements are significantly different from those in the other methods we have presented so far, they are fairly difficult to understand. Let us, therefore, consider an example to help clarify how this inexact reasoning method would be applied.

8.4.2 Example

Consider the following situation (adapted from [Spillman, 1990]). Four people (e.g., Bob, Jim, Sally, and Karen) are in a locked room when the lights suddenly go out. When the lights return, Karen is found dead from stabbing. If we assume that it is highly unlikely that Karen stabbed herself, the guilty party must be one of the remaining individuals (i.e., assuming that no more than one individual was involved). The group of these individuals forms our set of possible events:

$E = \{B$ (e.g, Bob is guilty), J (e.g., Jim is guilty), S (e.g., Sally is guilty)$\}$.

Our feelings about who committed this crime are expressed over the Frame of Discernment, which is the power set of E:

$2^E = \{\phi, \{B\}, \{J\}, \{S\}, \{B, J\}, \{B, S\}, \{J, S\}, \{B, J, S\}\}$.

These feelings express our portion of the total belief that is committed specifically to each of these sets of events. These numeric values are called mass probabilities since some of them express a belief in a set of events (i.e., $\{B, J\}$), not just an individual event (i.e., $\{B\}$), and cannot be further subdivided into our belief in each of the individuals contained within these sets. Note that the mass probability of ϕ is always zero (since this is the false hypothesis, e.g., none of these people killed her, and we know that these individuals were the only ones that could have done it) and the sum of all of these values is one (e.g., one of the three individuals did stab her since the door was locked).

Let us suppose that the detective investigating this crime, after reviewing the initial set of evidence at the crime scene (the location of the body, the location of each individual, etc.), assigns the following mass probabilities to the members of the Frame of Discernment:

EVENT	MASS
Bob is guilty $\{B\}$	0.1
Jim is guilty $\{J\}$	0.2
Sally is guilty $\{S\}$	0.1
Either Bob or Jim is guilty $\{B, J\}$	0.1
Either Bob or Sally is guilty $\{B, S\}$	0.1
Either Jim or Sally is guilty $\{J, S\}$	0.3
One of the three is guilty $\{B, J, S\}$	0.1

Using our definition from above, we can now compute our belief in a particular subset of events using these mass probability values. For example, our belief that the guilty party is either Jim or Bob is computed to be

$$Bel(\{B, J\}) = m(\{B\}) + m(\{J\}) + m(\{B,J\})$$

$$= 0.1 + 0.2 + 0.1$$

$$= 0.4$$

A summary of all of these computed belief values and the mass probability values is shown below, where A is the subset of the Frame of Discernment and m_{init} is the initial mass probability function:

A	{B}	{J}	{S}	{B, J}	{B, S}	{J, S}	{B, J, S}
$Bel(A)$	0.1	0.2	0.1	0.4	0.3	0.6	1.0
$m_{init}(A)$	0.1	0.2	0.1	0.1	0.1	0.3	0.1

While these belief values seem to indicate that Jim is the guilty party (all of the subsets containing Jim have higher belief values than the equivalent subsets without him), we cannot make that assumption yet, since these values only indicate that he might be guilty, they do not guarantee it. As more evidence is collected, the belief values will change and will hopefully identify a specific solution or some small subset that contains the solution. Our belief interval for Jim being guilty is

$$[Bel(\{J\})\ 1 - Bel(\{J\}^c)] = [0.2 \quad 1 - (m_{init}(\{B\}) + m_{init}(\{S\}) + m_{init}(\{B,S\}))]$$

$$= [0.2 \quad 1 - (0.1 + 0.1 + 0.1)]$$

$$= [0.2 \quad 0.7]$$

The width (e.g., difference of these values) is our amount of uncertainty that Jim is guilty, given this evidence.

Suppose that the detective investigating this crime has an opportunity to read Karen's will. Considering this information alone, a new belief function is generated:

A	{B}	{J}	{S}	{B, J}	{B, S}	{J, S}	{B, J, S}
$Bel(A)$	0.2	0.1	0.05	0.6	0.3	0.25	1.0
$m_{will}(A)$	0.2	0.1	0.05	0.3	0.05	0.1	0.2

Using Dempster's rule these two sets of belief values can be combined to form a composite belief function. How this rule actually works is best understood through a visual representation. Each of the mass probability distributions divide the interval [0,1] into segments as shown in Figure 8.5 [Spillman, 1990].

By placing these two distributions perpendicular to each other, we can determine their combined effect. The area of each rectangle provides a measure of the probability mass of the intersection of the two subsets forming that rectangle as shown in Figure 8.6 [Spillman, 1990].

Mass probability segments for m_{init}:

{B}	{J}	{S}	{B,J}	{B,S}	{J,S}	{B,J,S}
0.1	0.2	0.1	0.1	0.1	0.3	0.1

Mass probability segments for m_{will}:

{B}	{J}	{S}	{B,J}	{B,S}	{J,S}	{B,J,S}
0.2	0.1	.05	0.3	.05	0.1	0.2

FIGURE 8.5   Mass Probability Distributions

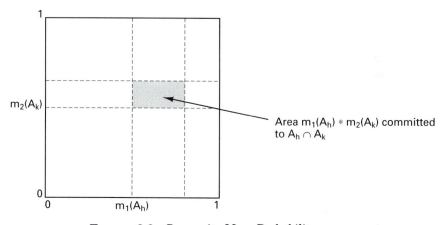

FIGURE 8.6   Composite Mass Probability

When this is done with m_{init} and m_{will}, we obtain the composite shown in Figure 8.7 [Spillman, 1990].

Note that a number of the rectangles that are obtained in this composite represent empty intersections. See Figure 8.8 [Spillman, 1990]. When computing the combined mass probability, Dempster's rule normalizes all of the results to account for these empty intersections. In this example, the empty intersections total 0.245 so all computed values are normalized by $1 - 0.245 = 0.755$.

Figure 8.9 [Spillman, 1990] illustrates all of the intersections that result in {B}. These intersections have a total area of 0.17, resulting in a combined evidence of

$$\frac{0.17}{0.755} = 0.225$$

for {B}. The following shows the mass probability and belief values resulting from this combination:

A	$\{B\}$	$\{J\}$	$\{S\}$	$\{B, J\}$	$\{B, S\}$	$\{J, S\}$	$\{B, J, S\}$
$Bel(A)$	0.225	0.219	0.25	0.580	0.484	0.600	1.00
$m_{end}(A)$	0.225	0.219	0.25	0.105	0.040	0.131	0.03

As you can tell from these values, Jim is no longer the prime suspect in the case. Sally has significantly increased as a suspect. Table 8.2 summarizes how the belief intervals have changed for Bob, Jim, and Sally.

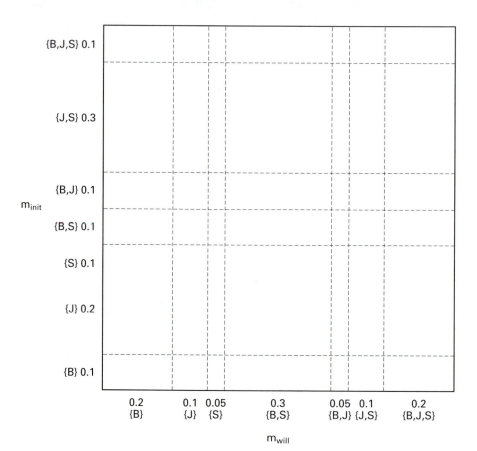

FIGURE 8.7 Composite of m_{init} and m_{will}

TABLE 8.2   SUMMARY OF BELIEF INTERVALS

	Bob	Jim	Sally
BI_{init}	[0.100 0.4]	[0.200 0.700]	[0.100 0.500]
BI_{end}	[0.225 0.4]	[0.215 0.485]	[0.250 0.451]

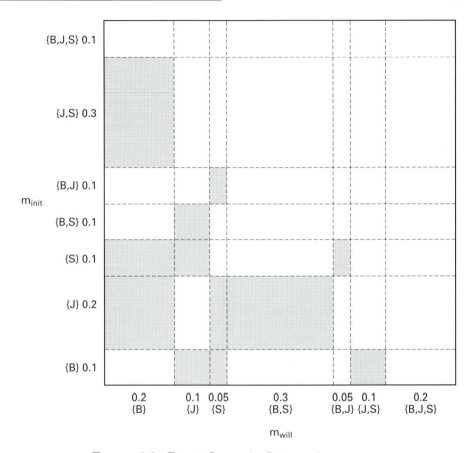

FIGURE 8.8   Empty Composite Intersections

8.4.3 Evaluation

Dempster-Shafer theory has one very important advantage not exhibited by most other uncertainty methods: It is able to represent our "certainty about certainty"—something the Bayesian method is criticized about not being able to represent. The commitment to a belief in some fact A, $Bel(A)$, does not imply that the remaining belief holds for A's complement, $Bel(A^c)$. It is instead the case that $Bel(A) + Bel(A^c) \leq 1$. The quantity $1 - [Bel(A) + Bel(A^c)]$ is the degree of ignorance concerning A.

The major difficulty with this theory is its complexity, requiring an exhaustive enumeration of all possible subsets in the frame of discernment in nearly all cases. Additionally, it offers no guidance on how the mass probability assignments should be computed or how to make decisions from the results.

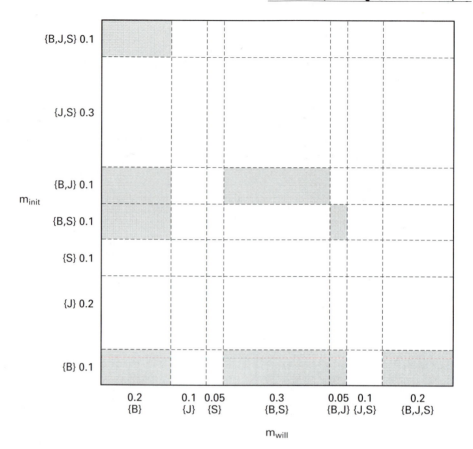

FIGURE 8.9   Intersections That Result in the Set {B}

8.5 FUZZY SETS AND FUZZY LOGICS

In the mid 1960s Lotfi Zadeh [Zadeh, 1965] developed the concept of "fuzzy sets" to account for the numerous concepts used in human reasoning which are intrinsically vague and imprecise (e.g., "tall," "old"). He later developed "fuzzy logic" to account for the imprecision of natural language quantifiers (e.g., "many") and statements (e.g., "not very likely"). Since many experts express knowledge using a similar set of imprecise and subjective quantifiers, his concepts appear to naturally apply within knowledge-based systems.

   Consider all of the animals in a zoo. For each animal, we can determine whether it is a mammal (reptile, bird, etc.) with absolute certainty based upon certain characteristics of the animals. The animals can be divided into two distinct, nonintersecting subsets based upon these characteristics. We can say that the predicate Mammal(X) returns a truth value determining X's membership within the set of mammals.

If we consider the students taking a particular class, we can apply a similar predicate to determine their membership in a certain ethnic category (e.g., German, Mexican, Lebanese). But this categorization is not as precise as our animal classifier since many individuals come from mixed backgrounds. We, therefore, must extend our predicates to return not an absolute truth value but rather a numeric value from the range [0 1] that expresses an individual's ethnic mix. So Kathy who has two French, one Vietnamese, and one native American grandparents might be considered to have a 0.5 "degree of membership" to the set of French individuals.

Other categorizations have even less precision. For example, consider the concept "tall." The degree to which an individual is a member of the set of "tall people" will depend upon the particular set of individuals about whom we are talking. Absolute membership (a 1.0 degree of membership) in the class "tall" might apply to all individuals above 6' if we are examining ninth grade students while 7'2" might apply for professional basketball players.

8.5.1 Definition of Terms

Given some set $S = \{s_1, s_2, \ldots, s_k\}$ of possible members of another set C, a fuzzy predicate F_P classifies the elements of S into the range [0 1] depending on their degree of membership in set C:

$$F_P(s_i)_{1 \leq i \leq k} \rightarrow [0\ 1]$$

$F_P(s_i) = 1$ denotes membership of s_i in set C as defined by predicate F_P and $F_P(s_i) = 0$ denotes nonmembership in C. The values between 0 and 1 denote a measure of the extent to which the particular element s_i satisfies that predicate F_P. The predicate, therefore, defines a fuzzy set:

$$S_P = \{ <s_i\ n_i> \mid s_i \in S, n_i \in [0\ 1], F_P(s_i) = n_i]$$

This fuzzy set, S_P, is empty if and only if (iff) n_i is zero for all elements of S.

All of the typical set operations have been extended to have fuzzy counterparts:

1. Two fuzzy sets, S_A and S_B, are said to be equal iff $A(s_i) = B(s_i)$ for all s_i in S.
2. The complement of the fuzzy set, S_P, is denoted $\sim S_P$ and has a predicate $F_{P\sim}(s_i) = 1 - F_P(s_i)$.
3. Fuzzy set S_A is a subset of S_B iff $A(s_i) \leq B(s_i)$ for all s_i in S.
4. The union of two fuzzy sets S_A and S_B is the fuzzy set S_C where $C(s_i) = \text{MAX}[A(s_i), B(s_i)]$ for all s_i in S.
5. The intersection of two fuzzy sets S_A and S_B is the fuzzy set S_C where $C(s_i) = \text{MIN}[A(s_i), B(s_i)]$ for all s_i in S.

To illustrate these relations, consider the fuzzy sets shown in Table 8.3 [Negoita, 1985]. We can see from this table that "tall" and "statuesque" are equal, "short" and "tall" are complements (e.g., not "short" equals "tall" and not "tall" equals "short"), and "giant" is a subset of "tall." We can also define two new concepts, "middle-sized" and not "middle-sized" to be the intersection and union of not "tall" and not "short," respectively. See Table 8.4 [Negoita, 1985].

If we have some fuzzy set, S_A, (e.g., tall people) that is a subset of S (e.g., all people) and we state the proposition that "X is S_A" (e.g., "John is a tall person") then we are associating a *possibility distribution*, Π_X, with S_A or $\Pi_X = S_A$. This is written:

$$X \text{ is } A \rightarrow \Pi_x = A$$

This proposition also makes an association between the membership function of S_A, F_A, and the possibility distribution function of X, $\Pi_X \cdot F_A = \Pi_X$.

The degree to which some individual item is a potential member in a fuzzy set is expressed through a possibility measure, $\text{Poss}\{x \in S_A\}$. This value is computed to be:

$$\text{Poss}\{x \in S_A\} = \text{MAX}_{y \in S_A}[\Pi_X(y)]$$

TABLE 8.3   FUZZY SETS TALL, STATUESQUE, SHORT, AND GIANT

Tall		Statuesque		Short		Giant	
5'0"	0.00	5'0"	0.00	5'0"	1.00	5'0"	0.00
5'4"	0.08	5'4"	0.08	5'4"	0.92	5'4"	0.04
5'8"	0.32	5'8"	0.32	5'8"	0.68	5'8"	0.08
6'0"	0.50	6'0"	0.50	6'0"	0.50	6'0"	0.18
6'4"	0.82	6'4"	0.82	6'4"	0.18	6'4"	0.32
6'8"	0.98	6'8"	0.98	6'8"	0.02	6'8"	0.50
7'0"	1.00	7'0"	1.00	7'0"	0.00	7'0"	0.75

TABLE 8.4   FUZZY SETS MIDDLE-SIZED AND NOT MIDDLE-SIZED FORMED FROM THE UNION AND INTERSECTION OF NOT TALL AND NOT SHORT

Not tall		Not short		Middle-sized		Not middle-sized	
5'0"	1.00	5'0"	0.00	5'0"	0.00	5'0"	1.00
5'4"	0.92	5'4"	0.08	5'4"	0.08	5'4"	0.92
5'8"	0.68	5'8"	0.32	5'8"	0.32	5'8"	0.68
6'0"	0.50	6'0"	0.50	6'0"	0.50	6'0"	0.50
6'4"	0.18	6'4"	0.82	6'4"	0.18	6'4"	0.82
6'8"	0.02	6'8"	0.98	6'8"	0.02	6'8"	0.98
7'0"	0.00	7'0"	1.00	7'0"	0.00	7'0"	1.00

For example, if I state the proposition that "John is between 5'7" and 6'1" in height" and the fuzzy set for tall person has been defined above to be

Tall = {<5'0", 0.0> <5'4", 0.08> <5'8", 0.32>

<6'0", 0.50> <6'4", 0.82> <6'8", 0.98> <7'0", 1.00>}

then Poss(John $\in$ Tall) = $\text{MAX}_{y \in \text{Tall}} [\Pi_X(y)]$ = 0.50.

Propositions are typically not stated singly so some method must be provided that allows the formation of compound statements through the use of the composition operators. The most common of these operators are defined as:

1. **Logical AND.** The proposition "A AND B" (where A and B are of the form "X is Y") is

   Poss(A & B) = MIN[Poss(A), Poss(B)]

2. **Logical OR.** The proposition "A OR B" is

   Poss(A + B) = MAX[Poss(A), Poss(B)]

3. **Implies.** The proposition "If A then B" is

   Poss(B | A) = MIN[1, (1 − Poss(A) + Poss(B))]

Finally, we have modifications caused by English language modifiers. If we have

$$X \text{ is } A \rightarrow \Pi_X = A,$$

$$\text{then } X \text{ is } mA \rightarrow \Pi_x = A^+$$

where m is a legal modifier that induces the modified possibility distribution A^+. Zadeh has suggested that the use of $A^+ = A^2$ for m = "very," $A^+ = 1 - A$ for m = "not" and $A^+ = \text{SQRT}(A)$ for m = "more or less." We might also define "extremely" as $A^+ = \text{INT}(A)$, where INT is the contrast intensification operation [Zadeh, 1973]:

$$\text{INT}(A) = 2A^2 \qquad \text{for values between 0 and 0.5}$$

$$= \text{not } 2(\text{not } A)^2 \qquad \text{for other values}$$

$$= (1 - 2(1 - A)^2)$$

This operation has the effect of reducing the fuzziness of A.

8.5.2 Example

Students at a university typically identify the difficulty level of the various courses that they take using fuzzy linguistic terms. Three possibility distributions, shown in Figure 8.5, are typically associated by these students with

TABLE 8.5   POSSIBILITY DISTRIBUTIONS

Low	{<A, 0.10>	<B, 0.30>	<C, 0.50>	<D, 0.90>	<F, 0.95>}
Standard	{<A, 0.20>	<B, 0.50>	<C, 0.90>	<D, 0.50>	<F, 0.20>}
High	{<A, 0.90>	<B, 0.70>	<C, 0.50>	<D, 0.10>	<F, 0.05>}

the linguistic terms used in describing their classes. These possibility distributions express the prospect that a student will receive a particular grade. Table 8.6 summarizes these linguistic terms in terms of these possibility distributions at Whatsamata University.

In examining these terms we can see that *impossible* is a subset of *hard*, *hard* is the complement of *easy*, and *moderate* equals *average*. We can also define two new terms, *simple* and *typical*, to be the union of *easy* and *moderate* and the intersection of *hard* and *moderate*, respectively, as shown in Table 8.7.

Once these various terms have been defined we can apply them to particular classes and talk about specific grades and their prospect of occurring within a class, that is, the degree to which the grade is a potential member of the various categories. For example, if we state that "ART 101 (basket

TABLE 8.6   FUZZY LINGUISTIC TERMS FOR UNIVERSITY GRADES

Impossible:	Very low = low^2
	= {<A, 0.01> <B, 0.09> <C, 0.25> <D, 0.81> <F, 0.90>}
Hard:	Low
	= {<A, 0.10> <B, 0.30> <C, 0.50> <D, 0.90> <F, 0.95>}
Easy:	High
	= {<A, 0.90> <B, 0.70> <C, 0.50> <D, 0.10> <F, 0.05>}
Moderate:	Standard
	= {<A, 0.20> <B, 0.50> <C, 0.90> <D, 0.50> <F, 0.20>}
Cake:	Extremely high = INT(A)
	= {<A, 0.98> <B, 0.82> <C, 0.50> <D, 0.02> <F, 0.005>}
Average:	Standard
	= {<A, 0.20> <B, 0.50> <C, 0.90> <D, 0.50> <F, 0.20>}

TABLE 8.7   DEFINITIONS OF THE FUZZY TERMS SIMPLE AND TYPICAL

Simple:	easy UNION moderate
	= {<A, 0.90> <B, 0.70> <C, 0.90> <D, 0.50> <F, 0.20>}
Typical:	hard INTERSECT moderate
	= {<A, 0.10> <B, 0.30> <C, 0.50> <D, 0.50> <F, 0.20>}

weaving) is an easy class" then the prospect of receiving a grade of "A" or "B" in this class:

$$\text{Poss("A" or "B" in ART 101 when ART 101} \in \text{easy})$$
$$= \text{MAX}_{y \in S}[\Pi_X(y)]$$
$$= \text{MAX}(_{\text{"A"} \in S}[\Pi_X(y)], _{\text{"B"} \in S}[\Pi_X(y)])$$
$$= 0.9$$

Other classes are defined as shown in Table 8.8.

TABLE 8.8   FUZZY DEFINITIONS FOR VARIOUS COURSES

MECH 310 (Statics) is a hard class.
GEOL 210 (Rocks for Jocks) is a cake class.
ART 102 (Underwater Basket Weaving) is an impossible class.
COMPSCI 201 (Artificial Intelligence) is a moderate class.

These definitions can be combined using the various logical operations to compute the prospects of various grades as shown below:

Poss["B" in Art 101 (an easy class) AND

MECH 310 (a hard class)] = 0.3

Poss["C" or "D" in ART 102 (an impossible class) OR

GEOL 210 (a cake class)] = 0.81

Poss["A" in COMPSCI 201 (a moderate class) AND

"A" or "B" in GEOL 201 (a cake class)] = 0.2

Poss[if "C" in ART 102 AND "D" in MECH 310 then "B" in GEOL 201]
$$= \text{MIN}[1, (1 - \text{MIN}(0.25, 0.90) + 0.82)]$$
$$= \text{MIN}[1, 1.57] = 1.0$$

8.5.3 Evaluation

While fuzzy techniques have been applied across a range of domains including medical diagnosis [Adlassnig, 1982; Bezdek, 1976; Fieschi, 1982], information retrieval [Kohout, 1987a, 1987b], process control [Mamdani, 1983; Oshima, 1988], and fault detection [Okada, 1988; Hayashi, 1988] there is wide debate about their viability because of some apparent inherent difficulties. The development of the membership functions is nontrivial, often taking significantly longer than the development of the knowledge base [Schwartz, 1990]. It is also argued [Cheeseman, 1986; Lindley, 1987] that fuzzy concepts can be just as accurately represented in normalized probability density functions though this is contested [Zadeh, 1986]. While these controversies remain, these techniques are receiving continued interest and are being applied in an increasing number of systems.

8.6 CHAPTER REVIEW

Uncertainty management is a critical issue in the development of knowledge-based systems. Since they mimic the heuristic knowledge of the experts, they should be able to incorporate a means of introducing and propagating uncertainty. This chapter described the four most popular numerically oriented methods: Bayesian probability, certainty factors, Dempster-Schafer, and fuzzy sets.

Each approach has particular advantages and disadvantages. The Bayesian probability approach has a sound theoretical foundation, but requires a significant amount of probability data to construct a knowledge base. Certainty factors do not require a statistical database since they rely on values obtained from the domain experts. However, they have difficulties when dealing with large quantities of nonindependent evidence. Dempster-Shafer theory of evidence is able to represent our "certainty about certainty," something none of the other methods can do, but the determination of the mass probability values is nonintuitive. Finally, fuzzy logic is able to deal with the numerous vague and imprecise concepts and terms which we use, but developing the required membership functions is nontrivial.

While many researchers, for simplicity's sake, use a form of certainty factors, neither this method nor any of the others has been found to be ideally suited for all applications and as stated in [Lemmer, 1988]:

> there continues to be no consensus concerning the "best" approach to uncertainty for AI systems. Moreover there is not agreement on how to measure "best". . . .

The method selected will likely depend on the nature and complexity of the domain of the knowledge-based system being developed, the nature of that uncertainty (mutually exclusive or not), the amount of historical data available to support the uncertainty (probabilities), and desire on the part of the developers to introduce a computationally complex propagation scheme. We hope that the explanations provided will allow the developers to make an informed selection of the uncertainty management method to use.

8.7 PROBLEMS

8-1. In Chapter 3 we discussed implication, A → B. If we know that A is true, then B is true. What is the certainty of B being true if we know that the certainty of A is 1? Suppose that we know that the certainty of A is only 0.6. What is the certainty of B? Does your answer change if we are talking of probabilities?

8-2. Suppose that we know the following:
    (a) The probability that we will see an alligator in Lake Alice is 0.7.
    (b) The probability that ducks are on Lake Alice given that we see an alligator in the lake is 0.05.
    (c) The probability that ducks are on Lake Alice given that we do not see an alligator in the lake is 0.2.
What is the probability that we will see an alligator, given that there are ducks on Lake Alice?

8-3. Why is it important that when certainty factors of the same sign are combined, the result asymptotically approach 1.0?

8-4. Give a verbal argument justifying the equation for combining certainty factors of differing signs.

8-5. Given the following set of rules and facts, compute the likelihood that Tim's car was stolen by Mike or that John stole the car:

```
RULE 1:   IF    the defendant has a
                motive AND the de-
                fendant has an op-
                portunity
          THEN  the defendant is
                guilty of the crime
                (CF = 0.6)

RULE 2:   IF    the defendant has
                an alibi
          THEN  the defendant is
                guilty
                (CF = -0.80)
```

```
RULE 3:   IF    the defendant's
                fingerprints are
                found on the car
          THEN  the defendant is
                guilty (CF = 0.4)

RULE 4:   IF    the keys are left
                in the car
          THEN  the defendant has
                an opportunity
                (CF = 0.9)

RULE 5:   IF    the defendant does
                not like Tim
          THEN  the defendant has a
                motive (CF = 0.5)

RULE 6:   IF    the defendant
                needed transporta-
                tion
          THEN  the defendant has a
                motive (CF = 0.9)

RULE 7:   IF    the defendant's
                fingerprints are
                found on the keys
          THEN  the defendant is
                guilty (CF = 0.7)
```

Mike's car is broken (therefore, he needed transportation) (CF = 1.0)
John's car is not broken (therefore, he did not need transportation) (CF = 1.0)
Mike's fingerprints are on the car (CF = 1.0)
John's fingerprints are not on the car (CF = 1.0)
Mike's fingerprints are not on the keys (CF = 1.0)
John's fingerprints are on the keys (CF = 1.0)
Tim's keys were left in the car (CF = 1.0)
Mike does not like Tim (CF = 0.6)
John likes Tim (CF = 0.8)

Mike was watching TV when the crime was committed (therefore, he has an alibi) (CF = 0.85)
John was sleeping when the crime was committed (therefore, he has a weak alibi) (CF = 0.2)

8-6. You are teaching a class and have given a "take home" examination. When grading the examination, you discover certain irregularities between Jason's and Sue's papers. Being a strong proponent of the Dempster-Shafer theory of evidence, you build the following table of frame of discernment values based on their answers:

Problem	They cheated	They didn't	Either
1	0.4	0.0	0.6
2	0.0	0.6	0.4
3	0.3	0.0	0.7
4	0.2	0.0	0.8

(a) Compute your belief interval after examining only Problem 1 that they cheated or that they did not.
(b) What are your belief intervals after examining all of the evidence associated with the four problems?

8-7. Suppose that I tell you that "Tim is between 5'11" and 6'4" in height." Compute the possibility measures based on Tables 8.3 and 8.4 that
(a) John is statuesque.
(b) John is not short.
(c) John is not middle-sized.
(d) John is short.

9 ■ Advanced Reasoning Techniques[1]

9.1 INTRODUCTION

At this point, you should have a clear understanding of the nature of the "traditional" knowledge-based systems. To complete your understanding, it is important to see what new developments lie on the horizon. Some of these developments could have a significant impact on the structure and use of the next generation of knowledge-based systems.

One constant in science and technology is that the state of the art is always progressing. Nowhere is this more apparent today than in computer science and engineering. The abductive and deductive reasoning systems discussed in most of the previous chapters were in the realm of research as late as the early to mid-1980s but are arguably no longer considered "research." The art of knowledge-based system development is now widely accepted to be a science. This does not mean that the field is static, however. Some researchers strive to find more efficient methods for pattern matching and search, others try to extend the realm of applications to domains where knowledge-based systems are not presently being applied; and research is being performed to relieve the knowledge engineering bottleneck by automating knowledge acquisition as is shown in Chapter 15. In this chapter we describe other techniques now considered "research," which could add considerable more power to the systems of today. These techniques are:

1. Model-based reasoning (MBR)
2. Qualitative reasoning (QR)
3. Case-based reasoning (CBR)

[1]In collaboration with Mark B. Fishman.

263

4. Temporal reasoning (TR)

5. Artificial neural networks

Model-based and qualitative reasoning are emerging as techniques that, hopefully, will correct some disadvantages of knowledge-based systems discussed in Chapter 2. Model-based reasoning attempts to relieve the knowledge acquisition bottleneck by eliminating the need for knowledge elicitation from experts. It represents physical systems, whether man-made or natural, by their structure and functionality. Thus, it reasons using first principles of engineering and science, (also called *deep knowledge*), rather than an expert's *associational* knowledge about the system's behavior. Qualitative reasoning, which is quite often associated with model-based reasoning, is a means of *qualitatively* simulating the behavior of a physical system.

Quantitative simulation has been the traditional technique used in computer simulation of physical systems. It models the exact behavior of the system or device in terms of a complete and deterministic description of all of its parameters. A qualitative simulation, on the other hand, does not attempt to model the exact behavior of a physical system or device, but rather will determine only its possible general states based on some defined general constraints.

To illustrate their difference, consider a simple home heating control system (a thermostat). Suppose the temperature setting is raised ten degrees. A quantitative simulation of its operation will account for fixed parameters such as the burner's efficiency, the blower capacity, the temperature of the warm air, the volume of the room(s) being heated, the room's heat loss factor, and so forth to calculate exactly what the temperature of the room air will be at any point in time. A qualitative simulation, on the other hand, will be able to determine only that, based on the general operating principles of the temperature control system, the room will get progressively warmer, until such a time as its temperature approaches the new set point. The time at which this will happen is not known, but it will be a significant landmark value. The room will then proceed slowly to cool until the thermostat starts the furnace again, and so forth.

Case-based reasoning is also an attempt to relieve the knowledge acquisition bottleneck by replacing the knowledge of an expert with a database of historical *cases*. These cases are examined for their significant features and, based on their resemblance to the present problem, their solutions are used to generate a solution to the present problem.

Temporal reasoning (i.e., reasoning with and about time) is not a complete reasoning technique in and by itself, but fills a real need in the many areas where time is a significant parameter to be considered. It unites well with model-based and qualitative reasoning and has applicability in many engineering and scientific tasks.

Artificial neural networks (ANNs) take an entirely different approach. ANNs represent a computer implementation of the human brain's physiological structure in an attempt to duplicate its functionality. Their capability to learn when properly trained provides a significant advantage over the traditional knowledge acquisition process described in the next few chapters.

There are many other techniques being developed to carry out intelligent reasoning. Some *such as constraint-based reasoning* are problem-solving techniques in themselves. Others such as *truth maintenance* systems (TMS) are designed for maintaining integrity in nonmonotonic logic systems. Space does not allow us to present all of these, however, so we present only the more significant alternatives to deductive and abductive reasoning discussed in the previous chapters.

9.2 MODEL-BASED REASONING IN DIAGNOSTIC APPLICATIONS

Diagnostic applications have always been well-suited domains for knowledge-based systems. The early research in knowledge-based systems was largely based on medical diagnosis (e.g., Mycin, INTERNIST) and on equipment diagnosis (e.g., GenAID, CATS, COOKER). In this section, we describe an alternative manner for performing diagnosis that eliminates some problems inherent in the rule-based (or *associational*) techniques described previously.

In this book we have described the concept of predicting a system's behavior by *associating* a set of inputs (i.e., sensors or user-entered information) to a set of observed faults. This mapping is based on the experience of experts in diagnosing the equipment and is usually expressed in terms of rules. Thus, we can often use black-box knowledge as described in Section 1.4.1 without really knowing the internal composition of the system being diagnosed (the *target* system). By historical information about past system behavior, we can determine future behavior to some level of certainty. This was illustrated through the example of an auto mechanic who may not really understand how a car works but who is nevertheless able to fix mechanical difficulties because of his acquired associational knowledge (gathered over an extended period) relating outward symptoms to specific causes. The mechanic illustrates the use of abductive reasoning (defined in Chapter 3). His experiential knowledge of a car's operation is "modeled" within a traditional system's knowledge base, giving a system its diagnostic capabilities.

However, abductive reasoning systems have traditionally been hindered by the difficulties faced with extracting the needed knowledge from its sources, namely, the human expert [Hoffman, 1987]. The two major reasons for this are that such knowledge is typically underdocumented and experts are often either unwilling or incapable of properly articulating their knowledge to a knowledge engineer. This is due in part to the knowledge possessed by experts being in a "compiled" form. That is, the experts themselves may be unaware of how their knowledge evolved and why it is correct from a theoretical point of view. They know only that it works because they have seen it work repeatedly throughout their years of experience.

Engineers, scientists, and skilled technicians, on the other hand, generally possess a much deeper understanding of the domain of interest. They do not treat the domain as a black box, but rather use a *model* to describe its behavior. This enables them to handle successfully problems and situations that they have never seen before.

Scarl [Scarl, 1991] describes three types of models as (1) equational, (2) stochastic, and (3) causal. Equational systems are mathematically based, stochastic systems are statistically based, and causal models are *device centered*, where a system is described by a representation of the devices that compose it.

Model-based reasoning systems attempt to solve problems by representing and reasoning with a deeper understanding of the application domain (such as provided by causal models). This domain is typically embodied in the context of a physical system (natural or man-made). The generic diagnostic procedures are embedded in an algorithmic process that makes use of a device-centered causal model of the target physical system. This model is used to identify possible causes of the failure, thus the name model-based reasoning. The problem of knowledge acquisition from an expert is altogether eliminated and replaced by the preparation of a representation of the system model often consisting of schematic diagrams. This effort, although nontrivial by any definition since it requires the development of a model, is considerably less complex due to the absence of the interaction with an expert.

The generic diagnostic procedures can be likened to the knowledge possessed by an experienced troubleshooter who, by using a few measuring devices and his knowledge of component behavior, can look at a schematic of a faulty system and identify the failed component(s). This technique, however, is not device dependent as it still requires the model of the target system to perform the diagnosis. Thus, the same model-based reasoning system can be used to diagnose other target systems by simply replacing the model.

The model can be likened to a knowledge base, while the model-based reasoning algorithm can be compared to a special-purpose inference engine in the more traditional abductive knowledge-based systems. In model-based reasoning systems, the generic diagnostic knowledge is incorporated in the inference engine, while the knowledge base (model) represents the schematic of the system being diagnosed.

Most of the early researchers in model-based techniques concentrated their efforts in the relatively simple area of combinatorial digital circuits [Genesereth, 1984; de Kleer, 1979; Davis, 1984]. One reason for this was that in such systems, the behavior of a component depends only on its immediate neighbor(s), making local behavior the limiting feature within the model. One of these systems called DART [Genesereth, 1984] generates for output a set of diagnostic tests to be performed by a technician.

Other researchers, such as Davis [Davis, 1984], reasoned about the model by looking for *discrepancies* between the behavior of the actual system and that predicted by the model under the same conditions. He reasoned that any discrepancies found were due to malfunction of a component in the actual system.

Rules have been found adequate to represent the *causal knowledge* of many model-based systems. Davis, in fact, found rules to be quite effective and separated them into two types: *simulation rules*, which simulate the physical constraints of the device (i.e., the flow of electricity), and *inference rules*, which represent conclusions that can be made about the device. Another research system called HOIST [Whitehead, 1987], which diagnoses the operation of mechanical devices, also uses rules as the main knowledge representation. More recently, other implementations of model-based reasoning, as described below, have used frames as the representation paradigm.

Research performed at NASA Kennedy Space Center [Scarl, 1987] has focused on the on-line monitoring of process systems. The result of this work is the Knowledge-based Autonomous Test Engineer (KATE). KATE has some features that are similar to the work of Davis. It is based on local behavior of components being used to describe the behavior of an entire system. Nevertheless, its application domain, the real-time monitoring, diagnosis, and control of process systems, introduces a significant difficulty: System behavior cannot be described solely through the local behavior of its components. This represents a significant leap forward from the combinatorial systems described above because in this domain, global behavior can influence the behavior of individual components. For example, the pressure drop through a valve is dependent not only on the geometry of the valve itself but also on the flow of the medium. The latter is heavily influenced by other system elements beyond the neighboring ones. Additionally, sensor failure, and not a component failure, is often the cause of the discrepancies. Lastly, real-time operation is typically quite demanding, requiring a solution in the order of one to two seconds.

Currently, research in model-based reasoning has taken many different directions. Nevertheless, we focus on KATE as an example of how model-based reasoning can be implemented. Let us, therefore, describe it in more detail.

9.2.1 Description of a Model-based Reasoning System

The basic premise behind KATE is that the fault-free operation of a physical system can be simulated under various conditions using a model that is based on:

1. The connectivity of the components in the system being modeled.
2. The functionality of each component within the system.

KATE works by continuously monitoring the sensors in the target system and comparing their readings to what would be expected based on the input conditions to the target system. The expected readings are obtained from the model by propagating the input values throughout the model using the local constraints imposed on the components of the system. As long as the physical system is operating normally, the parameters monitored should be in general agreement (within a properly chosen margin of error) with the model's expected values. Any disagreement, however, causes a discrepancy to be noted whose cause must be determined. The first discrepancy noted after a (long) period of normal operation is called the *original discrepancy (OD)*, and this label, OD, is assigned to the sensor that records it.

The KATE diagnoser is invoked immediately upon discovery of the OD. Its purpose is to identify all the *inputs*, *suspects*, and *siblings* of the OD. Using the natural constraints on each component connected to the OD, the diagnoser then tries to determine a *hypothetical value* (hv) for each component suspected of failure (called *suspects*) based on the OD. Since this is quite complex, let us first define what these terms mean.

KATE requires two types of inputs to generate a diagnostic conclusion: *commands* and *measurements*. A *command* is an input describing external parameters that affect the system's operation. Examples of commands include the pressure setting in a pump, the throttle setting on a valve, or the voltage setting on a variable power supply. These parameters are set by outside influences, and knowing their values is necessary to simulate the system operation properly. Commands are typically controlled by either humans or external systems.

The other input type consists of *measurements* from all the sensors within the system. These readings are compared to the predicted fault-free values of the corresponding parameters within the system's model.

Components that are deemed capable of causing the detected discrepancy are called *suspects*. The initial set of suspects is determined from the system's structure by considering all components structurally preceding the OD. KATE considers the OD sensor to be a suspect since it could also malfunction, thus providing an incorrect reading in an otherwise fault-free system. A sensor's *siblings* are those other sensors that depend in any way upon the inputs that affect that sensor.

As mentioned above, a component's *hypothetical value* (hv) describes the state of the component as implied by the observations made (i.e., sensor value or failed component). Thus, the hypothetical value is the value assigned to components and sensors based either on the value of the OD or the value of a suspect. A key process in KATE is the use of functional dependency *inversion* to calculate hypothetical values. Functional inversion is where the functional representations of the components are inverted and values are propagated throughout the system. Computing a hypothetical value using inversion requires understanding what the measurement of the OD is telling us about the state of one suspect.

Diagnosis is performed by taking the suspect components and exonerating them until one (or a limited set) is found that can either be demonstrably declared the culprit or cannot be exonerated. KATE uses a consistency algorithm to search for some fault that can explain what the sensors are showing [Scarl, 1987]. It does not, however, have to test all components against all sensors because it bases its search on the OD. Therefore, instead of randomly generating hypothetical faults for the suspect, the OD is used to determine possible faults.

Scarl [Scarl, 1985] describes the four criteria that declare a suspect to be *innocent* and, thus, exonerated as:

1. The suspect controls the OD only through components known to be innocent.
2. No hypothetical value can be established for the suspect because the functional dependency of the OD cannot be inverted.
3. The suspect's hypothetical value agrees with its expected value.
4. The assumption that the suspect actually has its hypothetical value does not cause all sensors to become consistent.

It must be noted that only one of the above has to be true for the suspect to be exonerated. KATE checks each suspect by considering what would happen if the component failed and calculating hv's for other components and sensors based on the failed value. The value of a failed discrete component is the negation of its normal value. Analog components are more difficult to represent because a failure mode has to be known *a priori*. If the simulated sensor's hypothetical value matches the physical system readings, then that suspect is considered a final suspect [Fulton, 1990].

KATE handles nonlocal phenomena through *pseudo-objects*. Pseudo-objects model system parameters by creating nonexisting components in the model whose attributes contain the system parameters. These parameters are used in calculations to determine global influences on the individual component. For example, the value of current in an electric circuit cannot be calculated from the functions of each component. The calculations require data about all the other components in the circuit and how these components are connected. Other parameters such as flow, resistance, pressure, temperature, and so forth also require pseudo-objects for them to be calculated throughout the system. Pseudo-objects are used to form a network that does not necessarily correspond to the way in which the actual components are physically connected, but that interacts with the components to simulate accurately the target system. This allows KATE to handle problems significantly more complex than local combinatorial problems.

Unlike other model-based systems that use rules to represent the model, KATE uses frames. Each component in the system is represented by an instantiation of a higher-level, more general frame corresponding to the type of component being represented. The structure of the system is expressed through slots in the frame that describe the neighboring component and serve as the input and receive its output. The functionality is also declared through the value of a slot, which is typically represented in a mathematical or logical form. Other information such as the component description, its units, its range, and so forth are also expressed through slots in the instantiation frame representing a component. The frame's relationship to more general classes is indicated through the *an-instance-of* (AIO) and a-kind-of (AKO) slots. Figure 9.1 shows a typical frame for the model-based system KATE.

```
(object 3-INPUT-RELAY
   (AKO RELAY)
   (NOMENCLATURE "relay")
   (INPUTS ((ELECTRICAL-INPUT-1 ANALOG-VALUE)
            (ELECTRICAL-INPUT-2 ANALOG-VALUE)
            (ELECTRICAL-COMMAND ANALOG-VALUE)))
   (OUTPUTS (ELECTRICAL-OUTPUT ANALOG-VALUE))
   (OUTPUT-FUNCTIONS
      (ELECTRICAL-OUTPUT
         (cond ((and ELECTRICAL-INPUT-1
                     (>ELECTRICAL-COMMAND THRESHOLD-VALUE))
                ELECTRICAL-INPUT-1)
               ((and ELECTRICAL-INPUT-2
                     (<ELECTRICAL-COMMAND THRESHOLD-VALUE))
                ELECTRICAL-INPUT-2)
               (t 0.0))))
   (PARAMETERS (THRESHOLD-VALUE 3.5))
   (TOLERANCE (ELECTRICAL-OUTPUT 0.2))
   (DELAY 0.1)
   (UNITS (ELECTRICAL-OUTPUT UNITS)) )
```

FIGURE 9.1   KATE Frame Representation

9.2.2 Example of Model-based Reasoning

The concepts of model-based reasoning, discrepancy, and suspects can be more easily described through a simple example developed by Scarl [Scarl, 1987]. Consider the network depicted in Figure 9.2 [Scarl, 1987] which details a hypothetical connection of components. In this diagram, commands are represented by rectangles at the top, measurements by rectangles at the bottom, and components by circles. Discrepant sensors are shaded and measurement *N* is the OD. The initial set of suspects can be determined by creating a list of all components whose output affects the value of N, either directly or indirectly. These are

$$(E\ F\ G\ I\ J)$$

This list is obtained by performing an analysis of the structure (connectivity) of the system. Each of these suspects is then individually hypothesized to be the culprit, and the consistency of this hypothesis is tested using the structure as well as the function of the other components and measurements ($L\ M\ O\ P$). The inconsistency of some suspects will cause them to be exonerated one by one until a minimal list of suspects remains. Let us now analyze the example to exonerate some suspects.

I is quickly exonerated because its hypothetical value cannot make the value indicated by O consistent with the original discrepancy identified since they are not connected. If G were the culprit, we would expect measurement P would be discrepant which it is not; thus, G is found innocent. If E and/or F were the culprits, then L and/or M also would be discrepant. Likewise, the presence of measurement O proves measurement N is innocent. This leaves component J as the last remaining suspect and no information exists that can exonerate it.

This example shows the interrelationships among the various components, and how the structure of the system can exonerate a suspect simply because the suspect is not connected to the original discrepancy. Note that the example does not take functionality into account. Functionality is used for

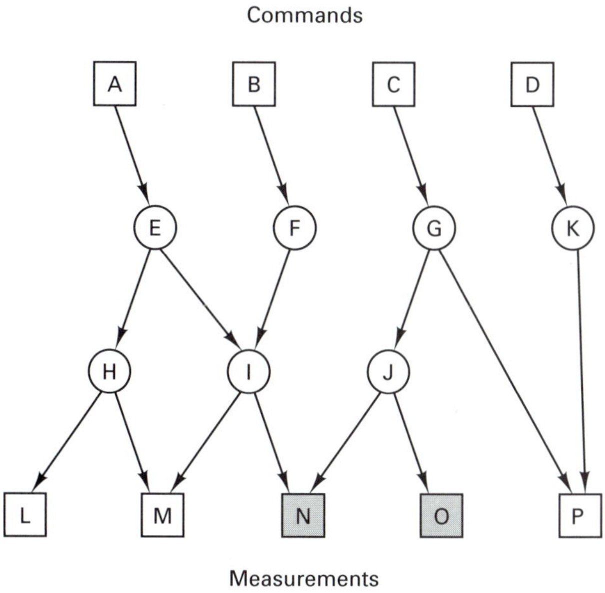

Commands

FIGURE 9.2 Model-based Reasoning Example Diagram

Measurements

modeling the system and determining the discrepancy. It is also used to exonerate some suspects when their quantitative behavior is found inconsistent with the OD.

9.2.3 Advantages and Disadvantages of Model-based Reasoning

Model-based reasoning reduces the burden of knowledge acquisition, shifting the work from acquiring all possible symptomatic behavior from an expert (associational knowledge) to that of developing a general model of underlying causes of the behavior. While this is frequently easier than the former, we should mention that for some systems, (those with a large branching factor, and/or those where the branches reconverge) this can pose significant model-development difficulties. Another advantage of model-based reasoning is that every possible malfunction does not need to be explicitly identified ahead of time, as required in abductive systems. By the nature of the model of the system, it is assumed that every possible component described can be a cause of a failure, regardless of whether it ever has been before.

While model-based systems have some significant advantages they are not without detractions. A primary weakness is their inability to manipulate heuristic knowledge. While this was previously listed as an advantage, it becomes a detraction when heuristic knowledge is a significant element of the problem domain. Additionally, model-based systems do not handle uncertainty easily. Although these features could be added, they represent a departure from the concept of reasoning from structure and function. Additionally, most model-based reasoning research has been based on the assumption that the system suffers only a single malfunction at any one time. While this is a reasonable assumption for most applications, it is nevertheless an issue that must be considered when determining the applicability of the model-based approach to some problem domain.

While many diagnostic problems are well suited to model-based reasoning, there are problems that do not make good applications for model-based reasoning techniques and for which the traditional abductive reasoning techniques can be superior in performance. These are problems where models either do not exist or cannot be easily described. To illustrate this, consider the following example.

An electrical turbine-generator is a large cylindrical device approximately 15 feet in diameter and 25 to 30 feet long. The device actually consists of two cylinders mounted one inside the other. The outer cylinder is held stationary while the smaller, inner cylinder rotates at speeds up to 60 revolutions per second. Electrical currents of thousands of amperes and up to 25,000 volts are generated in copper conductors mounted on the surfaces of these cylinders as they rotate by each other. To avoid overheating of their internal components, these generators are hermetically sealed and blanketed in an environment of hydrogen gas pressurized at up to 75 psi (pounds per square inch). Some larger generators also have internal water cooling systems. The potential for problems in these devices is significant, as is their potential cost of repair and the replacement of their power output while they are being repaired.

It should be obvious that the internal environment of these generators is quite hostile not only to direct human observation, but also to a lesser, yet still significant degree, to measurement devices. Thus, no one knows exactly what goes on inside a generator during its normal operation, much less when it is operating abnormally. This causes all measurements of the internal states of these generators to be indirect and provides a weak set of direct cause-and-effect relationships. As a result, to describe the process within the generator as it operates is quite difficult and an appropriate model cannot be formulated. Application of model-based reasoning to this problem is therefore inappropriate, making abductive reasoning with heuristic knowledge the most appropriate diagnostic technique.

9.3 QUALITATIVE REASONING

Like model-based reasoning, qualitative reasoning (also called qualitative simulation) is in its relative infancy as a research area of AI. It is closely related to model-based reasoning since some models that are developed are actually qualitative models. In the words of Forbus [Forbus, 1988]:

> *Qualitative simulation is crucial in the engineering applications of AI because it helps capture the common-sense understanding of the world that is the foundation of engineering knowledge.*

For example, when an object is tossed in the air, it is well known that it reaches a maximum height proportional to the force with which it was thrown and then it falls back to earth. If we are determining the trajectory of a ballistic missile, it is quite important to know how high the missile will rise and how fast it will reach the peak. But a qualitative understanding of the cause-and-effect relationships involved in this process is sufficient for 12-year-old Little League baseball players.

Many decisions made by engineers are based on this type of qualitative knowledge of systems instead of the more rigorous quantitative knowledge. While exact mathematical modeling of systems has existed for many years and is well understood, qualitative simulation can complement these techniques in several ways. In Forbus' [Forbus, 1988] view:

1. Qualitative simulation can provide answers when insufficient data are available for a quantitative simulation.
2. When a more detailed form of analysis is desired, qualitative simulation can provide an organizational structure for this task.

Given a structural representation of a system to be modeled as well as its initial conditions, qualitative simulations can predict many possible behaviors of the system. Whereas no theoretically possible behavior is overlooked by the simulation, other behaviors that are not really possible can also be predicted [Kuipers 1986]. For example, a qualitative simulation of a tossed ball could derive a possible behavior to be that the ball will continue rising forever. Yet, the actual behavior, the ball decelerating to zero velocity at the maximum height and then accelerating towards the ground, will not be missed as one possible behavior.

Qualitative simulation is advantageous whenever there is insufficient information to simulate the phenomenon quantitatively or when the nature of the problem precludes a detailed analysis. For example, in the design of a complex process such as a nuclear power plant, it may be desirable to know how a critical parameter (e.g., core temperature) will react to a change in the setting of some particular control valve. If it is only important to know whether this parameter will increase or decrease in magnitude, a qualitative simulation may prove adequate in lieu of modeling the entire system quantitatively.

The only disadvantage to a qualitative simulation is that it may not provide sufficient accuracy for the solution of some problems. This is not a problem with the technique itself, but rather with its proper application.

To illustrate qualitative simulation, the next section discusses QSIM, a qualitative simulation language developed by Kuipers. Most of the examples discussed in this section are taken from [Kuipers, 1986].

9.3.1 QSIM—A Qualitative Reasoning Language

QSIM, a qualitative simulation language, attempts to use physical constraints to describe what qualitative states are possible for the system being simulated. Qualitative states are defined as a set of parameters, each of which is either increasing, decreasing, or steady. This language describes a system through symbols that represent the system's *physical parameters* and *constraints* that define the relationships between the parameters. For example, to describe relationships such as

$$\text{Acceleration} = \frac{dv}{dt} \text{ , where } v \text{ is the velocity}$$

$$\text{Force} = \text{mass} * \text{acceleration,}$$

QSIM uses DERIV(vel acc) and MULT(mass acc force), where DERIV is the derivative relationship shown above, and MULT is the multiplication operation also shown above.

Other constraints simply describe a monotonically increasing or decreasing relationship between two parameters. For example, "larger wattage light bulbs produce more lumens" can be expressed as M+(wattage lumens) while "decreasing the size of a computer increases its processing speed" can be expressed as M−(computer-size speed).

Each physical parameter is represented as a function of time that has a finite number of *critical points*. A critical point is where the function representing the physical parameter changes value. The value of the function describing the physical parameter is represented qualitatively at the critical points. A totally ordered set of *landmark values* represents all the values of the physical parameter at its critical points.

Kuipers represents time as a set of *distinguished time points* on the time line. Only two types of time elements can be defined: (1) the time at a distinguished time point or (2) the interval between distinguished time points. The *initial state* of the system is defined by the qualitative values (i.e., increasing, decreasing, or steady) for the various physical parameters at a particular point in time or within an interval between points in time.

The basis of the qualitative simulation is the determination of all the possible combinations of values for all the physical parameters at a point or interval in time. This is defined as the *qualitative state* (QS) of the system being simulated. A sequence of qualitative states describes a qualitative behavior of the system. But the many combinations of qualitative values makes for a prohibitively large number of potential qualitative states. One important aspect of the qualitative simulation, therefore, is to apply the constraints that describe the system's behavior to prune the number of feasible qualitative states. If more than one qualitative change remains as feasible after the constraints have been applied, however, then the current qualitative state has multiple successors and the simulation produces a tree.

Kuipers more formally defines the qualitative state of a function, f, that represents a physical parameter at time t, by the pair $(qval, qdir)$. $qval$ is the qualitative value of the parameter. It is not represented as a number, but in terms of landmark values, such as a maximum height, minimum acceleration, and so forth, or as a value between two landmark values. $qdir$ is the direction of change of the qualitative value of the physical parameter. Thus, they can take the following values:

$$qval = l_j \qquad \text{if } f(t) = l_j \text{ (a landmark value)}$$
$$= (l_j, l_{j+1}) \qquad \text{if } f(t) \text{ is an element of } (l_j, l_{j+1})$$
$$qdir = \text{inc(reasing)} \qquad \text{if the derivative of } f > 0$$
$$= \text{std(eady)} \qquad \text{if the derivative of } f = 0$$
$$= \text{dec(reasing)} \qquad \text{if the derivative of } f < 0.$$

The qualitative state of f on (t_i, t_{i+1}) is, therefore, $QS(f, t)$ when t is an element of (t_i, t_{i+1}).

Likewise, the *qualitative behavior* of function f is the sequence of qualitative states of f:

$$QS(f, t_0), QS(f, t_0, t_1), QS(f, t_1), \ldots, QS(f, t_{n1}, t_n), QS(f, t_n)$$

Kuipers also defines a *system* as a set of functions F, such that

$$F = [f_1, f_2, \ldots, f_n]$$

where f_i is one physical parameter and the qualitative state of F at time t_1 is:

$$QS(F, t_1) = [QS(f_1, t_1), QS(f_2, t_1), QS(f_3, t_1), \ldots, QS(f_n, t_1)]$$

The *qualitative behavior* of the system is the sequence of qualitative states

$$QS(F, t_0), QS(F, t_0, t_1), QS(F, t_1), \ldots, QS(F, t_n)$$

The objective of qualitative simulation is to determine the next feasible qualitative state (or states) of the physical parameters. If the present QS is defined at a point, then the next state would naturally be in the interval between the present time point and the next distinguished time point. If, on the other hand, the present QS is defined in a time interval, then the next state will be at the distinguished time point that terminates the interval. A physical parameter is restricted to a predetermined set of possible transitions from one qualitative state to the next. There are two types of transitions: those moving from a time-point to a time interval, called *p transitions*, and those moving from an interval to a point, which are called *i-transitions*. Figure 9.3 [Kuipers, 1986] depicts these transitions.

The example in the following section illustrates the performance of qualitative simulation about a ball being thrown upwards [Kuipers, 1986].

9.3.2 A Qualitative Simulation Example Using QSIM

To illustrate qualitative simulation consider the simple act of throwing a ball upwards. The physical parameters that we must simulate are:

Y = the height to which the ball rises (not necessarily the maximum)

V = the speed of the ball as it rises and falls

A = acceleration acting on the ball

The constraints involved are

$$\text{DERIV}(Y, V): V = \frac{dY}{dt},$$

$$\text{DERIV}(V, A): A = \frac{dV}{dt}, \text{ and}$$

$$A(t) \qquad = g < 0 \text{ (acceleration = gravity as a constant).}$$

p-transition	From $QS(f, t_i)$	To $QS(f, t_i, t_{i+1})$
P_1	$<l_j, std>$	$<l_j, std>$
P_2	$<l_j, std>$	$<(l_j, l_{j+1}), inc>$
P_3	$<l_j, std>$	$<(l_{j-1}, l_j), dec>$
P_4	$<l_j, inc>$	$<(l_j, l_{j+1}), inc>$
P_5	$<(l_j, l_{j+1}), inc>$	$<(l_j, l_{j+1}), inc>$
P_6	$<l_j, dec>$	$<(l_{j-1}, l_j), dec>$
P_7	$<(l_j, l_{j+1}), dec>$	$<(l_j, l_{j+1}), dec>$

i-transition	From $QS(f, t_i, t_{i+1})$	To $QS(f, t_{i+1})$
I_1	$<l_j, std>$	$<l_j, std>$
I_2	$<(l_j, l_{j+1}), inc>$	$<l_{j+1}, std>$
I_3	$<(l_j, l_{j+1}), inc>$	$<l_{j+1}, inc>$
I_4	$<(l_j, l_{j+1}), inc>$	$<(l_j, l_{j+1}), inc>$
I_5	$<(l_j, l_{j+1}), dec>$	$<l_j, std>$
I_6	$<(l_j, l_{j+1}), dec>$	$<l_j, std>$
I_7	$<(l_j, l_{j+1}), dec>$	$<(l_j, l_{j+1}), dec>$
I_8	$<(l_j, l_{j+1}), inc>$	$<l^*, std>$
I_9	$<(l_j, l_{j+1}), dec>$	$<l^*, std>$

FIGURE 9.3 Transition Tables for QSIM

The first state is when the ball is initially accelerated (thrown) upwards. This takes place at time t_0. Let us, however, begin our simulation in the second state where the ball is moving upward toward a peak that is yet to be discovered. We can describe the qualitative state of each physical parameter (acceleration, velocity, and height) within the time interval $[t_0, t_1]$ as

QS(A, t_0, t_1) = (g, std), where qval = g, a landmark value, and qdir = std (constant).

QS(V, t_0, t_1) = ([0, ∞], dec), where velocity is decreasing in the time interval $[t_0, t_1]$ and the qualitative value of the velocity is somewhere between zero and the initial velocity, which could be any value.

QS(Y, t_0, t_1) = ([0, ∞], inc), where the height is increasing in the time interval of interest and its qualitative value is somewhere between the initial value (0) and the maximum value, which could be anything between 0 and infinity.

The interval $[t_0, t_1]$ is the time interval during which the ball is moving upward. The objective of this example is to compute the new qualitative state QS(F, t_1).

The first step is to determine the possible transitions from the present qualitative state to the next. This is done individually for each of the three physical parameters. Note that since the simulation is moving from a time interval to a time point, only the i-transitions of Figure 9.3 are applicable.

For QS(A, t_0, t_1) $\rightarrow$ QS(A, t_1): Since the gravitational acceleration is a constant, the only possible transition for this state change is I_1. Therefore, for A

$$A \quad I_1 \quad <g, std> \rightarrow <g, std>$$

For QS(V, t_0, t_1) $\rightarrow$ QS(V, t_1): The possible transitions are I_5, I_6, I_7, and I_9. These are the only ones whose middle column in the second table of Figure 9.3 matches the conditions during the interval [t_0, t_1]. Note that in I_9, QSIM discovers a new landmark value. The transitions are as follows:

$$V \quad I_5 \quad <(0, \infty), dec> \rightarrow <0, std>$$
$$I_6 \quad <(0, \infty), dec> \rightarrow <0, dec>$$
$$I_7 \quad <(0, \infty), dec> \rightarrow <(0, \infty), dec>$$
$$I_9 \quad <(0, \infty), dec> \rightarrow <L^*, std>$$

For QS(Y, t_0, t_1) $\rightarrow$ QS(Y, t_1): The possible transitions are I_4 and I_8. I_8 also allows for the discovery of a new landmark value.

$$Y \quad I_4 \quad <(0, \infty), inc> \rightarrow <(0, \infty), inc>$$
$$I_8 \quad <(0, \infty), inc> \rightarrow <L^*, std>$$

Note that since l_{j+1} is infinity, which is not a landmark value, I_2 and I_3 are not feasible. This is in contrast to parameter V, which, as it decreases in the interval [0, ∞], may decrease to 0.

The next step is to filter these possible new states by determining which are consistent with the individual constraints. Those found inconsistent are discarded. The remaining possible states are further filtered using progressively more restrictive constraints. Kuipers identifies that a variety of filters are used to accomplish this, such as constraint-based consistency criteria, the Waltz algorithm [Waltz, 1975], and global filters.

The above filtering process continues until the following global interpretations of the transitions to the next qualitative state remain:

Y	V	A
I_4	I_7	I_1
I_8	I_6	I_1

The first interpretation represents a qualitative state that is identical with the previous one. Since this is not an interesting new qualitative state, it can be discarded. The only other possibility specifies a unique successor state. The new qualitative state is therefore

$$QS(A, t_1) = [g, \text{std}]$$

$$QS(V, t_1) = [0, \text{dec}]$$

$$QS(Y, t_1) = [Y_{\text{new}}, \text{std}]$$

The last qualitative state indicates that a new landmark value has been discovered. If the simulation were to continue, then the next qualitative state would be $QS(F, t_1, t_2)$ and a procedure similar to the one above must be invoked again.

In many situations, however, QSIM may not be able to arrive at a unique next qualitative state such as was done for the above example. Instead, the simulation may identify several possible next states that are equally plausible. In such cases, a tree must be formed and all the qualitative states must be extended independently of one another.

The QSIM algorithm is not the only one that exists, but it is representative of the idea of qualitative modeling and simulation.

9.4 CASE-BASED REASONING

Human problem solving is based somewhat on the application of experiences to the current problem. Experts become experts by doing and experiencing. In the heuristic systems described in the last few chapters, an expert's knowledge is represented as compiled knowledge, that is, rules of thumb, shortcuts, and so forth. However, it is unlikely that when asked, an expert will be able to recall the details of more than a few problem-solving cases. Thus the experience represented is compiled, rather than explicit.

The concept of case-based reasoning, on the other hand, is founded on the idea of using explicit, documented experiences to solve new problems. Consider the following examples that illustrate this process [Klein 1985].

A fireground commander was coordinating his crew as they combatted a fire at a four-story apartment building. He looked up and noticed billboards on the roof, and recalled an earlier incident where the flames had burned through the wooden supports of the billboards, sending them crashing to the street below. He then ordered that the spectators be moved further back to prevent injury from falling billboards.

Another fireground commander noticed some peculiar properties in a cloud of smoke at a fire. He recalled an incident in which toxic smoke had been given off showing the same features of density, color, and heaviness as the cloud he saw. He ordered his crew to use breathing support systems.

In both of these examples, the decision maker used previous explicit experiences, called *cases*, to help him solve the present problem. He retrieved the appropriate cases from a larger set of cases. The similarities between the present problem and the retrieved case were the basis for the latter's selection.

A case-based reasoning system consists of three basic components:

1. A *library* of historical cases.
2. A means of using the key elements of the present problem to find and retrieve the most similar case(s) from the case library.
3. A means for making modifications to the proposed solution when the case on which the solution is based is not identical with the current problem.

The construction and organization of a library of cases is a critical task. The effect of retrieving an improperly matched case [Barletta, 1988] is often more computationally expensive than selecting the wrong rule to execute in a rule-based system. Inefficient searches through the case library due to its poor organization can result in unacceptable performance. The case library may be organized as a flat database or hierarchically based on some organizational structure within inputs or goals.

The cases in the library must be indexed to allow for efficient searches. How these indices are expressed is a key issue in case-based reasoning because if they are defined too broadly, too many cases may be retrieved as similar to the problem. Conversely, if they are expressed too specifically, there may be no case deemed similar. One way to approach this problem is to use *explanation-based indexing* [Barletta, 1988]. This technique addresses the indexing problem by providing a set of *observables* (features) of the problem description, both before and after an action. This set is coupled with an explanation of why they were given and a description of the goal for which the action was taken.

It seems natural that the application of parallel search methods would significantly decrease the case retrieval time. While this is quite likely, it must be understood that even this will not overcome poor indexing of cases [Kolodner, 1988].

Building a cased-based system involves the development of a fairly robust and well-indexed set of cases. These cases can be developed by an expert based on his experiences. Ideally, the case library would be composed of documented historical cases.

Using the system's knowledge consists of providing an input case (i.e., problem) and asking the system to provide the appropriate matching case from its library, an expert then compares the significant features of the case retrieved against those of the present problem. If the case retrieved is the same as the present problem, then the expert tries another test. Figure 9.4 shows a situation in which the target case T was not retrieved for the input

	Input	Target	Current	
Age	25	28	22	
Occupation	Carpenter	Systems analysis	Plumber	
Purpose of loan	Buy Pinto	Buy Horizon	Buy Continental	Importance
Amount of loan	$5200	$5000	$6400	
Years at residence	4	2	4	

FIGURE 9.4   Case Retrieval Example

case *I* [Riesbeck, 1988]. Instead, the system retrieved the current case *C*, which represents a mistake. This points to a problem in the matching and retrieval process.

One way to address this problem is to define the fields that are more important than others and assign greater weight to them in the matching process. Alternatively, tolerances specifying what constitutes a match for numeric fields can be specified. Lastly, additional fields could be added to the cases to index them better [Riesbeck, 1988].

9.4.1 Example of Case-based Reasoning

Case-based reasoning is an excellent technique to use when many well-documented histories of past problems and their solutions exist. For example, the legal profession thrives on judicial precedent, where a decision about a current case can be dependent on a landmark decision on a similar case. The similarities as well as the differences between the present and the landmark case have to be carefully considered before a decision is made by a judge, or an appeal is made by either the defendant or the plaintiff. As an example, the HYPO system [Ashley, 1988] is designed to assist in the analysis of court cases dealing with trade secret laws by using other cases that have been previously decided.

To illustrate the process of case-based reasoning, let us examine how real estate property is appraised. The value of a property is generally determined by the market price in the area where the property is located. A property similar in size, function, and features must be found in the same area so that the market price can be determined. There is a large library of cases readily available from the local realty association or the local government records that can be used to complete this task.

Property appraisal or valuation is a domain characterized by having a single parameter in its solution—the value of the property being appraised. This makes it different from most of other case-based reasoning domains, since these other domains require the satisfaction of multiple goals, which are related to one another. Because property appraisal has a single goal, it is particularly important to find the best possible answer. Additionally, due to the heuristic nature of the domain when even the experts may reach somewhat different answers while having the same data at their disposition, it is essential to achieve consistency.

Property appraisal is a time-consuming task requiring significant research and expense. There are three basic methods of appraisal (1) the cost approach, (2) the market data or sales comparison approach, and (3) the income approach.

The cost approach is based upon the reproduction cost of the building plus the value of the land; the market data approach is based upon the selling price of similar properties in the market; and the income approach is based upon the amount of net income the property can produce. For a more detailed description of the methods, see [Creteau, 1974; AIREA, 1988; Boyce, 1984]. While an appraiser uses a combination of these methods to make a property valuation, the most popular, especially in the appraisal of residential properties, is the market data approach.

The market data approach of appraisal operates on the premise that an informed buyer would pay for a property no more than the cost of acquiring an existing property with the same features [Boyce, 1984]. The sales price in a transaction is then a reflection of the knowledge that both the seller and the buyer have of the market. This justifies the use of similar properties that have been sold recently (i.e., *comparables*) to determine the market value. The principle involved is that each factor or element of comparison in a property has a contribution to value, and this contribution may be reflected in a sales price differential.

A knowledge-based system has been developed to determine automatically the appraised value of a property using case-based reasoning [Gonzalez, 1992]. This system uses the following elements of comparison:

Living area in square feet
Number of bedrooms
Number of bathrooms
Architectural style of the house
Age of the house
Location (neighborhood)
Date of sale
Type of cooling equipment

Type of heating equipment

Type of garage

Site or lot size

Availability of a swimming pool

The first step in the process is *case retrieval*. The case-based reasoner looks in a case library of recently sold properties, retrieves the ten best cases, and ranks them in order of decreasing similarity. The evaluation of a case is performed by assigning weights to each element of comparison and determining how to evaluate differences in these elements.

The next step is *case adaptation*. Since the retrieved properties are not precisely the same as the property being evaluated, even if the degree of similarity is high, each retrieved case must be *adapted* to compensate for its differences with the appraised property. This is done using *critics*. A critic is a rule that increases or decreases the actual sold price of a retrieved property based upon a difference between it and the property being appraised.

For example, let us assume that house A is the appraised property and house B is a recently sold case that the system retrieved as one of the top ten matches. The case-based reasoner adapts the sales price of B based on how well it matches A. If A has a swimming pool, but B does not, this represents a difference that must be compensated for. The swimming pool critic might indicate that the value of a pool is $5,000. Thus, if B sold for $75,000, its adapted sales price (which reflects an appropriate price for A) would now be $80,000.

The adaption process is cumulative and is done for all the elements of comparison. For instance, the critic for living area might specify a compensation of $500 for every 50 square feet of difference. If B has 2,000 square feet while A has 2,100 square feet, then the adapted cost of B would now be $81,000.

But too many adaptions to the cases can result in inaccuracies. The Property Appraisal System penalizes each case for the extent of adaptions made. The more adaptions, the higher the penalty. This leads to a *comfort factor* that tells the system which of the ten adapted cases is most applicable to the house being appraised. The system ranks the ten adapted cases in order of decreasing comfort factor and selects the top three, since that is the traditional number of comparisons used in the appraisal business. Lastly, it takes the average of the three and uses that value as the appraised value of the subject property.

9.4.2 Advantages and Disadvantages of Case-based Reasoning

Some advantages of case-based reasoning over the more traditional deductive rule-based systems are [Kovarik, 1988]:

1. Case-based reasoning is patterned after human reasoning. While rule-based systems depend on the prior experience of an expert, their knowledge is represented quite differently. A case library is a more formal and explicit representation of this knowledge, since it details the case history of the domain directly rather than through the interpretation and recollection of an expert. The problems faced before will be compared to the present problem and the solution to the past problem most similar to the present one is then adopted.

2. Case-based reasoning lends itself to analogical reasoning. The use of analogies with past cases is how it solves new problems.

3. The knowledge acquisition process is considerably simplified since the case library may already exist as corporate documentation, possibly even in an electronic database. If a library of cases does not exist, however, an expert can be asked to create it from his experience. This, however, may be more difficult to do than implementing the knowledge in a conventional deductive/abductive knowledge-based system, which, it can be argued, defeats the purpose of case-based reasoning.

4. The base of experience used can be that of an entire organization, rather than that of a single individual.

The disadvantages associated with this technique revolve around the computational cost of a solution. Doing a search in a large, poorly indexed case library can be quite expensive. Therefore, the issues of proper indexing, case library architecture, the "quality" of the cases included in the library, and the proper number of cases to use are of utmost importance in the development of a case-based system. But these are not inherent problems with the technique. They are merely temporary obstacles that require more investigation to be overcome.

9.5 TEMPORAL REASONING

Temporal reasoning is the ability to reason about the time relationships between events. Each of us has a well-developed ability to think in terms of time. Nearly all communication that we have with others makes reference to time and many forms of problem solving rely heavily on the temporal relations between events. As a result, it is recognized that some knowledge-based systems, as well as other AI systems, require temporal reasoning abilities (e.g., diagnostics, planning, intelligent simulation).

Several knowledge representation schemes have evolved for temporal relationships and events [Kovarik, 1989]. One of the most popular and widely accepted models for representing and manipulating time is the interval-based approach developed by Allen in the early 1980s [Allen, 1983]. In his approach, Allen defines all actions or events as *intervals* of time having a nonzero duration. We can mathematically describe an interval as a segment of the time line bounded by two real numbers, (t_1, t_2) where $t_1 < t_2$. Time point t_1 is called the *starting point* of the interval and t_2 its *end point*.

The relationship between two intervals is described by one of seven primitive binary relationships. Suppose that we have two events, E_1 and E_2, which occur in intervals i and j, respectively. See Figure 9.5 [Allen, 1983a]. If the interval i is defined by the ordered pair of time points $<a\ b>$ and j by the pair $<c\ d>$, these primitive binary relationships can be defined graphically as shown in Figure 9.6 [Allen, 1983a] or textually as follows [Allen, 1983b]:

Overlaps: Interval i *overlaps* interval j when they intersect (i.e., a portion of i occurs during j), but i neither wholly contains nor is wholly contained by j. That is, $a < c < b < d$.

Precedes: Interval i *precedes* interval j if i ends before j begins. That is, $a < b < c < d$. A finite duration gap between the two intervals is implied.

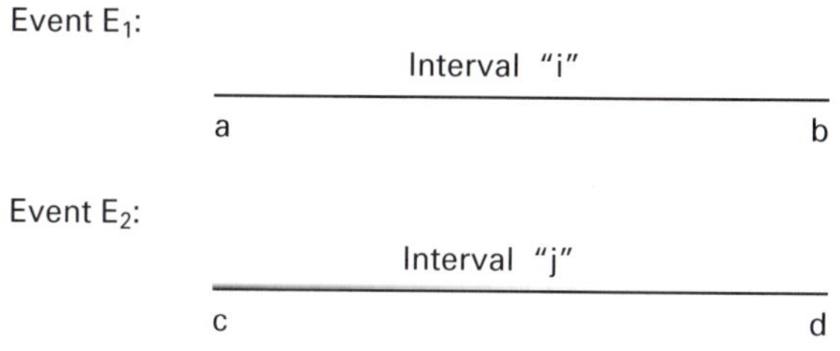

Event E_1:

Interval "i"

a   b

Event E_2:

Interval "j"

c   d

FIGURE 9.5   Time Intervals Associated with Events E_1 and E_2

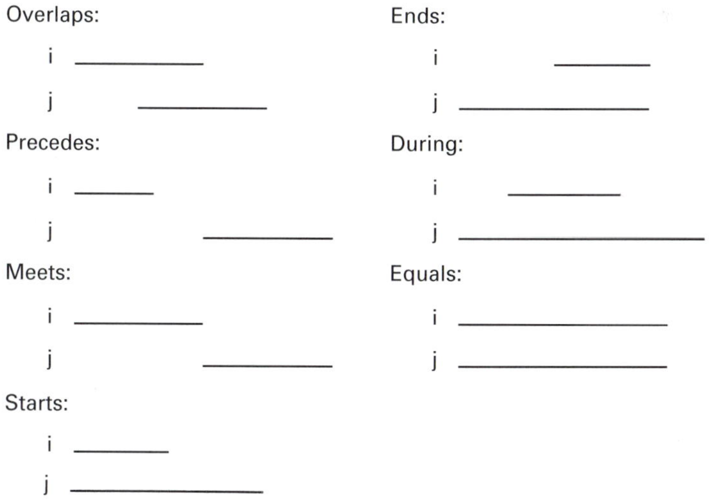

Overlaps: Ends:

i   i

j   j

Precedes: During:

i   i

j   j

Meets: Equals:

i   i

j   j

Starts:

i

j

FIGURE 9.6   Graphical Representation of the Seven Primitive Temporal Relationships

Meets: Interval i *meets* interval j when i ends at the same time j begins, or $a < b = c < d$. There is no gap between the two intervals.

Starts: Interval i *starts* interval j when they have the same starting point but i ends before j, or $a = c < b < d$.

Ends: Interval i *ends* interval j when they both have the same ending point, but i starts after j, or $c < a < b = d$.

During: Interval i is *during* interval j if it is entirely contained within j, but does not start or end j. That is $c < a < b < d$.

Equals: Interval i *equals* interval j if the two intervals are identical or $a = c < b = d$.

Additionally, each of these primitives R has a *converse* relation R', such that R' is the converse of R if and only if [Allen, 1983b]:

$$i \ R' \ j \ <\text{----}> \ j \ R \ i$$

See Figure 9.7 [Allen, 1983]. Since each of the seven primitive relations has one converse relation, there should be a total of 14 ways of ordering points on the time line. However, since the converse of Equal (Equal') is the same as the relation itself, there are only 13 nonequivalent relationships [Allen, 1983b]. Therefore, the entire list of relations is:

$$P, \ M, \ O, \ D, \ S, \ F, \ P', \ M', \ O', \ D', \ S', \ F', \ E$$

It should be obvious from the above discussion that [Ladkin, 1989]:

1. Two intervals i and j cannot exist such that their relationship to each other is not expressed by one of these thirteen relations.
2. Every pair of intervals that can be defined on the time line are related to each other by one and only one of these 13 relations.

Time intervals can also be represented by a *composition* of the relations. These compositions represent constraints between two intervals and an intermediate interval that can be used to deduce relations between the first two. For example [Ladkin, 1989],

$$i \ (\text{Overlaps or Ends}) \ k$$

is true if and only if there exists an intermediate interval j such that

$$(i \ \text{Overlaps} \ j) \ \text{and} \ (j \ \text{Ends} \ k)$$

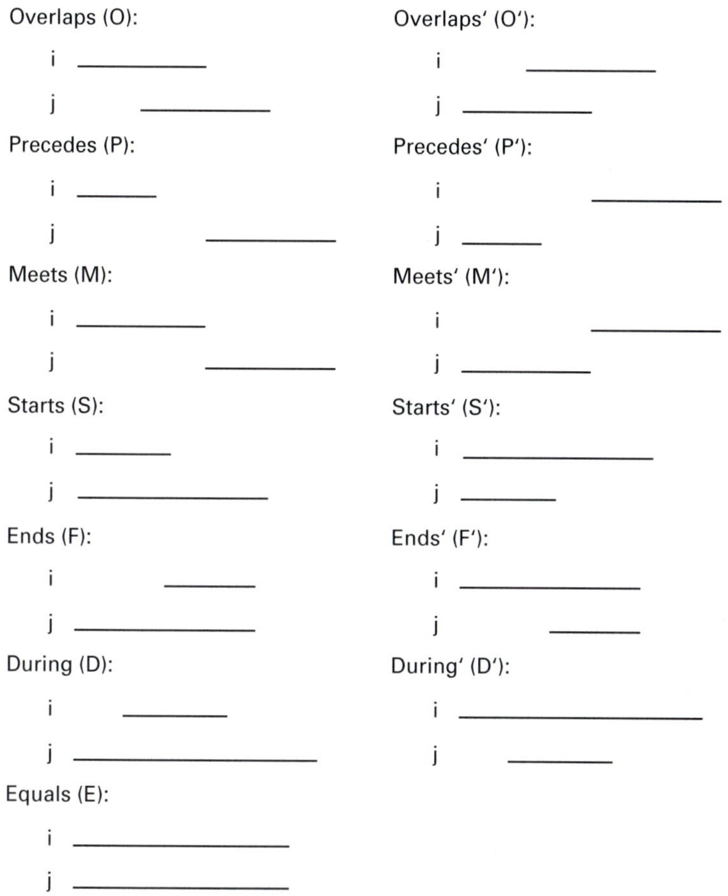

Overlaps (O):

i ————
j ————

Overlaps' (O'):

i ————
j ————

Precedes (P):

i ——
j ————

Precedes' (P'):

i ————
j ——

Meets (M):

i ————
j ————

Meets' (M'):

i ————
j ————

Starts (S):

i ——
j ————

Starts' (S'):

i ————
j ——

Ends (F):

i ————
j ————

Ends' (F'):

i ————
j ——

During (D):

i ————
j ————

During' (D'):

i ————
j ——

Equals (E):

i ————
j ————

FIGURE 9.7 The Complete Set of Primitive Relationships

The resulting interval graph is shown in Figure 9.8 [Ladkin, 1989]. As this figure shows, the starting point of interval k (e.g., point c) can occur at any one of three places:

1. $c < a$ in which case: (i During k)

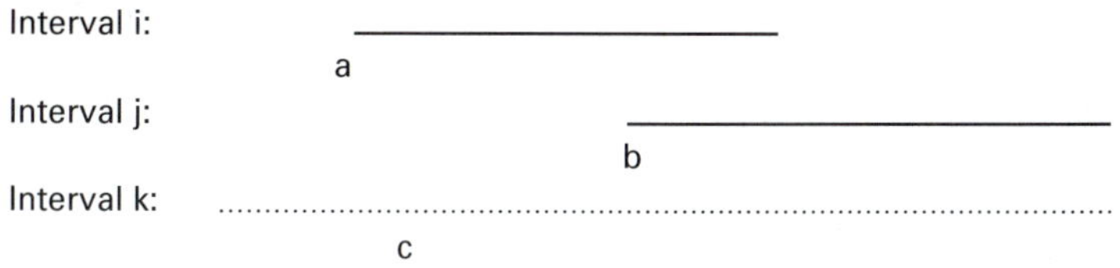

Interval i: ———————
                a
Interval j: ———————
                              b
Interval k: ··
                    c

FIGURE 9.8 The Interval Graph for the Relationship: i (Overlaps *or* Ends) k

2. $c = a$ in which case: (i Starts k)

3. $c > a$ (but $< b$) in which case: (i Overlaps k)

The actual relationship between i and k, therefore, is ambiguous and is represented by the composition of these three possibilities

$$i \ \text{(During or Starts or Overlaps)} \ k$$

Allen describes a transitivity table [Allen, 1983b] that computes these various compositions.

9.5.1 Intervals and Points of Time

The representation of discrete time points is perfectly consistent with interval-based temporal reasoning. While we can say that the measurement of any physical quantity is done in an *instant* of time, a practical definition of an instant is somewhat difficult to imagine. From a theoretical point of view, an instant of time is the temporal equivalent of an impulse function, which has an amplitude of infinity and a duration of zero, and clearly zero duration for an event that occurs is a practical impossibility. No matter how small an interval is, it is still an interval. Thus, we can define a time point as an arbitrarily small interval with respect to the length of the overall task.

Practically speaking, what makes an interval appear to be a point is its relation to the point of reference. For example, the interval of an hour can be looked upon as a point in time when compared to a task that spans several years. However, an interval of one hour cannot be considered a point when the frame of reference is one day. Likewise, when we talk about the earth's geologic periods, intervals of less than one million years are too short to be of interest. We can, therefore, think of intervals as time points within the context of the problem.

9.5.2 The Time Unit System

The Time Unit System is a natural way of representing intervals. Using the analogy of a digital watch [Ladkin, 1989], it displays the interval of time between the changes in the digits. For example, if a watch reads [7:20:18], it is in reality displaying the interval between 7:20:18 and 7:20:19. If it displays only the hours and the minutes, [7:20], then it is really displaying 60-second intervals of time.

Like a digital watch, the time unit system uses a sequence of integers to represent time intervals. These integers are ordered in the sequence to represent the year, month, day, hour, minute, and second of a particular event. For example,

93 represents the year 1993, which is an interval of one year.

93/6 represents the sixth month (June) of the year 1993, which is not only the interval of one month, but also of a very specific month.

93/6/23 represents the twenty-third day of June in 1993, likewise, a very specific interval of one day.

9.5.3 Temporal Reasoning Example

Temporal reasoning involves using a representation like the one presented in the last section to represent events occurring within some system and to use these representations to reason about the processes being represented and to make decisions. Figure 9.9 depicts a rather simple, generic closed-loop system used to cool a heat source. This heat source, shown at the top, could be a nuclear reactor or some piece of machinery.

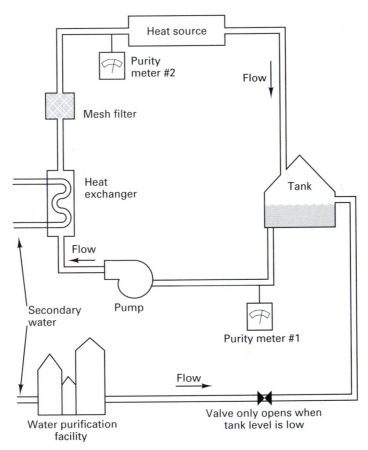

FIGURE 9.9   Simple Closed-loop Cooling System

The key feature of our example is that the purity of the cooling medium (in this case, water) within the system must be very high to prevent deterioration of the equipment being cooled. This is not atypical for industrial or power generating plants. The system pumps pure water throughout the system (from the holding tank through the secondary heat exchanger, the filter, and the heat source back into the tank). Assume that the holding tank is lined with an inert material and is pressurized with a high purity, inert gas, thereby eliminating it as a source of impurities. While the system is closed-looped, some loss of coolant does occur, so a source of replenishing water must be available. This source of water is of an unacceptably low purity and requires purification before it is added to the system. Thus, all make-up (replenishing) water is passed through a purifier before being fed into the holding tank. Our task is to develop a diagnostic knowledge-based system that quickly detects the causes of any impurities within the coolant to isolate the problem and avoid any equipment damage.

To simplify this situation, let us assume that only two sources of impurities exist:

1. **Impurities from the secondary heat exchanger.** The secondary heat exchanger removes heat from the primary coolant system, transferring it to a secondary water supply, which is highly impure. This is OK because it does not go through the sensitive equipment. Under normal circumstances, these two coolants never meet, but on occasion a rupture in the heat exchanger tubes permits a mixing of the two coolants resulting in a contamination of the primary coolant. When a rupture is discovered, the leaking tube must be found and plugged.

2. **Impurities from the purification process.** If the chemicals in the water purification plant are exhausted, the purification process becomes incapacitated. This allows impure water to enter the primary coolant.

Two "purity" sensors monitor the process system. Meter 1 is located in the outlet from the holding tank while meter 2 is located at the inlet to the heat source. Since these sensors are identical and any impurities will circulate through the entire system, they ultimately have identical readings. The key to determining what is the source of the impurity is ascertaining which sensor registers a discrepancy first. Additionally, the rate of increase of the impurity in the water dictates the severity of the situation and how quickly corrective action must be taken to avoid equipment damage. Thus, it is obvious that temporal reasoning is important for monitoring this system. Real systems of this variety are significantly more complicated than this example with numerous sources of impurities, making the need for sophisticated temporal reasoning more significant.

Representing this problem in a temporal knowledge-based system could be done as follows:

1. Begin a new time interval, I_1, when purity meter 1 first reaches an alarm level (t_1).
2. Begin a second time interval, I_2, when meter 2 first reaches alarm level (t_2).
3. Begin a third interval, I_3, at the time the first one of the two meters reaches alarm level.
4. When the second purity meter (chronologically) reaches alarm, end the first interval (either I_1 or I_2, but not I_3). Assume that the end time for the running intervals is the present time.

A problem with the purification plant is diagnosed if meter 1 is high first. See Figure 9.10. This is represented temporally as:

$(I_1$ starts $I_3)$ and $(I_1$ meets $I_2)$

Likewise, a leak in the heat exchanger is recognized by a jump in the level of meter 2, which is described by:

$(I_2$ starts $I_3)$ and $(I_2$ meets $I_1)$

Naturally, you would expect I_3 to overlap either I_1 or I_2. This overlap can signify that this is a true introduction of impurities. If the second meter (chronologically) does not reach alarm level after an appropriately long time, then it could be assumed that the meter is reading incorrectly. This is determined by:

$(I_1$ equals $I_3)$ or $(I_2$ equals $I_3)$

where the magnitude of I_1 exceeds a preset number. The severity of the leak could be calculated by the duration of the first time interval to have started and reach alarm $(I_1$ or $I_2)$.

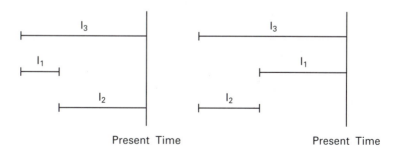

Meter #1 reaches alarm first   Meter #2 reaches alarm first

FIGURE 9.10   Temporal Description of Purity Meter Behavior

9.6 ARTIFICIAL NEURAL NETWORKS

Artificial neural nets in the era of *perceptrons* were an object of derision. Today they have turned out to be a viable, even if contentious, technology. In brief, they *work*. These varied simulations of human neural hardware have been successful in learning rules for synthesizing speech from text [Teasauro, 1989], in playing backgammon [Tesauro, 1989], and even for making decisions in that most grail-like of all nonlinear dynamic systems, the stock market [Fishman, 1991a].

If we view neural networks as functional, adaptive learning systems, the classical knowledge engineer (having her own demonstrably successful paradigm) asks "What is their advantage?" To respond, one has only to consider the limitations of a traditional knowledge-based system—knowledge elicitation. The knowledge elicited from a human expert was developed by that expert's own organic neural network (i.e., the brain) that was exposed to all of the raw data of numerous problems. No guarantee can be offered that every last bit of relational information in those data was captured and used to form the expert's domain view or that the expert's domain view is truly reflected within the elicited knowledge. Neural networks, however, use all of that raw data to arrive at the pertinent rules.

There are several types of neural nets, but their advantages relative to traditional instruments of knowledge engineering are all essentially the same: No rules need be elicited from a human. The data are explored automatically, systematically, and exhaustively to ferret out every last regularity and generality that may reside within them. Having made all these statements, it might be worthwhile now to explain what a neural network is.

An artificial neural network is a system loosely modeled on the human brain. It is an attempt to simulate within specialized hardware or sophisticated software, the multiple layers of simple processing elements called *neurons*. See Figure 9.11. Each neuron ($N1$ through $N12$) is linked to certain of its neighbors with varying coefficients of connectivity ($w1$ through $w32$) that represent the strengths of these connections. "Learning" is accomplished by adjusting these strengths to cause the overall network to output appropriate results. The network is fed a set of "training cases," each consisting of one vector of input values and one of output values. The inputs for each test case, modified by the appropriate coefficients, are propagated through the network, and the results are compared to the test case's output values. When the network generates a prediction that is discrepant from the actual desired output, "negative reinforcement" is applied, and the weights given to those connections that produced the undesirable output are reduced. Conversely, correct output may be rewarded by reinforcement of certain connections. Through this process the network attempts to synthesize a function capable of classifying patterns of input by their approximate output and, thus, to predict output for new patterns.

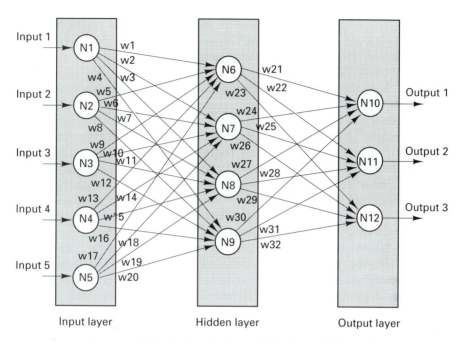

FIGURE 9.11   A Simple Three-layer Neural Network

The learning ability of a neural net is determined by its "architecture" (the number and the connectivity structure of the neurons) and by the algorithmic method chosen for training. In one respect, the fundamental architecture of all networks is the same: an *input layer*, a (usually distinct) *output layer*, and some (possibly zero) number of *hidden layers*. In general, the greater the number of hidden layers, the more complex the function or relationship that may be able to be detected by the network from the training set data. Note that too many hidden layers may result in computational intractability or "overlearning."

The training method is just as important as the architecture and usually consists of one of three schemes. In the first approach, called "unsupervised learning," the hidden neurons must find a way to organize themselves without help from the outside. In essence, the neurons are compelled to compete among themselves for the job of responding to a particular input. Eventually, the neuron or group of neurons best suited for particular tasks assume that role. In this approach, no sample outputs are provided to the network against which it can measure its predictive performance for a given vector of inputs. Instead, the vectors of inputs are merely grouped into similarity clusters representing classes for purposes of categorizing any new examples that are later encountered outside the training set.

The second learning scheme works on reinforcement from the outside. Here, the connections among the neurons in the hidden layer are randomly arranged, then reshuffled as the network is told how close it is to solving the problem.

Both unsupervised and reinforcement learning, however, suffer from relative slowness and inefficiency, relying on a random shuffling to find the proper connection weights. A third learning scheme called *back propagation* has proven highly successful in the training of multilayered neural nets. In back propagation, the network is given not just reinforcement for how it is doing on a task. Information about errors is also filtered back through the system and is used to adjust the connections between the layers, thus improving performance. Back propagation is a form of supervised learning and has proven much faster than some other learning schemes in training the hidden neurons of a multilayered neural net.

Neural networks have been used as a mechanism of knowledge acquisition for expert systems in stock market forecasting [Fishman, 1991b] with astonishingly accurate results. This system is currently managing $200 million in institutional assets without human intervention.

9.7 CHAPTER REVIEW

Several advanced reasoning techniques exist that can overcome some problems inherent with conventional abductive/deductive knowledge-based systems. These described techniques also have natural applicability to particular domains.

Model-based reasoning is applicable to diagnosis of physical systems that can be easily and accurately modeled. It uses deep knowledge about the structure and function of the system and its components to propose a fault mechanism that is consistent with the observed values in the monitored system. The fault mechanism is represented by a faulted component. The diagnostic process is started by the recognition of a discrepancy between the system simulation carried out with the use of the system model and the physical system being monitored. The advantages of model-based reasoning are that knowledge acquisition from an expert is eliminated altogether and is replaced by a model development process that can be more easily carried out by experts or semiexperts in the domain.

Qualitative reasoning is best used in reasoning about physical systems. It can be useful not only in diagnosis of complex systems, but also in design of systems. It provides an alternative to quantitative simulation whenever all the parameters required for the latter are not available. Many engineers and scientists think qualitatively when considering the behavior of a particular device or system, so it is something familiar to them.

Case-based reasoning, on the other hand, has a natural applicability in domains where there exists a significant historical database of prior problems and how they were solved. Examples of such domains are legal reasoning and property appraisal, where large, structured case libraries already exist and where decisions are heavily based on precedence. It employs the similarities between the present case and historical cases to adapt a solution to the present case based on what was done before.

Temporal reasoning, reasoning about time, has found applicability in many domains simply because time is a significant parameter in most aspects of life. One means of describing time is through an interval algebra in which all happenings are described as intervals of time. The algebra describes the relationships between the intervals.

Lastly, artificial neural networks altogether abandon the symbolic approach that is common to all other techniques described in this text and instead try to mimic the physical architecture of the human brain. In the process, the developers of these systems have succeeded in creating systems that learn by themselves.

We expect that these techniques will eventually be incorporated into conventional knowledge-based systems. This will result in tools that are significantly more powerful and easier to construct.

9.8 PROBLEMS

9-1. List five general features common to applications that would be suited for solution through model-based reasoning.

9-2. List five general features common to applications that would be suited for solution through case-based reasoning.

9-3. What do model-based reasoning and case-based reasoning have in common?

9-4. Not all occurrences in life take place in an interval. Some take place at a point in time. How does the interval-based temporal representation deal with points in time? Does it represent a contradiction?

9-5. Provide five real-world examples of applications of qualitative reasoning? How are they similar?

9-6. Do you feel that a specific diagnostic application would run more efficiently in a MBR implementation rather than with input/output type of reasoning? Why?

9-7. How suitable would MBR be if applied towards diagnosing illnesses in the human body (a biological system!)?

9-8. List and discuss five applications that are suitable for solution through MBR.

9-9. As seen in the chapter, model-based reasoning can be implemented with rules. Describe how you would do this.

9-10. List and discuss five applications suitable for solution through CBR.

10 ▐ The Knowledge-based System Lifecycle

10.1 INTRODUCTION

Knowledge engineering, like some other areas in AI, appears to many to be a black art practiced by only a chosen few. This appearance results from a lack of established procedures, such as those of conventional software, which guide the development of knowledge-based systems. This lack is partly due to the infancy of the knowledge-based systems area. Nevertheless, there are more similarities than differences between software engineering and knowledge engineering. The objective of this chapter is thus to set the stage for the rest of the book by describing and analyzing these differences and similarities. In the process, we define a set of steps known as the *knowledge engineering lifecycle*, which provides such a procedure.

10.2 THE LIFECYCLE OF CONVENTIONAL SOFTWARE

The lifecycle of conventional software has been traditionally described through the *waterfall model*. This popularly accepted model of software development, shown in Figure 10.1, contains the following six stages:

1. *Problem analysis:* In this stage, the problem is analyzed for its ability to be computationally solved. The costs and benefits of the proposed software system are determined to ascertain whether development of the system is justified. This requires either market research, if the product is to be developed for a specific market, or an in-depth examination of the customer's request for proposal (whether internal or external) to determine the cost effectiveness of the system.

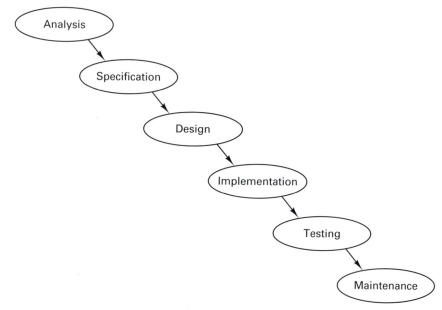

FIGURE 10.1   The Waterfall Model of Software Development

2. *Requirements specification:* Based on the analysis made during the previous stage, a specification document is generated that describes all desired goals and features of the proposed system. This requirements specification document should clearly describe the objectives of the system, the expected users of the system, the computational environment, and any constraints that may affect the success of the development effort or the final system itself.

3. *Design:* The design is a critical stage within the lifecycle. A properly designed system will be relatively easy to implement, test, verify, and maintain. Additionally, a well-designed system responds to the requirements detailed within the specification and, thus, to its ultimate user. The design encompasses the choice of tools (i.e., software and hardware), the user interface, the structure of the code, and the composition of a development team whose talents and personalities must properly blend together.

The design stage subdivides into *preliminary design* and *detailed design*. Preliminary design determines a high level architectural structure for the software. It includes a data flow diagram, structure (hierarchical) chart, and, possibly, the determination of the implementation language. Detailed design, on the other hand, specifies lower-level details within the design including flow diagrams of the various modules defined in the structure chart and the data structures to be used.

4. *Implementation:* This stage entails writing and debugging code for each module, integrating the different modules into a unified system, and interfacing the system to any outside components (e.g., a database). A proper design minimizes the debugging.

5. *Testing:* Testing ensures that the developed software meets the specification and provides the proper solution to the problem. This step involves comparing the system to its specification and testing the operation of the system, either in a simulated or real environment.

6. *Maintenance:* This stage encompasses any modifications to the software after its development. Maintenance includes the elimination of errors not discovered during the implementation and the testing stages, enhancements to the software, and/or modifications due to the changing nature of the problem. It is the most costly of the lifecycle stages, comprising an estimated 30 to 80 percent of the total effort [Shooman, 1983].

The advantage of the waterfall model is its clear, stepwise methodology from conception through development to implementation. This fosters an organized and methodical approach to development that can, hopefully, pay off in correct as well as timely software, developed (hopefully) within budget. The disadvantage, however, is its serial nature, which has two undesirable effects:

1. There is no quick way to allow a customer or developer to "feel" the system as it will be when finalized since the entire system is completed before evaluation or examination by the user. Thus, valuable user feedback is not available until the end of the implementation stage.

2. Because the entire system is composed of modules performing specific and interrelated operations, the entire system has to be completed and validated before it can be of any use to the customer. This can make for a long time between project conception and system implementation.

A second popular model for conventional software lifecycle is the *Boehm spiral model* [Boehm, 1988]. This model combines the best features of the waterfall lifecycle, the idea of prototyping, and the concept of risk analysis. See Figure 10.2 [Boehm, 1988]. This model views software development as a cyclic repetition of a sequence of steps. These steps are performed on each level of the development process from developing an operations document to coding a module. In this model the radial dimension represents the accumulated costs incurred in performing the steps so far, while the angular dimension represents the progress in completing a particular cycle. Each cycle consists of:

1. *Identification.* Determines the objectives of this cycle, the different alternatives that can be used to accomplish the objectives, and what constraints exist on these alternatives.

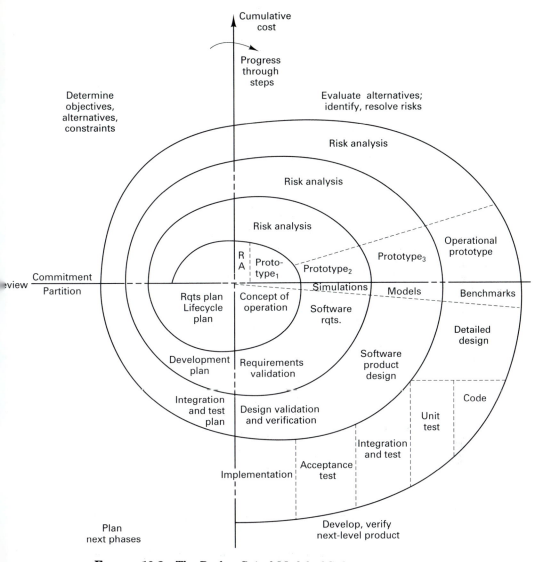

Figure 10.2   The Boehm Spiral Model of Software Development

2. *Evaluation*. Examines the various objectives and constraints imposed on the alternatives to uncover any uncertainties and risks involved.

3. *Formulation*. Develops a strategy that solves the uncertainties and risks. This may involve administering questionnaires, benchmarking, creating simulations, and/or prototyping.

4. *Assessment*. Evaluates what has been done to determine the remaining risks. This determines if evolutionary development should continue on

the current component or if the next component or step of development should be examined.

This model is an extremely realistic view of how most large-scale software systems should be developed. It builds upon the stepwise approach of the waterfall lifecycle by (a) imposing an iterative process that reflects what really happens in software development and (b) identifying, evaluating, and reducing risks at each stage of the development. While being very realistic, it is not without problems:

1. Management must be convinced that its evolutionary process can be controlled.
2. It relies heavily on risk assessment. If risks are not found early, development can be severely impacted just as it would be in the waterfall model.

Additional models have been developed that recognize the cyclic nature of software development. Some are very simplistic, providing little detail of the actual process, while others are extremely complex, providing so much detail that the process becomes lost in the minutiae. For a more in-depth discussion of software engineering refer to [Jones, 1990; Macro, 1987; Shooman, 1983; Summerville, 1982].

10.3 DIFFERENCES FROM KNOWLEDGE-BASED SYSTEMS

Knowledge-based systems, like other forms of software, have the objective of creating computational solutions to problems. Although knowledge-based systems rely largely on heuristics rather than algorithmic procedures, the development of a knowledge-based system has a lifecycle similar to conventional software.

There are some significant differences between knowledge engineering and software engineering. One major difference is the type of knowledge being represented. Software engineering involves representing well-known and well-defined algorithmic procedures that are typically known by many individuals, while knowledge engineering involves representing the extensive, imprecise, and ill-defined heuristic knowledge that is stored in the minds of a few experts. Since the heuristic knowledge is not widely known and understood, it somehow must be transferred from the minds of these individuals into a computerized representation. This transfer, called *knowledge acquisition*, is detailed and time consuming.

A second significant difference involves the nature and quantity of the knowledge. While the nature and quantity of knowledge required to solve a traditional algorithmic problem can be estimated reasonably well, such is not the case for knowledge-based systems. Typically, the nature and quantity of the problem-solving knowledge required within a knowledge-based system is not well known even by the experts themselves. This makes it difficult to predict the total effort required to develop a knowledge-based system. But more importantly, it can also make it difficult to arrive at a suitable design in the early stages of the project. This last situation can lead to what is commonly called a *paradigm shift*. See Figure 10.3 [Waterman, 1985].

The paradigm shift can arise during the development process when a knowledge engineer discovers that the knowledge representation structure, tool, and/or other design features of the system are inadequate. This discovery is generally due to either an initial misunderstanding of the complexities of the problem domain or an underestimation of its magnitude. It can be a serious problem if it happens well into the incremental development stage of the system. The knowledge engineer is then faced with the dilemma of either continuing development with an inadequate infrastructure that may result in serious difficulties later in the project or starting development again with, hopefully, the proper knowledge representation structure and/or other features. Either of these may place the project seriously behind schedule. A paradigm shift that takes place early in the development process, however, can be beneficial since mistakes can be corrected before great investment of time and money are put into the prior paradigm.

To overcome these obstacles and to provide the development team a feel for the breadth and depth of the required knowledge, knowledge-based system developers utilize development techniques called *rapid prototyping* and *incremental development*. While these two models are by no means limited to knowledge-based systems, they have become very popular in their development, since they have an added benefit—when the prototype system makes mistakes, they assist in drawing out the expert's knowledge.

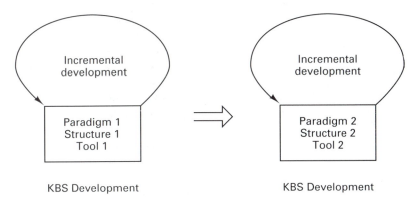

FIGURE 10.3   Paradigm Shift

Rapid prototyping uses the flexibility and power of LISP, PROLOG, and/or commercially available shells to quickly create a working prototype of the envisioned final system. By acquiring and representing knowledge from some limited aspect of the problem domain, the development team is able to create an initial prototype of the final system that exhibits a semblance of this system's capabilities. This allows early feedback to the development team about the scope of the knowledge, the customer's needs, and the validity of the decisions made during the design stage. Thus, if a paradigm shift is deemed necessary at that point, its impact will be minimal due to its early occurrence.

Note that the development of this initial prototype uses a modified lifecycle. The analysis and specification phases must be performed with a view of the complete system, but the design and implementation are performed in a shortened and more preliminary manner. This provides a working system that can be evaluated to obtain the needed feedback. This initial prototype can then either be discarded once the desired feedback is obtained or incrementally enhanced to serve as one subsystem of the final knowledge-based system. In most cases, it is discarded because of the difficulties in modifying it to accommodate all of the ideas generated during its development. It is typically easier to start the development process fresh, this time following the various lifecycle stages in more detail.

Once the initial prototype of the system's knowledge base is developed, its depth, breadth, and quality can be enhanced through the continuous cycle of additions, deletions, and modifications known as incremental development. This strategy is defined as:

> The iterative process of extracting, representing, and confirming knowledge in a limited subset of the problem domain with the objective of incrementally constructing the knowledge-based system in self-contained chunks.

Incremental development centers on two concepts: *divide-and-conquer*, where a manageable, yet complete, chunk of knowledge is selected and developed, and *iterative development*, where divide-and-conquer is applied iteratively across the various chunks that compose the complete problem. The application of incremental development, therefore, involves various cycles of eliciting knowledge from the expert(s), implementing the knowledge within the emerging system, reviewing the resulting implementation with the experts, and refining the implementation to correct any uncovered problems. By progressively adding independent chunks (i.e., modules) to the emerging system, a knowledge-based system can be quickly made partially functional and placed in use even though it is not yet completed. Conventional programs, on the other hand, because of their procedural nature, generally must be fully implemented before use.

Figure 10.4 depicts a knowledge-based system lifecycle model that permits the implementation of the incremental development concept. This approach divides the knowledge-based system into subsections, and subjects each to the development stages of design, implementation, and testing. The various subsections are integrated within the main system as they are developed, thus allowing increased usage of the knowledge-based system as these are progressively developed. The development of these subsections can be done either in series if there is only one knowledge engineer or in parallel should the project have multiple developers. The declarative nature of the knowledge contained within these systems permits relatively easy integration of the various subsections into the emerging system.

In the next section we describe the development phases presented in Figure 10.4 in more detail.

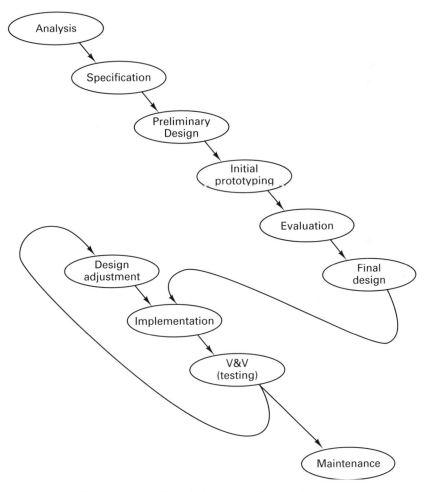

FIGURE 10.4   Knowledge-based System Lifecycle

10.4 THE KNOWLEDGE-BASED SYSTEM LIFECYCLE STAGES

The process of knowledge acquisition is most commonly associated with knowledge engineering. However, the latter is not merely interviewing experts and representing their knowledge. It involves much more, starting with the inception of the project to its final delivery. Developing a knowledge-based system can be a difficult and involved process. To be successful, many tasks have to fall properly into place including:

1. Selecting an application that will be appropriate for solution through a knowledge-based systems approach.
2. Determining the project resources, such as team members.
3. Choosing the correct implementation tool given the constraints of the particular application as well as those of the sponsoring organization (e.g., financial capability).
4. Developing an initial prototype.
5. Acquiring knowledge and incrementally developing the system until its completion.
6. Validating and verifying (i.e., testing) the system.
7. Documenting the system.
8. Maintaining the completed system.

In general, these tasks fit the descriptions of the conventional software lifecycle stages, assuming that the lifecycle model includes the development of a rapid prototype as well as the use of incremental development. But further refinement of the knowledge-based system lifecycle model is necessary to satisfy the different nature of knowledge-based systems. So let us describe anew the stages of a knowledge-based system lifecycle (as shown in Figure 10.4) given its special requirements:

1. *Problem analysis:* Evaluate the problem and the resources available to determine the applicability of a knowledge-based solution. The costs and benefits of the proposed knowledge-based system are determined to ascertain whether its development is warranted. This also requires either market research if the product is to be developed for a specific market or an in-depth examination of the customer's request for proposal (whether internal or external) to determine the cost effectiveness of the system.
2. *Requirements specification:* Formalize and put in writing what was learned during the analysis stage. This sets the objectives of the project in, hopefully, an unequivocal manner and outlines the means to obtain

these objectives. Cumulative experience in developing knowledge-based systems has shown that no significant knowledge-based system should be developed without a specification. Because of their heuristic nature, knowledge-based systems may actually derive greater benefit from such a document than traditional software projects. This is especially true where multiple knowledge engineers work in parallel. This document should discuss the objectives and the features of the system, its user environment, and its constraints.

3. *Preliminary design:* This stage deals with only the high level decisions necessary to begin the initial (and rapidly developed) prototype. Specifically, this stage determines the knowledge representation paradigm, the tool chosen for the prototype, and the selection of experts. Considerable acquisition of general knowledge from experts or from printed sources may be required at this stage to make sound decisions about the representation paradigm and, therefore, the tool.

4. *Initial (rapid) prototyping and evaluation:* This is a key stage since all of the preliminary design decisions must be either justified or overturned based on the knowledge elicited from the experts in the process of completing this stage. The initial prototype should look like the complete system except that it will be limited in breadth. It should include a fairly well-developed user interface and a reasonably robust knowledge subset so the intended users can judge its acceptability. Note that this does not mean that the prototype must be highly robust. It merely indicates that it reflects the ultimate system that will be developed. We recommend that the prototype be discarded upon the completion of its evaluation with the development of the final system starting from scratch, unless *all* of the decisions made in the preliminary design stage are shown to be justified by the initial prototype (a rather unlikely scenario). The key to the prototyping stage is that as much knowledge as reasonably possible needs to be extracted from the experts at this point to validate the design decisions. If mistakes are made in the preliminary design, they should be detected and corrected at this stage

5. *Final design:* The final design involves the selection of the tools and resources required to develop the delivered system. Knowledge-based systems differ from conventional software in that this stage also includes the selection of a knowledge representation paradigm, a choice that can greatly impact the tool selected. The development of a structure chart is not applicable due to the declarative nature of knowledge-based systems. Nevertheless, some high level description of the system architecture must be made. For example, the development of an automobile diagnostic system might identify different knowledge modules as the

Fuel system

Ignition system

Cooling system

Transmission

Electrical system

Lubrication system

Emission control system

among others.

For each of these knowledge subsections, the design would include the specification of typical inputs and conclusions that it would reach. Since overlaps will undoubtedly exist between some subsections (e.g., an input could be used in more than one module), a description of subsystem interfaces is essential.

6. *Implementation:* This stage is the most time consuming of the lifecycle stages in the development of knowledge-based systems, even when an excellent design exists. Implementation encompasses the complete knowledge acquisition process for all subsystems. It is in this stage that incremental development occurs.

7. *Validation and verification (V&V) or testing:* Since the objectives of V&V are the same in conventional software and knowledge-based systems development, their high-level description remains unchanged. Only when the implementation details are described do the significant differences between the process followed for knowledge-based systems differ from those of conventional software. This is discussed in more detail in Chapter 16.

8. *Design adjustment:* As the work progresses and the knowledge engineers have the benefit of "20-20 hindsight," there may be some adjustments made to the design of the system at the start of every iteration. As long as the adjustments are relatively minor in nature and not retroactive, this is good. If, however, the design changes are significant in scope and/ or retroactive to what has already been developed and validated, this can be a setback to the project, resulting in a paradigm shift.

9. *Maintenance:* This stage is quite similar to that of conventional software, and is not discussed further. Please refer to a software engineering text such as [Jones, 1990] or [Shooman, 1983] for a full description.

All of the above lifecycle stages (except design adjustment and maintenance) are described in greater detail in the following chapters. Chapter 11 covers problem analysis; chapter 12 describes project team selection and the functional specification, rapid prototyping, and the two design stages; chapters 13, 14, and 15 describe knowledge acquisition; and Chapter 16 discusses validation and verification.

10.5 CHAPTER REVIEW

There is a need for a strong flow of ideas from software engineering to knowledge engineering. In the past, knowledge engineering has been performed in an extemporaneous and improvised manner. Software engineering offers methodologies that have proven to be relatively successful. One of the most popular of the software engineering models is the waterfall model, which is serial in nature, consisting of the following stages:

1. Problem analysis
2. Requirements specification
3. Design
4. Implementation
5. Testing
6. Maintenance

This model, however, suffers from the lack of rapid prototyping and incremental development, two highly useful and popular development techniques traditionally used in knowledge-based systems development.

Boehm's spiral model combines the best features of the waterfall lifecycle, prototyping, and risk analysis. It considers software development to be a continual cycle of identifying objectives, evaluating the objectives for risks, formulating strategies to eliminate the risks, and assessing what remains to be done. Its biggest drawback is its heavy reliance on risk assessment.

We present a knowledge-based lifecycle model that combines rapid prototyping, incremental development, and a cyclical lifecycle. This model contains the following stages:

1. Problem analysis
2. Requirement specifications
3. Preliminary design
4. Initial prototype
5. Detailed design
6. Knowledge acquisition (implementation)
7. Validation and verification (return to 6)
8. Design adjustment
9. Maintenance

At this point, you should have the background needed to learn the art of knowledge engineering effectively. The following chapters describe this process and supply the guidelines necessary for successfully developing a knowledge-based system.

11 Feasibility Analysis

11.1 INTRODUCTION

Knowledge-based systems represent a means for solving very difficult and complicated problems. As the major thrust of this chapter we present a discussion of the criteria needed for a problem to be well suited to a knowledge-based approach. A problem that meets all (or most) of these criteria is probably a good application. Unfortunately, knowledge-based systems are often viewed as solutions looking for problems, and the criteria for a suitable application are not always properly considered.

In other cases, knowledge-based solutions are attempted where the more traditional programming techniques are better suited. This is sometimes done to appear to be "hi-tech" to impress customers or other important parties.

Choosing the right application for the right reason can have a significant positive influence on the ultimate success of the project. Choosing the right application for the wrong reason is also acceptable, although maybe not quite as satisfying.

The criteria for knowledge-based system feasibility analysis consist of many factors that must be considered when a particular problem is being evaluated. These can be grouped into two general categories: (1) the suitability of the application and, (2) the availability of the required resources.

Let us discuss each of these categories separately in the following two sections. But before we begin, we should note that these are merely guidelines. Some violations of these are acceptable provided they are few in number. The more violations that a potential application introduces, the less feasible it becomes for a solution through knowledge-based systems.

11.2 SUITABILITY OF THE APPLICATION

Many failed knowledge-based system application projects can probably be attributed to an inappropriate application of a knowledge-based approach. What makes a problem suitable for a knowledge-based approach? Why do some projects fail when similar projects succeed?

In this section, we provide guidelines that impart some indication as to the suitability of an application. Three main issues must be considered:

1. Does a problem really exist?
2. Is a knowledge-based technique suited?
3. Is a knowledge-based approach really justified?

Let us look at these issues in greater detail.

11.2.1 Does a Problem Really Exist?

When confronting any apparent problem, a knowledge engineer should first determine whether a problem really exists. The danger in solving a nonexisting problem is that the solution will have no real impact on the operation of the organization. Thus, interest in applying knowledge-based approaches will wane and possibly die before true applications are recognized. This may be mistakenly taken by some to indicate failure of the technology. Additionally, by forcing a problem onto a solution, the tendency is to skip all other steps that justify the development of a knowledge-based system.

As an illustration, let us consider the fictional Belchfire Equipment Corporation, a manufacturer of heavy equipment for industry. Belchfire has recently undergone some hard times because of its aging product line, which has not been updated in five years. Its competitors have made full use of new technology and are gaining the upper hand in the marketplace with more state-of-the-art products. Having belatedly recognized this, Belchfire recently hired a new president and a new sales manager to turn the situation around.

The new president called a meeting of his staff to discuss his strategy for the financial turnaround of the company. The main thrust of his presentation was that the staff needs to identify areas where new technology can improve the products or the operation of the company. He has heard about the new technology of artificial intelligence and wants to see where it can be applied.

After the engineering manager and the manufacturing manager suggest a few possible areas and agree to discuss this with their respective staffs later, the personnel manager mentions a problem that he has observed. Visitors are having an embarrassingly difficult time getting around Belchfire's two-square-mile factory. He suggests developing a knowledge-based guide to place in the security station at the plant entrance. This system will ask visitors which employee they want to visit, their country of citizenship, and other pertinent questions, and will determine if the visitor should be admitted and the best route to the employee's location. The sales manager immediately jumps up saying this is a great idea since it will demonstrate to all visitors how Belchfire is at the leading edge of technology. It is immediately decided, over the objections of the engineering manager, to develop this system and to call it PATHFINDER.

In reality, this difficulty of Belchfire's visitors does not represent a truly significant problem. Many alternative solutions could be used and while this proposed solution is novel, it will not have a likely impact on the company's operation or even on their sales. Once the really significant, technical problems begin to be addressed, it is probable that the manpower needed to solve them will be squandered tackling trivial issues of a visitor's problem. The resulting long-lasting effect could be the attitude that, "well, we tried knowledge-based systems, but it didn't really seem to work out."

This example illustrates a solution looking for a problem and not what is really required—a real problem looking for a solution. The question that must be asked whenever an application of knowledge-based technology is proposed is whether the solution to the problem represents considerable value to the organization. Note that the measure of considerable value may not necessarily always be monetary—prestige could be a great motivator. The higher the value, the greater the support that an organization will give to a development project, and the more patience it will show in waiting for a deliverable system. Several successful knowledge-based systems have severely taxed the patience of their organization's management at one time or another and could easily have been terminated before success was achieved.

11.2.2 Is a Knowledge-based Technique Suited?

Once we have established that a true problem really exists, we can then turn our attention toward how to solve it. Problems come in all shapes and sizes. Some clearly demand knowledge-based solutions while others obviously require conventional programming techniques. The most ambiguous area occurs with problems involving decision trees. While some types of decision tree analysis problems are excellent candidates for knowledge-based system implementations, there are many others that would be better solved using conventional computing techniques.

The confusion arises because decision trees usually employ IF-THEN statements that most people associate with rule-oriented knowledge-based systems. What is forgotten, however, is that conditional statements exist in all high level languages—they are not exclusive to the domain of knowledge-based systems. It is only when they are used in a declarative fashion with the other features of knowledge-based systems discussed in Chapter 1 that they can be defined as knowledge-based systems.

The following questions may assist in determining whether a knowledge-based approach is best. The answers to these questions as a whole must be used in this determination, since there is no absolute score or boundary that dictates that "now you must use a knowledge-based approach." In some organizations certain factors may have greater influence than others. This makes the process of determining if a knowledge-based approach is best, a heuristic, inexact process itself.

1. *Is human problem-solving knowledge being replicated in the solution of the problem?* An answer of "yes" implies that expert systems may be the proper solution. A "no" answer does not necessarily imply that this is a bad application, but it is certainly not a good omen. In our example of the Belchfire Equipment Corporation, the proposed PATHFINDER system would in fact entail human knowledge, albeit at a low level.

2. *Is the problem-solving knowledge heuristic in nature or is it predominantly algorithmic?* No task is purely one or the other. Most real-world problems contain elements of both. The key is which knowledge form is predominant. Heuristics imply the use of knowledge-based systems, while algorithms imply the use of conventional software. In our PATHFINDER example, most of the knowledge is algorithmic, since there are only a limited number of ways for getting from one place to another. A heuristic element does, however, occur in proposing shortcuts, taking into account the time of day to avoid employee traffic, and routing foreign visitors around sensitive areas.

3. *Does the knowledge or expertise periodically change or does it remain constant?* Knowledge that changes often is well suited for a knowledge-based system because of its inherent ease in incorporating changes. This can even justify knowledge-based systems solutions to problems that are predominantly algorithmic but whose rules change regularly (e.g., tax law). In our example of PATHFINDER, it is likely that some data would change frequently, as people transfer departments, move from office to office, leave the company, and so forth. Notice we used the word "data," because that is all that is involved. This information can be stored in a database and easily retrieved when trying to determine a particular path. The knowledge involved within this system describes how to get from one building to another and remains fairly constant provided there is no new construction on the plant property.

4. *If expertise is involved, is the expertise fairly well understood and accepted?* Knowledge-based systems are difficult to develop in domains that are not well understood. These systems are not intended to know more than humans, but only to use knowledge to solve problems that humans generally can solve (albeit less efficiently). It is fairly easy to identify, organize, and represent the expertise on how to diagnose a problem in an

automobile, but more difficult to do the same for expertise on extraterrestrial radio signal interpretation, winning strategies for the lottery, or astrology. On the other hand, if expertise can be adequately reduced to formulas or mathematical models, then a conventional program could be more advantageous. While human knowledge is used in PATHFINDER, it can hardly be considered expertise.

5. *Are the input data always complete and correct?* If the answer is "no," then knowledge-based systems solution may offer a distinct advantage. Conventional programming techniques have difficulty representing and reasoning with incomplete or inexact data. These are, however, precisely the types of input data for which knowledge-based systems are ideally suited. Given the simplicity of the responses presumably required in the PATHFINDER system, we would have to assume that the input data are complete and exact and, therefore, do not require a knowledge-based approach.

6. *Can the problem be solved better through other means?* Although knowledge-based systems offer excellent features to solve some types of problems, these features may not be necessary for others. For some problems, conventional software solutions may be highly appropriate. For others, a noncomputing solution may even be the best approach. In our example from the Belchfire Equipment Corporation, the "problem" could easily be solved by tying a small conventional program to a database containing the location of each employee. An even simpler solution would be to print maps of the complex and provide a telephone for visitors to call the parties being visited for instructions or a pick-up.

7. *Does it pass the telephone test?* This test asks whether an expert, by speaking with someone over the telephone, can gather sufficient information to allow him to solve the problem. The telephone test, of course, is not intended to be taken literally. Otherwise, any real-time monitoring/diagnostic knowledge-based system would not pass since the data are acquired automatically. The test is really a means of classifying the type of knowledge that is required to solve a problem. It ensures that the knowledge is not of a visual, audio, or tactile nature. While a limited amount of such data can be handled by a knowledge-based system if these data can be clearly categorized and organized, a predominant amount of such data can make the development of a knowledge-based system extremely difficult. The PATHFINDER example clearly passes this test.

11.2.3 Is a Knowledge-based Approach Justified?

The cost of developing a knowledge-based system is usually higher than most conventional software projects. Several explanations for these costs exist. First is the need for specialized hardware and software to support the special development requirements. Additionally, there is the need for experienced personnel. Such people are hard to find, expensive, and/or difficult to train.

Occasionally, a problem can be so complex that it defies even a practical solution through knowledge-based systems. From a technical standpoint, if a project is suitable according to the other criteria, sheer difficulty should not stop the development. However, it is possible that a project can require so much effort that it may not be economically justified. Knowledge-based system solutions should be evaluated for cost/benefit just like any other project.

11.3 AVAILABILITY OF RESOURCES

While a particular problem may meet all the criteria described in the section preceding for implementation of a knowledge-based systems solution, it may not become a successful implementation. Many factors can defeat a project. First, the individual assigned as the knowledge engineer, or system developer, has to be highly capable. This topic is explored in more depth in the next chapter. Second, since projects generally do not exist in a vacuum, they are subject to the same constraints commonly found in government, industry, and academic organizations that affect all other development projects. You should carefully answer the following questions to determine whether the resources for a successful knowledge-based system implementation exist in your organization.

11.3.1 Is There Management Support for the Project?

Unless the developer of the knowledge-based application owns the company or has an excellent relationship with its chief executive officer (CEO), contentions with management will always exist. Management's support for a project does not necessarily guarantee success of a well-suited project, but its lack means almost certain failure. Such support can take various forms, all of which are essential to the project's successful implementation.

1. *Availability of time:* This is definitely the first and most important means of organizational support. Needless to say, if the system developer(s) does not have time, then the system will never become a reality. There have been excellent knowledge-based systems applications that have never gotten off the ground due to lack of time of the knowledge engineer. Time, of course, equates to priority. Management must be made aware of the labor intensive nature of knowledge-based system development. Additionally, the knowledge engineering staff must realize that knowledge-based systems development is their top priority.

2. *Tools and training:* Second in priority is supplying the knowledge engineer with adequate tools and training on their use. The choice of development tools may often be constrained by parameters beyond realistic control of the management such as the installed hardware or available software. However, these tools should at least be adequate for the present task. Training may be as simple as providing adequate time for the knowledge engineer to study the manuals provided with a tool or as complex and expensive as an extensive formal training course. In either case the knowledge engineer must be given adequate time to become familiar with the features of the provided tools.

3. *Expert availability:* Since knowledge-based system development requires significant interaction with the domain expert(s), it is logical to require that the expert(s) be available. Two problems can occur. Domain experts, because they are experts in a limited area of expertise, are in high demand. Their time is very constrained and, therefore, a commitment must be made to provide the knowledge engineer adequate access to them. In most organizations, the domain experts reside in a different organizational unit than the knowledge engineering staff. Thus, management commitment must be at a high enough level to encompass both units. In some situations, the knowledge engineer's management is highly motivated to develop a system, only to face apathetic management in the expert's organization. The result, of course, is very likely to be failure.

11.3.2 Is There Support on the Part of the Expert?

Even if the expert's management fully supports the project and has allowed the knowledge engineer access to the expert, support by the expert(s) is critical. A cooperative expert who is excited by the idea of replicating his/her thinking in a knowledge-based system is ideal. Note, however, that this very concept can also appear threatening to the job security of an expert, causing him/her to be uncooperative. There are some steps that a knowledge engineer or the expert's management can take to mitigate this problem, but they are not foolproof. We discuss these in Chapters 13 and 14. Suffice it to say for now that an expert's cooperation can significantly affect the rate at which progress is made on the development of a knowledge-based system.

11.3.3 Is the Expert Competent?

The question of expert competency is a difficult one to treat. In almost all cases the knowledge engineer is in no position to know whether the expert is competent because of her own lack of knowledge of the domain. Additionally, it can be a rather touchy subject to broach with the expert's co-workers. Nevertheless, it is important to the ultimate success of the project that the expert truly be expert in the domain. Otherwise, the problem-solving ability of the system, once it is completed, will be less than desirable.

Once management has identified the person acting as the expert, the options for the knowledge engineer, who has found this expert to be incompetent, are rather limited short of explaining the situation to management. Although sometimes the latter can be appropriate, in most cases, it is not a realistic alternative.

There are some things that the knowledge engineer can do, however. The most important is to make sure that there is more than one source of expertise available. It would be ideal to have two or three experts assigned to a project, but in lieu of that, simply having other experts with whom to consult, or "bounce ideas," can be extremely helpful. This approach is, however, not risk-free. The main expert can take offense at someone else being consulted and different experts might derive the same results using radically different problem-solving approaches.

Remember that the competency of the expert involved is critical and should be a criterion in deciding whether a project is viable.

11.3.4 Is the Expert Articulate?

Having an individual who is truly an expert is very important in building a knowledge-based system, but it does not ensure that a system will be built. The expert must additionally be articulate—able to communicate not only "textbook" knowledge, but, more important, his problem-solving techniques. An expert who is highly skilled at problem solving who states "the solution is so obvious, any idiot can see that!" or "I cannot explain why this is the answer, it just is!" is not going to be of much assistance.

The expert must be able to verbalize the process used to examine a problem and determine the proper course of action. They must be able to explain their reasoning process—what facts did they consider, why were certain lines of reasoning quickly eliminated while others remained, how did they determine what were the important facts that were needed at particular points in their reasoning, and when did they become convinced that their answer was correct? The knowledge engineer has many techniques to aid in extracting this knowledge from the expert that we discuss in Chapter 13, but these are still limited by the natural ability of the expert to communicate.

11.3.5 Is the Expert in Physical Proximity?

A situation to be avoided if at all possible is one where the expert(s) are physically distant from the knowledge engineer. This distance will limit the knowledge engineer's access to the expert(s), which might in turn slow the development process. Although this handicap can be overcome if the expert is cooperative and there is strong management support, it does not represent an ideal situation.

11.4 SAMPLE APPLICATION

So far, this chapter has presented some criteria for determining the applicability of knowledge-based techniques to specific problems. We also discussed a sample application, PATHFINDER, which in many respects represented an inadequate application of knowledge-based systems. Let us now examine another application that we will evaluate using the criteria described above. To do this, we need to revisit our friends at Belchfire Equipment Corporation, who by now have realized their mistake in funding the PATHFINDER project.

While the PATHFINDER project was struggling along, the engineering manager and the manufacturing manager quietly looked for real problems whose solutions could significantly impact either their operations or their products. The results were three problems that appeared amenable to knowledge-based solutions. The first of these is described below, while the other two are posed as problems for you to investigate at the conclusion of the chapter.

The cost of manufacturing products has steadily risen over the last few years due to the increasing downtime of the manufacturing equipment as it gets older and wears out. Although some redundancy is available in the factory floor, the manual rescheduling process currently used is slow, often taking up to five days to determine an alternative manufacturing plan. This has necessitated keeping a large inventory to circumvent the delays in determining alternative plans. While the ultimate answer is clearly the replacement of the old equipment, the present financial status of the company precludes replacements for at least the next five years. One alternative is to determine an alternative manufacturing plan more quickly when a particular machine or workstation in the shop floor fails. If this succeeds, it may even decrease the maintained inventory.

At the present time, the scheduling is performed by an industrial engineer who has been with Belchfire since its founding. While he does an excellent job of rescheduling, he has many other duties, and rescheduling is not one of his priorities. This has led to some production delays. Other delays have occurred because many outages take place during the night or on weekends, when he is not readily available. In addition, his health has declined during the last two years. When his health problems are combined with his eight weeks of vacation per year, he has been absent more than present at work.

The engineering and manufacturing managers have had some discussions with the industrial engineer. These discussions have determined that many factors are utilized in rescheduling manufacturing including the stage of manufacturing a product, the type of failure on the machine (i.e., how long before it is back in service), the availability of other machines, the priority of other work in progress on the shop floor, the time of the year, and the personnel that are available.

Given all of this information, let us analyze this problem to determine whether this is a good candidate for a knowledge-based solution.

First, it is clear that this is a real problem. Although no figures are given in the description, it is easy to perceive that proper, rapid rescheduling of the factory floor can have a significant impact on production costs. It is also obvious that even when the old manufacturing equipment is replaced, this system will remain useful by forecasting the progress of products through the factory floor which will help maintain appropriately low inventory levels. These factors represent a significant value to the organization and would thus meet the test of suitability of the problem.

Let us now determine whether a knowledge-based system solution is the best approach possible by examining the various questions raised in Section 11.3:

1. *Will human problem-solving knowledge be replicated in the solution of the problem?* Clearly yes, the human involved is using a wide range of data and expertise that has been acquired over an extended time period to solve this problem.

2. *Is the problem-solving knowledge heuristic in nature?* Yes, it appears to be predominantly heuristic because there are many factors to consider and there is no definitive way to handle every situation.

3. *Does the knowledge or expertise often change?* At the present time probably not, but this will probably change drastically as new equipment is slowly added after five years.

4. *Is the domain of expertise well understood?* Although we cannot determine what happens inside the mind of the industrial engineer when he does the scheduling, it appears that he knows his job well.

5. *Are the input data always complete and correct?* This is difficult to determine given the short description of the problem. However, given the nature of factory floors, it is likely that the available data will often be incomplete. On the other hand, correctness may not be a problem here.

6. *Can this problem be solved adequately any other way?* This is always a difficult question to answer, but let us try by proposing alternative approaches:
   a. Develop a conventional program to create the scheduling. This is probably unrealistic due to the heuristic nature of the problem.
   b. Hire additional schedulers. This is not a good solution either because training new schedulers is time consuming, possibly taking a year or

two before they become really competent. Additionally, they will not really be required in five years when the new equipment is ordered.

   c. Relieve the present scheduler from his other duties so that he can spend more time rescheduling. This is not a good solution since because of his poor health, his inability to work evenings and weekends, and his accumulated vacation time, such an approach may be quite useless.

7. *Can this pass the telephone test?* Clearly yes. The expert can be given all the data he needs to solve the problem over the telephone.

There may be other possible solutions, but for the purposes of illustration let us stop here. It appears clear from the above analysis that no practical alternative exists other than continuing the present, unacceptable operation. But determining that this approach is well suited is only half the story. We must, additionally, investigate whether this approach is economically justified.

No financial numbers are supplied in this example, since all the information is qualitative in nature. Therefore, the judgment must be an educated guess. Nevertheless, it is usually the case that production delays can be very costly. Depending on the type of equipment being manufactured and the shop load, production delays can easily run into hundreds of thousands of dollars for any one year. On the other hand, the system described represents a small- to medium-sized system, which may require somewhere in the neighborhood of two man-years to develop. Assuming a personnel cost of $100,000 per man-year, and an additional $50,000 in travel costs, tools, and miscellaneous expenses, the final estimated cost of the system should be in the neighborhood of $250,000. Thus, based on this simplified analysis, we can surmise that the project is economically justified.

Our second task is to determine whether the resources necessary to successfully develop the system exist.

Is there management support for the project? Based upon the statements of the problem, there appears to be significant management support, up to and including the company president. Let us now examine all the issues that are pertinent:

1. *Availability of time:* Given the high level of management support for this project, there will likely be little difficulty making time available for the knowledge engineer.

2. *Tools and training:* Basically the same response applies here. Since there appears to be strong management support, there should be little problem in securing adequate tools and training. This is even truer since Belchfire has no prior involvement in AI development and thus does not have to contend with memories of old failed projects.

3. *Expert availability:* Once again, the expert most definitely exists, and, because of apparent management support, he will be given the time to work on this project.

The next issue to consider is whether the expert will support and be enthusiastic about the project. Whether the identified expert will cooperate or not is unknown, but considering his other responsibilities and the assistance this system will provide, it is likely that he will. This should be further clarified with the expert before a commitment is made to the project.

Is the expert competent and articulate? From the description given, it appears that he is competent in his job, but there is no indication of his verbal skills. This last issue should be determined with the expert before project commitment, but it is doubtful that it, by itself, would negatively affect a positive decision.

Is the expert in physical proximity? Assuming that the system is developed in-house by a member of the technical staff, the issue of physical proximity is not applicable. If, however, an outside consultant is chosen, then there may be a problem, depending on where the consultant is based.

In summary, this application appears to be well suited for a knowledge-based solution. There are, however, some potential obstacles that need further investigation. Some of these deal with the expert and have been noted above. Another is that the scheduling domain is a difficult domain in which to develop a system. Therefore, it is important that management understands this and that resources commensurate with this level of difficulty be made available to the development team.

11.5 CHAPTER REVIEW

The suitability of an application can have a major effect on the ultimate success of the project. We believe that the most significant cause for failure in such projects is the misapplication of the technology.

The criteria for determining if a knowledge-based system should be developed can be divided into two parts: (1) the suitability of application and (2) the availability of resources.

Suitability of application can be determined by answering the following questions:

1. Does a problem really exist?

2. Is a knowledge-based technique suited?

    a. Is human problem-solving knowledge being replicated?
    b. Is the knowledge heuristic in nature?
    c. Does the knowledge change periodically?
    d. Is the knowledge well understood and accepted by human experts?
    e. Are the input data always complete and correct?
    f. Can the problem be solved through other means?
    g. Does it pass the telephone test?
3. Is a knowledge-based approach really justified?

Availability of resources, on the other hand, can be described as follows:

1. Is there management support?
    a. Availability of time?
    b. Tools and training?
    c. Expert availability?
2. Is there support on the part of the expert?
3. Is the expert competent?
4. Is the expert articulate?
5. Is the expert in close physical proximity?

A sample application is analyzed for these characteristics. You should leave this chapter knowing how to determine whether a particular application is appropriate or not for a knowledge-based solution.

11.6 PROBLEMS

The following situations represent possible application areas for knowledge-based techniques. For each situation answer the questions asked.

11-1. Pierre, the head chef at the world renowned Le Petit Paris Restaurant in Chicago, has indicated his intention to retire. During his career, he has become known as one of the greatest masters of French cuisine in the Midwest. Jean-Claude, his capable assistant, is an excellent chef in his own right, but he has not worked with Pierre long enough to have learned *the magic*. He can follow Pierre's recipes to the letter, but he still cannot achieve quite the same results. The daughter of the owner of the restaurant is majoring in computer science at a nearby university and is currently taking a class in knowledge-based systems. She has suggested to her father that building a knowledge-based system to capture Pierre's knowledge before he retires will solve this problem. Is this correct? What are their chances of success?

11-2. Charlie Miller is the owner of Charlie's Auto Repair Shop in Muncie, Indiana. In the five years that he has owned his shop, his reputation as an expert mechanic has spread everywhere. To handle the resulting increased level of business, he recently hired two young mechanics.

Although he was very careful to choose competent individuals, he found their abilities to be significantly below his. He, therefore, spent a significant amount of time assisting them by answering their questions and even correcting some of their work. This greatly reduced his efficiency. After finally training them, one was recruited and hired by the dealership down the road. Charlie is now afraid that this will happen to the other.

Meanwhile, business has continued to increase to the point where he will need to have five mechanics in his shop by next year. At that point Charlie will be so busy teaching these new mechanics and checking their work that he will not have any time left to work on cars himself, something that he really enjoys. Charlie wonders if that is just the price of success, but his next-door neighbor Ted Johnson, a technician at a large local manufacturing plant, has told him about a new technology called knowledge-based systems that could possibly help him. After an initial description by Ted, Charlie is interested. Will the construction of a knowledge-based system provide the relief that Charlie desires?

11-3. Dr. John Smith, the chief scientist at Technoid, Inc., has built a career for himself in product design. He is nationally recognized as the father of the Widget A-100, which revolutionized the field of automated manufacturing. Dr. Smith has a reputation of being a highly creative individual who always finds ingenious solutions to problems. Where other bright and competent individuals find problem solutions that are adequate but far from ideal, Dr. Smith always seems to find better solutions. These solutions not only solve the problem better, but also do it less expensively and in an easier to implement manner.

As Technoid has grown Dr. Smith has found that the number of problems that he must examine is beginning to outstrip his available time. Being the creative individual he is and realizing that he has a unique talent for solving problems, he has decided to sponsor a project to develop a knowledge-based system that will capture his problem-solving expertise. Is this a good move? What are his chances for success?

11-4. As president of the Belchfire company, you have recently uncovered a new problem: the poor quality of the instruction manuals provided to the customer with the equipment purchased. The information in these manuals is poorly written, poorly organized, and almost devoid of any technical content. This has resulted in numerous customer calls to the service department about installation, operation, and especially troubleshooting the equipment. Customers are also continually complaining about the manuals to the field sales people.

Because of the large number of complaints, the company is spending a disproportionately large amount of money maintaining an artificially large service department. It is also highly suspected that this problem is resulting in lost sales. The most obvious solution is to rewrite the manual, an action that will definitely occur. Nevertheless, the service department feels that a knowledge-based system would be the most help to customers in troubleshooting their equipment.

They have proposed that a diskette be included with the manuals and be sent to existing owners of the equipment. This diskette would contain a compiled version of the knowledge-based system that would run on a personal computer. One side effect of this action would be the integration of all diagnostic knowledge into one source. The marketing manager thinks that this is a great idea for the same reason he thought PATHFINDER was a great idea, that is, it will impress the customers. As president of the company, what would you recommend? Why?

11-5. Another problem that the Belchfire Equipment Corporation recently discovered is that they have lost some orders due to the inappropriate selection of their products. It seems that either they quoted a product that did not meet the specifications which caused them to be disqualified on technical criteria, or they overdesigned a product which caused them to be uncompetitive in price. According to the engineering manager, the problem is not the lack of expertise. Instead it appears to be the lack of coordination or consistency in the selection of products to be offered. His staff of five individuals, while generally knowledgeable in the entire product line, appear to have specialized in different applications or specific equipment. As a result, the right technical specifications do not always reach the right individual. This is particularly exacerbated by the fact that Belchfire products are customized for every customer, and a certain amount of design is required with each product selected.

Because of these problems, the engineering manager proposes that a knowledge-based system be developed to encompass all of the corporate knowledge about the products and their preliminary design. This system could be used by the application engineers to insure the best possible fit between the customer's specification and the company's product line. Unfortunately, the marketing manager feels that what is necessary is for the engineering department to set down guidelines and force their people to stick to them.

As president of the company, what would you do? Would you approve this development project? If so, who would you select to be the knowledge engineer(s) on the project?

11-6. As president of Expert Systems Unlimited, a consulting firm that specializes in marketing various knowledge-based system shells, you have decided that the knowledge that your employees use in selecting and recommending a particular shell can be incorporated within a knowledge-based system. This system will examine the characteristics of the user's application, the amount of money that they can spend on a shell, and the hardware on which the shell must run. Based on these characteristics, it will recommend the purchase of a particular shell. Do you feel that this is a good application for a knowledge-based system? Why?

11-7. As a young, new business-applications consultant, you have noticed that many small companies have requested your services in developing business related programs that maintain databases on employee sales, customers, product inventory, and so forth. This is a very limited application domain; therefore, you feel that it would be a good candidate for a knowledge-based solution.

After many weeks of thought you have determined what this knowledge-based system should do. It will collect data on the application problem, verify that no inconsistencies exist within a user's specification, create the database structure, and assist the user in developing interface programs—in effect, the system will automate the coding of the entire application. What is the likelihood that such a knowledge-based system can be created, given that it is such a highly restricted domain within business applications' programming?

11-8. Your father works for a manufacturing company that produces a wide range of consumer products. You have talked with him about knowledge-based systems, their wide range of application, and their significant benefits. After hearing your description, he identifies a problem in the design of these products that he thinks might be a good candidate for a knowledge-based solution. Within each product, the various pieces that compose the product must be fastened together. Sometimes it is appropriate to use glues; other times rivets, welds, or snaps are employed. Not only is there a wide range of possible fasteners, but within each category there are also numerous possible choices. Is this a good candidate for a knowledge-based solution?

12 Requirements Specification and Design

12.1 INTRODUCTION

In the last chapter we discussed the evaluation of a problem—is it a good candidate for a knowledge-based system solution? Assuming that it is, our next two tasks are to prepare a specification of the solution to the problem based on its requirements, and to design the knowledge-based system that will solve the problem.

The specification of the requirements of a knowledge-based system is typically ignored by the AI community in favor of the rapid prototyping and incremental development process. Our position is that rapid prototyping and incremental development are complementary to a requirement specification and not contradictory.

Once a specification is generated, it is time to design the system. As we saw in Chapter 10, this step is composed of three stages:

1. Preliminary design
2. Initial prototyping
3. Detailed design

Preliminary design involves determining the basic resources required: the work force required to develop the system, the knowledge sources from which the knowledge will be gathered, and the tools used within the development. Two issues exist in selecting the development team. First, since the knowledge engineer is a key individual in the development of a successful system, it is important that the right knowledge engineer is chosen. Thus, we present the desirable traits and qualities for a qualified knowledge engineer.

Second are the staffing levels and the types of talents necessary for developing the knowledge-based system. Knowledge-based systems can vary widely in size. This chapter divides systems into small, medium, and large projects and discusses the different requirements for each.

We also present a detailed discussion on the selection of a development tool. Should a shell be used or should the application be developed from "scratch"? The pros and cons for each approach are presented. If a shell is to be used, then a decision must be made on which shell. This chapter lists a set of criteria to assist the development team in selecting a shell. Hardware tools are also briefly discussed, but only in the context that the software tool dictates its supporting environment.

This chapter also discusses the issues involved in the actual design of the knowledge-based system. Some of these issues include various instruments used to represent the design of the system: the *modified structure chart* (MSC) and the *knowledge diagram*. Although these are representation tools, these instruments are quite useful in helping the knowledge engineer design the system structure and the knowledge within the system.

12.2 REQUIREMENTS SPECIFICATION

A requirement specification should most importantly describe the problem and how the output of the knowledge-based system will actually solve the problem. It also needs to identify and set specific goals so the developers can determine when the system is complete and they are finished. This setting of goals is a tricky yet important task since knowledge-based systems have a tendency of expanding almost uncontrollably once development has begun. If opportunities for nonessential extensions of the system are discovered during development, they should be treated as just that, nonessential, and should not be considered part of the primary effort.

The specification document should also address the needs, desires, and concerns of the end users. A well-developed, technically excellent, and practical solution to a problem is worthless if it is not used by the ultimate customers. The only way to ensure its use is to meet the users' specific needs.

Finally, the specification should also address the issue of validation and verification. While this may later be superseded by a separate, more detailed treatment of the subject, some thought should be given to validation and verification at an early stage to avoid any later surprises as much as possible. We examine this topic further in Chapter 16.

Our objective is not to provide a specific blueprint for a requirements specification. The requirements specification can range from a simple statement of goals to an exhaustive analysis of the problem and its solution. It should not constrain a development team unnecessarily, but rather should set forth the *what's* and the *why's* of the system and should allow the development team to determine the *how's*. Critical, however, at this stage in the system development is a careful and deliberate organization of the goals and a description of the constraints *before* the initiation of the actual system implementation or coding. The organization and details of a functional specification depend mostly upon the development team and with what they are most comfortable. Nevertheless, for the sake of completeness, we put forth a template for a requirement specification borrowed from Jones [Jones, 1990] that is modified and tailored to knowledge-based systems. This template is displayed in the box.

Introduction

Problem overview: This is a textual description of the problem as understood by the developers and why this problem is important to solve. Most of this information can be obtained from the suitability analysis process performed in the analysis stage, described in Chapter 11.

User profile: This entry identifies the expected users of the knowledge-based system. Specific issues treated here are the user's level of education, his/her familiarity with computers, and his/her familiarity with the problem domain. Whether the system being contemplated will assist a human decision maker or whether it will make independent decisions is also relevant at this point. A proper description of the users will assist greatly in the design of the user interface.

Project goals: The project goals provide a clear definition of what the knowledge-based system is to accomplish. This is a very important consideration since without a clear set of goals you cannot evaluate the success of the development effort. The more detailed this description is, the better.

Knowledge-based System Functions

System outputs: This entry describes the nature of the system outputs, if it does not provide the list of outputs (which may not be known at this point). It is important to identify if the user desires only the most likely solution and nothing else, or whether he/she wants a list of all the various possible solutions. It is also important to identify the level of detail sought within the solution. For example, in an automobile diagnostic system, does it suffice to tell the mechanic that the problem is in the fuel injectors or should the system instead describe the fuel injector diagnosis in great detail providing a drawing showing where the injectors are and how to replace or fix them? Graphical display of the outputs, if required, must be identified. Is a measure of the certainty of the diagnosis applicable or important? Is an indication of the confidence or urgency (or both) of the situation necessary?

System inputs: The nature of the input data expected during problem solving should be discussed. Will they generally be complete and consistent? Will they

---

occasionally be erroneous? If so, how often? Are they predominantly numerical or symbolic? Are they subject to interpretation of a human? Will they carry some implicit uncertainty? Are preliminary calculations necessary to put the data in a usable form? Are the data supplied automatically from another computer or instrument?

Auxiliary features: Auxiliary features include any other features that affect the design of the system. For example, does the logic used by the system have to be explained to the user? If so, how much can we assume the user knows?

Implementation priorities: What features of the system should be developed first? A particular system may heavily utilize a specific small chunk of knowledge. It thus makes sense to implement that subsystem first.

Constraints

Hardware constraints: One significant constraint for any software system is the hardware platform on which the delivered product will run. If the customers typically have access to only personal computers, it would be unwise to develop a system to run on mainframes.

External interfaces: This entry should discuss any hardware, database, existing procedures, or networks that must interface with the knowledge-based system.

Compatibility with previous products: What relationships and capabilities must be maintained with previously developed products? What features are identical to those in previous products? What features have been changed? What features have been added? While this may not be a significant issue when initially developing a knowledge-based system, it will eventually become an important one.

Speed of execution: Nothing disturbs a user more than having to wait for an answer, except possibly having to wait for the wrong answer. Some prototype systems have acceptable performance, but their performance degrades significantly when expanded. Definition of realistic speed requirements is important to avoid problems arising later in the development process.

Reliability: What is the anticipated reliability of the system? How confident should the user be in the system's answers? It is preferable to quantify this, but it may not always be possible. Alternatively, a specification should contain a discussion of the consequence of an incorrect answer.

Maintainability: How dynamic is the knowledge? Does the knowledge change overnight, or can it be expected to remain unchanged for years? Will the problem itself or the knowledge used to solve the problem evolve over time? This discussion can affect the knowledge representation paradigm as well as the tool chosen.

Security: Is the knowledge classified or proprietary? Can the users make changes to the knowledge base or is a knowledge engineer the only one who is designated to do so?

Error identification: How are errors in the operation of the system to be handled? What about errors in the data? Or errors in the hardware or tool?

Miscellaneous Issues

Validation method: Describe the methods and techniques to be used in validating the system.

Verification method: Describe the methods and techniques to be used in verifying the system.

Documentation: Discuss the documentation requirements of the finalized system including the level of detail required in any user documentation. Should the knowledge base be included in the documentation or is it to be kept confidential? The documentation should also address the technical sophistication of the typical reader of the user's manual. Is it written for a computer-literate reader who is not AI-literate or is written for a computer-illiterate class of individuals?

Other: Discuss other issues that do not fit within any of the above prescribed headings of this suggested template.

12.3 PRELIMINARY DESIGN

The preliminary design is the next logical step in the development process. The basic decisions to be made here all involve the selection of components needed during the actual design and development: (1) the knowledge representation paradigm, (2) the reasoning method, (3) the tool, and (4) the development team.

12.3.1 Selection of a Knowledge Representation Paradigm

Selection of the knowledge representation paradigm is an important decision since the paradigm chosen affects the tool selection. A poor selection of either one can severely impact a system's success. It is therefore important to make the best possible initial selection to minimize any later effects.

The knowledge representation choice is essentially between rules, logic, frames, objects, or associative networks. Given the similarity between rules and logic on one hand, and between frames, objects, and associative networks on the other, we will simplify the discussion by considering only two general types of knowledge representation paradigms: *rules* and *structures*. As described in Chapters 2, 4, and 5, rules cause inferences to be made if the supporting facts are present. Diagnostic, classification, and interpretative tasks involving *shallow knowledge* are generally suited for the rule-based paradigm. Shallow knowledge is input-output knowledge (see Chapter 1) that is symptomatic in nature and does not attempt to understand the underlying principles of the problem, but only to solve it using its external features. Remember, however, that drawbacks do exist. One primary drawback is that facts, and the rules that use them, cannot efficiently represent the structure and relationships within even simple concepts or objects.

On the other hand, the structured paradigms discussed in Chapter 6 are ideally suited for domains that require the representation of deeper and more structurally related knowledge. Frames were designed specifically for representing the relationships that exist within or between ideas or objects. The difference between relationships expressed by rules and relationships explained through inheritance and demons is whether the relationship is between facts (or states) or between structured entities (or classes of entities). If the latter is true, then objects are a better means of representing this relationship. Often, however, it becomes intuitively obvious to the developer whether the knowledge in the domain is predominantly rule-based or structured based. Structured paradigms are best suited for domains consisting of a set of objects having interrelationships that need to be explicitly modeled. Through inheritance and demons, the structured paradigms can also express relationships between entities. However, like the rule paradigm, structures have their own drawback—the lack of an inferential capability.[1]

Hybrid systems are the best of both worlds, combining the rich representation environment offered by structures (typically frames) with the inferential capability found within rules. In hybrid systems, frame slots act as facts in a database, and rules make inferences based on the value of the slot. Yet the frames still maintain the inherited relationships as well as the procedural capability of demons. Hybrid systems are, however, generally more complex than rule-based systems, and therefore more expensive as well as more difficult to use.

12.3.2 Reasoning Method Selection

The choice of a knowledge representation paradigm does not happen in a vacuum. Its choice should occur concurrently with the selection of a reasoning methodology. For example if rules are selected as the representation paradigm, then the choices are clear: forward chaining, backward chaining, or bi-directional reasoning. These have been discussed extensively in Chapters 4 and 5.

If, however, the structured paradigm of frames is chosen, then we also must design a reasoning mechanism, since frames have no innate means of progressing from inputs to outputs. Some candidate techniques are described in Chapter 9.

[1] Some researchers argue, however, that demons, through their nature of filling a value in a slot whenever it is needed, provide that inferential capability in frames. This, however, makes reasoning about frames similar to rule-based reasoning, thus weakening the argument for using frames.

12.3.3 Tool Selection

Any tool selection made this early in the development process is really only tentative. As a result, no commitment of significant funds should be made to procure a full version of the intended tool. Most tool developers allow an evaluation period of a few months either free of charge or at a fraction of the cost of the full implementation of the tool.

Sometimes, however, the decision of the particular shell and hardware platform has already been made. Previous development projects may have evaluated the existing available systems, selecting a particular combination of hardware and software, which management is reluctant to change or modify due to expense (for both the equipment and training of personnel). Alternatively, the choice of tool may be limited by the computing hardware available at the developing organization.

For the purposes of this discussion, however, we assume that knowledge-based systems are a novelty to the company so no prior commitment has been made to particular hardware or software. Should this be true, two decisions must now be made:

1. Should a commercially available shell be used or should a customized shell be developed from scratch?
2. How do we evaluate and compare the various commercial shells or languages to determine which is best suited for our particular problem?

12.3.3.1 Custom or commercial shell?   The factor to consider when selecting a tool is whether effort should be expended to develop a custom shell or if a commercially available shell will be adequate. The rule of thumb to follow is if a commercial shell exists that satisfies the representation, performance, and support requirements of the project, then use that shell.

Assuming that there is a direct relationship between size and complexity (which is not always true), it is likely that such a suitable commercial shell exists for a small system; the problem merely becomes one of locating it. For medium-sized projects, some of the more sophisticated hybrid tools that support various reasoning mechanisms are good candidates.

For large projects, however, their sheer size and accompanying complexity make it less likely that a suitable commercially available shell exists. The development team must evaluate the trade off of living with a commercial shell that satisfies a portion of the project's requirements versus the time and effort that must be expended to develop a shell that is "perfect." The wrong choice can be very expensive to correct.

The major advantage of a shell is the limited time and effort required to develop an inferencing mechanism and auxiliary features since they already exist. The major disadvantage is that the knowledge engineer is limited by what the shell can and cannot do. Although vendors sometimes will modify their shells to suit a particular user under special circumstances, there is a limit to what they can do. Additionally, a shell often has features that are of no use for a particular project, yet whose overhead must be carried.

It must be noted that programming a knowledge-based system from scratch using LISP, C, or any other high level language is an arduous and time-consuming task. It does, however, allow the development team to build a shell that meets all of their specific requirements.

One possible scenario is for the development team to start a project using a commercial shell to build the initial prototype quickly. As the project develops and the system requirements evolve, this shell may fail to satisfy all of the emerging requirements. A change can then be made to an alternative— either another more suitable shell or an internally developed one.

This change does not occur without some discomfort, however. The electronic knowledge base is usually lost since no standards, like the graphic standards of CAD systems (e.g., IGES or EDS), exist to allow portability between shells. But while the current encoding of the knowledge may be lost, recoding the knowledge is a small cost when compared to the effort required originally to elicit and formulate the knowledge from the expert. This knowledge can be relatively easily restructured and recoded for the new host shell.

While this process might seem very painful, it is commonly known that during the development of most knowledge-based systems at least one major transformation or paradigm shift occurs [Hayes-Roth, 1983]. Most system development leaders would agree that if it was their choice, they would recode their systems because of subtle irregularities that have crept into their knowledge base over its development process.

12.3.3.2 Criteria for selecting commercially available shells. Choosing a shell that is poorly matched to your problem is analogous to forcing a person to walk a long distance in a pair of shoes that are several sizes too small. If the initial decision is made to use a commercially available shell, you must consider a number of issues, including:

1. *Knowledge representation and reasoning paradigm:* The most important criterion the shell must satisfy is supporting the knowledge representation paradigm and reasoning method chosen by the knowledge engineer. The selection of the knowledge representation paradigm has already been discussed. Another criterion that may be useful to check is whether the shell allows knowledge structuring. Knowledge structuring involves manipulating the relationships between the various chunks of knowledge. In a structured knowledge base, a chunk of knowledge consists of a group of related rules that can be kept separate from other rule groups and is called into action only when the context is appropriate. For example, an automobile diagnostic system, could consist of separate groups of

rules used to diagnose problems in the transmission, ignition system, electrical system, and so forth. Any particular rule group would only be "instantiated" when there is cause to believe that they are required (i.e., it is suspected that the car has a transmission malfunction). It is a significant advantage for systems with a substantial quantity of knowledge to be able to structure the knowledge, both from an organizational and performance standpoint.

2. *Flexibility:* Another issue to consider is the flexibility of the shell. Flexibility includes:

   a. User-defined functions: Does the shell permit user-defined functions? Are they easy to write, edit, and call?

   b. External routines: Can external routines in a different language be called from within the shell?

   c. Built-in functions: Does the shell have a sufficient quantity of commonly used functions? Must all simple calculations be accomplished with user-defined procedures?

   d. Rich data structure support: Does the shell support lists, arrays, and so forth? Are such data structures likely to be needed in the system being developed?

3. *Special requirements:* Some knowledge-based systems have special requirements not commonly found in knowledge-based system shells. These requirements include:

   a. Temporal reasoning: The ability to reason using time as a parameter.

   b. Real-time operation: The definition of real time depends upon the requirements of the process. Two examples of real-time processes with significantly different requirements are air traffic control, where the targets on the radar scope move rather slowly, and diagnosis of electrical power generators, where electrical transients occur in a matter of milliseconds. In the first case, decisions are required within minutes, whereas in the second case they are required within seconds. Clearly, the real-time requirements for each application are quite different.

   c. Uncertainty management: Reasoning about uncertainty is found in most shells to some degree or another. However, there are various methods for managing uncertainty and the one employed by the shell in question may not be appropriate for your domain. This can be a significant drawback that is easy to overlook when searching for the right tool.

   d. Delivery environment: Some systems have special requirements for their delivery format (e.g., color graphics). You must be certain that these are available in the shell being considered.

   e. Ability to access other external software: A feature that may be critical to some applications is the ability to access external software packages such as databases or spreadsheets. This feature is not supported by all shells, so do not overlook it when evaluating a potential shell.

f. Graphics: Graphical output is often required when querying the user or explaining the system's resulting conclusions.

g. Windows: Since user interactions with a developed system play an important role in the ultimate acceptance of a system, features like the ability to create pop-up windows might prove extremely valuable. This feature is generally available in the more sophisticated shells.

4. *Auxiliary features:* There are several auxiliary features that can make development of a knowledge base considerably easier. These have been discussed in Chapter 2, but are listed below for completeness.

a. Knowledge-base editor: Some shells include a user-friendly knowledge editor for entering and editing the knowledge base. Others simply use a screen editor such as Emacs. While some sophisticated users prefer to use a screen editor for its flexibility, a knowledge editor has the advantage of verifying consistency and completeness within the knowledge base as it is entered. One disadvantage to an editor is that it often creates its own names for segments of knowledge. This is undesirable since the developer often wants the freedom to label the knowledge as she sees fit to make the knowledge base easier to understand.

b. Trace feature: A trace feature is common in most shells. It permits the developer to observe the operation of the system while it is executing, allowing the developer to determine whether proper actions are being taken at the appropriate time. Due to its usefulness and importance in debugging a knowledge base, you should ensure that a trace facility is available in whatever shell you use.

c. Explanation feature: Explanation of the knowledge used to arrive at the problem solution is a standard feature within most backward-chaining knowledge-based system shells. It is not, however, a feature typically provided by forward-chaining systems. As noted in the discussion of the trace feature, we should ensure that this feature is available in any backward-chaining shell chosen.

d. Testing and verification aids: These aids come in many shapes and formats. The most commonly provided aid allows the developer to build a library of test cases to execute on the knowledge base. This aid typically includes the ability to create, save, replay (i.e., execute automatically on the knowledge base), and modify their parameters on-line. Another aid that is highly desirable, but not as common, is an automatic search facility within the knowledge base that identifies either contradictory or duplicated knowledge to the developer.

e. Graphic presentation of the knowledge base: This is also a highly desirable feature found in many shells. It consists of the shell graphically displaying the relationships between the knowledge components.

5. *Performance:* A shell may meet all of the above requirements and yet be unacceptable in its performance. Many shells have good performance when the knowledge base is small (i.e., with the initial prototypes). As the knowledge grows, however, the performance can quickly degrade. When the performance of a shell is evaluated, the test cases should approximate the size of the intended application to ensure that proper performance exists at the expected size and complexity of the final system.

6. *Vendor support:* We should realize that a developed knowledge-based system may possibly be used for several years. We should, therefore, expect that the shell be maintained and its creating organization remain solvent. For that reason we should keep in mind the following:
   a. Documentation: Just like any other piece of conventional software, a shell's documentation should be complete and easy to read. It should contain examples and, if possible, a tutorial.
   b. On-line help: Ideally, the shell should provide some form of on-line tutorial or assistance in its operation. While this is useful, it is not absolutely necessary.
   c. Hot-line support: Some vendors offer hot-line services to subscribers, which answer questions quickly and efficiently for any problems that occur. These services are particularly appreciated when knowledge engineers become hopelessly frustrated on a particular problem and are unable to determine the solution.
   d. Training: The availability of training is also important in most cases. Regardless of how well the documentation is written, many features are best learned in an interactive classroom situation. This is especially true for the more sophisticated shells.
   e. Consulting: Most major shell vendors will (for a fee) assist the purchaser in the development effort. This assistance can be as simple as a part-time consultant who helps in the initial structuring of a solution, or as complex as a team that actually develops the entire system.

7. *Cost:* The definition of high cost varies with each organization. But we should note that the cost of a shell does not always reflect its capability. Many inexpensive shells provide numerous features to aid the development process, while some very expensive shells are quite limited. When purchasing any shell, carefully analyze its performance/cost ratio.

In general, salespeople tell us what we want to hear, which is sometimes not necessarily the truth. It is, therefore, important for a development team to get objective reviews of any software from people who have used it or are using it. The vendor should, therefore, be asked for user references. Naturally, they will provide you with names of individuals who will give a good recommendation of the system. It is important to ask these initial references for others who use the shell and to contact these secondary references. The latter are likely to supply a more objective review of the shell. Additionally, trade magazines regularly contain columns that review new software. These columns should be regularly consulted.

12.3.4 Selection of Human Resources

The next step in the development process is choosing the team members. The size and composition of a development team varies greatly depending upon the various factors described above. Our discussion now turns to the qualities desired within the various team members.

12.3.4.1 Choosing the right knowledge engineer.   The actions taken by a knowledge engineer and a software engineer are highly related. As a result, both jobs have many common characteristics that the engineer must display including:

1. *Competence in her field:* Like a software engineer, a knowledge engineer must have the ability to interpret clearly the requirements of a task and design the structure of a solution in a logical manner. This trait implies competence in her field. A thorough understanding of knowledge and software engineering as well as the tools within these fields is a requirement.

2. *Organized thinking:* The ability to analyze the project requirements and plan a general solution to the problem at an early stage is important. The processes of rapid prototyping in knowledge engineering and top-down design in software engineering determine the validity of the proposed solution. If the solution is carefully organized and structured, the chances of it being incorrect are significantly diminished.

3. *Patience:* In spite of rapid prototyping and incremental development, system development can be a slow and tedious process. This is particularly true of medium and large projects. The time between a project's definition and its completion can be as long as three to four years. As a result, it takes a significant amount of patience to see a project through to completion.

   Moreover, turnover in personnel during project development can become a significant setback because a system's development depends greatly on the developer's interpretation of knowledge about the application. It is difficult for a new developer to quickly pick up where another left off. As with the development of any project, a developer begins to have a good understanding of the application domain only after considerable exposure to it. This understanding allows her to accelerate the development progress. Since a new developer requires time to build a rudimentary understanding of the problem domain, this has the potential to irritate the project leader and the experts. Therefore, patience is a great virtue for all involved in a development team.

In addition to the above requirements, the knowledge engineer must possess some traits that, while certainly desirable for a software engineer, are imperative for a knowledge engineer. This is what sets a knowledge engineer apart from a software engineer.

4. *Friendliness:* We cannot understate the importance of the ability of a knowledge engineer to interact easily with other people. Knowledge engineers spend a significant amount of time interviewing and interacting with experts. These experts may or may not willingly participate, but it is certain that in either case their patience will be pushed to the limit. Thus, a friendly disposition is a definite requirement.

5. *Interpersonal communication skills:* To be effective, knowledge engineers must have the interpersonal skills to effectively communicate with the expert under all circumstances, some of which may be very trying.

6. *Interest in expanding one's knowledge:* Prospective knowledge engineers who do not enjoy experiencing and learning about new subjects may quickly lose interest in a project. This can result in a turnover of personnel with the resulting difficulties described above. Note that the domains of expertise are sometimes not new or exciting and may often be difficult to understand.

7. *Confidence in her own abilities:* The role of the knowledge engineer is to extract facts, laws, principles, and information from an expert. It is sometimes awkward for her to continually play the role of a novice, asking very elementary questions of an expert. Eventually, over the lifetime of developing a system, the knowledge engineer develops a reasonable understanding of the domain. But once she gains this understanding, she moves on to the development of another system about whose domain she may once again have little understanding. This may become very frustrating to the knowledge engineer—forever being constrained to the role of a neophyte. She may lose sight of the fact that she is very much an expert in what she does—the extraction of knowledge from some domain expert. A knowledge engineer must recognize her role and have solid confidence in her own abilities to succeed in the field over the long term.

The ideal candidate for a knowledge engineer is someone who has an excellent understanding of knowledge-based systems as well as a rudimentary understanding about the domain of application. Such a person will likely not require the time-consuming early indoctrination in the domain to be conversant in it. Realistically, however, such a combination is quite rare, and thus, compromises have to be made.

An understudy to an expert in a particular domain who is also generally knowledgeable about computing techniques sometimes represents a reasonable choice. It is often easier to teach *quasi-experts* the art of knowledge engineering than to teach computer scientists the basics of a domain of expertise for which they may not be prepared. The danger, however, is that this newly trained knowledge engineer may not be interested in developing knowledge-based systems in other domains.

Sometimes, it is better for the knowledge engineer to be totally ignorant of the domain. Then her questions are totally naive and unbiased by any prior knowledge that she might have about the domain. This allows the domain to be treated more thoroughly, thus resulting in a higher quality knowledge base. However, a disadvantage does exist: The knowledge extraction process is likely to take longer because of the time required by the knowledge engineer to build an understanding of the domain to be able to effectively represent it.

In either case, it is imperative that the knowledge engineer have a good foundation in knowledge representation and extraction, since these are her primary responsibilities.

Finally, much has been said about the disadvantages of having an expert be the knowledge engineer. While some potential problems can indeed arise, namely that the system will not reflect the collective knowledge about the domain, but rather one person's opinion, and that the system's granularity (i.e., level of detail) may not be appropriate for the task (usually too detailed), one cannot make the blanket statement that experts should never be their own knowledge engineers. It depends on the domain and, more importantly, on the expert himself. The idea certainly has some advantages since interviewing is unnecessary and no learning curve on the domain knowledge will occur (although there might be on the concepts of knowledge-based systems). We have witnessed at least one occasion where an expert has successfully developed a large knowledge-based system.

The converse, however, is usually true. That is, the (nonexpert) knowledge engineer should never play the role of an expert and make decisions about the knowledge without consulting the expert. Knowledge engineers who have been working on a particular system for several years and have become knowledgeable in the domain, may begin to think of themselves as "experts" and find themselves making expert-like decisions. While they may very well be knowledgeable, one becomes a true expert by performing an expert's tasks and not by talking to one. This can be very dangerous and should be avoided.

12.3.4.2 Choosing the right team leader.   The most critical person in the team is, of course, the team leader. We find it very difficult to state unequivocally the optimal qualities for this person since different organizations operate disparately. We feel that the requirements for such a person will undoubtedly vary depending on the size of the team and the technical sophistication of the system under development.

Nevertheless, this person should have significant experience in developing knowledge-based systems. This includes having a good understanding of knowledge acquisition, sufficient experience in knowledge-based implementation and development, a good understanding of the language or shell being used, and if possible some perception and comprehension of the domain.

A more realistic requirement may be that the team leader be at least educationally compatible with the domain. For example, an individual with a background in electrical engineering would be a poor choice for a project leader of a system to assist homeowner's insurance adjusters. Likewise, an individual with a background in sociology would be a poor choice to lead a development team in a chemical process diagnostic system.

12.3.4.3 Choosing the right expert.   The selection of the expert is also quite important. The choice, however, is usually more constrained than that of selecting the other participants because, whereas a knowledge engineer or a team leader can be hired quite easily (albeit expensively!), experts from some domain are usually in limited supply at any price. In fact, in many cases the choice is predetermined since there may be only one expert in existence within the organization. Nevertheless, for the sake of completeness, let us assume that more than one expert is available to work on a project and a selection must be made. The following is a list of desirable traits that the selected expert should possess.

1. *Competence:* First and foremost, the expert must be unquestionably competent in his field. Developing a knowledge-based system based on incorrect knowledge is inexcusable. Competence can be measured in several ways: years of employment, publications, patents in the domain, reputation among peers, and so forth. This characteristic is as important as any other mentioned below.
2. *Articulate:* The expert should be articulate. This greatly eases the knowledge extraction task for the development team. The expert must be able to relate answers to the questions from the knowledge engineer completely as well as succinctly. He must be able to explain precisely how and why he reaches conclusions. It is not desirable to have a storyteller who repeatedly goes off on tangents, nor is it desirous to have an expert who states "Why are you asking me that! It's obvious!"
3. *Self-confidence:* The expert should be self-confident about his knowledge and his position within the organization. It is very difficult to work with an expert who is defensive about his role due to fear of being fired or demoted. Likewise, it is difficult to work with an expert who does not give straight answers for fear of being wrong. In situations where there are multiple experts, this issue is also significant, since one expert's opinion may contradict another's and you do not know who is correct.

4. *Availability:* Next to competence and articulation, this is the most significant characteristic of the expert. An ideal expert needs to be available to assist in the development of a knowledge-based system. This is a time-consuming task requiring a significant commitment from the expert. If the expert cannot make this commitment (i.e., due to overwork), no matter how willing he is, the project may be doomed to failure.

5. *Open-minded:* Having an open mind to the new technology of knowledge-based systems is important. Resistance by the expert can prove to be a major obstacle in the development of a system, while enthusiastic support can almost ensure success. Open-mindedness also applies to the expert's relationship with other experts. This is especially significant in multiexpert situations, where disagreements between the experts can develop.

6. *Personable:* Although this is not an absolute requirement (most people have at one time worked successfully with people they don't like), it greatly eases the development task. If there is a choice, a personable expert who treats other members of the development team as equals is a definite advantage.

7. *Enthusiastic:* Enthusiasm by the expert about the system and its potential is also not a requirement, but makes the development task significantly easier. An enthusiastic expert gladly devotes his time to the project. This assists not only the interview process but also, more importantly, the time between interviews when documentation or data compilation is necessary. The enthusiastic expert also acts as an advocate for the adaptation of the final system and for the development of other systems within the company.

12.3.5 Development Team Requirements

The most important factor determining the composition of the development team is the complexity of the knowledge-based system under development. The business culture (i.e., the business atmosphere or professional environment) of the sponsoring organization can also influence the formation of the development team, but it is very difficult to generalize this concept given the many different cultures that exist.

If we assume a direct relationship between the size of the knowledge-based system and its complexity (an assumption that is not always valid), the description of development teams breaks down into three classes of systems: (1) small, (2) medium, and (3) large. Let us examine the characteristics of each of these classes in turn.

12.3.5.1 Small knowledge-based systems.   Small systems are those requiring approximately 100 to 200 rules. The knowledge within these systems may be exclusively heuristic or a mixture of procedures and heuristics. The expertise used to develop these systems may be readily available from an expert and/or printed literature. Occasionally, this knowledge can be implemented as a simple decision tree.

A good example of this class of systems is the COOKER system described briefly in Chapter 1 [AInteractions, 1985], which consists of 151 rules. Other examples include simple diagnostic systems (e.g., verification of medical diagnosis [Dankel, 1988] and X-ray machine repair [Jenkins, 1986]); small motor design [Palmin, 1986]; simple selection-type systems (e.g., vacation planners [Personal Consultant User's Manual, 1986] and simple financial advisors [Gupta, 1987]); and others that simulate rather uncomplicated knowledge-based tasks [Mahler, 1989].

Some features of this class of knowledge-based system include the following:

1. They usually employs rules as the main knowledge representation paradigm.
2. They use simple commercially available shells.
3. They are normally developed and implemented on personal computers.
4. They are often developed by the expert himself.
5. They use a single expert if a knowledge engineer is required.

It is difficult to define the team requirements for this type of system because of their limited scope. As mentioned above, these systems do not always require a knowledge engineer, since experts themselves often undertake the development task if they are computer-oriented to any degree. If a knowledge engineer is required and used, there is certainly no more than one. The duration of the development process should be approximately six months.

These types of projects are ideal for training new knowledge engineers. Because of their relatively small size, it is entirely realistic that such systems be developed by students in a one academic semester course. For that reason, this book concentrates on this type of system in the examples and the exercises.

12.3.5.2 Medium systems.   Medium systems involve more complex domains where problem-solving knowledge is mostly heuristic in nature. While these systems typically contain between 250 and 1,000 rules, the number of rules does not always reflect the complexity of the system since other knowledge representation paradigms, such as frames, may alternatively be used. Nevertheless, the number of rules provides a convenient, though not perfect, measurement for classifying systems. It is in these size systems where drastic midstream corrections begin to become costly and should be avoided if possible.

Medium systems have been developed in the areas of diagnosis (KATE [Cornell, 1986], SOPHIE [Brown, 1975], and MUD [Khan, 1984]), planning (MOLGEN [Stefik, 1981a, 1981b]), analysis (CONGEN [Carhart, 1979]), and scheduling (ISIS [FOX, 1984]) to name a few. These systems typically:

1. Solve moderately complex problems.
2. Are implemented using a custom developed or sophisticated hybrid shell.
3. Are developed using a specialized workstations or larger computer.
4. Can possibly be delivered on a personal computer.
5. Probably used multiple experts in their development.
6. Had the developers greatly concerned with the structuring of the knowledge due to its magnitude.
7. Employ expertise not completely found in printed material.

The development team requirements for this type of system are significantly more demanding than for small knowledge-based systems. These projects require at least one knowledge engineer and sometimes more. A typical development team might be composed of a senior knowledge engineer acting as team leader, a junior knowledge engineer, at least one domain expert, and possibly the part-time assistance of a conventional system's analyst.

The senior technical leader, experienced in developing knowledge-based systems, is employed in structuring the system so that little time is wasted once the project has begun. This also minimizes the possibility of midstream corrections. With the junior knowledge engineer, the leader interviews the domain expert, often directing these interviews. The junior knowledge engineer is responsible for structuring the knowledge, implementing the knowledge base, and testing and validating the system and its documentation. The system analyst assists the knowledge engineers in interfacing the knowledge-based system to other software packages such as a database or to another computer system, if applicable. While multiple domain experts might be used in the development of a system, it is important that one expert act as the main source of knowledge. The other experts can serve to verify as well as clarify the implemented knowledge. This, however, can be a tricky situation, one discussed in greater depth in Chapter 13.

One important consideration should be noted about the individuals employed. When developing a medium or large system, it can be dangerous if an expert is used as a knowledge engineer. This danger occurs because that individual will often tend to reflect his personal biases and opinions within the system and not those of other experts in the field. Although this may be acceptable for many small systems developed by the expert himself, this is usually not true for medium or large systems where a wide class of knowledge is to be represented.

The duration of medium-sized systems, from their initial conception to implementation, is typically one to two years.

12.3.5.3 Large systems.   Large systems typically contain more than 1,000 rules or their equivalent. They can be characterized partially by their mixture of knowledge representation paradigms and procedural algorithms that are required to express their highly heuristic problem-solving knowledge. These additional paradigms and algorithms are necessary in highly technical fields because of the inefficiencies in most circumstances of expressing all knowledge as rules. Examples of systems include GenAID [Gonzalez, 1986], DENDRAL [Lindsay, 1980], PROSPECTOR [Duda, 1978], XCON [McDermott, 1982], and GEMS (another electrical machinery diagnostic system developed at SRI International and Ontario Hydroelectric of Canada) [Lloyd, 1989]. Each of these systems has more than 1000 rules or their equivalent. Other features of large knowledge-based systems include:

1. An intricate and complex problem.
2. A likely requirement to interface with other software and/or hardware.
3. A potentially serious problem with the management of the knowledge.
4. A need for multiple experts.
5. A requirement for a special purpose, custom shell or a sophisticated, commercially available shell.
6. A workstation or special purpose computer as a development vehicle.
7. A delivery vehicle similar to the development machine.

Because of the size of these projects, the development team is significantly larger. A team typically consists of various junior knowledge engineers under the supervision of the technical leader, who should be an experienced knowledge engineer herself, a full-time system analyst, and an overall project manager. The logistics for a large system are such that the team would probably need to divide the problem into various components, which would be developed independently by the various knowledge engineers. Hopefully, these components would be independent of each other but, should they not be, the technical leader has to define clearly the boundaries of the different components and how the components interface with each other. Wherever they overlap, she should create guidelines so that no knowledge is duplicated or falls through the proverbial cracks. Some of these components may require knowledge from different experts, so it is important for the leader to have a presence in all knowledge-acquisition interviews at least initially.

Needless to say, the responsibilities of the technical leader are much greater for these projects than for medium-size projects because of the many people involved. Consequently, it is desirable that the leader have some background in the domain of the knowledge-based system. This will greatly aid her in designing, structuring, and organizing her team and its solution. However, this is often not realistic.

Another significant difference in large systems is that the development team may require some full-time expertise in system engineering. This is due to the likelihood that a large system, especially in technical domains, requires some type of interface to another computer system.

The biggest difference, however, is that the development team should include an overall project manager to deal with budgets as well as the organizational politics that are likely to exist in any large development effort. As we can suspect, the technical leader will not have the time to perform these functions. The project manager should, hopefully, have technical background in knowledge-based systems so he/she will understand the problems associated with knowledge-based systems development, but this is not an absolute requirement. The technical expertise in knowledge-based systems development will be provided by the technical leader.

12.4 INITIAL PROTOTYPE (IP)

The main objective of the initial prototype is to implement immediately the design decisions made in the previous step and test their validity within the context of the problem. If a paradigm shift or a tool change is required, it can then be carried out as early as possible to minimize wasted effort as well as expenditures for unnecessary hardware and software. The development of the initial prototype should be performed in the same fashion as that of the real system. The IP should, of course, follow the requirement specifications as closely as the actual system will.

As mentioned above, it is quite possible that the IP will ultimately become one part of the final system. Usually, however, the IP will be set aside (or thrown away!) because some decisions made during its development will prove to be less than optimal, and it would require too much effort to fix the IP to reflect the revised thinking of the development team.

The significant decision to be made, therefore, is to define the scope of the IP. The following comments should aid in making this decision.

1. The main objective of the IP is to learn firsthand about the knowledge in the domain. Thus, its most important component should be a prototype knowledge base.

2. The prototype knowledge base should be deep enough to solve some complete subproblems from input to output, but be very narrow so as not to present a significant effort. For example, in the development of an automotive diagnostic system, an appropriate scope for the IP might be to implement the knowledge required to solve problems within a car's fuel system.

3. Once the knowledge, the inputs, and the outputs for five to ten different subproblems have been implemented and you can see that to do any more would be carrying out the same process repeatedly, then the prototype knowledge base is probably complete.
4. The development team should learn as much as possible about the entire domain during the development of the IP. Thus, it is important to try to set the IP within the context of the entire system. For example, the IP might represent 5 percent of the knowledge required for the final system. This can assist in getting a better estimate of system cost and schedule.
5. The expected effort for an IP should be about two to four weeks for a small system, and two to four months for medium and large systems.
6. The user interface is important and a prototype version should be implemented in the IP. However, the development team should not spend a disproportionately large amount of effort developing the interface, to the exclusion of developing the prototype knowledge base.
7. The prototype should be validated and verified in the same fashion as the entire system. Representatives of the user population should be allowed, nay, encouraged, to use the IP and provide feedback.
8. A report should be written at the completion of the IP addressing the validity of the decisions made in the preliminary design stage of the knowledge engineering process.

Upon revising any decisions made in the preliminary design stage, the development process can proceed to the detailed design.

12.5 DETAILED DESIGN

Just as data flow diagrams and a hierarchical (structure) charts provide road maps for conventional software systems, the detailed design of a knowledge-based system uses similar instruments. The importance of these instruments in the simplification of the system maintenance is significant.

While data flow diagrams and structure (hierarchy) charts, because of their procedural nature, are not readily applicable to knowledge-based systems, two important instruments for representing the design of a knowledge-based system are available:

1. *Modified structure charts* (MSC): The objective of *modified structure charts* is to depict the overall structure of the system, specifically the modules of knowledge within the knowledge base. While they may look quite similar to a conventional structure chart, they do not follow a conventional structure chart's strict requirements (e.g., one-entry–one-exit, sequential flow of control). Each module may represent some component

of related knowledge that is to be kept together and, possibly, subdivided. Some tools provide a mechanism for subdividing a knowledge base into manageable "chunks." Higher level rules are then provided that identify when particular "chunks" are to be utilized during problem solving. PC Plus provides a feature like this called *frames* (an unfortunate and confusing misnomer because it has nothing to do with the concept of frames introduced in Chapter 6). In earlier versions of the Personal Consultant series, this feature was called *contexts,* a more properly descriptive name.

The modules should follow the principles of loose coupling and functional cohesion. Loose coupling means that the modules are as independent of each other as possible, while functional cohesion means that the knowledge within each module pertains to a single, specific purpose.

The concept of code reuse is rather inapplicable within knowledge-based systems because the knowledge contained within these systems is very specific and domain dependent. To illustrate their structure, Figure 12.1 depicts a MSC for an automobile diagnostic system.

2. *Knowledge diagrams:* The *knowledge diagram* is the second instrument that can assist in the detailed design of the knowledge-based system. This diagram represents the detailed knowledge expressed in the paradigm of choice, (i.e., rules, frames). This is not always easy to do, but we feel it is necessary for proper control of the knowledge-base contents.

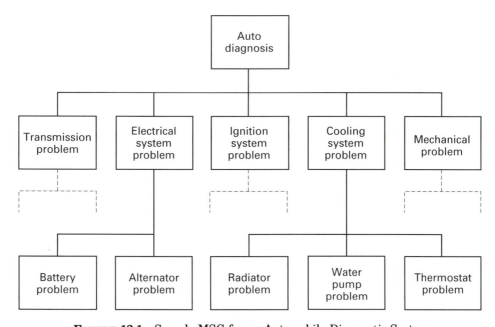

FIGURE 12.1   Sample MSC for an Automobile Diagnostic System

Some tools graphically display the relationship between the pieces of knowledge in a knowledge base. If your tool provides such displays, then knowledge diagrams may not be needed. Nevertheless, a separate hard copy documentation of the knowledge should be part of the system documentation. Maintenance of the system without it can be a painful process. The knowledge diagram is discussed in more depth in Chapter 13.

12.6 CHAPTER REVIEW

There are many important issues at the initial stages of a knowledge-based system development project. The most important of these are the preparation of a specification to identify the requirements of the project and the design of the system. The system design includes a preliminary design stage in which some general decisions about the knowledge representation paradigm, the reasoning method, and the tool are made. The preliminary design additionally involves the determination of the composition of the development team. The *initial prototype* provides a means for verifying the appropriateness of these decisions before it becomes too costly to revise them. The detailed design stage is where we design the architecture of the system, much like the structured chart provides a design of conventional software.

At the completion of Chapter 12, you should be ready to begin the task of acquiring the knowledge from the experts and to implement that knowledge in the chosen tool. These tasks are covered in Chapter 13 and 14.

12.7 PROBLEMS

12-1. You are the owner of a sporting goods store in Ft. Lauderdale, FL. Customers come to you all the time to buy deep-sea fishing gear, and these sales represents a sizable portion of your business. However, the out-of-town customers who have never been deep-sea fishing continually ask questions about the proper type of baits, lures, rods, and reels, as well as about the right time of day or night to catch a particular type of fish. This is taking quite a bit of your time, and you would like to pass this task along to someone (or something) else to do. Since you are a part-time computer science student at the local university, you feel that this is something that a knowledge-based system could do well. As a class project, you undertake this task. Write a specification and prepare a modified structure chart for this project. Determine and justify your choice of a knowledge representation paradigm and determine an appropriate reasoning mechanism. Decide which tool you would prefer for this application: PC Plus or CLIPS.

12-2. You are working your way through engineering school by teaching deer hunters in Northwestern Pennsylvania the art of "bagging a buck." You include tracking the prey through the snow, where and how to wait for it, how to shoot a gun, gun safety, and hunting regulations. You certainly do not want to limit your lucrative instruction business, but you feel it could be enhanced through a knowledge-based system. Develop a specification and a modified structure chart for this system. Use your imagination if you are not a hunter. Choose a knowledge representation paradigm and reasoning mechanism, and select a shell between PC Plus and CLIPS. Besides the domain, how else is this problem different from the one above? How is it similar?

12-3. Select a problem in which you consider yourself an expert. Then, prepare a specification, a modified structure chart for a limited subproblem of the domain. Determine the knowledge representation paradigm, the reasoning mechanism, and appropriate tool (either PC Plus or CLIPS) required with justifications for your choices.

12-4. For any of the preceding problems, determine whether the system would be small, medium, or large. Justify your answer. Define a properly sized team to carry out the project. Estimate the time to develop it.

12-5. For the problem chosen in Problems 12-3 and 12-4, select people from among your friends and/or classmates to fill the team members' job descriptions and justify the selection.

12-6. Choose the problem descriptions from Chapter 11 that you considered good applications of knowledge-based systems. Confirm your decision by developing the following for each:
(**a**) Specification.
(**b**) Modified structure chart.
(**c**) Knowledge representation paradigm.
(**d**) Reasoning mechanism.
(**e**) Tool.
(**f**) Expected size of the system.

12-7. Consider the job of an automobile mechanic. When a mechanic diagnoses the problem in an automobile, his task has only begun. He knows what part must be replaced, the time involved, and the procedure that must be performed. But there are many types of automobiles that share common parts. These parts are shared, not only across different models, but also across different years. In short, it can be difficult for a mechanic to determine if a particular part available in stock is appropriate without actually trying the part out. If you were in charge of developing a knowledge-based system to solve this problem, would you use a rule-based system? If so, what features would you require it to possess? If not, why not, and what would you use instead?

13 ▮ Knowledge Acquisition and System Implementation

13.1 INTRODUCTION

Knowledge acquisition and incremental development are normally the most time-consuming phases in the development of a knowledge-based system. These two steps involve an iterative process of knowledge extraction, representation, and confirmation that can seemingly continue forever. Thus, it is of utmost importance that this cycle proceed as smoothly as possible to limit the number of iterations that must be taken to create a system.

This chapter examines the topic of knowledge acquisition and the many issues involved. Within this chapter we cover the chronology or sequence of events that occurs when a single knowledge engineer interfaces with one domain expert, the different types of interview structures used, and techniques used during these interviews.

13.2 KNOWLEDGE ACQUISITION

The real task of developing a knowledge-based system begins after selecting and justifying the application, preparing a requirements specification, and designing the knowledge-based system as described in the previous two chapters. Employing incremental development, also called "proto-cycling," this task develops and expands the system's knowledge base. A key process in the incremental development phase is the acquisition of knowledge. Knowledge acquisition is composed of (1) *knowledge elicitation* of the knowledge from the sources and (2) *representation* of this knowledge within the tool.

Knowledge elicitation encompasses many facets. Through this process a knowledge engineer extracts expertise so that it can later be represented electronically. Note that there is a subtle difference between knowledge elicitation and knowledge acquisition that we defined previously. The former specifically refers to the elicitation of knowledge by the knowledge engineer from various sources (e.g., primarily an expert but also books, reports, drawings, visual inspection). Knowledge acquisition, on the other hand, refers to the elicitation *and* internal representation of the knowledge within the tool.

The main vehicle for knowledge elicitation is face-to-face discussions between the expert who possesses the domain knowledge and the knowledge engineer who asks questions, observes the expert solving problems, and determines what knowledge is being used. These discussions, or *interviews*, occur repeatedly over several weeks or months making this a rigorous but tedious process. As a result, this phase represents a significant portion of the knowledge-based system development effort. Thus care should be taken to perform it efficiently to minimize its effect.

Consider the following statement:

> In general, the knowledge engineer has a greater stake in the success of the project than does the expert.

Despite who is at fault, should a project be canceled due to lack of progress or any other difficulty, the expert will probably not be held responsible and will still have a job. That may not be the case for the knowledge engineer, who at the very least would find herself explaining this failure to suspicious superiors and peers. Thus, we begin our discussion with the premise that the burden of success, which requires establishing a good working relationship with the expert, falls largely on the knowledge engineer.

The following sections discuss the interview process. Interviewing is first described as a sequence of different types of sessions each having separate and distinct objectives. We then concentrate on other issues in the process, for example, techniques for extracting knowledge from the expert(s).

13.3 THE BASIC UNSTRUCTURED ONE-ON-ONE INTERVIEW

Interviews can take many different formats, as presented below. No matter what format is used, in most knowledge-based systems, knowledge elicitation is performed one-on-one. This simply means that one knowledge engineer and one expert meet and interact in an unstructured manner. All other interview formats are variations of this theme. Ideally, the one-on-one interview process consists of a series of interview sessions, each having slightly different objectives.

13.3.1 Kickoff Interview

The main objective in this first meeting is the creation of a good rapport with the expert. If this is the first extensive meeting between the knowledge engineer and the expert, the knowledge engineer should attempt to make a good first impression.

This can be achieved by demonstrating to the expert that an honest attempt has been made by the knowledge engineer to gain familiarization with the domain before the meeting. Therefore, when preparing for this initial interview, the knowledge engineer should acquaint herself with the discipline. Extensive familiarization is not required nor desired since the expert's guidance should be used in learning about the domain and significant prior knowledge might cause important relationships to be ignored (since they might appear to be "obvious" facts or relationships about the domain to both the expert and knowledge engineer).

A typical agenda for the initial interview consists of:

1. An introduction and light conversation.
2. An explanation of what knowledge-based systems are and their relationship to this project.
3. A discussion of the importance of the project (if applicable).
4. A discussion of what is expected of the expert as well as what the expert can expect from the knowledge engineer.
5. A discussion of what reading materials the expert recommends for the knowledge engineer to review to familiarize herself with the domain.
6. The scheduling of the next meeting.

We now discuss each of these critical agenda items in greater detail.

After a few minutes of introduction in which the knowledge engineer and expert get to know each other, the conversation should shift to a discussion of the project. The knowledge engineer should explain what a knowledge-based system is and how this technology relates to the expert's domain. The advantages of a successful project should be identified and discussed. The depth of this discussion should be determined by the knowledge that the expert possesses about computers. If the expert is computer literate, the knowledge engineer might assume prior familiarity with knowledge-based systems in general and thus talk about new knowledge representation techniques, hardware platforms, software tools, and so forth. Alternatively, a nontechnical expert may require definitions of simple terminology (e.g., knowledge base) and not be interested in hearing the details of the technology. A key to this discussion is getting the expert familiar with *what* is going to be done, not the specifics of *how* it will be done. When the system is actually being developed, the expert should be spared all implementation details.

The discussion should eventually shift to the documentation the expert recommends that the knowledge engineer read to gain more familiarity with the domain. This allows the knowledge engineer to use documentation familiar to the expert (i.e., textbooks, reports, illustrations) that describes the domain in terms appropriate for the knowledge engineer. The advantage of reading material recommended by the expert is that it provides the knowledge engineer with a common set of concepts, terminology, and vocabulary with the expert. This greatly assists the knowledge elicitation process.

The ground rules of the system development should be discussed next. A major requirement for building rapport is the early identification of the expectations of both the expert and the knowledge engineer. It is critical that the expert know from the beginning what is required of him in terms of time, effort, and cooperation. Likewise, it is important that the expert know what he should expect from the knowledge engineer. For example, is the expert going to have to spoon-feed the knowledge engineer? Or, will the knowledge engineer simply take a general direction supplied by the expert and work on her own? Advantages and disadvantages exist for both approaches, so it is important that they clearly identify each other's roles so their working relationship is firmly established early in the process. If the expert, due to other commitments, cannot or does not want to make the required commitment toward this project, then it is better to know this up front so alternatives can be explored. Included within these discussions should be a description of the interview process, an explanation of the concepts of incremental development, and possibly a short dialogue on verification and testing.

It is important that the length of the kickoff interview be kept short (i.e., to not more than one hour). Remember that the most significant accomplishment of the kickoff session is establishing rapport. All other goals should be secondary.

13.3.2 Knowledge Elicitation Sessions

These sessions, following the kickoff interview, begin the actual knowledge elicitation process. We can categorize them into one of two types by the types of knowledge gathered: (1) general knowledge-gathering sessions and (2) specific problem-solving knowledge-gathering sessions.

The knowledge engineer uses the first category to learn general principles about the domain from the expert. The knowledge she gathers, while important and educational, will probably not be explicitly coded within the knowledge base since it is primarily used to gain a basic understanding of the domain. She requires this knowledge to understand the more specific problem-solving knowledge learned in the later sessions.

The knowledge engineer uses the second category of sessions to understand and gather the specific problem-solving knowledge used by the expert. It is this knowledge that she must represent within the knowledge base. In the next two subsections we describe these sessions in more detail as well as some useful techniques in extracting knowledge.

13.3.2.1 General knowledge-gathering sessions.

The first few sessions after the kickoff interview are general knowledge-gathering sessions. The main objectives for the knowledge engineer at this point are to:

1. Understand the problem domain better.
2. Understand the expert's opinions and viewpoints on the domain.
3. Continue building rapport with the expert.

Before the first of these sessions, the knowledge engineer should be well read in the domain, having not only reviewed the literature suggested by the expert, but also other documents she could locate that were not mentioned. After reading this information, she has a vocabulary and basic understanding of the domain that enables her to converse with the expert. This relieves some of the burden from the expert, since he will not be required to continually define every term that he uses. It also facilitates the major task of these sessions: knowledge gathering through an interview consisting of *open-ended* questions.

Open-ended questions are similar to essay questions on an examination. They require discussion and cannot be answered simply with yes, no, a term, or a number. Using these questions is effective because they give the expert an opportunity to talk freely about the domain and, thus, serve as a concentrated learning experience for the knowledge engineer. Experts generally enjoy an opportunity to speak openly about their domain and show how much they know. This can help a reluctant or distrustful expert relax and feel more at ease sharing his knowledge and skills. Even experts who are either reluctant or mistrustful become more cooperative. An astute knowledge engineer also benefits from such dialogues by gaining insight into how the mind of the expert works. This verifies and strengthens her understanding of the domain. If she does not understand certain concepts or terminology, this is the proper time to ask questions.

The danger in asking open-ended questions is that the expert may take *uncontrolled walks* or tangents through the domain. While these digressions may appear very interesting, they can result in wasted time, a feeling of frustration for the knowledge engineer, and difficulty bringing the expert back to the main path or topic of the interview. While *controlled walks* are desirable, only a fine line separates them from uncontrolled walks, making it often very difficult for the domain-naive knowledge engineer to direct the interview. Remember that open-ended questions require great tact and patience. Failure to use tact and patience can make it difficult for the knowledge engineer to maintain control of the interview without angering or losing patience with the expert.

Interviews such as these may range from one to three hours in duration. It is often difficult and undesirable to schedule longer periods with the expert. Experts are in high demand; thus it is often difficult to find extended periods of time when they are free.

Concentration abilities also decrease quickly after two to three hours. If you have an option, it is best to hold these interviews in the early morning because everyone will be fresh and there is less chance that the expert will already be involved with a problem from which he cannot break away.

Open-ended questioning should continue for enough sessions to satisfy the objectives of obtaining a better understanding of the problem domain, the expert's opinions and viewpoints on the domain, and a continued building of rapport with the expert. During this time the knowledge engineer is also digesting and attempting to understand the knowledge presented with the objective of identifying subproblems that are appropriate for further examination.

13.3.2.2 Specific problem-solving, knowledge-gathering sessions.   Once the knowledge engineer understands the basics of the domain, the process of incremental development can be started by selecting a subarea that will serve as the first chunk of knowledge to be extracted from the expert and represented within the system. Specific subareas can be difficult to identify since a definition of what is appropriate for further examination is somewhat nebulous. It can depend greatly on nontechnical issues such as schedule requirements or customer preferences. However, this subarea should involve problems that are

1. Well understood by the particular expert being interviewed.
2. Fairly well understood by the knowledge engineer.
3. Of sufficient breadth and depth to truly represent the difficulties of problems within this domain.
4. Small enough to require only two to three months of development effort without trivializing the scope of this domain's problems.

Now that the expert has (hopefully) shed his inhibitions about the project, the knowledge engineer has become comfortable with the domain, and an initial subproblem has been identified, it is time to shift the focus of the interviews from general fact gathering and learning to more specific knowledge identification. Whereas the previous interviews were of a wide-ranging nature, these are highly directed, emphasizing depth instead of breadth of coverage.

The objective of these interviews is to explore how the expert solves specific problems. More specific questions are asked, many of which result in yes/no or numeric answers. Such questions are called *close-ended questions*.

During these interviews, care must be taken to keep the expert focused on the problem at hand, diplomatically not allowing him to digress from the question being posed. Efforts should be made to relate interviews to each other. The first part of any interview should summarize the subject and knowledge gained during the previous interview. This review process allows the expert to verify the correctness of the knowledge and promotes continuity throughout the knowledge acquisition process. A more detailed discussion of this step follows in Chapter 14, Section 3.3.1.

13.3.3 Knowledge Organization

One knowledge organization technique commonly used is the *output-input-middle* method. This technique consists of the following sequence:

1. Identifying the answer(s) or solution(s) to the problem being discussed— the system's *outputs*. These represent the goal(s) that the expert and the knowledge-based system reach when searching for an answer. In the case where more than one exists, they should all be defined with their subtle differences clearly identified. These differences should be understood by the knowledge engineer.
2. Identifying the sources of information that the expert uses to deduce the solution—the system *inputs*. How these inputs are identified, determined, and generated should also be known and understood by the knowledge engineer.
3. Finally and most important, determining the links between the inputs and the outputs—the *middle*. These connections represent the core of the expert's knowledge. Some inputs may not be required initially, but are requested later after the initial inputs are interpreted. Additionally, intermediate goals or hypotheses may be required to complete the connections.

The boxed example illustrates this concept for an automotive diagnostics knowledge-based system.

Output-Input-Middle Example

An expert mechanic system is being designed that will allow motorists to call and obtain a diagnosis of their automobile's cooling system malfunction. The motorist is assumed to be not mechanically inclined and, therefore, unable to inspect obvious parts like hoses or belts. All communication with the motorist takes place over the telephone (i.e., the expert does not actually see the automobile). The builder of this sample knowledge base first compiled a list of all the possible problems that can occur with the cooling system of an automobile.

OUTPUTS: The possible outputs expected in this domain are:

> leak in radiator
> broken fan belt
> defective water pump
> loss of coolant through evaporation due to a loose radiator cap
> broken or cracked water hose
> frozen coolant

Then she determines the various inputs used to discover these problems.

INPUTS: The inputs necessary for an expert mechanic to diagnose the cooling system malfunction are:

> temperature indicator on the dashboard
> steam coming out of the hood
> weather conditions
> puddles of coolant underneath engine compartment

Last, the expert determines the relationships between the inputs and the outputs. This may require some intermediate goals or states that she may have to define. These relationships are translated into the rules of the system. A sample of the set of rules that the expert might have determined are needed for diagnosing cooling systems is provided below. Note that these rules are just a representative sample, not the complete set required.

MIDDLE: Since the knowledge of this domain is mostly heuristic, the appropriate format for representing it is rules. Some rules determined to be applicable are:

> Rule 1: The presence of a "hot" reading on the dashboard temperature gauge generally implies that at least one problem exists.

> Rule 2: The absence of a "hot" reading on the temperature gauge does not necessarily imply absence of a problem.

> Rule 3: A large pool of coolant under the engine compartment can indicate radiator leaks, broken hoses, and/or a defective water pump.

> Rule 4: A relatively small pool of coolant under the engine compartment usually implies a defective water pump.

> Rule 5: Absence of a pool of coolant under the engine compartment, and a "hot" reading on the dashboard temperature gauge indicates a broken fan belt.

> Rule 6: An ambient temperature below 10° Fahrenheit implies that the coolant is frozen.

> Rule 7: The presence of a hissing sound accompanied by a small pool of coolant under the engine compartment indicates a radiator and/or hose leak.

Another technique to consider that may assist in structuring the interview is to determine whether there is a standard script that describes the process that the expert typically performs. If the task is a common one, a standard script may already be in existence. If not, it may be useful to create one if it is going to be used heavily. For example, a script for going to the restaurant is to enter and be greeted by a host; proceed to the table and be given a menu; order the food; eat the food (which may be subdivided into a description of the different courses); receive and pay the bill; and exit the restaurant.

An example of a more realistic situation that could occur in a knowledge-based system exists in our diagnosis of an automobile's problems. For example, this includes the analysis of symptoms to determine the faulty subsystem; performing tests to obtain more information; using this information to narrow the problem further to a set of two or three possibilities; using experience or other tests to further segregate the possibilities, possibly narrowing the scope to a single possibility; verifying that the possibility being considered is the particular problem; and repairing the problem.

13.3.4 Knowledge Documentation

In Chapter 12 we discussed the knowledge diagram as an instrument for documenting elicited knowledge. Documenting knowledge is an important facet of the implementation stage, since the knowledge must somehow be represented before it can be implemented. The documentation also serves as a permanent "paper" record of the knowledge. However, because of the advanced display features available in some commercial shells, having a permanent, external record of the knowledge may not be a significant issue.

There are a number of graphical representations for knowledge including tables, decision trees, and flow diagrams. Each has minor differences from the others in how the knowledge is presented and what portion of the knowledge is emphasized. But despite these differences, any knowledge diagram should be capable of displaying all of the significant components of the knowledge (e.g., all rules of a rule-based system or each network node/frame/object of a structure-based system). Since there is no universally accepted best method for representing knowledge, the methods discussed below merely represent the authors' preferences.

A rule-based system's knowledge diagram details how the rules connect facts together. This is typically detailed as a network of interconnected nodes where each node represents a single fact or a parameter. The directed arcs connecting nodes identify which parameters are used to derive values for others. For example the arc between nodes A and B in Figure 13.1a identifies that A is the premise of rule 1 while B is its conclusion. Conjunctions and disjunctions are diagrammed as shown in Figures 13.1b and 13.1c. Rules involving multiple conclusions can be diagrammed as a set of rules (Figure 13.1d) or as shown in Figure 13.1e.

(a)   A simple rule

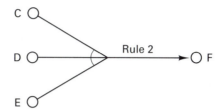

(b)   Conjunctive rule

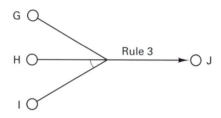

(c)   Disjunctive rule

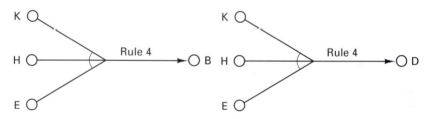

(d)   Set of rules diagramming multiple conclusions

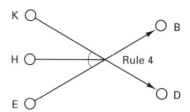

(e)   Single rule diagramming multiple conclusions

FIGURE 13.1   The Structure of Rule-based Knowledge Diagrams

Since a knowledge diagram contains many rules, the input parameters are generally shown on one side of the diagram with outputs on the opposite side for ease in understanding. Note that the structure of the diagram is independent of whether the rule-based system uses forward, backward, or bidirectional reasoning. The diagram merely shows the causal direction, not the direction of inference. See Figure 13.2.

It is considerably easier to represent the rules of an inference net system than those of a pattern-matching system because of the variability provided within the pattern-matching rules. Nevertheless, pattern-matching systems can be described. Each node of the network represents a particular fact that can be derived and the rules simply connect the nodes that satisfy the patterns that they contain. Two problems exist with this approach. First, you might not be able to create nodes describing every possible fact. And second, multiple copies of each rule must be placed in diagram: one for each set of facts that it matches. As the patterns become complex, the diagram can become unwieldy. As a result, diagrams are rarely developed for any but the simplest of pattern-matching systems.

It is often easy to document frames because of their structured nature. In many applications a network of frames can be diagrammed as a set of nodes interconnected by their inheritance relationships as shown in Figure 13.3a. If more detailed information must be included, the noninheritance slot/value pairs can be displayed within each node as shown in Figure 13.3b. Should the inheritance diagram be complex or if each frame contains numerous slots, these slot/value pairs might be described through separate diagrams, one for each frame.

Often the relationships between frames that are not inherited must be depicted to properly convey the represented knowledge. For example, Figure 13.4

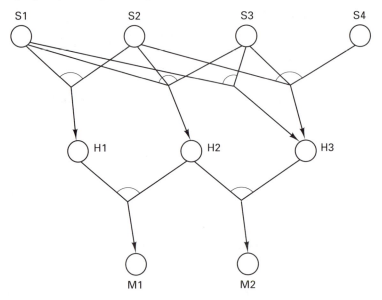

FIGURE 13.2   A Simple Rule-based Knowledge Diagram

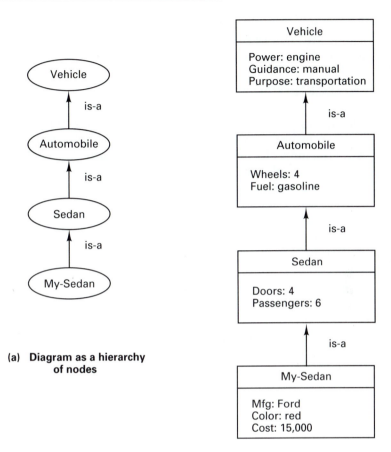

(a) **Diagram as a hierarchy of nodes**

(b) **Diagram as a hierarchy of nodes detailing slot values**

FIGURE 13.3   Frame-based Knowledge Diagrams

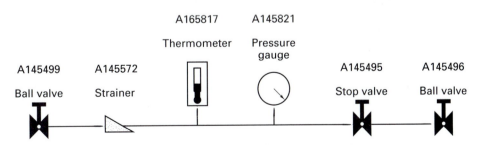

FIGURE 13.4   Diagram of a Process System Path

shows the components of a simple process system and their interconnections. These are expressed using the *connected-to* relationship as shown in Figure 13.5.

13.4 KNOWLEDGE ELICITATION TECHNIQUES

The unstructured question-and-answer interview described above is the most common means of extracting knowledge from an expert. However, it is not always the most efficient. There are other knowledge elicitation techniques besides the simple question-and-answer interview that can be more effective under certain circumstances. In some domains, significant quantities of expertise are documented in instruction manuals or books. Consider automobile diagnosis. There are literally dozens of maintenance manuals published for every type of automobile. Some are published by the manufacturer, while others are written by third parties. A significant portion of knowledge about automobile diagnosis can be obtained from such manuals by someone who understands the basics of that domain.

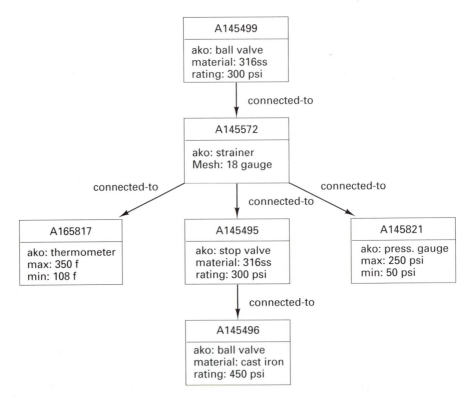

FIGURE 13.5 Knowledge Diagram of the Objects Depicted in Figure 13.4

Some experts, cooperative as they may be, often have a hard time verbalizing their expertise. Part of the reason is that they perform the tasks so automatically and subconsciously that they do not really know how they do it. They do, however, know what to do when it comes time to solve the problem. A good analogy to this is when Tom asks Joe for directions to a location to which Joe has often been. Joe's answer often is something like "I know how to get there, but I can't explain it to you."

In cases such as this, alternative techniques must be used that do not rely as heavily on the question-and-answer routine. These can be broken down into two different methods:

1. *Observational,* where the knowledge engineer observes the expert at work and tries to understand and duplicate his problem-solving methods
2. *Intuitive,* where the knowledge engineer attempts to become a pseudo-expert and implement her pseudo-knowledge about the problem domain

Both techniques are applied in an iterative fashion. The knowledge engineer gathers knowledge, implements this knowledge in the tool, and then verifies its correctness by showing the expert the resulting implementation. We next discuss each of these methods in more detail.

13.4.1 Observational Techniques

The technique of observation simply means looking over the shoulders of an expert while he does his job. This gives an indication of the data the expert uses to solve a particular (and real) problem. There are many variations of the observation technique, some of which are discussed in the following subsections.

13.4.1.1 Quiet on-site observation.   This type of observation does not permit the knowledge engineer to question the expert while he is solving a real problem. Because the expert's train of thought is not continually being interrupted by questions, he is able to proceed at his most effective as well as realistic form. One way of doing this is to have the expert think aloud as he performs a task. There is clearly something to be learned from this.

The disadvantage to this technique is that the lack of interaction leaves the knowledge engineer wondering about the solution approaches taken by the expert. Consequently, the technique of quiet observation should be used only when there is a need simply to get a feel for the total magnitude of the problem-solving process or to verify that a hypothesized approach is being used (see box for example). It is usually not a good technique for obtaining details about the process.

Pattie, a graduate student at the University of Florida, was interacting with an agricultural extension agent to build an expert system that would offer advice about when pesticides should be applied to a crop. The expert explained that he performed a field survey and counted the number of insects that fell into five size categories. Based upon the number of insects in each category and the age of the crop, he determined whether pesticides were economically warranted.

Pattie gathered knowledge from this expert and built a series of rules that described his approach. Because there were several cases not covered by the examples that they discussed, she prepared a simple written test that would uncover additional rules.

When this test was administered to the expert, Pattie discovered that the expert was reducing the five categories that he said he used to three by adding several counts together. This quiet on-site observation of the expert's problem solving allowed her to uncover the true technique that he was using, not the technique that he though he used.

13.4.1.2 On-site observation with discussion.   This is, of course, the process of observation described above without a gag order on the knowledge engineer. While this interaction does not allow the expert to be himself, thereby clouding full visibility of the problem-solving process, the inclusion of questions does permit the knowledge engineer to better probe the process that she observes. Hopefully, the difference between the real process and this interrupted process is not very significant.

If the observed task does not significantly challenge the expert's problem-solving abilities (i.e., the problem is routine for the expert), the expert will be free to devote significant time and effort toward providing a detailed explanation of his approach. A perceptive knowledge engineer can acquire significant knowledge from this exercise, because the expert will feel quite at ease and perform his task relatively uninhibited.

If the problem is significantly more involved (i.e., difficult), then the expert may have difficulty in reaching a solution. Some symptoms of this are uneasiness, hesitation in making a decision, or simply refusing to create a solution in front of the knowledge engineer. With a cooperative expert, however, such situations can provide a wealth of information. The expert will typically verbalize his problem-solving process because the problem and its solution approach are so uncertain to him. The various alternatives will be overtly explored. It is important that a question-and-answer session follow so the knowledge engineer can satisfy whatever questions were raised during the exercise, whether the observation period included questions or not.

13.4.1.3 Exercising the expert.   One disadvantage of the pure observation method is that real problems have to be used. While experts in some domains solve several problems every day, in other domains problems arise only seldomly and unpredictably. Even in domains where problems are abundant, the difficulty level of these problems may not be sufficiently high, limiting their usefulness.

One method to alleviate this difficulty is to prepare cases of varying difficulty from historical data. These can then be presented to the expert in an "off-line" environment to observe the expert's methodology.

One difficulty with this technique, especially in small organizations, is that the expert may already be familiar with most of the historical cases, having actually been involved with their solutions or knowing their results. In such situations, the effectiveness of this technique can be limited. Alternatively, since the solution is already known, he may resent being "tested."

One way to circumvent this situation is to provide what Hoffman [Hoffman, 1987] calls *limited information tasks* and *constrained processing tasks*. These are defined as follows:

Limited information tasks: A routine task is performed, but the expert is not provided certain information that is typically available [Hoffman, 1987].

Constrained processing tasks: A routine task is performed, but the expert must execute it under some constraint, for example, within a limited amount of time [Hoffman, 1987].

These techniques examine the expert's abilities to provide additional information about his problem-solving talents. Both require observation, making them special cases of the techniques described above.

13.4.1.4 Problem description and analysis.

This category does not consist of posed problems, whether real or historical, but rather classical problems. These problems are best characterized as ones typically discussed and analyzed by instructors in a classroom situation. Their importance is demonstrated by their use in the teaching environment—they illustrate important or significant relationships within the domain that every problem solver should possess. Normally, these are selected by the expert since he has been exposed to a wealth of these problems during his career, but occasionally they are selected by the knowledge engineer when she questions the approach of the expert.

In examining these problems, the expert explains the rationale behind distinguishing these problems as classics. Why are they used for teaching purposes? What are the important relationships and features that make each of these problems significant? This examination is typically performed as a case study where the expert describes the setting and then identifies the significant features that are present that make this problem important. This methodical approach clearly illustrates to the knowledge engineer what is significant and important, so she can concentrate on how it should be represented within the system.

13.4.2 Intuitive Techniques

Intuitive techniques are ideally suited for situations where the knowledge engineer already has a significant understanding of the problem-solving process and wishes to verify its correctness. These techniques are generally not used for extracting knowledge, but rather for verifying knowledge previously obtained before it is electronically represented.

A knowledge engineer using intuitive techniques attempts to become a pseudo-expert in the domain. She studies the techniques and approaches used by the expert and builds a set of protocols on how to attack problems. Then with the aid of the expert, she tests her abilities using the concept of *role playing*.

Role playing employs the idea of role reversal, where the knowledge engineer acts as the expert and vice versa. The pseudo-expert attempts to solve a problem in the presence of the true expert who questions her about what she is doing and why. In effect, this is the process of observation with questions where the roles have been reversed. With the right expert and appropriate problems, this process can clarify and modify approaches that were thought to be appropriate and can provide significant new problem-solving information not previously uncovered by the knowledge engineer.

13.5 CHAPTER REVIEW

Knowledge acquisition is the process of eliciting the knowledge from an expert and implementing it within the shell. Knowledge acquisition is the primary operation in implementing a knowledge-based system and is the longest and most arduous of the development tasks.

The basic process consists of selecting a chunk of knowledge, eliciting the knowledge, implementing this knowledge, then testing it for validity. Once this chunk is developed, another chunk is chosen and the process begins again. When the next chunk of knowledge is properly represented, it is then merged with the rest of the emerging knowledge-based system. This process is called incremental development.

The most basic means of carrying out knowledge acquisition involves a series of question-and-answer sessions with domain experts that are designed to elicit the knowledge from these experts. Such sessions, called interviews, are commonly performed one-on-one between a single expert and one knowledge engineer. The interviewing process consists into three phases:

1. The kickoff interview consisting of one initial session to set the ground rules.

2. The general knowledge-gathering interviews where the knowledge engineer tries to become familiar with the domain.

3. Specific knowledge-gathering sessions where the knowledge engineer tries to elicit more specific knowledge about solving problems.

Other knowledge elicitation techniques besides the basic question-and-answer interview are (1) observation of the expert at work and (2) intuition. The former consists of watching the expert perform a real problem-solving activity and observing his actions, either quietly, or with discussion. It can also mean exercising the expert when real problems are not readily available. Intuition involves attempting to become a pseudo-expert and trying to solve the problems faced by an expert (with his oversight). This allows the knowledge engineer to think like an expert as much as possible.

13.6 PROBLEMS

13-1. Team up with a classmate or peer who is an expert at some task (almost everybody is expert in some form of problem solving) and try to elicit their knowledge, even if it does not represent a good application for knowledge-based systems. Employ the basic one-on-one interview techniques discussed in this chapter. Begin with general knowledge acquisition. List what worked and what did not. What was the greatest difficulty faced? How did you get around it?

13-2. With the same partner, perform specific problem-solving knowledge acquisition. Use the output-input-middle method to organize the elicited knowledge. How does this differ from general knowledge acquisition? List what worked and what did not. What was the greatest difficulty faced? How did you get around it?

13-3. Team up with another classmate or peer who is an expert at some task and quietly observe how he/she solves problems or makes decisions in that domain. Do not ask questions during the problem-solving process. How does this technique compare in effectiveness to the question-and-answer interview?

13-4. Repeat the process described in Problem 13-3 allowing questions to be asked during the problem-solving process. Does this improve your ability to elicit the knowledge? What effect does it have on the expert's ability to concentrate?

13-5. After interviewing your expert using any or all of the above techniques, try solving a problem supplied to you by your expert partner. Does solving this problem provide you with a greater insight into what the expert's thinking process is? Justify your answer.

13-6. Reverse roles with your partner. List all actions that the knowledge engineer partner did that were effective in eliciting your knowledge. Also list those that were not.

13-7. Develop a knowledge diagram for the knowledge contained in the following transcript of an interview.

> *There can be many reasons why an automobile won't start. The most basic one is that it is out of fuel. This is also the simplest one to detect and recognize, but depending on where you are, it is not always*

the easiest one to fix. By looking at the fuel gauge, you can easily determine whether this is the problem or not.

From this point on, it gets somewhat more complicated. A weak or dead battery is typically the most likely cause of the problem. If the engine turns over, but does so weakly, then that is a good indication that you have a battery problem. The lights can confirm this if they are dim because a weak battery will result in either dim lights or no lights at all.

Occasionally, however, the battery may be too weak to crank up the engine properly, but it will have enough residual capacity to turn on the lights, brightly, for a short period of time. While this will happen only rarely, the presence of the bright lights might seem to contradict the dead battery assumption. What you have to consider in this case is the age of the battery. An old battery will have significantly decreased capacity, whereas a new battery should be quite vigorous. If the battery is two years old or less, then I would consider that a new battery. If the age of the battery is between two and four years, then I still say that it is new, but I say that much less confidently. On the other hand, any battery older than four years is in its last legs.

The ambient temperature also has an effect. The hotter it is, the better the battery will operate. Thus, if the temperature is below 20° F, then you can be surer of the battery problem, even though there may not be anything really wrong with the battery. The ultimate test, if you happen to have a voltmeter handy, is to measure its voltage. If the voltage across the posts is 13 volts or greater, then your battery is in good shape. Between 8 and 13, it is probably normal, but it is less so as you get closer to 8. Any voltage less than 8 means that you are beating a dead horse.

If the engine turns over and the battery does not appear to be dead, then it could be fuel starvation. This could be the result of carburetor flooding. If the carburetor is flooded, a strong smell of gasoline will be noticeable. A defective solenoid could also prohibit the car from starting. The symptoms involved here would be either a clicking sound when the ignition is operated, or no sound at all. The latter could also be due to a totally dead battery, so you have to eliminate the latter before you can be sure of the former. Nevertheless, a totally dead battery is not likely unless you left the lights on for two days straight, and I think you would probably know if you did. The last possibility is the starter motor. A good indication of a bad starter motor is if the car tries to turn over and a screeching sound comes from the motor. It could fail in other ways, but this is the most likely one.

14 ■ Practical Considerations in Knowledge Acquisition

14.1 INTRODUCTION

This chapter presents issues to consider when the knowledge acquisition process is either underway or being planned. These hints, based primarily on our experience and simple common sense, include such issues as team interviewing and its pro's and con's, optimal locations for interviews, scheduling interviews, and planning and conducting interviews. Included in this last topic is a discussion on how to deal with problem experts.

14.2 TEAM INTERVIEWING

All of the discussions about knowledge extraction interviews in the last chapter were based on one-on-one interviews between a single expert and one knowledge engineer. Another option, however, does exist that, under certain circumstances, can be extremely beneficial—team interviewing. There are three types of team interviewing:

1. One knowledge engineer and multiple experts (one-on-many)
2. Multiple knowledge engineers and one expert (many-on-one)
3. Multiple knowledge engineers and multiple experts (many-on-many)

Each has its own advantages and disadvantages.

14.2.1 One-on-many Interviews

One-on-many interviews are common when several experts work closely together. If the experts are compatible, such meetings can be very fruitful because of the synergism of the situation. Each expert may be specialized in slightly different areas, thereby complementing each other and assuring that the most complete set of knowledge is being captured. If differences in opinion arise during a discussion, chances are good that they can be resolved at that point. Usually, differences of opinion that are resolved amicably result in the uncovering of a higher level of knowledge, benefiting both the knowledge engineer and the experts. If circumstances exist for the use of one-on-many interviews, it is highly encouraged.

Problems can arise, however, if the experts do not get along with each other. Some disagreements can be very useful and productive since they help to clarify subtle issues within the domain, but an undercurrent of uncooperativeness can undermine the productivity of any interview. If the knowledge engineer detects such conflicts, she should conclude the discussion as early and as smoothly as possible. She can then take measures either to exclude the problematic expert(s) from further group discussions or, if that is impossible, revert to one-on-one interviews for all future knowledge-extraction sessions. In no case should she take sides with one expert over another. This could seriously jeopardize her working relations with the other.

There are other situations in which one-on-many interviews are not appropriate. The first is a generic knowledge-gathering session. This situation is analogous to attending an introductory computer science lecture with two or more instructors present. All of them are simply not required. Under some circumstances, such one-on-many sessions can help the experts get to know each other better if they are not from the same location and can assist the participants get into the mode of working together toward a common goal. By and large, however, multiple experts at a generic knowledge-gathering session are not a good idea since they will tend to be bored and may resent the time imposition.

The second situation where one-on-many interviews are not appropriate is when the knowledge engineer is inexperienced or introverted. A knowledge engineer of this type can easily feel overwhelmed by multiple experts. This can inhibit her from asking provocative questions, resulting in a less productive and possibly ineffective interview.

Third, it can also be fairly easy for discussions to drift away from the current subject as the experts discuss particular incidents in greater detail than may be necessary or stray into areas irrelevant to the knowledge-based system. Because the experts are talking about something that is important to them, it can be difficult for the knowledge engineer to bring the discussion back into focus. She might also not be able to recognize this deviation because of her limited knowledge of the domain.

These last two situations call for a strong knowledge engineer who can diplomatically maintain control of the meeting and not be easily intimidated by the experts. Knowledge engineers should not attempt one-on-many meetings unless they are confident of themselves, their rapport with the experts, and their understanding of the domain. Additionally, such interviews can be mentally taxing to the knowledge engineer since her concentration is required for the entire length of the meeting. While an expert can drift in and out of the conversation, the knowledge engineer must maintain continual attention not only with the topic being discussed, but also the multiple sources of knowledge (experts).

14.2.2 Many-on-one Interviews

Many-on-one interviews are normally not as advantageous as one-on-many, since the single expert may feel overwhelmed by the multitude of knowledge engineers and may thus be more defensive. There is also little chance for synergism because no one else is present with the expert's level of understanding of the domain.

One situation where a many-on-one interview is valuable is when a senior knowledge engineer or project leader conducts an interview session in the presence of one or more junior engineers who will implement the knowledge. This is certainly better than the senior knowledge engineer conducting a one-on-one interview and then explaining what to do to the junior engineers, since in such cases the senior person would presumably act as a pseudo-expert relaying (possibly incorrectly) the knowledge gained at the interview. When a many-on-one interview is directed by a senior knowledge engineer, it can additionally serve as training for the junior knowledge engineers in knowledge-acquisition techniques.

Another advantage to this approach is that multiple sets of eyes and ears are most always better than one. The junior knowledge engineers can observe the expert carefully and can identify many subtle issues that a single knowledge engineer might miss. Each can provide an alternative perspective about what happened during the interview, thereby clarifying the meeting's results.

However, the development team must be careful to not overwhelm the expert. They must refrain from discussing implementation details since these details are of little interest to the expert and may confuse him. They should also limit their discussions with each other since the purpose of the interview is to obtain knowledge from the expert and the expert's time is a valuable resource that should not be squandered. Disagreements between the knowledge engineers should also be eliminated. These can give the expert an impression of a lack of organization by the development team.

Also remember that while the different knowledge engineers can share in the gathering of knowledge (i.e., while one knowledge engineer asks questions, the others all listen), the lone expert is answering all the questions himself.

He will, therefore, become mentally exhausted long before any one of the knowledge engineers. Thus, care must be taken to keep the length of many-on-one sessions to a reasonable limit (e.g., under two hours).

14.2.3 Many-on-many Interviews

Many-on-many interviews can range from massive interviews with a roomful of experts and knowledge engineers to simple two-on-two meetings. We unequivocally do *not* recommend the former, since the larger the group, the harder it will be to accomplish the current task. Nevertheless, there are times when large interviews are unavoidable due to political pressures. If such meetings occur, a strong leader must be chosen who can control the flow of the discussion closely so that it doesn't degrade into multiple simultaneous meetings. More acceptable are few-on-few meetings (e.g., two-on-two or two-on-three) where the advantages of synergism and multiple observers combine.

14.3 PLANNING INTERVIEWS

The most important aspect of an interview occurs before it takes place—its planning. The location, time, topic, and structure of the knowledge-acquisition session all need to be considered. We begin by discussing the time and location of interviews, a seemingly trivial task that can be surprisingly significant in the overall success of the session.

14.3.1 Interview Location

The location of an interview can play an important role in its success or failure. Thus it is important that this aspect of a meeting be considered carefully when planning the interview.

One of the most important objectives in the early stages of the knowledge-acquisition process is to build rapport and gain the confidence of the expert. Because it is natural for people to feel most comfortable in familiar surroundings, the ideal location of the kickoff interview, as well as the general knowledge-gathering sessions, should be the expert's work area. Not only will the expert be more at ease, but it is also much more practical due to its proximity to the expert's sources of information (i.e., books, reports, photographs). The only caveat is interruptions. When meeting in the expert's area, you may be subject to frequent interruptions by telephone calls or visitors. The number of interruptions to which the expert will be subjected can be gauged somewhat during the kickoff meeting. If the expert does not make an effort or is unable to limit interruptions, then an alternative strategy should be established and employed.

One possible alternative is to schedule meetings in a conference room or a neutral office near the expert's workplace. This allows the expert to feel that he is within his own territory, while simultaneously limiting interruptions. Another option is to schedule meetings before or after normal working hours or during lunch when interruptions are again minimized. This alternative, however, is certainly less desirable since fatigue may occur quicker and the expert may personally find such hours unacceptable.

Once specific knowledge-gathering sessions start, the expert should feel comfortable with the knowledge engineer as well as the interview process. A shift in meeting location to the knowledge engineer's work area is often justified at this point since portions of the existing computerized knowledge-based system may need to be shown to the expert. This shift may not always be needed, especially if computer access is available in the expert's area, the knowledge engineer is from out of town, or the knowledge engineer does not have an adequate work area.

14.3.2 Interview Schedules

Interviews should, if possible, be scheduled no more than two or three working days apart. If they occur more often, the knowledge engineer will not have sufficient time to digest the acquired information, while any less frequently may introduce a loss of continuity. It is best if a routine schedule is kept (e.g., every Monday and Thursday), but in reality this can be difficult because of travel schedules and other problems the expert and/or the knowledge engineer may face.

The duration of interviews should not exceed three hours and preferably should be kept to two. Knowledge elicitation can be an intense process, and mental fatigue comes on quickly.

These above are simply guidelines. Actual situations are so diverse that following some of these guidelines may be impossible. For example, the knowledge engineer and the expert may live in different cities. Such a situation may necessitate several closely spaced marathon sessions. These sessions can be advantageous in that they require total immersion into the problem, but the loss of efficiency can become significant.

14.3.3 Preparation of Interview

Preparation for an interview session is of utmost importance. Being properly prepared demonstrates to the expert that the knowledge engineer is competent and serious about the project. Misusing the expert's valuable time during a session because of poor preparation gives the expert an impression of indifference or unprofessionalism that may affect the expert's incentive to participate.

Before the structure of any interview can be planned, the knowledge engineer needs to do some homework. This preparation is very important and consists of the following:

1. The "digesting" of the knowledge obtained during the last interview. This involves going over the recorded proceedings of the last interview and trying to understand their meaning and the knowledge contained therein.
2. The transfer of this knowledge into a representation that can be easily understood by the expert(s). This could be a paper diagram, a set of rules, or a computer implementation (preferably all three). This helps to ensure the correctness of the knowledge.

Upon completion of this work for the previous interview, the knowledge engineer is now ready to prepare the upcoming interview. This encompasses two steps: reviewing the prior work and defining the objectives for the upcoming session.

We next examine these steps.

14.3.3.1 Review of prior work.   This process does not necessarily have to be performed formally, but it is important that the knowledge engineer and the expert are satisfied that the knowledge that was gathered during the last session is valid and correct before exploring and gathering additional knowledge.

It is at this point that the knowledge engineer should introduce the evolving prototype of the knowledge-based system which includes the knowledge elicited during the previous interview(s). Demonstrating the prototype to the expert at the beginning of the interviews can be a powerful mechanism to verify the correctness of the knowledge elicited in the previous interview as well as to show the expert the amount of progress being made. Nevertheless, it must be used judiciously to avoid getting "bogged down" in its internal details during the interview. Consequently, we recommend that the evolving prototype be presented to the expert only as a black box that receives a set of inputs and provides a response to be analyzed by the expert. Any error or inaccuracy should be discussed until the knowledge engineer understands its cause. Correction of the error should wait until a later time (unless it is a very simple change).

Techniques such as role playing (see Chapter 13) can also be useful in accomplishing this verification. We should emphasize, however, that the process is altogether separate from the formal validation and verification of the system and should not replace the latter. Formal validation of the knowledge base is covered in Chapter 16.

14.3.3.2 Setting session objectives.   Once the work from previous sessions has been verified, it is time to move on to new problems. The knowledge organization recommended for use in this situation is described in the next section.

The expert needs to know the objectives of each session. It will help him to organize his thoughts and will help both the expert and knowledge engineer keep the discussion on track. As noted above, experts have a tendency to deviate from the designated path of the discussion. If they know and are reminded of the objectives, they will stay focused on the day's topic.

Typically a session involves choosing one or two new problems within the same overall chunk of knowledge and examining these problems in detail. These problems need to be clearly defined and should be realistically given the time allotted for the session. For example, consider the diagnosis of a problem within an automobile. A general class or context of problems involves the diagnosis of problems within the electrical system. One session attacking this problem context might have the objective of discussing the knowledge required to detect a dead battery (which must be replaced) and how this condition is distinguished from a battery that is discharged (and only needs to be recharged).

Some thought should be also given to the objectives of the succeeding interview. This is often difficult to do because of the uncertainty of what is going to happen in the current session. Nevertheless, it is quite advantageous to have a general road map of where the effort is going because if these can be identified at the end of the interview, it will give the expert time to prepare. Additionally, it has the side effect of showing the expert that there is an overall strategy to the process.

Carrying out these objectives is the process of conducting the interview, which we cover in the next section.

14.4 CONDUCTING THE INTERVIEW

Conducting a productive meeting is analogous to conducting a symphony. There are various forces present that, if harnessed cohesively, can result in beautiful music; otherwise, discord results. It is thus incumbent upon the knowledge engineer to maintain control to maximize the interview's productivity and achieve the interview's desired objectives.

By continually monitoring an interview's progress, the knowledge engineer can enhance its efficiency and effectiveness as well as the expert's good will. If knowledge extraction begins to seriously falter, the interview should be discontinued gracefully, even if the objectives have not yet been accomplished. There comes a point in all interviews when the concentration powers of the participants are reduced below what even a coffee break can restore. A perceptive knowledge engineer recognizes this situation and discontinues the interview before the expert suggests it.

Other important issues in conducting the interview are described in the following subsections.

14.4.1 Interpersonal Communications

A very important aspect of the interview process is the interpersonal communication between the expert and the knowledge engineer. Many knowledge-based projects have failed because of a lack of communication, while some have succeeded in spite of this barrier. If any improvement is warranted in the interviewing technique of a knowledge engineer, it is likely to be in the area of communication.

Good communication is established through good listening habits. Unfortunately, human beings are generally poor listeners. The human brain processes information more rapidly than any person can speak, leaving idle capacity to be filled with other thoughts. These thoughts can distract the listener from the current task.

At other times, people are so busy formulating the next question or rebuttal that they fail to comprehend what was said. Nonverbal as well as verbal cues indicate these poor listening habits. For example, a person who doodles while listening does not give the speaker the impression of interest to the discussion topic. Lack of eye contact by the listener may also indicate to the expert a lack of attentiveness and/or comprehension. Verbal cues include asking questions that the speaker just answered or forgetting a statement made by the speaker only moments before.

Without digressing into an in-depth examination of the art of listening, which is beyond the scope of this book, we suggest the following tasks to improve a knowledge engineer's listening habits.

1. Eye contact with the expert should be maintained as much as possible when he is speaking. The only exception to this should be when it is necessary to take notes.
2. Interruptions should be minimized.
3. If a question arises, it should be noted and asked later, rather than interrupting the expert. The expert should be allowed to complete his thought before he is asked new questions.
4. Concise notes should be taken, concentrating on the expert's important points rather than furiously writing every word he utters.
5. The use of reflective listening is encouraged; paraphrase what the expert states to confirm its validity.

Of course, listening to the spoken word is only part of the interaction process. A significant amount of nonverbal communication occurs in the typical interview. How clearly the knowledge engineer interprets this is in direct relationship to how successful the knowledge extraction process will be. For example, an expert could unequivocally confirm the truth of a particular rule while exhibiting gestures (e.g., scratching his chin, avoiding eye contact, and clearing his throat) which contradict this verbal communication. This should alert the knowledge engineer that this rule may not be as certain as the expert verbally indicates. For a light discussion on the subject of nonverbal communication, refer to [Nierenberg, 1971].

14.4.2 Recording the Information Gained in Meetings

How to preserve the knowledge extracted during an interview session can be a problem for a knowledge engineer. Needless to say, attempting to commit everything to memory will fail. There are, however, some reasonable alternatives available.

The most common option is to take written notes. Experts are rarely bothered by this process and, except for sometimes slowing the knowledge-extraction process, it is an effective way to record significant points about the topic of discussion. Notes should never be verbatim, but should be indexes that will trigger the knowledge engineer's memory. Too much note taking can be burdensome and, chances are, not necessary if the knowledge engineer goes over the notes very soon after the interview has ended (i.e., within a day or two). More extensive notes should be taken only if the knowledge engineer will not get back to the notes until several days later, during which time she may have forgotten what the expert meant. In that case, recording the interview electronically may be prudent.

To capture as much of the discussion as possible, a video recorder can be used. An advantage to this approach is that a complete record of the interview is maintained. Often, remarks made in a meeting do not appear terribly meaningful at the time, but gain in significance later. If the meeting is recorded, then these tidbits of information are saved.

If there is only one expert and no visual information is pertinent (i.e., drawings, maps, graphs, etc.), then an audio recording is preferable. If, however, visual tasks are involved or there are various experts whose voices are not easily recognized, it is best to make a video recording. Video taping has the advantage of capturing nonverbal cues that experts often supply. We recommend that even if electronic recording occurs, the knowledge engineer should take a good set of notes as a backup in case of difficulties with the recording (e.g., poor sound quality).

A disadvantage of recording is that the expert may be reluctant to allow it. Sometimes he may agree to allow it, but because of his discomfort, he will not fully cooperate in the knowledge-extraction process. We strongly recommend that the expert(s) be consulted about any decision to use electronic recording.

Once a recording has been made, it must be reviewed. This review, while often providing a wealth of information, typically takes two to three times longer than the original session, making the review a tedious and time-consuming process. Alternatively, someone can be hired to transcribe the recording, but this (at least for video recorded sessions) does not take full advantage of the power of the recording.

14.5 HANDLING PROBLEM EXPERTS

The expert's personality and how it matches that of the knowledge engineer are obvious potential sources of difficulty in the knowledge-extraction process. While many books and papers express the view that experts are difficult people with whom to work, it is our experience from several years of performing knowledge engineering as well as directing other knowledge engineers, that this is rarely true. This includes interfacing with dozens of experts in different domains.

Nevertheless, problem experts do exist, who for various reasons impede the development of a system. The most common types are profiled below with suggestions on how to deal with them.

14.5.1 The Wimp Expert

Wimp experts fear the loss of their job or status within their organization should a knowledge-based system be developed that can perform their functions. As a result, they rarely provide a straight answer to any question, since the sharing of knowledge will, in their mind, lead to their downfall. This is probably the most difficult type of expert with whom to work initially, but often the one easiest to change (unless, of course, it is true that his employer wants to get rid of him!).

A knowledge-based system is typically being built to free the expert for other more pressing tasks. The knowledge engineer must convince the expert of this fact. Some arguments that the knowledge engineer might use are:

1. The knowledge-based system will allow the expert to concentrate on the more challenging aspects of his job, thereby allowing him to better justify his existence.
2. Knowledge-based systems cannot totally replace humans. These systems lack common sense and creativity, limiting them to the performance of only a subset of the tasks normally carried out by the expert.
3. Knowledge-based systems cannot discover new knowledge. That is still the task of a human with the right expertise, just like him.
4. The importance and significance of the expert's accomplishments are exemplified by his company's desire to codify his knowledge.
5. The area of artificial intelligence represents a new technology, one with which he should find it exciting to work.

Most importantly, the knowledge engineer should be extra careful in dealing with this expert's fragile ego. Whatever she says or does during the course of the project should not in any way inspire insecurity in the expert's mind.

14.5.2 The Cynical Expert

A cynical expert, in the extreme case, is a person who hates his job, despises his boss, and detests his organization. He may have been passed over for promotion several times and, as a result, resents performing tasks for the organization. But for some reason (e.g., seniority, salary, benefits), he does not want to leave. He resents being forced to work on this project after the company treated him so shabbily.

Most cynical experts, of course, are not that extreme. Unfortunately, this makes them difficult to detect. Clues that a cynical expert is present may include the expert's steadfast refusal to have any electronic recording devices present, criticism of peers and/or superiors, and other signs of bitterness. He might share accurate knowledge grudgingly or (on rare occasions) provide incorrect knowledge willingly, thus making interacting with him fraught with perils.

If there is no choice but to work with such an individual, there are a few actions that a knowledge engineer can take that may ease the situations. These include:

1. Carefully examining all provided knowledge, since the expert may attempt to sabotage the project by providing incorrect knowledge. The knowledge engineer should take extraordinary steps to ensure that the knowledge is correct. This can be done by performing extensive testing and validations of the knowledge base, and using other experts as reviewers of the test cases that the knowledge engineer suspects as being incorrect. Otherwise, the knowledge engineer may be viewed as responsible for the ultimate low quality of the knowledge.

2. Showing sympathy for the expert. If the expert sees the knowledge engineer as another fellow "victim" of the organization, he may identify with the knowledge engineer and be more cooperative. He may then be quite cooperative as a favor for a friend.

3. Appealing to the expert's professionalism. This can be done through example by being conscientious, thorough, and precise. This is especially effective if the knowledge engineer is employed by the same organization (as opposed to an outside consultant).

14.5.3 The High Priest of the Domain Expert

This expert considers himself to be the high priest of the domain. He views the knowledge engineer as an ignoramus who wastes his time with mundane questions, daring to think that he, the expert, can be replaced with a machine. Knowledge-based technology in his mind will be extremely underdeveloped without his personal assistance and can never approach his level of competence. Because of this arrogance, he can be an extremely difficult individual with whom to interact: he is never available for meetings, he allows numerous interruptions during the few audiences granted, and he is unwilling to do any tasks for the project between meetings.

The knowledge engineer must be patient in dealing with this expert. She must gain his confidence in her intellectual capacity through the development of a competent first prototype. This will gain his respect and, hopefully, convince him of the viability of this technology. Complaining to his superiors is not likely to result in any improvements due to the expert's probable high stature in the domain as well as in the organization. In fact, it may even do more harm than good. Thus, this should be used only as a last resort.

14.5.4 The Paternalistic Expert

This expert is analogous to the gentle, old professor who wants to assist and welcomes a willing listener to his tales of prowess. The paternalistic expert is a difficult individual with whom to work because of his good intentions and willingness to help. He tends to talk too much, telling stories revolving around his achievements. He relishes having someone as a captive audience whom he can teach. This forms a teacher-student relationship that can be very beneficial to knowledge extraction if handled correctly, but can conversely be quite burdensome if not.

Dealing with this expert requires much patience by the knowledge engineer, as well as a strong but delicate touch in executing interviews. She must minimize the expert's discourses, attempting to turn them into useful information. She must be skilled to halt his lengthy discourses diplomatically and proceed to other questions. Very often a sense of humor can achieve the desired effect with this type of expert.

14.5.5 The Uncommunicative Expert

The uncommunicative expert poses some special problems. He speaks in short sentences and does not offer elaborations on his answers—a fact that can greatly frustrate the knowledge engineer. He does not intend any harm; he is simply a quiet, introspective individual. Patience is extremely important when working with this expert. The knowledge engineer must carefully probe for answers and explanations and must examine these with great attention. She is forced to study the domain diligently to try to uncover new problems that may arise or angles that may not be immediately obvious to her.

14.5.6 The Uncaring Expert

This variation of the uncommunicative expert never disagrees with anything the knowledge engineer proposes, simply because it will take too much time to explain. This may be due to unassertiveness, complacency, or simply a lack of interest with the project. The result is always the same—the inability to gather appropriate and complete knowledge. The knowledge engineer is forced to take extra care in understanding the domain so she can attempt to verify the expert's knowledge, even if only to a limited extent. The use of recording devices with this type of person (if he agrees) may force him to think more about the answers given.

14.5.7 The Pseudo–AI-literate Expert

This type of expert has read an article or two about knowledge-based systems and thinks he knows it all. This can be quite a dangerous type because they can undermine the knowledge acquisition process by getting involved in the gory internal details of the system which are the domain of the knowledge engineer. He may also continually make suggestions about improving the interview process and attempt to lead and direct the knowledge engineer. The way to get around this is to gently let him know who is and who is not the knowledge engineer.

14.6 CHAPTER REVIEW

Various alternatives to the one-on-one interview described in the previous chapter exist. These are

1. the one-on-many
2. the many-on-one
3. the many-on-many

Each can be useful under certain circumstances either because it brings together the knowledge of many experts or the advantage of more than one pair of eyes and ears to elicit knowledge from experts. At the very least, these alternatives help spread the load of knowledge elicitation and acquisition among many individuals. But these interviews can also be quite difficult to manage and may result in considerable conflict among the experts and/or the knowledge engineers.

The interview is an important set of meetings that represent the main effort in interacting with the expert. Since the expert's time is usually a scarce resource, these interviews must be optimized. This can be accomplished by carefully planning the interview and effectively managing the process itself.

The location of an interview should, at the start of the knowledge-acquisition process, be at the expert's workspace. This can and should (if possible) be moved to the knowledge engineer's work area as the project unfolds. The latter will provide a more continuous elicitation process (i.e., fewer interruptions). Interviews should be kept to about two hours and, under normal circumstances, should never exceed three.

Planning is an important issue, and the overall success of an interview will likely depend heavily on the amount of planning done by the knowledge engineer. Planning should consist of reviewing the prior work (last interview session) to see what remains to be done and setting objectives for the next interview. But planning is useless unless the knowledge engineer adheres to the plan. The expert(s) must be told what the objectives are and must be reminded of it if the session begins to get derailed.

Various means exist for recording the proceedings of an interview. The most common one is to take notes. Nevertheless, other alternatives may present better choices under some circumstances. These are

1. audio recording
2. video recording
3. direct manual transcription of the interview by a trained transcriber, either during the meeting itself, or preferably, from the tapes

Many types of experts are commonly found and the way to deal with them is important because it can have a serious effect on how the entire knowledge-acquisition process develops. The problem experts discussed are

1. the wimp expert
2. the cynical expert
3. the high priest of the domain expert
4. the paternalistic expert
5. the uncommunicative expert
6. the uncaring expert
7. the pseudo–AI-literate expert

15 ▨ Alternative Knowledge Acquisition Means

15.1 THE KNOWLEDGE ACQUISITION BOTTLENECK

In the previous two chapters we discussed the traditional methods of extracting knowledge from an expert to develop a knowledge base. Most existing knowledge-based systems today were developed using these techniques. However, anyone who has gone through the process of developing a nontrivial system can attest to how painstaking and time consuming the knowledge engineering process can be. Feigenbaum [Feigenbaum, 1979] has aptly named this the *knowledge acquisition bottleneck.*

One of the reasons for this is the frequent inability of an expert to verbalize, or even to recognize, the problem-solving process that he uses. Psychological studies have suggested that this difficulty occurs from the existence of cognitive defenses by the experts that result in knowledge not being accessible [Parsaye, 1988]. While in most cases these difficulties can be overcome by a competent knowledge engineer using the techniques described in the previous chapter, the interview process seems quite archaic in our current age of automation. While these techniques are destined to remain the primary methods of knowledge-based system development for the foreseeable future, alternative methods should and are being investigated that can help relieve this bottleneck.

This chapter examines three alternative methods that can be used alone or in combination with more traditional acquisition techniques. These methods are

1. *Knowledge engineering facilitators:* These programs interact with a user (i.e., expert or knowledge engineer) to help him/her structure the

knowledge in a logical manner thereby facilitating the generation of a set of domain specific rules.

2. *Inductive tools:* These systems aid the knowledge acquisition effort by creating a set of rules from example cases presented by an expert or a knowledge engineer.

3. *Automated knowledge extraction from databases:* This approach represents the ultimate concept where human intervention is either very limited or nonexistent.

15.2 FACILITATING THE KNOWLEDGE ACQUISITION PROCESS

Efforts to facilitate the knowledge acquisition process are primarily based on George Kelly's theory of personal constructs in clinical psychology [Kelly, 1955]. This theory was designed to improve the effectiveness of clinical sessions with a patient. Since every person perceives the world from a different and changing perspective, a model is built for a particular person that represents his/her view of the world. As the person changes his/her perspective of the world, this person's model is modified to represent the person's revised beliefs about the world.

Kelly proposed a tool called *repertory grids* for the implementation of the Personal Construct Theory. Shaw and Gaines adapted the repertory grids for use as an aid in knowledge elicitation and demonstrated its use in a system called PLANET [Shaw, 1982]. Since then, other systems have been developed including Expertise Transfer System (or ETS) [Boose, 1984; Boose, 1985], MORE [Kahn, 1985], SALT [Marcus, 1985], ICONKAT [Ford, 1991], and Auto-Intelligence [Parsaye, 1988].

These systems ask questions of the user (either the expert or the knowledge engineer) about the domain with the goal of assisting the user in developing a more adequate knowledge structure. It is claimed [Parsaye, 1988] that this process often leaves the experts feeling that they have learned more about their own knowledge.

A repertory grid, as applied to knowledge elicitation, is a matrix that relates certain characteristics of the problem domain (called *elements*) with the *constructs* that represent the person's (the expert) ability to evaluate accurately the degree of presence or absence of these elements [Ford, 1988]. The rating assigned by the expert to an element for a given construct can be either binary (0 or 1) or a range of values. Some implementations of the multivalued rating for an element provide an indication of that element's degree of membership to a fuzzy set defined by the construct [Boose, 1985] and [Shaw, 1987]. This provides the expert with greater flexibility in expressing his/her knowledge about the domain.

The repertory grid shown in Figure 15.1 represents the personal construct for a typical staff consisting of a superior (the manager) and ten sub-

ELEMENTS 10, CONSTRUCTS 14, RANGE 1-5
PURPOSE: Staff appraisal

		1	2	3	4	5	6	7	8	9	10		
1	intelligent	1	1	4	5	3	3	5	2	3	5	1	dim
2	willing	1	2	4	5	1	1	4	3	1	2	2	unwilling
3	new boy	1	2	3	5	4	4	4	1	4	3	3	old sweats
4	little supervision	3	1	4	5	2	1	5	2	2	3	4	needs supervision
5	motivated	1	1	4	5	2	2	5	3	3	2	5	less motivated
6	reliable	3	2	2	5	1	1	5	1	2	3	6	not so reliable
7	mild	3	4	5	2	2	3	1	5	4	5	7	abrasive
8	ideas men	1	1	5	4	2	3	1	3	4	4	8	staid
9	selfstarters	2	1	5	5	1	3	5	3	4	5	9	need a push
10	creative	1	1	5	5	2	3	4	3	4	5	10	non-creative
11	helpful	4	3	4	2	3	5	1	4	5	5	11	unhelpful
12	professional	1	2	3	3	2	1	5	2	4	4	12	less professional
13	overall high	2	1	3	4	1	2	5	2	3	4	13	overall rating low
14	messers	2	2	5	4	3	5	1	5	3	1	14	tidy

	1	2	3	4	5	6	7	8	9	10

FIGURE 15.1   Repertory Grid

ordinates [Shaw, 1987]. Each member of the staff is characterized by the superior through 14 categories, each of which has 2 extreme and diametrically opposed characteristics (i.e., intelligent - dim). This is done by assigning a number that accurately describes the person's standing in relation to the opposing extremes.

The concept of this idea is best illustrated through an example. This example uses repertory grids to automatically elicit and represent expert knowledge involving the classification of various types of automobiles according to their characteristics. We indicate the system queries in CAPITAL LETTERS and the user responses in *italics*.

Initially, the system queries the user about the problem domain and the objective of the knowledge base. This is followed by a request for a list of the automobiles and the typical places where these could be found. We pick up the dialogue at this point with the user's response (this example is based on an example in [Parsaye, 1988]):

Porsche 911	*Road racing*
Dodge Caravan	*Family vacations*
Oldsmobile 98	*Golf club parking lot*

Ford Escort   *Factory parking lot*

Mazda Miata   *Sunday drive*

Mercedes Benz   *Estate entrance*

Jeep   *Dirt roads*

Pick-up truck   *Farmhouse*

PLEASE THINK OF:

PORSCHE 911   ROAD RACING

DODGE CARAVAN   FAMILY VACATIONS

OLDSMOBILE 98   GOLF CLUB PARKING LOT

IS ONE OF THEM SOMEHOW DIFFERENT FROM THE OTHER TWO?

Yes, Porsche 911

WHAT IS A TRAIT WHICH CHARACTERIZES THIS DIFFERENCE?

High performance

WHAT IS THE OPPOSITE TRAIT OF HIGH PERFORMANCE?

Flabby

PLEASE THINK OF:

DODGE CARAVAN   FAMILY VACATIONS

OLDSMOBILE 98   GOLF CLUB PARKING LOT

FORD ESCORT   FACTORY PARKING LOT

IS ONE OF THEM SIGNIFICANTLY DIFFERENT FROM THE OTHER TWO?

Yes, Ford Escort

WHAT IS THE TRAIT WHICH CHARACTERIZES THIS DIFFERENCE?

Small

WHAT IS THE OPPOSITE OF SMALL?

Large

PLEASE THINK OF:

PORSCHE 911   ROAD RACING

MAZDA MIATA   SUNDAY DRIVE

MERCEDES BENZ   COUNTRY ESTATE

IS ONE OF THEM SOMEHOW DIFFERENT FROM THE OTHER TWO?

Mercedes Benz, Sedan

WHAT IS THE OPPOSITE OF SEDAN?

Coupe

This question-and-answer process may continue for a longer period, taking three cases at a time. If three-by-three is not effective in distinguishing some types of automobiles from each other, the system reverts to two-by-two comparisons. For example,

PLEASE THINK OF:

PORSCHE 911   ROAD RACING

DODGE CARAVAN   FAMILY VACATIONS

IS THERE A TRAIT WHICH DISTINGUISHES THEM?

Yes, functional

WHAT IS THE OPPOSITE TRAIT OF FUNCTIONAL?

Fun-to-drive.

Once these traits have been identified, the system allows the user to specify how well each automobile matches the characteristics defined above. The system performs this step by presenting a template to the user that must be filled with relative weights. We again pick up the dialogue:

PLEASE THINK OF A FORD ESCORT. PLEASE PROVIDE A NUMBER BE-TWEEN 0 AND 100 SHOWING HOW WELL IT MATCHES (100 MEANS A COMPLETE MATCH AND 0 MEANS NO MATCH AT ALL):

HIGH-PERFORMANCE: *20*

INEXPENSIVE: *80*

SMALL: *90*

FUNCTIONAL: *60*

SEDAN: *40*

FUEL-EFFICIENT: *80*

FAST: *40*

LUXURIOUS: *10*

PLEASE THINK OF PORSCHE 911. PLEASE PROVIDE A NUMBER BE-
TWEEN 0 AND 100 SHOWING HOW WELL IT MATCHES (100 MEANS A
COMPLETE MATCH AND 0 MEANS NO MATCH AT ALL.):

HIGH-PERFORMANCE: *100*

INEXPENSIVE: *10*

SMALL: *40*

FUNCTIONAL: *20*

SEDAN: *0*

FUEL-EFFICIENT: *50*

FAST: *95*

This type of questioning continues until all the automobiles and traits
are correlated. This information can be represented in a grid as shown in Figure 15.2, where each automobile defines a row and each trait defines a column.
Pattern matching can utilized to apply this represented knowledge to the classification of a particular automobile.

Car	Hi-Perf	Cost	Size	Funct.	Type	Fuel	Speed
P911	yes	hi	sm	no	cpe	no	fast
Van	no	med	lrg	yes	van	yes	slow
Olds	no	hi	lrg	yes	sdn	no	med
Ford	no	low	sm	yes	sdn	yes	slow
Miata	yes	hi	sm	no	cpe	yes	fast
M-B	yes	hi	lrg	yes	sdn	no	fast
Jeep	no	med	sm	no	off-rd	no	slow
truck	no	low	med	yes	truck	yes	slow

FIGURE 15.2   Automobile Selection Grid

While the knowledge represented within this grid is not sufficient to build a complete knowledge-based system, it provides a good starting point from which to proceed in its development.

15.3 MACHINE LEARNING

Ideally, we would prefer to connect a computer directly to the brain of an expert. This connection would allow the computer to somehow acquire the expert's knowledge, immediately incorporating it into its knowledge base. Recognizing that this is highly unlikely to ever occur, we employ knowledge engineers to act as the "connection" between the computer and the expert. These engineers use the techniques discussed in the last two chapters to acquire the expert's knowledge by asking questions and observing the expert at work. In reality, what the knowledge engineers are doing is *learning* the concepts and techniques of the expert's domain, developing representations of these, and then transferring these representations from their own minds into the computer. This ability to learn new concepts and techniques is one characteristic that some researchers say defines human intelligence [Fischler, 1987]. If computers, however, were able to learn directly from the knowledge sources, this would have a significant effect on the development of knowledge-based systems and many other fields.

The topic of machine learning is significant in its size and scope, so significant that any detailed discussion is clearly beyond the scope of this book. However, because of its potential benefits to knowledge-based systems, we must provide a short description. Learning can be defined as

The improvement in the performance of a specific task (intellectual or physical) after previous exposure to that task or a related one.

Humans are very adept at learning through observation, especially when combined with questions and/or exploration. This is clearly evident to anyone who has raised preschool children. While they are (generally!) not able to read or write, they show an astounding capacity for learning. As they grow older and acquire reading skills, some learning occurs through printed material (i.e., textbooks, notes, etc.). Examples still remain extremely useful, and teachers aid learning by answering questions.

Learning advanced concepts always depends on the mastery of more simplistic ideas. Thus, as William A. Martin said, "you can't learn anything unless you almost know it already" [Winston, 1992]. For example, to comprehend quantum mechanics, knowledge of advanced mathematics must be assumed. Similarly, we identified in Chapter 13 that a knowledge engineer should become conversant in the domain through reading as well as questioning the expert before any attempt is made to gather more specific knowledge.

15.3.1 Inductive Reasoning—Learning from Examples

According to Webster's dictionary [Webster, 1960], the definition of induction is:

Reasoning from particular facts or individual cases to general conclusion.

In the classical artificial intelligence paradigm, inductive learning is performed by presenting to a machine a series of examples and the conclusion that should be drawn from each example. The machine, through a set of predefined induction heuristics, analyzes each example and builds an internal representation of the domain characteristics that are present.

Winston [Winston, 1992], an early researcher in the field of learning, defined these inductive heuristics to be rules that examine a series of examples to capture the presence or absence of specific features and that induce the important relationships and features from these examples. In his approach, a series of true examples and *near misses* (i.e., examples that fail to exhibit all of the required characteristics) are presented to the learning procedure one at a time. By applying the inductive heuristics and observing the features of all examples, his system learns which features distinguish true examples from near misses.

A second inductive approach, called the ID3 algorithm [Quinlan, 1983], examines a set of objects described in terms of a fixed collection of properties. This algorithm produces a decision tree based on these attributes that correctly classifies all the given objects.

Consider a set of objects, S, which belong to one of two classes, C_1 or C_2. Each of these objects is described by a set of attributes. One of three situations exist:

1. If the set of objects is empty, it could arbitrarily be associated with either class.
2. If all objects in S belong to the same class, the decision tree reduces to a leaf node bearing the name of that class (i.e., C_1 or C_2).
3. S contains representatives of both classes.

In the last case, we select an attribute and partition S into disjoint sets $S_1, S_2, S_3, \ldots, S_n$, where each partition contains the members of the original set that have the same value for the chosen attribute. Each of these subcollections is then examined to see if all of its members belong to the same class. If they do not, another attribute is selected and the process is repeated. The resulting leaves of the tree carry the name of each class.

This process can easily be extended to handle the case where the original set of objects, S, contains objects from several classes. This is illustrated by the following example.

Suppose that we are attempting to select a knowledge-based system shell for some application. Each shell is designed with particular features (i.e., development language, memory requirements, monetary cost, reasoning schemes, external interfaces) that help us classify the shell as acceptable or unacceptable for the application. Our original set of objects (i.e., the shells) can be described by a set of vectors. Each vector describes one combination of features associated with a particular knowledge-based system shell. Note that because each shell can have multiple reasoning schemes and external interfaces, a particular shell might be described by more than one vector.

For this example, let us suppose that we are considering the following (hypothetical) knowledge-based system shells: ThoughtGen, OffSite, Genie, Silverworks, XS, and MilliExpert. The attributes with their possible values are

Development Language: {Pascal, C, LISP}

Reasoning Method: {Forward, Backward}

External Interfaces: {dBase, 1-2-3, ASCII file, Devices}

Cost: any positive number

Memory: any positive number

The collection, *S*, is shown in Figure 15.3. Note that an asterisk is used to signify that all of the values for this attribute are acceptable. Since all of these objects do not all belong to the same classification, we must apply Quinlan's partitioning method.

The first step in the algorithm is to select an attribute and form a tree with the name of the attribute at its root. If we select "Language" as our attribute, we have three branches emanating from this root, each labeled for one

Language	Reasoning method	Interface method	Cost	Memory	Classification
Pascal	Backward	1-2-3	50	128K	MilliExpert
Pascal	Backward	ASCII	50	128K	MilliExpert
Pascal	Backward	dBase	195	256K	ThoughtGen
Pascal	*	Devices	685	512K	OffSite
C	Forward	*	6500	640K	Genie
LISP	Forward	*	5000	5000K	Silverworks
C	Backward	*	395	200K	XS
LISP	Backward	*	395	200K	XS

FIGURE 15.3   Collection of Objects Described by Vectors of Attributes

of the three possible values of that attribute. All of the objects having the same value for the selected attribute are placed at the end of the corresponding branch. This results in the tree shown in Figure 15.4.

Note that all of the leaf nodes in the tree shown in Figure 15.4 have multiple associated values. Therefore, the process must be repeated on all of these nodes with a new attribute. Suppose that we now select the attribute "Reasoning Method." This results in the tree shown in Figure 15.5. Note that all but

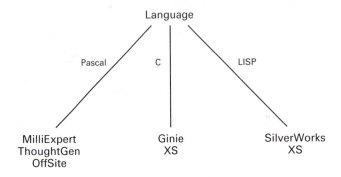

FIGURE 15.4 Resulting Decision Tree from Selection of the Language Attribute

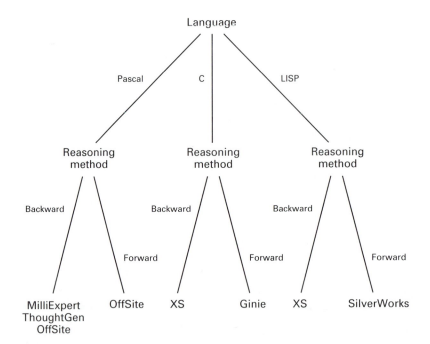

FIGURE 15.5 Resulting Decision Tree from the Addition of the Reasoning Method Attribute

the leftmost leaf node contain the names of single systems, so they must be considered no longer.

At this point we have three attributes to select from for further refining of this tree—"Interface Method," "Cost," and "Memory Requirements." Suppose that the "Interface Method" attribute is selected. After making this last application of the classification algorithm we discover that each leaf node contains single objects, therefore the process halts. Figure 15.6 displays the final resulting tree that can easily be used to derive a set of rules to assist us in selecting a particular knowledge-based system for some application or identifying a knowledge-based system given its characteristics.

Note, however, that the appearance of the tree varies according to which attribute is chosen first, second, and so forth. These differences have a distinct

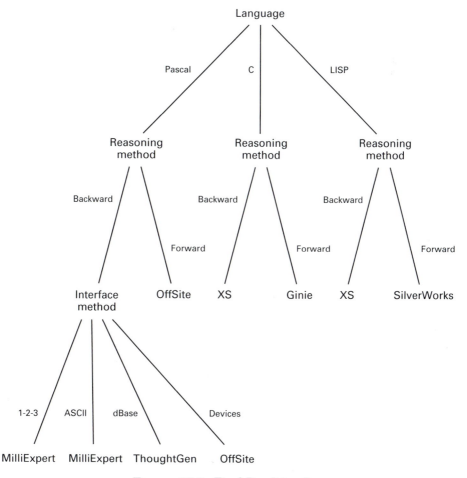

FIGURE 15.6   Final Resulting Tree

effect on how the rules will be written. Naturally, derivation of a minimal decision tree will minimize the complexity of the rules because the number of tests (premises) required to classify an object using the rule(s) derived from the decision tree will be the least possible. Therefore, our objective when selecting the attribute to use in partitioning the remaining cases might be to derive the minimal tree. Other objectives, such as avoiding expensive or dangerous distinguishing tests, are also possible to implement within this algorithm.

ID3 accomplishes the development of a minimal tree by using an information-theoretic approach [Quinlan, 1983]. The path through a decision tree, which an object follows when being classified, can be viewed as a message. The measure of the information content of this message determines how the object is classified. ID3 bases the selection of the best attribute to use on the plausible assumption that the complexity of the decision tree is strongly related to the amount of information conveyed by this message [Quinlan, 1983]. By determining the amount of information that can be gained by testing each possible attribute and selecting the one containing the largest amount of information, our tree can be optimized. To do this, we first need to calculate the overall information content of the final messages. We then compare this number to that calculated in a similar fashion from the partial trees created when a particular attribute is tested.

To see how this optimization algorithm works, we will now introduce a second (and simpler) example involving aircraft identification. Given images of various aircraft such as those shown in Figures 15.7 and 15.8, we are being

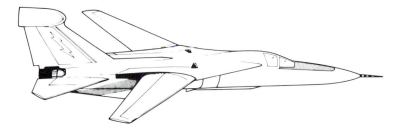

FIGURE 15.7   Domestic Aircraft

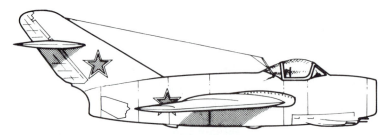

FIGURE 15.8   Foreign Aircraft

asked to develop a system that can classify an aircraft as either domestic or foreign made. To simplify this example, let us assume that we are not dealing with the image understanding process. A machine vision preprocessor examines our images of aircraft to extract the relevant features that we must examine to classify them. Our concern in this example is strictly with the acquisition of the knowledge that allows a computer to perform this classification.

The process starts by identifying the attributes of the aircraft that are of interest, as well as their possible values. This is shown in Figure 15.9.

The set of examples used to derive the rules must be developed by the knowledge engineer or the expert. In our example, each image is described by the relevant features that it possesses and its classification (domestic or foreign). This is depicted in Figure 15.10. This matrix of examples is called the *induction file*. Using the ID3 algorithm our inductive learning system reviews this file to generate a set of rules that allows it to classify aircraft encountered during actual operation. It must be noted, however, that all the data for each attribute must be available for each case. Additionally, noise (i.e., cases with the same data but different classification) is not acceptable.

If our system generates these rules at random, there will be five rules, one for each case in the induction file. But our main purpose in introducing this example was to generate the minimal tree and thus the simplest possible rules. The optimization algorithm determines which of the attributes that have not yet been represented contain the greatest amount of information, and represents this attribute next in the optimal tree. Let us see how this is done using the ID3 algorithm.

Feature	Possible values
Wing_mount	High, Mid, Low
Engines	1 to 3
Nose	Flat, Snub, Pointed
Intake	Nose, Body
Fuselage	Cigar, Sleek, Thick

FIGURE 15.9 Attributes and Possible Values for the Aircraft Recognition Case Study

Wing_Mnt.	Engs	Nose	Intake	Fuselage	Classif
mid	1	flat	nose	cigar	foreign
mid	1	flat	nose	sleek	foreign
low	1	snub	nose	sleek	foreign
high	2	point	body	thick	domestic
high	1	point	body	thick	domestic

FIGURE 15.10 Induction Table for Aircraft Identification Case Study

Since only two classes of aircraft are possible, the probabilities of each of these messages being generated are respectively

$$P_f \text{ for foreign and}$$
$$P_d \text{ for domestic.}$$

These probabilities can be estimated by using relative frequencies in the case of a known set of objects. In our example, the relative frequency of "domestic" is two out of the five possibilities, or a P_f of 2/5. Likewise, the P_d is 3/5.

The expected information content of the message over a set C of objects is:

$$M(C) = -P_f \log_2(P_f) - P_d \log_2(P_d)$$

or, for our example,

$$M(C) = -.6*\log_2(.6) - .4*\log_2(.4)$$

$$= .971$$

Next, we calculate the information content of the partial tree if a particular attribute is selected for testing. In our example, we use the "Engines" attribute. The partial tree resulting from this selection can be seen in Figure 15.11. The expected information content for this partial tree is calculated to be the probability that the value of the attribute is 1, times the message content of the subgroup of objects that match this attribute value, plus the same calculation for an attribute value of 2:

B(C,"Engines") = [(probability that the value of Engines is "1") *(M(C) for the four objects that satisfy the attribute)] + [(probability that the value of Engines is "2") *(M(C) for the single object that satisfies this attribute)]

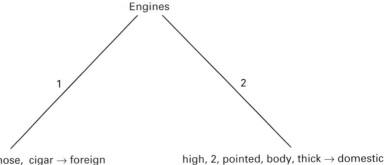

mid, 1, flat, nose, cigar → foreign
mid, 1, flat, nose, sleek → foreign
low, 1, snub, nose, sleek → foreign
high, 1, pointed, body, thick → domestic

high, 2, pointed, body, thick → domestic

FIGURE 15.11   Partial Tree Resulting from Selecting the Attribute Engines

For our example:

$$B(C,\text{"Engines"}) = [P_1 * M(C_1)] + [P_2 * M(C_2)]$$

$$P_1 = 4/5 \text{ (4 of 5 cases are "1")}$$

$$P_2 = 1/5 \text{ (1 of 5 cases is "2")}$$

Next, we have to calculate the expected information content value of each sub-tree created by the two branches of the attribute "Engines". For the branch with the value of "1":

$$M(C_1) = -P'_f \log_2(P'_f) - P'_d \log_2(P'_d)$$

where $P'_f = 3/4$ (3 of 4 are foreign) and $P'_d = 1/4$ (1 of 4 are domestic), giving

$$M(C_1) = -[3/4 \log_2 (3/4)] - [1/4 \log_2 (1/4)]$$

$$= -[.75 * (-.4)] - [.25 * (-2)]$$

$$= .80$$

For the expected information of the other branch:

$$M(C_2) = -P''_f \log_2(P''_f) - P''_d \log_2(P''_d)$$

where $P''_f = 0$ (no cases are foreign) and $P''_d = 1$ (only 1 case is domestic), giving:

$$M(C_2) = 0$$

Therefore, the new expected information from the selection of the attribute "Engines" for testing is:

$$B(C,\text{"Engines"}) = .80 + 0 = .80$$

Finally, the information contribution of this selection is the total information content of the original tree (0.971), minus the content of the subtree when the selection is made (0.80). Thus:

$$M(C) - B(C,\text{"Engines"}) = .971 - .80$$

$$= .171$$

The same procedure must be performed with all the other possible selections. The one that contributes the most information is the one that should be chosen next. In our example, let us next select the attribute "Intake," and repeat the process. The tree generated with this choice is shown in Figure 15.12. As can be seen, this represents a terminal tree because all the objects in each side are of the same class.

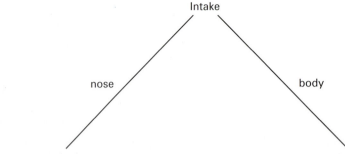

mid, 1, flat, nose, cigar → foreign   high, 2, pointed, body, thick → domestic
mid, 1, flat, nose, sleek → foreign   high, 1, pointed, body, thick → domestic
low, 1, snub, nose, sleek → foreign

FIGURE 15.12 Partial Tree Resulting from the Selection of the Attribute Intake

$$B(C,\text{"Intake"}) = [P_n * M(C_n)] + [P_b * M(C_b)]$$

where

$$P_n = 3/5 \text{ (3 of 5 are "nose")}$$

$$P_b = 2/5 \text{ (2 of 5 are "body")}$$

$$M(C_n) = -[P'_f \log_2(P'_f)] - [P'_d \log_2(P'_d)]$$

but since $P'_f = 1$ and $P'_d = 0$, we get

$$M(C_n) = 0$$

Similarly, we can derive the value for $M(C_b)$

$$M(C_b) = 0$$

When these values are substituted above, we derive the information content for the subtree, $B(C,\text{"Intake"})$, to be 0. Thus,

$$M(C) - B(C,\text{"Intake"}) = .971 - 0$$

$$= .971$$

This number is clearly greater than the 0.171 calculated previously; therefore the attribute "Intake" should be chosen over the attribute "Engines." The same calculation should be made for the other attributes with the selection of which attribute to use being made after all these results have been compared.

15.3.2 Knowledge Acquisition through Inductive Tools

The ID3 algorithm described above forms the basis for a type of knowledge engineering tool, called an *induction tool,* which can be used to assist in the knowledge acquisition process. These tools can be quite useful when a significant quantity of knowledge exists as examples or cases. For instance, in the diagnosis of sophisticated equipment such as turbine generators, whenever a serious problem arises, maintenance engineers investigate the problem thoroughly and, upon satisfactory correction, extensively document the observations found as well as the cause of the malfunction. Such a database of the repair history of various other products is typically available and can be used as the source of the knowledge to be interpreted by the induction tool.

As illustrated in the examples of the previous section, an inductive tool accepts a collection of objects (i.e., examples) described by a set of attributes and their values and generates a *minimal* decision tree that uniquely classifies the objects. A set of inference rules is then generated for use in a knowledge-based system.

To illustrate how such systems operate, let us examine how a typical inductive tool, or expert system shell that includes an inductive learning feature, handles the above problem dealing with aircraft identification from images. The inductive systems chosen for this illustration are V-P Expert, an expert system shell developed and marketed by Paperback Software, and First Class, developed and marketed by Programs in Motion. Two differences exist between these systems: First Class contains an inductive learning feature patterned after Quinlan's ID3 and while V-P Expert does not optimize the tree, First Class will give the user the option. Figures 15.13 and 15.14 represent, respectively, the rules derived for the aircraft identification program by V-P Expert (nonoptimized) and by First Class (optimized).

Although these inductive tools can often assist in the development of a knowledge-based system, they are not useful in all cases. Inductive techniques are appropriate for classification tasks only. Diagnosis, as a form of classification, fits under this category.

Moreover, our experience indicates that they are most helpful in the development of small systems where an expert acts as his own knowledge engineer. Medium-sized and large systems would still require the services of a knowledge engineer(s) since the creation of the inductive tables would become unwieldy. Nevertheless, more and more shell developers are providing inductive learning features within their shells as an additional and useful feature.

15.4 AUTOMATED KNOWLEDGE EXTRACTION FROM DATABASES

Databases often contain embedded knowledge that might be extracted for use in a knowledge-based system. Consider the process of engineering design: This process generally uses both algorithmic and heuristic knowledge to formulate a design. Knowledge is, therefore, embedded within the graphical representation of the device or system being designed. If the design representation (drawing) is performed on a Computer-Aided Design (CAD) system, then the

```
ACTIONS
    FIND Classifications:

    RULE 0  IF    Wing-mount = mid AND
                  Engines = 1 AND
                  Nose = flat AND
                  Intake = nose AND
                  Fuselage = cigar
            THEN Classification = foreign;

    RULE 1  IF    Wing-mount = mid AND
                  Engines = 1 AND
                  Nose = flat AND
                  Intake = nose AND
                  Fuselage = sleek
            THEN Classification = foreign;

    RULE 2  IF    Wing-mount = low AND
                  Engines = 1 AND
                  Nose = snub AND
                  Intake = nose AND
                  Fuselage = sleek
            THEN Classification = foreign;

    RULE 3  IF    Wing-mount = high AND
                  Engines = 2 AND
                  Nose = point AND
                  Intake = body AND
                  Fuselage = thick
            THEN Classification = domestic;

    RULE 4  IF    Wing-mount = high AND
                  Engines = 1 AND
                  Nose = point AND
                  Intake = body AND
                  Fuselage = thick
            THEN Classification = domestic;
```

FIGURE 15.13   Nonoptimized Rule Base Developed by V-P Expert for Aircraft Classification (in rule format)

knowledge already exists in an electronic form. Sometimes this knowledge is shown explicitly (e.g., the formula used to derive parts of the design is shown in the drawing itself) and sometimes it is implicit (e.g., no justification of the design exists on the drawing).

Unfortunately, the majority of engineering designs are of the second category. This makes the automated knowledge acquisition of design knowledge considerably more difficult, since some knowledge of general engineering de-

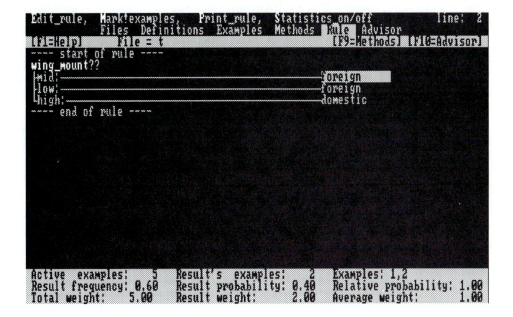

FIGURE 15.14 Optimized Rule Base Developed by First Class for Aircraft Classification (in tree format)

sign must exist to understand the new knowledge expressed within the current developing design. Recall a statement that we made earlier in this chapter: To learn something, you almost have to know it already.

A type of knowledge that can be extracted from a CAD database is that which is embodied in a *model* description of an engineering system (e.g., a chemical process system or an electronic circuit). Knowledge about the components that compose such systems and how these components are interconnected can be used to diagnose any misoperations or faults within the target system. Such a model constitutes the knowledge base for a *model-based system*. As described in Chapter 9, model-based systems are knowledge-based systems that use the deep causal knowledge contained in these models to overcome some of the deficiencies of abductive reasoning in traditional rule-based knowledge-based systems.

More generally, the systems that are applicable to model-based reasoning include those that can be represented in a *one-line diagram* or a *schematic drawing*. These drawings depict systems from a functional perspective, showing all the general features of the components as well as their connections, while skipping over their detailed connections (i.e., which wire goes to which terminal). Systems that lend themselves to such representations include hydraulic, pneumatic, gas, or chemical process systems as well as electrical or electronic circuits. The model is normally described using frames, where each frame represents each of the components in the system.

The knowledge required by a model can consist of two different parts:

1. *The system connectivity:* This defines how each component in the system is connected to the other system components and in which direction the medium (e.g., gas, fluid or electric current) flows.

2. *The functionality:* A specification of the functionality of the various components in the system allows each component to be modeled. Typically this functionality includes the component's transfer function, units, tolerance, range of operation, time delay in reacting (if any), and so forth.

System connectivity can be obtained from the CAD system database. Usually each component is represented as an object with connection terminals (input and output ports) that define the object's location within the system.

Because connectivity data typically exist in a CAD system database, it is normally unnecessary to know what the nature of the component is to establish its connectivity. Nevertheless, to completely define a model, information that is not present in the CAD system database must be integrated into a model being generated by an automated knowledge elicitation system. Such information must therefore be retrieved from an external database of generic components and their attributes. This database is called the *component knowledge base* and can be quite extensive.

The knowledge base on components is continually growing as new components are included. This knowledge base is generally updated by a human, although some updates can be made by the knowledge acquisition system automatically, with the help of a human. Included in the form of constraints is information about how a component would be applied in the model of the system being extracted. For example, this database would know that a valve or filter could be connected to the output of a water pump, while an electrical transformer could not, or that a three-way valve would have three ports and, therefore, three connections.

Identifying the proper information within this database may be rather simple in cases where the component is adequately labeled. A parser can examine the description information contained in the CAD database and extract the component's identity from its description. Once the component is identified, a search is made of the component knowledge base to locate an entry that matches as closely as possible the component's description. A certainty factor can be assigned to this description to reflect how well it matches the actual component.

Occasionally, however, a component description is inadequately specified in the CAD database. This may occur through an abbreviation or a synonym that makes the identification process much more difficult. It is imperative that the parser be able to compensate for these shortcomings in the CAD system.

On rare occasions a component within the database will be incorrectly specified or not described at all. These situations generate conflicts within the knowledge extraction system, which must be resolved before a consistent and correct knowledge base can be generated. Ultimately, a human can assist in resolving these inconsistencies, but there are some actions that the system can take before requesting assistance. For example, let us assume that the system has knowledge of the connectivity of the unknown component(s) as well as the existing constraints applicable to all known components as found in the component database. All components can be assigned a certainty factor that describes how certain their identification is, based on the various sources of information described above. Working from known components (i.e., those with high certainty factors) and using the *relaxation labeling* technique [Price, 1985; Thathachar, 1986], the system can begin to propagate the constraints from these *islands of certainty,* thus narrowing the number of possibilities for the unknown components. This process is very similar to that followed by a process engineer in identifying an unknown component in the drawing.

Another technique that can be used to identify the components is to make use of the icons that represent the components within the drawing. The American National Standards Institute (ANSI) has defined all the icons and their interpretations. The knowledge generation system can search the library used by the CAD system in creating the drawing or can interpret the shape of the icon directly in an attempt to correctly identify it. Unfortunately, this approach is not always foolproof either because not all companies use the standard library of icons.

As an example of automated knowledge acquisition from CAD databases, let us look at extracting the model description from the electronic circuit shown in Figure 15.15 [Gonzalez, 1991].

The CAD system database stores a set of lists that (usually) identify each component and describe their connectivity. For our example, the first is called the COMPU list and is shown in Figure 15.16 [Gonzalez, 1991]. This list

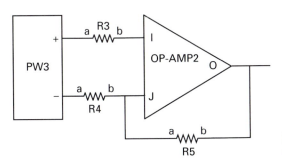

FIGURE 15.15   A Partial Electrical Circuit

Component Name	Description	Units
PW3	Power Supply	VDC
OP-AMP2	Operational Amplifier	volts
R3	Resistor	Ohms
R4	Resistor	Ohms
R5	Resistor	Ohms

FIGURE 15.16   COMPU List Obtained for Example Problem

supplies the component name, its description (which is often optional and at the whim of the draftsperson), and the units that are often not specified by the draftsperson. Figure 15.17 [Gonzalez, 1991] depicts the *to-from* list that details the connections for each component listed in the COMPU list. A third list, the NODELIST, indicates the connection points for each component. See Figure 15.18. Other sources of knowledge are available from the CAD system, but the ones above are the most important.

Comp. name	Connect pt.	Comp. name	Connect pt.
PW3	+	R3	a
PW3	−	R4	a
R3	b	OP-AMP2	I
R4	b	OP-AMP2	J
R4	b	R5	a
OP-AMP2	O	R5	b

FIGURE 15.17   TO/FROM List for the Example Problem

Net#	Component name	Connect point
026	PW3	+
026	R3	a
027	R3	b
027	OP-AMP2	I
028	OP-AMP2	O
028	R5	b
029	R5	a
029	OP-AMP2	J
029	R4	b
030	R4	a
030	PW3	−

FIGURE 15.18   NODELIST for the Example Problem

The objective of the automated knowledge acquisition system is to create a set of frames, each representing a system component, which contain the structural as well as the functional description of the applicable component. Thus, some slots that need to be filled correspond to

input
output
transfer-function
description
an-instance-of
units
delay
tolerance
current-value

Of the slots above, the *input* and *output* slots deal mainly with the structure of the system and, as mentioned above, can be generally obtained from the CAD database. Conversely, the *transfer-function, delay,* and *tolerance* slots represent the functional description of the component, which must be obtained from the component knowledge base. The *description* and the *unit* slots are some of the means through which the component is identified and a match within the component knowledge base is made. Figure 15.19 [Gonzalez, 1991] shows the frames generated by the system for two of the components and Figure 15.20 shows the portion of the component knowledge base that is applicable to some elements in the sample system.

In our example, the components have been properly documented by the draftsperson, thus easing the problem of identification. The challenge exists when the description for some components is either incorrect or nonexistent. In such cases, our automated knowledge extraction system tries to find

```
(DEFRAME R3
         (NOMENCLATURE    "RESISTOR R3")
         (AIO   RESISTOR)
         (SOURCE    PW3)
         (SOURCE-PATH   CSTATUS-PW3)
         (IN-PATH-OF   OP-AMP2)
         (UNITS   "OHMS")
         (STATUS   (/   (CSTATUS   PW3)
                        (CSTATUS   R3))  )
         (CVALUE   150)  )
```

FIGURE 15.19   Frames Generated by System for Components R4 and R5

```
(object   ANAL-DIFF-PRESS-TRANSDUCER
  (type   MEASUREMENT)
  (my-parents   (DIFFERENTIAL-PRESSURE-TRANSDUCER))
  (inputs  ((PRESSURE-INPUT-1   ANALOG-VALUE)
            (PRESSURE-INPUT-2   ANALOG-VALUE)))
  (outputs  (ELECTRICAL-OUTPUT   ANALOG-VALUE))
  (output-functions
    (ELECTRICAL-OUTPUT  (*  (-   PRESSURE-INPUT-1
                                 PRESSURE-INPUT-2)
                         SCALE)))
  (parameters  (SCALE   1.0))
  (strong-constraint  (TYPE-OF-OUTPUTS
                       TYPE-OF-OUTPUTS
                       NUMBER-OF-OUTPUTS))
  (normal-constraint  (NUMBER-OF-OUTPUTS   UNITS))
  (weak-constraint  (RATING))
  (support-constraint  (TOLERANCE))
  (tolerance  (ELECTRICAL-OUTPUT 0.35))
  (rating  PSI)
  (description  "pressure-input-1 == upstream pressure)
  (units  ((ELECTRICAL-OUTPUT   VOLTS)
           (PRESSURE-INPUT   PSI)))  )

(object   ANALOG-PRESSURE-TRANSDUCER
  (type   MEASUREMENT)
  (my-parents  (PRESSURE-TRANSDUCER))
  (inputs  (PRESSURE-INPUT   ANALOG-VALUE))
  (outputs  (ELECTRICAL-OUTPUT   ANALOG-VALUE))
  (output-functions
    (ELECTRICAL-OUTPUT  (*   PRESSURE-INPUT   SCALE)))
  (parameters  (SCALE   1.0))
  (strong-constraint
    (TYPE-OF-OUTPUTS   TYPE-OF-INPUTS))
  (normal-constraint  (NUMBER-OF-OUTPUTS   UNITS))
  (weak-constraint  (RATING))
  (support-constraint  (TOLERANCE))
  (tolerance  (ELECTRICAL-OUTPUT   0.35))
  (rating  PSI)
  (units  ((ELECTRICAL-OUTPUT VOLTS)
           (PRESSURE-INPUT   PSI)))  )
```

FIGURE 15.20 Portion of Component Knowledge Base Used in Example

```
(object RESISTOR
  (inputs  ((CURRENT-INPUT   ANALOG-VALUE)
            (VOLTAGE-INPUT   ANALOG-VALUE)))
  (outputs ((CURRENT-OUTPUT  ANALOG-VALUE)
            (VOLTAGE-OUTPUT  ANALOG-VALUE)))
  (output-functions
    ((CURRENT-OUTPUT  CURRENT-INPUT)
     (VOLTAGE-OUTPUT  (*  CURRENT-INPUT  RESISTANCE))))
  (parameters  (RESISTANCE  1.0  OHMS))
  (strong-constraint
    (UNITS  NUMBER-OF-INPUTS  NUMBER-OF-OUTPUTS
            TYPE-OF-INPUTS  TYPE-OF-OUTPUTS  RATING))
  (weak-constraint  (RANGE))
  (rating OHMS)
  (units  ((CURRENT-OUTPUT  AMPS)
           (VOLTAGE-OUTPUT  VOLTS)))  )
```

FIGURE 15.20   (Continued)

islands of certainty within the target system and, using constraints, propagates the belief outwardly to "discover" the nature of other, unknown components without having to resort to human intervention.

Suppose that resistor R4 was not labeled at all, giving its identity a low certainty factor, while the power supply PW3 and the OP-AMP2 components are properly described, making their identity and acquired functional attribute values highly certain. Looking at the component knowledge base entry for resistors, we see that one of their constraints is that they are electrical in nature, which our unknown component is. Another characteristic they possess is that they are used to limit electric current in a circuit, that is, they can be connected to a power source. Using such constraints, heuristics, and supporting facts (such as the units of the unknown component are in ohms), the conflict resolution algorithm can determine that the most likely identity of the unknown component is a resistor and endow the unknown component with all the functional characteristics of the resistor entry in the component knowledge base. A detailed description of this *resolver* algorithm is beyond the scope of this book. See [Myler, 1989] for details.

15.5 CHAPTER REVIEW

Various alternative means of acquiring or generating knowledge exist besides the traditional techniques described in the previous two chapters. Three different methods are described.

1. *Facilitation of the elicitation:* This technique consists of asking questions of the expert through a dialogue with an automatic knowledge acquisition tool and organizing the responses into a knowledge base. The most popular technique for implementing this is the repertory grid, a template of the expert's thinking on the domain. This grid can assist in the early stages of the knowledge acquisition process when the knowledge structure is being designed.

2. *Inductive learning:* This is the concept of learning from examples. There is an algorithm that can derive a minimal classification tree from examples prepared by an expert. This algorithm is called ID3 and has been used in commercial inductive tools. Learning from examples (induction) can be quite useful if the examples exist in an electronic format and can be easily presented to the inductive system.

3. *Automated generation of knowledge from databases:* This technique can be used to build models of engineered systems from CAD drawings. It comprises the examination of a design database for a schematic of a system, the identification of the components included therein, the resolution of any conflicting information, and the final creation of a knowledge base (i.e., a model) for use in a model-based reasoning system. It employs constraint propagation and an external knowledge base of domain elements to carry out the task. The automated generation of knowledge from a CAD design database can be powerful, although limited in its applications.

Although these methods, in general, do not replace the traditional interview method, they provide useful alternatives for some problem domains at various stages of the knowledge acquisition process. Research is continuing in these topics, and we expect that significant advances will be made in the area in the relatively near future.

15.6 PROBLEMS

15-1. Pick a classmate who has expertise in some topic (almost everyone has expertise in some area). Interview him/her and draw a repertory grid from the results of the interview.

15-2. Take the repertory grid developed in Problem 15-1 and generate a set of rules from it. Is this easier than using the techniques shown in Chapters 13 and 14? Justify your answer.

15-3. Pick a topic about which you consider yourself to be knowledgeable. Develop a set of examples based on your experience. Now use the ID3 algorithm to develop a minimal tree and, therefore, a rule base for your knowledge.

15-4. Develop a minimal tree from the set of examples shown below for the diagnosis of an automobile that will not start.

lights	sound	turn-over	fuel-gauge	smell	problem
dim	howl	yes	not-empty	normal	battery
normal	screech	no	not-empty	normal	starter
normal	click	no	not-empty	normal	solenoid
normal	normal	yes	empty	normal	out-of-gas
normal	normal	yes	not-empty	gas	flooding

15-5. Do the same as in Problem 15-4 for the set of examples shown below for the classification of certain types of trees in the southern temperate zone (lve = leaf).

lve-shape	lve-size	fruit	wood	deci-duous	type
broad	large	brown-balls	hard	yes	sycamore
needle	short	acorn	fine	no	pine
thin	long	nut	fibrous	no	coconut
simple	small	acorn	hard	no	live-oak
lobed	large	samara	hard	yes	maple

16 ■ Verification and Validation[1]

16.1 INTRODUCTION

The subject of ensuring quality in software has taken on considerably more importance with the exponential increase in the size and complexity of modern software systems. The critical nature of some applications (e.g., air traffic control) also requires the highest quality in software. Knowledge-based systems should be no different.

Until recently, the issues of quality and/or reliability of knowledge-based systems had been addressed in a sketchy manner. Validation of existing knowledge-based systems, with a few exceptions, was done in an ad hoc and informal manner [O'Keefe, 1987]. During the past few years we have seen more formal and precise techniques being developed [Stachowitz, 1987; Nguyen, 1987; Gupta, 1990; Preece, 1992; Zlatareva, 1992], but additional work in the area remains.

Future growth of knowledge-based systems will be severely hampered if developers do not come to grips with the problem of reliability. The reliability of a knowledge-based system in critical-use (e.g., diagnostic and/or control of a nuclear power plant, space vehicle) and many noncritical-use applications (e.g., crop pesticide treatment, manufacturing process control) must be assured before employing a system for these tasks. Additionally, since a knowledge-based system is supposed to be "intelligent," loss of credibility by the user could result from mistaken conclusions drawn by the system. This can lead to decreased use of the system and its ultimate failure.

As we saw in Chapter 13, a certain amount of testing is naturally done as part of the incremental development process. This is a sensible component of

---

[1]In collaboration with Uma Gupta.

any software development project. Nevertheless, a formal evaluation of the knowledge-based system should be done over and above the error elimination carried out during development. *Verification and validation* (V&V) provide the mechanism for performing the needed formal evaluation.

The terms verification and validation are often loosely used. Whereas the main objective of both processes is to ensure that the knowledge-based system provides the correct answer in the correct form when called upon to solve a problem, they also involve other objectives such as ensuring the maintainability, safety, security, and usability of the system. To do this, we must discover and then eliminate any errors or inadequacies from the system.

Errors are the bane of any software product, including knowledge-based systems. They are introduced into a knowledge-based system during the design of the system or during knowledge acquisition. The major causes of errors in a knowledge-based system are

1. The lack of system specifications or, where they exist, lack of adherence to them. In a survey reported by Hamilton [Hamilton, 1991], 52 percent of the respondents indicated that no requirements were documented for their systems, while 43 percent reported that the initial prototype was used to define the requirements.
2. Semantic as well as syntactic errors introduced during the implementation of the system (bugs).
3. The incorrect representation of the domain knowledge, resulting in an erroneous solution or the inability to find any solution to a problem.

Verification addresses the first two causes. It examines the issue of compliance with the specifications (if they exist). It also serves to ensure the consistency and completeness of a knowledge base, which are affected by syntactic and semantic errors. Validation addresses many issues such as those described above but, most importantly, it ensures that the domain knowledge is correct and the system solves problems within the domain correctly and accurately.

Since validating and verifying knowledge-based systems are new, the challenges are many. Much confusion exists about what V&V are, how they differ from each other, and how V&V of knowledge-based systems differ from those of conventional software. This chapter defines these terms and clarifies these issues. We start this discussion by examining V&V in conventional software to provide a basis of comparison for our discussion.

16.2 A COMPARISON OF THE V&V OF KNOWLEDGE-BASED SYSTEMS AND CONVENTIONAL SOFTWARE

It is appropriate to draw a parallel between the validation of knowledge-based systems and conventional software. Ken Penderson [Penderson, 1989] states:

Many developers think of knowledge-based system projects as completely outside the context of traditional software development. Many developers ignore standard systems analysis techniques that should be used in all software applications. Knowledge-based systems are still software, even though they employ new ideas and techniques.

Conventional software testing traditionally involves the execution of a set of test cases whose results are precisely known: The calculations of a mathematical program can often be verified through hand calculations while the behavior of physical phenomena can be observed in an actual system and compared to that of the software's mathematical models of the same phenomenon. If the software produces the correct results for a given set of inputs, then it has correctly solved the test case. If this continues for the entire set of test cases, then the software system can be considered valid. Benchmarks are special test cases that check the performance of a system in very special circumstances. These are special because they represent critical circumstances or because they demonstrate a specified level of performance.

While the test case approach has and continues to work satisfactorily for traditional software, it has not proven totally adequate for knowledge-based systems. What is it that makes V&V of knowledge-based systems different from those of conventional software? Part of the reason stems from how knowledge-based systems differ from conventional software:

1. Knowledge-based systems are not completely objective in nature. The problem-solving knowledge that they contain is based on the subjective impressions and thoughts of a human expert. In fact, for some applications, if you give the same situation to two experts of equal competence, each may decide to approach the problem in a different, yet correct, fashion resulting in two different, but adequate, solutions. While both solution approaches are appropriate, each expert may consider his/her approach to be the best while labeling the other expert's solution less than optimal.

2. A certain amount of uncertainty is tolerated in knowledge-based systems. As we discussed in Chapter 8, expert solutions are not always precise and exact, but rather have some associated uncertainty and imprecision due to either the data used or the domain knowledge itself. Whereas some numerical imprecision is tolerated in conventional software when numerical analysis problems or simulations are implemented, the acceptable tolerance is typically distinctly bound.

3. For some applications, conventional software can be verified by performing laboratory experiments on the process that the software models. If the results of the tests agree with the output of the software for an appropriately wide range of inputs, then the software simulation model is considered verified. Knowledge-based systems, on the other hand, cannot

be easily verified in the laboratory. This is because they generally do not model a physical system but rather the experts' compiled interpretation about the physical system.

4. In conventional software, the question of the correctness of the results of a test case is generally not an issue. A system verifier can always clearly determine whether the answer provided by the program is correct or not. Since knowledge-based systems model the expert's knowledge about a domain, a human expert is inextricably involved. This means that an expert (or a group of experts) is the final arbiter of the correctness of the knowledge-based system. This, of course, introduces the variations of opinion described above, which tend to complicate the V&V of knowledge-based systems.

Given these differences, new methods of evaluating knowledge-based systems are necessary to ensure their reliability. No single technique has been developed that has gained universal acceptance, nor is a single method likely ever to do so. But several approaches exist that, in combination with each other, can serve to accomplish many of our desired goals.

16.3 VERIFICATION

Many definitions of verification exist in the literature including:

Verification is building the system right. [O'Keefe, 1987]

It is a demonstration of the consistency and completeness of a system. [Adrion, 1982]

One objective of verification is to ensure the existence of a match between the specifications of the system and what the system actually does. Ideally, the specifications accurately reflect the requirements of the system, but unfortunately that is not always the case. Verification also ensures that the system is free of errors introduced by the developers during the implementation stage. Verification of knowledge-based systems is, for the most part, quite similar to the verification of software programs.

When verifying a knowledge-based system, we must consider both of its major components: the inference engine as well as the knowledge base. If a commercial shell is used, it is hoped that its verification would be a moot issue since it should already have been verified by the developer. However, this is not always the case. Many commercial tools are less than reliable, and this issue should be addressed by the system developers when selecting the tool. Nevertheless, verification of the tool is not normally the responsibility of the knowledge engineer and, other than purchasing another tool, is beyond her control.

If, on the other hand, you have developed your own inference engine, then you should apply conventional software verification techniques since the tool is really a piece of conventional software. As a result, we concentrate our discussion on the verification of the knowledge base.

Two steps compose knowledge base verification: (1) checking for compliance with the system specifications and (2) checking for semantic and syntactic errors in the knowledge base. We discuss these in the following sections.

16.3.1 Specification Compliance

A check for compliance with the specification has traditionally been a paper exercise in which an objective third party, or, a team of developers, users, and experts as well as objective third parties, evaluate the knowledge base to determine its compliance with the specifications. While the advent of Computer-Aided Software Engineering tools (CASE) has allowed for significant automation of this process in conventional software, migration of these advances to the knowledge-based system field has been slow. Some issues to be considered are whether

1. The proper knowledge representation paradigm was implemented.
2. The proper reasoning technique was employed.
3. Modularity was used in the design and implementation.
4. The system interfaces properly to external software.
5. The user interface meets the specification.
6. The explanation facility is appropriate for the intended users.
7. The real-time performance requirements of the system are met.
8. The system is maintainable to the degree specified.
9. The system meets the security specifications.
10. Appropriate security measures have been implemented into the system to protect against unauthorized modification of the knowledge base.

16.3.2 Developer-induced Errors

The second step in knowledge base verification is to check for semantic and syntactic errors that may have been introduced by the knowledge engineer when developing the knowledge base. Such errors can affect the completeness and consistency of the knowledge base with respect to the domain. While a verified knowledge-based system (complete and consistent) is not an implication that it will provide the correct answers, it does ensure that the knowledge-based system was properly designed and implemented. A verified knowledge-based system, as far as the knowledge engineer is concerned, correctly represents the knowledge elicited from the expert(s).

Most research in V&V of knowledge-based systems has been performed on rule-based systems. As a result, we concentrate our discussion on the verification of these systems unless otherwise noted. This is not to say, however, that systems built with other paradigms do not require V&V (they do!) or that it is not possible to verify them (it is!) [Cheng, 1989].

A check for syntactic errors in a rule base means that the rule base must be checked for

1. redundant rules
2. conflicting rules
3. subsumed rules
4. circular rules
5. unnecessary IF conditions
6. dead-end rules
7. missing rules
8. unreachable rules

The first five of these errors involve the consistency of the knowledge base while the last three affect its completeness. The next few sections discuss each of these in more detail.

16.3.2.1 Redundant rules.   Two rules are considered *syntactically redundant* if they have identical premises and reach identical conclusions. For example, the following two rules

```
RULE 1: IF    The humidity is high AND
              The temperature is hot
        THEN  There will be thunderstorms

RULE 2: IF    The temperature is hot AND
              The humidity is high
        THEN  There will be thunderstorms
```

will always succeed under the same circumstances; both assert that "There will be thunderstorms." As a result, they are considered redundant. Redundant rules can be harmful in knowledge-based systems that employ certainty factors because they can unwittingly influence the certainty factor of their conclusions.

Semantic redundancy occurs when the premises or the conclusions of otherwise redundant rules are not identical in syntax, but convey the same meaning. For instance, RULE3 and RULE4 below are semantically redundant

```
RULE 3: IF    The humidity is high AND
              The temperature is hot
        THEN  There will be thunderstorms
```

```
RULE 4: IF    The temperature is hot AND
              The humidity is high
        THEN  There will be electrical storms
```

Semantic redundancies are less common, but more difficult to detect because the system does not know that thunderstorms and electrical storms are identical.

16.3.2.2 Conflicting rules.   *Conflicting* rules occur when the premises of two rules are identical, yet their conclusions contradict. For example

```
RULE 5: IF    The temperature is hot AND
              The humidity is high
        THEN  There will be sunshine

RULE 6: IF    The temperature is hot AND
              The humidity is high
        THEN  There will not be sunshine
```

16.3.2.3 Subsumed rules.   One rule is considered *subsumed* by another if it has more constraints in the premise while having identical conclusions. For example, given the following rules

```
RULE 7: IF    The temperature is hot AND
              The humidity is high AND
              The barometric pressure is low
        THEN  There will be thunderstorms

RULE 8: IF    The temperature is hot AND
              The humidity is high
        THEN  There will be thunderstorms
```

we can state that RULE7 is subsumed by RULE8 because the former has one more constraint than the latter.

16.3.2.4 Circular rules.   If care is not taken in the construction of a knowledge base, it is possible to specify a sequence of rules that employs *circular* reasoning. This situation can be explained with the simple forward reasoning case shown below

```
RULE 9:  IF    X and Y are brothers
         THEN  X and Y have the same parents

RULE 10: IF    X and Y have the same parents
         THEN  X and Y are brothers
```

If RULE9 finds a match and fires, its conclusion will cause RULE10 to match and subsequently fire. But RULE10's conclusion will match RULE9's premise causing it to fire again beginning an infinite loop of useless rule firings. This looping occurs because forward-reasoning systems rarely check to see if rule conclusions have been previously derived.

Another form of circularity takes the following form

```
RULE 11: IF    X is bald
         THEN  X's son is bald
```

If we know that John is bald, this rule will derive that John's son is bald. That in turn satisfies the rule which causes it to derive Johns' son's son is bald, and so forth. This situation can occur in both forward and backward reasoning.

16.3.2.5 Unnecessary IF conditions. An *unnecessary IF condition* exists when two rules with identical conclusions have almost identical premises. The premises of these rules are identical except one in each rule that contradicts. Consider the following example taken from Nguyen [Nguyen, 1987]

```
RULE 12: IF    the patient has pink spots AND
               The patient has a fever
         THEN  The patient has measles

RULE 13: IF    the patient has pink spots AND
               The patient does not have fever
         THEN  the patient has the measles
```

If the second premises of each rule are truly unnecessary, these two rules can be collapsed into the single rule

```
RULE 14: IF    the patient has pink spots
         THEN  the patient has the measles
```

An additional comment should be made about this situation. Conflicting rules are not always so easy to correct. Very often a conflict does not signify unnecessary IF conditions but rather missing premises within the rules or incorrect knowledge expressed within a rule.

16.3.2.6 Dead-end rules. *Dead-end rules* in forward chaining systems are those that have actions that do not affect any conclusions and are not used by other rules to generate any other conclusion. Consider an automobile diagnostic system. Suppose that this system contained the rule

```
RULE 15: IF    the gauge reads empty
         THEN  the gas tank is empty
```

But, if the conclusion "The gas tank is empty" is not a goal of the system and if this fact is not utilized by any other rules, then this rule would be considered a *dead-end rule*. Such rules indicate conclusions that are being drawn unnecessarily or the presence of a missing rule (or rules) that would make use of that conclusion.

A similar situation exists in backward-chaining systems. For example, if RULE15 occurs in a backward-chaining automobile diagnostics system, it is using the input from the car's gas gauge to derive how much gas is left in the car's gas tank. This would be considered a dead-end rule if the premise of the rule does not have an input or the input never matches the value specified in the premise. In other words, whereas this type of rule can be traced, it will never affect the conclusion it is trying to make. Its presence also indicates that the rule itself may be unnecessary, that there is a missing rule, or that the premise's specified value is incorrect (i.e., is misspelled or inappropriate).

16.3.2.7 Missing rules. *Missing rules* are characterized by facts that are not used within the inference process, conclusions not affected by any rules or procedures, or a failure to cover all legal values of some input. To illustrate this problem consider RULE15 of the automobile diagnostic system example above. This rule could be a result of a missing rule that would use the output of the now dead-end rule to reach another useful conclusion. Suppose that this system additionally has a defined input for the amount of gasoline left in the tank, but does not use this datum to draw any conclusions. It would appear in this situation that a rule is missing that ties a problem with starting the automobile's engine to the amount of gasoline when the tank is empty.

16.3.2.8 Unreachable rules. This type of syntactic error, which is different for forward and backward chainers, is the inverse of the dead-end rules. In a forward-chainer, an *unreachable rule* has a premise that will never be matched by the system under any circumstances, either due to missing rules or to lack of input data. This is the equivalent to a dead-end rule in a backward-chaining system.

In backward chainers the situation is somewhat different. The consequence of an unreachable rule does not match any of the goals defined for the system or any intermediate hypothesis. This would make RULE15 untraceable in a backward chainer, which is equivalent to a dead-end rule in a forward-chaining system.

16.3.3 When Semantic Errors Are Not Errors

The use of uncertainty management in a rule base changes the nature of some of the above descriptions. For example, subsumed rules have occasionally been used purposely by knowledge engineers to increase the confidence in a conclusion when an unnecessary, but helpful, piece of evidence is present.

To illustrate this, let us assume the following: (1) The presence of high humidity is sufficient to reach a conclusion of "thunderstorms" and (2) high ambient temperature increases the confidence of "thunderstorms" if it happens simultaneously with the high humidity, but is not by itself sufficient to conclude it. These two statements can be represented by the following (purposely) subsumed rules:

```
RULE 16:IF    The humidity is high
         THEN Thunderstorms are likely    CF=.70

RULE 17:IF    The humidity is high AND
              The ambient temperature is high
         THEN Thunderstorms are likely    CF=.50
```

Note that in high temperature and high humidity, both rules will fire, having a combined CF of 0.85. Yet, if there is only high humidity, the CF is 0.70. However, the conclusion of "Thunderstorms" will not be reached if there is only high ambient temperature. Thus, semantic "errors" need to be evaluated in terms of how the inference engine operates and the intent of the knowledge engineer.

16.3.4 Verification Tools

Several automated tools exist that can examine a rule base and identify all of the syntactic errors described above. One example is CHECK [Nguyen, 1987]. Developed for use with the Lockheed Expert System (LES), a rule-based, knowledge-based system shell, CHECK identifies inconsistencies in knowledge bases by searching for redundant rules, conflicting rules, subsumed rules, unnecessary IF conditions, and circular rule chains. It verifies completeness by probing for unreferenced or illegal attribute values, unreachable goals, missing rules, and dead-end rules. CHECK is capable of handling any knowledge base developed under LES: those using forward- as well as backward-chaining rules and knowledge bases using certainty factors. CHECK [Nguyen, 1987] partitions the knowledge into "sets" of rules pertaining to particular portions of the problem domain. To determine the relationships between the clauses making up the premises and the conclusions as well as the relationships between the rules themselves, CHECK then compares

1. The clauses in the premises and the conclusions of every rule individually with one another.

2. The entire premises of rules with the premises of other rules.

3. The entire conclusions of rules with those of other rules.

4. The entire premises of rules with the conclusions of other rules.

Each comparison is labeled as a *subset,* a *superset,* the *same as, different from,* or *in conflict with*. These classified comparisons are represented in tables of relationships. Based on these comparisons, CHECK can then determine which rules are subsumed, conflicting, and so forth.

Other automated verification tools exist that perform similar functions. TEIRESIAS [Davis, 1976] was the earliest attempt to debug a knowledge base automatically. A rule checker was developed for the knowledge-based system ONCOCIN that attempted to find inconsistencies and incompleteness in its knowledge bases [Suwa, 1982]. Unlike CHECK and TEIRESIAS, the rule checker in ONCOCIN is not a generic tool and checks the consistency of every rule as it enters the system. Another system developed at Lockheed, the Expert system Validation Associate (EVA) [Stachowitz, 1987], also attempts to perform the same function of rule-base verification as CHECK.

The research trend is now to include the ability to detect syntactic and semantic errors within a knowledge-based system's development environment.

16.4 VALIDATION

Validation is inherently more complicated than verification. Some definitions of validation are:

> *It refers to the process of building the right system.* [O'Keefe, 1987]
>
> *It involves the determination of the correctness of the final system with respect to user needs and requirements.* [Adrion, 1982]

In simple terms, validation is the final quality control step of knowledge-based systems. Validation ensures that the output of the system is correct (however that is defined) and that the developed system is what the users want and need [Nguyen, 1987]. Assuming that a knowledge base has been verified, validation ensures that the knowledge it contains correctly represents and simulates the domain knowledge.

16.4.1 Significant Issues in Validation

O'Keefe [O'Keefe, 1987] defines some important issues in the validation of a system as

1. What is being validated.
2. Validation methodology.
3. Validation criteria.
4. When validation should occur.

16.4.1.1 What to validate.   Validation of a knowledge base can be accomplished by validating [O'Keefe, 1987]

1. The intermediate results.
2. The final results.
3. Some combination of the two.

Obviously, the production of correct final results is the ultimate goal, so these results should never be omitted from a validation effort. However, the validation of intermediate results can provide deep insight into the operation of the system and allow quick correction of problems at the cost of additional effort expended.

16.4.1.2 Validation methodology.   Many methods can be employed in the validation of knowledge-based systems. The methods described here are not mutually exclusive. In fact, we recommend that several of these be applied concurrently to provide depth as well as breadth within the validation effort. The practicality, advantages, and disadvantages of each of these varies, depending on the type and intended use of the knowledge-based system being developed.

1. *Informal validation:* As the name suggests, informal validation represents a superficial and qualitative process that may consist of the system developers meeting with one or more domain experts and users to discuss the validity of each conclusion reached by the system. While this technique can be useful as a quality check during the development of a knowledge-base module, it cannot generally be considered satisfactory as the sole means of validating a knowledge-based system.
2. *Validation by testing:* This method requires prepared test cases. These test cases are processed by the knowledge-based system, and the resulting answers are compared for *agreement* with those of an expert or a panel of experts who try to solve the same problem. This method is a black-box approach where only the system inputs and the produced outputs are significant. It represents a more formal and quantitative alternative to informal validation.

    There are various ways to implement the comparison between the system's results and the opinion of the experts/users. One is to have the experts present the system with the test cases and determine whether they agree or disagree with the results. This agreement can be a simple *yes* or *no* or a more flexible set of opinions like *strongly agree, agree, acceptable, disagree, strongly disagree*. Alternatively, a continuous range of values could be used where a zero indicates total disagreement and a ten total agreement. The opinions of the various experts/users can then be tallied and a quantitative determination made of the accuracy and adequacy of the system. If this approach is employed, the developers must ensure that the experts/users have no trouble operating the system, either by assisting them with the system's execution or by implementing an easy-to-use user interface. Alternatively, the experts/users could simply be provided with hard copy results of the knowledge-based system operation.

A second way to perform the comparison, which eliminates the experts' operating the system and the potentially difficult problem of resolving differences in experts' opinions, is to present the test case results to the validation panel as a whole. Our experience has generally been that when disagreements among experts arise, they tend to be resolved quite successfully.

One major problem with these two approaches is bias by the experts/users for or against the computer. This problem is discussed by O'Keefe [1987] and was also a concern of the developers of MYCIN [Buchanan, 1984a]. It is very important to maintain objectivity during the validation process. If the development team is charged with the validation task, they might skew the process to ensure validation should no outside oversight be provided. At the other extreme, an external set of validators might be too critical because of personality conflicts with members of the development team or because they feel that they should have been consulted during the system's development (i.e., they will now make management see their mistake by showing them that the system is all wrong). These individuals may be critical of the system for reasons other than its technical merits, such as dislike for the user interface, the graphics output, or the language used in the explanations.

Steps can be taken to manage such destructive bias. For example, populate the validation panel with experts/users who were not originally involved with the development process, as well as some who were. This blend provides objectivity (by including outside individuals) while precluding incorrect and preconceived ideas (through the presence of developers).

Another technique that can assist in the elimination of bias is the *Turing test*. This method was used successfully in the validation of MYCIN [Yu, 1984]. In this variation of the original test designed by Alan Turing in the 1950s, an evaluator is presented with both the system's and an expert's results in a similar format to disguise which is which. Structured as a blind test, this technique allows the evaluator(s) to appraise the knowledge-based system without knowing the source of the results. The idea behind this technique is conceptually simple, but can be somewhat complicated to implement. The output format of the system has to be such that it lends itself to this type of dialogue. Additionally, an elaborate scheme must be created for the experts to obtain maximum benefit. The advantage of this approach is the elimination of pro- or anti-computer bias by the expert, since the expert is never sure which results are being examined.

In summary, the test case validation technique is the most popular of the validation techniques. Nevertheless, two major concerns exist when using this approach. First is the issue of how to define agreement between the knowledge-based system's solution and that of the expert (or even between the various experts in a multiexpert panel). Second, as the number of rules, frames, or other knowledge elements grow, the number of required test cases grow exponentially, quickly getting out of control. Thus, an exhaustive set of test cases cannot be used in any but the simplest systems. Therefore, some criteria for preparing a comprehensive yet nonexhaustive set of test cases needs to be determined.

3. *Field tests:* In general, field tests are a good idea because they allow the developer to see the system perform in its actual operating environment. No matter how extensively the system is validated through other means, and how much input is provided by the expert and the users during the development process, field testing always uncovers unexpected errors or undesirable side effects. However, field testing on incomplete prototypes presents one inherent danger: The system may lose credibility before the users get a chance to see the final product. Regaining their lost confidence can be difficult. There are steps to take to mitigate this, however: First, the users evaluating the system should be receptive to the concept of knowledge-based systems beforehand to avoid user hostility. This helps ensure that the prototype receives a complete and fair evaluation. Second, the users should be aware that they are testing only a prototype, which may not be as complete or as intelligent as they might expect. Therefore, the system may commit some errors, which will be eliminated in the production version. Field testing should occur late in the validation process and should represent only a portion of the process rather than the entire validation effort.

4. *Subsystem validation:* This method requires partitioning the knowledge-based system into subsystems (e.g., modules), which are validated individually using the other methodologies described here. Good design

methodology requires that systems be modular in nature, thus allowing the subsystems to be validated as they are built. This "divide and conquer" technique should make errors easier to fix, but has two significant disadvantages: (a) Not all systems easily decompose into clear-cut, independent subsystems and (b) validation of all the subsystems does not equate to validation of the entire system. Thus, subsystem validation should not be entire scope of the validation effort.

5. *Sensitivity analysis:* Sensitivity analysis utilizes techniques similar to those employed when validating simulation models. In this technique the system is given sets of inputs containing slight variations. The impact of the variations in the inputs is studied by observing the resulting changes in the output. This is a very powerful technique that is especially useful in systems relying heavily on uncertainty management since the impact of changes in certainty factors on intermediate results and final conclusions can be effectively studied.

16.4.1.3 Validation criteria.   Determining the appropriate validation criteria is an important consideration. It can safely be said that all knowledge-based systems are valid against some criteria, while invalid against others. Given this fact, how do we determine which criteria are correct for evaluating a particular system? This is a difficult question to answer because all knowledge-based systems have different purposes and goals. Certainly, significantly more stringent validation criteria would apply to a medical diagnosis system than a system that assists in the selection of a wine for dinner. So, instead of trying to answer this question directly, let us discuss some different types of validation criteria that can be used.

1. *Comparison against known results:* The results of the knowledge-based system can be compared to historical cases. For example, the validation of a medical diagnostic system can involve presenting data captured from a patient to the knowledge-based system and comparing its conclusion to the actual incident. This can be likened to 20/20 hindsight.

2. *Comparison against expert performance:* This approach differs from *comparison against known results* by including a tolerance for mistakes made by an expert. Therefore, the system is not compared to actual historical results but, rather, to the expert's prediction of the final results. This criterion is less strict as well as more realistic, since most knowledge-based systems are designed to model an expert's knowledge and thus should not be expected to be perfect. Remember that a knowledge-based system that performs as well as an expert, but that is not 100 percent accurate, can be highly beneficial in many cases.

3. *Comparison against theoretical possibility:* In cases where a knowledge-based system is modeling a physical process, the performance of the

knowledge-based system could be compared to the theoretical behavior of the physical system. This is not always possible in domains where heuristic reasoning predominates and algorithmic model validation is more suitable.

All the criteria mentioned above are simply gross metrics. Varying levels of stringency can be built into each, as may be called for by the application. As with any other software product, however, it is impractical and infeasible to provide 100 percent performance guarantees on any knowledge-based system. This problem is further compounded by inaccuracies within the knowledge itself on which such systems are based. Therefore, validation of knowledge-based systems is really a quest to determine if the system is performing acceptably, rather than perfectly. The definition of acceptable performance, furthermore, may vary widely depending on the particular application. Two important system parameters to consider here are: *accuracy* and *adequacy*.

Accuracy can be defined as the proportion of "acceptable" answers that the knowledge-based system generates. Likewise, acceptability can be defined as those solutions that agree with those proposed by an expert faced with the same problem [Marcot, 1987]. Statistical tests such as the chi-square test can then be used to derive a quantitative measure of the accuracy of the system's performance.

Adequacy, on the other hand, measures how much of the problem domain is covered by the system. This is referred to as *coverage* [Marcot, 1987]. For instance, a classification system for species of insects that correctly classifies 120 of 145 total species would have an adequacy of nearly 83 percent. As an alternative, a weighted adequacy can be computed by assigning weights to each possible answer to distinguish those that are more critical within the domain.

16.4.1.4 When is validation appropriate?   At what stage in the development process should a knowledge-based system be validated? Experts differ in their opinion regarding the timing of validation [O'Keefe, 1987]. One argument [Bachant, 1984a] is that to validate anything but a nearly complete system against stringent criteria is foolish because it is only then that the system has sufficient knowledge to make accurate decisions. On the other hand, Buchanan and Shortliffe [Buchanan, 1984] argue that the validation process should begin with the specification of the system and continue throughout the development process. This last point of view has become the more widely accepted of the two, resulting in validation becoming ingrained in the development process, rather than being simply a phase within it. Nevertheless, the broader implication of the first statement is that there still needs to be some final validation process that evaluates the performance of the system against its most stringent criteria.

The consensus, therefore, is to expect some level of acceptable performance (dependent on the complexity and criticalness of the system) in the early stages of development. This level of performance is expected to increase as the system development progresses towards completion.

The initial prototype lays the foundation for formal and rigorous validation. Several important steps in the validation process should be achieved in this phase. The performance criteria to evaluate the system should be finalized; the accuracy and adequacy of the prototype system should be measured; and the type and rigorousness of the techniques that will be used to validate the system should also be determined.

The timing of validation is also related to a system's development cycle. You should expect different levels of performance based upon the current stage of development. Formal validation, however, should begin as soon as the initial prototype has been developed. At this point, often called the *alpha-test* stage, the initial objectives of building the system are usually reconsidered and any necessary modifications are made. Subsystem validation can also answer this question by suggesting that validation be started as soon as any one of the modules is complete.

16.4.2 Errors

Knowledge-based system errors in representing the domain knowledge can be categorized as either *errors of commission* or *errors of omission*. Either or both of these types of errors can be present within a given system.

1. *Errors of commission* occur when a knowledge-based system arrives at an incorrect conclusion for a given set of input values. These errors affect the accuracy of the system and are fairly easy to detect, but often difficult to locate and correct.

2. *Errors of omission* exist when a set of input values fails to cause the system to reach a conclusion. In other words, the knowledge necessary to solve a particular problem within the domain is not found in the knowledge base. These are often more difficult to detect because the test case to locate this omission may not be obvious to the developer. Such errors affect the adequacy of the system.

Errors can also be made in the validation process. There are two generally recognized types of validation errors [O'Keefe, 1987]: (1) *builder's risk,* where a valid system is incorrectly rejected and (2) *user's risk,* where an invalid system is accepted as valid. Some systems may be able to tolerate one type of error but not the other. For instance, due to the serious consequences of any errors, a medical diagnostic system can tolerate builder's risk, but not user's risk. On the other hand, a desperately needed system to diagnose automobiles at a large repair shop could tolerate user's risk, but not builder's risk.

16.5 CASE STUDIES—MYCIN AND R1

The primary validation method used for Mycin was validation by testing. As reported by Buchanan and Shortliffe [Buchanan, 1984a], some testing of the system was being performed during the development process. Nevertheless, the developers felt a need to formally validate the system and proceeded to perform three studies.

The first study was carried out by Shortliffe as a part of his dissertation [Shortliffe, 1974] and is discussed in [Buchanan, 1984a]. It involved five faculty and fellows in the Stanford University Division of Infectious Diseases who were asked to review and critique 15 test cases for which Mycin had offered therapy advise. They were asked to comment on the following issues concerning Mycin:

1. Its ability to evaluate a patient's need for treatment.
2. Its ability to gauge the importance of isolated organisms.
3. Its ability to identify the organisms that were affecting the patient.
4. Its ability to prescribe the appropriate cure.
5. Its overall performance.

The results of this first test were that Mycin received an "approval rating" of 75 percent. Although certainly good, this was not seen to be expert performance against the "gold standard" of the performance of true experts. There were also some concerns that all the experts were part of the same university community, which could lead to provincialism, since some parts of the country treat the same disease differently. Lastly, the experts knew they were evaluating a computer system, which could have produced biased results.

The second study addressed some of the above problems by selecting experts from other centers around the United States (five from Stanford, five from elsewhere). In this study, charts of 15 patients were given to the evaluators and the experts were asked to select a therapy for each patient, which was compared to Mycin's recommendation. Again, the experts knew that they were evaluating a computer program and, although the knowledge had been significantly refined since the first study, the results again showed a 75 percent approval rating. This result was disappointing, given the significant refinements that had been made in the system. The problem with this form of evaluation was no one knew how these experts would have rated the results of other experts. It could very well have been that 75 percent represented a ceiling of expert performance as evaluated by other experts in a field where inexact reasoning is very significant.

The third study addressed this last issue. It was carried out using the Turing test described earlier. Ten patients with meningitis were chosen by a physician who was not aware of Mycin. All cases had been identified as diagnostically challenging. The clinical summaries for each of the ten patients were presented to a control group of five Stanford faculty members, a medical student, a postdoctoral fellow in infectious diseases, a resident physician, a treating physician at the patients' hospital, and Mycin. This made for ten different diagnoses for each patient, resulting in a total of 100 diagnoses.

Eight infectious disease experts from various centers around the country were then presented with identical summaries for each patient, as well as the 100 different diagnoses, without identifying which was Mycin's. The team of evaluators was to evaluate each diagnosis and label each as "Equivalent" to what they would prescribe, "Acceptable alternative" to what they would prescribe, or "Not acceptable." At this point there were 800 evaluations (100 prescriptions times eight evaluators). Mycin provided either an equivalent or acceptable alternative in 65 percent of the cases. Although this value might not be considered good by itself, it was actually higher than any of the other nine prescribers with the next highest receiving a rating of 62.5 percent. Figure 16.1 summarizes the results of this test [Yu, 1984]. In all other categories that were evaluated, Mycin outperformed all of the human experts.

Prescribers	No. (%) of items in which therapy was rated acceptable* by an evaluator (n = 80)	No. (%) of items in which therapy was rated acceptable* by majority of evaluators (n = 10)	No. of cases in which therapy failed to cover a treatable pathogen (n = 10)
Mycin	52 (65)	7 (70)	0
Faculty-1	50 (62.5)	5 (50)	1
Faculty-2	48 (60)	5 (50)	1
Infectious disease fellow	48 (60)	5 (50)	1
Faculty-3	46 (57.5)	4 (40)	0
Actual therapy	46 (57.5)	7 (70)	0
Faculty-4	44 (55)	5 (50)	0
Resident	36 (45)	3 (30)	1
Faculty-5	34 (42.5)	3 (30)	0
Student	24 (30)	1 (10)	3

*Therapy was classified as acceptable if an evaluator rated it as equivalent or as an acceptable alternative.

FIGURE 16.1   Ratings of Antimicrobial Selection Based on Evaluator Rating and Etiologic Diagnosis [Buchanan, 1984]

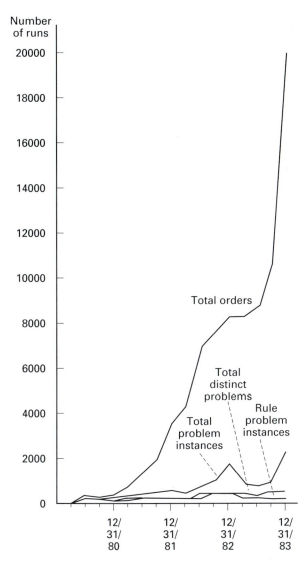

FIGURE 16.2   R1's Performance by Quarter (in graphical form) [Bachant, 1984]

In contrast, R1 [Bachant, 1984] was continuously field tested during its development. Its results were continually being checked by experts and problem reports were entered whenever it was found to disagree with the experts. There was no effort, however, to hide the identity of the computer's conclusion from the experts. The percent of "distinct problems" reports decreased as the development went on, from approximately 53 percent early in the testing and development phase, to 2.8 percent four years later [Bachant 1984]. This project benefited from the numerous test cases evaluated by the system (82,995 from first quarter 1980 to fourth quarter 1983). Figure 16.2 [Bachant, 1984] depicts this improving performance.

R1 is now a commercially used system. Its operation has been critical for a major corporation heavily committed to knowledge-based systems. Thus, it can be justifiably argued that the validation process was a success. Mycin, on the other hand, was never commercialized and never progressed beyond a research prototype. However, we cannot argue that this occurred because of an inadequate validation process. Nevertheless, these different experiences do suggest that for ultimate acceptance it is important to carry out an extensive (but not necessarily exhaustive) validation effort. Furthermore, using actual "field" data, as R1 did, is preferable to "made-up" cases, even though the latter may have been based on actual situations.

Other systems have used a combination of test case validation with field testing. GenAID, for example, employed both techniques, but unfortunately, due to the infrequency of problems with the monitored equipment, there were not nearly as many cases examined during field testing. Nevertheless, the ones that were tested were very significant, and the validation effort proved to be successful.

16.6 A PRACTICAL APPROACH TO V&V

So far we have talked about the issues as well as some methods involved within V&V, but how do we put them into practice? This is difficult to answer because of the many different kinds of systems and their various objectives. Nevertheless, we shall try to define how V&V could be accomplished for a system that uses rules as its sole representation scheme. The technique described is based on the experience in validating and verifying the GenAID system [Osborne, 1985].

First, the system must be verified to

1. Determine whether the system conforms to specifications.
2. Determine the completeness and consistency of the knowledge base by checking the syntactic and semantic correctness of the knowledge base.

This evaluation can generally be done by the development team with no need for outside involvement. Implementation of the first step is currently the subject of research and thus beyond the scope of this book. Let us, therefore, assume that the system does conform to its specifications.

Checking the syntactic correctness of the knowledge base can be relatively easy if an automated tool is available and applicable. Otherwise, a qualitative review should occur: Manually look for the errors that may result when the system is exercised.

Upon successful completion of verification, the development team can be certain that the system was designed and developed according to the specifications and is free of programmer-introduced errors. No statements, however, can yet be made of the absolute correctness of the answers provided or the system's usability. This is done in validation, which is typically performed in collaboration with outsiders.

Validation involves three phases.

1. Design a validation plan by determining the various validation techniques that are appropriate for the system. For example, based on the problem domain, the performance criteria, the critical nature of the conclusions, and the complexity of the model, the test case validation technique may be recommended. Alternatively, a combination of the test case validation technique and the Turing test may be best.

    The heart and soul of the validation process is test case validation. But while this technique is extremely valuable and widely used in some form or another [Buchanan, 1984], it should not be used as the only method for a comprehensive validation effort, but rather in combination with other techniques. Sensitivity analysis should be used to examine the results of the system for the critical test cases (i.e., those inputs that indicate serious or critical conclusions). This can be used to ensure the system reacts properly at critical times.

    The combinatorial explosion of test case development makes this a difficult technique to employ exhaustively. Thus, where applicable, field testing is used together with test case validation to expose the system to other test cases possibly not included in the test case validation stage [Osborne, 1985; Bachant, 1984]. This use of field testing for partial validation can serve as the final seal on the system's validity.

    Another issue to treat in the design of the validation process is whether it is appropriate to decompose the validation effort into a series of subsystem validations.

2. Once the validation technique or techniques are determined, the validation criteria should be established. If test case validation is to be implemented, some issues are raised.

    a. How many test cases will suffice?
    b. How should test cases be generated without creating any bias?
    c. If test cases should be a mixture of easy, medium, and hard cases, then what determines the proportion of each?
    d. Should the results of the test cases be compared against human expert performance or against another measure?
    e. How is human performance measured in this domain?
    f. If multiple experts having different opinions exist how should the system be evaluated?

g. If a test case generates multiple responses (e.g., with different confidence factors), how should these responses be integrated into the validation process?

The nature, scope, number, and complexity of the test cases should be determined first, with testing of the system to follow. As mentioned above, 100 percent certainty in validation, although commendable, is an unrealistic goal for even medium-sized systems since this would require a nearly exhaustive set of test cases, which would be prohibitively costly.

In summary, the issues that we should address in this phase are:

a. How many test cases are sufficient to validate the system to the desired confidence?
b. What should the test cases be?
c. How should the results of the test cases be analyzed? Should a panel of experts be used to directly evaluate the output of the knowledge-based system, or should the Turing test be employed to minimize the evaluator bias?

3. Implement the procedures identified above. For test case validation this phase will involve the generation of the actual test cases, their implementation, and the analysis of the results. Lastly, it must be determined whether the validation process is rigorous enough to instill the desired confidence in the system's performance.

Admittedly, the above steps are easier said than done. Once again, how to accomplish this is still the subject of research. While no general procedure exists at this time, there are many different ways to approach the validation and verification of a system. One reason for the variety is the great differences between the systems being developed. Hamilton [Hamilton, 1991] provides an enlightening review of the current state of the art in V&V.

Lastly, it must be remembered that validation never really ends. It is an on-going effort that must continue throughout the life of the system. Maintaining an up-to-date library of test cases with their anticipated results is an important aspect of this process.

16.7 RECOMMENDED PROCEDURE FOR V&V

One suggested algorithm for V&V of a knowledge-based system, which admittedly makes several assumptions about the nature of the system being developed, is as follows:

1. Perform the following steps for each module in the system, independently of each other:

a. Verify compliance of the knowledge base (module) with the specification.

b. Verify that the module is complete and consistent, that is, no semantic or syntactic errors exist. This can be done either manually or with an automated tool if one is available.

c. Determine the validation criteria to be used by a panel of outside experts judging a comprehensive set of test cases. The Turing test could be employed if desired but, at the very least, the evaluation of the test cases should be done in parallel. That is, the experts evaluate the input data without access to the conclusion reached by the system. All of the test cases should be correctly solved by the knowledge-based system. Corrective action should be taken on all cases that do not arrive at a correct answer as determined by the panel of experts. If inexact reasoning is being used, then a proper error margin should be defined on both sides of the ideal number.

d. The test cases should be prepared, so that they completely cover all of the critical conclusions expected to be made by the system, plus provide incomplete coverage of all others. This step is the one most subject to the nature of the system being evaluated.

e. The test cases should be executed on the system and presented to a validation panel for evaluation.

f. Those test cases not correctly solved should be flagged for future correction.

g. Sensitivity analysis should be performed on all test cases that represent critical problems.

h. The panel is asked to generate additional test cases that represent gaps in the set of cases presented and that could lead to critical conclusions. This is an attempt to eliminate errors of omission. These test cases are run through the system and corrective action is determined if the system is found wanting.

i. A process is instituted to ensure completion of all corrective action to the satisfaction of the expert panel.

2. Test the entire system (the collection of all the modules) in the manner described in step 1. Test cases have only to be presented in cases where there is an overlap between different modules. Additionally, some general system cases should be also executed but they do not need to be comprehensive at this point.

3. Field test the entire system.

Figure 16.3 shows the flow diagram of the above procedure.

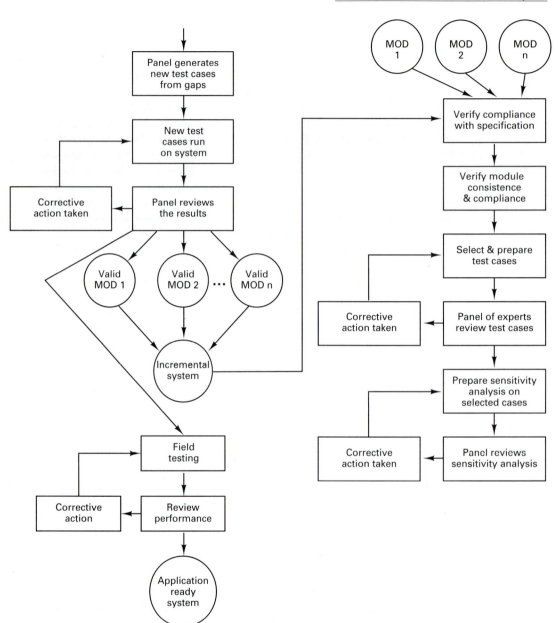

FIGURE 16.3 Block Diagram of Recommended V&V Procedure

16.8 CHAPTER REVIEW

The quality assurance of knowledge-based systems has taken on greater significance as the size, complexity, and critical nature of the applications have grown in the past few years. This is manifested in the process of validation and verification. These two elements are quite different in nature, and they are both necessary. Three types of errors can be introduced into a knowledge-based system and each is addressed by either validation or verification. These are:

1. Lack of adherence to the system specifications, if these exist, (verification).
2. Semantic as well as syntactic errors introduced during the implementation of the system, that is, bugs (verification).
3. Incorrect representation of the domain knowledge, resulting in an erroneous solution or the inability to find any solution to a problem (validation).

Verification can be defined as "building the system right" [O'Keefe, 1987]. It consists of two basic processes; checking for compliance with the specification and checking for the consistency and completeness of the knowledge base (i.e., syntactic and semantic errors). The latter can consist of the following set of common errors:

1. Redundant rules
2. Conflicting rules
3. Subsumed rules
4. Circular rules
5. Unnecessary IF conditions
6. Dead-end rules
7. Missing rules
8. Unreachable rules

A few automated knowledge base verification tools such as CHECK and EVA can be used to facilitate the verification process.

Validation is defined as building the right system [O'Keefe, 1987]. It includes a discussion of the significant issues of validation, such as,

1. What is being validated
2. Validation methodology
3. Validation criteria
4. When validation should occur

This chapter proposes a general methodology and procedure for the V&V of a knowledge-based system. It finally describes how two classic systems such as MYCIN and R1 were validated.

Based on the literature, the area of V&V of knowledge-based systems is a challenging field that has room for exploring many new ideas.

17 Legal Issues in Knowledge-based Systems

17.1 INTRODUCTION

In our highly litigious modern society, a thorough understanding of the technical structure of complex products is often insufficient for a successful developer or user. It is, unfortunately, quite important that the legal implications of the technology be understood as well. The legal issues within computing have increasingly become a subject of great interest to people in the industry during the past several years. Given the ambiguous of computers (specifically, computer programs) when compared to more traditional products, the courts of the United States have been unable to develop a satisfactory theory that is uniformly applicable. Knowledge-based systems, due to their ability to capture and represent human expertise, have served to exacerbate this problem.

When discussing the legal issues of computing, two significant topics come to mind immediately:

1. *Liability:* How liable are the developers of software for errors that cause injuries to a person or property?
2. *Protection:* How do you protect software from unauthorized use?

We conclude our book with a discussion of these issues. It is not our purpose to provide the wealth of information to enable you to make independent decisions regarding when liability exists or when protection is certain. Rather, we aim to alert you to the significant issues, so appropriate advice can be sought when needed or, even better, so that legal action can be avoided altogether by taking preventive steps in the development of your knowledge-based system.

Before examining the issue of liability, we need to provide a general description of the *law of torts*.

17.2 THE LAW OF TORTS

The judicial systems derived from English law consist of two types: *criminal* law and *civil* law. Criminal law is "the law of prevention, punishment and rehabilitation" [Wienerman, 1978]. Statutory laws are created by the *state*. These laws represent the standards of that community of people and clearly define what is a crime. Any violation of these laws victimizes the state and represents cause for prosecution. In criminal cases, the plaintiff is the state and the victim of the crime simply assumes the role of witness against the perpetrator.

Civil law, on the other hand, does not deal with crimes, but with disputes among persons. Its objective is to mediate and find remedy for wrongs caused by actions (or inactions) of one or more persons against another person or group to "return the victim to the same position he was in before the . . . offense was committed" [Wienerman, 1978]. *Torts*, derived from the French word for "wrongs," are the actions that cause the injury and can include injury to property as well as to persons. Torts are not necessarily crimes, and the notion of moral right or wrong has only peripheral influence in the determination of the remedy.

Within the realm of computer science, we have an interest in torts involving injury suffered because of using a product or service. It should be noted that injury is interpreted to mean injury to property as well as to a person's being. When deciding cases dealing with torts, courts apply one of three theories:

1. The theory of strict liability
2. The theory of negligence
3. The publication theory

The *theory of strict liability* "provides that a manufacturer of any product in a defective condition dangerous to the ultimate user is liable for resulting physical harm if the maker is in the business of selling the product" [Trubow, 1991]. The concept of strict liability is that the manufacturer is in a better position than the consumer to recognize potential dangers within a product and thus correct them. Additionally, the manufacturer, through its ability to spread corrective costs to all consumers through higher prices, is typically better able financially to withstand the remedy than is the victim.

Strict liability has occasionally been applied to the defendant in cases where the product is inherently dangerous, regardless of whether there was any fault by the manufacturer. This is considered part of the cost of doing business for the manufacturer [Frank, 1988b].

One key element of strict liability is that it is generally applicable to tangible products sold to the consumer at large. As we will discuss, this has a significant implication for computer programs.

The *theory of negligence*, on the other hand, applies to services and is considerably less burdensome on the defendant. This is because the plaintiff must prove negligence by the defendant to merit a remedy. Negligence is the failure to act within the standard of care expected of a person in the position of the service provider. The standard of care is usually determined according to the defendant's industry or profession, but also considers what the defendant was asked to do. For example, innkeepers are held to the highest degree of care and even the slightest negligence can be held against them [Frank, 1988b]. On the other hand, an auto mechanic who is asked to repair a computer by its owner would be held to a much lower standard of care.

The reason that negligence is applied to services is that services tend to be more specific and personal than physical products and, as a result, generally entail less value to the provider. It therefore would be quite burdensome to service providers to recover the cost of a remedy by increasing the prices to all subsequent customers.

The *publication theory* is not considered a theory per se, but only how the courts have treated publishers of books and reference manuals. In general, courts have not found publishers, authors of books, or lecturers (e.g., instructors) liable for errors in their publications or lectures. This is true only if no contract existed between the user of the information and the publisher, and if the statements were neither defamatory or fraudulent [Gemignani, 1988]. Nevertheless, there is some indication that courts are beginning to allow recovery from publishers in cases where personal injury is involved, as happened when a high school student was injured when conducting a chemistry experiment incorrectly described in a textbook [Gemignani, 1988].

Now that we have a rudimentary understanding of the laws that could apply, let us discuss how the courts are likely to consider computer programs, and more specifically, knowledge-based systems.

17.3 ARE COMPUTER PROGRAMS PRODUCTS OR SERVICES?

In the introduction we spoke of the "ambiguous nature" of computer programs. This refers to the fact that computer programs have aspects of both a product and a service. Because of the discussion about strict liability and negligence, how a court classifies a program becomes a significant question.

The argument can be made that a computer program is not a tangible product, since it consists only of a series of zeros and ones representing electrical impulses within the computer hardware. Yet, these programs are bought and sold in a medium that is tangible (e.g., magnetic disks or tape). On the other hand, programs provide an information-related service. The programmer uses her talents, training, and skills to implement a procedure inside the program. The use of her talents and skills is considered a service.

To resolve the product/service ambiguity, some courts have looked at the essence of the transaction to determine the type of liability. For example, is the purchaser interested in the developer's skill to implement a procedure as a program, or is the purchaser mainly interested in the product itself [Trubow, 1991]?

The relationship between the buyer and the developer also influences whether the program is considered a product or a service. When a software development company is expressly hired to develop custom software, this company is clearly providing a service. Typically, the courts have treated this situation in this manner unless there are other complicating circumstances. Similarly, if a company sells a software product in mass distribution where there is no direct interaction with the customer, the court may have an argument for treating the software as a product even if it is in fact "intangible" [Frank, 1988b].

To complicate the issue further, professionals, such as physicians, engineers, accountants, and so forth, generally provide services. They are typically held to a high standard of care when providing their services and, therefore, have generally not been subject to strict liability [Trubow, 1991]. So, if the programmer is considered a professional, only the theory of negligence would apply.

If the theory of negligence applies, proving that the programmer was negligent could be difficult. A programming "bug" would have to be found and then proven to represent an error that should have been detected using reasonable care, and whose effect was foreseeable [Zeide, 1992]. This can be difficult to do. However, if the programmer failed to include error checking code for foreseeable errors, then proving negligence could be rather easy.

17.4 WHAT ABOUT KNOWLEDGE-BASED SYSTEMS?

Moving away from computer programs in general, consider knowledge-based systems and other "intelligent" programs capable of making judgmental decisions similar to those made by humans. Such systems clearly have the potential to cause significant harm if not properly developed or if misused. A prime example of this is medical diagnostic systems. An incorrect or even misleading conclusion could put a patient in imminent danger. Similarly, other applications (e.g., air traffic control or the diagnosis and control of a nuclear power plant) can potentially bring harm to many people. Since our interest is to discuss knowledge-based systems that represent expertise, we will now cease using the term *knowledge-based* and instead refer to these systems as *expert systems*. The implications of this label would presumably influence the courts somewhat.

The legal treatment of knowledge-based systems is a subset of that for general computer programs. If a tort results from the use of an expert system under strict liability, no further meaningful discussion exists unless you are a lawyer. But, if it is treated under the theory of negligence, there are other issues that need to be considered. These deal with the intelligent nature of expert systems.

To date, no case dealing with expert systems has been brought before the courts. Therefore, this discussion represents conjecture by legal experts. Nevertheless, most experts believe that it is just a matter of time before such a case comes before a court.

Three major issues exist:

1. Can the expert system be considered similar to a reference book that provides advice that, occasionally, is quite specific? The argument can be made that a reference book represents the expertise of the authors. Since the expert system is merely providing advice, it should be held to no higher standard of care than the authors of the book. One difference exists, however. An expert system usually is interactive, providing a dialogue with the user, thus making it more personal in appearance. How this difference will be interpreted by the courts is anyone's guess.

2. Are experts known to make mistakes in judgment even when not guilty of negligence? It is one thing for an expert system to make a mistake that is the result of a programming error that should have been detected if the program had been verified more carefully. It is another when an error is a consequence of incorrect judgment, therefore, falling within the realm of professionalism. The mere fact that an incorrect diagnosis is made should not always indicate a malfunction of the system. For example, physicians are human and medicine is an inexact science. As a result, physicians often produce incorrect diagnoses, even though they have carefully considered all the factors.

3. How is the expert system to be used? An expert system used autonomously to make decisions and perform actions related to that decision would be more susceptible to strict liability than one that simply provides advice. But, merely providing advice does not limit liability. It depends upon who is receiving the advice. Is the individual a member of the general public, implying higher liability, or a highly trained professional, who must evaluate the advice based on his/her professionalism?

   In a field such as medicine, providing advice to nonprofessionals is highly unlikely, at least in the United States, because the practice of medicine requires a regulatory license. It could be argued that an expert system that dispenses medical advice is acting as an unlicensed physician. However, such a scenario is indeed possible in financial planning where an individual can make independent decisions about what to buy, sell, or trade. Another likely situation is that of a tax preparation system, where the wrong advice could result in penalties from the IRS.

Expert systems, however, are more likely to act as intelligent assistants to professionals. Such people will look upon the expert system as a decision-making tool and not as an infallible source of expertise. Consequently, it may be difficult for the professional to "hide" behind the system. Consider a case where a physician provides improper treatment to a patient that results in injury (e.g., prescribing an inappropriate drug therapy that results in neurological damage). If the physician were to blame the expert system for the incorrect diagnosis, this would amount to an admission of an abrogation of his/her duty as a physician. As described by Frank [Frank, 1988b], "the price of limiting the practice of a profession to a select group of peers is accepting complete responsibility for professional misjudgment." Thus it is likely that such an attempt to hide behind an expert system would be unsuccessful and the physician would probably be held responsible for his/her actions.

Furthermore, should the physician be held responsible for a misdiagnosis, it is questionable whether the physician can sue the developer of the expert system for the losses. This is because courts generally permit strict liability recovery only in cases resulting in physical injury or property damage, not for economic loss [Frank, 1988b]. While the patient suffered injury, the physician suffered only economic loss. Thus, the doctor's tort suit must be based on negligence. Negligence would be difficult to prove if the developer has exercised reasonable care in debugging the system and included a statement warning of the system's limitations.

Lastly, while we have discussed the concept of misuse of an expert system by a professional (whether through his fault or that of the developer), a very interesting paradox exists with the use of expert systems as intelligent providers of advice to professionals. If these systems become standard tools of a particular trade and a practitioner in that trade makes an incorrect assessment without consulting an available expert system, then liability could be applied against the practitioner. Conversely, a practitioner who relies too much on such tools without using her judgment could be equally liable.

17.5 SOFTWARE PROTECTION

Computer programs are expensive to develop. To provide an incentive to developers, the laws provide a means of protecting programs from unauthorized users or from those who would make unauthorized use of the intellectual properties contained within them. Unfortunately, computer programs, copy protection notwithstanding, are easy to copy, making the mechanisms of protection inadequate.

Therefore, the second important issue facing developers of knowledge-based systems (going back to our old terminology) is how to protect them from unauthorized use and to protect the intellectual property contained within them. Protection of knowledge-based systems is treated similarly to conventional software.

Three different ways exist to protect software: (1) copyright, (2) patents, and (3) trade secrets.

17.5.1 Copyright Protection

Copyright protection was not originally designed for protection of computer programs and therein lies its problems. Its original purpose was to protect the literary works of authors and publishers. To quote the code itself (the 1976 Act, Title 17 of the U. S. Code), as contained in [Frank, 1988a], "copyright protection and registration are made available for 'original works of authorship fixed in any tangible medium of expression.' "

Registration of a copyright is a simple process. In fact, it is not even necessary for a copyrighted work to be registered with the government for the copyright to be valid. It is only sufficient to state in the work itself that it is copyrighted. A copyright generally lasts for the lifetime of the author plus 50 years, which is a significant length of time. One problem is that while copyright protects the work from being reproduced, it does not protect the ideas contained within the work itself. It protects only the expression of those ideas. Therefore, the ideas contained in a protected program can be taken and implemented into another program without violating the copyright if the new expression of those ideas is significantly different from those of the copyrighted work. Since most ideas within a program can be expressed in code in many different forms, the protection of the ideas through a copyright is weak. In fact, as indicated by Frank, [1988a], "courts will not support a (copyright) infringement action if too few alternative means of expression exist."

Nevertheless, it is not necessary that two programs be identical for one to be a copyright infringement of the other. It needs only to be proven that "substantial similarity" between the two exists. The issue at this point becomes subjective and, therefore, open to the interpretation of the individual courts. This effectively provides a certain degree of protection of the ideas within the program.

17.5.2 Patent Protection

Whereas copyrights protect only the expression of an idea, patents are intended to protect the idea itself. However, there are some caveats.

1. To be patentable, an idea not only has to be expressed in a written form, but it also has to be reduced to practice. This is done to encourage inventors to put their ideas to good use and not keep them from providing a service to the public.

2. Protection under a patent, while comprehensive, lasts for only 17 years. After that time, the idea becomes public for anyone to use.

3. While a copyright can be achieved by simply marking the work as copyrighted, the process for the granting of a patent is quite arduous and expensive. The process takes years and costs thousands of dollars to carry out. Before a patent is granted, the United States Patent Office must review the application to determine if the idea is patentable and has not yet been patented. This discourages many inventors from going through the process.

4. Once a patent is granted, the details of the idea are said to be in the public domain and, thus, can be inspected by anyone. If the idea is not patented in other countries, the inventor may not be able to protect his idea from being copied and commercialized in other countries without renumeration. Additionally, some details that may be necessary to describe the invention may include certain trade secrets that the inventor may not wish to disclose.

In addition to these obstacles which could discourage developers from patenting software, the courts have refused to uphold patents of mathematical and logical algorithms. Nevertheless, under the right circumstances, a patent can represent appropriate protection of knowledge-based systems. The nuances of patent law, however, are many, and clearly beyond the scope of this book. The reader is encouraged to refer to [Frank, 1988a] for more details.

17.5.3 Trade Secret Protection

As mentioned before, there may be some processes critical to the operation of a company or to the manufacture of a product or system that are deemed, for whatever reason, to be either unpatentable or unable to be protected through copyrights. For example, a process control algorithm could be unpatentable because it could be easily implemented in many different forms, thus invalidating copyright protection. In such cases, it is to the benefit of the owner of these ideas to keep them secret from competitors. As described by Frank [Frank, 1988a], " the basic purpose of trade secret laws is to maintain proper standards of commercial ethics. . . . "

The biggest difference between trade secret laws and patents and copyrights is that patents and copyrights require public disclosure of the idea, while the trade secret laws absolutely prohibit it. In fact, if the owner of a trade secret fails to take reasonable measures to prevent the ideas from being misappropriated, then he/she may lose protection from the trade secret laws.

One important consideration is that the secret cannot be discernible from inspection of the commercial product. If it is, it is considered legally disclosed and protection under the trade secret laws vanishes. It is therefore important to a software developer who chooses to use trade secrets that any disclosures of the idea to potential costumers or other individuals outside the company be bound by a nondisclosure agreement. Likewise, any proposals that disclose the idea must be accompanied by assurances that the idea will not be divulged.

Employees of the company where the secret ideas exist are implicitly bound to nondisclosure of the idea, not only while they are employed by the company, but also after they leave. It is also customary for employers to ask departing employees to sign an affidavit of nondisclosure upon their departure to emphasize their duty. The length of this nondisclosure term should be agreed upon at the time of departure and will vary in length depending upon the product lifecycle.

Trade secrets are a good way to maintain protection of computer programs that are often not adequately protected by the copyright or patent laws. This is partly because they do not fit the mold of a device (for which patents were designed) or literary works (for which copyrights were designed). But as noted above, precautions must be taken by the owner of the ideas to protect them.

In summary, there is no single, best way to protect knowledge-based and expert systems. Each developer must weight the pro's and con's of each protection method and decide which is best for the given circumstances. We recommend that appropriate counsel be sought to aid in determining your best avenue whenever these important issues arise.

17.6 CHAPTER REVIEW

The issue of liability for personal injury or property damage resulting from the use of a knowledge-based or expert system is certainly one whose time is near. Although no such case appears to have been brought to trial yet, we can expect that in our highly litigious society, it will not be long before that happens. Expert systems, which operate in the areas of diagnosis (especially in medicine), design, and possibly even law, have the potential to cause such injury to users. Thus, it is imperative that developers of systems become familiar with the issues involved and how they could be affected.

There are many complicated and involved issues. At this point no one knows how they will be resolved until a case comes to court. The most significant issue is whether the knowledge-based or expert system will be considered a product or a service. If it is considered a product, the theory of strict liability could be applied; this states that despite the care taken, a defective or dangerous product is the responsibility of the manufacturer. If the program is considered a service, then negligence must be proven by the defendant under the theory of negligence. This is a much less burdensome theory for the software developer, as negligence is more difficult to prove. However, there are other complicating circumstances applying to expert systems, in particular, that make the situation less predictable.

There are no solid answers to the question of liability because the theories, as they apply to knowledge-based and expert systems, have not been tested in court. Nevertheless, it likely that before long, this will become a significant issue for system developers.

On the topic of protection, three potential means of protecting software exist: copyrights, patents, and trade secrets. Copyright affords protection for the expression of the idea embodied in the program, but only limited protection for the idea itself. Patents are designed to protect the idea, but the idea must be reduced to practice to be patentable. Additionally, the procedure for patenting an idea is long and arduous. Trade secrets allow the owner of an idea to keep his idea from being used by his competitors. Nevertheless, certain precautions must be taken to ensure that protection under these laws will be applicable to his ideas.

No single best way exists to protect a knowledge-based or expert system. Each developer must weight the pro's and con's of each protection route and decide which is best under the circumstances.

A ▌ The CLIPS System

A.1 INTRODUCTION

This appendix examines CLIPS, a forward-chaining, pattern-matching knowledge-based system shell. This system differs significantly from the Texas Instruments' Personal Consultant (discussed in Appendix B) in both its structure and its interface with users and developers. Included with this book is the compiled version of the full CLIPS system, Version 5.1. Details on how to obtain the user's manual and the source code for CLIPS are included at the end of this appendix.

CLIPS stands for *C Language Implementation Production System*. Developed by the Artificial Intelligence Section of the Johnson Space Center of NASA, CLIPS is a forward-chaining rule-based system based on the pattern-matching algorithm (the Rete algorithm) developed for the OPS-5 system. The system provides high portability, low cost, and high degree of integration with external programs.

This appendix provides sufficient information to allow you to develop small knowledge-based systems using CLIPS. For a complete tutorial on the use of CLIPS or for information on how to develop advanced and detailed knowledge bases, you should consult the *CLIPS User's Manual* [Giarratano, 1991], as well as the *CLIPS Reference Manual* [STB, 1991].

A.2 THE CLIPS SYSTEM

CLIPS is a forward-reasoning system as described in Chapter 4. This appendix provides sufficient details of some of CLIPS' specific features to enable you to start developing small knowledge bases. Five topics must be discussed to give you a good understanding of CLIPS: facts, rules, variables and functions, input and output, and the user interface. Each is discussed in the following sections.

To start the execution of CLIPS you must select the disk drive on which the file "CLPDSSZ.EXE" resides and simply enter

```
CLPDSSZ
```

Once CLIPS is loaded into memory, the system prompt appears

```
CLIPS>
```

All commands entered at this level are top-level CLIPS' commands. One such command is the exit command

```
(exit)
```

which returns you to the operating system.

It is interesting that while CLIPS is written in C, the format of CLIPS' commands and rules is very similar to LISP. This leads many users to mistakenly believe that CLIPS was written in LISP.

Now that we know how to get in and out of CLIPS, let us examine each of its important features.

A.3 FACTS

CLIPS defines a fact to be "one or more fields enclosed within matching left and right parentheses" [Giarratano, 1991]. The following subsections discuss the mechanics of creating, using, and deleting facts.

A.3.1 Assertion of Facts

Facts are added to CLIPS' fact list through the *assert* command. Facts can be asserted by issuing an *assert* command at the top level of CLIPS or within a rule consequent. For example, to assert that Ivan plays tennis we would enter

```
(assert (play Ivan tennis))
```

This causes the fact (play Ivan tennis) to be added to the set of facts within the facts list.

The set of facts within the facts list can be inspected by entering the top-level *facts* command

```
(facts)
```

which causes all of the facts in the facts list to be displayed on the screen along with their *fact identifier*. This identifier is a symbol that contains a fact *index*, identifying when the fact was asserted during execution. This index starts initially at zero and is incremented by one whenever a new fact is asserted. (Note: The index of zero is reserved for a special fact, "(initial-fact)," described below.) For example, suppose that we enter the following set of commands:

```
(assert (play Ivan tennis))
(assert (play Martina tennis))
(facts)
```

The system will respond with the following output

```
f-0  (initial-fact)
f-1  (play Ivan tennis)
f-2  (play Martina tennis)
```

where f-1 and f-2 are fact identifiers, and the numbers 1 and 2 are the indexes.

It is good programming practice to use the first field of a fact to describe the relationships of the subsequent fields [Giarratano, 1991]. When used this way, the first field is called the *relation* of the fact. For example, the relation between tennis and Ivan is that the latter "plays" the former.

The alternative way to assert facts is to place an *assert* command in the consequent of a rule. Further details on this use of the assert command are provided in Section A.4, which discusses rules.

A.3.2 Retracting Facts

Deleting facts from CLIPS' facts list is performed by the *retract* command. Like the *assert* command, *retract* can occur both at the top level of CLIPS and within rules.

The top-level *retract* command can delete any fact from the fact list. This command requires that the particular fact being deleted be identified by its *fact index*. If our fact list contains the following facts

```
f-1  (play Ivan tennis)
f-2  (play Martina tennis)
```

and we issue the commands

```
(retract 1)
(facts)
```

we will see that the fact list now contains only

```
f-0  (initial-fact)
f-2  (play Martina tennis)
```

If you attempt to retract a fact that does not exist, CLIPS issues an error message.

The entire facts list can be erased by using the *clear* command

```
(clear)
```

This command has the effect of eliminating not only all of the facts, but also the entire knowledge base, resetting CLIPS to its initial, start-up state [Giarratano, 1991].

A.3.3 Initial Facts

An alternative manner for entering facts into the system's fact list is through the *deffacts* function. These facts are called initial facts and the utility of this alternative will become clear during our discussion of rules in the next section. The format of the *deffacts* function is

```
(deffacts fact-defn-name comment fact-1 . . . fact-n)
```

where the fields are

fact-defn-name: The name of the fact definition list. This must be a symbol, not a number.

comment: A string describing the set of facts as a comment. It must be enclosed in double quotes and is optional.

fact-1 . . . fact-n: A set of sublists each of which describes an initial fact. An upper limit on the number of facts is not specified.

The following example illustrates a deffacts statement

```
(deffacts tennis-players
          "list of tennis players"
          (athlete Ivan very-good)
          (play Ivan tennis)
          (athlete Martina very-good)
          (play Martina tennis) )
```

Facts contained in a *deffacts* statement are asserted into a system's fact list through the execution of the *reset* command

```
(reset)
```

This command has several results. First, any facts currently on the facts list (e.g., due to the execution of some previous program) are deleted. Second, all facts described in the *deffacts* statement are created on the facts list. Finally, this command additionally asserts the fact

$$(\texttt{initial-fact})$$

with an identifier of f-0. This last fact is typically used by CLIPS' programmers to start the execution of their programs.

If a *reset* command is issued in the presence of the above tennis-players' *deffacts*, the facts list will contain the following facts

```
f-0    (initial-fact)
f-1    (athlete Ivan very-good)
f-2    (play Ivan tennis)
f-3    (athlete Martina very-good)
f-4    (play Martina tennis)
```

A particular *deffacts* statement can be removed from memory through the *undeffacts* command

```
(undeffacts tennis-players)
```

When the *reset* command is now issued, the facts list will contain only

```
f-0    (initial-fact)
```

Similarly, you can inhibit (initial-fact) from being placed in the facts list by issuing the command

```
(undeffacts initial-fact)
```

If a reset command is now issued, the facts list will be completely empty.

A.4 RULES

Rules are defined using the top-level *defrule* command. This command has the syntax

```
(defrule  r-name comment
          patt-1 . . . patt-n
          =>
          act-1 . . . act-m)
```

where the fields are

  r-name : The rule name, which identifies that particular rule.

  comment : An optional comment field. This text must be surrounded with double quotes.

  patt-1 . . . patt-n : The sublists representing the antecedent of the rule. Each sublist is a pattern intended to match a fact in the facts list. There is no limit on the number of antecedents that can be used in a rule.

  => : The delimiting *arrow* that indicates to the system that the antecedent is complete. It is read as "implies".

  act-1 . . . act-m : The sublists representing the consequent of the rule. Each of these represent some action to take when the rule is executed.

Additional comments are highly recommended and can be added to any line of a CLIPS rule. These comments, like comments in LISP, must be placed on the end of a line and are separated from the CLIPS code by a semicolon.

CLIPS attempts to match the patterns contained in a rule antecedent (also called the left-hand side or LHS) with facts in the fact list. If all the patterns in the rule's antecedent match facts, then the rule is placed on the *agenda.* The agenda is a priority list of rules that have satisfied antecedents and are awaiting execution. Once the CLIPS control mechanism selects a rule for execution, it is *fired* and the actions in the consequent (also called the right-hand side of the rule or RHS) are carried out. You can inspect the contents of the agenda by entering the top-level *agenda* command

(agenda)

CLIPS executes a single rule from the agenda on each execution cycle. This rule is the one with the highest priority value. Priorities are designated by the knowledge engineer through the *salience* feature of a rule. Salience is represented by a number ranging from $-10,000$ (lowest priority) to $+10,000$ (highest priority). If a rule does not have a specified salience, then CLIPS assumes a default value of 0.

Salience is assigned to a rule through a salience declaration. For example

(declare (salience 25))

specifies a salience value of 25. This declaration is placed immediately following the optional comment, before the first pattern of the antecedent.

CLIPS employs the Rete algorithm described in Chapter 4 to determine if a rule is capable of firing. All rules that are satisfied (i.e., able to execute) are placed on the agenda, which is structured as a priority queue. The position of a rule within the agenda is determined by the rule's salience. Rules having the highest salience value are fired based upon their position within the agenda, which is organized on a last-in-first-out basis.

The description of a rule can be requested by entering the *pprule* command

```
(pprule r-name)
```

where *r–name* is the name of a particular rule. This command causes the rule description to appear on the screen in an easily readable format.

Rules can be selectively eliminated from the system through the *excise* command

```
(excise r-name)
```

where *r-name* is the name of a particular rule.

A.5 VARIABLES, OPERATORS, AND USER-DEFINED FUNCTIONS

CLIPS provides several features that aid rules in manipulating patterns. These features include the use of variables, special symbols, and user-defined functions.

A.5.1 Variables

The use of variables in patterns greatly expands the pattern-matching capabilities of CLIPS. As identified in Section 4.7, variables must begin with the character "?". This character is then immediately followed by a symbolic name. During pattern matching when a pattern is found to match a fact, the variables in the pattern are bound to their corresponding values within the fact. These bindings are valid only within that particular rule—they are not carried between rules.

We have seen that retraction of facts from the facts list is a common operation in forward-chaining systems like CLIPS. As we learned in Section A.3, to retract a fact from the top level using the *retract* command, the index number of a fact must be known. Unfortunately, when facts are being asserted by rule execution, it is difficult to keep track of their indices. Facts can, however, be retracted without knowing their indices using variables and the *left arrow* (i.e., <-). The left arrow binds a variable to an entire fact from the facts list. This variable can subsequently be retracted without knowing that fact's index number. This is illustrated in the following example.

Suppose that we have a friend named Harry who is presently 17 years old (i.e., considered to be a child), but who has a birthday today. Thus, Harry is described in our fact list by the following

```
(child harry)
(birthday harry August-15)
(age harry 17)
```

We can define a rule that will make Harry an adult by updating his age, retracting that he is a child, and asserting that he is an adult:

```
(defrule become-adult
          (child harry)
          (birthday harry August-15)
          (age harry 17)
          (date today August-15)
    =>
          (assert (adult harry))
          (retract (child harry))
          (retract (age harry 17))
          (assert (age harry 18))
          (fprintout t "harry is now an adult" crlf))
```

But this does not work because the retract statements require an index number. Therefore, we must structure the rule using the left arrow and variables

```
(defrule become-adult
          ?child <- (child harry)
          (birthday harry August-15)
          ?age <- (age harry 17)
          (date today August-15)
    =>
          (assert (adult harry))
          (retract ?child)
          (retract ?age)
          (assert (age harry 18))
          (fprintout t "harry is now an adult" crlf))
```

If we want to change other individuals into adults, it would be extremely tedious to create separate rules for each. Instead, we would replace all references to Harry and all references to the date, August 15, with variables (e.g., *?person* and *?date*). Any individual having the appropriate facts on the facts list would then be converted into an adult. Note that the output statement (i.e., fprintout) requires some special modifications to print the names properly. This is discussed in Section A.6.1.

A.5.2 Special Symbols in Pattern

There are many different symbols and features available within CLIPS that can extend the power of its pattern matcher. These include a wildcard, field constraints, mathematical operations, test features, and pattern connectives.

A.5.2.1 The wildcard. Occasionally when pattern matching, fields exist in a fact that we are not interested in matching. These fields are superfluous to our interests, but because they exist they must be accounted for within our pattern. Rather than binding them to a variable, we can use the *wildcard* symbol to identify their presence and our lack of interest in their specific value.

The wildcard is a general pattern that represents a single field within a fact. The wildcard ensures that something is in the field without worrying about its actual value. CLIPS uses the question mark, ?, without a following name as the wildcard symbol.

To illustrate its use, let us assume that we are looking for a fact containing the name of a person. This name consists of a first name, middle name, and family name. For example

```
(name John Fitzgerald Kennedy)
```

To match anyone whose family name was Kennedy, regardless of their first and middle names, we would use the pattern

```
(name ? ? Kennedy)
```

where each wildcard represents a single field.

Suppose, however, that we do not know how many middle names a person has. CLIPS provides a special multifield wildcard, $?, which is capable of matching zero or more fields. For example

```
(name ? $? Smith)
```

would match any of the following

```
(name John Smith)
(name Suzie Jane Smith)
(name John James Jones Smith)
```

but would not match

```
(name Smith)
(name John Jones Smith Rogers)
```

This wildcard can also be used with a variable name to remember the names actually matched (e.g., $?middlename).

A.5.2.2 Field constraints.   The concept of pattern matching as presented so far is lacking some important features. Occasionally, we may want to match something that is *not* present; in others, we may wish to match any value from a subset of possibilities. These situations require the use of *field constraints* that restrict the possible values of a field when making a match.

One type of field constraint is the *negation* constraint. This prefix constraint is represented by the tilde symbol, "~" [Giarratano, 1991]. It states that the field can take any value except the one shown. For example, the rule

```
(defrule apply–heat
          (temperature water ~boil)
     =>
          (adjust heat maximum); a function call
          (fprintout t "Turn the heat to the maximum
                          setting" crlf))
```

identifies that if you are cooking and the water is not yet boiling, you should apply more heat.

Another field constraint is the *or* constraint, represented by a vertical bar "|." This infix constraint is used to identify alternative values. For example, the rule

```
(defrule apply–heat
          (temperature water cold|cool|warm)
     =>
          (adjust heat medium); a function call
          (fprintout t "Turn the heat to a medium
                          setting" crlf))
```

matches a water temperature of either cold, cool, or warm.

The last constraint is the *and* operation, represented by the ampersand, "&." This infix constraint states that a match can be made only if the value of the field is all of the specified values. Although this appears too restrictive, it is particularly useful when binding a value to a variable in the presence of other constraints. For example, the pattern

```
(temperature water ?temp&hot|boil)
```

will match either of the following facts

```
(temperature water hot)
(temperature water boil)
```

with *temp* being bound to the value that is matched.

A.5.2.3 Mathematical operators. CLIPS is also capable of performing mathematical calculations within the consequent of a rule. All of the basic operations (i.e., addition, subtraction, multiplication, and division) are supported as well as trigonometric, logarithmic, and exponential functions. For a complete list, consult Section 10.6 of the *CLIPS Reference Manual*, Vol. 1, *Basic Programming Guide* [STB, 1991].

Mathematical operations are specified using prefix notation with parentheses surrounding every operation. There is no natural precedence of operations since all operations are performed outward from the innermost parentheses with operations on the same parenthesis level performed from left to right.

Mathematical expressions are evaluated in either an *assert* or *bind* command. Within an *assert*, the evaluation of numeric expressions is specified by using the prefix "=" operator. This operator tells CLIPS that the following expression should be evaluated and its result used as the value of a field within the fact to be asserted. For example, the following *assert* command

```
(assert (answer =(* 3 4)))
```

places the fact

```
(answer 12)
```

on the facts list, while

```
(assert (answer (- 8 4)))
```

results in an error since the = operator was not used and CLIPS cannot assert an embedded list such as (- 8 4).

An alternative manner of evaluating mathematical expressions is through the *bind* function. *Bind* is used whenever the result of the operation is to be printed or displayed rather than asserted to the facts list. The *bind* function does not need the = operator because CLIPS assumes that *bind*'s second argument should be evaluated. For example, the rule

```
(defrule subtraction
        (numbers ?x ?y)
    =>
        (bind ?answer (- ?x ?y) )
        (fprintout t "the answer is " ?answer crlf))
```

performs the operation of subtraction on two numbers found in a matched fact. Note the use of the variable in the output statements and that the variables used in the subtraction operation imbedded within the *bind* must be bound before the expression is evaluated.

A.5.2.4 The test feature.   The test feature is an extension of the field constraints. Since it is a rather important feature for building patterns in a rule,
we treat it separately. The *test* function allows the knowledge engineer to specify a comparison between variables, strings, and/or numbers within a pattern
of a rule. This very useful feature has the format of

```
(test (function arg-1 arg-2 . . . arg-n))
```

where *function* is a predefined function and *arg-1 arg-2 . . . arg-n* are the zero
or more arguments required by this function. These predefined functions are
predicates already made available in CLIPS including *eq* (equal); *neq* (not
equal); = (numeric equal); != (numeric not equal); >=; >; <=; and <; and
the logical functions of *!* or *not*, *&&* or *and*, and *||* or *or*.

A simple example illustrates the use of the test function. Suppose that
we wish to examine the dimensions of an object determining if its length and
width are equal so we can declare that it is a square. The following rule, taken
from [Giarratano, 1991], accomplishes this task.

```
(defrule square
        (width ?obj ?w)
        (length ?obj ?l)
        (test (= ?l ?w))
    =>
        (fprintout t ?obj "is a square" crlf))
```

A.5.2.5 Pattern connectives.   Whenever a set of patterns is placed in the antecedent of a rule, it is implied that they are connected through an *implicit
logical AND*. That is, *all* of the patterns must be successfully matched before
the antecedent is completely satisfied. In most applications, the use of a logical AND is what is desired. Nevertheless, CLIPS allows patterns to be connected in alternative manners.

The first of these alternatives is the *explicit logical OR*. Occasionally, applications require any one of a set of patterns to be true. Individual rules can
be written for each of these patterns or they can be combined using an explicit
logical OR. By combining these patterns into a single rule our code becomes
more efficient and readable.

An OR can combine all or just some portion of the patterns in a
rule's antecedent. A group of patterns connected through an OR, which
does not comprise all the patterns in an antecedent, is called a *logical
block*. Such logical blocks can be connected with other blocks using other
connectives.

Note that a rule containing a logical OR is satisfied once any pattern
within the OR is matched. Should multiple patterns of the OR be satisfied, it

is possible that the rule can execute several times. For example, if we have the following rule in our knowledge base [STB, 1991]

```
(defrule big-obj
            (width ?obj ?w)
            (length ?obj ?l)
            (height ?obj ?h)
            (or
                    (test (> ?w 50))
                    (test (> ?l 50))
                    (test (> ?h 50)))
    =>
            (fprintout t ?obj "is a large object" crlf))
```

where the first three patterns and the OR are connected by an implicit AND, and our facts list contains

```
                    (width box-15 100)
                    (length box-15 75)
                    (height box-15 65)
```

this rule can execute three times.

CLIPS also provides an *explicit logical AND* as illustrated in the following rule

```
(defrule example
            (analyze portfolio)
            (or   (and
                            (key-rate prime)
                            (rate prime stable) )
                    (and (key-rate t-bill)
                            (rate increasing) )   )
    =>
            (fprintout t "stable portfolio" crlf))
```

The last pattern connective is *negation* or *NOT*. This connective states that for a match to be made, the specified pattern must not be in the facts list. The syntax for this connective is

$$(not \ patt)$$

where *patt* specifies the pattern to be matched by a fact from the facts list.

Note the difference between the pattern connectives described above and the field constraints described in Section A.5.2.2. Whereas pattern connectives deal with individual patterns, field constraints deal with possible values for one or more fields within a pattern.

A.5.3 User-defined Functions

Functions required to perform some special action that are not predefined in CLIPS can be defined by the user. These *external functions* must be explicitly described to CLIPS through a modification of the *UserFunctions* function. Each user-defined function is declared within a call to this function using the *DefineFunction* routine. This topic is considered an advanced feature of CLIPS so you are referred to the *CLIPS Reference Manual,* Vol. II, *Advanced Programming Guide* [STB, 1991] for additional details. Since CLIPS is written in C, most user-defined functions are also written in C, though CLIPS does support the use of several other languages.

A.6 INPUT/OUTPUT IN CLIPS

We have already seen the *fprintout* function of CLIPS in the examples given above, although we have not explicitly discussed it. This section provides a discussion of this function as well as the other input/output functions.

A.6.1 The fprintout Function

CLIPS allows the knowledge engineer to specify the output of any desired information through a call to the *fprintout* function. The format of this function call is

```
(fprintout dev item-1 item-2 . . . item-n)
```

where the fields are

> *dev:* The name indicating the device to which the output is directed. The character "t" identifies the computer's primary output device (usually the terminal). Output to other devices such as a printer, a modem, or a file is allowed, but these devices must be specified by their logical name and must be enabled (e.g., opened for output).

> *item-1 item-2... item-n:* The information to be printed. These can be strings (enclosed in double quotes), variables with bound values, or even function calls. All items are evaluated before printing. Note that carriage return/line feeds are considered printable items. These are specified by the symbol *crlf.*

A *format* function exists that permits more flexibility in customizing output. The use of this function is considered an advanced feature, so for details refer to the *CLIPS Reference Manual,* Vol. I, *Basic Programming Guide* [STB, 1991].

A.6.2 File I/O

CLIPS also provides the knowledge engineer with some commonly used file accessing capabilities through several predefined functions. For example, the *open* function allows the user to open a file by assigning it a logical name. This function can be used only in a rule's consequent and has the following syntax

$$(\text{open } ''file-name'' \ logical-name \ [mode])$$

where the fields are

file-name: The actual name of the file as seen by the operating system. Note that the backslash character, \, is a special symbol in CLIPS (i.e., it states that the following symbol is to be taken literally, not as CLIPS normally interprets it) and must be used with care. If the backslash is to be used in the *file-name*, then a second backslash symbol must be placed in front of it.

logical-name: This logical name assigned to the file. This name is used in any patterns to refer to the file.

mode: The optional mode specifier. This determines the type of access available to the file: "r" is read access only, "w" is write access only, "r+" is read and write access, and "a" is append access only.

Files that have been opened must be closed by a call to the *close* function. The syntax for this function is simply

$$(\text{close } logical-name)$$

where *logical-name* is the logical name assigned to the file to be closed.

A.6.3 Terminal Inputs

The final form of input/output to be discussed is that of input from the terminal. Two functions, *read* and *readline*, accomplish this.

The *read* function allows the user to provide a single data value (delimited by a blank), while *readline* allows an entire string (delimited by a carriage return, a semicolon, or an end of file). The value returned by *read* is an atom, while *readline*'s value is a quoted string.

The syntax for both functions is identical

$$(\text{read } [logical-name])$$
$$(\text{readline } [logical-name])$$

where *logical-name* is an optional parameter identifying an attached file. If *logical-name* is either omitted or set to "t," then CLIPS assumes that the input is read from the standard input device (i.e., the terminal).

A.6.4 The MicroEMACS Editor

CLIPS provides the developer with a screen editor called MicroEMACS. This is a public domain screen editor that has been integrated into CLIPS so that knowledge bases can be constructed more easily. This editor is called from the top level of CLIPS through the edit command

$$(\texttt{edit}\ [\ ''file-name''\ ])$$

where *file-name* is optional and specifies the name of a file. Figure A.1 contains some of the more important MicroEMACS commands. For more information about the MicroEMACS editor, you should refer to Appendix B of the *CLIPS Reference Manual*, Vol. 1, *Basic Programming Guide* [STB, 1991].

A.7 THE CLIPS USER INTERFACE

CLIPS provides two execution environments. The basic environment is entered by typing *CLIPS* at the operating system prompt. The alternative menu-based environment available for DOS-based computers is entered by typing *CLPDSSZ*.[1] Both environments respond with the standard CLIPS prompt

                              CLIPS>

You can define rules and facts or enter any top-level commands to this prompt in either interface. The menu-based environment is somewhat simpler to use since it uses windows to present menus and can be used with either the keyboard or a mouse. Consequently, it is the interface that we discuss in this section. Figure A.2 presents its top-level screen interface. We discuss next the various operations that can be initiated from this menu.

    If your computer does not have a mouse, you can obtain a simulated mouse by pressing function key <F1>. The arrow keys are then enabled to move you from position to position in the various menus on the screen and the <enter> or <return> key executes the currently selected item. Pressing the escape key, <esc>, in a submenu returns you to the top menu without performing any action. Pressing <esc> in the top-level menu turns the simulated mouse off. If you do not care to use the simulated mouse, you can execute any of the commands by pressing <alt> and the highlighted letter of the command. Submenu commands are selected using the up and down arrow keys, then pressing <return> or merely entering the highlighted letter of the command.

---

[1]There are actually two window environments, CLPDSSZ and CLPDSSDP, but only CLPDSSZ is included with this book. CLPDSSZ sacrifices speed for additional memory, while CLPDSSDP executes faster but provides less working space.

Control Commands

<ctrl-@>	Set mark at current position
<ctrl-A>	Move cursor to beginning of line
<ctrl-B>	Move cursor BACK one character
<ctrl-D>	DELETE character under cursor
<ctrl-E>	Move cursor to END of line
<ctrl-F>	Move cursor FORWARD one character
<ctrl-G>	Abort any command
<ctrl-H>	(backspace) delete previous character
<ctrl-K>	KILL (delete to end of line)
<ctrl-L>	Redisplay screen
<ctrl-M>	Insert a CRLF
<ctrl-N>	Move cursor to NEXT line
<ctrl-O>	OPEN a new line
<ctrl-P>	Move to PREVIOUS line
<ctrl-Q>	QUOTE (insert) the next character
<ctrl-S>	Forward SEARCH
<ctrl-V>	VIEW the next screen
<ctrl-Z>	Quick save of file in current buffer (only) and exit
<ctrl-X> =	Show current cursor column and line number
<ctrl-X>:	Go to specific line number
<ctrl-X>M	MATCH parenthesis
<ctrl-X>S	Global SEARCH and replace
<ctrl-X><ctrl-C>	Exit without saving
<ctrl-X><ctrl-R>	RENAME file
<ctrl-X><ctrl-S>	SAVE
<esc> >	Move cursor to end of buffer
<esc> <	Move cursor to start of buffer
<esc> B	Move cursor BACK one work
<esc> D	DELETE next word
<esc> F	Move cursor FORWARD one word
<esc> S	Query SEARCH and replace
<esc> V	VIEW the previous screen
<esc> W	Copy region into kill buffer
<esc> Z	Save current buffer into file
<esc> <del>	DELETE previous word

FIGURE A.1   Summary of MicroEMACS Editor Commands

The top level interface of CLIPS contains four selections: File, Execution, Browse, and Window. Selecting any of these causes a second level menu to appear. Note that the bottom line of the interface always provides a help summary.

Selection of the File option causes the pop-down menu of Figure A.3 to appear. This menu has ten options. New and Open place you in the editor. New allows you to create a new knowledge base while Open first prompts you for

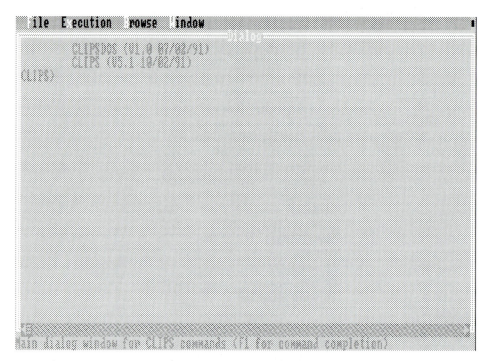

FIGURE A.2   CLIPS Top-level Screen Interface

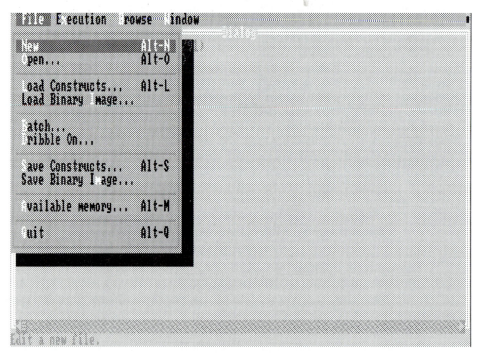

FIGURE A.3   The *File* Menu

462

the file that you would like to edit. This prompt is similar to the one shown in Figure A.4, which is for the Load Constructs ... menu option. Load Binary Image ... loads a previously compiled version of a knowledge base, Batch ... loads a file of batch commands, Dribble On ... allows you to specify a file in which a copy of all screen output will be placed, Save Constructs ... saves a knowledge base to a file, Save Binary Image ... saves a compiled version of the knowledge base to a file, Available memory ... displays the amount of free memory, and Quit exits CLIPS.

Selection of the Execution option from the initial screen causes the pop-down menu of Figure A.5 to appear. This menu contains seven options. Reset initializes the knowledge base in preparation for Run or Step. Reset performs three actions:

1. It removes existing facts from the facts list, which may remove activated rules from the agenda.
2. It asserts (initial-fact).
3. It asserts facts from existing (deffacts) statements.

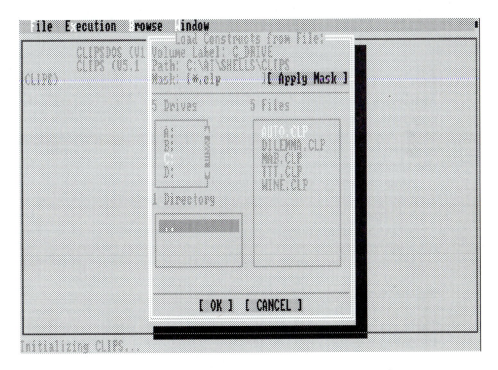

FIGURE A.4 The Load Constructs ... Option from the File Menu

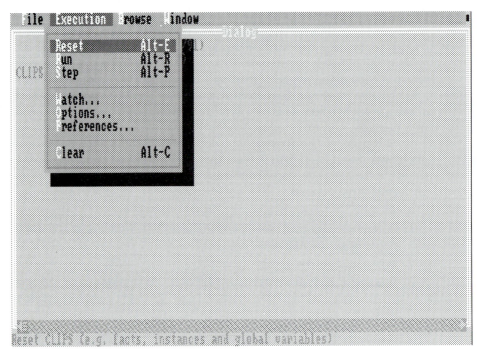

FIGURE A.5 File Command Options

Although it not absolutely necessary to call Reset before executing the knowledge base, it is highly recommended, especially if the knowledge base has already been executed during the current session. Otherwise, you are responsible for deleting the old facts from the facts list and asserting the initial facts that are required.

Run causes the knowledge base to execute. Step allows CLIPS to execute a limited number of rule firings (i.e., it is Run with the rule firing limit discussed above).

Watch displays another menu of the various watch flags. See Figure A.6. An X in the brackets before an option identifies that flag as being set. These options control the display of output on the screen when a knowledge base is loaded and executed. Selecting the All option will set all flags, while selecting the None option will turn all flags off.

Options displays the menu in Figure A.7 of the Execution Options. These options control the knowledge-base search strategy, the evaluation of the salience values, and the checking of conditions during execution.

Preferences displays a small menu that allows you to set three user options: the type of scrolling, the display of warning messages before clearing or resetting the knowledge base, and the size of the step increment.

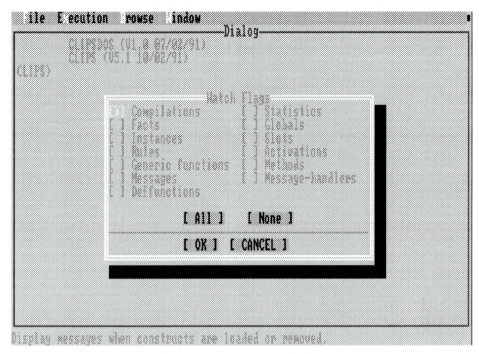

FIGURE A.6 The Watch Flags

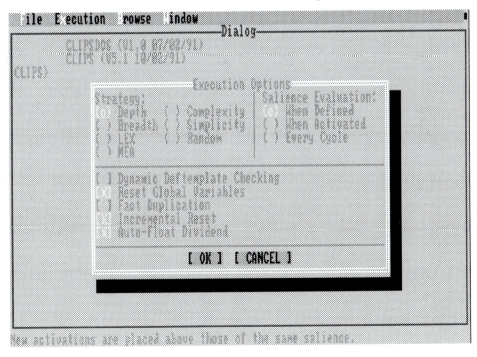

FIGURE A.7 The Execution Options

Finally, *Clear* clears the knowledge base from memory. All rules and facts are destroyed. This is unlike *Reset*, which only initializes the system by erasing unwanted facts and loading initial facts. This option is useful when some corrections have been made to the knowledge base and a revised knowledge base must be loaded.

Figure A.8 displays the browse managers obtained by selecting the *Browse* option from the initial screen. These managers display the names of the various items that are currently loaded in memory. Only those managers that have items are highlighted. The managers allow you to see what is in the knowledge base and, in some cases change and delete this information. Figure A.9 illustrates the options available in the Defrule Manager.

The final option available from the initial screen is the *Window* option. Selecting this option displays the menu in Figure A.10. The first four items in this window (*Agenda, Facts, Instances,* and *Globals*) control the addition of debug subwindows to the screen. The following two items (*All* and *None*) cause all or none of the debug windows to appear. The final option, *Clear Dialog Window*, clears all information displayed in the main display window. Figure A.11 shows the initial screen with the addition of all four debug windows.

FIGURE A.8 The Browse Options

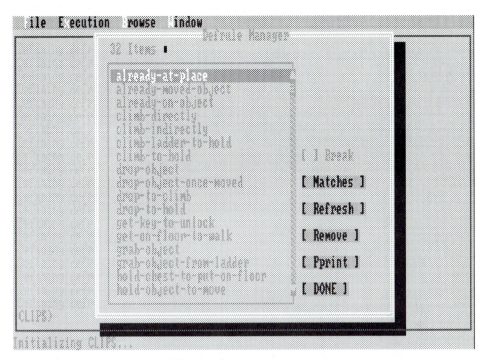

FIGURE A.9 The Defrule Manager for the Monkey and Bananas Sample Knowledge Base

FIGURE A.10 The Window Options

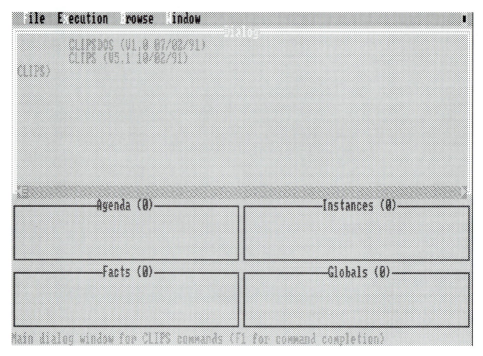

FIGURE A.11   The Initial Screen with All Four Debug Windows

Figures A.4 and A.12 through A.15 illustrate the use of CLIPS. Figure A.4 shows the selection a particular knowledge base from a directory containing five knowledge bases. When MAB.CLP is selected from the file list in Figure A.4, that knowledge base is loaded into memory. Figure A.12 shows what is displayed once that knowledge base has been loaded. We then selected from the Window option to include in the display debug subwindows for the Agenda and Facts. See Figure A.13. Figure A.14 shows the results of executing (reset): A single fact is added to the fact list, (initial-fact), and the agenda identifies that only the rule startup matches facts in the fact list. Figure A.15 shows the result from single stepping the execution. The fact base now contains 14 facts and a single rule, hold-to-eat, is capable of execution and it matches facts f-13 and f-1 from the fact base.

A.8 SOME FINAL NOTES ON CLIPS

This purpose of this appendix was to introduce you to a forward-chaining, pattern-matching knowledge-based system shell called CLIPS. This system represents a significantly different approach than that of Personal Consultant

FIGURE A.12 The Display after Loading the Monkey and Bananas Knowledge Base

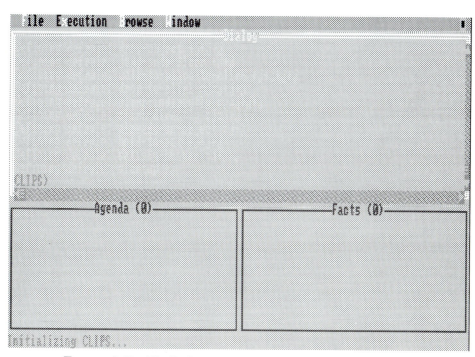

FIGURE A.13 The Inclusion of Agenda and Facts Subwindows

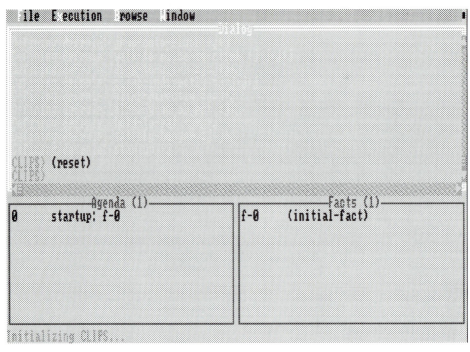

FIGURE A.14 The Result of Resetting the Knowledge Base

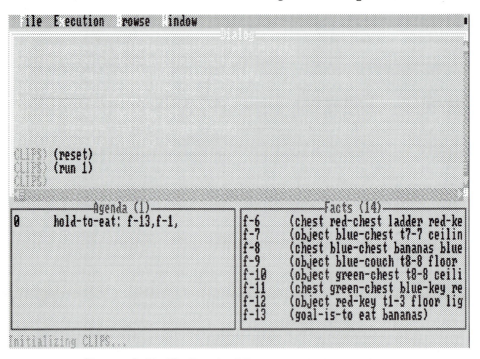

FIGURE A.15 The Result of Execution of a Single Rule

covered in Appendix B. Together, these two systems are representative of the two basic types of shells available today.

We provided you with a minimal introduction to CLIPS, including facts, rules, variables, operators, I/O, and the user interface. This introduction should be sufficient to allow you to use the system at a basic level. You are strongly encouraged, however, to obtain the *CLIPS User's Guide* and the *CLIPS Reference Manual*. These manuals provide additional details on all of the topics discussed above and other more advanced features.

The version of CLIPS included with this textbook is CLIPS Version 5.1. It is the latest version of this shell available at the time of publication. NASA is continually improving this system and providing new releases that include advanced functionality like the CLIPS object-oriented language (COOL). This object-oriented extension to CLIPS is contained in Version 5.1. It was not discussed in this appendix because its structure and organization are not central to the concepts discussed in the book.

B ■ The Personal Consultant Plus Shell System

B.1 INTRODUCTION

The objective of this appendix is to introduce a knowledge-based system shell based on the classic E-MYCIN system called Personal Consultant. Personal Consultant was developed by Texas Instruments (TI) of Austin, Texas using Scheme, a variation of LISP. It is a backward-chaining, rule-based system that supports limited forward chaining and uses an inference network to represent its knowledge base internally.

This appendix is *not* intended to replace the User's manual or the Reference Guide published by Texas Instruments.[1] Rather, it is designed to provide a quick introduction to a backward-reasoning, rule-based system. This tool can be used to develop the small knowledge-based systems posed in the problems at the end of the chapters or class projects. To fully appreciate and use all of the power of the system, you should consult the Texas Instruments' documents mentioned above.

This textbook provides a small version of the Personal Consultant Plus system (PC Plus).[2] TI refers to this system as a demonstration diskette. Although limited in scope (e.g., you can build only knowledge bases that contain ten or fewer rules), it does allow exploration of the basic functions of a rule-based, backward-chaining, inference-networked shell, as well as development of very small systems.

The direction of chaining in PC-Easy is specific to each rule and must be set by the knowledge engineer when the knowledge base is being developed. PC Plus refers to backward-chaining rules as *consequent* rules, while *antecedent* rules are another name for forward-chaining rules.

---

[1]The material contained in this Appendix is obtained with permission from PC Plus Reference Guide.

[2]The enclosed disk is PC Demo, not PC Plus and does not contain the full set of functions of PC Plus.

B.2 PARAMETERS

In Personal Consultant, *parameters* are named items that represent the facts of the problem domain [Texas Instruments, 1986]. Parameters obtain values during a consultation just as variables obtain values in conventional languages. Values of parameters can be determined by any one of the following methods [Texas Instruments, 1986]

1. Asking the user through the keyboard interface
2. Using rules to infer the value
3. Obtaining values from an external file or program
4. Using a default value

The value(s) of a parameter in PC Plus are assigned a *certainty factor* (CF), which provides an indication of the confidence in that parameter's value being true. Certainty factor values range from -100 (an absolutely false value) to $+100$ (an absolutely true value). A certainty factor of 0 indicates complete uncertainty in the particular value.

The PC Plus system automatically calculates certainty factors as beliefs that propagate throughout the inference network. This propagation of certainty factors is discussed further in Section B.5.

A parameter is identified by its *name*. Names are similar to variables in that they must start with a character and can be followed by any number of alphanumerics. Numeric names are not allowed. If a name consists of several words, these words must be linked together using either hyphens or underscores. The following are all acceptable parameter names: "pressure," "color-of-car," "#5TEST," and "$-2.3A$."

Like many other software systems, there are words reserved for use by the system that cannot be used for other purposes. These reserved words are shown in Figure B.1.

abs	cond	frame	not	sequence
access	cons	freeze	plus	substring
alias	define	length	quote	syntax
apply	delay	let	quotient	tally
assert	difference	macro	rec	text
assoc	do	maxval	remainder	times
car	error	member	reset	truncate
case	float	minus	reverse	val
ceiling	floor	minval	round	when
conclude	fluid	modulo	same	

FIGURE B.1   PC Plus Reserved Words

B.2.1 Parameter Properties

A parameter in PC Plus is internally composed of properties that determine its characteristics. These properties are grouped into three categories:

1. Required properties
2. Internal properties
3. User-supplied (optional) properties

B.2.2 Required Properties

Of the many possible properties of a parameter, the most important is its *type*. This property tells PC Plus what kind of values the parameter is allowed to have [Texas Instruments, 1986] and is the only property required for every parameter.

The four possible parameter types are

1. YES/NO
2. SINGLEVALUED
3. MULTIVALUED
4. ASK-ALL

B.2.2.1 The YES/NO parameter.   This commonly used parameter type is limited to values of either YES or NO. Certainty factors can be assigned to any value of this type.

B.2.2.2 The SINGLEVALUED parameter.   A SINGLEVALUED parameter can actually have several values, but as the name implies, only one of these values can have a certainty value that is absolute (i.e., +100 or −100). A parameter of this type is also required to have an EXPECT property. The EXPECT property has one of six possible values

1. SINGLE-LINE-INPUT
2. MULTI-LINE-INPUT
3. INTEGER
4. NUMBER
5. POSITIVE-NUMBER
6. User-defined

The first five of these values are self-explanatory. The last one, however, merits some discussion. If a parameter has an EXPECT property value of *user-defined,* another property must be examined: CERTAINTY-

FACTOR-RANGE. If the CERTAINTY-FACTOR-RANGE property has not been defined for this parameter, only one value can be selected as the parameter's value and it is assigned a certainty factor value of +100 (i.e., absolute confidence in the parameter's value being true). Should the CERTAINTY-FACTOR-RANGE property be defined for this parameter, users are allowed to specify how confident they are in the value they have selected and are permitted to select more than one value. If PC Plus detects that more than one value has been selected with +100 certainty, then it will deselect all but the most recently selected value with a certainty of 100.

B.2.2.3 The MULTIVALUED parameter.   A MULTIVALUED parameter can be assigned more than one value with absolute certainty. It offers the developer a convenient way to ask the user about several related items instead of using separate YES/NO parameters for each item [Texas Instruments, 1986]. For example, in a medical knowledge-based system the user would be queried about the symptoms displayed by the patient. A MULTIVALUED parameter would allow all of these symptoms to be expressed at once since they are all obviously present (i.e., there is no uncertainty about them). A MULTIVALUED parameter cannot be used when there is some degree of confidence that must be expressed in each value (e.g., the system asks the user what diseases are suspected. If there is some doubt associated with each of these, separate parameters must be used for each).

A PROMPT property is not required with MULTIVALUED parameters but, if present, PC Plus queries the user for the values of the parameter one at a time.

B.2.2.4 The ASK-ALL type.   Like MULTIVALUED, an ASK-ALL parameter can have more than one value with absolute certainty. These parameters must have both an EXPECT property and a PROMPT property. They differ from the MULTIVALUED parameters in how the user is prompted. The MULTI-VALUED parameter requires that the user enter values by responding to a series of questions, while an ASK-ALL parameter presents a list of possible values to the user from which the user makes selections (i.e., MULTIVALUED parameters query the user through a series of questions while ASK-ALL parameters query all at once through a list of possible values).

The differences among the parameter types are best illustrated through Figure B.2 [Texas Instruments, 1986], which displays the prompts presented by each of the four types of parameters when asking the user about sports preferences.

B.2.2.5 Parameter example.   A simple example helps to clarify further the differences among the various types of parameters. Consider the three-rule thunderstorm forecasting system described in Chapter 4. This system would require three parameters in PC Plus: temperature (the outdoor temperature

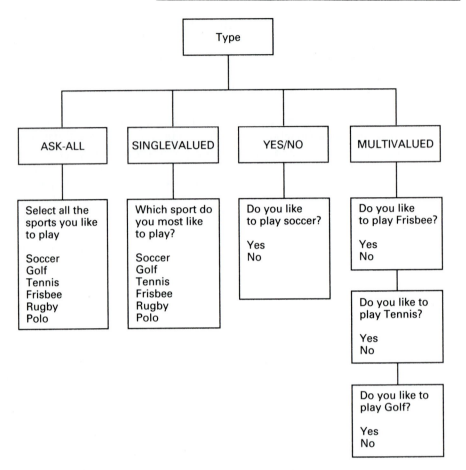

FIGURE B.2   Graphical Description of Parameter Types

in degrees Fahrenheit), atmosphere (the relative humidity), and forecast (the weather that is likely to occur).

Clearly, there is only one current temperature and we would have absolute confidence in its value (assuming we have what we know to be an accurate thermometer). The temperature parameter would, therefore, be designated SINGLEVALUED. Its EXPECT property would naturally be NUMBER because the temperature is generally a real number and it can be negative as well as positive.

The second parameter, atmosphere, is very similar to temperature. This parameter would be designated SINGLEVALUED with an EXPECT property of POSITIVE-NUMBER because relative humidity is never negative.

The third parameter could be handled in several different manners. This parameter could be SINGLEVALUED if we are concerned only about the chances of a thunderstorm, a snowstorm, or a hurricane. If we want to include in our forecast an indication of the expected high and low temperatures of the day or other data, then we may want to make it a MULTIVALUED parameter. If, on the other hand, we are concerned solely about the possibility of a thunderstorm and nothing else, we could make it a simple YES/NO parameter.

B.2.3 Internal Parameter Properties

Internal parameter properties provide PC Plus with the ability to perform the traces that compose the backward-chaining system. As we saw in Chapter 5, each node of the inference network identifies its connections to other nodes. These connections are identified by specifying for each node the rules that use this node to derive values for other nodes and the rules that contribute toward deriving this node's value.

The five properties described in this section provide these interconnections. Note that these properties are created and maintained internally by PC Plus. The knowledge engineer has no responsibilities in their maintenance. The description of these properties is provided as an aid toward understanding how the tracing process is performed. These properties are:

1. *UPDATED-BY:* This property contains a list of all the backward-chaining rules that are capable of determining a value for this parameter. PC Plus uses this list to begin the tracing process for each goal parameter.
2. *USED-BY:* This property lists all the backward-chaining rules that utilize this parameter within their premise (IF part).
3. *ANTECEDENT-IN:* This property lists all the forward-chaining rules that reference this particular parameter within their premise. This list is used when the parameter is given a value. Each rule in the list is then examined to see if one of its premises is satisfied so the rule's derived results can be propagated through the inference network.
4. *UPDATED-IN:* This property lists all the forward-chaining rules that derive a value for this parameter.
5. *CONTAINED-IN:* All the rules, whether forward or backward chaining, which reference this parameter as an action but are unable to set the parameter's value, are listed in this property. Note that this is different from UPDATED-BY and UPDATED-IN which respectively contain the rules that reference a parameter as an action and set the value for a parameter.

B.2.4 Optional Parameter Properties

A multitude of other parameter properties are optional. Some are rather significant in the way in which they assist the user in interfacing with the system. These include:

1. *CERTAINTY-FACTOR-RANGE:* If this property has a value, the user is allowed to designate the level of confidence that he has in the parameter's value(s).

2. *DEFAULT.* This property allows the knowledge engineer to provide a default value for the parameter if the user does not know the answer to a question.

3. *HELP* and *GHELP:* These properties contain more detailed information to provide to the users regarding a particular question when the users do not understand what is being asked. HELP contains text, while GHELP contains graphics.

4. *RANGE:* This useful property provides a built-in check on the values entered by a user in response to questions. For example, a parameter describing the current outdoor temperature might have a specified range from $-40°$ to $+120°$ degrees Fahrenheit. If the user responds to a question about the current temperature with a value of $1500°$, then this property will cause PC Plus to question the user about the accuracy of his response. This property applies only to parameters expecting numeric values, and the acceptable range must be specified by the knowledge engineer.

5. *PROMPT* and *GPROMPT.* These properties specify the format of the questions posed to the user when obtaining the value of a parameter. PROMPT is used for textual prompts, while GPROMPT is used to display graphics.

6. *DICTIONARY* and *TRANSLATION:* These properties contain text strings that describe the parameter. DICTIONARY is a brief description used to formulate an answer in response to HOW and REVIEW (see Section B.6.2). Translation is used for WHY queries. How the description is phrased can be somewhat tricky, depending on what the description is. Take care in specifying these phrases properly; otherwise, PC Plus's response will seem awkward.

B.3 RULES

The rules are the most important element in PC Plus because through them we represent our problem-solving knowledge. Rules show the relationships that exist between various facts. They show how these facts are interconnected to define knowledge within some domain. In this section we describe the syntax for rules within PC Plus and discuss some of their more advanced features.

PC Plus allows the rules of a knowledge base to be divided into rule groups. This permits the knowledge engineer to separate the large number of rules typically found in a knowledge base into logical divisions.

Rules are similar to parameters in that they use properties, both required and optional, to describe their important features. We examine the required properties and some optional ones below. The two most important properties of a rule are, of course, the PREMISE and the ACTION, which we examine first. Before we do this, however, it is advantageous to introduce the syntax used to define these properties called the abbreviated rule language (ARL).

B.3.1 The Abbreviated Rule Language

The *abbreviated rule language* (ARL) allows us to define rules without having to use LISP-like syntax. It is a shortcut that permits us to describe the rules in an English-like syntax, which is easy for us to understand, before they are converted into their internal representation. ARL contains a set of predefined functions that represent most of the tasks normally performed in a knowledge-based system, thus easing the knowledge base development task.

The ARL syntax for both the PREMISE and the ACTION of a rule is identical. The basic clause, describing the relationship between a parameter and one of its values, consists of a parameter name, an ARL function, and a value in infix notation as shown below:

```
parameter    ARL function    value
```

Several such clauses can be combined through the logical operators of AND and OR into statements. For example

```
parameter1    ARL function1    value    AND
parameter2    ARL function2    value
```

The logical operators AND and OR are discussed further later in this section.

The ARL functions are separated into seven groups:

1. Arithmetic
2. Predicate
3. Text
4. Graphics
5. Conclusion
6. External access
7. Auxiliary.

The order in which PC Plus evaluates the ARL functions is similar to that of other programming languages. Since the precedence of functions is applicable only in arithmetic and predicate functions, let us begin by discussing these first.

B.3.1.1 Arithmetic functions in ARL.

The arithmetic functions perform the basic operations commonly performed on numbers in most languages. These include addition (+), subtraction (−), multiplication (∗), division (/), exponential (∧), and truncation (FIX). The precedence of operations is identical with that of most programming languages.

Suppose we need to write a rule that states "if the item to be purchased is a piece of jewelry, then there is a value-added tax on that item equal to 8 percent of its value." If the cost of the item is to be represented in a parameter called "item-cost," the rule would be

```
RULE 89  PREMISE:  item-type = jewelry and
                   item-cost = is known
         ACTION:   total-cost = item-cost +
                                    item-cost * .08
```

The meaning of "is known," although seemingly self-explanatory, will become clear in the next section.

B.3.1.2 Predicate functions.

Predicate functions return a value of true or false. They are subdivided into numeric and nonnumeric functions. The numeric predicate functions include less-than (<), greater-than (>), between (BT), greater than or equal to (≥), and less than or equal to (≤).

Consider two of the rules introduced in the weather forecasting example from Chapter 3

```
RULE 1: IF   the ambient temperature is above 90 degrees F
        THEN the weather is hot

RULE 2: IF   the relative humidity is greater than 65%
        THEN the atmosphere is humid
```

Numeric predicate functions are found in these rules where the temperature and relative humidity are tested in the premises. These rules would be expressed in ARL as

```
RULE 1   PREMISE: temperature > 90
         ACTION:  weather = hot

RULE 2   PREMISE: humidity > 65
         ACTION:  atmosphere = humid
```

The nonnumeric predicate functions are divided into two groups. The first group's functions test whether a specified parameter has a designated value and whether the certainty factor associated with that value is within the correct range. Rather than describe these functions one by one (which is done in the Reference Guide), we graphically illustrate their ranges in Figure B.3 [Texas Instruments, 1986]. These functions are applicable to ASK-ALL, MULTIVALUED, and SINGLEVALUED parameter types. YES/NO parameters, however, are a special case. These parameters use positive certainty factors with the word NO on the left-hand side of the number line rather than negative certainty factors. This means that a YES with a certainty factor of -100 is the same as a NO with a certainty factor of $+100$. To illustrate the use of these predicates, consider the following example.

Suppose that we have developed a home medical advising system. This system advises on common diseases and their treatment. One rule in this system might state

```
RULE 75: IF    the diagnosis is definitely a common cold
         THEN  take two aspirin
```

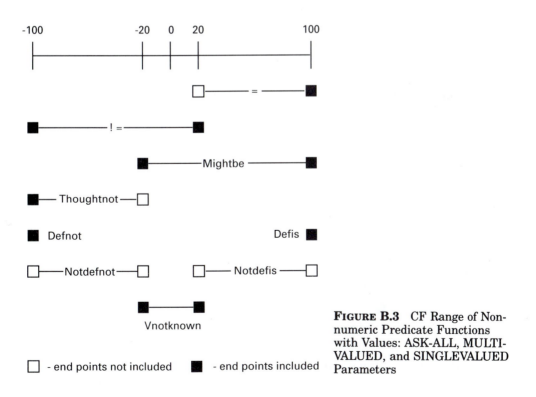

FIGURE B.3 CF Range of Non-numeric Predicate Functions with Values: ASK-ALL, MULTI-VALUED, and SINGLEVALUED Parameters

Since this rule identifies that the premise requires absolute certainty of its value, we can use the predicate function IS DEFIS to test its value. This rule would then be expressed as

```
RULE 75  PREMISE: diagnosis is defis common- cold
         ACTION:  remedy = take-two-aspirins
```

The second group of nonnumeric predicate functions is similar to those in the first group except that they test whether the certainty factor associated with the parameter (irrespective of the parameter's value) falls within a certain predefined range. Figures B.4 and B.5 [Texas Instruments, 1986] details the ranges for these functions. YES/NO parameters have the same restriction applied as the first group of functions discussed above and illustrated in Figures B.2 and B.3.

An illustration of these functions was given in the last section during the discussion of the item-cost parameter in the value-added tax example.

```
RULE 89  PREMISE: item-type = jewelry and
                  item-cost = is known
```

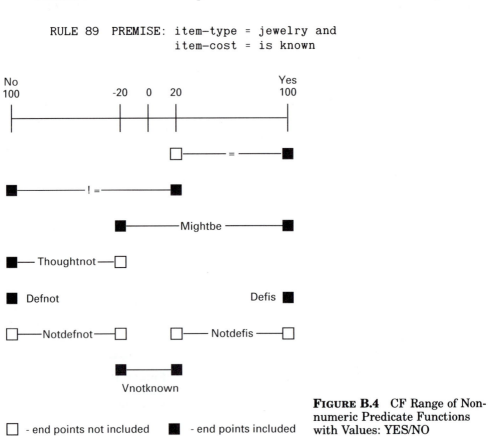

FIGURE B.4   CF Range of Nonnumeric Predicate Functions with Values: YES/NO

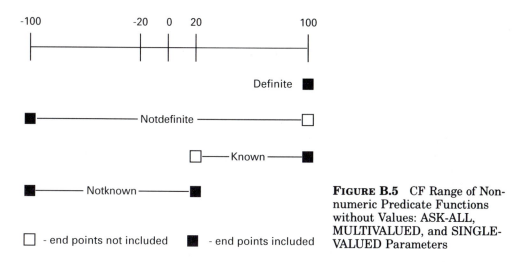

FIGURE B.5   CF Range of Non-numeric Predicate Functions without Values: ASK-ALL, MULTIVALUED, and SINGLE-VALUED Parameters

The test on the item-cost parameter's value stated that it does not matter what the value of the parameter is, only that it *is known*. This means that the parameter's value has to have a confidence factor within a specific certainty factor range (greater than 20 and less than or equal to 100).

B.3.1.3 Text and graphics ARL functions.
Text and Graphics ARL functions are used to display items on the screen. These functions include: PRINT, SHOW, TEXTUAL, = G, and PICTURE. The discussion of these functions has been combined since there are few of them and they all deal with display.

The PRINT function displays parameter values, numbers, or text strings. The items to be printed are listed after the word PRINT. Text strings must be enclosed in double parentheses. For example, consider the third rule of thunderstorm forecasting illustrated in Chapter 3

```
RULE 3: IF    the ambient temperature is hot and
              the atmosphere is humid
        THEN  thunderstorms are likely to develop
```

Suppose that we also wish to display a message to the user when this rule is executed that states that thunderstorms are likely. This would be accomplished by the following encoding of the rule

```
RULE 3    PREMISE: temperature = hot and
                   atmosphere = humid
          ACTION:  forecast = thunderstorm CF 80
                   print "Thunderstorms are
                   likely to develop"
```

The function SHOW prints the value of a parameter. Its format is

```
SHOW parameter header [IFUNKNOWN]
```

where *parameter* is the name of the parameter whose value is to be displayed and *header* is an optional set of text to display before the parameter's value. This text is typically used to describe the displayed value. If *T* is used instead of text, PC Plus generates a standard message. If the *header* is omitted, no accompanying text is displayed. The keyword IFUNKNOWN is valid only when the *header* is present. Should the parameter not have a value (i.e., its value is unknown), this keyword causes a message to be printed that states that the value of the parameter is not known.

Consider the rule given below, which we created in the value-added tax example

```
RULE 89  PREMISE: item-type = jewelry and
                  item-cost = is known
         ACTION:  total-cost = item-cost +
                               item-cost * .08
```

Suppose that we want the total cost displayed for the user when it is calculated. This is done by adding a SHOW action, changing the rule to

```
RULE 89  PREMISE: item-type = jewelry and
                  item-cost = is known
         ACTION:  total-cost = item-cost +
                               item-cost * .08 and
                  show total-cost "The total
                       cost for your jewelry
                       item will be" ifunknown
```

If the rule is executed and calculates a total-cost of the jewelry item to be $751.98, the SHOW action prints the following

```
The total cost for your jewelry item will be 751.98
```

If the total-cost cannot be computed for whatever reason, the IFNOTKNOWN option causes the following message to be printed

```
I was unable to make any conclusions regarding the total cost
of the item.
```

The function TEXTVAL assigns a text value to a parameter. It allows for easier formatting of text.

The graphics functions are =G and PICTURE. =G makes a picture appear in the conclusion screen. The PICTURE function makes a picture appear whenever the function is executed as an action of a rule. The pictures must have been produced previously. This is an advanced topic, so the Reference Guide should be consulted for additional information if desired.

B.3.1.4 The conclusion ARL function.   The equal (=) function is used to set the value of a parameter within the action of a rule. Its syntax is

$$parameter \; = \; value \; [\text{CF} \; cf\text{-}value]$$

where *parameter* is the name of the parameter being assigned the value, *value*. A confidence in the parameter's value is expressed by following the above expression with the function CF and the *cf-value*, an integer between −100 and +100. We discuss certainty factors in more detail in subsequent sections of this appendix.

B.3.1.5 The auxiliary ARL functions.   The auxiliary ARL functions are used within the premise and action statements to help PC Plus evaluate predicate and conclusion functions. These functions include AND, OR, and CERTAINTY.

The AND function can be used to join both premises and actions. When used between two premise clauses, the AND function ensures that both clauses evaluate to a positive result. Should either clause evaluate to false, the entire statement is considered to be false and PC Plus ceases evaluation. Used between action statements, the AND function indicates multiple actions to be performed.

The OR function is used between premises. Only when both premise clauses joined by an OR evaluate to false is the entire statement considered to be false. If a premise contains a combination of ANDs and ORs (with no parentheses to specify precedence), PC Plus evaluates the clauses joined by ORs before those joined by ANDs.

The CERTAINTY function returns the highest certainty factor associated with the parameter. Consider our medical diagnostic system that prescribed two aspirins if we had a common cold. Suppose the doctor decided that aspirin should be prescribed in all cases where he is 70 percent confident in the diagnosis (note that this is any diagnosis, not just a common cold). The rule would be rewritten as follows using the CERTAINTY function

```
Rule 75   PREMISE: certainty diagnosis > 70
          ACTION:  remedy  = take-two-aspirins
```

B.3.2 Rule Properties

Rules, like all other entities within PC Plus, also have properties. The only required properties are the PREMISE and the ACTION. We have already discussed these and we have seen how we can specify their values by using ARL functions. The IF (PREMISE) and THEN (ACTION) statements are automatically requested when a rule is being specified.

Curiously enough, PC Plus does not allow the knowledge engineer to name rules. Instead, it simply assigns names sequentially (RULE001, RULE002, RULE003, . . . etc.). While this liberates the knowledge engineer from having to create names, it does take away considerable flexibility.

The most significant optional rule property is the ANTECEDENT. The presence of this property makes this rule a forward-chaining rule, while the lack of this property (the default state) makes the rule a backward-chaining rule.

The second most important property is the UTILITY of a rule. This integer value between -100 and $+100$ determines the order in which rules are examined. PC Plus tries to satisfy rules with high UTILITY before those with lower values. The default value of UTILITY is 0. Rules with UTILITY values less than zero are not tried at all. Rules with the same UTILITY value are tried in the order of their goal parameter's UPDATED-BY property value.

EXPLANATION and DESCRIPTION are used to describe the rule in English. If a rule has an EXPLANATION value, PC Plus uses it to respond to the WHY and HOW commands [Texas Instruments, 1986]. The DESCRIPTION property allows a short description to be specified that will appear on the bottom of the rulegroup screen when you select a particular rule name. It is an advantage when you do not remember the rules by name.

B.3.3 Meta-rules

Meta-rules are rules associated with parameters, system properties, and rules. They can dynamically change a list of GOAL parameters or the UTILITY value of a rule. This feature is typically used to dynamically change the execution of a knowledge base based on new facts that have been discovered. For example, when performing diagnosis on an automobile we have several potential problems listed as system GOALS. These range from simple problems (e.g., a dead battery) to potentially very complicated problems (e.g., electrical and transmission problems). If, however, early in the diagnostic process, we discover that the car's problem falls into a specific category that precludes the possibility of other problems, it would then be advantageous to temporarily eliminate these other problems from the GOALS list so they are not unnecessarily traced.

B.4 THE KNOWLEDGE BASE PROPERTIES

Knowledge base *Properties* contain information about the knowledge base as a whole, or control a knowledge base characteristic [Texas Instruments, 1986].

The values for these Properties are defined when creating a knowledge base and can be changed directly through the editor in the user interface.

Knowledge base Properties should not be confused with parameter properties described in the previous section. To avoid confusion, the first letter of the word Property for knowledge base Properties will be capitalized. Numerous knowledge base Properties exist, but we cover only a limited number significant to our discussion. More detailed information about these Properties is found in the Reference Guide.

B.4.1 The GOALS Property

GOALS is a required Property that indicates which parameters, called *goal parameters*, represent final conclusions. The goal parameters are a key concept in backward-chaining systems. They are used to initiate backward tracing, the backbone of PC Plus's consultation process. If a knowledge base has more than one goal parameter, PC Plus traces each in the order in which they are listed in the GOALS Property. Every knowledge base must have at least one goal parameter.

B.4.2 The INITIALDATA Property

The INITIALDATA Property is a list of all parameters that should have an initial value. PC Plus prompts the user for the values of all these parameters when it starts a consultation. These parameters are ones whose values are typically required from the user in all consultations, whatever the nature of the problem. For example, a medical system would require the name, age, sex, and social security number of all patients while a crop pest management system would require the name of the farm and type of crop.

Sometimes the knowledge engineer is able to build rules to derive values for INITIALDATA parameters in cases when the user does not know their value (e.g., a patient's sex). In other cases no rules can be constructed (e.g., a patient's social security number).

The INITIALDATA Property is not required. PC Plus can begin the tracing process without having any initial data by prompting for values when they are needed. However, this feature provides the developer some control over the structure of a consultation, allowing it to appear highly organized and directed, similar to what a human expert would do.

B.4.3 The DOMAIN Property

The DOMAIN Property is a required Property that is displayed at the top of every screen when you interact with a knowledge base. This 64-character string provides a short heading or description of this knowledge base to both the users and the knowledge engineer. It is used solely for identification purposes. Its value must be entered when starting to build the knowledge base and can be changed at any time through the editing facility.

B.4.4 The TITLE Property

The optional TITLE Property specifies text or graphics to be displayed at the beginning of a consultation. This feature is typically used to provide the title of the system, the copyright notice, and any trademark credits. The TITLE Property is added through the editing features of PC Plus.

B.4.5 The PROMPTEVER and GPROMPTEVER Properties

These two optional Properties control text or graphics that appear in the *Objective* screen. This screen serves as a more extensive introduction to the knowledge-based system than the title and is typically used to provide a short introduction to the operation and function of the knowledge-based system. The *Objective* screen appears at the beginning of a consultation session after the optional title screen. PROMPTEVER controls text on the Objective screen while GPROMPTEVER controls graphics.

B.4.6 The DISPLAYRESULTS Property

The DISPLAYRESULTS Property causes the results of a consultation to be displayed at its conclusion. The form of the message depends on the type and the value of the goal parameter in question.

DISPLAYRESULTS is an optional Property that is normally enabled. It can be suppressed by simply erasing this Property from the system.

B.5 CERTAINTY FACTOR PROPAGATION

A knowledge-based system may encounter two different kinds of uncertainty [Texas Instruments, 1986]

1. The user-entered information may include uncertainty as to its truth or accuracy.
2. The facts and relationships of the domain involve uncertainty.

The theoretical basis for the representation of uncertainty is covered in Chapter 8. In this appendix we briefly present how PC Plus internally manipulates certainty factors (CFs).

B.5.1 Certainty Factors

PC Plus allows both uncertainty about user-entered information and uncertainty about facts and relationships. Uncertainty about user-entered information is simply assigned by the user when the user enters a piece of information in response to a system query. This can only be done to parameters that have a CERTAINTY-FACTOR-RANGE property with a value of either FULL or POSITIVE. Note that MULTIVALUED parameters cannot have such a property.

Figure B.6 depicts a screen with a prompt for a SINGLEVALUED parameter with a CERTAINTY-FACTOR-RANGE of POSITIVE. The certainty factor can be specified by moving the cursor laterally to its proper location before pressing the enter key. A similar screen would appear for a CERTAINTY-FACTOR-RANGE of FULL, except that the line next to the value would only go from −100 (or no) to 100 (or YES). An ASK-ALL parameter would allow the user to specify more than one value at 100, while a SINGLEVALUED would not.

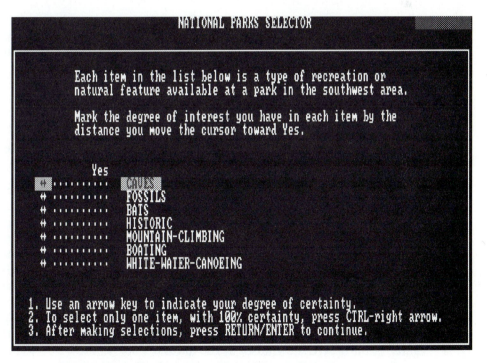

FIGURE B.6 Prompt for a SINGLEVALUED Parameter with a CERTAINTY-FACTOR-RANGE of POSITIVE

Certainty Factors can also be assigned within the action of a rule. This is done by specifying the keyword "CF." after the parameter's value and assigning an integer value between −100 and +100. For example, let's say that when the temperature is hot and the atmosphere is humid, there is an 80 percent chance of a thunderstorm. We can express this as

```
RULE 3   PREMISE: temperature = hot and
                  atmosphere = humid
         ACTION:  forecast = thunderstorm CF 80
```

But expressing our confidence in the conclusion is only part of the issue. Our confidence in the forecast of thunderstorm is obviously affected by our confidence in how hot or humid it is. Additionally, there may be factors expressed in other rules that also affect the probability of thunderstorms, such as the atmospheric pressure or high-level winds. Thus, the combination of certainty factors, called *belief propagation*, is an important issue.

B.5.2 Belief Propagation

To understand the propagation of belief in PC Plus requires, first, understanding how certainty factors combine. The certainty factor associated with a parameter's value is typically produced by a rule that derives this value. The certainty factor is computed by combining the following certainty factors [Texas Instruments, 1986]

1. The certainty factor of the rule's PREMISE.
2. The certainty factor of the rule's ACTION.
3. Any certainty factor previously existing for that particular value of the parameter (due possibly to the effects of another rule).

If the PREMISE of a rule evaluates to true, the certainty factor of this PREMISE is determined by two factors: the certainty factor of each individual premise clause and the logical operator(s) used to combine these premise clauses. The certainty factor of each individual premise clause depends on the function used within the clause. The THOUGHTNOT and = predicate functions return the certainty factor of the tested parameter's value. All other predicate functions return true or false, which are considered to have certainty factors of 100.

Two logical are used to combine clauses: OR and AND. The certainty factor of OR'ed clauses is the highest of the individual clauses, while the certainty factor of AND'ed clauses is the lowest.

The certainty factor of each action clause within a rule is specified directly by the knowledge engineer. The = function is used to set the parameter's value. This is followed by the letters CF and an integer between −100 and +100.

A previous certainty factor does not exist for a parameter's value when [Texas Instruments, 1986]:

1. The parameter being assigned a value has not had any value assigned to it previously in the consultation.
2. The parameter being assigned a value has a previous value with an associated certainty factor of zero.

In these two cases a new certainty factor, CF_{new}, is computed to be

$$CF_{new} = \frac{(cf_{premise} * cf_{action} + 50)}{100}$$

where $cf_{premise}$ is the computed certainty factor of the rule's PREMISE and cf_{action} is the certainty factor of the ACTION clause.

If the parameter's value already exists, then a new certainty factor, CF_{rev}, must be computed based upon this old value, CF_{prev}, and the new one derived by the current rule, CF_{new}. This is done through four equations. The equation used depends upon the signs of CF_{prev} and CF_{new}

If $CF_{prev} \geq 0$ and $CF_{new} \geq 0$, then

$$CF_{rev} = CF_{prev} + \frac{CF_{new} * (100 - CF_{prev}) + 50}{100}$$

If $CF_{prev} < 0$ and $CF_{new} < 0$, then

$$CF_{rev} = CF_{prev} + \frac{CF_{new} * (100 + CF_{prev}) - 50}{100}$$

If $CF_{prev} * CF_{new} < 0$ and $CF_{prev} + CF_{new} > 0$, then

$$CF_{rev} = \frac{(CF_{prev} + CF_{new}) * 100 + \frac{100 - MIN}{2}}{100 - MIN}$$

where MIN is the lesser of the absolute values of CF_{prev} and CF_{new}.

Lastly, if $CF_{prev} * CF_{new} < 0$ and $CF_{prev} + CF_{new} < 0$, then

$$CF_{rev} = \frac{(CF_{prev} + CF_{new}) * 100 - \frac{100 - MIN}{2}}{100 - MIN}$$

B.6 INTERFACING WITH PC PLUS

PC Plus provides two views or interfaces to the knowledge base. The developer's interface acts as a knowledge acquisition tool, supplying the knowledge engineer with a view of the knowledge base during the development process. The user's interface, on the other hand, provides a view of the knowledge base for the typical user. In this section we discuss the developer's interface in full detail. The user's interface is then discussed briefly.

B.6.1 The Developer's Interface

The knowledge base development process with PC Plus begins at the *Knowledge bases screen*. This screen is shown in Figure B.7. This screen displays a list of all the knowledge bases contained in the file directory. To load an existing knowledge base for further development, editing, or consultation, you move the cursor, using the arrow keys, over the item and hit return/enter. The last entry in the knowledge base list reads

Create new knowledge base

Select this item when you want to begin developing a new knowledge base. The system responds by prompting you, the knowledge engineer, for the name of the knowledge base to be developed. The text that you type is the title that always appears at the top of the screen whenever you are working with

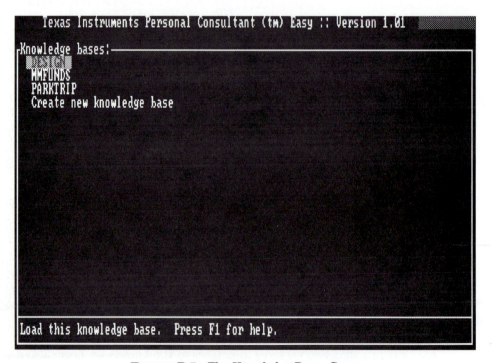

FIGURE B.7   The Knowledge Bases Screen

this knowledge base. This prompt appears only when the knowledge base is initially created. The title's value can be changed by editing the system Property DOMAIN.

You are next requested to designate the GOALS of the knowledge base. Each of these is specified on the command line separated by a space. No parentheses are needed around the group. PC Plus responds by now asking you to define each of these parameters. You are first asked for the TYPE of parameter (i.e., SINGLEVALUED, YES/NO). If the TYPE chosen requires further parameters (i.e., EXPECT), then values for these are also requested.

Next, the TRANSLATION property is requested. Since this property is optional, simply hit return/enter if you do not want to define it or would like to do so later. When all the GOALS parameters have been defined, PC Plus places you on the activities screen. We should note that additional GOALS can be defined at any time by editing the knowledge base, so it is not critical that all the GOALS be known when you start this development process.

B.6.1.1 The activities screen.   The *activities screen*, shown in Figure B.8, displays a menu of two items representing the two possible activities that you may now wish to perform

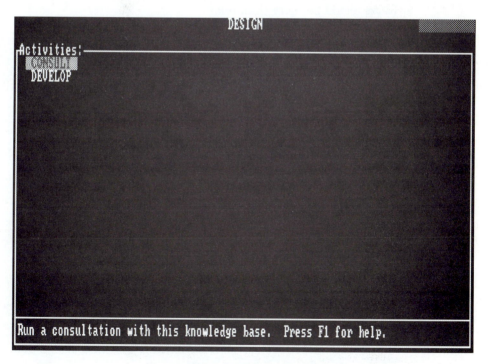

FIGURE B.8   The Activities Screen

1. Consult with a knowledge base

2. Develop a knowledge base

If you had requested the loading of an existing knowledge base from the *knowledge bases screen*, PC Plus would have taken you directly to this activities screen. If you select the second item, you will be placed in the knowledge editor (i.e., the *knowledge base screen*) to continue developing this knowledge base. Note the singular nature of "Base" as opposed to plural in the *knowledge bases screen* described previously. This distinction is important since the *knowledge bases screen* allows you to load a knowledge base from the set of defined knowledge bases while the *knowledge base screen* permits the development of an individual knowledge base. Selection of the first item places you into the execution of the knowledge base, performing an actual consultation.

B.6.1.2 The knowledge base screen.   The *knowledge base screen*, shown in Figure B.9, contains at least three entries

1. System Properties

2. Parameters (could be more than one)

3. Rules (could be more than one)

FIGURE B.9   The Knowledge Base Screen

System Properties is selected to either view or change the global characteristics of the knowledge base. Parameters or rules are selected to either add or modify parameters or rules respectively. No matter which item is selected, PC Plus displays an appropriate screen for the item chosen. These screens display a list of all the system Properties, parameters, and rules that have already been defined. Whereas the parameters screen and the rules screen show only a list of the names, the properties screen shows the Properties that exist as well as their values. We describe these screens in more detail in the following sections.

B.6.1.3 The properties screen.   The *properties screen* shows all the system properties that have been defined or that have a default value which has not been changed (see Figure B.10). The knowledge engineer can either change, add, or delete these properties as she sees fit. The set of commands applicable to this screen can be obtained by pressing the function key <F2>.

Figure B.11 shows the *Properties Screen* with the command menu window superimposed. These commands are MODIFY, ADD, ERASE, and QUIT. Each is self-explanatory: modify an existing Property, add a new Property, eliminate an existing Property, or quit, returning to the activities screen. A shortcut to activating these commands is pressing the **alt** key, <alt>, at the same time as the first letter of the desired command. For example, if a new

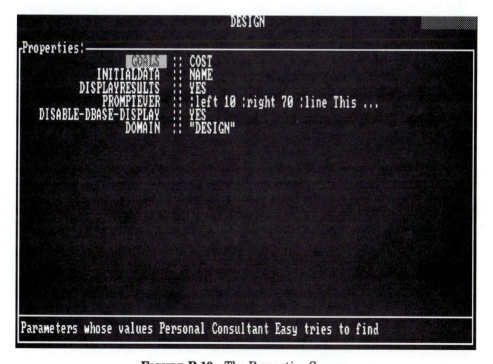

FIGURE B.10   The Properties Screen

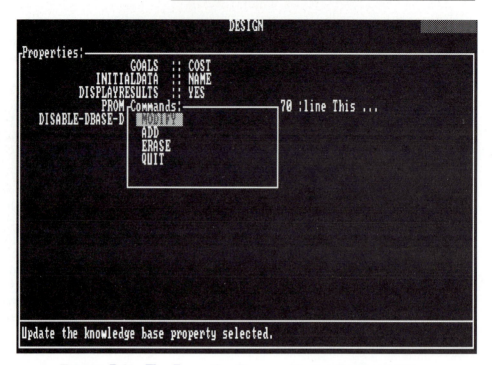

FIGURE B.11 The Properties Screen with the Command Menu Window

Property is to be added, then the keystroke <**alt**> **a** pops-up a window containing all the possible choices of Properties to be added. To change a Property you need only place the cursor over the desired Property and press return/ enter. After a Property is changed, the *Properties screen* redisplays itself to include the newly changed Property.

To delete a Property, simply place the cursor over the Property to be deleted and enter <**alt**> **e.**

B.6.1.4 The parameters screen.   The *Parameters Screen* acts similarly to the Properties screen, except that only a list of the parameters already defined in the system is displayed (see Figure B.12). The command menu applicable to parameters is obtained through F2 (see Figure B.13), or individual commands, can be referenced through the **alt** key shortcut. When adding a parameter, PC Plus prompts you for the information in much the same manner that it did when defining the GOALS parameters. You are asked for the parameter's NAME, TRANSLATION, and TYPE, as well as any other information required for the specified TYPE. Deletion of parameters can be accomplished by placing the cursor over the name and entering <**alt**> **e.**

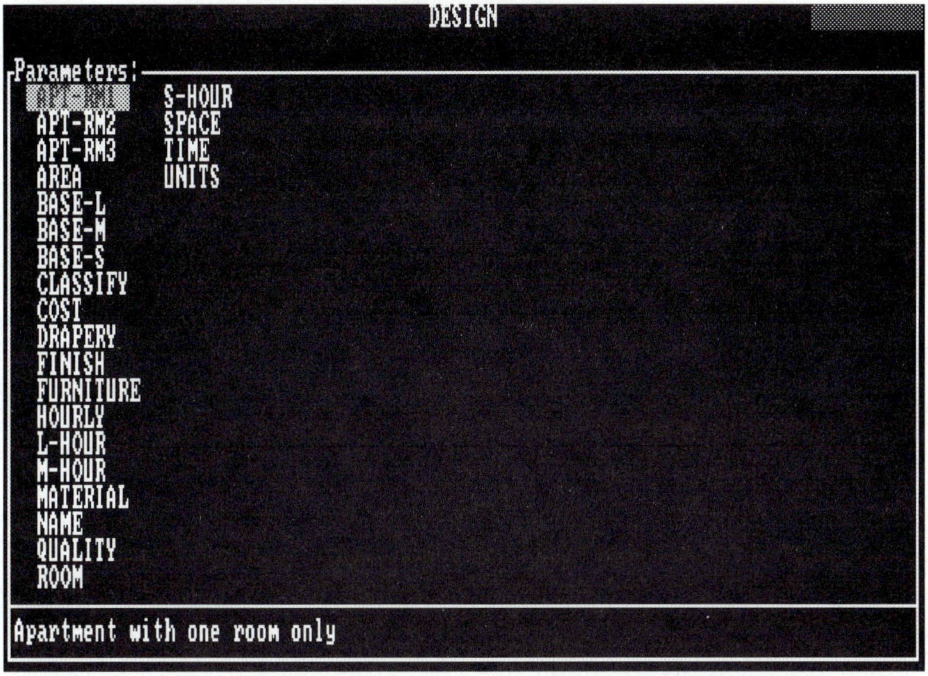

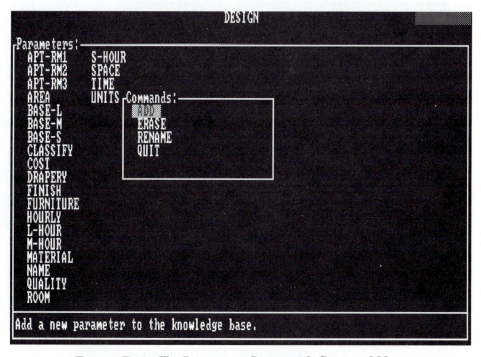

FIGURE B.12 The Parameters Screen

FIGURE B.13 The Parameters Screen with Command Menu

Modification of parameters, whether to correct errors or to add properties to existing ones, is done by selecting the appropriate parameter (using the cursor) and pressing RETURN. PC Plus displays all the properties of the parameter, in a fashion similar to the *Parameters screen* seen in the last section. You select the property to modify by placing the cursor over the property to be edited and hitting return/enter. The system then prompts you for the new value. The QUIT command returns you to the Activities screen.

B.6.1.5 The rules screen. Analogous to the Parameter screen, the rules screen displays a list of all the rules that are presently defined. See Figure B.14. Using <F2> or the **alt** key shortcut, the commands functional for this screen are accessible. Figure B.15 displays the Rules screen with the applicable menu superimposed in a pop-up window, similar to that done for the Parameters screen. The operation of adding new rules is identical with adding new parameters except that PC Plus assigns names to the rules. If a rule is deleted, its rule number is not reused. When a rule is to be added, PC Plus asks for the PREMISE and ACTION properties. These properties are entered using ARL as described in the rules's section of this appendix. If a rule references a parameter that has not yet been defined, PC Plus immediately prompts you for its definition.

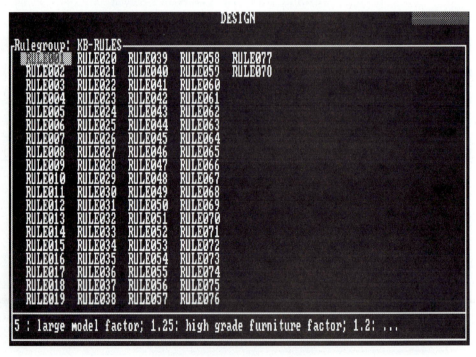

FIGURE B.14 The Rules Screen

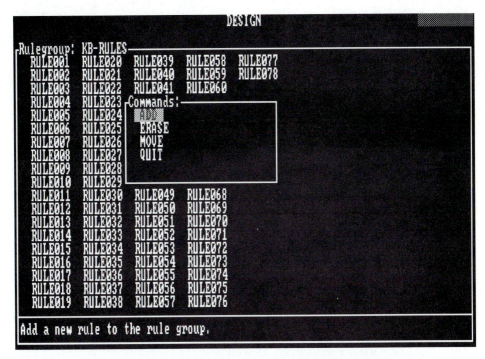

FIGURE B.15   The Rules Screen with Command Menu

Editing of the PREMISE and ACTION occurs by simply selecting the rule in question, placing the cursor on the property to be modified, and pressing return/enter. PC Plus then prompts you for the new clauses.

New properties are added to a rule by entering the F2 function key when the cursor is placed on the name of the rule. PC Plus then provides a menu containing all the possible new properties that can be added.

The <esc> key always take you back one screen. <**alt**> **q** (for QUIT), ends the development session and takes you back to the *Activities screen.* You can also go back to the *Activities screen* by placing the cursor over the word QUIT in the menu that appears when <F2> is depressed.

B.6.2 Additional Features of PC Plus

There are three more features that provide the user or developer a better interaction with the knowledge-based system. These are the *HOW*, the *RE-VIEW*, and the *WHY* functions. They are very useful not only for the user who may want to know more about the logic being followed by the program, but also for a knowledge engineer trying to debug the knowledge base. The following three sub-sections describe these commands in more detail.

B.6.2.1 The HOW command.   One important feature of knowledge-based systems that we mentioned in Chapter 1 was the ability to explain to a user how conclusions were derived. This is the function of the HOW command.

This function lists the parameters whose values have been derived by the system (i.e., obtained by a means other than prompting the user). The user selects any parameter from the list and in response obtains information on how the selected parameter's value(s) and certainty factor(s) were determined.

The HOW command is available from any prompt or at the end of the consultation. It can be accessed by using <F2>, or <**alt**> **h**.

B.6.2.2 The WHY command.   The WHY command allows the user to question PC Plus for the reason why a particular piece of information is needed. PC Plus specifies the rule currently being evaluated, identifies the parameter that caused this rule to be selected, and explains what the rule is about.

Like the HOW command, the WHY is available from any prompt in the consult mode. It can be accessed through the <F2> key. The keystroke <**alt**> **w** achieves the same results without <F2>.

B.6.2.3 The REVIEW command.   This command allows the user to review the responses made to prompts during a consultation and modify them if desired. The command is available at any prompt in a consultation through the <F2> or the <**alt**> **r** keystroke, as well as in the conclusions screen at the very end of the consultation. It is very useful in determining the sensitivity of the result by allowing the developer or user to change some answers originally provided and observe its effect on the results.

B.7 FINAL NOTES ABOUT PC PLUS

This appendix provides a brief introduction to the PC Plus shell. It covers some salient aspects of inference net systems, backward chaining, and how PC Plus implements these concepts. Our aim has been to provide an introduction to this system without completely duplicating its Reference Manual. Hopefully, this appendix has given you the ability to use the enclosed demonstration diskette for PC Plus with minimum inconvenience.

References

[ADLASSNIG, 1982] Adlassnig, K. P., and G. Kolarz. "Cagiag-2: Computer-Assisted Medical Diagnosis using Fuzzy Subsets." In *Approximate Reasoning in Decision Analysis,* ed. M. M. Gupta and E. Sanchez. New York, NY: Elsevier, pp. 219–247.

[ADRION, 1982] Adrion, W., M. Branstad, and J. Cherniavsky. "Validation, Verification and Testing of Computer Software." *ACM Computing Surveys,* vol. 14, no. 2, pp. 159–192.

[AIKINS, 1983] Aikins, J. S., J. C. Kunz, and E. H. Shortliffe. "PUFF: An Expert System for Interpretation of Pulmonary Function Data." *Computers and Biomedical Research,* vol. 16, pp. 199–208.

[AINTERACTIONS, 1985] AInteractions. "Campbell's Keeps Kettles Boiling With Personal Consultant." *AI Interactions,* vol. 1, no. 1 (August), pp. 3–4.

[AIREA, 1988] American Institute of Real Estate Appraisers. *Appraising Residential Properties.* Chicago, IL: AIREA.

[ALLEN, 1983a] Allen, J., and J. A. Koomen. "Planning Using a Temporal World Model." *Proceedings of the Eighth International Joint Conference on Artificial Intelligence.* San Mateo, CA: Morgan Kaufmann, pp. 741–747.

[ALLEN, 1983b] Allen, J. "Maintaining Knowledge about Temporal Intervals." *Communications of the ACM,* vol. 26, no. 11 (November), pp. 832–843.

[ANDERSON, 1987] Anderson, J. R., A. T. Corbett, and B. J. Reiser. *Essential LISP.* Reading, MA: Addison-Wesley.

[ASHLEY, 1988] Ashley, K. D., E. L. Rissland. "A Case-based Approach to Modeling Legal Expertise." *IEEE Expert* (Fall), pp. 70–77.

[BACHANT, 1984] Bachant, J., and J. McDermott. "R1 Revisited: Four Years in the Trenches." *AI Magazine,* vol. 5, no. 3 (Fall), pp. 21–33.

[BARLETTA, 1988] Barletta, R., and W. Mark. "Explanation-based Indexing of Cases." *Proceedings of the Seventh National Conference on Artificial Intelligence.* San Mateo, CA: Morgan Kaufmann, pp. 541–546.

[BENNETT, 1978] Bennett, J., L. Creary, R. Engelmore, and R. Melosh. "A Knowledge-Based Consultant for Structural Analysis." Report No. 78–23. Computer Science Department, Stanford University, Stanford, CA, September.

[BERLINER, 1980] Berliner, H. "Backgammon Program Beats World Champ." *SIGART Newsletter,* no. 69 (January), pp. 6–9.

[BEZDEK, 1976] Bezdek, J. C. "Feature Selection for Binary Data-Medical Diagnosis with Fuzzy Sets." *Proceedings of AFIPS,* vol. 45, pp. 1057–1068.

[BOBROW, 1977] Bobrow, D. G., and T. Winograd. "An Overview of KRL, A Knowledge Representation Language." *Cognitive Science,* vol. 1, no. 1 (January), pp. 3–46.

[BOEHM, 1988] Boehm, B. W., and P. N. Papaccio. "Understanding and Controlling Software Costs." *IEEE Transactions on Software Engineering,* vol. 14, no. 10 (October), pp. 1462–1477.

[BONISSONE, 1983] Bonissone, P. P., and H. E. Johnson. "Expert System for Diesel Electric Automotive Repair." *Knowledge-based System Report.* The General Electric Co., Schenectady, NY.

[BONNET, 1983] Bonnet, A., and C. Dahan. "Oil-Well Data Interpretation Using Expert System and Pattern Recognition Technique." *Proceedings of the Eighth International Conference of Artificial Intelligence.* Menlo Park, CA: The American Association for Artificial Intelligence, pp. 185–189.

[BOOSE, 1984] Boose, J. H. "Personal Construct Theory and the Transfer of Human Expertise." *Proceedings of the National Conference on Artificial Intelligence.* Menlo Park, CA: The American Association for Artificial Intelligence, pp. 27–33.

[BOOSE, 1985] Boose, J. H. "A Knowledge Acquisition Program for Expert Systems Based on Personal Construct Theory." *International Journal of Man-Machine Studies,* vol. 23, no. 5 (November), pp. 495–525.

[BOYCE, 1984] Boyce, B. N., and W. N. Kinnard. *Appraising Real Property.* Lexington, MA: D. C. Heath and Co.

[BRACHMAN, 1979] Brachman, R. J. "On the Epistemological Status of Semantic Networks." In *Associative Networks,* ed. N. V. Findler. New York, NY: Academic Press, pp. 3–50.

[BRACHMAN, 1983] Brachman, R. J., R. E. Fikes, and H. J. Levesque. "KRYPTON: A Functional Approach to Knowledge Representation." *IEEE Computer,* vol. 16, no. 10 (October), pp. 67–73.

[BROWN, 1975] Brown, J. S., R. R. Burton, and A. G. Bell. "SOPHIE: A Step Towards Creating a Reactive Learning Environment." *International Journal of Man-Machine Studies,* vol. 7, no. 5, pp. 675–696.

[BROWNSTON, 1985] Brownston, L., R. Farrell, and E. Kant. *Programming Expert Systems in OPS-5: An Introduction to Rule-Based Programming.* Reading, MA: Addison-Wesley.

[BUCHANAN, 1984a] Buchanan, B. G., and E. H. Shortliffe. "Uncertainty and Evidential Support." In *Rule-Based Expert Systems: The MYCIN Experiments of the Stanford Heuristic Programming Project,* ed. B. G. Buchanan and E. H. Shortliffe. Reading, MA: Addison-Wesley, pp. 209–232.

[BUCHANAN, 1984b] Buchanan, B. G., and E. H. Shortliffe. *Rule-Based Expert Systems.* Reading, MA: Addison-Wesley.

[CARHART, 1979] Carhart, R. E. "CONGEN: An Expert System Aiding the Structural Chemist." In *Expert Systems in the Microelectronic Age,* ed. D. Michie. Edinburgh, Scotland: Edinburgh University Press, pp. 65–82.

[CHARNIAK, 1985] Charniak, E., and D. McDermott. *Introduction to Artificial Intelligence.* Reading, MA: Addison-Wesley.

[CHEESEMAN, 1986] Cheeseman, P. "Probabilistic versus Fuzzy Reasoning." In *Uncertainty in Artificial Intelligence,* ed. L. N. Kanal and J. F. Lemmer. New York, NY: Elsevier, pp. 85–102.

[CHENG, 1989] Cheng, A. M. "Expert System Validation as it Applies to Expert Systems Utilizing a Frame-Based Knowledge Representation." Master's Thesis, Department of Computer Science and Engineering, University of South Florida, Tampa, FL.

[CLANCEY, 1979] Clancey, W. J. "Tutoring Rules for Guiding a Case Method Dialogue." *International Journal of Man-Machine Studies,* vol. 11, no. 1 (January), pp. 25–49

[CLANCEY, 1981a] Clancey, W. J. "The Epistemology of a Rule-Based Expert System: A Framework for Explanation." Report No. 81-17. Department of Computer Science, Stanford University, Stanford, CA.

[CLANCEY, 1981b] Clancey, W. J. "Methodology for Building an Intelligent Tutoring System." Report No. 81-18. Department of Computer Science, Stanford University, Stanford, CA.

[CLANCEY, 1983] Clancey, W. J. "GUIDON." *Journal of Computer-Based Instruction,* vol. 10, no. 1-2 (Summer), pp. 8–15.

[CLARK, 1990] Clark, D. A. "Uncertainty Management in AI." *Artificial Intelligence Review,* vol. 4, no. 2, pp. 109–146.

[CLARK, 1978] Clark, K. "Negation as Failure." In *Logic and Databases,* ed. H. Gallaire and A. J. Minker. New York, NY: Plenum, pp. 293–322.

[COHEN, 1985] Cohen, P. *Heuristic Reasoning about Uncertainty: An Artificial Intelligence Approach.* London: Pitman.

[COLMERAUER, 1973] Colmerauer, A., H. Kanoui, R. Pasero, and P. Roussel. "Une Systeme de Communication Homme-machine en Francais." Research Report. Groupe d'Intelligence Artificielle, Univ. d'Aix-Marseille, Luminy, France.

[CORKILL, 1988] Corkill, D. D., K. Q. Gallagher, and K. E. Murray. "GBB: A Generic Blackboard Development System." In *Blackboard Systems,* ed. R. Englemore and T. Morgan. Reading, MA: Addison-Wesley, pp. 503–517.

[CORNELL, 1986] Cornell, M. "Knowledge-Based Automatic Test Equipment." *The Second Annual Workshop on Robotics and Expert Systems.* Houston, TX: NASA, Lyndon B. Johnson Space Center, pp. 97–104.

[CRETEAU, 1974] Creteau, P. G. *Real Estate Appraising (Step-by-step),* 2d ed. Portland, ME: Castle Publishing.

[DANKEL, 1988] Dankel, D. D., and G. Russo. "Verification of Medical Diagnoses using a Microcomputer." In *Microcomputer-Based Expert Systems,* ed. A. Gupta and B. E. Prasad. New York, NY: IEEE Press, pp. 329–334.

[DAVIS, 1976] Davis, R. "Applications of Meta-level Knowledge to the Construction, Maintenance, and Use of Large Knowledge Bases." Doctoral Dissertation, Computer Science Dept., Stanford University, Stanford, CA.

[DAVIS, 1982] Davis, R., and D. B. Lenat. *Knowledge-Based Systems in Artificial Intelligence.* New York, NY: McGraw-Hill.

[DAVIS, 1983] Davis, R., and C. Rich. "Expert Systems: Part 1-Fundamentals." Tutorial No. 4. *The Third National Conference on Artificial Intelligence.* Menlo Park, CA: American Association for Artificial Intelligence.

[DAVIS, 1984] Davis, R. "Diagnostic Reasoning Based on Structure and Behavior." *Artificial Intelligence,* vol. 24, no. 1-3, pp. 347–410.

[DE KLEER, 1979] de Kleer, J. "Causal and Teleological Reasoning in Circuit Recognition." TR-529. Artificial Intelligence Laboratory, MIT, Cambridge, MA.

[DEMPSTER, 1967] Dempster, A. "Upper and Lower Probabilities Induced by a Multivalued Mapping." *Annals of Mathematical Statistics,* vol. 38, no. 2, pp. 325–399.

[DUDA, 1978] Duda, R., P. E. Hart, N. J. Nilsson, R. Reboh, J. Slocum, and G. Sutherland. "Development of the PROSPECTOR Consultation System for Mineral Exploration." SRI Report. Stanford Research Institute, Menlo Park, CA, October.

[DUNGAN, 1983] Dungan, C. "A Model of an Audit Judgment in the Form of an Expert System." Ph.D. Dissertation, University of Illinois at Urbana-Champaign, Urbana, IL.

[ERMAN, 1980] Erman, D. L., F. Hayes-Roth, V. R. Lesser, and D. R. Reddy. "The HEARSAY-II Speech Understanding System: Integrating Knowledge to Resolve Uncertainty." *ACM Computing Survey,* vol. 12, no. 2 (June), pp. 213–253.

[ERMAN, 1988] Erman, D. L., F. Hayes-Roth, V. R. Lesser, and D. R. Reddy. "The HEARSAY-II Speech Understanding System: Integrating Knowledge to Resolve Uncertainty." In *Blackboard Systems,* ed. R. Engelmore and T. Morgan. Reading, MA: Addison-Wesley, pp. 31–86.

[FEIGENBAUM, 1963] Feigenbaum, E. A., and J. Feldman. *Computers and Thought.* New York, NY: McGraw-Hill.

[FEIGENBAUM, 1979] Feigenbaum, E. A. "Themes and Case Studies of Knowledge Engineering." In *Expert Systems in the Micro-Electronic Age,* ed. D. Michie. Edinburgh, Scotland: Edinburgh University Press, pp. 3–25.

[FEIGENBAUM, 1982] Feigenbaum, E. A. "Knowledge Engineering for the 1980's." Computer Science Department, Stanford University, Stanford, CA.

[FEIGENBAUM, 1988] Feigenbaum, E. A., P. McCorduck, and H. P. Nii. *The Rise of the Expert Company.* New York, NY: Times Books.

[FIESCHI, 1982] Fieschi, M., M. Joubert, D. Fieschi, and M. Roux. "SPHINX-A System for Computer-aided Diagnosis." *Methods of Information in Medicine,* vol. 21, no. 3 (July), pp. 143–148.

[FIKES, 1985] Fikes, R., and T. Kehler. "The Role of Frame-Based Representation in Reasoning." *Communications of the ACM,* vol. 28, no. 9 (September), pp. 904–920.

[FININ, 1986] Finin, T. "Understanding Frame Languages, Part 2." *AI Expert,* vol. 1, no. 4 (December), pp. 51–56.

[FISCHLER, 1987] Fischler, M. A., and O. Firschein. *Intelligence: The Eye, the Brain, and the Computer.* Reading, MA: Addison-Wesley.

[FISHMAN, 1991a] Fishman, M. B., D. S. Barr, and E. Heavner. "A New Perspective on Conflict Resolution in Market Forecasting." *Proceedings of the First International Conference on Artificial Intelligence Applications on Wall Street.* Los Alamitos, CA: IEEE Computer Society Press, pp. 97–102.

[FISHMAN, 1991b] Fishman, M. B., and D. S. Barr. "A Hybrid System for Market Timing," *Technical Analysis of Stocks and Commodities,* vol. 9, no. 8 (August), pp. 26–34.

[FORBUS, 1988] Forbus, K. D. "Intelligent Computer-Aided Engineering." *AI Magazine,* vol. 9, no. 3 (Fall), pp. 23–36.

[FORD, 1988] Ford, K. M. "An Approach to the Automated Acquisition of Expert System Rules." *Proceedings of the First Florida Artificial Intelligence Research Symposium.* St. Petersburg, FL: FLAIRS, pp. 86–90.

[FORD, 1991] Ford, K. M., H. Stahl, J. R. Adams-Webber, A. J. Canas, J. Novak, and J. C. Jones. "ICONKAT: An Integrated Constructivist Knowledge Acquisition Tool." *Knowledge Acquisition,* vol. 3, pp. 215–236.

[Fox, 1983] Fox, M. S., P. Kleinosky, and S. Lowenfeld. "Techniques for Sensor-based Diagnosis." *Proceedings of the Eighth International Joint Conference on Artificial Intelligence.* San Mateo, CA: Morgan Kaufmann, pp. 158–163.

[Fox, 1984] Fox, M. S., and S. F. Smith. "ISIS: A Knowledge-based System for Factory Scheduling." *Expert Systems,* vol. 1, no. 1, pp. 25–49.

[Fox, 1986a] Fox, J. "Knowledge, Decision Making and Uncertainty." In *Artificial Intelligence and Statistics,* ed. A. Gale. Reading, MA: Addison-Wesley, pp. 57–76.

[Fox, 1986b] Fox, J. "Three Arguments for Extending the Framework of Probability." In *Uncertainty and Artificial Intelligence,* ed. N. Kanal and J. F. Lemmer. New York, NY: Elsevier, pp. 447–458.

[Fox, 1989] Fox, J. et al. "Decision Making as a Logical Process." In *Research and Development in Expert Systems V,* ed. B. Kelly and A. Rector. Cambridge: Cambridge University Press, pp. 160–175.

[FRANK, 1988a] Frank, S. J. "What AI Practitioners Should Know about the Law—Part 1." *AI Magazine,* vol. 9, no. 1 (Spring), pp. 63–75.

[FRANK, 1988b] Frank, S. J. "What AI Practitioners Should Know about the Law—Part 2." *AI Magazine,* vol. 9, no. 2 (Summer), pp. 109–114.

[FULTON, 1990] Fulton, S. L., and C. O. Pepe. "An Introduction to Model-based Reasoning." *AI Expert,* vol. 5, no. 1 (January), pp. 48–55.

[GALLIER, 1986] Gallier, J. H. *Logic for Computer Science: Foundations of Automatic Theorem Proving.* New York, NY: Harper & Row.

[GASCHNIG, 1979] Gaschnig, J. "Preliminary Performance Analysis of the Prospector Consultant System for Mineral Exploration." *The Sixth International Joint Conference on Artificial Intelligence.* San Mateo, CA: Morgan Kaufmann, pp. 308–310.

[GEMIGNANI, 1988] Gemignani, M. "Potential Liability for Use of Expert Systems." *IDEA—The Journal of Law and Technology,* vol. 29, pp. 120–127.

[GENESERETH, 1984] Genesereth, M. R. "The Use of Design Descriptions in Automated Diagnosis." *Artificial Intelligence,* vol. 24, no. 1-3, pp. 411–436.

[GEVARTER, 1984] Gevarter, W. B. *Artificial Intelligence, Expert Systems, Computer Vision, and Natural Language Processing.* Park Ridge, NJ: Noyes Publications.

[GIARRATANO, 1991] Giarratano, J. C. *CLIPS User's Guide, Volume 1, Rules.* NASA, Lyndon B. Johnson Space Center, Information Systems Directorate, Software Technology Branch, Houston, TX.

[GOLDBERG, 1981] Goldberg, A. "Introducing the Smalltalk-80 System." *BYTE,* vol. 6, no. 8 (August), pp. 14–26.

[GOLDBERG, 1983] Goldberg, A., and D. Robson. *Smalltalk-80, The Language and Its Implementation.* Reading, MA: Addison-Wesley.

[GOLDSTEIN, 1977] Goldstein, I. P., and R. B. Roberts. "NUDGE, A Knowledge-Based Scheduling Program." *The Fifth International Joint Conference on Artificial Intelligence.* San Mateo, CA: Morgan Kaufmann, pp. 257–263.

[GONZALEZ, 1986] Gonzalez, A. J., R. L. Osborne, C. Kemper, and S. Lowenfeld. "On-Line Diagnosis of Turbine Generators Using Artificial Intelligence." *IEEE Transactions on Energy Conversion,* vol. EC-1, no. 2 (June), pp. 68–74.

[GONZALEZ, 1988] Gonzalez, A. J., H. R. Myler, B. C. Owen, and M. Towhidnejad. "Automated Generation of Knowledge from CAD Design Databases." *Proceedings of the First Florida Artificial Intelligence Research Symposium.* St. Petersburg, FL: FLAIRS, pp. 75–80.

[GONZALEZ, 1991] Gonzalez, A. J., and H. R. Myler. "Issues in Automating the Extraction of a System Model from CAD Databases for Use in Model-Based Reasoning." *International Journal of Expert Systems, Research and Applications,* vol. 4, no. 1, pp. 29–50.

[GONZALEZ, 1992] Gonzalez, A. J., and R. Laureano. "A Case-Based Reasoning Approach to Real Estate Property Appraisal." *Expert Systems with Applications, An International Journal,* vol. 4, no. 2, pp. 229–246.

[GORDON, 1984] Gordon, J., and E. H. Shortliffe. "The Dempster-Shafer Theory of Evidence." In *Rule-Based Expert Systems: The MYCIN Experiments of the Stanford Heuristic Programming Project,* ed. B. G. Buchanan and E. H. Shortliffe. Reading, MA: Addison-Wesley, pp. 272–292.

[GUPTA, 1987] Gupta, U. G. "Financial Advisor Expert System, User's Documentation." Department of Computer Engineering, University of Central Florida, Orlando, FL.

[GUPTA, 1989] Gupta, U. G. "Validation and Verification of Expert Systems." Term Research Report. Department of Computer Engineering, University of Central Florida, Orlando, FL.

[GUPTA, 1990] Gupta, U. G. "RITCaG: Rule-based Intelligent Test Case Generator." Doctoral Dissertation, University of Central Florida, Orlando, FL.

[HAMILTON, 1991] Hamilton, D., K. Kelley, and C. Culbert. "State-of-the-Practice in Knowledge-Based System Validation and Verification." *Expert Systems with Applications, An International Journal,* vol. 3, no. 4, pp. 403–410.

[HAYASHI, 1988] Hayashi, Y., and M. Nakai. "Efficient Method for Multi-dimensional Fuzzy Reasoning and Its Application to Fault Diagnosis." *International Workshop on Artificial Intelligence for Industrial Applications 1988.* New York, NY: IEEE Press, pp. 27–32.

[HAYES-ROTH, 1977] Hayes-Roth, F., and V. R. Lesser. "Focus of Attention in the Hearsay-II System." *Proceedings of the 5th International Joint Conference on Artificial Intelligence.* San Mateo, CA: Morgan Kaufmann, pp. 27–35.

[HAYES-ROTH, 1983] Hayes-Roth, F., D. A. Waterman, and D. Lenat. "An Overview of Expert Systems." In *Building Expert Systems,* ed. F. Hayes-Roth, D. A. Waterman, and D. Lenat. Reading, MA: Addison-Wesley.

[HAYES-ROTH, 1988a] Hayes-Roth, B., and M. Hewett. "BB1: An Implementation of the Blackboard Control Architecture." In *Blackboard Systems,* ed. R. Englemore and T. Morgan. Reading, MA: Addison-Wesley, pp. 297–313.

[HAYES-ROTH, 1988b] Hayes-Roth, B., M. V. Johnson, A. Garvey, and M. Hewett. "Building Systems in the BB* Environment." In *Blackboard Systems,* ed. R. Englemore and T. Morgan. Reading, MA: Addison-Wesley, pp. 543–560.

[HAMILTON, 1991] Hamilton, D., K. Kelley, and C. Culbert. "State-of-the-Practice in Knowledge-Based System Validation and Verification." *Expert Systems with Applications,* vol. 3, no. 4, pp. 403–410.

[HECKERMAN, 1986] Heckerman, D. E. "Probabilistic Interpretation of Mycin's Certainty Factors." In *Uncertainty in Artificial Intelligence,* ed. L. N. Kanal and J. F. Lemmer. New York, NY: Elsevier, pp. 167–196.

[HECKERMAN, 1987] Heckerman, D. E., and E. J. Horvitz. "On the Expressiveness of Rule-Based Systems for Reasoning under Uncertainty." *Proceedings of the Sixth National Conference on Artificial Intelligence.* Menlo Park, CA: American Association for Artificial Intelligence, pp. 121–126.

[HECKERMAN, 1988] Heckerman, D. E., and E. J. Horvitz. "The Myth of Modularity in Rule-Based Systems for Reasoning with Uncertainty." In *Uncertainty in Artificial Intelligence 2,* ed. J. F. Lemmer and L. N. Kanal. New York, NY: Elsevier, pp. 23–34.

[HOFFMAN, 1987] Hoffman, R. R. "The Problem of Extracting the Knowledge of Experts from the Perspective of Experimental Psychology." *AI Magazine,* vol. 8, no. 2 (Summer), pp. 53–67.

[HOLLAN, 1984] Hollan, J. D., E. L. Hutchins, and L. Weitzman. "STEAMER: An Interactive, Inspectable, Simulation-Based Training System." *AI Magazine,* vol. 5, no. 2 (Summer), pp. 15–27.

[HOLLAND, 1986] Holland, J. H., K. F. Holyoak, R. E. Nisbett, and P. R. Thagard. *Induction-Processes of Inference, Learning and Discovery.* Cambridge, MA: MIT Press.

[HSU, 1990] Hsu, F., T. Anantharaman, M. Campbell, and A. Nowatzyk. "A Grandmaster Chess Machine." *Scientific American,* vol. 263, no. 4 (October), pp. 44–50.

[INOUE, 1985] Inoue, H. "Building a Bridge Between AI and Robotics." *Proceedings of the Ninth International Joint Conference on Artificial Intelligence.* San Mateo, CA: Morgan Kaufmann, pp. 1231–1237.

[JENKINS, 1986] Jenkins, A. "Artificial Intelligence Meets Practicality." *PC Week,* September 23, pp. 37–40.

[JONES, 1990] Jones, G. W. *Software Engineering,* New York, NY: John Wiley & Sons.

[KAHN, 1984] Kahn, G., and J. McDermott. "The MUD System." *Proceedings of the First Conference on Artificial Intelligence Applications.* Los Alamitos, CA: IEEE Computer Society, pp. 116–122.

[KAHN, 1985] Kahn, G., S. Nowlan, and J. McDermott. "MORE: An Intelligent Knowledge Acquisition Tool." *Proceedings of the Ninth International Joint Conference on Artificial Intelligence,* Vol. 1. San Mateo, CA: Morgan Kaufmann, pp. 581–584.

[KEARSLEY, 1987] Kearsley, G. *Artificial Intelligence and Instruction.* Reading, MA: Addison-Wesley.

[KEENE, 1988] Keene, S. E. *Object-Oriented Programming in Common Lisp.* Reading, MA: Addison-Wesley.

[KELLY, 1955] Kelly, G. A. *The Psychology of Personal Constructs, Vol. 1—A Theory of Personality.* New York, NY: W. W. Norton.

[KIREMIDJIAN, 1983] Kiremidjian, G., A. Clarkson, and D. Lenat. "Expert System for Tactical Indications and Warning (I&W) Analysis." *Proceedings of the Army Conference on the Application of AI to Battlefield Information Management.* Report AD-A139 685. Battelle Columbus Laboratories, Washington, DC.

[KLEIN, 1985] Klein, G., and R. Calderwood. "How Do People Use Analogues to Make Decisions." *Proceedings of the 1988 Case-Based Reasoning Workshop.* San Mateo, CA: Morgan Kaufmann, pp. 209–223.

[KOHONEN, 1988] Kohonen, T. *Self-Organization and Associative Memory.* New York, NY: Springer-Verlag.

[KOHOUT, 1987a] Kohout, L. J., and W. Bandler. "The Use of Fuzzy Information Retrieval Techniques in Construction of Multi-centre Knowledge-Based Systems." In *Uncertainty in Knowledge-Based Systems,* ed. B. Bouchon and R. R. Yager. New York, NY: Springer-Verlag, pp. 257–264.

[KOHOUT, 1987b] Kohout, L. J., and M. Kallala. "The Use of Fuzzy Information Retrieval in Knowledge-Based Management of Patient's Clinical Profiles." In *Uncertainty in Knowledge-Based Systems,* ed. B. Bouchon and R. R. Yager. New York, NY: Springer-Verlag, pp. 275–282.

[KOLODNER, 1988] Kolodner, J. "Retrieving Events from Case Memory: A Parallel Implementation." *Proceedings of the Case-Based Reasoning Workshop.* San Mateo, CA: Morgan Kaufmann, pp. 233–249.

[KOVARIK, 1988] Kovarik, V. J. "Case-Based Reasoning." Technical Report. University of Central Florida, Orlando, FL, November.

[KOVARIK, 1989] Kovarik, V. J. "Temporal Representation and Reasoning." Research Report. University of Central Florida, Orlando, FL.

[KRASNER, 1983] Krasner, G. *Smalltalk-80: Bits of History, Words of Advice.* Reading, MA: Addison-Wesley.

[KUIPERS, 1986] Kuipers, B. "Qualitative Simulation." *Artificial Intelligence,* vol. 29, no. 3, pp. 289–338.

[LADKIN, 1989] Ladkin, P. B. "Temporal Reasoning and Constraint Satisfaction." Tutorial. *Florida Artificial Intelligence Research Symposium.* St. Petersburg, FL: FLAIRS.

[LEMMER, 1988] Lemmer, J. F., and L. N. Kanal. *Uncertainty in Artificial Intelligence 2.* New York, NY: Elsevier.

[LENAT, 1977] Lenat, D. B., and J. McDermott. "Less than General Production System Architectures." *The Fifth International Joint Conference on Artificial Intelligence.* San Mateo, CA: Morgan Kaufmann, pp. 928–932.

[LEONARD-BARTON, 1988] Leonard-Barton, D., and J. J. Sviokla. "Putting Expert Systems to Work." *The Harvard Business Review* (March-April), pp. 91–98.

[LINDLEY, 1987] Lindley, D. V. "The Probability Approach to the Treatment of Uncertainty in Artificial Intelligence." *Statistical Science,* vol. 2, no. 1, pp. 17–24.

[LINDSAY, 1980] Lindsay, R. K., B. G. Buchanan, E. A. Feigenbaum, and J. Lederberg. *Applications of Artificial Intelligence for Organic Chemistry.* New York, NY: McGraw-Hill.

[LLOYD, 1989] Lloyd, B., W. Park, J. White, and M. Divakaruni. "A Generator Expert Monitoring System." *Proceedings of the Conference on Expert System Applications for the Electric Power Industry.* Palo Alto, CA: Electric Power Research Institute.

[LUGER, 1989] Luger, G. F., and W. A. Stubblefield. *Artificial Intelligence and the Design of Expert Systems.* Redwood City, CA: Benjamin/Cummings.

[MACRO, 1987] Macro, A., and J. Burton. *The Craft of Software Engineering.* Reading, MA: Addison-Wesley.

[MAHLER, 1989] Mahler, E. and L. Shipman. "Experts Creating Expert Systems at Du-Pont." *Scientific Computing and Automation* (April), pp. 49–54.

[MAIER, 1988] Maier, D., and D. S. Warren. *Computing with Logic: Logic Programming with Prolog.* Reading, MA: Addison-Wesley.

[MAMDANI, 1983] Mamdani, E. H. "Process Control Using Fuzzy Logic." In *Designing for Human-Computer Communication,* ed. M. E. Sime and M. J. Coombs. New York, NY: Academic Press, pp. 311–336.

[MAMDANI, 1985] Mamdani, E. H., and H. J. Efstathiou. "Higher-order Logics for Handling Uncertainty in Expert Systems." *International Journal of Man-Machine Studies,* vol. 22, no. 3 (March), pp. 283–293.

[MARCOT, 1987] Marcot, B. "Testing Your Knowledge Base," *AI Expert,* vol. 2, no. 8 (August), pp. 42–47.

[MARCUS, 1985] Marcus, S., J. McDermott, and T. Wang. "Knowledge Acquisition for Constructive Systems." *Proceedings of the Ninth International Joint Conference on Artificial Intelligence,* Vol. 1. San Mateo, CA: Morgan Kaufmann, pp. 581–584.

[McDERMOTT, 1982] McDermott, J. "R1: A Rule-Based Configurer of Computer Systems." *Artificial Intelligence,* vol. 19, no. 1 (September), pp. 39–88.

[MEYER, 1988] Meyer, B. *Object-Oriented Software Construction.* New York, NY: Prentice Hall.

[MICHALSKI, 1983] Michalski, R. S., J. G. Carbonell, and T. M. Mitchell. *Machine Learning: An Artificial Intelligence Approach.* San Mateo, CA: Tioga.

[MICHALSKI, 1986] Michalski, R. S., J. G. Carbonell, and T. M. Mitchell. *Machine Learning: An Artificial Intelligence Approach,* Vol. II. San Mateo, CA: Morgan Kaufmann.

[MILLER, 1982] Miller, R. A., H. E. Pople Jr., and J. D. Myers. "INTERNIST-I, an Experimental Computer-based Diagnostic Consultant for General Internal Medicine." *New England Journal of Medicine,* vol. 37, no. 8 (August), pp. 468–476.

[MINSKY, 1975] Minsky, M. "A Framework for Representing Knowledge." In *The Psychology of Computer Vision,* ed. P. H. Winston. New York, NY: McGraw-Hill, pp. 211–277.

[MITCHELL, 1986] Mitchell, T. M., J. G. Carbonell, and R. S. Michalski. *Machine Learning: A Guide to Current Research.* Boston, MA: Kluwer Academic.

[MYLER, 1989] Myler, H. R., A. J. Gonzalez, M. Towhidnejad, F. D. McKenzie, and R. R. Kladke. "Automated Knowledge Generation from Incomplete CAD Data: Research Results." *Proceedings of the Second Florida Artificial Intelligence Research Symposium.* St. Petersburg, FL: FLAIRS, pp. 10–15.

[NEGOITA, 1985] Negoita, C. V. *Expert Systems and Fuzzy Systems.* Menlo Park, CA: Benjamin/Cummings.

[NELSON, 1982] Nelson, W. R. "REACTOR: An Expert System for Diagnosis and Treatment of Nuclear Reactor Accidents." *Proceedings of the Second National Conference on Artificial Intelligence.* San Mateo, CA: Morgan Kaufmann, pp. 296–301.

[NEWELL, 1962] Newell, A. "Some Problems of Basic Organization in Problem-Solving Programs." In *Conference on Self-Organizing Systems,* ed. M. C. Yovits, G. T. Jacobi, and G. D. Goldstein. Washington, DC: Spartan Book, pp. 393–423.

[NEWELL, 1963] Newell, A., and H. A. Simon. "GPS, A Program that Simulates Human Thought." In *Computers and Thought,* ed. E. A. Feigenbaum and J. Feldman. New York, NY: McGraw-Hill, pp. 279–296.

[NGUYEN, 1987] Nguyen, T. A., W. A. Perkins, T. J. Laffey, and D. Pecora. "Knowledge Base Verification." *AI Magazine,* vol. 8, no. 2 (Summer), pp. 69–75.

[NIERENBERG, 1971] Nierenberg, G. I., and H. H. Calero. *How to Read a Person Like a Book.* New York, NY: Hawthorn Books.

[NII, 1986] Nii, P. "The Blackboard Model of Problem Solving." *AI Magazine,* vol. 7, no. 2 (Summer), pp. 38–53.

[NII, 1988] Nii, H. P., and N. Aiello. "AGE (Attempt to GEneralize): A Knowledge-Based Program for Building Knowledge-Based Programs." In *Blackboard Systems,* ed. R. Engelmore and T. Morgan. Reading, MA: Addison-Wesley, pp. 251–280.

[O'KEEFE, 1987] O'Keefe, R. M., O. Balci, and E. P. Smith. "Validating Expert System Performance." *IEEE Expert,* vol. 2, no. 4 (Winter), pp. 81–90.

[O'KEEFE, 1989] O'Keefe, R., and D. O'Leary. "Verifying and Validating Expert Systems." Tutorial MP-4. *The Eleventh International Joint Conference on Artificial Intelligence.* San Mateo, CA: Morgan Kaufmann.

[OKADA, 1988] Okada, K., K. Urasawa, K. Kanemaru, and H. Kanoh. "Knowledge-based Fault Location System for Electric Power Transmission Lines." *International Workshop on Artificial Intelligence for Industrial Applications 1988.* New York, NY: IEEE Press, pp. 52–57.

[OSBORNE, 1985] Osborne, R. L., A. J. Gonzalez, J. C. Bellows, and J. D. Chess. "On-line Diagnosis of Instrumentation through Artificial Intelligence." *Proceedings of the Power Instrumentation Symposium.* Research Triangle Park, NC: Instrument Society of America, pp. 89–94.

[OSHIMA, 1988] Oshima, H., S. Yasunobu, and S. Sekino. "Automatic Train Operation System Based on Predictive Fuzzy Control." *International Workshop on Artificial Intelligence for Industrial Applications 1988.* New York, NY: IEEE Press, pp. 485–489.

[PALMIN, 1986] Palmin, S. "Mini-Expert System Simplifies Stepping Motor System Design." *PCIM* (December), pp. 44–50.

[PARK, 1988] Park, W. Personal communication.

[PARSAYE, 1988] Parsaye, K. "Acquiring and Verifying Knowledge Automatically." *AI Expert,* vol. 3, no. 5 (May), pp. 48–63.

[PENDERSON, 1989] Penderson, K. "Well-Structured Knowledge Bases-Part I." *AI Expert,* vol. 4, no. 4 (April), pp. 44–55.

[PETERSON, 1991] Peterson, I. "The Checkers Challenge." *Science News,* vol. 140, no. 3 (July 20), pp. 40–41.

[POST, 1943] Post, E. L. "Formal Reductions of the General Combinatorial Decision Problem." *American Journal of Mathematics,* vol. 65, pp. 197–268.

[PREECE, 1992] Preece, A. D., R. Shingal, and A. Batarekh. "Verifying Expert Systems: A Logical Framework and a Practical Tool." *Expert Systems with Applications,* vol. 5, no. 2/3, pp. 421–436.

[PRICE, 1985] Price, K. E. "Relaxation Matching Techniques-A Comparison." *IEEE Transactions on Pattern Analysis and Machine Intelligence,* vol. PAMI-7, no. 5 (September), pp. 617–623.

[QUILLIAN, 1968] Quillian, M. R. "Semantic Memory." In *Semantic Information Processing,* ed. M. Minsky. Cambridge, MA: MIT Press, pp. 271–270.

[QUINLAN, 1983] Quinlan, J. R. "Learning Efficient Classification Procedures and Their Application to Chess Games." In *Machine Learning,* ed. R. S. Michalski, J. G. Carbonell, and T. M. Mitchell. Palo Alto, CA: Tioga Press, pp. 463–482.

[REIGER, 1977] Reiger, C., and M. Grinberg. "The Declarative Representation and Procedural Simulation of Causality in Physical Mechanisms." *Proceedings of the Fifth International Joint Conference on Artificial Intelligence.* San Mateo, CA: Morgan Kaufmann, pp. 250–256.

[REITER, 1978] Reiter, R. "On Reasoning by Default." *Proceedings of Theoretical Issues in Natural Language Processing-2.* New York, NY: ACM, pp. 210–218.

[REITER, 1980] Reiter, R. "A Logic for Default Reasoning." *Artificial Intelligence,* vol. 13, nos. 1-2, pp. 81–132.

[REYNOLDS, 1988] Reynolds, D. "MUSE: A Toolkit for Embedded Real-Time AI." In *Blackboard Systems,* ed. R. Englemore and T. Morgan. Reading, MA: Addison-Wesley, pp. 519–532.

[RICH, 1991] Rich, E., and K. Knight. *Artificial Intelligence,* 2d Ed. New York, NY: McGraw-Hill.

[RIESBECK, 1988] Riesbeck, C. "An Interface for Case-based Knowledge Acquisition." *Proceedings of the Case-Based Reasoning Workshop.* San Mateo, CA: Morgan Kaufmann, pp. 312–326.

[ROBINSON, 1965] Robinson, J. A. "A Machine-Oriented Logic Based on the Resolution Principle." *Journal of the ACM,* vol. 12, no. 1, pp. 23–41.

[RUMELHART, 1987] Rumelhart, D. E., J. L. McClelland, and the PDP Research Group. *Parallel Distributed Processing.* Cambridge, MA: MIT Press.

[SAFFIOTTI, 1987] Saffiotti, A. "An AI View of the Treatment of Uncertainty." *The Knowledge Engineering Review,* vol. 2, no. 2, pp. 75–97.

[SAMUEL, 1963] Samuel, A. L. "Some Studies in Machine Learning Using the Game of Checkers." In *Computers and Thought,* ed. E. A. Feigenbaum and J. Feldman. New York, NY: McGraw-Hill, pp. 71–105.

[SCARL, 1985] Scarl, E. A., J. R. Jamieson, and C. I. Delaune. "A Fault Detection and Isolation Method Applied to Liquid Oxygen Loading for the Space Shuttle." *Proceedings of the Ninth International Joint Conference on Artificial Intelligence.* San Mateo, CA: Morgan Kaufmann, pp. 414–416.

[SCARL, 1987] Scarl, E. A., J. R. Jamieson, and C. I. Delaune. "Diagnosis and Sensor Validation through Knowledge of Structure and Function." *IEEE Transactions on Systems, Man and Cybernetics,* vol. SMC-17, no. 3 (May-June), pp. 360–368.

[SCARL, 1991] Scarl, E. A. "Tutorial on Model Based Reasoning." *Florida Artificial Intelligence Research Symposium.* St. Petersburg, FL: FLAIRS.

[SCHAEFFER, 1991] Schaeffer, J., J. Culberson, N. Treloar, B. Knight, P. Lu, and D. Szafron. "Checkers Program to Challenge for World Championship." *SIGART Bulletin,* vol. 2, no. 2, pp. 3–5.

[SCHANK, 1977] Schank, R. C., and R. P. Abelson. *Scripts, Plans, Goals, and Understanding.* Hillsdale, NJ: Lawrence Erlbaum.

[SCHWARTZ, 1990] Schwartz, T. J. "Fuzzy Systems in the Real World." *AI Expert,* vol. 5, no. 8 (August), pp. 29–36.

[SCHWEICKERT, 1987] Schweickert, R., A. M. Burton, N. K. Taylor, E. N. Corlett, N. R. Shadbolt, and A. P. Hedgecock. "Comparing Knowledge Elicitation Techniques: A Case Study." *Artificial Intelligence Review,* vol. 1, no. 4, pp. 245–253.

[SELFRIDGE, 1959] Selfridge, O. "Pandemonium: A Paradigm for Learning." *Proceedings of Symposium of Mechanisation of Thought and Processes.* Teddington, UK: National Physics Laboratory, pp. 511–529.

[SHAFER, 1976] Shafer, G. *A Mathematical Theory of Evidence.* Princeton, NJ: Princeton University Press.

[SHAW, 1982] Shaw, M. L. G. "PLANET: Some Experience in Creating an Integrated System for Repertory Grid Application on a Microcomputer." *International Journal of Man-machine Studies,* vol. 17, no. 3, pp. 345–360.

[SHAW, 1987] Shaw, M. L. G., and B. R. Gaines. "An Interactive Knowledge Elicitation Technique Using Personal Construct Technology." In *Knowledge Acquisition for Expert Systems,* ed. A. L. Kidd. New York, NY: Plenum Press, pp. 109–136.

[SHOOMAN, 1983] Shooman, M. L. *Software Engineering: Design, Reliability, and Management.* New York, NY: McGraw-Hill.

[SHORTLIFFE, 1974] Shortliffe, E. A. "MYCIN: A Rule-based Computer Program for Advising Physicians Regarding Antimicrobial Therapy Selection." Ph.D. Dissertation, Stanford University, Stanford, CA.

[SHORTLIFFE, 1976] Shortliffe, E. H. *Computer-Based Medical Consultations: Mycin.* New York, NY: American Elsevier.

[SHORTLIFFE, 1979] Shortliffe, E. H., B. G. Buchanan, and E. A. Feigenbaum. "Knowledge Engineering for Medical Decision Making: A Review of Computer-Based Clinical Decision Aids." *Proceedings of IEEE,* vol. 67, no. 9, pp. 1207–1224.

[SHORTLIFFE, 1982] Shortliffe, E. H., and L. W. Fagan. "Expert Systems Research: Modeling the Medical Decision Making Process." Report 82-03. Department of Computer Science, Stanford University, Stanford, CA.

[SIMON, 1977] Simon, H. A. "Scientific Discovery and the Psychology of Problem Solving." In *Models of Discovery,* ed. H. A. Simon. Boston, MA: Reidel, pp. 286–303.

[SLAGLE, 1971] Slagle, J. R. *Artificial Intelligence: The Heuristic Programming Approach.* New York, NY: McGraw-Hill.

[SOWA, 1984] Sowa, J. F. *Conceptual Structures: Information Processing in Mind and Machine.* Reading, MA: Addison-Wesley.

[SPILLMAN, 1990] Spillman, R. "Managing Uncertainty with Belief Functions." *AI Expert,* vol. 5, no. 3 (May), pp. 44–49.

[STACHOWITZ, 1987] Stachowitz, R. A., J. B. Combs, and C. L. Chang. "Validation of Knowledge-Based Systems." *Proceedings of the Twentieth Annual Hawaii Conference on Systems Science.* Honolulu, HI: University of Hawaii Press, pp. 686–695.

[STANAT, 1977] Stanat, D. F., and D. F. McAllister. *Discrete Mathematics in Computer Science.* Englewood Cliffs, NJ: Prentice Hall.

[STB, 1991] Software Technology Branch. *CLIPS Reference Manual*. Houston, TX: NASA, Lyndon B. Johnson Space Center, Information Systems Directorate, Software Technology Branch.

[STEFIK, 1981a] Stefik, M. J. "Planning with Constraints, MOLGEN: Part 1." *Artificial Intelligence,* vol. 16, no. 2 (May), pp. 111–140.

[STEFIK, 1981b] Stefik, M. J. "Planning and Meta-planning, MOLGEN: Part 2." *Artificial Intelligence,* vol. 16, no. 2 (May), pp. 141–170.

[STEFIK, 1983] Stefik, M. J. et al. "Knowledge Engineering in Loops." *AI Magazine,* vol. 4, no. 3 (Fall), pp. 3–13.

[STEFIK, 1986] Stefik, M. J., and D. G. Bobrow. "Object-Oriented Programming: Themes and Variations." *AI Magazine,* vol. 6, no. 4 (Fall), pp. 40–62.

[SUMMERVILLE, 1982] Summerville, I. *Software Engineering*. Reading, MA: Addison-Wesley.

[SUWA, 1982] Suwa, M., A. C. Scott, and E. H. Shortliffe. "An Approach to Verifying Completeness and Consistency in a Rule-Based Expert System." *AI Magazine,* vol. 3, no. 4 (Fall), pp. 16–21.

[TANIMOTO, 1987] Tanimoto, S. L. *The Elements of Artificial Intelligence*. New York, NY: Computer Science Press.

[TAILOR, 1988] Tailor, A. "MXA: A Blackboard Expert System Shell." In *Blackboard Systems,* ed. R. Englemore and T. Morgan. Reading, MA: Addison-Wesley, pp. 315–333.

[TERRY, 1983] Terry, A. "The CRYSALIS Project: Hierarchical Control of Production Systems." Technical Report HPP-83-19. Stanford, CA: Stanford University.

[TERRY, 1988] Terry, A. "Using Explicit Strategic Knowledge to Control Expert Systems." In *Blackboard Systems,* ed. R. Engelmore and T. Morgan. Reading, MA: Addison-Wesley, pp. 159–188.

[TESAURO, 1989] Tesauro, G., and T. J. Sejnowski. "A Parallel Network that Learns to Play Backgammon." *Artificial Intelligence,* vol. 39, no. 3, pp. 357–390.

[TEXAS Instruments, 1986] Texas Instruments Inc. *Personal Consultant Easy, Getting Started Manual*. Austin, TX: Texas Instruments Inc.

[TEXAS Instruments, 1987] Texas Instruments Inc. *Personal Consultant Plus Reference Guide*. Austin, TX: Texas Instruments Inc.

[THATHACHAR, 1986] Thathachar, M. A., and P. S. Sastry. "Relaxation Labeling with Learning Automata." *IEEE Transactions on Pattern Analysis and Machine Intelligence,* vol. PAMI-8, no. 2 (March), pp. 256–267.

[TREMBLAY, 1984] Tremblay, J. P., and P. G. Sorenson. *An Introduction to Data Structures with Applications*. New York, NY: McGraw-Hill.

[TRUBOW, 1991] Trubow, G. B. "How Liable are You for your Software?" *IEEE Software,* vol. 8, no. 4 (July), pp. 94–95.

[TURNER, 1984] Turner, R. *Logics for Artificial Intelligence*. West Sussex, England: Ellis Horwood Limited.

[UNDERWOOD, 1981] Underwood, W. E., and J. P. Summerville. "PROJCON: A Prototype Project Management Consultant." *Proceedings of the International Conference on Cybernetics and Society*. Los Alamitos, CA: IEEE Computer Society (October), pp. 149–155.

[WALTZ, 1975] Waltz, D. "Understanding Line Drawings of Scenes with Shadows." In *The Psychology of Computer Vision,* ed. P. H. Winston. New York, NY: McGraw Hill, pp. 19–91.

[WATERMAN, 1978] Waterman, D. A., and F. Hayes-Roth. *Pattern-Directed Inference Systems.* New York, NY: Academic Press.

[WATERMAN, 1986a] Waterman, D. A. *A Guide to Expert Systems.* Reading, MA: Addison-Wesley.

[WATERMAN, 1986b] Waterman, D. A., and B. M. Jenkins. "Developing Expert Systems to Combat International Terrorism." In *Expert Systems,* ed. P. Klahr and D. A. Waterman. Reading, MA: Addison-Wesley, pp. 95–134.

[WEBSTER, 1960] *Webster's New World Dictionary of the American Language.* New York, NY: World.

[WEINERMAN, 1978] Weinerman, C. S. *Practical Law: A Layperson's Handbook.* Englewood Cliffs, NJ: Prentice Hall.

[WHITEHEAD, 1987] Whitehead, J. D., and J. W. Roach. "Expert Systems Without an Expert: Fault Diagnosis Based on Causal Reasoning." *Texas Instruments Technical Journal* (Winter), pp. 19–29.

[WINSTON, 1992] Winston, P. H. *Artificial Intelligence,* 3d Ed. Reading, MA: Addison-Wesley.

[WOODS, 1975] Woods, W. A. "What's in a Link: Foundations for Semantic Networks." In *Representation and Understanding,* ed. D. G. Bobrow and A. Collins. New York, NY: Academic Press, pp. 35–82.

[WRIGHT, 1983] Wright, J. M., and M. S. Fox. "SRL/1.5 User Manual." Pittsburgh, PA: Robotics Institute, Carnegie-Mellon University (December).

[YU, 1984] Yu, V. L., L. M. Fagan, S. W. Bennett, W. J. Clancey, A. C. Scott, J. F. Hanigan, R. L. Blum, B. G. Buchanan, and S. N. Cohen. "An Evaluation of MYCIN's Advice." In *Rule-Based Expert Systems: The MYCIN Experiment of the Stanford Heuristic Programming Project,* ed. B. G. Buchanan and E. H. Shortliffe. Reading, MA: Addison-Wesley, pp. 589–596.

[ZADEH, 1965] Zadeh, L. A. "Fuzzy Sets." *Information and Control,* vol. 8, no. 3, pp. 338–353.

[ZADEH, 1973] Zadeh, L. A. "Outline of a New Approach to the Analysis of Complex Systems and Decision Processes." *IEEE Transactions on Systems, Man, and Cybernetics,* vol. SMC-3, no. 1 (January), pp. 28–44.

[ZADEH, 1986] Zadeh, L. A. "Is Probability Theory Sufficient for Dealing with Uncertainty in AI: A Negative View." In *Uncertainty in Artificial Intelligence 2,* ed. J. F. Lemmer and L. N. Kanal. New York, NY: Elsevier, pp. 103–116.

[ZANCONATO, 1988] Zanconato, R. "BLOBS: An Object-Oriented Blackboard System Framework for Reasoning in Time." In *Blackboard Systems,* ed. R. Englemore and T. Morgan. Reading, MA: Addison-Wesley, pp. 335–345.

[ZEIDE, 1992] Zeide, J. S., and J. Liebowitz. "Institutionalizing Expert Systems: Guidelines and Legal Concerns." *Proceedings of the Fifth Annual Florida Artificial Intelligence Research Symposium.* St. Petersburg, FL: FLAIRS, pp. 6–9.

[ZLATAREVA, 1992] Zlatareva, N. P. "A Framework for Knowledge-based System Verification, Validation and Refinement: The VVR System." *Proceedings of the Fifth Florida Artificial Intelligence Research Symposium,* St. Petersburg, FL: FLAIRS, pp. 10–14.

Index

Personal Computer with PC-DOS or MS-DOS 3.3   two 3-1/2" 800kB HD disks
by Avelino J. Gonzalez and Douglas D. Dankel   Prentice-Hall